# Reasoning about Uncert

# Reasoning about Uncertainty

Joseph Y. Halpern

The MIT Press
Cambridge, Massachusetts
London, England

First MIT Press paperback edition, 2005

© 2003 Massachusetts Institute of Technology

This book was set in Times Roman by Windfall Software (using ZzTEX) and was printed and bound in the United States of America.

Library of Congress Cataloging-in-Publication Data

Halpern, Joseph Y., 1953–
   Reasoning about uncertainty / Joseph Y. Halpern.
    p.   cm.
   Includes bibliographical references and index.
   ISBN 978-0-262-08320-1 (hc. : alk. paper) — 978-0-262-58259-9 (pb. : alk. paper)
   1. Uncertainty (Information theory)  2. Reasoning.  3. Logic, Symbolic and mathematical.
 I. Title.

Q375.H35 2003
003'.54—dc21

                                               2003044565

10  9  8  7  6  5  4

*To Daniel, a low probability event of unbounded utility, without whom this book would have undoubtedly been finished a little earlier; and to all my collaborators over the years, without whom there would have been no book to write.*

# Contents

# Preface

This is a highly biased view of uncertainty. I have focused on topics that I found interesting and with which I was familiar, with a particular emphasis on topics on which I have done some research. (This is meant to be a partial apology for the rather large number of references in the bibliography that list "Halpern" as a coauthor. It gives a rather unbalanced view of the influence I have had on the field!)

I hope the book will be read by researchers in a number of disciplines, including computer science, artificial intelligence, economics (particularly game theory), mathematics, philosophy, and statistics. With this goal in mind, I have tried to make the book accessible to readers with widely differing backgrounds. Logicians and philosophers may well be comfortable with all the logic and have trouble with probability and random variables. Statisticians and economists may have just the opposite problem. The book should contain enough detail to make it almost completely self-contained. However, there is no question that having some background in both propositional logic and probability would be helpful (although a few weeks of each in a discrete mathematics course ought to suffice); for Chapter 11, a basic understanding of limits is also necessary.

This book is mathematical, in the sense that ideas are formalized in terms of definitions and theorems. On the other hand, the emphasis on the book is not on proving theorems. Rather, I have tried to focus on a certain philosophy for representing and reasoning about uncertainty. (References to where proofs of theorems can be found are given in the notes to each chapter; in many cases, the proofs are discussed in the exercises, with hints.)

Now comes the paragraph in the book that was perhaps the most pleasurable to write: the acknowledgments. I'd particularly like to thank my collaborators over the years on topics related to reasoning about uncertainty, including Fahiem Bacchus, Francis Chu, Ron Fagin, Nir Friedman, Adam Grove, Peter Grünwald, Daphne Koller, Yoram Moses, Riccardo Pucella, Mark Tuttle, and Moshe Vardi. There would have been no book to write if it hadn't been for the work we did together, and I wouldn't have been inspired to write the book if the work hadn't been so much fun. Thanks to many students and colleagues who gave me comments and found typos, including Fokko von de Bult, Willem Conradie, Francis Chu, Christine Chung, Dieter Denneberg, Pablo Fierens, Li Li, Lori Lorigo, Fabrice Nauze, Sabina Petride, Riccardo Pucella, Joshua Sack, Richard Shore, Sebastian Silgardo, Jan de Vos, Peter Wakker, and Eduardo Zambrano. Riccardo, in particular, gave detailed comments and went out of his way to make suggestions that greatly improved the presentation. Of course, the responsibility for all remaining bugs are mine. (I don't know of any as I write this, but I am quite sure there are still some there.) Thanks to those who funded much of the research reported here: Abe Waksman at AFOSR, Ralph Wachter at ONR, and Larry Reeker and Ephraim Glinert at NSF. I would also like to acknowledge a Fulbright Fellowship and a Guggenheim Fellowship, which provided me with partial support during a sabbatical in 2001–2002, when I put the finishing touches to the book. And last but far from least, thanks to my family, who have put up with me coming home late for so many years. I'll try to be better.

# Chapter 1

# Introduction and Overview

*When one admits that nothing is certain one must, I think, also add that some things are more nearly certain than others.*

—Bertrand Russell

*It is not certain that everything is uncertain.*

—Blaise Pascal

Uncertainty is a fundamental—and unavoidable—feature of daily life. In order to deal with uncertainty intelligently, we need to be able to represent it and reason about it. How to do that is what this book is about.

Reasoning about uncertainty can be subtle. If it weren't, this book would be much shorter. The puzzles and problems described in the next section hint at some of the subtleties.

## 1.1  Some Puzzles and Problems

**The second-ace puzzle**   A deck has four cards: the ace and deuce of hearts, and the ace and deuce of spades. After a fair shuffle of the deck, two cards are dealt to Alice. It is easy to see that, at this point, there is a probability of 1/6 that Alice has both aces, a probability of 5/6 that Alice has at least one ace, a probability of 1/2 that Alice has the ace of spades, and a probability of 1/2 that Alice has the ace of hearts: of the six possible deals of two cards out of four, Alice has both aces in one of them, at least one ace in five of them, the ace of hearts in three of them, and the ace of spades in three of them. (For readers unfamiliar with probability, there is an introduction in Chapter 2.)

Alice then says, "I have an ace." Conditioning on this information (by discarding the possibility that Alice was dealt no aces), Bob computes the probability that Alice holds both aces to be 1/5. This seems reasonable. The probability, according to Bob, of Alice having two aces goes up if he learns that she has an ace. Next, Alice says, "I have the ace of spades." Conditioning on this new information, Bob now computes the probability that Alice holds both aces to be 1/3. Of the three deals in which Alice holds the ace of spades, she holds both aces in one of them. As a result of learning not only that Alice holds at least one ace, but that the ace is actually the ace of spades, the conditional probability that Alice holds both aces goes up from 1/5 to 1/3. But suppose that Alice had instead said, "I have the ace of hearts." It seems that a similar argument again shows that the conditional probability that Alice holds both aces is 1/3.

Is this reasonable? When Bob learns that Alice has an ace, he knows that she must have either the ace of hearts or the ace of spades. Why should finding out which particular ace it is raise the conditional probability of Alice having two aces? Put another way, if this probability goes up from 1/5 to 1/3 whichever ace Alice says she has, and Bob knows that she has an ace, then why isn't it 1/3 all along?

**The Monty Hall puzzle**    The Monty Hall puzzle is very similar to the second-ace puzzle. Suppose that you're on a game show and given a choice of three doors. Behind one is a car; behind the others are goats. You pick door 1. Before opening door 1, host Monty Hall (who knows what is behind each door) opens door 3, which has a goat. He then asks you if you still want to take what's behind door 1, or to take instead what's behind door 2. Should you switch? Assuming that, initially, the car was equally likely to be behind each of the doors, naive conditioning suggests that, given that it is not behind door 3, it is equally likely to be behind door 1 and door 2, so there is no reason to switch. On the other hand, the car is equally likely to be behind each of the doors. If it is behind door 1, then you clearly should not switch; but if it is not behind door 1, then it must be behind door 2 (since it is obviously not behind door 3), and you should switch to door 2. Since the probability that it is behind door 1 is 1/3, it seems that, with probability 2/3, you should switch. But if this reasoning is correct, then why exactly is the original argument incorrect?

The second-ace puzzle and the Monty Hall puzzle are the stuff of puzzle books. Nevertheless, understanding exactly why naive conditioning does not give reasonable answers in these cases turns out to have deep implications, not just for puzzles, but for important statistical problems.

**The two-coin problem**    Suppose that Alice has two coins. One of them is fair, and so has equal likelihood of landing heads and tails. The other is biased, and is twice as likely to land heads as to land tails. Alice chooses one of her coins (assume she can tell them apart by their weight and feel) and is about to toss it. Bob knows that one coin is fair and the other is twice as likely to land heads as tails. He does not know which coin Alice has chosen, nor is he given a probability that the fair coin is chosen. What is the probability, according to Bob, that the outcome of the coin toss will be heads? What is the probability according to Alice? (Both of these probabilities are for the situation *before* the coin is tossed.)

**A coin with unknown bias**   Again, suppose that Alice has two coins, one fair and the other with a probability 2/3 of landing heads. Suppose also that Bob can choose which coin Alice will flip, and he knows which coin is fair and which is biased toward heads. He gets $1 if the coin lands heads and loses $1 if the coin lands tails. Clearly, in that case, Bob should choose the coin with a probability 2/3 of landing heads.

But now consider a variant of the story. Instead of knowing that the first coin is fair, Bob has no idea of its bias. What coin should he choose then? If Bob represents his uncertainty about the first coin using a single probability measure, then perhaps the best thing to do is to say that heads and tails are equally likely, and so each gets probability 1/2. But is this in fact the best thing to do? Is using a single probability measure to represent Bob's uncertainty even appropriate here?

Although this example may seem fanciful, it is an abstraction of what are called *exploitation vs. exploration* decisions, which arise frequently in practice, especially if it is possible to play the game repeatedly. Should Bob choose the first coin and try to find out something about its bias (this is *exploration*), or should Bob *exploit* the second coin, with known bias?

**The one-coin problem**   Suppose instead that both Bob and Alice know that Alice is using the fair coin. Alice tosses the coin and looks at the outcome. What is the probability of heads (after the coin toss) according to Bob? One argument would say that the probability is still 1/2. After all, Bob hasn't learned anything about the outcome of the coin toss, so why should he change his valuation of the probability? On the other hand, runs the counterargument, once the coin has been tossed, does it really make sense to talk about the probability of heads? The coin has either landed heads or tails, so at best, Bob can say that the probability is either 0 or 1, but he doesn't know which.

**A medical decision problem**   On a more serious note, consider a doctor who is examining a patient Eric. The doctor can see that Eric has jaundice, no temperature, and red hair. According to his medical textbook, 90 percent of people with jaundice have hepatitis and 80 percent of people with hepatitis have a temperature. This is all the information he has that is relevant to the problem. Should he proceed under the assumption that Eric has hepatitis?

There is clearly some ambiguity in the presentation of this problem (far more than, say, in the presentation of the second-ace puzzle). For example, there is no indication of what other options the doctor has. Even if this ambiguity is ignored, this problem raises a number of issues. An obvious one is how the doctor's statistical information should affect his beliefs regarding what to do. There are many others though. For example, what does it mean that the doctor has "no other relevant information"? Typically the doctor has a great deal of information, and part of the problem lies in deciding what is and is not relevant. Another issue is perhaps more pragmatic. How should the doctor's information be represented? If the doctor feels that the fact that Eric has red hair is irrelevant to the question of whether he has hepatitis, how should that be represented?

In many cases, there is no quantitative information, only qualitative information. For example, rather than knowing that 90 percent of people with jaundice have hepatitis and 80 percent of people with hepatitis have a temperature, the doctor may know only that people with jaundice typically have hepatitis, and people with hepatitis typically have a temperature. How does this affect things?

## 1.2    An Overview of the Book

I hope that the puzzles and problems of the preceding section have convinced you that reasoning about uncertainty can be subtle and that it requires a careful formal analysis.

So how do we reason about uncertainty? The first step is to appropriately *represent* the uncertainty. Perhaps the most common representation of uncertainty uses probability, but it is by no means the only one, and not necessarily always the best one. Motivated by examples like the earlier one about a coin with unknown bias, many other representations have been considered in the literature. In Chapter 2, which sets the stage for all the later material in the book, I examine a few of them. Among these are probability, of course, but also *Dempster-Shafer belief functions, possibility measures,* and *ranking functions.* I also introduce a very general representation of uncertainty called *plausibility measures;* all the other representations of uncertainty considered in this book can be viewed as special cases of plausibility measures. Plausibility measures provide a vantage point from which to understand basic features of uncertainty representation. In addition, general results regarding uncertainty can often be formulated rather elegantly in terms of plausibility measures.

An agent typically acquires new information all the time. How should the new information affect her beliefs? The standard way of incorporating new information in probability theory is by *conditioning.* This is what Bob used in the second-ace puzzle to incorporate the information he got from Alice, such as the fact that she holds an ace or that she holds the ace of hearts. This puzzle already suggests that there are subtleties involved with conditioning. Things get even more complicated if uncertainty is not represented using probability, or if the new information does not come in a nice package that allows conditioning. (Consider, e.g., information like "people with jaundice typically have hepatitis.") Chapter 3 examines conditioning in the context of probability and considers analogues of conditioning for the representations of uncertainty discussed in Chapter 2. It also considers generalizations of conditioning, such as *Jeffrey's Rule*, that apply even when the new information does not come in the form to which standard conditioning can be applied. A more careful examination of when conditioning is appropriate (and why it seems to give unreasonable answers in problems like the second-ace puzzle) is deferred to Chapter 6.

Chapter 4 considers a related topic closely related to updating: *independence*. People seem to think in terms of dependence and independence when describing the world. Thinking in terms of dependence and independence also turns out to be useful for getting a well-structured and often compact representation of uncertainty called a *Bayesian network*. While Bayesian networks have been applied mainly in the context of probability, in Chapter 4 I discuss general conditions under which they can be applied to uncertainty represented in terms of plausibility. Plausibility measures help explain what it is about a representation of uncertainty that allows it to be represented in terms of a Bayesian network.

Chapter 5 considers *expectation*, another significant notion in the context of probability. I consider what the analogue of expectation should be for various representations of uncertainty. Expectation is particularly relevant when it comes to decision making in the presence of uncertainty. The standard rule—which works under the assumption that uncertainty is represented using probability, and that the "goodness" of an outcome is represented in terms of what is called *utility*—recommends maximizing the *expected utility*. Roughly speaking, this is the utility the agent expects to get (i.e., how happy the agent expects to be) on average, given her uncertainty. This rule cannot be used if uncertainty is not represented using probability. Not surprisingly, many alternative rules have been proposed. Plausibility measures prove useful in understanding the alternatives. It turns out that all standard decision rules can be viewed as a plausibilistic generalization of expected utility maximization.

All the approaches to reasoning about uncertainty considered in Chapter 2 consider the uncertainty of a single agent, at a single point in time. Chapter 6 deals with more dynamic aspects of belief and probability; in addition, it considers interactive situations, where there are a number of agents, each reasoning about each other's uncertainty. It introduces the *multi-agent systems* framework, which provides a natural way to model time and many agents. The framework facilitates an analysis of the second-ace puzzle.

It turns out that in order to represent the puzzle formally, it is important to describe the *protocol* used by Alice. The protocol determines the set of *runs,* or possible sequences of events that might happen. The key question here is what Alice's protocol says to do after she has answered "yes" to Bob's question as to whether she has an ace. Roughly speaking, if her protocol is "if I have the ace of spades, then I will say that, otherwise I will say nothing," then 1/3 is indeed Bob's probability that Alice has both aces. This is the conditional probability of Alice having both aces given that she has the ace of spades. On the other hand, suppose that her protocol is "I will tell Bob which ace I have; if I have both, I will choose at random between the ace of hearts and the ace of spades." Then, in fact, Bob's conditional probability should not go up to 1/3 but should stay at 1/5. The different protocols determine different possible runs and so result in different probability spaces. In general, it is critical to make the protocol explicit in examples such as this one.

In Chapter 7, I consider formal logics for reasoning about uncertainty. This may seem rather late in the game, given the title of the book. However, I believe that there is no point in designing logics for reasoning about uncertainty without having a deep understanding of various representations of uncertainty and their appropriateness. The term "formal logic" as I use it here means a *syntax* or *language*—that is, a collection of well-formed formulas, together with a *semantics*—which typically consists of a class of structures, together with rules for deciding whether a given formula in the language is true or false in a world in a structure.

But not just any syntax and semantics will do. The semantics should bear a clear and natural relationship to the real-world phenomena it is trying to model, and the syntax should be well-suited to its purpose. In particular, it should be easy to render the statements one wants to express as formulas in the language. If this cannot be done, then the logic is not doing its job. Of course, "ease," "clarity," and "naturalness" are in the eye of the beholder. To complicate the matter, expressive power usually comes at a price. A more expressive logic, which can express more statements, is typically more complex than a less expressive one. This makes the task of designing a useful logic, or choosing among several preexisting candidates, far more of an art than a science, and one that requires a deep understanding of the phenomena that we are reasoning about.

In any case, in Chapter 7, I start with a review of propositional logic, then consider a number of different propositional logics for reasoning about uncertainty. The appropriate choice depends in part on the underlying method for representing uncertainty. I consider logics for each of the methods of representing uncertainty discussed in the preceding chapters.

Chapter 8 deals with *belief, defaults,* and *counterfactuals.* Default reasoning involves reasoning about statements like "birds typically fly" and "people with hepatitis typically have jaundice." Such reasoning may be *nonmonotonic:* stronger hypotheses may lead to altogether different conclusions. For example, although birds typically fly, penguins typically do not fly. Thus, if an agent learns that a particular bird is a penguin, she may want to retract her initial conclusion that it flies. Counterfactual reasoning involves reasoning about statements that may be counter to what actually occurred. Statements like "If I hadn't slept in (although I did), I wouldn't have been late for my wedding" are counterfactuals. It turns out that both defaults and counterfactuals can be understood in terms of conditional beliefs. Roughly speaking, (an agent believes that) birds typically fly if he believes that given that something is a bird, then it flies. Similarly, he believes that if he hadn't slept in, then he wouldn't have been late for his wedding if he believes that, given that he hadn't slept in, he wouldn't have been late for the wedding. The differences between counterfactuals and defaults can be captured by making slightly different assumptions about the properties of belief. Plausibility measures again turn out to play a key role in this analysis. They can be used to characterize the crucial properties needed for a representation of uncertainty to be able to represent belief appropriately.

In Chapter 9, I return to the multi-agent systems framework discussed in Chapter 6, using it as a tool for considering the problem of *belief revision* in a more qualitative setting. How should an agent revise her beliefs in the light of new information, especially when the information contradicts her old beliefs? Having a framework where time appears explicitly turns out to clarify a number of subtleties; these are addressed in some detail. Belief revision can be understood in terms of conditioning, as discussed in Chapter 3, as long as beliefs are represented using appropriate plausibility measures, along the lines discussed in Chapter 8.

Propositional logic is known to be quite weak. The logics considered in Chapters 7, 8, and 9 augment propositional logic with *modal operators* such as knowledge, belief, and probability. These logics can express statements like "Alice knows $p$," "Bob does not believe that Alice believes $p$," or "Bob ascribes probability .3 to $q$," thus providing a great deal of added expressive power. Moving to first-order logic also gives a great deal of additional expressive power, but along a different dimension. It allows reasoning about individuals and their properties. In Chapter 10 I consider *first-order modal logic,* which, as the name suggests, allows both modal reasoning and first-order reasoning. The combination of first-order and modal reasoning leads to new subtleties. For example, with first-order logics of probability, it is important to distinguish two kinds of "probabilities" that are often confounded: statistical information (such as "90 percent of birds fly") and degrees of belief (such as "My degree of belief that Tweety—a particular bird—flies is .9."). I discuss an approach for doing this.

Once these two different types of probability are distinguished, it is possible to ask what the connection between them should be. Suppose that an agent has the statistical information that 90 percent of birds fly and also knows that Tweety is a bird. What should her degree of belief be that Tweety flies? If this is all she knows about Tweety, then it seems reasonable that her degree of belief should be .9. But what if she knows that Tweety is a yellow bird? Should the fact that it is yellow affect her degree of belief that Tweety flies? What if she also knows that Tweety is a penguin, and only 5 percent of penguins fly? Then it seems more reasonable for her degree of belief to be .05 rather than .9. But how can this be justified? More generally, what is a reasonable way of computing degrees of belief when given some statistical information? In Chapter 11, I describe a general approach to this problem. The basic idea is quite simple. Given a knowledge base *KB*, consider the set of possible worlds consistent with *KB* and treat all the worlds as equally likely. The degree of belief in a fact $\phi$ is then the fraction of the worlds consistent with the *KB* in which $\phi$ is true. I examine this approach and some of its variants, showing that it has some rather attractive (and some not so attractive) properties. I also discuss one application of this approach: to default reasoning.

I have tried to write this book in as modular a fashion as possible. Figure 1.1 describes the dependencies between chapters. An arrow from one chapter to another indicates that it is necessary to read (at least part of) the first to understand (at least part of) the second. Where the dependency involves only one or two sections, I have labeled the arrows. For example, the arrow between Chapter 2 and Chapter 6 is labeled 2.2, 2.8 → 6.10. That means that the only part of Chapter 2 that is needed for Chapter 6 is Section 2.2, except that for Section 6.10, Section 2.8 is needed as well; similarly, the arrow labeled 5 → 7.8 between Chapter 5 and Chapter 7 indicates that Chapter 5 is needed for Section 7.8, but otherwise Chapter 5 is not needed for Chapter 7 at all.

In a typical thirteen-week semester at Cornell University, I cover most of the first eight chapters. In a short eight-week course in Amsterdam (meeting once a week for two hours), I covered large parts of Chapters 1, 2, 3, 6, and 7, moving quite quickly and leaving out (most of) Sections 2.2.1, 2.7, 3.2.1, 3.5–3.9, 7.7, and 7.8. It is possible to avoid logic altogether by just doing, for example, Chapters 1–6. Alternatively, a course that focuses more on logic could cover (all or part of) Chapters 1, 2, 3, 7, 8, 10, and 11.

Formal proofs of many of the statements in the text are left as exercises. In addition, there are exercises devotedx to a more detailed examination of some tangential (but still interesting!) topics. I strongly encourage the reader to read over all the exercises and attempt as many as possible. This is the best way to master the material!

Each chapter ends with a section of notes, which provides references to material and, occasionally, more details on some material not covered in the chapter. Although

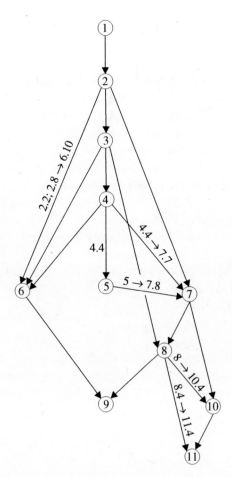

Figure 1.1   The dependence between chapters.

the bibliography is extensive, reasoning about uncertainty is a huge area. I am sure that I have (inadvertently!) left out relevant references. I apologize in advance for any such omissions. There is a detailed index and a separate glossary of symbols at the end of the book. The glossary should help the reader find where, for example, the notation $\mathcal{L}_n^K(\Phi)$ is defined. In some cases, it was not obvious (at least, to me) whether a particular notation should be listed in the index or in the glossary; it is worth checking both.

## Notes

Many books have been written recently regarding alternative approaches to reasoning about uncertainty. Shafer [1976] provides a good introduction to the Dempster -Shafer approach; Klir and Folger [1988] provide a good introduction to fuzzy logic; [Shafer and Pearl 1990] contains a good overview of a number of approaches.

There are numerous discussions of the subtleties in probabilistic reasoning. A particularly good one is given by Bar-Hillel and Falk [1982], who discuss the second-ace puzzle (and the related three-prisoners puzzle, discussed in Section 3.3). Freund [1965] and Shafer [1985] also discuss the second-ace puzzle. The Monty Hall puzzle is also an old problem [Mosteller 1965]; it has generated a great deal of discussion since it was discussed by vos Savant in *Parade Magazine* [1990]. Morgan et al. [1991] provide an interesting counterpoint to vos Savant's discussion. The two-coin problem is discussed in [Fagin and Halpern 1994]; the one-coin problem is discussed in [Halpern and Tuttle 1993]. Sutton and Barto [1998] discuss exploration vs. exploitation.

See the notes at the ends of later chapters for more references on the specific subjects discussed in these chapters.

# Chapter 2

# Representing Uncertainty

*Do not expect to arrive at certainty in every subject which you pursue. There are a hundred things wherein we mortals . . . must be content with probability, where our best light and reasoning will reach no farther.*

—Isaac Watts

How should uncertainty be represented? This has been the subject of much heated debate. For those steeped in probability, there is only one appropriate model for numeric uncertainty, and that is probability. But probability has its problems. For one thing, the numbers aren't always available. For another, the commitment to numbers means that any two events must be comparable in terms of probability: either one event is more probable than the other, or they have equal probability. It is impossible to say that two events are incomparable in likelihood. Later in this chapter, I discuss some other difficulties that probability has in representing uncertainty.

Not surprisingly, many other representations of uncertainty have been considered in the literature. I examine a number of them here, including sets of probability measures, *Dempster-Shafer belief functions, possibility measures,* and *ranking functions.* All these representations are numeric. Later in the chapter I also discuss approaches that end up placing a nonnumeric relative likelihood on events. In particular, I consider *plausibility measures,* an approach that can be viewed as generalizing all the other notions considered.

Considering so many different approaches makes it easier to illustrate the relative advantages and disadvantages of each approach. Moreover, it becomes possible to examine how various concepts relevant to likelihood play out in each of these representations. For example, each of the approaches I cover in this chapter has associated with it a notion of *updating,* which describes how a measure should be updated in the

light of additional information. In the next chapter I discuss how likelihood can be updated in each of these approaches, with an eye to understanding the commonalities (and
thus getting a better understanding of updating, independent of the representation of
uncertainty). Later chapters do the same thing for *independence* and *expectation*.

## 2.1    Possible Worlds

Most representations of uncertainty (certainly all the ones considered in this book)
start with a set of *possible worlds,* sometimes called *states* or *elementary outcomes.*
Intuitively, these are the worlds or outcomes that an agent considers possible. For
example, when tossing a die, it seems reasonable to consider six possible worlds, one for
each of the ways that the die could land. This can be represented by a set $W$ consisting
of six possible worlds, $\{w_1, \ldots, w_6\}$; the world $w_i$ is the one where the die lands $i$, for
$i = 1, \ldots, 6$. (The set $W$ is often called a *sample space* in probability texts.)

For the purposes of this book, the objects that are known (or considered likely or
possible or probable) are *events* (or *propositions*). Formally, an event or proposition
is just a set of possible worlds. For example, an event like "the die landed on an
even number" would correspond to the set $\{w_2, w_4, w_6\}$. If the agent's uncertainty
involves weather, then there might be an event like "it is sunny in San Francisco,"
which corresponds to the set of possible worlds where it is sunny in San Francisco.

The picture is that in the background there is a large set of possible worlds (all
the possible outcomes); of these, the agent considers some subset possible. The set of
worlds that an agent considers possible can be viewed as a qualitative measure of her
uncertainty. The more worlds she considers possible, the more uncertain she is as to the
true state of affairs, and the less she knows. This is a very coarse-grained representation
of uncertainty. No facilities have yet been provided for comparing the likelihood of one
world to that of another. In later sections, I consider a number of ways of doing this. Yet,
even at this level of granularity, it is possible to talk about knowledge and possibility.

Given a set $W$ of possible worlds, suppose that an agent's uncertainty is represented
by a set $W' \subseteq W$. The agent considers $U$ *possible* if $U \cap W' \neq \emptyset$; that is, if there is a
world that the agent considers possible which is in $U$. If $U$ is the event corresponding
to "it is sunny in San Francisco," then the agent considers it possible that it is sunny
in San Francisco if the agent considers at least one world possible where it is sunny in
San Francisco. An agent *knows* $U$ if $W' \subseteq U$. Roughly speaking, the agent knows $U$ if
in all worlds the agent considers possible, $U$ holds. Put another way, an agent knows
$U$ if the agent does not consider $\overline{U}$ (the complement of $U$) possible.

What an agent knows depends to some extent on how the possible worlds are chosen and the way they are represented. Choosing the appropriate set of possible worlds can sometimes be quite nontrivial. There can be a great deal of subjective judgment involved in deciding which worlds to include and which to exclude, and at what level of detail to model a world. Consider again the case of throwing a fair die. I took the set of possible worlds in that case to consist of six worlds, one for each possible way the die might have landed. Note that there are (at least) two major assumptions being made here. The first is that all that matters is how the die lands. If, for example, the moods of the gods can have a significant impact on the outcome (if the gods are in a favorable mood, then the die will never land on 1), then the gods' moods should be part of the description of a possible world. More realistically, perhaps, if it is possible that the die is not fair, then its possible bias should be part of the description of a possible world. (This becomes particularly relevant when more quantitative notions of uncertainty are considered.) There will be a possible world corresponding to each possible (bias, outcome) pair. The second assumption being made is that the only outcomes possible are $1, \ldots, 6$. While this may seem reasonable, my experience playing games involving dice with my children in their room, which has a relatively deep pile carpet, is that a die can land on its edge. Excluding this possibility from the set of possible worlds amounts to saying that this cannot happen.

Things get even more complicated when there is more than one agent in the picture. Suppose, for example, that there are two agents, Alice and Bob, who are watching a die being tossed and have different information about the outcome. Then the description of a world has to include, not just what actually happens (the die landed on 3), but what Alice considers possible and what Bob considers possible. For example, if Alice got a quick glimpse of the die and so was able to see that it had at least four dots showing, then Alice would consider the worlds $\{w_4, w_5, w_6\}$ possible. In another world, Alice might consider a different set of worlds possible. Similarly for Bob. For the next few chapters, I focus on the single-agent case. However, the case of multiple agents is discussed in depth in Chapter 6.

The choice of the set of possible worlds encodes many of the assumptions the modeler is making about the domain. It is an issue that is not one that is typically discussed in texts on probability (or other approaches to modeling uncertainty), and it deserves more care than it is usually given. Of course, there is not necessarily a single "right" set of possible worlds to use. For example, even if the modeler thinks that there is a small possibility that the coin is not fair or that it will land on its edge, it might make sense to ignore these possibilities in order to get a simpler, but still quite useful, model of the situation. In Sections 4.4 and 6.3, I give some tools that may help a modeler in deciding on an appropriate set of possible worlds in a disciplined way. But even with these tools, deciding which possible worlds to consider often remains a difficult task (which, by and large, is not really discussed any further in this book, since I have nothing to say about it beyond what I have just said).

**Important assumption**    For the most part in this book, I assume that the set $W$ of possible worlds is finite. This simplifies the exposition. Most of the results stated in the book hold with almost no change if $W$ is infinite; I try to make it clear when this is not the case.

## 2.2    Probability Measures

Perhaps the best-known approach to getting a more fine-grained representation of uncertainty is probability. Most readers have probably seen probability before, so I do not go into great detail here. However, I do try to give enough of a review of probability to make the presentation completely self-contained. Even readers familiar with this material may want to scan it briefly, just to get used to the notation.

Suppose that the agent's uncertainty is represented by the set $W = \{w_1, \ldots, w_n\}$ of possible worlds. A probability measure assigns to each of the worlds in $W$ a number—a *probability*—that can be thought of as describing the likelihood of that world being the actual world. In the die-tossing example, if each of the six outcomes is considered equally likely, then it seems reasonable to assign to each of the six worlds the same number. What number should this be?

For one thing, in practice, if a die is tossed repeatedly, each of the six outcomes occurs roughly 1/6 of the time. For another, the choice of 1/6 makes the sum 1; the reasons for this are discussed in the next paragraph. On the other hand, if the outcome of 1 seems much more likely than the others, $w_1$ might be assigned probability 1/2, and all the other outcomes probability 1/10. Again, the sum here is 1.

Assuming that each elementary outcome is given probability 1/6, what probability should be assigned to the event of the die landing either 1 or 2, that is, to the set $\{w_1, w_2\}$? It seems reasonable to take the probability to be 1/3, the sum of the probability of landing 1 and the probability of landing 2. Thus, the probability of the whole space $\{w_1, \ldots, w_6\}$ is 1, the sum of the probabilities of all the possible outcomes. In probability theory, 1 is conventionally taken to denote certainty. Since it is certain that there will be some outcome, the probability of the whole space should be 1.

In most of the examples in this book, all the subsets of a set $W$ of worlds are assigned a probability. Nevertheless, there are good reasons, both technical and philosophical, for not *requiring* that a probability measure be defined on all subsets. If $W$ is infinite, it may not be possible to assign a probability to all subsets in such a way that certain natural properties hold. (See the notes to this chapter for a few more details and references.) But even if $W$ is finite, an agent may not be prepared to assign a numerical probability to all subsets. (See Section 2.3 for some examples.) For technical reasons, it is typically assumed that the set of subsets of $W$ to which probability is assigned satisfies some closure properties. In particular, if a probability can be assigned to both $U$ and $V$, then it is useful to be able to assume that a probability can also be assigned to $U \cup V$ and to $\overline{U}$.

**Definition 2.2.1** An *algebra over* $W$ is a set $\mathcal{F}$ of subsets of $W$ that contains $W$ and is closed under union and complementation, so that if $U$ and $V$ are in $\mathcal{F}$, then so are $U \cup V$ and $\overline{U}$. A *$\sigma$-algebra* is closed under complementation and countable union, so that if $U_1, U_2, \ldots$ are all in $\mathcal{F}$, then so is $\cup_i U_i$. ∎

Note that an algebra is also closed under intersection, since $U \cap V = \overline{\overline{U} \cup \overline{V}}$. Clearly, if $W$ is finite, every algebra is a $\sigma$-algebra.

These technical conditions are fairly natural; moreover, assuming that the domain of a probability measure is a $\sigma$-algebra is sufficient to deal with some of the mathematical difficulties mentioned earlier (again, see the notes). However, it is not clear why an agent should be willing or able to assign a probability to $U \cup V$ if she can assign a probability to each of $U$ and $V$. This condition seems more reasonable if $U$ and $V$ are disjoint (which is all that is needed in many cases). Despite that, I assume that $\mathcal{F}$ is an algebra, since it makes the technical presentation simpler; see the notes at the end of the chapter for more discussion of this issue.

A *basic* subset of $\mathcal{F}$ is a minimal nonempty set in $\mathcal{F}$; that is, $U \in \mathcal{F}$ is basic if (a) $U \neq \emptyset$ and (b) $U' \subset U$ and $U' \in \mathcal{F}$ implies that $U' = \emptyset$. (Note that I use $\subseteq$ for subset and $\subset$ for strict subset; thus, if $U' \subset U$, then $U' \neq U$, while if $U' \subseteq U$, then $U'$ and $U$ may be equal.) It is not hard to show that, if $W$ is finite, then every set in $\mathcal{F}$ is the union of basic sets. This is no longer necessarily true if $W$ is infinite (Exercise 2.1(a)). A *basis* for $\mathcal{F}$ is a collection $\mathcal{F}' \subseteq \mathcal{F}$ of sets such that every set in $\mathcal{F}$ is the union of sets in $\mathcal{F}'$. If $W$ is finite, the basic sets in $\mathcal{F}$ form a basis for $\mathcal{F}$ (Exercise 2.1(b)).

The domain of a probability measure is an algebra $\mathcal{F}$ over some set $W$. By convention, the range of a probability measure is the interval $[0, 1]$. (In general, $[a, b]$ denotes the set of reals between $a$ and $b$, including both $a$ and $b$, that is, $[a, b] = \{x \in \mathbb{R} : a \leq x \leq b\}$.)

**Definition 2.2.2** A *probability space* is a tuple $(W, \mathcal{F}, \mu)$, where $\mathcal{F}$ is an algebra over $W$ and $\mu : \mathcal{F} \to [0, 1]$ satisfies the following two properties:

P1.   $\mu(W) = 1$.

P2.   $\mu(U \cup V) = \mu(U) + \mu(V)$ if $U$ and $V$ are disjoint elements of $\mathcal{F}$. ∎

The sets in $\mathcal{F}$ are called the *measurable sets*; $\mu$ is called a *probability measure on W* (or on $\mathcal{F}$, especially if $\mathcal{F} \neq 2^W$). Notice that the arguments to $\mu$ are not elements of $W$ but subsets of $W$. If the argument is a singleton subset $\{w\}$, I often abuse notation and write $\mu(w)$ rather than $\mu(\{w\})$. I occasionally omit the $\mathcal{F}$ if $\mathcal{F} = 2^W$, writing just $(W, \mu)$. These conventions are also followed for the other notions of uncertainty introduced later in this chapter.

It follows from P1 and P2 that $\mu(\emptyset) = 0$. Since $\emptyset$ and $W$ are disjoint,

$$1 = \mu(W) = \mu(W \cup \emptyset) = \mu(W) + \mu(\emptyset) = 1 + \mu(\emptyset),$$

so $\mu(\emptyset) = 0$.

Although P2 applies only to pairs of sets, an easy induction argument shows that if $U_1, \ldots, U_k$ are pairwise disjoint elements of $\mathcal{F}$, then

$$\mu(U_1 \cup \ldots \cup U_k) = \mu(U_1) + \cdots + \mu(U_k).$$

This property is known as *finite additivity*. It follows from finite additivity that if $W$ is finite and $\mathcal{F}$ consists of all subsets of $W$, then a probability measure can be characterized as a function $\mu : W \to [0, 1]$ such that $\sum_{w \in W} \mu(w) = 1$. That is, if $\mathcal{F} = 2^W$, then it suffices to define a probability measure $\mu$ only on the elements of $W$; it can then be uniquely extended to all subsets of $W$ by taking $\mu(U) = \sum_{u \in U} \mu(u)$. While the assumption that all sets are measurable is certainly an important special case (and is a standard assumption if $W$ is finite), I have taken the more traditional approach of not requiring all sets to be measurable; this allows greater flexibility.

If $W$ is infinite, it is typically required that $\mathcal{F}$ be a $\sigma$-algebra, and that $\mu$ be $\sigma$-additive or countably additive, so that if $U_1, U_2, \ldots$ are pairwise disjoint sets in $\mathcal{F}$, then $\mu(\cup_i U_i) = \mu(U_1) + \mu(U_2) + \cdots$. For future reference, note that, in the presence of finite additivity, countable additivity is equivalent to the following "continuity" property:

> If $U_i, i = 1, 2, \ldots$ is an increasing sequence of sets (i.e.,
> $U_1 \subseteq U_2 \subseteq \ldots$) in $\mathcal{F}$, then $\lim_{i \to \infty} \mu(U_i) = \mu(\cup_{i=1}^{\infty} U_i)$          (2.1)

(Exercise 2.2). This property can be expressed equivalently in terms of decreasing sequences of sets:

> If $U_i, i = 1, 2, \ldots$ is an decreasing sequence of sets (i.e.,
> $U_1 \supseteq U_2 \supseteq \ldots$) all in $\mathcal{F}$, then $\lim_{i \to \infty} \mu(U_i) = \mu(\cap_{i=1}^{\infty} U_i)$          (2.2)

(Exercise 2.2). (Readers unfamiliar with limits can just ignore these continuity properties and all the ones discussed later; they do not play a significant role in the book.)

To see that these properties do not hold for finitely additive probability, let $\mathcal{F}$
consist of all the finite and *cofinite* subsets of $\mathbb{N}$ ($\mathbb{N}$ denotes the natural numbers,
$\{0, 1, 2, \ldots\}$). A set is cofinite if it is the complement of a finite set. Thus, for example,
$\{3, 4, 6, 7, 8, \ldots\}$ is cofinite since its complement is $\{1, 2, 5\}$. Define $\mu(U)$ to be 0 if
$U$ is finite and 1 if $U$ is cofinite. It is easy to check that $\mathcal{F}$ is an algebra and that $\mu$ is a
finitely additive probability measure on $\mathcal{F}$ (Exercise 2.3). But $\mu$ clearly does not satisfy
any of the properties above. For example, if $U_n = \{0, \ldots, n\}$, then $U_n$ increases to $\mathbb{N}$,
but $\mu(U_n) = 0$ for all $n$, while $\mu(\mathbb{N}) = 1$, so $\lim_{n \to \infty} \mu(U_n) \neq \mu(\cup_{i=1}^{\infty} U_i)$.

For most of this book, I focus on finite sample spaces, so I largely ignore the issue
of whether probability is countably additive or only finitely additive.

## 2.2.1 Justifying Probability

If belief is quantified using probability, then it is important to explain what the numbers
represent, where they come from, and why finite additivity is appropriate. Without such
an explanation, it will not be clear how to assign probabilities in applications, nor how
to interpret the results obtained by using probability.

The classical approach to applying probability, which goes back to the seventeenth
and eighteenth centuries, is to reduce a situation to a number of elementary outcomes. A
natural assumption, called the *principle of indifference,* is that all elementary outcomes
are equally likely. Intuitively, in the absence of any other information, there is no reason
to consider one more likely than another. Applying the principle of indifference, if there
are $n$ elementary outcomes, the probability of each one is $1/n$; the probability of a set
of $k$ outcomes is $k/n$. Clearly this definition satisfies P1 and P2 (where $W$ consists of
all the elementary outcomes).

This is certainly the justification for ascribing to each of the six outcomes of the toss
of a die a probability of 1/6. By using powerful techniques of combinatorics together
with the principle of indifference, card players can compute the probability of getting
various kinds of hands, and then use this information to guide their play of the game.

The principle of indifference is also typically applied to handle situations with
statistical information. For example, if 40 percent of a doctor's patients are over 60,
and a nurse informs the doctor that one of his patients is waiting for him in the waiting
room, it seems reasonable for the doctor to say that the likelihood of that patient being
over 60 is .4. Essentially what is going on here is that there is one possible world (i.e.,
basic outcome) for each of the possible patients who might be in the waiting room.
If each of these worlds is equally probable, then the probability of the patient being

over 60 will indeed be .4. (I return to the principle of indifference and the relationship between statistical information and probability in Chapter 11.)

While taking possible worlds to be equally probable is a very compelling intuition, the trouble with the principle of indifference is that it is not always obvious how to reduce a situation to elementary outcomes that seem equally likely. This is a significant concern, because different choices of elementary outcomes will in general lead to different answers. For example, in computing the probability that a couple with two children has two boys, the most obvious way of applying the principle of indifference would suggest that the answer is 1/3. After all, the two children could be either (1) two boys, (2) two girls, or (3) a boy and a girl. If all these outcomes are equally likely, then the probability of having two boys is 1/3.

There is, however, another way of applying the principle of indifference, by taking the elementary outcomes to be $(B, B)$, $(B, G)$, $(G, B)$, and $(G, G)$: (1) both children are boys, (2) the first child is a boy and the second a girl, (3) the first child is a girl and the second a boy, and (4) both children are girls. Applying the principle of indifference to this description of the elementary outcomes gives a probability of 1/4 of having two boys.

The latter answer accords better with observed frequencies, and there are compelling general reasons to consider the second approach better than the first for constructing the set of possible outcomes. But in many other cases, it is far from obvious how to choose the elementary outcomes. What makes one choice right and another one wrong?

Even in cases where there seem to be some obvious choices for the elementary outcomes, it is far from clear that they should be equally likely. For example, consider a biased coin. It still seems reasonable to take the elementary outcomes to be heads and tails, just as with a fair coin, but it certainly is no longer appropriate to assign each of these outcomes probability 1/2 if the coin is biased. What are the "equally likely" outcomes in that case? Even worse difficulties arise in trying to assign a probability to the event that a particular nuclear power plant will have a meltdown. What should the set of possible events be in that case, and why should they be equally likely?

In light of these problems, philosophers and probabilists have tried to find ways of viewing probability that do not depend on assigning elementary outcomes equal likelihood. Perhaps the two most common views are that (1) the numbers represent relative frequencies, and (2) the numbers reflect subjective assessments of likelihood.

The intuition behind the relative-frequency interpretation is easy to explain. The justification usually given for saying that the probability that a coin lands heads is 1/2 is that if the coin is tossed sufficiently often, roughly half the time it will land heads. Similarly, a typical justification for saying that the probability that a coin has *bias* .6 (where the bias of a coin is the probability that it lands heads) is that it lands heads roughly 60 percent of the time when it is tossed sufficiently often.

While this interpretation seems quite natural and intuitive, and certainly has been used successfully by the insurance industry and the gambling industry to make significant amounts of money, it has its problems. The informal definition said that the probability of the coin landing heads is .6 if "roughly" 60 percent of the time it lands heads, when it is tossed "sufficiently often." But what do "roughly" and "sufficiently often" mean? It is notoriously difficult to make these notions precise. How many times must the coin be tossed for it to be tossed "sufficiently often"? Is it 100 times? 1,000 times? 1,000,000 times? And what exactly does "roughly half the time" mean? It certainly does not mean "exactly half the time." If the coin is tossed an odd number of times, it cannot land heads exactly half the time. And even if it is tossed an even number of times, it is rather unlikely that it will land heads *exactly* half of those times.

To make matters worse, to assign a probability to an event such as "the nuclear power plant will have a meltdown in the next five years," it is hard to think in terms of relative frequency. While it is easy to imagine tossing a coin repeatedly, it is somewhat harder to capture the sequence of events that lead to a nuclear meltdown and imagine them happening repeatedly.

Many attempts have been made to deal with these problems, perhaps the most successful being that of von Mises. It is beyond the scope of this book to discuss these attempts, however. The main message that the reader should derive is that, while the intuition behind relative frequency is a very powerful one (and is certainly a compelling justification for the use of probability in some cases), it is quite difficult (some would argue impossible) to extend it to all cases where probability is applied.

Despite these concerns, in many simple settings, it is straightforward to apply the relative-frequency interpretation. If $N$ is fixed and an experiment is repeated $N$ times, then the probability of an event $U$ is taken to be the fraction of the $N$ times $U$ occurred. It is easy to see that the relative-frequency interpretation of probability satisfies the additivity property P2. Moreover, it is closely related to the intuition behind the principle of indifference. In the case of a coin, roughly speaking, the possible worlds now become the outcomes of the $N$ coin tosses. If the coin is fair, then roughly half of the outcomes should be heads and half should be tails. If the coin is biased, the fraction of outcomes that are heads should reflect the bias. That is, taking the basic outcomes to be the results of tossing the coin $N$ times, the principle of indifference leads to roughly the same probability as the relative-frequency interpretation.

The relative-frequency interpretation takes probability to be an objective property of a situation. The (extreme) subjective viewpoint argues that there is no such thing as an objective notion of probability; probability is a number assigned by an individual representing his or her subjective assessment of likelihood. Any choice of numbers is all right, as long as it satisfies P1 and P2. But why should the assignment of numbers even obey P1 and P2?

There have been various attempts to argue that it should. The most famous of these arguments, due to Ramsey, is in terms of betting behavior. I discuss a variant of Ramsey's argument here. Given a set $W$ of possible worlds and a subset $U \subseteq W$, consider an agent who can evaluate bets of the form "If $U$ happens (i.e., if the actual world is in $U$) then I win $\$100(1 - \alpha)$ while if $U$ doesn't happen then I lose $\$100\alpha$," for $0 \le \alpha \le 1$. Denote such a bet as $(U, \alpha)$. The bet $(\overline{U}, 1 - \alpha)$ is called the *complementary* bet to $(U, \alpha)$; by definition, $(\overline{U}, 1 - \alpha)$ denotes the bet where the agent wins $\$100\alpha$ if $\overline{U}$ happens and loses $\$100(1 - \alpha)$ if $U$ happens.

Note that $(U, 0)$ is a "can't lose" proposition for the agent. She wins $\$100$ if $U$ is the case and loses 0 if it is not. The bet becomes less and less attractive as $\alpha$ gets larger; she wins less if $U$ is the case and loses more if it is not. The worst case is if $\alpha = 1$. $(U, 1)$ is a "can't win" proposition; she wins nothing if $U$ is true and loses $\$100$ if it is false. By way of contrast, the bet $(\overline{U}, 1 - \alpha)$ is a can't lose proposition if $\alpha = 1$ and becomes less and less attractive as $\alpha$ approaches 0.

Now suppose that the agent must choose between the complementary bets $(U, \alpha)$ and $(\overline{U}, 1 - \alpha)$. Which she prefers clearly depends on $\alpha$. Actually, I assume that the agent may have to choose, not just between individual bets, but between sets of bets. More generally, I assume that the agent has a *preference order* defined on sets of bets. "Prefers" here should be interpreted as meaning "at least as good as," not "strictly preferable to." Thus, for example, an agent prefers a set of bets to itself. I do *not* assume that all sets of bets are comparable. However, it follows from the rationality postulates that I am about to present that certain sets of bets are comparable. The postulates focus on the agent's preferences between two sets of the form $\{(U_1, \alpha_1), \ldots, (U_k, \alpha_k)\}$ and $\{(\overline{U_1}, 1 - \alpha_1), \ldots, (\overline{U_k}, 1 - \alpha_k)\}$. These are said to be *complementary sets of bets*. For singleton sets, I often omit set braces. I write $B_1 \succeq B_2$ if the agent prefers the set $B_1$ of bets to the set $B_2$, and $B_1 \succ B_2$ if $B_1 \succeq B_2$ and it is not the case that $B_2 \succeq B_1$.

Define an agent to be *rational* if she satisfies the following four properties:

RAT1. If the set $B_1$ of bets is guaranteed to give at least as much money as $B_2$, then $B_1 \succeq B_2$; if $B_1$ is guaranteed to give more money than $B_2$, then $B_1 \succ B_2$.

By "guaranteed to give at least as much money" here, I mean that no matter what happens, the agent does at least as well with $B_1$ as with $B_2$. This is perhaps best understood if $B_1$ consists of just $(U, \alpha)$ and $B_2$ consists of just $(V, \beta)$. There are then four cases to consider: the world is in $U \cap V$, $U \cap \overline{V}$, $\overline{U} \cap V$, or $\overline{U} \cap \overline{V}$. For $(U, \alpha)$ to be guaranteed to give at least as much money as $(V, \beta)$, the following three conditions must hold:

- If $U \cap V \neq \emptyset$, it must be the case that $\alpha \leq \beta$. For if $w \in U \cap V$, then in world $w$, the agent wins $100(1 - \alpha)$ with the bet $(U, \alpha)$ and wins $100(1 - \beta)$ with the bet $(V, \beta)$. Thus, for $(U, \alpha)$ to give at least as much money as $(V, \beta)$ in $w$, it must be the case that $100(1 - \alpha) \geq 100(1 - \beta)$, that is, $\alpha \leq \beta$.

- If $\overline{U} \cap V \neq \emptyset$, then $\alpha = 0$ and $\beta = 1$.

- If $\overline{U} \cap \overline{V} \neq \emptyset$, then $\alpha \leq \beta$.

Note that there is no condition corresponding to $U \cap \overline{V} \neq \emptyset$, for if $w \in U \cap \overline{V}$ then, in $w$, the agent is guaranteed not to lose with $(U, \alpha)$ and not to win with $(V, \beta)$. In any case, note that it follows from these conditions that $(U, \alpha) \succ (U, \alpha')$ if and only if $\alpha < \alpha'$. This should seem reasonable.

If $B_1$ and $B_2$ are sets of bets, then the meaning of "$B_1$ is guaranteed to give at least as much money as $B_2$" is similar in spirit. Now, for each world $w$, the sum of the payoffs of the bets in $B_1$ at $w$ must be at least as large as the sum of the payoffs of the bets in $B_2$. I leave it to the reader to define "$B_1$ is guaranteed to give more money than $B_2$."

The second rationality condition says that preferences are transitive.

RAT2. Preferences are transitive, so that if $B_1 \succeq B_2$ and $B_2 \succeq B_3$, then $B_1 \succeq B_3$.

While transitivity seems reasonable, it is worth observing that transitivity of preferences often does not seem to hold in practice.

In any case, by RAT1, $(U, \alpha) \succeq (\overline{U}, 1 - \alpha)$ if $\alpha = 0$, and $(\overline{U}, 1 - \alpha) \succeq (U, \alpha)$ if $\alpha = 1$. By RAT1 and RAT2, if $(U, \alpha) \succeq (\overline{U}, 1 - \alpha)$, then $(U, \alpha') \succ (\overline{U}, 1 - \alpha')$ for all $\alpha' < \alpha$. (It clearly follows from RAT1 and RAT2 that $(U, \alpha') \succeq (\overline{U}, 1 - \alpha')$. But if it is not the case that $(U, \alpha') \succ (\overline{U}, 1 - \alpha')$, then $(\overline{U}, 1 - \alpha') \succeq (U, \alpha')$. Now applying RAT1 and RAT2, together with the fact that $(\overline{U}, 1 - \alpha) \succeq (U, \alpha)$, yields $(\overline{U}, 1 - \alpha') \succeq (\overline{U}, 1 - \alpha)$, which contradicts RAT1.) Similarly, if $(\overline{U}, 1 - \beta) \succeq (U, \beta)$, then $(\overline{U}, 1 - \beta') \succ (U, \beta')$ for all $\beta' > \beta$.

The third assumption says that the agent can always compare complementary bets.

RAT3. Either $(U, \alpha) \succeq (\overline{U}, 1 - \alpha)$ or $(\overline{U}, 1 - \alpha) \succeq (U, \alpha)$.

Since "$\succeq$" means "considers at least as good as," it is possible that both $(U, \alpha) \succeq (\overline{U}, 1 - \alpha)$ and $(\overline{U}, 1 - \alpha) \succeq (U, \alpha)$ hold. Note that I do not presume that all sets of bets are comparable. RAT3 says only that complementary bets are comparable. While RAT3 is not unreasonable, it is certainly not vacuous. One could instead imagine an agent who had numbers $\alpha_1 < \alpha_2$ such that $(U, \alpha) \succeq (\overline{U}, 1 - \alpha)$ for $\alpha < \alpha_1$ and $(\overline{U}, 1 - \alpha) \succeq (U, \alpha)$ for $\alpha > \alpha_2$, but in the interval between $\alpha_1$ and $\alpha_2$, the agent wasn't sure which of the complementary bets was preferable. (Note that "incomparable" here does not mean "equivalent.") This certainly doesn't seem so irrational.

The fourth and last rationality condition says that preferences are determined point-wise.

> RAT4. If $(U_i, \alpha_i) \succeq (V_i, \beta_i)$ for $i = 1, \ldots, k$, then $\{(U_1, \alpha_1), \ldots, (U_k, \alpha_k)\} \succeq$
> $\{(V_1, \beta_1), \ldots, (V_k, \beta_k)\}$.

While RAT4 may seem reasonable, again there are subtleties. For example, compare the bets $(W, 1)$ and $(U, .01)$, where $U$ is, intuitively, an unlikely event. The bet $(W, 1)$ is the "break-even" bet: the agent wins 0 if $W$ happens (which will always be the case) and loses \$100 if $\emptyset$ happens (i.e., if $w \in \emptyset$). The bet $(U, .01)$ can be viewed as a lottery: if $U$ happens (which is very unlikely), the agent wins \$99, while if $U$ does not happen, then the agent loses \$1. The agent might reasonably decide that she is willing to pay \$1 for a small chance to win \$99. That is, $(U, .01) \succeq (W, 1)$. On the other hand, consider the collection $B_1$ consisting of 1,000,000 copies of $(W, 1)$ compared to the collection $B_2$ consisting of 1,000,000 copies of $(U, .01)$. According to RAT4, $B_2 \succeq B_1$. But the agent might not feel that she can afford to pay \$1,000,000 for a small chance to win \$99,000,000.

These rationality postulates make it possible to associate with each set $U$ a number $\alpha_U$, which intuitively represents the probability of $U$. It follows from RAT1 that $(U, 0) \succeq (\overline{U}, 1)$. As observed earlier, $(U, \alpha)$ gets less attractive as $\alpha$ gets larger, and $(\overline{U}, 1 - \alpha)$ gets more attractive as $\alpha$ gets larger. Since, by RAT1, $(\overline{U}, 0) \succeq (U, 1)$, it easily follows that there is there is some point $\alpha^*$ at which, roughly speaking, $(U, \alpha^*)$ and $(\overline{U}, 1 - \alpha^*)$ are in balance. I take $\alpha_U$ to be $\alpha^*$.

I need a few more definitions to make this precise. Given a set $X$ of real numbers, let sup $X$, the *supremum* (or just *sup*) of $X$, be the *least upper bound of X*—the smallest real number that is at least as large as all the elements in $X$. That is, sup $X = \alpha$ if $x \leq \alpha$ for all $x \in X$ and if, for all $\alpha' < \alpha$, there is some $x \in X$ such that $x > \alpha'$. For example, if $X = \{1/2, 3/4, 7/8, 15/16, \ldots\}$, then sup $X = 1$. Similarly, inf $X$, the *infimum* (or just *inf*) of $X$, is the greatest lower bound of $X$—the largest real number that is less than or equal to every element in $X$. The sup of a set may be $\infty$; for example, the sup of $\{1, 2, 3, \ldots\}$ is $\infty$. Similarly, the inf of a set may be $-\infty$. However, if $X$ is bounded (as will be the case for all the sets to which sup and inf are applied in this book), then sup $X$ and inf $X$ are both finite.

Let $\alpha_U = \sup\{\beta : (U, \beta) \succeq (\overline{U}, 1 - \beta)\}$. It is not hard to show that if an agent satisfies RAT1–3, then $(U, \alpha) \succeq (\overline{U}, 1 - \alpha)$ for all $\alpha < \alpha_U$ and $(\overline{U}, 1 - \alpha) \succeq (U, \alpha)$ for all $\alpha > \alpha_U$ (Exercise 2.5). It is not clear what happens at $\alpha_U$; the agent's preferences could go either way. (Actually, with one more natural assumption, the agent is indifferent between $(U, \alpha_U)$ and $(\overline{U}, 1 - \alpha_U)$; see Exercise 2.6.)

Intuitively, $\alpha_U$ is a measure of the likelihood (according to the agent) of $U$. The more likely she thinks $U$ is, the higher $\alpha_U$ should be. If she thinks that $U$ is certainly the case (i.e., if she is certain that the actual world is in $U$), then $\alpha_U$ should be 1. That is, if she feels that $U$ is certain, then for any $\alpha > 0$, it should be the case that $(U, \alpha) \succeq (\overline{U}, 1 - \alpha)$, since she feels that with $(U, \alpha)$ she is guaranteed to win $\$100(1 - \alpha)$, while with $(\overline{U}, 1 - \alpha)$ she is guaranteed to lose the same amount.

Similarly, if she is certain that $U$ is not the case, then $\alpha_U$ should be 0. More significantly, it can be shown that if $U_1$ and $U_2$ are disjoint sets, then a rational agent should take $\alpha_{U_1 \cup U_2} = \alpha_{U_1} + \alpha_{U_2}$. More precisely, as is shown in Exercise 2.5, if $\alpha_{U_1 \cup U_2} \neq \alpha_{U_1} + \alpha_{U_2}$, then there is a set $B_1$ of bets such that the agent prefers $B_1$ to the complementary set $B_2$, yet the agent is guaranteed to lose money with $B_1$ and guaranteed to win money with $B_2$, thus contradicting RAT1. (In the literature, such a collection $B_1$ is called a *Dutch book*. Of course, this is not a literary book, but a book as in "bookie" or "bookmaker.") It follows from all this that if $\mu(U)$ is defined as $\alpha_U$, then $\mu$ is a probability measure.

This discussion is summarized by the following theorem:

**Theorem 2.2.3**   *If an agent satisfies RAT1–4, then for each subset $U$ of $W$, a number $\alpha_U$ exists such that $(U, \alpha) \succeq (\overline{U}, 1 - \alpha)$ for all $\alpha < \alpha_U$ and $(\overline{U}, 1 - \alpha) \succeq (U, \alpha)$ for all $\alpha > \alpha_U$. Moreover, the function defined by $\mu(U) = \alpha_U$ is a probability measure.*

**Proof**   See Exercise 2.5.   ∎

Theorem 2.2.3 has been viewed as a compelling argument that if an agent's preferences can be expressed numerically, then they should obey the rules of probability. However, Theorem 2.2.3 depends critically on the assumptions RAT1–4. The degree to which the argument is compelling depends largely on how reasonable these assumptions of rationality seem. That, of course, is in the eye of the beholder.

It might also seem worrisome that the subjective probability interpretation puts no constraints on the agent's subjective likelihood other than the requirement that it obey the laws of probability. In the case of tossing a fair die, for example, taking each outcome to be equally likely seems "right." It may seem unreasonable for someone who subscribes to the subjective point of view to be able to put probability .8 on the die landing 1, and probability .04 on each of the other five possible outcomes. More generally, when it seems that the principle of indifference is applicable or if detailed frequency information is available, should the subjective probability take this into account? The standard responses to this concern are (1) indeed frequency information and the principle of indifference should be taken into account, when appropriate, and (2) even if they are not taken into account, all choices of initial subjective probability will eventually converge to the same probability measure as more information is received; the measure that they converge to will in some sense be the "right" one (see Example 3.2.2).

Different readers will probably have different feelings as to how compelling these and other defenses of probability really are. However, the fact that philosophers have come up with a number of independent justifications for probability is certainly a strong point in its favor. Much more effort has gone into justifying probability than any other approach for representing uncertainty. Time will tell if equally compelling justifications can be given for other approaches. In any case, there is no question that probability is currently the most widely accepted and widely used approach to representing uncertainty.

## 2.3    Lower and Upper Probabilities

Despite its widespread acceptance, there are some problems in using probability to represent uncertainty. Three of the most serious are (1) probability is not good at representing ignorance, (2) while an agent may be prepared to assign probabilities to some sets, she may not be prepared to assign probabilities to all sets, and (3) while an agent may be willing in principle to assign probabilities to all the sets in some algebra, computing these probabilities requires some computational effort; she may simply not have the computational resources required to do it. These criticisms turn out to be closely related to one of the criticisms of the Dutch book justification for probability mentioned in Section 2.2.1. The following two examples might help clarify the issues.

**Example 2.3.1**    Suppose that a coin is tossed once. There are two possible worlds, *heads* and *tails*, corresponding to the two possible outcomes. If the coin is known to be fair, it seems reasonable to assign probability 1/2 to each of these worlds. However, suppose that the coin has an unknown bias. How should this be represented? One approach might be to continue to take heads and tails as the elementary outcomes and, applying the principle of indifference, assign them both probability 1/2, just as in the case of a fair coin. However, there seems to be a significant qualitative difference between a fair coin and a coin of unknown bias. Is there some way that this difference can be captured? One possibility is to take the bias of the coin to be part of the possible world (i.e., a basic outcome would now describe both the bias of the coin and the outcome of the toss), but then what is the probability of *heads*?  ∎

**Example 2.3.2**   Suppose that a bag contains 100 marbles; 30 are known to be red, and the remainder are known to be either blue or yellow, although the exact proportion of blue and yellow is not known. What is the likelihood that a marble taken out of the bag is yellow? This can be modeled with three possible worlds, *red*, *blue*, and *yellow*, one for each of the possible outcomes. It seems reasonable to assign probability .3 to the outcome to choosing a red marble, and thus probability .7 to choosing either blue or yellow, but what probability should be assigned to the other two outcomes?  ∎

Empirically, it is clear that people do *not* use probability to represent the uncertainty in examples such as Example 2.3.2. For example, consider the following three bets. In each case a marble is chosen from the bag.

- $B_r$ pays \$1 if the marble is red, and 0 otherwise;

- $B_b$ pays \$1 if the marble is blue, and 0 otherwise;

- $B_y$ pays \$1 if the marble is yellow, and 0 otherwise.

People invariably prefer $B_r$ to both $B_b$ and $B_y$, and they are indifferent between $B_b$ and $B_y$. The fact that they are indifferent between $B_b$ ad $B_y$ suggests that they view it equally likely that the marble chosen is blue and that it is yellow. This seems reasonable; the problem statement provides no reason to prefer blue to yellow, or vice versa. However, if blue and yellow are equally probable, then the probability of drawing a blue marble and that of drawing a yellow marble are both .35, which suggests that $B_y$ and $B_b$ should both be preferred to $B_r$. Moreover, any way of ascribing probability to blue and yellow either makes choosing a blue marble more likely than choosing a red marble, or makes choosing a yellow marble more likely than choosing a red marble (or both). This suggests that at least one of $B_b$ and $B_y$ should be preferred to $B_r$, which is simply not what the experimental evidence shows.

There are a number of ways of representing the uncertainty in these examples. As suggested in Example 2.3.1, it is possible to make the uncertainty about the bias of the coin part of the possible world. A possible world would then be a pair $(a, X)$, where $a \in [0, 1]$ and $X \in \{H, T\}$. Thus, for example, $(1/3, H)$ is the world where the coin has bias 1/3 and lands heads. (Recall that the bias of a coin is the probability that it lands heads.) The problem with this approach (besides the fact that there are an uncountable number of worlds, although that is not a serious problem) is that it is not clear how to put a probability measure on the whole space, since there is no probability given on the coin having, say, bias in [1/3, 2/3]. The space can be partitioned into subspaces $W_a$, $a \in [0, 1]$, where $W_a$ consists of the two worlds $(a, H)$ and $(a, T)$. In $W_a$, there is an obvious probability $\mu_a$ on $W_a$: $\mu_a(a, H) = a$ and $\mu_a(a, T) = 1 - a$. This just says that in a world in $W_a$ (where the bias of the coin is $a$), the probability of heads is $a$ and the probability of tails is $1 - a$. For example, in the world $(1/3, H)$, the probability measure is taken to be on just $(1/3, H)$ and $(1/3, T)$; all the other worlds are ignored. The probability of heads is taken to be $1/3$ at $(1/3, H)$. This is just the probability of $(1/3, H)$, since $(1/3, H)$ is the intersection of the event "the coin lands heads" (i.e., all worlds of the form $(a, H)$) with $W_{1/3}$.

This is an instance of an approach that will be examined in more detail in Sections 3.4 and 6.9. Rather than there being a global probability on the whole space, the space $W$ is partitioned into subsets $W_i$, $i \in I$. (In this case, $I = [0, 1]$.) On each subset $W_i$, there is a separate probability measure $\mu_i$ that is used for the worlds in that subset. The probability of an event $U$ at a world in $W_i$ is $\mu_i(W_i \cap U)$.

For Example 2.3.2, the worlds would have the form $(n, X)$, where $X \in \{red, blue, yellow\}$ and $n \in \{0, \ldots, 70\}$. (Think of $n$ as representing the number of blue marbles.) In the subset $W_n = \{(n, red), (n, blue), (n, yellow)\}$, the world $(n, red)$ has probability .3, $(n, blue)$ has probability $n/100$, and $(n, yellow)$ has probability $(70 - n)/100$. Thus, the probability of *red* is *known* to be .3; this is a fact true at every world (even though a different probability measure may be used at different worlds). Similarly, the probability of *blue* is known to be between 0 and .7, as is the probability of *yellow*. The probability of *blue* may be .3, but this is not known.

An advantage of this approach is that it allows a smooth transition to the purely probabilistic case. Suppose, for example, that a probability on the number of blue marbles is given. That amounts to putting a probability on the sets $W_n$, since $W_n$ corresponds to the event that there are $n$ blue marbles. If the probability of $W_n$ is, say, $b_n$, where $\sum_{n=0}^{70} b_n = 1$, then the probability of $(n, blue) = b_n \times (n/70)$. In this way, a probability $\mu$ on the whole space $W$ can be defined. The original probability $\mu_n$ on $W_n$ is the result of conditioning $\mu$ on $W_n$. (I am assuming that readers are familiar with conditional probability; it is discussed in much more detail in Chapter 3.)

This approach turns out to be quite fruitful. However, for now, I focus on two other approaches that do not involve extending the set of possible worlds. The first approach, which has been thoroughly studied in the literature, is quite natural. The idea is to simply represent uncertainty using not just one probability measure, but a set of them. For example, in the case of the coin with unknown bias, the uncertainty can be represented using the set $\mathcal{P}_1 = \{\mu_a : a \in [0, 1]\}$ of probability measures, where $\mu_a$ gives *heads* probability $a$. Similarly, in the case of the marbles, the uncertainty can be represented using the set $\mathcal{P}_2 = \{\mu'_a : a \in [0, .7]\}$, where $\mu'_a$ gives *red* probability .3, *blue* probability $a$, and *yellow* probability $.7 - a$. (I could restrict $a$ to having the form $n/100$, for $n \in \{0, \ldots, 70\}$, but it turns out to be a little more convenient in the later discussion not to make this restriction.)

A set $\mathcal{P}$ of probability measures, all defined on a set $W$, can be represented as a single space $\mathcal{P} \times W$. This space can be partitioned into subspaces $W_\mu$, for $\mu \in \mathcal{P}$, where $W_\mu = \{(\mu, w) : w \in W\}$. On the subspace $W_\mu$, the probability measure $\mu$ is used. This, of course, is an instance of the first approach discussed in this section. The first approach is actually somewhat more general. Here I am assuming that the space has the form $A \times B$, where the elements of $A$ define the partition, so that there is a probability $\mu_a$ on $\{a\} \times B$ for each $a \in A$. This type of space arises in many applications (see Section 3.4).

The last approach I consider in this section is to make only some sets measurable. Intuitively, the measurable sets are the ones to which a probability can be assigned. For example, in the case of the coin, the algebra might consist only of the empty set and $\{heads, tails\}$, so that $\{heads\}$ and $\{tails\}$ are no longer measurable sets. Clearly, there is only one probability measure on this space; for future reference, call it $\mu_1$. By considering this trivial algebra, there is no need to assign a probability to $\{heads\}$ or $\{tails\}$.

Similarly, in the case of the marbles, consider the algebra

$$\{\emptyset, \{red\}, \{blue, yellow\}, \{red, yellow, blue\}\}.$$

There is an obvious probability measure $\mu_2$ on this algebra that describes the story in Example 2.3.2: simply take $\mu_2(red) = .3$. That determines all the other probabilities.

Notice that, with the first approach, in the case of the marbles, the probability of *red* is .3 (since all probability measures $\mathcal{P}_2$ give *red* probability .3), but all that can be said about the probability of *blue* is that it is somewhere between 0 and .7 (since that is the range of possible probabilities for *blue* according to the probability measures in $\mathcal{P}_2$), and similarly for *yellow*. There is a sense in which the second approach also gives this answer: any probability for *blue* between 0 and .7 is compatible with the probability measure $\mu_2$. Similarly, in the case of the coin with an unknown bias, all that can be said about the probability of *heads* is that it is somewhere between 0 and 1.

Recasting these examples in terms of the Dutch book argument, the fact that, for example, all that can be said about the probability of the marble being blue is that it is between 0 and .7 corresponds to the agent definitely preferring $(\overline{blue}, 1 - \alpha)$ to $(blue, \alpha)$ for $\alpha > .7$, but not being able to choose between the two bets for $0 \leq \alpha \leq .7$. In fact, the Dutch book justification for probability given in Theorem 2.2.3 can be recast to provide a justification for using sets of probabilities. Interestingly, with sets of probabilities, RAT3 no longer holds. The agent may not always be able to decide which of $(U, \alpha)$ and $(\overline{U}, 1 - \alpha)$ she prefers.

Given a set $\mathcal{P}$ of probability measures, all defined on an algebra $\mathcal{F}$ over a set $W$, and $U \in \mathcal{F}$, define

$$\mathcal{P}_*(U) = \inf\{\mu(U) : \mu \in \mathcal{P}\}, \text{ and}$$
$$\mathcal{P}^*(U) = \sup\{\mu(U) : \mu \in \mathcal{P}\}.$$

$\mathcal{P}_*(U)$ is called the *lower probability* of $U$, and $\mathcal{P}^*(U)$ is called the *upper probability* of $U$. For example, $(\mathcal{P}_2)_*(blue) = 0$, $(\mathcal{P}_2)^*(blue) = .7$, and similarly for *yellow*, while $(\mathcal{P}_2)_*(red) = (\mathcal{P}_2)^*(red) = .3$.

Now consider the approach of taking only some subsets to be measurable. An algebra $\mathcal{F}$ is a *subalgebra* of an algebra $\mathcal{F}'$ if $\mathcal{F} \subseteq \mathcal{F}'$. If $\mathcal{F}$ is a subalgebra of $\mathcal{F}'$, $\mu$ is a probability measure on $\mathcal{F}$, and $\mu'$ is a probability measure on $\mathcal{F}'$, then $\mu'$ is an *extension* of $\mu$ if $\mu$ and $\mu'$ agree on all sets in $\mathcal{F}$. Notice that $\mathcal{P}_1$ consists of all the extensions of $\mu_1$ to the algebra consisting of all subsets of $\{heads, tails\}$ and $\mathcal{P}_2$ consists of all extensions of $\mu_2$ to the algebra of all subsets of $\{red, blue, yellow\}$.

If $\mu$ is a probability measure on the subalgebra $\mathcal{F}$ and $U \in \mathcal{F}' - \mathcal{F}$, then $\mu(U)$ is undefined, since $U$ is not in the domain of $\mu$. There are two standard ways of extending $\mu$ to $\mathcal{F}'$, by defining functions $\mu_*$ and $\mu^*$, traditionally called the *inner measure* and *outer measure induced by* $\mu$, respectively. For $U \in \mathcal{F}'$, define

$$\mu_*(U) = \sup\{\mu(V) : V \subseteq U, V \in \mathcal{F}\}, \text{ and}$$
$$\mu^*(U) = \inf\{\mu(V) : V \supseteq U, V \in \mathcal{F}\}.$$

These definitions are perhaps best understood in the case where the set of possible worlds (and hence the algebra $\mathcal{F}$) is finite. In that case, $\mu_*(U)$ is the measure of the largest measurable set (in $\mathcal{F}$) contained in $U$, and $\mu^*(U)$ is the measure of the smallest measurable set containing $U$. That is, $\mu_*(U) = \mu(V_1)$, where $V_1 = \cup\{B \in \mathcal{F}' : B \subseteq U\}$ and $\mu^*(U) = \mu(V_2)$, where $V_2 = \cap\{B \in \mathcal{F}' : U \subseteq B\}$ (Exercise 2.7). Intuitively, $\mu_*(U)$ is the best approximation to the actual probability of $U$ from below and $\mu^*(U)$ is the best approximation from above. If $U \in \mathcal{F}$, then it is easy to see that $\mu_*(U) = \mu^*(U) = \mu(U)$. If $U \in \mathcal{F}' - \mathcal{F}$ then, in general, $\mu_*(U) < \mu^*(U)$. For example, $(\mu_2)_*(blue) = 0$ and $(\mu_2)^*(blue) = .7$, since the largest measurable set contained in $\{blue\}$ is the empty set, while the smallest measurable set containing *blue* is $\{blue, yellow\}$. Similarly, $(\mu_2)_*(red) = (\mu_2)^*(red) = \mu_2(red) = .3$. These are precisely the same numbers obtained using the lower and upper probabilities $(\mathcal{P}_2)_*$ and $(\mathcal{P}_2)^*$. Of course, this is no accident.

**Theorem 2.3.3**  *Let $\mu$ be a probability measure on a subalgebra $\mathcal{F} \subseteq \mathcal{F}'$ and let $\mathcal{P}_\mu$ consist of all extensions of $\mu$ to $\mathcal{F}'$. Then $\mu_*(U) = (\mathcal{P}_\mu)_*(U)$ and $\mu^*(U) = (\mathcal{P}_\mu)^*(U)$ for all $U \in \mathcal{F}'$.*

**Proof**  See Exercise 2.8. Note that, as the discussion in Exercise 2.8 and the notes to this chapter show, in general, the probability measures in $\mathcal{P}_\mu$ are only finitely additive. The result is not true in general for countably additive probability measures. A variant of this result does hold even for countably additive measures; see the notes for details.

∎

Note that whereas probability measures are additive, so that if $U$ and $V$ are disjoint sets then $\mu(U \cup V) = \mu(U) + \mu(V)$, inner measures are *superadditive* and outer measures are *subadditive*, so that for disjoint sets $U$ and $V$,

$$\mu_*(U \cup V) \geq \mu_*(U) + \mu_*(V), \text{ and}$$
$$\mu^*(U \cup V) \leq \mu^*(U) + \mu^*(V). \tag{2.3}$$

In addition, the relationship between inner and outer measures is defined by

$$\mu_*(U) = 1 - \mu^*(\overline{U}) \tag{2.4}$$

(Exercise 2.9).

The inequalities in (2.3) are special cases of more general inequalities satisfied by inner and outer measures. These more general inequalities are best understood in terms of the *inclusion-exclusion* rule for probability, which describes how to compute the probability of the union of (not necessarily disjoint) sets. In the case of two sets, the rule says

$$\mu(U \cup V) = \mu(U) + \mu(V) - \mu(U \cap V). \tag{2.5}$$

To see this, note that $U \cup V$ can be written as the union of three disjoint sets, $U - V$, $V - U$, and $U \cap V$. Thus,

$$\mu(U \cup V) = \mu(U - V) + \mu(V - U) + \mu(U \cap V).$$

Since $U$ is the union of $U - V$ and $U \cap V$, and $V$ is the union of $V - U$ and $U \cap V$, it follows that

$$\mu(U) = \mu(U - V) + \mu(U \cap V) \text{ and}$$
$$\mu(V) = \mu(V - U) + \mu(U \cap V).$$

Now (2.5) easily follows by simple algebra.

In the case of three sets $U_1$, $U_2$, $U_3$, similar arguments show that

$$\mu(U_1 \cup U_2 \cup U_3) = \mu(U_1) + \mu(U_2) + \mu(U_3) - \mu(U_1 \cap U_2)$$
$$- \mu(U_1 \cap U_3) - \mu(U_2 \cap U_3) + \mu(U_1 \cap U_2 \cap U_3). \tag{2.6}$$

That is, the probability of the union of $U_1$, $U_2$, and $U_3$ can be determined by adding the probability of the individual sets (these are one-way intersections), subtracting the probability of the two-way intersections, and adding the probability of the three-way intersections.

The full-blown inclusion-exclusion rule is

$$\mu(\cup_{i=1}^{n} U_i) = \sum_{i=1}^{n} \sum_{\{I \subseteq \{1,\dots,n\}:|I|=i\}} (-1)^{i+1} \mu(\cap_{j \in I} U_j). \tag{2.7}$$

Equation (2.7) says that the probability of the union of $n$ sets is obtained by adding the probability of the one-way intersections (the case when $|I| = 1$), subtracting the probability of the two-way intersections (the case when $|I| = 2$), adding the probability of the three-way intersections, and so on. The $(-1)^{i+1}$ term causes the alternation from addition to subtraction and back again as the size of the intersection set increases. Equations (2.5) and (2.6) are just special cases of the general rule when $n = 2$ and $n = 3$. I leave it to the reader to verify the general rule (Exercise 2.10).

For inner measures, there is also an inclusion-exclusion rule, except that $=$ is replaced by $\geq$. Thus,

$$\mu_*(\cup_{i=1}^{n} U_i) \geq \sum_{i=1}^{n} \sum_{\{I \subseteq \{1,\dots,n\}:|I|=i\}} (-1)^{i+1} \mu_*(\cap_{j \in I} U_j) \tag{2.8}$$

(Exercise 2.12). For outer measures, there is a dual property that holds, which results from (2.8) by (1) switching the roles of intersection and union and (2) replacing $\geq$ by $\leq$. That is,

$$\mu^*(\cap_{i=1}^{n} U_i) \geq \sum_{i=1}^{n} \sum_{\{I \subseteq \{1,\dots,n\}:|I|=i\}} (-1)^{i+1} \mu^*(\cup_{j \in I} U_j) \tag{2.9}$$

(Exercise 2.13). Theorem 7.4.1 in Section 7.4 shows that there is a sense in which these inequalities characterize inner and outer measures.

Theorem 2.3.3 shows that for every probability measure $\mu$ on an algebra $\mathcal{F}$, there exists a set $\mathcal{P}$ of probability measures defined on $2^W$ such that $\mu_* = \mathcal{P}_*$. Thus, inner measure can be viewed as a special case of lower probability. The converse of Theorem 2.3.3 does not hold; not every lower probability is the inner measure that arises from a measure defined on a subalgebra of $2^W$. One way of seeing that lower probabilities are more general is by considering the properties that they satisfy.

It is easy to see that lower and upper probabilities satisfy analogues of (2.3) and (2.4) (with $\mu_*$ and $\mu^*$ replaced by $\mathcal{P}_*$ and $\mathcal{P}^*$, respectively). If $U$ and $V$ are disjoint, then

$$\mathcal{P}_*(U \cup V) \geq \mathcal{P}_*(U) + \mathcal{P}_*(V),$$
$$\mathcal{P}^*(U \cup V) \leq \mathcal{P}^*(U) + \mathcal{P}^*(V), \tag{2.10}$$

and

$$\mathcal{P}_*(U) = 1 - \mathcal{P}^*(\overline{U}). \tag{2.11}$$

However, they do not satisfy the analogues of (2.8) and (2.9) in general (Exercise 2.14). Note that if $\mathcal{P}_*$ does not satisfy the analogue of (2.8), then it cannot be the case that $\mathcal{P}_* = \mu_*$ for some probability measure $\mu$, since all inner measures do satisfy (2.12).

While (2.10) and (2.11) hold for all lower and upper probabilities, these properties do not completely characterize them. For example, the following property holds for lower probabilities and upper probabilities if $U$ and $V$ are disjoint:

$$\mathcal{P}_*(U \cup V) \leq \mathcal{P}_*(U) + \mathcal{P}^*(V) \leq \mathcal{P}^*(U \cup V); \tag{2.12}$$

moreover, this property does not follow from (2.10) and (2.11) (Exercise 2.15). However, even adding (2.12) to (2.10) and (2.11) does not provide a complete characterization of upper and lower probabilities. The property needed is rather complex. Stating it requires one more definition: A set $\mathcal{U}$ of subsets of $W$ *covers a subset $U$ of $W$ exactly $k$ times* if every element of $U$ is in exactly $k$ sets in $\mathcal{U}$. Consider the following property:

If $\mathcal{U} = \{U_1, \ldots, U_k\}$ covers $U$ exactly $m + n$ times and covers $\overline{U}$ exactly
$m$ times, then $\sum_{i=1}^{k} \mathcal{P}_*(U_i) \leq m + n\mathcal{P}_*(U)$. $\tag{2.13}$

It is not hard to show that lower probabilities satisfy (2.13) and that (2.10) and (2.12) follow from (2.13) and (2.11) (Exercise 2.16). Indeed, in a precise sense (discussed in Exercise 2.16), (2.13) completely characterizes lower probabilities (and hence, together with (2.11), upper probabilities as well), at least if all the probability measures are only finitely additive.

If all the probability measures in $\mathcal{P}$ are countably additive and are defined on a $\sigma$-algebra $\mathcal{F}$, then $\mathcal{P}_*$ has one additional continuity property analogous to (2.2):

If $U_1, U_2, U_3, \ldots$ is a decreasing sequence of sets in $\mathcal{F}$, then
$\lim_{i \to \infty} \mathcal{P}_*(U_i) = \mathcal{P}_*(\cap_{i=1}^{\infty} U_i)$ $\tag{2.14}$

(Exercise 2.18(a)). The analogue of (2.1) does *not* hold for lower probability. For example, suppose that $\mathcal{P} = \{\mu_0, \mu_1, \ldots\}$, where $\mu_n$ is the probability measure on $\mathbb{N}$ such that $\mu_n(n) = 1$. Clearly $\mathcal{P}_*(U) = 0$ if $U$ is a strict subset of $\mathbb{N}$, and $\mathcal{P}_*(\mathbb{N}) = 1$. Let $U_n = \{1, \ldots, n\}$. Then $U_n$ is an increasing sequence and $\bigcup_{i=1}^{\infty} U_i = \mathbb{N}$, but $\lim_{i \to \infty} \mathcal{P}_*(U_i) = 0 \neq \mathcal{P}_*(\mathbb{N}) = 1$. On the other hand, the analogue of (2.1) does hold for upper probability, while the analogue of (2.2) does not (Exercise 2.18(b)).

Although I have been focusing on lower and upper probability, it is important to stress that sets of probability measures contain more information than is captured by their lower and upper probability, as the following example shows:

**Example 2.3.4**   Consider two variants of the example with marbles. In the first, all that is know is that there are at most 50 yellow marbles and at most 50 blue marbles in a bag of 100 marbles; no information at all is given about the number of red marbles. In the second case, it is known that there are exactly as many blue marbles as yellow marbles. The first situation can be captured by the set $\mathcal{P}_3 = \{\mu : \mu(blue) \leq .5, \mu(yellow) \leq .5\}$. The second situation can be captured by the set $\mathcal{P}_4 = \{\mu : \mu(b) = \mu(y)\}$. These sets of measures are obviously quite different; in fact $\mathcal{P}_4 \subset \mathcal{P}_3$. However, it is easy to see that $(\mathcal{P}_3)_* = (\mathcal{P}_4)_*$ and, hence, that $\mathcal{P}_3^* = \mathcal{P}_4^*$ (Exercise 2.19). Thus, the fact that blue and yellow have equal probability in every measure in $\mathcal{P}_4$ has been lost. I return to this issue in Section 2.8.   ∎

## 2.4   Dempster-Shafer Belief Functions

The Dempster-Shafer theory of evidence, originally introduced by Arthur Dempster and then developed by Glenn Shafer, provides another approach to attaching likelihood to events. This approach starts out with a *belief function* (sometimes called a *support function*). Given a set $W$ of possible worlds and $U \subseteq W$, the belief in $U$, denoted $\text{Bel}(U)$, is a number in the interval $[0, 1]$. (Think of Bel as being defined on the algebra $2^W$ consisting of all subsets of $W$. The definition can easily be generalized so that the domain of Bel is an arbitrary algebra over $W$, although this is typically not done in the literature.) A belief function Bel defined on a space $W$ must satisfy the following three properties:

B1.    $\text{Bel}(\emptyset) = 0$.

B2.    $\text{Bel}(W) = 1$.

B3.    $\text{Bel}(\bigcup_{i=1}^{n} U_i) \geq \sum_{i=1}^{n} \sum_{\{I \subseteq \{1, \ldots, n\} : |I| = i\}} (-1)^{i+1} \text{Bel}(\bigcap_{j \in I} U_j)$,
       for $n = 1, 2, 3, \ldots$.

If $W$ is infinite, Bel is sometimes assumed to satisfy the continuity property that results by replacing $\mu$ in (2.2) by Bel:

If $U_1, U_2, U_3, \ldots$ is a decreasing sequence of subsets of $W$, then
$$\lim_{i \to \infty} \text{Bel}(U_i) = \text{Bel}(\cap_{i=1}^{\infty} U_i). \tag{2.15}$$

The reason that the analogue of (2.2) is considered rather than (2.1) should shortly become clear. In any case, like countable additivity, this is a property that is not always required.

B1 and B2 just say that, like probability measures, belief functions follow the convention of using 0 and 1 to denote the minimum and maximum likelihood. B3 is just the inclusion-exclusion rule with = replaced by $\geq$. Thus, every probability measure defined on $2^W$ is a belief function. Moreover, from the results of the previous section, it follows that every inner measure is a belief function as well. The converse does not hold; that is, not every belief function is an inner measure corresponding to some probability measure. For example, if $W = \{w, w'\}$, $\text{Bel}(w) = 1/2$, $\text{Bel}(w') = 0$, $\text{Bel}(W) = 1$, and $\text{Bel}(\emptyset) = 0$, then Bel is a belief function, but there is no probability measure $\mu$ on $W$ such that $\text{Bel} = \mu_*$ (Exercise 2.20). On the other hand, Exercise 7.11 shows that there is a sense in which every belief function can be identified with the inner measure corresponding to some probability measure.

A probability measure defined on $2^W$ can be characterized by its behavior on singleton sets. This is not the case for belief functions. For example, it is easy to construct two belief functions $\text{Bel}_1$ and $\text{Bel}_2$ on $\{1, 2, 3\}$ such that $\text{Bel}_1(i) = \text{Bel}_2(i) = 0$ for $i = 1, 2, 3$ (so that $\text{Bel}_1$ and $\text{Bel}_2$ agree on singleton sets) but $\text{Bel}_1(\{1, 2\}) \neq \text{Bel}_2(\{1, 2\})$ (Exercise 2.21). Thus, a belief function cannot be viewed as a function on $W$; its domain must be viewed as being $2^W$ (or some algebra over $W$). (The same is also true for $\mathcal{P}^*$ and $\mathcal{P}_*$. It is easy to see this directly; it also follows from Theorem 2.4.1, which says that every belief function is $\mathcal{P}_*$ for some set $\mathcal{P}$ of probability measures.)

Just like an inner measure, $\text{Bel}(U)$ can be viewed as providing a lower bound on the likelihood of $U$. Define $\text{Plaus}(U) = 1 - \text{Bel}(\overline{U})$. Plaus is a *plausibility function*; $\text{Plaus}(U)$ is the *plausibility* of $U$. A plausibility function bears the same relationship to a belief function that an outer measure bears to an inner measure. Indeed, every outer measure is a plausibility function. It follows easily from B3 (applied to $U$ and $\overline{U}$, with $n = 2$) that $\text{Bel}(U) \leq \text{Plaus}(U)$ (Exercise 2.22). For an event $U$, the interval $[\text{Bel}(U), \text{Plaus}(U)]$ can be viewed as describing the range of possible values of the likelihood of $U$. Moreover, plausibility functions satisfy the analogue of (2.9):

$$\text{Plaus}(\cap_{i=1}^{n} U_i) \geq \sum_{i=1}^{n} \sum_{\{I \subseteq \{1,\ldots,n\} : |I| = i\}} (-1)^{i+1} \text{Plaus}(\cup_{j \in I} U_j) \qquad (2.16)$$

(Exercise 2.13). Indeed, plausibility measures are characterized by the properties $\text{Plaus}(\emptyset) = 0$, $\text{Plaus}(W) = 1$, and (2.16).

These observations show that there is a close relationship among belief functions, inner measures, and lower probabilities. Part of this relationship is made precise by the following theorem:

**Theorem 2.4.1** *Given a belief function* Bel *defined on a space* $W$, *let* $\mathcal{P}_{\text{Bel}} = \{\mu : \mu(U) \geq \text{Bel}(U) \text{ for all } U \subseteq W\}$. *Then* $\text{Bel} = (\mathcal{P}_{\text{Bel}})_*$ *and* $\text{Plaus} = (\mathcal{P}_{\text{Bel}})^*$.

**Proof**   See Exercise 2.23. ∎

Theorem 2.4.1 shows that every belief function on $W$ can be viewed as a lower probability of a set of probability measures on $W$. That is why (2.15) seems to be the appropriate continuity property for belief functions, rather than the analogue of (2.1).

The converse of Theorem 2.4.1 does not hold. It follows from Exercise 2.14 that lower probabilities do not necessarily satisfy the analogue of (2.8), and thus there is a space $W$ and a set $\mathcal{P}$ of probability measures on $W$ such that no belief function Bel on $W$ with $\text{Bel} = \mathcal{P}_*$ exists. For future reference, it is also worth noting that, in general, there may be sets $\mathcal{P}$ other than $\mathcal{P}_{\text{Bel}}$ such that $\text{Bel} = \mathcal{P}_*$ and $\text{Plaus} = \mathcal{P}^*$ (Exercise 2.24).

In any case, while belief functions can be understood (to some extent) in terms of lower probability, this is not the only way of understanding them. Belief functions are part of a theory of *evidence*. Intuitively, evidence supports events to varying degrees. For example, in the case of the marbles, the information that there are exactly 30 red marbles provides support in degree .3 for *red*; the information that there are 70 yellow and blue marbles does not provide any positive support for either *blue* or *yellow*, but does provide support .7 for {*blue, yellow*}. In general, evidence provides some degree of support (possibly 0) for each subset of $W$. The total amount of support is 1. The belief that $U$ holds, $\text{Bel}(U)$, is then the sum of all of the support on subsets of $U$.

Formally, this is captured as follows. A *mass function* (sometimes called a *basic probability assignment*) on $W$ is a function $m : 2^W \rightarrow [0, 1]$ satisfying the following properties:

M1.    $m(\emptyset) = 0$.

M2.    $\sum_{U \subseteq W} m(U) = 1$.

Intuitively, $m(U)$ describes the extent to which the evidence supports $U$. This is perhaps best understood in terms of making observations. Suppose that an observation $U$ is accurate, in that if $U$ is observed, the actual world is in $U$. Then $m(U)$ can be viewed as the probability of observing $U$. Clearly it is impossible to observe $\emptyset$ (since the actual world cannot be in $\emptyset$), so $m(\emptyset) = 0$. Thus, M1 holds. On the other hand, since *something* must be observed, M2 must hold.

Given a mass function $m$, define the belief function based on $m$, $\mathrm{Bel}_m$, by taking

$$\mathrm{Bel}_m(U) = \sum_{\{U':U'\subseteq U\}} m(U'). \tag{2.17}$$

Intuitively, $\mathrm{Bel}_m(U)$ is the sum of the probabilities of the evidence or observations that guarantee that the actual world is in $U$. The corresponding plausibility function $\mathrm{Plaus}_m$ is defined as

$$\mathrm{Plaus}_m(U) = \sum_{\{U':U'\cap U\neq\emptyset\}} m(U').$$

(If $U = \emptyset$, the sum on the right-hand side of the equality has no terms; by convention, it is taken to be 0.) $\mathrm{Plaus}_m(U)$ can be thought of as the sum of the probabilities of the evidence that is compatible with the actual world being in $U$.

**Example 2.4.2**  Suppose that $W = \{w_1, w_2, w_3\}$. Define $m$ as follows:

- $m(w_1) = 1/4$;

- $m(\{w_1, w_2\}) = 1/4$;

- $m(\{w_2, w_3\}) = 1/2$;

- $m(U) = 0$ if $U$ is not one of $\{w_1\}$, $\{w_1, w_2\}$, or $\{w_1, w_3\}$.

Then it is easy to check that

$\mathrm{Bel}_m(w_1) = 1/4$; $\qquad$ $\mathrm{Bel}_m(w_2) = \mathrm{Bel}_m(w_3) = 0$;
$\mathrm{Bel}_m(\{w_1, w_2\}) = 1/2$; $\qquad$ $\mathrm{Bel}_m(\{w_2, w_3\}) = 1/2$; $\qquad$ $\mathrm{Bel}_m(\{w_1, w_3\}) = 1/4$;
$\mathrm{Bel}_m(\{w_1, w_2, w_3\}) = 1$;
$\mathrm{Plaus}_m(w_1) = 1/2$; $\qquad$ $\mathrm{Plaus}_m(w_2) = 3/4$; $\qquad$ $\mathrm{Plaus}_m(w_3) = 1/2$;
$\mathrm{Plaus}_m(\{w_1, w_2\}) = 1$; $\qquad$ $\mathrm{Plaus}_m(\{w_2, w_3\}) = 3/4$; $\qquad$ $\mathrm{Plaus}_m(\{w_1, w_3\}) = 1$;
$\mathrm{Plaus}_m(\{w_1, w_2, w_3\}) = 1$. $\blacksquare$

Although I have called $\mathrm{Bel}_m$ a belief function, it is not so clear that it is. While it is obvious that $\mathrm{Bel}_m$ satisfies B1 and B2, it must be checked that it satisfies B3. The following theorem confirms that $\text{Bel}_m$ is indeed a belief function. It shows much more though: it shows that every belief function is $\text{Bel}_m$ for some mass function $m$. Thus, there is a one-to-one correspondence between belief functions and mass functions.

**Theorem 2.4.3**    *Given a mass function $m$ on a finite set $W$, the function $\text{Bel}_m$ is a belief function and $\text{Plaus}_m$ is the corresponding plausibility function. Moreover, given a belief function $\text{Bel}$ on $W$, there is a unique mass function $m$ on $W$ such that $\text{Bel} = \text{Bel}_m$.*

**Proof**    See Exercise 2.25.    ∎

$\text{Bel}_m$ and its corresponding plausibility function $\text{Plaus}_m$ are the belief function and plausibility function *corresponding to* the mass function $m$.

Theorem 2.4.3 is one of the few results in this book that depends on the set $W$ being finite. While it is still true that to every mass function there corresponds a belief function even if $W$ is infinite, there are belief functions in the infinite case that have no corresponding mass functions (Exercise 2.26).

Since a probability measure $\mu$ on $2^W$ is a belief function, it too can be characterized in terms of a mass function. It is not hard to show that if $\mu$ is a probability measure on $2^W$, so that every set is measurable, the mass function $m_\mu$ corresponding to $\mu$ gives positive mass only to singletons and, in fact, $m_\mu(w) = \mu(w)$ for all $w \in W$. Conversely, if $m$ is a mass function that gives positive mass only to singletons, then the belief function corresponding to $m$ is in fact a probability measure on $\mathcal{F}$ (Exercise 2.27).

Example 2.3.2 can be captured using the function $m$ such that $m(red) = .3$, $m(blue) = m(yellow) = m(\{red, blue, yellow\}) = 0$, and $m(\{blue, yellow\}) = .7$. In this case, $m$ looks like a probability measure, since the sets that get positive mass are disjoint, and the masses sum to 1. However, in general, the sets of positive mass may not be disjoint. It is perhaps best to think of $m(U)$ as the amount of belief committed to $U$ that has not already been committed to its subsets. The following example should help make this clear:

**Example 2.4.4**    Suppose that a physician sees a case of jaundice. He considers four possible hypotheses regarding its cause: hepatitis (*hep*), cirrhosis (*cirr*), gallstone (*gall*), and pancreatic cancer (*pan*). For simplicity, suppose that these are the only causes of jaundice, and that a patient with jaundice suffers from exactly one of these problems. Thus, the physician can take the set $W$ of possible worlds to be $\{hep, cirr, gall, pan\}$. Only some subsets of $2^W$ are of diagnostic significance. There are tests whose outcomes support each of the individual hypotheses, and tests that support *intrahepatic cholestasis*, $\{hep, cirr\}$, and *extrahepatic cholestasis*, $\{gall, pan\}$; the latter two tests do not provide further support for the individual hypotheses.

If there is no information supporting any of the hypotheses, this would be represented by a mass function that assigns mass 1 to $W$ and mass 0 to all other subsets of
$W$. On the other hand, suppose there is evidence that supports intrahepatic cholestasis to degree .7. (The degree to which evidence supports a subset of $W$ can be given
both a relative frequency and a subjective interpretation. Under the relative frequency
interpretation, it could be the case that 70 percent of the time that the test had this outcome, a patient had hepatitis or cirrhosis.) This can be represented by a mass function
that assigns .7 to {*hep, cirr*} and the remaining .3 to $W$. The fact that the test provides
support only .7 to {*hep, cirr*} does not mean that it provides support .3 for its complement, {*gall, pan*}. Rather, the remaining .3 is viewed as uncommitted. As a result,
Bel({*hep, cirr*}) $= .7$ and Plaus({*hep, cirr*}) $= 1$.  ∎

Suppose that a doctor performs two tests on a patient, each of which provides some
degree of support for a particular hypothesis. Clearly the doctor would like some way of
combining the evidence given by these two tests; the Dempster-Shafer theory provides
one way of doing this.

Let $Bel_1$ and $Bel_2$ denote two belief functions on some set $W$, and let $m_1$ and $m_2$
be their respective mass functions. *Dempster's Rule of Combination* provides a way
of constructing a new mass function $m_1 \oplus m_2$, provided that there are at least two sets
$U_1$ and $U_2$ such that $U_1 \cap U_2 \neq \emptyset$ and $m_1(U_1)m_2(U_2) > 0$. If there are no such sets $U_1$
and $U_2$, then $m_1 \oplus m_2$ is undefined. Notice that, in this case, there must be disjoint
sets $V_1$ and $V_2$ such that $Bel_1(V_1) = Bel_2(V_2) = 1$ (Exercise 2.28). Thus, $Bel_1$ and $Bel_2$
describe diametrically opposed beliefs, so it should come as no surprise that they cannot
be combined.

The intuition behind the Rule of Combination is not that hard to explain. Suppose
that an agent obtains evidence from two sources, one characterized by $m_1$ and the other
by $m_2$. An observation $U_1$ from the first source and an observation $U_2$ from the second
source can be viewed as together providing evidence for $U_1 \cap U_2$. Roughly speaking
then, the evidence for a set $U_3$ should consist of the all the ways of observing sets
$U_1$ from the first source and $U_2$ from the second source such that $U_1 \cap U_2 = U_3$. If the
two sources are independent (a notion discussed in greater detail in Chapter 4), then the
likelihood of observing both $U_1$ and $U_2$ is the product of the likelihood of observing each
one, namely, $m_1(U_1)m_2(U_2)$. This suggests that the mass of $U_3$ according to $m_1 \oplus m_2$
should be $\sum_{\{U_1, U_2: U_1 \cap U_2 = U_3\}} m_1(U_1)m_2(U_2)$. This is almost the case. The problem is
that it is possible that $U_1 \cap U_2 = \emptyset$. This counts as support for the true world being
in the empty set, which is, of course, impossible. Such a pair of observations should
be ignored. Thus, $m_3(U)$ is the sum of $m_1(U_1)m_2(U_2)$ for all pairs $(U_1, U_2)$ such
that $U_1 \cap U_2 \neq \emptyset$, conditioned on not observing pairs whose intersection is empty.

(Conditioning is discussed in Chapter 3. I assume here that the reader has a basic understanding of how conditioning works, although it is not critical for understanding the Rule of Combination.)

Formally, define $(m_1 \oplus m_2)(\emptyset) = 0$ and for $U \neq \emptyset$, define

$$(m_1 \oplus m_2)(U) = \sum_{\{U_1, U_2 : U_1 \cap U_2 = U\}} m_1(U_1) m_2(U_2)/c,$$

where $c = \sum_{\{U_1, U_2 : U_1 \cap U_2 \neq \emptyset\}} m_1(U_1) m_2(U_2)$. Note that $c$ is can be thought of as the probability of observing a pair $(U_1, U_2)$ such that $U_1 \cap U_2 \neq \emptyset$. If $m_1 \oplus m_2$ is defined, then $c > 0$, since there are sets $U_1, U_2$ such that $U_1 \cap U_2 \neq \emptyset$ and $m_1(U_1) m_2(U_2) > 0$. Conversely, if $c > 0$, then it is almost immediate that $m_1 \oplus m_2$ is defined and is a mass function (Exercise 2.29). Let $\text{Bel}_1 \oplus \text{Bel}_2$ be the belief function corresponding to $m_1 \oplus m_2$.

It is perhaps easiest to understand how $\text{Bel}_1 \oplus \text{Bel}_2$ works in the case that $\text{Bel}_1$ and $\text{Bel}_2$ are actually probability measures $\mu_1$ and $\mu_2$, and all sets are measurable. In that case, $\text{Bel}_1 \oplus \text{Bel}_2$ is a probability measure, where the probability of a world $w$ is the product of its probability according to $\text{Bel}_1$ and $\text{Bel}_2$, appropriately normalized so that the sum is 1. To see this, recall that the corresponding mass functions $m_1$ and $m_2$ assign positive mass only to singleton sets and $m_i(w) = \mu_i(w)$ for $i = 1, 2$. Since $m_i(U) = 0$ if $U$ is not a singleton for $i = 1, 2$, it follows easily that $(m_1 \oplus m_2)(U) = 0$ if $U$ is not a singleton, and $(m_1 \oplus m_2)(w) = \mu_1(w)\mu_2(w)/c$, where $c = \sum_{w \in W} \mu_1(w)\mu_2(w)$. Since $m_1 \oplus m_2$ assigns positive mass only to singletons, the belief function corresponding to $m_1 \oplus m_2$ is a probability measure. Moreover, it is immediate that $(\mu_1 \oplus \mu_2)(U) = \sum_{w \in U} \mu_1(w)\mu_2(w)/c$.

It has been argued that the Dempster rule of combination is appropriate when combining two *independent* pieces of evidence. Independence is viewed as an intuitive, primitive notion here. Essentially, it says the sources of the evidence are unrelated. (See Section 4.1 for more discussion of this issue.) The rule has the attractive feature of being commutative and associative:

$$m_1 \oplus m_2 = m_2 \oplus m_1, \text{ and}$$
$$m_1 \oplus (m_2 \oplus m_3) = (m_1 \oplus m_2) \oplus m_3.$$

This seems reasonable. Final beliefs should be independent of the order and the way in which the evidence is combined. Let $m_{vac}$ be the *vacuous mass function* on $W : m_{vac}(W) = 1$ and $m(U) = 0$ for $U \subset W$. It is easy to check that $m_{vac}$ is the neutral element in the space of mass functions on $W$; that is, $m_{vac} \oplus m = m \oplus m_{vac} = m$ for every mass function $m$ (Exercise 2.30).

Rather than going through a formal derivation of the Rule of Combination, I consider two examples of its use here, where it gives intuitively reasonable results. In Section 3.2, I relate it to the probabilistic combination of evidence.

**Example 2.4.5**   Returning to the medical situation in Example 2.4.4, suppose that two tests are carried out. The first confirms hepatitis to degree .8 and says nothing about the other hypotheses; this is captured by the mass function $m_1$ such that $m_1(hep) = .8$ and $m_1(W) = .2$. The second test confirms intrahepatic cholestasis to degree .6; it is captured by the mass function $m_2$ such that $m_2(\{hep, cirr\}) = .6$ and $m_2(W) = .4$. A straightforward computation shows that

$$(m_1 \oplus m_2)(hep) = .8,$$
$$(m_1 \oplus m_2)(\{hep, cirr\}) = .12,$$
$$(m_1 \oplus m_2)(W) = .08. \quad \blacksquare$$

**Example 2.4.6**   Suppose that Alice has a coin and she knows that it either has bias 2/3 ($BH$) or bias 1/3 ($BT$). Initially, she has no evidence for $BH$ or $BT$. This is captured by the vacuous belief function $\mathrm{Bel}_{init}$, where $\mathrm{Bel}_{init}(BH) = \mathrm{Bel}_{init}(BT) = 0$ and $\mathrm{Bel}_{init}(W) = 1$. Suppose that Alice then tosses the coin and observes that it lands heads. This should give her some positive evidence for $BH$ but no evidence for $BT$. One way to capture this evidence is by using the belief function $\mathrm{Bel}_{heads}$ such that $\mathrm{Bel}_{heads}(BH) = \alpha > 0$ and $\mathrm{Bel}_{heads}(BT) = 0$. (The exact choice of $\alpha$ does not matter.) The corresponding mass function $m_{heads}$ is such that $m_{heads}(BT) = 0$, $m_{heads}(BH) = \alpha$, and $m_{heads}(W) = 1 - \alpha$. Mass and belief functions $m_{tails}$ and $\mathrm{Bel}_{tails}$ that capture the evidence of tossing the coin and seeing tails can be similarly defined. Note that $m_{init} \oplus m_{heads} = m_{heads}$, and similarly for $m_{tails}$. Combining Alice's initial ignorance regarding $BH$ and $BT$ with the evidence results in the same beliefs as those produced by just the evidence itself.

Now what happens if Alice observes $k$ heads in a row? Intuitively, this should increase her degree of belief that the coin is biased toward heads. Let $m^k_{heads} = m_{heads} \oplus \cdots \oplus m_{heads}$ ($k$ times). A straightforward computation shows that $m^k_{heads}(BT) = 0$, $m^k_{heads}(BH) = 1 - (1 - \alpha)^k$, and $m^k_{heads}(W) = (1 - \alpha)^k$. Observing heads more and more often drives Alice's belief that the coin is biased toward heads to 1.

Another straightforward computation shows that

$$m_{heads} \oplus m_{tails}(BH) = m_{heads} \oplus m_{tails}(BT) = \alpha(1 - \alpha)/(1 - \alpha^2).$$

Thus, as would be expected, after seeing heads and then tails (or, since $\oplus$ is commutative, after seeing tails and then heads), Alice assigns an equal degree of belief to $BH$

and $BT$. However, unlike the initial situation where Alice assigned no belief to either $BH$ or $BT$, she now assigns positive belief to each of them, since she has seen some evidence in favor of each.  ∎

## 2.5   Possibility Measures

*Possibility measures* are yet another approach to assigning numbers to sets. They are based on ideas of *fuzzy logic*. Suppose for simplicity that $W$, the set of worlds, is finite and that all sets are measurable. A *possibility measure* Poss associates with each subset of $W$ a number in $[0, 1]$ and satisfies the following three properties:

Poss1.  $\text{Poss}(\emptyset) = 0$.

Poss2.  $\text{Poss}(W) = 1$.

Poss3.  $\text{Poss}(U \cup V) = \max(\text{Poss}(U), \text{Poss}(V))$ if $U$ and $V$ are disjoint.

The only difference between probability and possibility is that if $A$ and $B$ are disjoint sets, then $\text{Poss}(U \cup V)$ is the maximum of $\text{Poss}(U)$ and $\text{Poss}(V)$, while $\mu(U \cup V)$ is the sum of $\mu(U)$ and $\mu(V)$. It is easy to see that Poss3 holds even if $U$ and $V$ are not disjoint (Exercise 2.31). By way of contrast, P2 does not hold if $U$ and $V$ are not disjoint.

It follows that, like probability, if $W$ is finite and all sets are measurable, then a possibility measure can be characterized by its behavior on singleton sets; $\text{Poss}(U) = \max_{u \in U} \text{Poss}(u)$. For Poss2 to be true, it must be the case that $\max_{w \in W} \text{Poss}(w) = 1$; that is, at least one element in $W$ must have maximum possibility.

Also like probability, without further assumptions, a possibility measure cannot be characterized by its behavior on singletons if $W$ is infinite. Moreover, in infinite spaces, Poss1–3 can hold without there being any world $w \in W$ with $\text{Poss}(w) = 1$, as the following example shows:

**Example 2.5.1**   Consider the possibility measure $\text{Poss}_0$ on $\mathbb{N}$ such that $\text{Poss}_0(U) = 0$ if $U$ is finite, and $\text{Poss}(U) = 1$ if $U$ is infinite. It is easy to check that $\text{Poss}_0$ satisfies Poss1–3, even though $\text{Poss}_0(n) = 0$ for all $n \in \mathbb{N}$ (Exercise 2.32(a)).  ∎

Poss3 is the analogue of finite additivity. The analogue of countable additivity is

Poss3′.  $\text{Poss}(\cup_{i=1}^{\infty} U_i) = \sup_{i=1}^{\infty} \text{Poss}(U_i)$ if $U_1, U_2, \ldots$ are pairwise disjoint sets.

It is easy to see that $\text{Poss}_0$ does not satisfy Poss3′ (Exercise 2.32(b)). Indeed, if $W$ is countable and Poss satisfies Poss1 and Poss3′, then it is immediate that $\text{Poss}(W) = 1 =$

$\sup_{w \in W}$ Poss($w$). Thus, there must be worlds in $W$ with possibility arbitrarily close to 1. However, there may be no world in $W$ with possibility 1.

**Example 2.5.2** If $\text{Poss}_1$ is defined on $\mathbb{N}$ by taking $\text{Poss}_1(U) = \sup_{n \in U}(1 - 1/n)$, then it satisfies Poss1, Poss2, and Poss3', although clearly there is no element $w \in W$ such that $\text{Poss}(w) = 1$ (Exercise 2.32(c)). ∎

If $W$ is uncountable, then even if Poss satisfies Poss1, Poss2, and Poss3', it is consistent that all worlds in $W$ have possibility 0. Moreover, Poss1, Poss2, and Poss3' do not suffice to ensure that the behavior of a possibility measure on singletons determines its behavior on all sets.

**Example 2.5.3** Let $\text{Poss}_2$ be the variant of $\text{Poss}_0$ defined on $\mathbb{R}$ by taking $\text{Poss}_2(U) = 0$ if $U$ is countable and $\text{Poss}_2(U) = 1$ if $U$ is uncountable. Then $\text{Poss}_2$ satisfies Poss1, Poss2, and Poss3', even though $\text{Poss}_2(w) = 0$ for all $w \in W$ (Exercise 2.32(d)). Now let $\text{Poss}_3$ be defined on $\mathbb{R}$ by taking

$$\text{Poss}_3(U) = \begin{cases} 0 & \text{if } U \text{ is countable,} \\ 1/2 & \text{if } U \text{ is uncountable but } U \cap [1/2, 1] \text{ is countable,} \\ 1 & \text{if } U \cap [1/2, 1] \text{ is uncountable.} \end{cases}$$

Then $\text{Poss}_3$ is a possibility measure that satisfies Poss1, Poss2, and Poss3' (Exercise 2.32(e)). Clearly $\text{Poss}_2$ and $\text{Poss}_3$ agree on all singletons ($\text{Poss}_2(w) = \text{Poss}_3(w) = 0$ for all $w \in \mathbb{R}$), but $\text{Poss}_2([0, 1/2]) = 1$ while $\text{Poss}_3([0, 1/2]) = 1/2$, so $\text{Poss}_2 \neq \text{Poss}_3$. ∎

To ensure that a possibility measure is determined by its behavior on singletons, Poss3' is typically strengthened further so that it applies to arbitrary collections of sets, not just to countable collections:

Poss3$^+$. For all index sets $I$, if the sets $U_i$, $i \in I$, are pairwise disjoint, then $\text{Poss}(\cup_{i \in I} U_i) = \sup_{i \in I} \text{Poss}(U_i)$.

Poss1 and Poss3$^+$ together clearly imply that there must be elements in $W$ of possibility arbitrarily close to 1, no matter what the cardinality of $W$. Moreover, since every set is the union of its elements, a possibility measure that satisfies Poss3$^+$ is characterized by its behavior on singletons; that is, if two possibility measures satisfying Poss3$^+$ agree on singletons, then they must agree on all sets.

Both Poss3' and Poss3$^+$ are equivalent to continuity properties in the presence of Poss3. See Exercise 2.33 for more discussion of these properties.

It can be shown that a possibility measure is a plausibility function, since it must satisfy (2.16) (Exercise 2.34). The dual of possibility, called *necessity*, is defined in the obvious way:

$$\mathrm{Nec}(U) = 1 - \mathrm{Poss}(\overline{U}).$$

Of course, since Poss is a plausibility function, it must be the case that Nec is the corresponding belief function. Thus, $\mathrm{Nec}(U) \leq \mathrm{Poss}(U)$. It is also straightforward to show this directly from Poss1–3 (Exercise 2.35).

There is an elegant characterization of possibility measures in terms of mass functions, at least in finite spaces. Define a mass function $m$ to be *consonant* if it assigns positive mass only to an increasing sequence of sets. More precisely, $m$ is a consonant mass function if $m(U) > 0$ and $m(U') > 0$ implies that either $U \subseteq U'$ or $U' \subseteq U$. The following theorem shows that possibility measures are the plausibility functions that correspond to a consonant mass function:

**Theorem 2.5.4**  *If $m$ is a consonant mass function on a finite space $W$, then $\mathrm{Plaus}_m$, the plausibility function corresponding to $m$, is a possibility measure. Conversely, given a possibility measure Poss on $W$, there is a consonant mass function $m$ such that Poss is the plausibility function corresponding to $m$.*

**Proof**   See Exercise 2.36.   ∎

Theorem 2.5.4, like Theorem 2.4.3, depends on $W$ being finite. If $W$ is infinite, it is still true that if $m$ is a consonant mass function on $W$, then $\mathrm{Plaus}_m$ is a possibility measure (Exercise 2.36). However, there are possibility measures on infinite spaces that, when viewed as plausibility functions, do not correspond to a mass function at all, let alone a consonant mass function (Exercise 2.37).

Although possibility measures can be understood in terms of the Dempster-Shafer approach, this is perhaps not the best way of thinking about them. Why restrict to belief functions that have consonant mass functions, for example? Many other interpretations of possibility measures have been provided, for example, in terms of degree of surprise (see the next section) and betting behavior. Perhaps the most common interpretation given to possibility and necessity is that they capture, not a degree of likelihood, but a (subjective) degree of uncertainty regarding the truth of a statement. This is viewed as being particularly appropriate for vague statements such as "John is tall." Two issues must be considered when deciding on the degree of uncertainty appropriate for such a statement. First, there might be uncertainty about John's actual height. But even if an agent knows that John is 1.78 meters (about 5 foot 10 inches) tall, he might still be uncertain about the truth of the statement "John is tall." To what extent should 1.78 meters count as tall? Putting the two sources of uncertainty together, the agent might decide that he believes the statement to be true to degree at least .3 and at most .7. In this case, the agent can take the necessity of the statement to be .3 and its possibility to be .7.

Possibility measures have an important computational advantage over probability: they are compositional. If $\mu$ is a probability measure, given $\mu(U)$ and $\mu(V)$, all that can be said is that $\mu(U \cup V)$ is at least $\max(\mu(U), \mu(V))$ and at most $\min(\mu(U) + \mu(V), 1)$. These, in fact, are the best bounds for $\mu(U \cup V)$ in terms of $\mu(U)$ and $\mu(V)$ (Exercise 2.38). On the other hand, as Exercise 2.31 shows, Poss($U \cup V$) is determined by Poss($U$) and Poss($V$): it is just the maximum of the two.

Of course, the question remains as to why max is the appropriate operation for ascribing uncertainty to the union of two sets. There have been various justifications given for taking max, but a discussion of this issue is beyond the scope of this book.

## 2.6   Ranking Functions

Another approach to representing uncertainty, somewhat similar in spirit to possibility measures, is given by what are called *(ordinal) ranking functions*. I consider a slightly simplified version here. A ranking function $\kappa$ again assigns to every set a number, but this time the number is a natural number or infinity; that is, $\kappa : 2^W \rightarrow \mathbb{N}^*$, where $\mathbb{N}^* = \mathbb{N} \cup \{\infty\}$. The numbers can be thought of as denoting degrees of surprise; that is, $\kappa(U)$ is the degree of surprise the agent would feel if the actual world were in $U$. The higher the number, the greater the degree of surprise. 0 denotes "unsurprising," 1 denotes "somewhat surprising," 2 denotes "quite surprising," and so on; $\infty$ denotes "so surprising as to be impossible." For example, the uncertainty corresponding to tossing a coin with bias 1/3 can be captured by a ranking function such as $\kappa(heads) = \kappa(tails) = 0$ and $\kappa(edge) = 3$, where *edge* is the event that the coin lands on edge.

Given this intuition, it should not be surprising that ranking functions are required to satisfy the following three properties:

Rk1.   $\kappa(\emptyset) = \infty$.

Rk2.   $\kappa(W) = 0$.

Rk3.   $\kappa(U \cup V) = \min(\kappa(U), \kappa(V))$ if $U$ and $V$ are disjoint.

(Again, Rk3 holds even if $U$ and $V$ are not disjoint; see Exercise 2.31.) Thus, with ranking functions, $\infty$ and 0 play the role played by 0 and 1 in probability and possibility, and min plays the role of $+$ in probability and max in possibility.

As with probability and possibility, a ranking function is characterized by its behavior on singletons in finite spaces; $\kappa(U) = \min_{u \in U} \kappa(u)$. To ensure that Rk2 holds, it must be the case that $\min_{w \in W} \kappa(w) = 0$; that is, at least one element in $W$ must have a rank of 0. And again, if $W$ is infinite, this is no longer necessarily true. For example, if $W = \mathbb{N}$, a ranking function that gives rank 0 to all infinite sets and rank $\infty$ to all finite sets satisfies Rk1–3.

To ensure that the behavior of rank is determined by singletons even in infinite sets, Rk3 is typically strengthened in a way analogous to Poss3$^+$:

Rk3$^+$. For all index sets $I$, if the sets $U_i$, $i \in I$, are pairwise disjoint, then $\kappa(\cup_{i \in I} U_i) = \min\{\kappa(U_i) : i \in I\}$.

In infinite domains, it may also be reasonable to allow ranks that are infinite ordinals, not just natural numbers or $\infty$. (The *ordinal* numbers go beyond the natural numbers and deal with different types of infinity.) However, I do not pursue this issue.

Ranking functions as defined here can in fact be viewed as possibility measures in a straightforward way. Given a ranking function $\kappa$, define the possibility measure Poss$_\kappa$ by taking Poss$_\kappa(U) = 1/(1 + \kappa(U))$. (Poss$_\kappa(U) = 0$ if $\kappa(U) = \infty$.) It is easy to see that Poss$_\kappa$ is indeed a possibility measure (Exercise 2.39). This suggests that possibility measures can be given a degree-of-surprise interpretation similar in spirit to that given to ranking functions, except that the degrees of surprise now range over $[0, 1]$, not the natural numbers.

Ranking functions can also be viewed as providing a way of doing order-of-magnitude probabilistic reasoning. Given a finite set $W$ of possible worlds, choose $\epsilon$ so that $\epsilon$ is significantly smaller than 1. (I am keeping the meaning of "significantly smaller" deliberately vague for now.) Sets $U$ such that $\kappa(U) = k$ can be thought of as having probability roughly $\epsilon^k$—more precisely, of having probability $\alpha \epsilon^k$ for some positive $\alpha$ that is significantly smaller than $1/\epsilon$ (so that $\alpha \epsilon^k$ is significantly smaller than $\epsilon^{k-1}$). With this interpretation, the assumptions that $\kappa(W) = 0$ and $\kappa(U \cup U') = \min(\kappa(U), \kappa(U'))$ make perfect probabilistic sense.

The vagueness regarding the meaning of "significantly smaller" can be removed by using nonstandard probability measures. It can be shown that there exist what are called *non-Archimedean fields*, fields that contain the real numbers and also *infinitesimals*, where an infinitesimal is an element that is positive but smaller than any positive real number. If $\epsilon$ is such an infinitesimal, then $\alpha\epsilon < 1$ for all positive real numbers $\alpha$. (If $\alpha\epsilon$ were greater than 1, then $\epsilon$ would be greater than $1/\alpha$, contradicting the assumption that $\epsilon$ is less than all positive real numbers.) Since multiplication is defined in non-Archimedean fields, if $\epsilon$ is an infinitesimal, then so is $\epsilon^k$ for all $k > 0$. Moreover, since $\alpha\epsilon < 1$ for all positive real numbers $\alpha$, it follows that $\alpha\epsilon^k < \epsilon^{k-1}$ for all real numbers $\alpha$.

Define a *nonstandard probability measure* to be a function associating with sets an element of a non-Archimedean field in the interval $[0, 1]$ that satisfies P1 and P2. Fix an infinitesimal $\epsilon$ and a nonstandard probability measure $\mu$. Define $\kappa(U)$ to be the smallest natural number $k$ such that $\mu(U) > \alpha\epsilon^k$ for some standard real $\alpha > 0$. It can be shown that this definition of $\kappa$ satisfies Rk1–3 (Exercise 2.40). However, in more practical order-of-magnitude reasoning, it may make more sense to think of $\epsilon$ as a very small positive real number, rather than as an infinitesimal.

## 2.7 Relative Likelihood

All the approaches considered thus far have been numeric. But numbers are not always so easy to come by. Sometimes it is enough to have just relative likelihood. In this section, I consider an approach that again starts with a set of possible worlds, but now ordered according to likelihood.

Let $\succeq$ be a reflexive and transitive relation on a set $W$ of worlds. Technically, $\succeq$ is a *partial preorder*. It is *partial* because two worlds might be incomparable as far as $\succeq$ goes; that is, it is possible that $w \not\succeq w'$ and $w' \not\succeq w$ for some worlds $w$ and $w'$. It is a partial *preorder* rather than a partial *order* because it is not necessarily *antisymmetric*. (A relation $\succeq$ is antisymmetric if $w \succeq w'$ and $w' \succeq w$ together imply that $w = w'$; that is, the relation is antisymmetric if there cannot be distinct equivalent worlds.) I typically write $w \succeq w'$ rather than $(w, w') \in \succeq$. (It may seem strange to write $(w, w') \in \succeq$, but recall that $\succeq$ is just a binary relation.) I also write $w \succ w'$ if $w \succeq w'$ and it is not the case that $w' \succeq w$. The relation $\succ$ is the *strict* partial order *determined by* $\succeq$: it is irreflexive and transitive, and hence also antisymmetric (Exercise 2.41). Thus, $\succ$ is an order rather than just a preorder.

Think of $\succeq$ as providing a likelihood ordering on the worlds in $W$. If $w \succeq w'$, then $w$ is at least as likely as $w'$. Given this interpretation, the fact that $\succeq$ is assumed to be a partial preorder is easy to justify. Transitivity just says that if $u$ is at least as likely as $v$, and $v$ is at least as likely as $w$, then $u$ is at least as likely as $w$; reflexivity just says that world $w$ is at least as likely as itself. The fact that $\succeq$ is partial allows for an agent who is not able to compare two worlds in likelihood.

Having an ordering $\succeq$ on worlds makes it possible to say that one world is more likely than another, but it does not immediately say when an event, or *set* of worlds, is more likely than another event. To deal with events, $\succeq$ must be extended to an order

$\triangleright$ on sets. Unfortunately, there are many ways of doing this; it is not clear which is "best." I consider two ways here. One is quite natural; the other is perhaps less natural, but has interesting connections with some material discussed in Chapter 8. Lack of space precludes me from considering other methods; however, I don't mean to suggest that the methods I consider are the only interesting approaches to defining an order on sets.

Define $\succeq^e$ (the superscript $e$ stands for *events,* to emphasize that this is a relation on events, not worlds) by taking $U \succeq^e V$ iff (if and only if) for all $v \in V$, there exists some $u \in U$ such that $u \succeq v$. Let $\succ^e$ be the strict partial order determined by $\succeq^e$. Clearly $\succeq^e$ is a partial preorder on sets, and it extends $\succeq$: $u \succeq v$ iff $\{u\} \succeq^e \{v\}$. It is also the case that $\succ^e$ extends $\succ$.

I now collect some properties of $\succeq^e$ that will prove important in Chapter 7; the proof that these properties hold is deferred to Exercise 2.42. A relation $\triangleright$ on $2^W$

- *respects subsets* if $U \supseteq V$ implies $U \triangleright V$;

- has the *union property* if, for all index sets $I$, if $U \triangleright V_i$ for all $i \in I$, then $U \triangleright \cup_i V_i$;

- is *determined by singletons* if $U \triangleright \{v\}$ implies that there exists some $u \in U$ such that $\{u\} \triangleright \{v\}$;

- is *conservative* if $\emptyset \not\triangleright V$ for $V \neq \emptyset$.

It is easy to check that $\succeq^e$ has all of these properties. How reasonable are these as properties of likelihood? It seems that any reasonable measure of likelihood would make a set as least as likely as any of its subsets. The conservative property merely says that all nonempty sets are viewed as possible; nothing is a priori excluded. The fact that $\succeq^e$ has the union property makes it quite different from, say, probability. With probability, sufficiently many "small" probabilities eventually can dominate a "large" probability. On the other hand, if a possibility measure satisfies Poss3$^+$, then likelihood as determined by possibility does satisfy the union property. It is immediate from Poss3$^+$ that if $\mathrm{Poss}(U) \geq \mathrm{Poss}(V_i)$ for all $i \in I$, then $\mathrm{Poss}(U) \geq \mathrm{Poss}(\cup_i V_i)$. Determination by singletons also holds for possibility measures restricted to finite sets; if $U$ is finite and $\mathrm{Poss}(U) \geq \mathrm{Poss}(v)$, then $\mathrm{Poss}(u) \geq \mathrm{Poss}(v)$ for some $u \in U$. However, it does not necessarily hold for infinite sets, even if Poss3$^+$ holds. For example, if $\mathrm{Poss}(0) = 1$ and $\mathrm{Poss}(n) = 1 - 1/n$ for $n > 0$, then $\mathrm{Poss}(\{1, 2, 3, \ldots\}) = 1 \geq \mathrm{Poss}(0)$, but $\mathrm{Poss}(n) < \mathrm{Poss}(0)$ for all $n > 0$. Determination by singletons is somewhat related to the union property. It follows from determination by singletons that if $U \cup U' \succeq^e \{v\}$, then either $U \succeq^e \{v\}$ or $U' \succeq^e \{v\}$.

Although I have allowed $\succeq$ to be a partial preorder, so that some elements of $W$ may be incomparable according to $\succeq$, in many cases of interest, $\succeq$ is a *total* preorder. This means that for all $w$, $w' \in W$, either $w \succeq w'$ or $w' \succeq w$. For example, if $\succeq$ is determined by a possibility measure Poss, so that $w \succeq w'$ if $\text{Poss}(w) \geq \text{Poss}(w')$, then $\succeq$ is total. It is not hard to check that if $\succeq$ is total, then so is $\succeq^e$.

The following theorem summarizes the properties of $\succeq^e$:

**Theorem 2.7.1** *The relation $\succeq^e$ is a conservative partial preorder that respects subsets, has the union property, and is determined by singletons. In addition, if $\succeq$ is a total preorder, then so is $\succeq^e$.*

**Proof**   See Exercise 2.42.   ∎

Are there other significant properties that hold for $\succeq^e$? As the following theorem shows, there are not. In a precise sense, these properties actually characterize $\succeq^e$.

**Theorem 2.7.2**   *If $\rhd$ is a conservative partial preorder on $2^W$ that respects subsets, has the union property, and is determined by singletons, then there is a partial preorder $\succeq$ on $W$ such that $\rhd = \succeq^e$. If in addition $\rhd$ is total, then so is $\succeq$.*

**Proof**   Given $\rhd$, define a preorder $\succeq$ on worlds by defining $u \succeq v$ iff $\{u\} \rhd \{v\}$. If $\rhd$ is total, so is $\succeq$. It remains to show that $\rhd = \succeq^e$. I leave the straightforward details to the reader (Exercise 2.43).   ∎

If $\succeq$ is total, $\succ^e$ has yet another property that will play an important role in modeling belief, default reasoning, and counterfactual reasoning (see Chapter 8). A relation $\rhd$ on $2^W$ is *qualitative* if, for disjoint sets $V_1$, $V_2$, and $V_3$, if $(V_1 \cup V_2) \rhd V_3$ and $(V_1 \cup V_3) \rhd V_2$, then $V_1 \rhd (V_2 \cup V_3)$. If $\rhd$ is viewed as meaning "much more likely," then this property says that if $V_1 \cup V_2$ is much more likely than $V_3$ and $V_1 \cup V_3$ is much more likely than $V_2$, then most of the likelihood has to be concentrated in $V_1$. Thus, $V_1$ must be much more likely than $V_2 \cup V_3$.

It is easy to see that $\succeq^e$ is not in general qualitative. For example, suppose that $W = \{w_1, w_2\}$, $w_1 \succeq w_2$, and $w_2 \succeq w_1$. Thus, $\{w_1\} \succeq^e \{w_2\}$ and $\{w_2\} \succeq^e \{w_1\}$. If $\succeq^e$ were qualitative, then (taking $V_1$, $V_2$, and $V_3$ to be $\emptyset$, $\{w_1\}$, and $\{w_2\}$, respectively), it would be the case that $\emptyset \succeq^e \{w_1, w_2\}$, which is clearly not the case. On the other hand, it is not hard to show that $\succ^e$ is qualitative if $\succeq$ is total. I did not include this property in Theorem 2.7.1 because it actually follows from the other properties (see Exercise 2.44). However, $\succ^e$ is not in general qualitative if $\succeq$ is a partial preorder, as the following example shows:

**Example 2.7.3**    Suppose that $W_0 = \{w_1, w_2, w_3\}$, where $w_1$ is incomparable to $w_2$ and $w_3$, while $w_2$ and $w_3$ are equivalent (so that $w_3 \succeq w_2$ and $w_2 \succeq w_3$). Notice that $\{w_1, w_2\} \succ^e \{w_3\}$ and $\{w_1, w_3\} \succ^e \{w_2\}$, but $\{w_1\} \not\succ^e \{w_2, w_3\}$. Taking $V_i = \{w_i\}$, $i = 1, 2, 3$, this shows that $\succ^e$ is not qualitative.    ∎

The qualitative property may not seem so natural, but because of its central role in modeling belief, I am interested in finding a preorder $\succeq^s$ on sets (the superscript $s$ stands for *set*) that extends $\succeq$ such that the strict partial order $\succ^s$ determined by $\succeq^s$ has the qualitative property. Unfortunately, this is impossible, at least if $\succeq^s$ also respects subsets. To see this, consider Example 2.7.3 again. If $\succeq^s$ respects subsets, then $\{w_1, w_2\} \succeq^s \{w_1\}$ and $\{w_1, w_2\} \succeq^s \{w_2\}$. Thus, it must be the case that $\{w_1, w_2\} \succ^s \{w_2\}$, for if $\{w_2\} \succeq^s \{w_1, w_2\}$, then by transitivity, $\{w_2\} \succeq^s \{w_1\}$, which contradicts the fact that $\succeq^s$ extends $\succeq$. (Recall that $w_1$ and $w_2$ are incomparable according to $\succeq$.) Since $\{w_1, w_2\} \succ^s \{w_2\}$ and $\{w_2\} \succeq^s \{w_3\}$, it follows by transitivity that $\{w_1, w_2\} \succ^s \{w_3\}$. A similar argument shows that $\{w_1, w_3\} \succ^s \{w_2\}$. By the qualitative property, it follows that $\{w_1\} \succ^s \{w_2, w_3\}$. But then, since $\succeq^s$ respects subsets, it must be the case that $\{w_1\} \succ^s \{w_2\}$, again contradicting the fact that $\succeq^s$ extends $\succeq$.

Although it is impossible to get a qualitative partial preorder on sets that extends $\succeq$, it is possible to get the next best thing: a qualitative partial preorder on sets that extends $\succ$. I do this in the remainder of this subsection. The discussion is somewhat technical and can be skipped on a first reading of the book.

Define a relation $\succeq^s$ on sets as follows:

$U \succeq^s V$ if for all $v \in V - U$, there exists $u \in U$ such that $u \succ v$ and $u$ dominates $V - U$, where $u$ *dominates* a set $X$ if it is not the case that $x \succ u$ for any element $x \in X$.

Ignoring the clause about domination (which is only relevant in infinite domains; see Example 2.7.4), this definition is not far off from that of $\succeq^e$. Indeed, it is not hard to check that $U \succeq^e V$ iff for all $v \in V - U$, there exists $u \in U$ such that $u \succeq v$ (Exercise 2.45). Thus, all that has really happened in going from $\succeq^e$ to $\succeq^s$ is that $\succeq$ has been replaced by $\succ$. Because of this change, $\succeq^s$ just misses extending $\succeq$. Certainly if $\{u\} \succeq^s \{v\}$ then $u \succeq v$; in fact, $u \succ v$. Moreover, it is almost immediate from the definition that $\{u\} \succ^s \{v\}$ iff $u \succ v$. The only time that $\succeq^s$ disagrees with $\succeq$ on singleton sets is if $u$ and $v$ are distinct worlds equivalent with respect to $\succeq$; in this case, they are incomparable with respect to $\succeq^s$. It follows that if $\succeq$ is a partial *order*, and not just a preorder, then $\succeq^s$ does extend $\succeq$. Interestingly, $\succ^e$ and $\succ^s$ agree if $\succeq$ is total. Of course, in general, they are different (Exercise 2.46).

As I said, the requirement that $u$ dominate $V$ is not relevant if $W$ is finite (Exercise 2.47); however, it does play a significant role if $W$ is infinite. Because of it, $\succeq^s$ does not satisfy the full union property, as the following example shows:

**Example 2.7.4**   Let $V_\infty = \{w_0, w_1, w_2, \ldots\}$, and suppose that $\succeq$ is a total preorder on $W$ such that

$$\ldots \succ w_3 \succ w_2 \succ w_1 \succ w_0.$$

Let $W_0 = \{w_0, w_2, w_4, \ldots\}$ and $W_1 = \{w_1, w_3, w_5, \ldots\}$. Then it is easy to see that $W_0 \succ^s \{w_j\}$ for all $w_j \in W_1$; however, it is not the case that $W_0 \succeq^s W_1$, since there is no element in $W_0$ that dominates $W_1$. Thus, $\succeq^s$ does not satisfy the union property.   ∎

It is easy to check that $\succeq^s$ satisfies a finitary version of the union property; that is, if $U \succeq^s V_1$ and $U \succeq^s V_2$, then $U \succeq^s V_1 \cup V_2$. It is only the full infinitary version that causes problems.

The following theorem summarizes the properties of $\succeq^s$:

**Theorem 2.7.5**   *The relation $\succeq^s$ is a conservative, qualitative partial preorder that respects subsets, has the finitary union property, and is determined by singletons. In addition, if $\succeq$ is a total preorder, then so is $\succeq^s$.*

**Proof**   See Exercise 2.48.   ∎

The original motivation for the definition of $\succeq^s$ was to make $\succ^s$ qualitative. Theorem 2.7.5 says only that $\succeq^s$ is qualitative. In fact, it is not hard to check that $\succ^s$ is qualitative too. (See Exercise 2.49 for further discussion of this point.)

The next theorem is the analogue of Theorem 2.7.2, at least in the case that $W$ is finite.

**Theorem 2.7.6**   *If $W$ is finite and $\rhd$ is a conservative, qualitative partial preorder that respects subsets, has the finitary union property, and is determined by singletons, then there is a partial preorder $\succeq$ on $W$ such that $\rhd = \succeq^s$. If in addition $\rhd$ is a total preorder, then $\succeq^s$ can be taken to be a total as well.*

**Proof**   Given $\rhd$, define a preorder $\succeq$ on worlds by defining $u \succeq v$ iff $\{u\} \rhd \{v\}$. If $\rhd$ is total, modify the definition so that $u \succeq v$ iff $\{v\} \not\rhd \{u\}$. I leave it to the reader to check that $\rhd = \succeq^s$, and if $\rhd$ is total, then so is $\succeq$ (Exercise 2.50).   ∎

I do not know if there is an elegant characterization of $\succeq^s$ if $W$ is infinite. The problem is that characterizing dominance seems difficult. (It is, of course, possible to characterize $\succeq^s$ by essentially rewriting the definition. This is not terribly interesting though.)

Given all the complications in the definitions of $\succeq^e$ and $\succeq^s$, it seems reasonable to ask how these definitions relate to other notions of likelihood. In fact, $\succeq^e$ can be seen as a qualitative version of possibility measures and ranking functions. Given a possibility measure Poss on $W$, define $w \succeq w'$ if $\text{Poss}(w) \geq \text{Poss}(w')$. It is easy to see that, as long as Poss is conservative (i.e., $\text{Poss}(w) > 0$ for all $w \in W$), then $U \succeq^e V$ iff $\text{Poss}(U) \geq \text{Poss}(V)$ and $U \succ^e V$ iff $\text{Poss}(U) > \text{Poss}(V)$ (Exercise 2.51). Since $\succeq$ is a total preorder, $\succ^s$ and $\succ^e$ agree, so $\text{Poss}(U) > \text{Poss}(V)$ iff $U \succ^s V$. It follows that Poss is qualitative; that is, if $\text{Poss}(U_1 \cup U_2) > \text{Poss}(U_3)$ and $\text{Poss}(U_1 \cup U_3) > \text{Poss}(U_2)$, then $\text{Poss}(U_1) > \text{Poss}(U_2 \cup U_3)$. (It is actually not hard to prove this directly; see Exercise 2.52.) Ranking functions also have the qualitative property. Indeed, just like possibility measures, ranking functions can be used to define an ordering on worlds that is compatible with relative likelihood (Exercise 2.53).

## 2.8   Plausibility Measures

I conclude this chapter by considering an approach that is a generalization of all the approaches mentioned so far. This approach uses what are called *plausibility measures,* which are unfortunately not the same as the plausibility functions used in the Dempster-Shafer approach (although plausibility functions are instances of plausibility measures). I hope that the reader will be able to sort through any confusion caused by this overloading of terminology.

The basic idea behind plausibility measures is straightforward. A probability measure maps sets in an algebra $\mathcal{F}$ over a set $W$ of worlds to $[0, 1]$. A *plausibility measure* is more general; it maps sets in $\mathcal{F}$ to some arbitrary partially ordered set. If Pl is a plausibility measure, $\text{Pl}(U)$ denotes the plausibility of $U$. If $\text{Pl}(U) \leq \text{Pl}(V)$, then $V$ is at least as plausible as $U$. Because the ordering is partial, it could be that the plausibility of two different sets is incomparable. An agent may not be prepared to order two sets in terms of plausibility.

Formally, a *plausibility space* is a tuple $S = (W, \mathcal{F}, \text{Pl})$, where $W$ is a set of worlds, $\mathcal{F}$ is an algebra over $W$, and Pl maps sets in $\mathcal{F}$ to some set $D$ of *plausibility values* partially ordered by a relation $\leq_D$ (so that $\leq_D$ is reflexive, transitive, and antisymmetric). $D$ is assumed to contain two special elements, $\top_D$ and $\bot_D$, such that $\bot_D \leq_D d \leq_D \top_D$ for all $d \in D$. As usual, the ordering $<_D$ is defined by taking $d_1 <_D d_2$ if $d_1 \leq_D d_2$ and $d_1 \neq d_2$. I omit the subscript $D$ from $\leq_D$, $<_D$, $\top_D$, and $\bot_D$ whenever it is clear from context.

There are three requirements on plausibility measures. The first two just enforce the standard convention that the whole space gets the maximum plausibility and the empty set gets the minimum plausibility ($\top$ and $\bot$). The third requirement says that a set must be at least as plausible as any of its subsets; that is, plausibility respects subsets.

Pl1.   $\mathrm{Pl}(\emptyset) = \bot$.

Pl2.   $\mathrm{Pl}(W) = \top$.

Pl3.   If $U \subseteq V$, then $\mathrm{Pl}(U) \leq \mathrm{Pl}(V)$.

Clearly probability measures, lower and upper probabilities, inner and outer measures, Dempster-Shafer belief functions and plausibility functions, and possibility and necessity measures are all instances of plausibility measures, where $D = [0, 1]$, $\bot = 0$, $\top = 1$, and $\leq_D$ is the standard ordering on the reals. Ranking functions are also instances of plausibility measures; in this case, $D = \mathbb{N}^*$, $\bot = \infty$, $\top = 0$, and the ordering $\leq_{\mathbb{N}^*}$ is the opposite of the standard ordering on $\mathbb{N}^*$; that is, $x \leq_{\mathbb{N}^*} y$ if and only if $y \leq x$ under the standard ordering.

In all these cases, the plausibility values are totally ordered. But there are also cases of interest where the plausibility values are *not* totally ordered. Two examples are given by starting with a partial preorder $\succeq$ on $W$ as in Section 2.7. The partial preorders $\succeq^e$ and $\succeq^s$ derived from $\succeq$ can be used to define plausibility measures, although there is a minor subtle issue. Given $\succeq$, consider the plausibility space $(W, 2^W, \mathrm{Pl}_{\succeq e})$. Roughly speaking, $\mathrm{Pl}_{\succeq e}$ is the identity, and $\mathrm{Pl}_{\succeq}(U) \geq \mathrm{Pl}_{\succeq e}(V)$ iff $U \succeq^e V$. There is only one problem with this. The set of plausibility values is supposed to be a partial order, not just a preorder.

One obvious way around this problem is to allow the order $\leq_D$ of plausibility values to be a preorder rather than a partial order. There would be no conceptual difficulty in doing this, and in fact I do it (briefly) for technical reasons in Section 5.4.3. I have restricted to partial orders here partly to be consistent with the literature and partly because there seems to be an intuition that if the likelihood of $U$ is at least as great as that of $V$, and the likelihood of $V$ is as great as that of $U$, then $U$ and $V$ have equal likelihoods. In any case, the particular problem of capturing $\succeq^e$ using plausibility measures can easily be solved. Define an equivalence relation $\sim$ on $2^W$ by taking $U \sim V$ if $U \succeq^e V$ and $V \succeq^e U$. Let $[U]$ consist of all the sets equivalent to $U$; that is, $[U] = \{U' : U \sim U'\}$. Let $W/\sim = \{[U] : U \in W\}$. Define a partial order on $W/\sim$ in the obvious way: $[U] \geq [V]$ iff $U \succeq^e V$. It is easy to check that this order on $W/\sim$ is well-defined and makes $W/\sim$ a partial order (Exercise 2.54). Now taking $E = W/\sim$ and defining $\mathrm{Pl}_{\succeq e}(U) = [U]$ gives a well-defined plausibility measure. Exactly the same technique works for $\succeq^s$.

For a perhaps more interesting example, suppose that $\mathcal{P}$ is a set of probability measures on $W$. Both $\mathcal{P}_*$ and $\mathcal{P}^*$ give a way of comparing the likelihood of two subsets $U$ and $V$ of $W$. These two ways are incomparable; it is easy to find a set $\mathcal{P}$ of probability measures on $W$ and subsets $U$ and $V$ of $W$ such that $\mathcal{P}_*(U) < \mathcal{P}_*(V)$ and $\mathcal{P}^*(U) > \mathcal{P}^*(V)$ (Exercise 2.55(a)). Rather than choosing between $\mathcal{P}_*$ and $\mathcal{P}^*$, it is possible to associate a different plausibility measure with $\mathcal{P}$ that captures both. Let $D_{int} = \{(a, b) : 0 \le a \le b \le 1\}$ (the $int$ is for interval) and define $(a, b) \le (a', b')$ iff $b \le a'$. This puts a partial order on $D_{int}$, with $\perp_{D_{int}} = (0, 0)$ and $\top_{D_{int}} = (1, 1)$. Define $\mathrm{Pl}_{\mathcal{P}_*, \mathcal{P}*}(U) = (\mathcal{P}_*(U), \mathcal{P}^*(U))$. Thus, $\mathrm{Pl}_{\mathcal{P}_*, \mathcal{P}*}$ associates with a set $U$ two numbers that can be thought of as defining an interval in terms of the lower and upper probability of $U$. It is easy to check that $\mathrm{Pl}_{\mathcal{P}_*, \mathcal{P}*}(U) \le \mathrm{Pl}_{\mathcal{P}_*, \mathcal{P}*}(V)$ if the upper probability of $U$ is less than or equal to the lower probability of $V$. Clearly $\mathrm{Pl}_{\mathcal{P}_*, \mathcal{P}*}$ satisfies Pl1–3, so it is indeed a plausibility measure, but one that puts only a partial (pre)order on events. A similar plausibility measure can be associated with a belief/plausibility function and with an inner/outer measure.

The trouble with $\mathcal{P}_*$, $\mathcal{P}^*$, and even $\mathrm{Pl}_{\mathcal{P}_*, \mathcal{P}*}$ is that they lose information. Example 2.3.4 gives one instance of this phenomenon; the fact that $\mu(r) = \mu(b)$ for every measure $\mu \in \mathcal{P}_4$ is lost by taking lower and upper probabilities. It is easy to generate other examples. For example, it is not hard to find a set $\mathcal{P}$ of probability measures and subsets $U$, $V$ of $W$ such that $\mu(U) \le \mu(V)$ for all $\mu \in \mathcal{P}$ and $\mu(U) < \mu(V)$ for some $\mu \in \mathcal{P}$, but $\mathcal{P}_*(U) = \mathcal{P}_*(V)$ and $\mathcal{P}^*(U) = \mathcal{P}^*(V)$. Indeed, there exists an infinite set $\mathcal{P}$ of probability measures such that $\mu(U) < \mu(V)$ for all $\mu \in \mathcal{P}$ but $\mathcal{P}_*(U) = \mathcal{P}_*(V)$ and $\mathcal{P}^*(U) = \mathcal{P}^*(V)$ (Exercise 2.55(b)). If all the probability measures in $\mathcal{P}$ agree that $U$ is less likely than $V$, it seems reasonable to conclude that $U$ is less likely than $V$. However, none of the plausibility measures $\mathcal{P}_*$, $\mathcal{P}^*$, or $\mathrm{Pl}_{\mathcal{P}_*, \mathcal{P}*}$ will necessarily draw this conclusion.

Fortunately, it is not hard to associate yet another plausibility measure with $\mathcal{P}$ that does not lose this important information (and does indeed conclude that $U$ is less likely than $V$).

To explain this representation, it is easiest to consider first the case that $\mathcal{P}$ is finite. Suppose $\mathcal{P} = \{\mu_1, \ldots, \mu_n\}$. Then the idea is to define $\mathrm{Pl}_{\mathcal{P}}(U) = (\mu_1(U), \ldots, \mu_n(U))$. That is, the plausibility of a set $U$ is represented as a tuple, consisting of the probability of $U$ according to each measure in $\mathcal{P}$. The ordering on tuples is pointwise: $(a_1, \ldots, a_n) \le (b_1, \ldots, b_n)$ if $a_i \le b_i$ for $i = 1, \ldots, n$. There are two minor problems with this approach, both easily fixed. The first is that a set is unordered. Although the subscripts suggest that $\mu_1$ is the "first" element in $\mathcal{P}$, there is no first element in $\mathcal{P}$. On the other hand, there really is a first element in a tuple. Which probability measure in $\mathcal{P}$ should be first, second, and so on? Another minor problem comes if $\mathcal{P}$ consists of an uncountable number of elements; it is not clear how to represent the set of measures in $\mathcal{P}$ as a tuple.

These problems can be dealt with in a straightforward way. Let $D_{\mathcal{P}}$ consist of all functions from $\mathcal{P}$ to $[0, 1]$. The standard pointwise ordering on functions—that is, $f \leq g$ if $f(\mu) \leq g(\mu)$ for all $\mu \in \mathcal{P}$—gives a partial order on $D_{\mathcal{P}}$. Note that $\perp_{D_{\mathcal{P}}}$ is the function $f : \mathcal{P} \rightarrow [0, 1]$ such that $f(\mu) = 0$ for all $\mu \in \mathcal{P}$ and $\top_{D_{\mathcal{P}}}$ is the function $g$ such that $g(\mu) = 1$ for all $\mu \in \mathcal{P}$. For $U \subseteq W$, let $f_U$ be the function such that $f_U(\mu) = \mu(U)$ for all $\mu \in \mathcal{P}$. Define the plausibility measure $\text{Pl}_{\mathcal{P}}$ by taking $\text{Pl}_{\mathcal{P}}(U) = f_U$. Thus, $\text{Pl}_{\mathcal{P}}(U) \leq \text{Pl}_{\mathcal{P}}(V)$ iff $\mu(U) \leq \mu(V)$ for all $\mu \in \mathcal{P}$. It is easy to see that $f_{\emptyset} = \perp_{D_{\mathcal{P}}}$ and $f_W = \top_{D_{\mathcal{P}}}$. Clearly $\text{Pl}_{\mathcal{P}}$ satisfies Pl1–3. Pl1 and Pl2 follow since $\text{Pl}_{\mathcal{P}}(\emptyset) = f_{\emptyset} = \perp_{D_{\mathcal{P}}}$ and $\text{Pl}_{\mathcal{P}}(W) = f_W = \top_{D_{\mathcal{P}}}$, while Pl3 holds because if $U \subseteq V$, then $\mu(U) \leq \mu(V)$ for all $\mu \in \mathcal{P}$. Note that if $\mathcal{P} = \{\mu_1, \ldots, \mu_n\}$, then $\text{Pl}_{\mathcal{P}}(U)$ is the function $f$ such that $f(\mu_i) = \mu_i(U)$. This function can be identified with the tuple $(\mu_1(U), \ldots, \mu_n(U))$.

To see how this representation works, consider Example 2.3.2 (the example with a bag of red, blue, and yellow marbles). Recall that this was modeled using the set $\mathcal{P}_2 = \{\mu_a : a \in [0, .7]\}$ of probabilities, where $\mu_a(red) = .3$, $\mu_a(blue) = a$, and $\mu_a(yellow) = .7 - a$. Then, for example, $\text{Pl}_{\mathcal{P}_2}(blue) = f_{blue}$, where $f_{blue}(\mu_a) = \mu_a(blue) = a$ for all $a \in [0, .7]$. Similarly,

- $\text{Pl}_{\mathcal{P}_2}(red) = f_{red}$, where $f_{red}(\mu_a) = .3$,

- $\text{Pl}_{\mathcal{P}_2}(yellow) = f_{yellow}$, where $f_{yellow}(\mu_a) = .7 - a$,

- $\text{Pl}_{\mathcal{P}_2}(\{red, blue\}) = f_{\{red,blue\}}$, where $f_{\{red,blue\}}(\mu_a) = .3 + a$.

The events *yellow* and *blue* are incomparable with respect to $\text{Pl}_{\mathcal{P}_2}$ since $f_{yellow}$ and $f_{blue}$ are incomparable (e.g., $f_{yellow}(\mu_{.7}) < f_{blue}(\mu_{.7})$ while $f_{yellow}(\mu_0) > f_{blue}(\mu_0)$).

On the other hand, consider the sets $\mathcal{P}_3$ and $\mathcal{P}_4$ from Example 2.3.4. Recall that $\mathcal{P}_3 = \{\mu : \mu(blue) \leq .5, \mu(yellow) \leq .5\}$, and $\mathcal{P}_4 = \{\mu : \mu(b) = \mu(y)\}$. It is easy to check that $\text{Pl}_{\mathcal{P}_4}(blue) = \text{Pl}_{\mathcal{P}_4}(yellow)$, while $\text{Pl}_{\mathcal{P}_3}(blue)$ and $\text{Pl}_{\mathcal{P}_3}(yellow)$ are incomparable.

This technique for defining a plausibility measure that represents a set of probability measures is quite general. The same approach can be used essentially without change to represent any set of plausibility measures as a single plausibility measure.

Plausibility measures are very general. Pl1–3 are quite minimal requirements, by design, and arguably are the smallest set of properties that a representation of likelihood should satisfy. It is, of course, possible to add more properties, some of which seem quite natural, but these are typically properties that some representation of uncertainty does not satisfy (see, e.g., Exercise 2.57).

What is the advantage of having this generality? This should hopefully become clearer in later chapters, but I can make at least some motivating remarks now. For one thing, by using plausibility measures, it is possible to prove general results about properties of representations of uncertainty. That is, it is possible to show that all representations of uncertainty that have property $X$ also have property $Y$. Since it may be clear that, say, possibility measures and ranking functions have property $X$, then it immediately follows that both have property $Y$; moreover, if Dempster-Shafer belief functions do not have property $X$, the proof may well give a deeper understanding as to why belief functions do not have property $Y$.

For example, it turns out that a great deal of mileage can be gained by assuming that there is some operation $\oplus$ on the set of plausibility values such that $\text{Pl}(U \cup V) = \text{Pl}(U) \oplus \text{Pl}(V)$ if $U$ and $V$ are disjoint. (Unfortunately, the $\oplus$ discussed here has nothing to do with the $\oplus$ defined in the context of Dempster's Rule of Combination. I hope that it will be clear from context which version of $\oplus$ is being used.) If such an $\oplus$ exists, then Pl is said to be *additive* (with respect to $\oplus$). Probability measures, possibility measures, and ranking functions are all additive. In the case of probability measures, $\oplus$ is $+$; in the case of possibility measures, it is max; in the case of ranking functions, it is min. For the plausibility measure $\text{Pl}_{\mathcal{P}}$, $\oplus$ is essentially pointwise addition (see Section 3.9 for a more careful definition). However, belief functions are not additive; neither are plausibility functions, lower probabilities, or upper probabilities. There exist a set $W$, a belief function Bel on $W$, and pairwise disjoint subsets $U_1, U_2, V_1, V_2$ of $W$ such that $\text{Bel}(U_1) = \text{Bel}(V_1)$, $\text{Bel}(U_2) = \text{Bel}(V_2)$, but $\text{Bel}(U_1 \cup U_2) \neq \text{Bel}(V_1 \cup V_2)$ (Exercise 2.56). It follows that there cannot be a function $\oplus$ such that $\text{Bel}(U \cup V) = \text{Bel}(U) \oplus \text{Bel}(V)$. Similar arguments apply to plausibility functions, lower probabilities, and upper probabilities. Thus, in the most general setting, I do not assume additivity. Plausibility measures are of interest in part because they make it possible to investigate the consequences of assuming additivity. I return to this issue in Sections 3.9, 5.3, and 8.4.

## 2.9   Choosing a Representation

Before concluding this chapter, a few words are in order regarding the problem of modeling a real-world situation. It should be clear that, whichever approach is used to model uncertainty, it is important to be sensitive to the implications of using that approach. Different approaches are more appropriate for different applications.

- Probability has the advantage of being well understood. It is a powerful tool; many technical results have been proved that facilitate its use, and a number of arguments suggest that, under certain assumptions (whose reasonableness can be debated), probability is the only "rational" way to represent uncertainty.

- Sets of probability measures have many of the advantages of probability but may be more appropriate in a setting where there is uncertainty about the likelihood.

- Belief functions may prove useful as a model of evidence, especially when combined with Dempster's Rule of Combination.

- In Chapter 8, it is shown that possibility measures and ranking functions deal well with default reasoning and counterfactual reasoning, as do partial preorders.

- Partial preorders on possible worlds may be also more appropriate in setting where no quantitative information is available.

- Plausibility measures provide a general approach that subsumes all the others considered and thus are appropriate for proving general results about ways of representing uncertainty.

In some applications, the set of possible worlds is infinite. Although I have focused on the case where the set of possible worlds is finite, it is worth stressing that all these approaches can deal with an infinite set of possible worlds with no difficulty, although occasionally some additional assumptions are necessary. In particular, it is standard to assume that the algebra of sets is closed under countable union, so that it is a $\sigma$-algebra. In the case of probability, it is also standard to assume that the probability measure is countably additive. The analogue for possibility measures is the assumption that the possibility of the union of a countable collection of disjoint sets is the sup of the possibility of each one. (In fact, for possibility, it is typically assumed that the possibility of the union of an arbitrary collection of sets is the sup of the possibility of each one.) Except for the connection between belief functions and mass functions described in Theorem 2.4.3, the connection between possibility measures and mass functions described in Theorem 2.5.4, and the characterization result for $\succeq^s$ in Theorem 2.7.6, all the results in the book apply even if the set of possible worlds is infinite. The key point here is that the fact that the set of possible worlds is infinite should not play a significant role in deciding which approach to use in modeling a problem.

See Chapter 12 for more discussion of the choice of the representation.

## Exercises

**2.1**   Let $\mathcal{F}$ be an algebra over $W$.

(a) Show by means of a counterexample that if $W$ is infinite, sets in $\mathcal{F}$ may not be the union of basic sets. (Hint: Let $\mathcal{F}$ consist of all finite and cofinite subsets of $W$, where a set is *cofinite* if its complement is finite.)

(b) Show that if $W$ is finite, then every set in $\mathcal{F}$ is the union of basic sets. (That is, the basic sets in $\mathcal{F}$ form a basis for $\mathcal{F}$ if $W$ is finite.)

**2.2**   This exercise examines countable additivity and the continuity properties (2.1) and (2.2). Suppose that $\mathcal{F}$ is a $\sigma$-algebra.

(a) Show that if $U_1, U_2, U_3, \ldots$ is an increasing sequence of sets all in $\mathcal{F}$, then $\bigcup_{i=1}^{\infty} U_i \in \mathcal{F}$.

(b) Show that if $U_1, U_2, U_3, \ldots$ is a decreasing sequence of sets, then $\bigcap_{i=1}^{\infty} U_i \in \mathcal{F}$.

(c) Show that the following are equivalent in the presence of finite additivity:

   (i) $\mu$ is countably additive,

   (ii) $\mu$ satisfies (2.1),

   (iii) $\mu$ satisfies (2.2).

**2.3**   Show that if $\mathcal{F}$ consists of the finite and cofinite subsets of $\mathbb{N}$, and $\mu(U) = 0$ if $U$ is finite and 1 if $U$ is cofinite, then $\mathcal{F}$ is an algebra and $\mu$ is a finitely additive probability measure on $\mathcal{F}$.

**2.4**   Show by using P2 that if $U \subseteq V$, then $\mu(U) \leq \mu(V)$.

*__2.5__   Let $\alpha_U = \sup\{\beta : (U, \beta) \succeq (\overline{U}, 1 - \beta)\}$. Show that $(U, \alpha) \succeq (\overline{U}, 1 - \alpha)$ for all $\alpha < \alpha_U$ and $(\overline{U}, 1 - \alpha) \succeq (U, \alpha)$ for all $\alpha > \alpha_U$. Moreover, if $U_1$ and $U_2$ are disjoint sets, show that if the agent is rational, then $\alpha_{U_1} + \alpha_{U_2} = \alpha_{U_1 \cup U_2}$. More precisely, show that if $\alpha_{U_1} + \alpha_{U_2} \neq \alpha_{U_1 \cup U_2}$, then there is a set of bets (on $U_1$, $U_2$, and $U_1 \cup U_2$) that the agent should be willing to accept given her stated preferences, according to which she is guaranteed to lose money. Show exactly where RAT4 comes into play.

**2.6**   Suppose that (a) if $(V, \beta) \succeq (U, \alpha)$ for all $\alpha > \alpha^*$ then $(V, \beta) \succeq (U, \alpha^*)$ and (b) if $(U, \alpha) \succeq (V, \beta)$ for all $\alpha < \alpha^*$ then $(U, \alpha^*) \succeq (V, \beta)$. Show that it follows that the agent must be indifferent between $(U, \alpha_U)$ and $(\overline{U}, 1 - \alpha_U)$ (i.e., each is preferred to the other).

**2.7**    Show that if $W$ is finite then $\mu_*(U) = \mu(V_1)$, where $V_1 = \cup\{B \in \mathcal{F} : B \subseteq U\}$ and $\mu^*(U) = \mu(V_2)$, where $V_2 = \cap\{B \in \mathcal{F} : U \subseteq B\}$.

**\*2.8**    This exercise examines the proof of Theorem 2.3.3.

(a) Show that if $\mathcal{F} \subseteq \mathcal{F}'$, $\mu$ is defined on $\mathcal{F}$, and $\mu'$ is an extension of $\mu$ defined on $\mathcal{F}'$, then $\mu_*(U) \le \mu'(U) \le \mu^*(U)$ for all $U \in \mathcal{F}'$.

(b) Given $U \in \mathcal{F}' - \mathcal{F}$, let $\mathcal{F}(U)$ be the smallest subalgebra of $\mathcal{F}'$ containing $U$ and $\mathcal{F}$. Show that $\mathcal{F}(U)$ consists of all sets of the form $(V \cap U) \cup (V' \cap \overline{U})$ for $V$, $V' \in \mathcal{F}$.

(c) Define $\mu_U$ on $\mathcal{F}(U)$ by setting $\mu_U((V \cap U) \cup (V' \cap \overline{U})) = \mu_*(V \cap U) + \mu^*(V' \cap \overline{U})$. Show that $\mu_U$ is a probability measure on $\mathcal{F}(U)$ that extends $\mu$. Moreover, if $\mu$ is countably additive, then so is $\mu_U$. Note that $\mu_U(U) = \mu_*(W \cap U) + \mu^*(\emptyset \cap \overline{U}) = \mu_*(U)$.

(d) Show that a measure $\mu'_U$ can be defined on $\mathcal{F}(U)$ such that $\mu'_U(U) = \mu^*(U)$.

It follows from part (a) that, if $\mathcal{P}_\mu \ne \emptyset$, then $\mu_*(U) \le (\mathcal{P}_\mu)_*(U)$ and $(\mathcal{P}_\mu)^*(U) \le \mu^*(U)$. It follows from part (c) that as long as the probability measure $\mu_U$ can be extended to $\mathcal{F}'$, then $\mu_*(U) = (\mathcal{P}_\mu)_*(U)$; similarly, part (d) shows that as long as $\mu'_U$ can be extended to $\mathcal{F}'$, then $\mu^*(U) = \mathcal{P}^*(U)$. Thus, Theorem 2.3.3 follows under the assumption that both $\mu_U$ and $\mu'_U$ can be extended to $\mathcal{F}'$. It easily follows from the construction of parts (b) and (c) that $\mu_U$ and $\mu'_U$ can indeed be extended to $\mathcal{F}'$ if there exist finitely many sets, say $U_1, \ldots, U_n$, such that $\mathcal{F}'$ is the smallest algebra containing $\mathcal{F}$ and $U_1, \ldots, U_n$. This is certainly the case if $W$ is finite. Essentially the same argument works even if $W$ is not finite. However, in general, the measure $\mu'$ on $\mathcal{F}'$ is not countably additive, even if $\mu$ is countably additive. Indeed, in general, there may not be a countably additive measure $\mu'$ on $\mathcal{F}'$ extending $\mu$. (See the notes for further discussion and references.)

**2.9**    Show that inner and outer measures satisfy (2.3) and (2.4).

**2.10**    Prove the inclusion-exclusion rule (Equation (2.7)). (Hint: Use induction on $n$, the number of sets in the union.)

**\*2.11**    Show that if $\mu$ is a $\sigma$-additive probability measure on a $\sigma$-algebra $\mathcal{F}$, then there exists a function $g : 2^W \to \mathcal{F}$ such that $g(U) \subset U$ and $\mu(g(U)) = \mu_*(U)$, for all $U \in \mathcal{F}$. Moreover, for any finite subset $\mathcal{F}'$ of $\mathcal{F}$, $g$ can be defined so that $g(U \cap U') = g(U) \cap g(U')$ for all $U$, $U' \in \mathcal{F}'$. If $W$ is finite, this result follows easily from Exercise 2.7. Indeed, that exercise shows that $g(U)$ can be taken to be $\cup\{B \in \mathcal{F} : U \subseteq B\}$, so that $g(U \cap U) = g(U) \cap g(U')$ for all $U$, $U' \in \mathcal{F}$. If $W$ is infinite, then $g(U)$ is not necessarily $\cup\{B \in \mathcal{F} : U \subseteq B\}$. The problem is that the latter set may not even be in $\mathcal{F}$, even if $\mathcal{F}$ is a $\sigma$-algebra; it may be a union over uncountably many sets. In the case that $W$ is infinite, the assumptions that $\mathcal{F}$ is a $\sigma$-algebra and $\mu$ is countably additive are necessary. (Your proof is probably incorrect if it does not use them!)

**2.12**    Prove Equation (2.8). (You may assume the results of Exercises 2.10 and 2.11.)

* **2.13**    Show that (2.9) follows from (2.8), using the fact that $\mu^*(U) = 1 - \mu_*(U)$. (Hint: Recall that by the Binomial Theorem, $0 = (1 + (-1))^n = \sum_{i=0}^{n} \binom{n}{i}(-1)^i$.) Indeed, note that if $f$ is an arbitrary function on sets that satisfies (2.8) and $g(U) = 1 - f(\overline{U})$, then $g$ satisfies the analogue of (2.9).

**2.14**    Show that lower and upper probabilities satisfy (2.10) and (2.11), but show by means of a counterexample that they do not satisfy the analogues of (2.8) and (2.9) in general. (Hint: It suffices for the counterexample to consider four possible worlds and a set consisting of two probability measures; alternatively, there is a counterexample with three possible worlds and a set consisting of three probability measures.)

* **2.15**    This exercise and the following one examine the properties that characterize upper and lower probabilities. This exercise focuses on (2.12).

 (a) Show that upper and lower probabilities satisfy (2.12).

 (b) Show that (2.12) does not follow from (2.10) and (2.11) by defining a set $W$ and functions $f$ and $g$ associating with each subset of $W$ a real number in $[0, 1]$ such that (i) $f(\emptyset) = 0$, (ii) $f(W) = 1$, (iii) $f(U) = 1 - g(\overline{U})$, (iv) $f(U \cup V) \geq f(U) + f(V)$ if $U$ and $V$ are disjoint, (v) $g(U \cup V) \leq g(U) + g(V)$ if $U$ and $V$ are disjoint, but (vi) there exist disjoint sets $U$ and $V$ such that $f(U) + g(V) > g(U \cup V)$. Note that (iii) and (iv) say that $f$ and $g$ satisfy analogues of (2.10) and (2.11), while (vi) says that $f$ and $g$ do not satisfy the analogue of (2.12).

* **2.16**    This exercise focuses on (2.13).

 (a) Show that lower probabilities satisfy (2.13).

 (b) Show that (2.10) and (2.12) follow from (2.13) and (2.11).

 (c) Show that $\mathcal{P}_*(\emptyset) = 0$ and $\mathcal{P}_*(W) \leq 1$ follow from (2.13).

   It can be shown that (2.13) characterizes lower probability in that if $g$ is an arbitrary real-valued function defined on subsets of $W$ that satisfies the analogue of (2.13), that is, if $\mathcal{U} = \{U_1, \ldots, U_k\}$ covers $U$ exactly $m + n$ times and covers $\overline{U}$ exactly $m$ times, then $\sum_{i=1}^{k} g(U_i) \leq m + n g(U)$ and, in addition, $g(W) \geq 1$, then $g = \mathcal{P}_*$ for some set $\mathcal{P}$ of probability measures on $W$. (See the notes to this chapter for references.)

**\* 2.17**  Show that the following property of upper probabilities follows from (2.11) and (2.13).

> If $\mathcal{U} = \{U_1, \ldots, U_k\}$ covers $U$ exactly $m + n$ times and covers $\overline{U}$ exactly $m$ times, then $\sum_{i=1}^{k} \mathcal{P}^*(U_i) \geq m + n\mathcal{P}^*(U)$.   (2.18)

An almost identical argument shows that (2.13) follows from (2.11) and (2.18). This shows that it is possible to take either upper probabilities or lower probabilities as basic.

**\* 2.18**  Suppose that $\mathcal{F}$ is a $\sigma$-algebra and all the probability measures in $\mathcal{P}$ are countably additive.

  (a) Show that (2.14) holds.

  (b) Show that the analogue of (2.1) holds for upper probability, while the analogue of (2.2) does not.

**2.19**  Show that $(\mathcal{P}_3)_* = (\mathcal{P}_4)_*$ in Example 2.3.4.

**2.20**  Let $W = \{w, w'\}$ and define $\mathrm{Bel}(\{w\}) = 1/2$, $\mathrm{Bel}(\{w'\}) = 0$, $\mathrm{Bel}(W) = 1$, and $\mathrm{Bel}(\emptyset) = 0$. Show that Bel is a belief function, but there is no probability $\mu$ on $W$ such that $\mathrm{Bel} = \mu_*$. (Hint: To show that Bel is a belief function, find a corresponding mass function.)

**2.21**  Construct two belief functions $\mathrm{Bel}_1$ and $\mathrm{Bel}_2$ on $\{1, 2, 3\}$ such that $\mathrm{Bel}_1(i) = \mathrm{Bel}_2(i) = 0$ for $i = 1, 2, 3$ (so that $\mathrm{Bel}_1$ and $\mathrm{Bel}_2$ agree on singleton sets) but $\mathrm{Bel}_1(\{1, 2\}) \neq \mathrm{Bel}_2(\{1, 2\})$. (Hint: Again, to show that the functions you construct are actually belief functions, find the corresponding mass functions.)

**2.22**  Show that $\mathrm{Bel}(U) \leq \mathrm{Plaus}(U)$ for all sets $U$.

**\* 2.23**  Prove Theorem 2.4.1.

**2.24**  Construct a belief function Bel on $W = \{a, b, c\}$ and a set $\mathcal{P} \neq \mathcal{P}_{\mathrm{Bel}}$ of probability measures such that $\mathrm{Bel} = \mathcal{P}_*$ (and hence $\mathrm{Plaus} = \mathcal{P}^*$).

**\* 2.25**  Prove Theorem 2.4.3. (Hint: Proving that $\mathrm{Bel}_m$ is a belief function requires proving B1, B2, and B3. B1 and B2 are obvious, given M1 and M2. For B3, proceed by induction on $n$, the number of sets in the union, using the fact that $\mathrm{Bel}_m(A_1 \cup \ldots \cup A_{n+1}) = \mathrm{Bel}_m((A_1 \cup \ldots \cup A_n) \cup A_{n+1})$. To construct $m$ given Bel, define $m(\{w_1, \ldots, w_n\})$ by induction on $n$ so that (2.17) holds. Note that the induction argument does not apply if $W$ is infinite. Indeed, as observed in Exercise 2.26, the theorem does not hold in that case.)

\* **2.26**   Show that Theorem 2.4.3 does not hold in general if $W$ is infinite. More precisely, show that there is a belief function Bel on an infinite set $W$ such that there is no mass function $m$ on $W$ such that $\text{Bel}(U) = \sum_{\{U':U'\subseteq U\}} m(U)$. (Hint: Define $\text{Bel}(U) = 1$ if $U$ is cofinite, i.e., $\overline{U}$ is finite, and $\text{Bel}(U) = 0$ otherwise.)

**2.27**   Show that if $W$ is finite and $\mu$ is a probability measure on $2^W$, then the mass function $m_\mu$ corresponding to $\mu$ gives positive mass only to singletons, and $m_\mu(w) = \mu(w)$. Conversely, if $m$ is a mass function that gives positive mass only to singletons, then the belief function corresponding to $m$ is in fact a probability measure. (This argument can be generalized so as to apply to probability measures defined only on some algebra $\mathcal{F}$, provided that belief functions defined only on $\mathcal{F}$ are allowed. That is, if $\mu$ is a probability measure on $\mathcal{F}$, then it can be viewed as a belief function on $\mathcal{F}$. There is then a corresponding mass function defined only on $\mathcal{F}$ that gives positive measure only to the basic sets in $\mathcal{F}$. Conversely, if $m$ is a mass function on $\mathcal{F}$ that gives positive mass only to the basic sets in $\mathcal{F}$, then $\text{Bel}_m$ is a probability measure on $\mathcal{F}$.)

**2.28**   Suppose that $m_1$ and $m_2$ are mass functions, $\text{Bel}_1$ and $\text{Bel}_2$ are the corresponding belief functions, and there do not exist sets $U_1$ and $U_2$ such that $U_1 \cap U_2 \neq \emptyset$ and $m_1(U_1)m_2(U_2) > 0$. Show that there must then be sets $V_1$, $V_2$ such that $\text{Bel}_1(V_1) = \text{Bel}_2(V_2) = 1$ and $V_1 \cap V_2 = \emptyset$.

**2.29**   Show that the definition of $\oplus$ in the Rule of Combination guarantees that $m_1 \oplus m_2$ is defined iff the renormalization constant $c$ is positive and that, if $m_1 \oplus m_2$ is defined, then it is a mass function (i.e., it satisfies M1 and M2).

**2.30**   Show that $\oplus$ is commutative and associative, and that $m_{vac}$ is the neutral element for $\oplus$.

**2.31**   Poss3 says that $\text{Poss}(U \cup V) = \max(\text{Poss}(U), \text{Poss}(V))$ for $U$, $V$ disjoint. Show that $\text{Poss}(U \cup V) = \max(\text{Poss}(U), \text{Poss}(V))$ even if $U$ and $V$ are not disjoint. Similarly, if $\kappa$ is a ranking function, show that $\kappa(U \cup V) = \min(\kappa(U), \kappa(V))$ even if $U$ and $V$ are not disjoint.

**2.32**   This exercise and the next investigate properties of possibility measures defined on infinite sets.

   (a) Show that if $\text{Poss}_0$ is defined as in Example 2.5.1, then it satisfies Poss1–3.

   (b) Show that $\text{Poss}_0$ does not satisfy Poss3$'$.

   (c) Show that if $\text{Poss}_1$ is defined as in Example 2.5.2, then it satisfies Poss1, Poss2, and Poss3$'$.

(d) Show that if $Poss_2$ is defined as in Example 2.5.3, it satisfies Poss1, Poss2, and Poss3′, but does not satisfy Poss3$^+$.

(e) Show that if $Poss_3$ is defined as in Example 2.5.3, then it satisfies Poss1, Poss2, and Poss3′.

* **2.33** This exercise considers Poss3′ and Poss3$^+$ in more detail.

(a) Show that Poss3′ and Poss3$^+$ are equivalent if $W$ is countable. (Note that the possibility measure $Poss_2$ defined in Example 2.5.3 and considered in Exercise 2.32 shows that they are not equivalent in general; $Poss_2$ satisfies Poss3′, but not Poss3$^+$.)

(b) Consider the following continuity property:

$$\text{If } U_1, U_2, U_3, \ldots \text{ is an increasing sequence, then}$$
$$\lim_{i \to \infty} Poss(U_i) = Poss(\cup_i U_i). \tag{2.19}$$

Show that (2.19) together with Poss3 is equivalent to Poss3′.

(c) Show that the following stronger continuity property together with Poss3 is equivalent to Poss3$^+$:

$$\text{If } U_\alpha, \alpha \le \beta \text{ is an increasing sequence of sets indexed by ordinals (so that if}$$
$$\alpha < \alpha' \le \beta, \text{ then } U_\alpha \subseteq U_{\alpha'}), \text{ then } Poss(\cup_\alpha U_\alpha) = \sup_\alpha Poss(U_\alpha).$$

* **2.34** Show that possibility measures satisfy (2.16) and hence are plausibility functions. (Hint: Show that

$$\sum_{i=1}^{n} \sum_{\{I \subseteq \{1,\ldots,n\}:|I|=i\}} (-1)^{i+1} Poss(\cup_{j \in I} U_j) = \min\{Poss(U_1), \ldots, Poss(U_n)\},$$

by induction on $n$.)

**2.35** Show that $Nec(U) \le Poss(U)$ for all sets $U$, using Poss1–3.

* **2.36** Prove Theorem 2.5.4. In addition, show that the argument that $Plaus_m$ is a possibility measure works even if $W$ is infinite.

* **2.37** Define Poss on $[0, 1]$ by taking $Poss(U) = \sup U$ if $U \neq \emptyset$, $Poss(\emptyset) = 0$. Show that Poss is a possibility measure and that $Poss(\cup_\alpha U_\alpha) = \sup_\alpha Poss(U_\alpha)$, where $\{U_\alpha\}$ is an arbitrary collection of subsets of $[0, 1]$. However, show that there is no mass function $m$ such that $Poss = Plaus_m$.

**2.38**    Show that $\max(\mu(U), \mu(V)) \le \mu(U \cup V) \le \min(\mu(U) + \mu(V), 1)$. Moreover, show that these bounds are optimal, in that there is a probability measure $\mu$ and sets $U_1$, $V_1$, $U_2$, and $V_2$ such that $\mu(U_1 \cup V_1) = \max(U_1, V_1)$ and $\mu(U_2 \cup V_2) = \min(\mu(U_2) + \mu(V_2), 1)$.

**2.39**    Show that $\mathrm{Poss}_\kappa$ (as defined in Section 2.5) is a possibility measure.

**2.40**    Fix an infinitesimal $\epsilon$ and a nonstandard probability measure $\mu$. Define $\kappa(U)$ to be the smallest natural number $k$ such that $\mu(U) > \alpha \epsilon^k$ for some standard real $\alpha > 0$. Show that $\kappa$ is a ranking function (i.e., $\kappa$ satisfies Rk1–3).

**2.41**    Show that if $\succeq$ is a partial preorder, then the relation $\succ$ defined by $w \succ w'$ if $w \succeq w'$ and $w' \not\succeq w$ is irreflexive, transitive, and antisymmetric.

**2.42**    Prove Theorem 2.7.1.

**2.43**    Prove Theorem 2.7.2. Moreover, show that if $\rhd$ is a total preorder, then the assumption that $\rhd$ is determined by singletons can be replaced by the assumption that the strict partial order determined by $\rhd$ has the union property. That is, show that if $\rhd$ is a total preorder on $2^W$ that respects subsets and has the union property, such that the strict partial order determined by $\rhd$ also has the union property, then there is a total preorder $\succeq$ such that $\succeq^e = \rhd$.

\* **2.44**    Show directly that $\succ^e$ has the qualitative property if $\succeq$ is total.

**2.45**    Show that $U \succeq^e V$ iff for all $v \in V - U$, there exists $u \in U$ such that $u \succeq v$.

**2.46**    Show that if $U \succ^s V$ then $U \succ^e V$. Note that Example 2.7.3 shows that the converse does not hold in general. However, show that the converse does hold if $\succeq$ is total. (Thus, for total preorders, $\succ^s$ and $\succ^e$ agree on finite sets.)

**2.47**    Show that if $W$ is finite, and for all $v \in V$ there exists $u \in U$ such that $u \succ v$, then for all $v \in V$ there exists $u \in U$ such that $u \succ v$ and $u$ dominates $V$. Show, however, that if $W$ is infinite, then even if $\succeq$ is a total preorder, there can exist disjoint sets $U$ and $V$ such that for all $v \in V$, there exists $u \in U$ such that $u \succ v$, yet there is no $u \in U$ that dominates $V$.

\* **2.48**    Prove Theorem 2.7.5.

**2.49**    Show that if $\rhd$ is a conservative qualitative relation and $\rhd'$ is the strict partial order determined by $\rhd$, then $\rhd$ and $\rhd'$ agree on disjoint sets (i.e., if $U$ and $V$ are disjoint, the $U \rhd V$ iff $U \rhd' V$.) Since $\succeq^s$ is a conservative qualitative relation, it follows that $\succeq^s$ and $\succ^s$ agree on disjoint sets and hence that $\succ^s$ is qualitative.

**2.50** Complete the proof of Theorem 2.7.6.

**2.51** Suppose that Poss is a possibility measure on $W$. Define a partial preorder $\succeq$ on $W$ such that $w \succeq w'$ if $\text{Poss}(w) \geq \text{Poss}(w')$.

(a) Show that $U \succeq^e V$ implies $\text{Poss}(U) \geq \text{Poss}(V)$.

(b) Show that $\text{Poss}(U) > \text{Poss}(V)$ implies $U \succ^e V$.

(c) Show that the converses to parts (a) and (b) do not hold in general. (Hint: Consider the case where one of $U$ or $V$ is the empty set.)

(d) Show that if $\text{Poss}(w) > 0$ for all $w \in W$, then the converses to parts (a) and (b) do hold.

**2.52** Show directly (without using Theorem 2.7.1) that Poss is qualitative; in fact, show that if $\text{Poss}(U_1 \cup U_2) > \text{Poss}(U_3)$ and $\text{Poss}(U_1 \cup U_3) > \text{Poss}(U_2)$, then $\text{Poss}(U_1) > \text{Poss}(U_2 \cup U_3)$. (This is true even if $U_1$, $U_2$, and $U_3$ are not pairwise disjoint.) An almost identical argument shows that ranking functions have the qualitative property.

**2.53** State and prove an analogue of Exercise 2.51 for ranking functions.

**2.54** Show that $\succeq$ as defined on $W/\sim$ in Section 2.8 is well defined (i.e., if $U$, $U' \in [U]$ and $V$, $V' \in [V]$ that $U \succeq V$ iff $U' \succeq V'$.

**2.55** Suppose that $|W| \geq 4$. Show that there exists a set $\mathcal{P}$ of probability measures on $W$ and subsets $U$, $V$ of $W$ such that

(a) $\mathcal{P}_*(U) < \mathcal{P}_*(V)$ and $\mathcal{P}^*(U) > \mathcal{P}^*(V)$; and

(b) $\mu(U) < \mu(V)$ for all $\mu \in \mathcal{P}$ but $\mathcal{P}_*(U) = \mathcal{P}_*(V)$ and $\mathcal{P}^*(U) = \mathcal{P}^*(V)$.

**2.56** Show that there exist a set $W$, a belief function Bel on $W$, and pairwise disjoint subsets $U_1$, $U_2$, $V_1$, $V_2$ of $W$ such that $\text{Bel}(U_1) = \text{Bel}(V_1)$, $\text{Bel}(U_2) = \text{Bel}(V_2)$, but $\text{Bel}(U_1 \cup U_2) \neq \text{Bel}(V_1 \cup V_2)$.

**2.57** Consider the following property of plausibility measures:

Pl3'. If $V$ is disjoint from both $U$ and $U'$ and $\text{Pl}(U) \leq \text{Pl}(U')$, then $\text{Pl}(U \cup V) \leq \text{Pl}(U' \cup V)$.

(a) Show that Pl3' implies Pl3.

(b) Show that probability measures, possibility measures, and ranking functions satisfy Pl3'.

(c) Show that probability measures satisfy the converse of P13' (if $\mu(U \cup V) \leq \mu(U' \cup V)$, then $\mu(U) \leq \mu(U')$), but possibility measures and ranking functions do not.

(d) Show by example that belief functions, and similarly lower probability measures and inner measures, do not satisfy P13' or its converse.

## Notes

There are many texts on all facets of probability; four standard introductions are by Ash [1970], Billingsley [1986], Feller [1957], and Halmos [1950]. In particular, these texts show that it is impossible to find a probability measure $\mu$ defined on all subsets of the interval [0, 1] in such a way that (1) the probability of an interval [a, b] is its length $b - a$ and (2) $\mu(U) = \mu(U')$ if $U'$ is the result of translating $U$ by a constant. (Formally, if $x$ mod 1 is the fractional part of $x$, so that, e.g., 1.6 mod 1 = .6, then $U'$ is the result of translating $U$ by the constant $c$ if $U' = \{(x + c) \bmod 1 : x \in U\}$.) There is a translation-invariant countably additive probability measure $\mu$ defined on a large $\sigma$-algebra of subsets of [0, 1] (that includes all intervals so that $\mu([a, b]) = b - a$) such that $\mu([a, b]) = b - a$. That is part of the technical motivation for taking the domain of a probability measure to be an algebra (or a $\sigma$-algebra, if $W$ is infinite).

Billingsley [1986, p. 17] discusses why, in general, it is useful to have probability measures defined on algebras (indeed, $\sigma$-algebras). *Dynkin systems* [Williams 1991] (sometimes called $\lambda$ *systems* [Billingsley 1986, p. 37]) are an attempt to go beyond algebras. A Dynkin system is a set of subsets of a space $W$ that contains $W$ and that is closed under complements and *disjoint* unions (or countable disjoint unions, depending on whether the analogue of an algebra or a $\sigma$-algebra is desired); it is not necessarily closed under arbitrary unions. That is, if $\mathcal{F}$ is a Dynkin system, and $U, V \in \mathcal{F}$, then $U \cup V$ is in $\mathcal{F}$ if $U$ and $V$ are disjoint, but if $U$ and $V$ are not disjoint, then $U \cup V$ may not be in $\mathcal{F}$. Notice that properties P1 and P2 make perfect sense in Dynkin systems, so a Dynkin system can be taken to be the domain of a probability measure. It is certainly more reasonable to assume that the set of sets to which a probability can be assigned form a Dynkin system rather than an algebra. Moreover, most of the discussion of probability given here goes through if the domain of a probability measure is taken to be a Dynkin system.

The use of the principle of indifference in probability is associated with a number of people in the seventeenth and eighteenth centuries, chief among them perhaps Bernoulli and Laplace. Hacking [1975] provides a good historical discussion. The term *principle of indifference* is due to Keynes [1921]; it has also been called the *principle of insufficient reason* [Kries 1886].

Many justifications for probability can be found in the literature. As stated in the text, the strongest proponent of the relative-frequency interpretation was von Mises [1957]. A recent defense of this position was given by van Lambalgen [1987].

Ramsey's [1931b] is perhaps the first careful justification of the subjective viewpoint; the variant of his argument given here is due to Paris [1994]. De Finetti [1931, 1937, 1972] proved the first Dutch book arguments. The subjective viewpoint often goes under the name *Bayesianism* and its adherents are often called *Bayesians* (named after Reverend Thomas Bayes, who derived Bayes' Rule, discussed in Chapter 3).

The notion of a bet considered here is an instance of what Walley [1991] calls a *gamble:* a function from the set $W$ of worlds to the reals. (Gambles will be studied in more detail in Chapter 4.) Walley [1991, p. 152] describes a number of rationality axioms for when a gamble should be considered *acceptable;* gamble $X$ is then considered preferable to $Y$ if the gamble $X - Y$ is acceptable. Walley's axioms D0 and D3 correspond to RAT1 and RAT4; axiom D3 corresponds to a property RAT5 considered in Chapter 3. RAT2 (transitivity) follows for Walley from his D3 and the definitions. Walley deliberately does not have an analogue of RAT3; he wants to allow incomparable gambles.

Another famous justification of probability is due to Cox [1946], who showed that any function that assigns degrees to events and satisfies certain minimal properties (such as the degree of belief in $\overline{U}$ is a decreasing function in the degree of belief in $U$) must be isomorphic to a probability measure. Unfortunately, Cox's argument is not quite correct as stated; his hypotheses need to be strengthened (in ways that make them less compelling) to make it correct [Halpern 1999a; Halpern 1999b; Paris 1994].

Yet another justification for probability is due to Savage [1954], who showed that a rational agent (where "rational" is defined in terms of a collection of axioms) can, in a precise sense, be viewed as acting as if his beliefs were characterized by a probability measure. More precisely, Savage showed that a rational agent's preferences on a set of actions can be represented by a probability measure on a set of possible worlds combined with a utility function on the outcomes of the actions; the agent then prefers action $a$ to action $b$ if and only if the expected utility of $a$ is higher than that of $b$. Savage's approach has had a profound impact on the field of *decision theory* (see Section 5.4).

The behavior of people on examples such as Example 2.3.2 has been the subject of intense investigation. This example is closely related to the *Ellsberg paradox*; see the references for Chapter 5.

The idea of modeling imprecision in terms of sets of probability measures is an old one, apparently going back as far as Boole [1854, Chapters 16–21] and Ostrogradsky

[1838]. Borel [1943, Section 3.8] suggested that upper and lower probabilities could be measured behaviorally, as betting rates on or against an event. These arguments were formalized by Smith [1961]. In many cases, the set $\mathcal{P}$ of probabilities is taken to be convex (so that if $\mu_1$ and $\mu_2$ are in $\mathcal{P}$, then so is $a\mu_1 + b\mu_2$, where $a, b \in [0, 1]$ and $a + b = 1$)—see, for example, [Campos and Moral 1995; Cousa, Moral, and Walley 1999; Gilboa and Schmeidler 1993; Levi 1985; Walley 1991] for discussion and further references. It has been argued [Cousa, Moral, and Walley 1999] that, as far as making a decision goes, a set of probabilities is behaviorally equivalent to its convex hull (i.e., the least convex set that contains it). However, a convex set does not seem appropriate for representing say, the uncertainty in the two-coin problem from Chapter 1. Moreover, there are contexts other than decision making where a set of probabilities has very different properties from its convex hull (see Exercise 4.12). Thus, I do not assume convexity in this book.

Walley [1991] provides a thorough discussion of a representation of uncertainty that he calls *upper* and *lower previsions*. They are upper and lower bounds on the uncertainty of an event (and are closely related to lower and upper probabilities); see the notes to Chapter 5 for more details.

The idea of using inner measures to capture imprecision was first discussed in [Fagin and Halpern 1991b]. The inclusion-exclusion rule is discussed in most standard probability texts, as well as in standard introductions to discrete mathematics (e.g., [Maurer and Ralston 1991]). Upper and lower probabilities were characterized (independently, it seems) by Wolf [1977], Williams [1976], and Anger and Lembcke [1985]. In particular, Anger and Lembcke show that (2.18) (see Exercise 2.17) characterizes upper probabilities. (It follows from Exercise 2.17 that (2.13) characterizes lower probabilities.) Further discussion of the properties of upper and lower probabilities can be found in [Halpern and Pucella 2001].

The proof of Theorem 2.3.3 is sketched in Exercise 2.8. The result seems to be due to Horn and Tarski [1948]. As mentioned in the discussion in Exercise 2.8, if countable additivity is required, Theorem 2.3.3 may not hold. In fact, if countable additivity is required, the set $\mathcal{P}_\mu$ may be empty! (For those familiar with probability theory and set theory, this is why: Let $\mathcal{F}$ be the Borel subsets of $[0, 1]$, let $\mathcal{F}'$ be all subsets of $[0, 1]$, and let $\mu$ be Lebesgue measure defined on the Borel sets in $[0, 1]$. As shown by Ulam [1930], under the continuum hypothesis (which says that there are no cardinalities in between the cardinality of the reals and the cardinality of the natural numbers), there is no countably additive measure extending $\mu$ defined on all subsets of $[0, 1]$.) A variant of Proposition 2.3.3 does hold even for countably additive measures. If $\mu$ is a probability measure on an algebra $\mathcal{F}$, let $\mathcal{P}'_\mu$ consist of all extensions of $\mu$ to some algebra $\mathcal{F}' \supseteq \mathcal{F}$ (so that the measures in $\mathcal{P}'_\mu$ may be defined on different algebras). Define $(\mathcal{P}'_\mu)_*(U) = \inf\{\mu'(U) : \mu \in \mathcal{P}'_\mu, \ \mu' \text{ is defined on } U\}$. Then essentially the same arguments as those given in Exercise 2.8 show that $\mu_* = (\mathcal{P}'_\mu)_*$. These arguments hold even if all the probability measures in $\mathcal{P}'_\mu$ are required to be countably additive (assuming that $\mu$ is countably additive).

Belief functions were originally introduced by Dempster [1967, 1968], and then extensively developed by Shafer [1976]. Choquet [1953] independently and earlier introduced the notion of *capacities* (now often called *Choquet capacities*); a *k-monotone* capacity satisfies B3 for $n = 1, \ldots, k$; infinitely-monotone capacities are mathematically equivalent to belief functions. Theorem 2.4.1 was originally proved by Dempster [1967], while Theorem 2.4.3 was proved by Shafer [1976, p. 39]. Examples 2.4.4 and 2.4.5 are taken from Gordon and Shortliffe [1984] (with slight modifications). Fagin and I [1991b] and Ruspini [1987] were the first to observe the connection between belief functions and inner measures. Exercise 2.12 is Proposition 3.1 in [Fagin and Halpern 1991b]; it also follows from a more general result proved by Shafer [1979]. Shafer [1990] discusses various justifications for and interpretations of belief functions. He explicitly rejects the idea of belief function as a lower probability.

Possibility measures were introduced by Zadeh [1978], who developed them from his earlier work on fuzzy sets and fuzzy logic [Zadeh 1975]. The theory was greatly developed by Dubois, Prade, and others; a good introduction can be found in [Dubois and Prade 1990]. Theorem 2.5.4 on the connection between possibility measures and plausibility functions based on consonant mass functions is proved, for example, by Dubois and Prade [1982].

Ordinal conditional functions were originally defined by Spohn [1988], who allowed them to have values in the ordinals, not just values in $\mathbb{N}^*$. Spohn also showed the relationship between his ranking functions and nonstandard probability, as sketched in Exercise 2.40. (For more on nonstandard probability measures and their applications to decision theory and game theory, see, e.g., [Hammond 1994].) The degree-of-surprise interpretation for ranking functions goes back to Shackle [1969].

Most of the ideas in Section 2.7 go back to Lewis [1973], but he focused on the case of total preorders. The presentation (and, to some extent, the notation) in this section is inspired by that of [Halpern 1997a]. What is called $\succeq^s$ in [Halpern 1997a] is called $\succeq^e$ here; $\succ'$ in [Halpern 1997a] is $\succ^e$ here. The ordering $\succeq^s$ is actually taken from [Friedman and Halpern 2001]. Other ways of ordering sets have been discussed in the literature; see, for example, [Dershowitz and Manna 1979; Doyle, Shoham, and Wellman 1991]. (A more detailed discussion of other approaches and further references can be found in [Halpern 1997a].) The characterizations in Theorems 2.7.2 and 2.7.6 are typical of results in the game theory literature. These particular results are inspired by similar results in [Halpern 1999c]. These "set-theoretic completeness" results should be compared to the axiomatic completeness results proved in Section 7.5.

As observed in the text, the properties of $\succeq^e$ are quite different from those satisfied by the (total) preorder on sets induced by a probability measure. A *qualitative probability preorder* is a preorder on sets induced by a probability measure. That is, $\succeq$ is a qualitative probability preorder if there is a probability measure $\mu$ such that $U \succeq V$ iff $\mu(U) \geq \mu(V)$. What properties does a qualitative probability preorder $\succeq$ have? Clearly, $\succeq$ must be a total preorder. Another obvious property is that if $V$ is disjoint from both $U$ and $U'$, then $U \succeq U'$ iff $U \cup V \succeq U' \cup V$ (i.e., the analogue of property P13$'$ in Exercise 2.57). It turns out that it is possible to characterize qualitative probability preorders, but the characterization is nontrivial. Fine [1973] discusses this issue in more detail.

Plausibility measures were introduced in [Friedman and Halpern 1995; Friedman and Halpern 2001]; the discussion in Section 2.8 is taken from these papers. Weber [1991] independently introduced an equivalent notion. Schmeidler [1989] has a notion of *nonadditive probability*, which is also similar in spirit, except that the range of a nonadditive probability is [0, 1] (so that $\nu$ is a nonadditive probability on $W$ iff (1) $\nu(\emptyset) = 0$, (2) $\nu(W) = 1$, and (3) $\nu(U) \leq \nu(V)$ if $U \subseteq V$).

The issue of what is the most appropriate representation to use in various setting deserves closer scrutiny. Walley [2000] has done one of the few serious analyses of this issue; I hope there will be more.

# Chapter 3

# Updating Beliefs

*God does not play dice with the Universe.*

—Albert Einstein

*Not only does God play dice, but sometimes he throws the dice where we can't see them.*

—Stephen Hawking

Agents continually obtain new information and then must update their beliefs to take this new information into account. How this should be done obviously depends in part on how uncertainty is represented. Each of the methods of representing uncertainty considered in Chapter 2 has an associated method for updating. In this chapter, I consider issues raised by updating and examine how they play out in each of the representations of uncertainty.

## 3.1 Updating Knowledge

I start by examining perhaps the simplest setting, where an agent's uncertainty is captured by a set $W$ of possible worlds, with no further structure. I assume that the agent obtains the information that the actual world is in some subset $U$ of $W$. (I do not consider more complicated types of information until Sections 3.10 and 3.11.) The obvious thing to do in that case is to take the set of possible worlds to be $W \cap U$. For example, when tossing a die, an agent might consider any one of the six outcomes to be possible. However, if she learns that the die landed on an even number, then she would consider possible only the three outcomes corresponding to 2, 4, and 6.

Even in this simple setting, three implicit assumptions are worth bringing out. The first is that this notion seems to require that the agent does not forget. To see this, it is helpful to have a concrete model.

**Example 3.1.1**    Suppose that a world describes which of 100 people have a certain disease. A world can be characterized by a tuple of 100 0s and 1s, where the $i$th component is 1 iff individual $i$ has the disease. There are $2^{100}$ possible worlds. Take the "agent" in question to be a computer system that initially has no information (and thus considers all $2^{100}$ worlds possible), then receives information that is assumed to be true about which world is the actual world. This information comes in the form of statements like "individual $i$ is sick or individual $j$ is healthy" or "at least seven people have the disease." Each such statement can be identified with a set of possible worlds. For example, the statement "at least seven people have the disease" can be identified with the set of tuples with at least seven 1s. Thus, for simplicity, assume that the agent is given information saying "the actual world is in set $U$," for various sets $U$.

Suppose at some point the agent has been told that the actual world is in $U_1, \ldots, U_n$. The agent should then consider possible precisely the worlds in $U_1 \cap \ldots \cap U_n$. If it is then told $V$, it considers possible $U_1 \cap \ldots \cap U_n \cap V$. This seems to justify the idea of capturing updating by $U$ as intersecting the current set of possible worlds with $U$.

But all is not so simple. How does the agent keep track of the worlds it considers possible? It certainly will not explicitly list the $2^{100}$ possible worlds it initially considers possible! Even though storage is getting cheaper, this is well beyond the capability of any imaginable system. What seems much more reasonable is that it uses an implicit description. That is, it keeps track of what it has been told and takes the set of possible worlds to be the ones consistent with what it has been told. But now suppose that it has been told $n$ things, say $U_1, \ldots, U_n$. In this case, the agent may not be able to keep all of $U_1, \ldots, U_n$ in its memory after learning some new fact $V$. How should updating work in this case? That depends on the details of memory management. It is not so clear that intersection is appropriate here if forgetting is allowed.  ∎

The second assumption is perhaps more obvious but nonetheless worth stressing. In the example, I have implicitly assumed that what the agent is told is true (i.e., that the actual world is in $U$ if the agent is told $U$) and that it initially considers the actual world possible. From this it follows that if $U_0$ is the system's initial set of possible worlds and the system is told $U$, then $U_0 \cap U \neq \emptyset$ (since the actual world is in $U_0 \cap U$).

It is not even clear how to interpret a situation where the system's set of possible worlds is empty. If the agent can be told inconsistent information, then clearly intersection is simply not an appropriate way of updating. Nevertheless, it seems reasonable to try to model a situation where an agent can believe that the actual world is in $U$ and later discover that it is not. This topic is discussed in more detail in Chapter 9. For now, I just assume that the information given is such that the sets that arise are always nonempty.

The third assumption is that the way an agent obtains the new information does not itself give the agent information. An agent often obtains new information by observing an event. For example, he may learn that it is sunny outdoors by looking out a window. However, making an observation may give more information than just the fact that what is observed is true. If this is not taken into account, intersecting may give an inappropriate answer. The following example should help to clarify this point:

**Example 3.1.2**   Suppose that Alice is about to look for a book in a room. The book may or may not be in the room and the light may or may not be on in the room. Thus, according to this naive description, there are four possible worlds. Suppose that, initially, Bob considers all four worlds possible. Assume for simplicity that if the book is in the room, it is on the table, so that Alice will certainly see it if the light is on. When Bob is told that Alice saw the book in the room, he clearly considers only one world possible: the one where the book is in the room and the light is on. This is obviously not the result of intersecting the four worlds he initially considered possible with the two worlds where the book is in the room. The fact that Alice saw the book tells Bob not only that the book is in the room, but also that the light is on. In this case, there is a big difference between Bob being told that Alice *saw* the book and Bob being told that the book is in the room (perhaps Alice remembered leaving it there).

If $W$ is augmented to include a relative likelihood on worlds, then even the relative likelihood of worlds could change if the observation gives more information than just what is observed. For example, suppose that Bob initially thinks that the light in the room is more likely to be off than on. Further suppose that there may be some light from outdoors filtering through the curtain, so that it is possible for Alice to see the book in the room even if the light is off. After hearing that Alice saw the book, Bob considers only the two worlds where a book is in the room to be possible, but now considers it more likely that the light is on. Bob's relative ordering of the worlds has changed.  ∎

The situation gets even more complicated if there are many agents, because now the model needs to take into account what other agents learn when one agent learns $U$. I defer further discussion of these issues to Chapter 6, where a model is provided that handles many agents, in which it is relatively straightforward to make precise what it means that an observation gives no more information than the fact that it is true (see Section 6.8).

## 3.2    Probabilistic Conditioning

Suppose that an agent's uncertainty is represented by a probability measure $\mu$ on $W$ and then the agent observes or learns (that the actual world is in) $U$. How should $\mu$ be updated to a new probability measure $\mu|U$ that takes this new information into account? Clearly if the agent believes that $U$ is true, then it seems reasonable to require that

$$\mu|U(\overline{U}) = 0; \tag{3.1}$$

all the worlds in $\overline{U}$ are impossible. What about worlds in $U$? What should their probability be? One reasonable intuition here is that if all that the agent has learned is $U$, then the relative likelihood of worlds in $U$ should remain unchanged. (This presumes that the way that the agent learns $U$ does not itself give the agent information; otherwise, as was shown in Example 3.1.2, relative likelihoods may indeed change.) That is, if $V_1$, $V_2 \subseteq U$ with $\mu(V_2) > 0$, then

$$\frac{\mu(V_1)}{\mu(V_2)} = \frac{\mu|U(V_1)}{\mu|U(V_2)}. \tag{3.2}$$

Equations (3.1) and (3.2) completely determine $\mu|U$ if $\mu(U) > 0$.

**Proposition 3.2.1**    *If $\mu(U) > 0$ and $\mu|U$ is a probability measure on $W$ satisfying (3.1) and (3.2), then*

$$\mu|U(V) = \frac{\mu(V \cap U)}{\mu(U)}. \tag{3.3}$$

**Proof**    Since $\mu|U$ is a probability measure and so satisfies P1 and P2, by (3.1), $\mu|U(U) = 1$. Taking $V_2 = U$ and $V_1 = V$ in (3.2), it follows that $\mu|U(V) = \mu(V)/\mu(U)$ for $V \subseteq U$. Now if $V$ is not a subset of $U$, then $V = (V \cap U) \cup (V \cap \overline{U})$. Since $V \cap U$ and $V \cap \overline{U}$ are disjoint sets, $\mu|U(V) = \mu|U(V \cap U) + \mu|U(V \cap \overline{U})$. Since $V \cap \overline{U} \subseteq \overline{U}$ and $\mu|U(\overline{U}) = 0$, it follows that $\mu|U(V \cap \overline{U}) = 0$ (Exercise 2.4). Since $U \cap V \subseteq U$, using the previous observations,

$$\mu|U(V) = \mu|U(V \cap U) = \frac{\mu(V \cap U)}{\mu(U)},$$

as desired.    ∎

Following traditional practice, I often write $\mu(V \mid U)$ rather than $\mu|U(V)$; $\mu|U$ is called a *conditional probability (measure)*, and $\mu(V \mid U)$ is read "the probability of $V$

*given* (or *conditional on*) $U$." Sometimes $\mu(U)$ is called the *unconditional* probability of $U$.

Using conditioning, I can make precise a remark that I made in Section 2.2: namely, that all choices of initial probability will eventually converge to the "right" probability measure as more and more information is received.

**Example 3.2.2**   Suppose that, as in Example 2.4.6, Alice has a coin and she knows that it has either bias $2/3$ (*BH*) or bias $1/3$ (*BT*). She considers it much more likely that the bias is $1/3$ than $2/3$. Thus, initially, she assigns a probability $.99$ to *BT* and a probability of $.01$ to *BH*.

Alice tosses the coin 25 times to learn more about its bias; she sees 19 heads and 6 tails. This seems to make it much more likely that the coin has bias $2/3$, so Alice would like to update her probabilities. To do this, she needs to construct an appropriate set of possible worlds. A reasonable candidate consists of $2^{26}$ worlds—for each of the two biases Alice considers possible, there are $2^{25}$ worlds consisting of all the possible sequences of 25 coin tosses. The prior probability (i.e., the probability before observing the coin tosses) of the coin having bias $1/3$ and getting a particular sequence of tosses with $n$ heads and $25 - n$ tails is $.99 \left(\frac{1}{3}\right)^n \left(\frac{2}{3}\right)^{25-n}$. That is, it is the probability of the coin having bias $1/3$ times the probability of getting that sequence given that the coin has bias $1/3$. In particular, the probability of the coin having bias $1/3$ and getting a particular sequence with 19 heads and 6 tails is $.99 \left(\frac{1}{3}\right)^{19} \left(\frac{2}{3}\right)^6$. Similarly, the probability of the coin having bias $2/3$ and getting the same sequence is $.01 \left(\frac{2}{3}\right)^{19} \left(\frac{1}{3}\right)^6$.

Since Alice has seen a particular sequence of 25 coin tosses, she should condition on the event corresponding to that sequence—that is, on the set $U$ consisting of the two worlds where that sequence of coin tosses occurs. The probability of $U$ is $.99 \left(\frac{1}{3}\right)^{19} \left(\frac{2}{3}\right)^6 + .01 \left(\frac{2}{3}\right)^{19} \left(\frac{1}{3}\right)^6$. The probability that the coin has bias $1/3$ given $U$ is then $.99 \left(\frac{1}{3}\right)^{19} \left(\frac{2}{3}\right)^6 / \mu(U)$. A straightforward calculation shows that this simplifies to $\frac{99}{99+2^{13}}$, which is roughly $.01$. Thus, although initially Alice gives *BT* probability $.99$, she gives *BH* probability roughly $.99$ after seeing the evidence.

Of course, this is not an accident. Technically, as long as Alice gives the correct hypothesis (*BH*—that the bias is $2/3$) positive probability initially, then her *posterior probability* of the correct hypothesis (after conditioning) will converge to 1 after almost all sequences of coin tosses. (A small aside: It is standard in the literature to talk about an agent's "prior" and "posterior" probabilities. The implicit assumption is that there is some fixed initial time when the analysis starts. The agent's probability at this time is her prior. Then the agent gets some information and conditions on it; the resulting probability is her posterior.) In any case, to make this claim precise, note that there are certainly times when the evidence is "misleading." That is, even if the bias is 2/3, it is possible that Alice will see a sequence of 25 coin tosses of which 6 are heads and 19 tails. After observing that, she will consider that her original opinion that the bias 1/3 has been confirmed. (Indeed, it is easy to check that she will give *BH* probability greater than .999998.) However, if the bias is actually 2/3, the probability of Alice seeing such misleading evidence is very low. In fact, the *Law of Large Numbers,* one of the central results of probability theory, says that, as the number $N$ of coin tosses increases, the fraction of sequences in which the evidence is misleading goes to 0. As $N$ gets large, in almost all sequences of $N$ coin tosses, Alice's belief that the bias is 2/3 approaches 1.

In this sense, even if Alice's initial beliefs were incorrect, the evidence almost certainly forces her beliefs to the correct bias, provided she updates her beliefs by conditioning. Of course, the result also holds for much more general hypotheses than the bias of a coin. ∎

Conditioning is a wonderful tool, but it does suffer from some problems, particularly when it comes to dealing with events with probability 0. Traditionally, (3.3) is taken as the definition of $\mu(V \mid U)$ if $\mu$ is an unconditional probability measure and $\mu(U) > 0$; if $\mu(U) = 0$, then the conditional probability $\mu(V \mid U)$ is undefined. This leads to a number of philosophical difficulties regarding worlds (and sets) with probability 0. Are they really impossible? If not, how unlikely does a world have to be before it is assigned probability 0? Should a world ever be assigned probability 0? If there are worlds with probability 0 that are not truly impossible, then what does it mean to condition on sets with probability 0?

Some of these issues can be sidestepped by treating conditional probability, not unconditional probability, as the basic notion. A *conditional probability measure* takes *pairs U, V* of subsets as arguments; $\mu(V, U)$ is generally written $\mu(V \mid U)$ to stress the conditioning aspects. What pairs $(V, U)$ should be allowed as arguments to $\mu$? The intuition is that for each fixed second argument $U$, the function $\mu(\cdot, U)$ should be a probability measure. Thus, for the same reasons discussed in Section 2.2, I assume that the set of possible first arguments form an algebra (or $\sigma$-algebra, if $W$ is infinite). In fact, I assume that the algebra is the same for all $U$, so that the domain of $\mu$ has the form $\mathcal{F} \times \mathcal{F}'$ for some algebra $\mathcal{F}$. For simplicity, I also assume that $\mathcal{F}'$ is a nonempty subset of $\mathcal{F}$ that is closed under supersets, so that if $U \in \mathcal{F}'$, $U \subseteq V$, and $V \in \mathcal{F}$, then $V \in \mathcal{F}'$. Formally, a *Popper algebra* over $W$ is a set $\mathcal{F} \times \mathcal{F}'$ of subsets of $W \times W$ such that (a) $\mathcal{F}$ is an algebra over $W$, (b) $\mathcal{F}'$ is a nonempty subset of $\mathcal{F}$, and (c) $\mathcal{F}'$ is closed under supersets in $\mathcal{F}$; that is, if $V \in \mathcal{F}'$, $V \subseteq V'$, and $V' \in \mathcal{F}$, then $V' \in \mathcal{F}'$. (Popper algebras are named after Karl Popper, who was the first to consider formally conditional probability as the basic notion; see the notes for further details.) Notice that $\mathcal{F}'$ need not be an algebra (in the sense of Definition 2.2.1); indeed, in general it is not an algebra.

Although, for convenience, I assume that the arguments of a conditional probability measure are in a Popper algebra throughout the book, the reasonableness of this assumption is certainly debatable. In Section 2.2 I already admitted that insisting that the domain of a probability measure be an algebra is somewhat questionable. Even more concerns arise here. Why should it be possible to condition only on elements of $\mathcal{F}'$? And why should it be possible to condition on a superset of $U$ if it is possible to condition on $U$? It may well be worth exploring the impact of weakening this assumption (and, for that matter, the assumption that the domain of a probability measure is an algebra); see Chapter 12 for further discussion of this issue.

**Definition 3.2.3**   A *conditional probability space* is a tuple $(W, \mathcal{F}, \mathcal{F}', \mu)$ such that $\mathcal{F} \times \mathcal{F}'$ is a Popper algebra over $W$ and $\mu : \mathcal{F} \times \mathcal{F}' \to [0, 1]$ satisfies the following conditions:

> CP1.   $\mu(U \mid U) = 1$ if $U \in \mathcal{F}'$.
>
> CP2.   $\mu(V_1 \cup V_2 \mid U) = \mu(V_1 \mid U) + \mu(V_2 \mid U)$ if $V_1 \cap V_2 = \emptyset$, $V_1$, $V_2 \in \mathcal{F}$, and $U \in \mathcal{F}'$.
>
> CP3.   $\mu(U_1 \cap U_2 \mid U_3) = \mu(U_1 \mid U_2 \cap U_3) \times \mu(U_2 \mid U_3)$ if $U_2 \cap U_3 \in \mathcal{F}'$ and $U_1 \in \mathcal{F}$. ∎

CP1 and CP2 are just the obvious analogues of P1 and P2. CP3 is perhaps best understood by considering the following two properties:

> CP4.   $\mu(V \mid U) = \mu(V \cap U \mid U)$ if $U \in \mathcal{F}'$, $V \in \mathcal{F}$.
>
> CP5.   $\mu(U_1 \mid U_3) = \mu(U_1 \mid U_2) \times \mu(U_2 \mid U_3)$, if $U_1 \subseteq U_2 \subseteq U_3$, $U_2, U_3 \in \mathcal{F}'$ and $U_1 \in \mathcal{F}$.

CP4 just says that, when conditioning on $U$, everything should be relativized to $U$. CP5 says that if $U_1 \subseteq U_2 \subseteq U_3$, it is possible to compute the conditional probability of $U_1$ given $U_3$ by computing the conditional probability of $U_1$ given $U_2$, computing the conditional probability of $U_2$ given $U_3$, and then multiplying them together. It is best to think of CP5 (and CP3) in terms of proportions. For example, the proportion of female minority students at a university is just the fraction of minority students who are female multiplied by the fraction of students in the department who are minority students.

It is easy to see that both CP4 and CP5 follow from CP3 (and CP1 in the case of CP4); in addition, CP3 follows immediately from CP4 and CP5 (Exercise 3.1). Thus, in the presence of CP1, CP3 is equivalent to CP4 and CP5.

If $\mu$ is a conditional probability measure, then I usually write $\mu(U)$ instead of $\mu(U \mid W)$. Thus, in the obvious way, an conditional probability measure determines an unconditional probability measure. What about the converse?

Given an unconditional probability measure $\mu$ defined on some algebra $\mathcal{F}$ over $W$, let $\mathcal{F}'$ consist of all sets $U$ such that $\mu(U) \neq 0$. Then (3.3) can be used to define a conditional probability measure $\mu^e$ on $\mathcal{F} \times \mathcal{F}'$ that is an extension of $\mu$, in that $\mu^e(U \mid W) = \mu(U)$. (This notion of extension is compatible with the one defined in Section 2.3; if an unconditional probability measure $\mu$ is identified with a conditional probability measure defined on $\mathcal{F} \times \{W\}$, then $\mu^e$ extends $\mu$ to $\mathcal{F} \times \mathcal{F}'$.) However, taking conditional probability as primitive is more general than starting with unconditional probability and defining conditional probability using (3.3). That is, in general, there are conditional probability measures that are extensions of $\mu$ for which, unlike the case of $\mu^e$, $\mathcal{F}'$ includes some sets $U$ such that $\mu(U) = 0$.

One family of examples can be obtained by considering *nonstandard probability measures*, as defined in Section 2.6. Recall from that discussion that infinitesimals are numbers that are positive but smaller than any positive real number. For every element $\alpha'$ in a non-Archimedean field such that $-r < \alpha' < r$ for some real number $r$, it is not hard to show that there is a unique real number $\alpha$ that is closest to $\alpha'$; moreover, $|\alpha - \alpha'|$ is an infinitesimal (or 0). In fact, $\alpha$ is just $\inf\{r \in \mathbb{R} : r > \alpha'\}$. Let $st(\alpha')$ denote the closest real number to $\alpha'$. (*st* is short for *standard;* that is because elements of a non-Archimedean field that are not reals are often called *nonstandard reals,* while real numbers are called *standard reals.*) Note that if $\epsilon$ is an infinitesimal, then $st(\epsilon^k) = 0$ for all $k > 0$. (The requirement that $-r < \alpha' < r$ is necessary. For if $\epsilon$ is an infinitesimal, then $1/\epsilon$, which is not bounded by any real number, does not have a standard real closest to it.)

Let $\mu^{ns}$ be a nonstandard probability measure defined on an algebra $\mathcal{F}$ with the property that $\mu^{ns}(U) \neq 0$ if $U \neq \emptyset$. $\mu^{ns}$ can be extended to a conditional probability measure defined on $\mathcal{F} \times (\mathcal{F} - \{\emptyset\})$ using definition (3.3). Let $\mu^s$ be the *standardization* of $\mu^{ns}$, that is, the conditional probability measure such that $\mu^s(V \mid U) = st(\mu^{ns}(V \mid U))$ for all $V \in \mathcal{F}$, $U \in \mathcal{F} - \{\emptyset\}$. It may well be that $\mu^s(U) = 0$ for some sets $U$ for which $\mu^{ns}(U) \neq 0$, since $\mu^{ns}(U)$ may be infinitesimally small. It is easy to see that $\mu^s$ defined this way satisfies CP1–3 (Exercise 3.2). By definition, $\mu^s$ is defined on $\mathcal{F} \times (\mathcal{F} - \{\emptyset\})$. If there are nonempty sets $U \in \mathcal{F}$ such that $\mu^s(U) = 0$, then $\mu^s$ is not the result of starting with a standard unconditional probability measure and extending it using (3.3). The following example gives a concrete instance of how this construction works:

**Example 3.2.4** Let $W_0 = \{w_1, w_2, w_3\}$ and let $\mu_0^{ns}(w_1) = 1 - \epsilon - \epsilon^2$, $\mu_0^{ns}(w_2) = \epsilon$, and $\mu_0^{ns}(w_3) = \epsilon^2$; , where $\epsilon$ is an infinitesimal. Notice that $\mu_0^{ns}(w_2 \mid \{w_2, w_3\}) = 1/(1 + \epsilon)$, while $\mu_0^{ns}(w_3 \mid \{w_2, w_3\}) = \epsilon/1 + \epsilon$. Thus, if $\mu_0^s$ is the standard approximation to $\mu_0^{ns}$, then $\mu_0^s(w_2) = \mu_0^s(w_3) = \mu_0^s(\{w_2, w_3\}) = \mu_0^s(w_3 \mid \{w_2, w_3\}) = 0$ and $\mu_0^s(w_2 \mid \{w_2, w_3\}) = 1$.

Although all the conditional probabilities that arise in the case of $\mu_0^s$ are either 0 or 1, it is easy to construct variants of $\mu_0^s$ where arbitrary conditional probabilities arise. For example, if $W_1 = \{w_1, w_2, w_3\}$, and $\mu_1^{ns}(w_1) = 1 - 2\epsilon$, $\mu_1^{ns}(w_2) = \epsilon$, and $\mu_1^{ns}(w_3) = \epsilon$, then $\mu_1^{ns}(w_2 \mid \{w_2, w_3\}) = \mu_1^s(w_3 \mid \{w_2, w_3\}) = 1/2$. ∎

### 3.2.1 Justifying Probabilistic Conditioning

Probabilistic conditioning can be justified in much the same way that probability is justified. For example, if it seems reasonable to apply the principle of indifference to $W$ and then $U$ is observed or learned, it seems equally reasonable to apply the principle of indifference again to $W \cap U$. This results in taking all the elements of $W \cap U$ to be equally likely and assigning all the elements in $\overline{W \cap U}$ probability 0, which is exactly what (3.3) says. Similarly, using the relative-frequency interpretation, $\mu(V \mid U)$ can be viewed as the fraction of times that $V$ occurs of the times that $U$ occurs. Again, (3.3) holds.

Finally, consider a betting justification. To evaluate $\mu(V \mid U)$, only worlds in $U$ are considered; the bet is called off if the world is not in $U$. More precisely, let $(V \mid U, \alpha)$ denote the following bet:

> If $U$ happens, then if $V$ also happens, then I win \$100(1 − α), while if $\overline{V}$ also happens, then I lose \$100α. If $U$ does not happen, then the bet is called off (I do not win or lose anything).

As before, suppose that the agent has to choose between bets of the form $(V \mid U, \alpha)$ and $(\overline{V} \mid U, 1 - \alpha)$. For worlds in $\overline{U}$, both bets are called off, so they are equivalent.

With this formulation of a conditional bet, it is possible to prove an analogue of Theorem 2.2.3, showing that an agent who is rational in the sense of satisfying properties RAT1–4 from Section 2.2 must use conditioning.

**Theorem 3.2.5** *If an agent satisfies RAT1–4, then for all subsets $U$, $V$ of $W$ such that $\alpha_U > 0$, there is a number $\alpha_{V \mid U}$ such that $(V \mid U, \alpha) \succeq (\overline{V} \mid U, 1 - \alpha)$ for all $\alpha < \alpha_{V \mid U}$ and $(\overline{V} \mid U, 1 - \alpha) \succeq (V \mid U, \alpha)$ for all $\alpha > \alpha_{V \mid U}$. Moreover, $\alpha_{V \mid U} = \alpha_{V \cap U}/\alpha_U$.*

**Proof** Assume that $\alpha_U \neq 0$. For worlds in $U$, just as in the unconditional case, $(V \mid U, \alpha)$ is a can't-lose proposition if $\alpha = 0$, becoming increasingly less attractive as $\alpha$

increases, and becomes a can't-win proposition if $\alpha = 1$. Let $\alpha_{V|U} = \sup\{\beta : (V|U, \beta) \succeq (\overline{V}|U, 1 - \beta)\}$. The same argument as in the unconditional case (Exercise 2.5) shows that if an agent satisfies RAT1 and RAT2, then $(V|U, \alpha) \succeq (\overline{V}|U, 1 - \alpha)$ for all $\alpha < \alpha_{V|U}$ and $(\overline{V}|U, 1 - \alpha) \succeq (V|U, \alpha)$ for all $\alpha > \alpha_{V|U}$.

It remains to show that if $\alpha_{V|U} \neq \alpha_{V \cap U}/\alpha_U$, then there is a collection of bets that the agent would be willing to accept that guarantee a sure loss. First, suppose that $\alpha_{V|U} < \alpha_{V \cap U}/\alpha_U$. By the arguments in the proof of Theorem 2.2.3, $\alpha_{V \cap U} \leq \alpha_U$, so $\alpha_{V \cap U}/\alpha_U \leq 1$. Thus, there exist numbers $\beta_1, \beta_2, \beta_3 \in [0, 1]$ such that $\beta_1 > \alpha_{V|U}$, $\beta_2 > \alpha_U$ (or $\beta_2 = 1$ if $\alpha_U = 1$), $\beta_3 < \alpha_{V \cap U}$, and $\beta_1 < \beta_3/\beta_2$ (or, equivalently, $\beta_1\beta_2 < \beta_3$).

By construction, $(\overline{V}|U, 1 - \beta_1) \succeq (V|U, \beta_1)$, $(\overline{U}, 1 - \beta_2) \succeq (U, \beta_2)$, and $(V \cap U, \beta_3) \succeq (\overline{V \cap U}, 1 - \beta_3)$. Without loss of generality, $\beta_1, \beta_2$, and $\beta_3$ are rational numbers, over some common denominator $N$; that is, $\beta_1 = b_1/N$, $\beta_2 = b_2/N$, and $\beta_3 = b_3/N$. Given a bet $(U, \alpha)$, let $N(U, \alpha)$ denote $N$ copies of $(U, \alpha)$. By RAT4, if $B_1 = \{N(\overline{V}|U, 1 - \beta_1), N(\overline{U}, 1 - \beta_2), b_1(\overline{U}, 1 - \beta_2)\}$ and $B_2 = \{N(V|U, \beta_1), N(U, \beta_2), b_1(U, \beta_2)\}$, then $B_1 \succeq B_2$. However, $B_1$ results in a sure loss, while $B_2$ results in a sure gain, so that the agent's preferences violate RAT1. To see this, three cases must be considered. If the actual world is in $\overline{U}$, then with $B_1$, the agent is guaranteed to win $N\beta_1\beta_2$ and lose $N\beta_3$, for a guaranteed net loss (since $\beta_1\beta_2 < \beta_3$), while with $B_2$, the agent is guaranteed a net gain of $N(\beta_3 - \beta_1\beta_2)$. The arguments are similar if the actual world is in $V \cap U$ or $\overline{V} \cap U$ (Exercise 3.3). Thus, the agent is irrational.

A similar argument works if $\alpha_{V|U} > \alpha_{V \cap U}/\alpha_U$ (Exercise 3.3).  ■

This justification can be criticized on a number of grounds. The earlier criticisms of RAT3 and RAT4 still apply, of course. An additional subtlety arises when dealing with conditioning. The Dutch book argument implicitly takes a static view of the agent's probabilities. It talks about an agent's current preference ordering on bets, including *conditional* bets of the form $(V|U, \alpha)$ that are called off if a specified event—$U$ in this case—does not occur. But for conditioning what matters is not just the agent's current beliefs regarding $V$ *if* $U$ were to occur, but also how the agent would change his beliefs regarding $V$ if $U$ actually did occur. If the agent currently prefers the conditional bet $(V|U, \alpha)$ to $(\overline{V}|U, 1 - \alpha)$, it is not so clear that he would still prefer $(V, \alpha)$ to $(\overline{V}, 1 - \alpha)$ if $U$ actually did occur. This added assumption must be made to justify conditioning as a way of updating probability measures.

Theorems 2.2.3 and 3.2.5 show that if an agent's betting behavior does not obey P1 and P2, and if he does not update his probabilities according to (3.3), then he is liable to have a Dutch book made against him. What about the converse? Suppose that an agent's betting behavior does obey P1, P2, and (3.3)—that is, suppose that it is characterized by a probability measure, with updating characterized by conditional probability. Is it still possible for there to be a Dutch book?

Say that an agent's betting behavior is *determined by* a probability measure if there is a probability measure $\mu$ on $W$ such that for all $U \subseteq W$, then $(U, \alpha) \succeq (\overline{U}, 1 - \alpha)$ iff $\mu(U) \geq \alpha$. The following result shows that there cannot be a Dutch book if an agent updates using conditioning:

**Theorem 3.2.6**   *If an agent's betting behavior is determined by a probability measure, then there do not exist sets $U_1, \ldots, U_k$, $\alpha_1, \ldots, \alpha_k \in [0, 1]$, and natural numbers $N_1, \ldots, N_k \geq 0$ such that (1) $(U_j, \alpha_j) \succeq (\overline{U}_j, 1 - \alpha_j)$, (2) the agent suffers a sure loss with $B = \{N_1(U_1, \alpha_1), \ldots, N_k(U_k, \alpha_k)\}$, and (3) the agent has a sure gain with the complementary connection collection of bets $B' = \{N_1(\overline{U}_1, 1 - \alpha_1), \ldots, N_k(\overline{U}_k, 1 - \alpha_k)\}$.*

**Proof**   See Exercise 3.4.   ∎

### 3.2.2   Bayes' Rule

One of the most important results in probability theory is called *Bayes' Rule*. It relates $\mu(V \mid U)$ and $\mu(U \mid V)$.

**Proposition 3.2.7**   (Bayes' Rule) *If $\mu(U)$, $\mu(V) > 0$, then*

$$\mu(V \mid U) = \frac{\mu(U \mid V)\mu(V)}{\mu(U)}.$$

**Proof**   The proof just consists of simple algebraic manipulation. Observe that

$$\frac{\mu(U \mid V)\mu(V)}{\mu(U)} = \frac{\mu(V \cap U)\mu(V)}{\mu(U)\mu(V)} = \frac{\mu(V \cap U)}{\mu(U)} = \mu(V \mid U).   ∎$$

Although Bayes' Rule is almost immediate from the definition of conditional probability, it is one of the most widely applicable results of probability theory. The following two examples show how it can be used:

**Example 3.2.8**   Suppose that Bob tests positive on an AIDS test that is known to be 99 percent reliable. How likely is it that Bob has AIDS? That depends in part on what "99 percent reliable" means. For the purposes of this example, suppose that it means that, according to extensive tests, 99 percent of the subjects with AIDS tested positive and 99 percent of subjects that did not have AIDS tested negative. (Note that, in general, for reliability data, it is important to know about both false positives and false negatives.)

As it stands, this information is insufficient to answer the original question. This is perhaps best seen using Bayes' Rule. Let $A$ be the event that Bob has AIDS and $P$ be the event that Bob tests positive. The problem is to compute $\mu(A \mid P)$. It might seem that, since the test is 99 percent reliable, it should be .99, but this is not the case. By Bayes' Rule, $\mu(A \mid P) = \mu(P \mid A) \times \mu(A)/\mu(P)$. Since 99 percent of people with AIDS test positive, it seems reasonable to take $\mu(P \mid A) = .99$. But the fact that $\mu(P \mid A) = .99$ does not make $\mu(A \mid P) = .99$. The value of $\mu(A \mid P)$ also depends on $\mu(A)$ and $\mu(P)$.

Before going on, note that while it may be reasonable to take $\mu(P \mid A) = .99$, a nontrivial leap is being made here. $A$ is the event that *Bob* has AIDS and $P$ is the event that *Bob* tests positive. The statistical information that 99 percent of people with AIDS test positive is thus being identified with the probability that Bob would test positive if Bob had AIDS. At best, making this identification involves the implicit assumption that Bob is like the test subjects from which the statistical information was derived in all relevant respects. See Chapter 11 for a more careful treatment of this issue.

In any case, going on with the computation of $\mu(A \mid P)$, note that although Bayes' Rule seems to require both $\mu(P)$ and $\mu(A)$, actually only $\mu(A)$ is needed. To see this, note that

- $\mu(P) = \mu(A \cap P) + \mu(\overline{A} \cap P)$,

- $\mu(A \cap P) = \mu(P \mid A)\mu(A) = .99\mu(A)$,

- $\mu(\overline{A} \cap P) = \mu(P \mid \overline{A})\mu(\overline{A}) = (1 - \mu(\overline{P} \mid \overline{A}))(1 - \mu(A)) = .01(1 - \mu(A))$.

Putting all this together, it follows that $\mu(P) = .01 + .98\mu(A)$ and thus

$$\mu(A \mid P) = \mu(P \mid A) \times \mu(A)/\mu(P) = \frac{.99\mu(A)}{.01 + .98\mu(A)}.$$

Just as $\mu(P \mid A)$ can be identified with the fraction of people with AIDS that tested positive, so $\mu(A)$, the unconditional probability that Bob has AIDS, can be identified with the fraction of the people in the population that have AIDS. If only 1 percent of the population has AIDS, then a straightforward computation shows that $\mu(A \mid P) = 1/2$. If only .1 percent (i.e., one in a thousand) have AIDS, then $\mu(A \mid P) \approx .09$. Finally, if the incidence of AIDS is as high as one in three (as it is in some countries in Central Africa), then $\mu(A \mid P) \approx .98$—still less than .99, despite the accuracy of the test. ∎

The importance of $\mu(A)$ in this case can be understood from a less sensitive example.

**Example 3.2.9**   Suppose that there is a huge bin full of coins. One of the coins in the bin is double-headed; all the rest are fair. A coin is picked from the bin and tossed 10 times.

The coin tosses can be viewed as a test of whether the coin is double-headed or fair. The test is positive if all the coin tosses land heads and negative if any of them land tails. This gives a test that is better than 99.9 percent reliable: the probability that the test is positive given that the coin is double-headed is 1; the probability that the test is negative given that the coin is not double-headed (i.e., fair) is $1023/1024 > .999$. Nevertheless, the probability that a coin that tests positive is double-headed clearly depends on the total number of coins in the bin. In fact, straightforward calculations similar to those in Example 3.2.8 show that if there are $N$ coins in the bin, then the probability that the coin is double-headed given that it tests positive is $1024/(N + 1023)$. If $N = 10$, then a positive test makes it very likely that the coin is double-headed. On the other hand, if $N = 1{,}000{,}000$, while a positive test certainly increases the likelihood that the coin is double-headed, it is still far more likely to be a fair coin that landed heads 10 times in a row than a double-headed coin. ∎

## 3.3 Conditioning with Sets of Probabilities

Suppose that an agent's uncertainty is defined in terms of a set $\mathcal{P}$ of probability measures. If the agent observes $U$, the obvious thing to do is to condition each member of $\mathcal{P}$ on $U$. This suggests that after observing $U$, the agent's uncertainty should be represented by the set $\{\mu|U : \mu \in \mathcal{P}\}$. There is one obvious issue that needs to be addressed: What happens if $\mu(U) = 0$ for some $\mu \in \mathcal{P}$? There are two choices here: either to say that conditioning makes sense only if $\mu(U) > 0$ for all $\mu \in \mathcal{P}$ (i.e., if $\mathcal{P}_*(U) > 0$) or to consider only those measures $\mu$ for which $\mu(U) > 0$. The latter choice is somewhat more general, so that is what I use here. Thus, I define

$$\mathcal{P}|U = \{\mu|U : \mu \in \mathcal{P}, \ \mu(U) > 0\}.$$

(Note that if the uncertainty in this case is represented using the sample space $\mathcal{P} \times W$, as discussed in Section 2.3, then what is going on here is that, just as in Section 3.1, all worlds incompatible with the observation are eliminated. However, now the set of worlds incompatible with observation $U$ consists of all pairs $(\mu, w)$ such that either $\mu(U) = 0$ or $w \notin U$.)

Once the agent has a set $\mathcal{P}|U$ of conditional probability measures, it is possible to consider lower and upper conditional probabilities. However, this is not the only way to represent the update of a set of probability measures. In particular, it is also possible to consider updating the plausibility measure $\mathrm{Pl}_\mathcal{P}$ discussed in Section 2.8. This is done in Section 3.9, where there is a general discussion of updating plausibility measures. For now, I just consider how sets of probabilities can be used to deal with the *three-prisoners puzzle*.

**Example 3.3.1**    The three-prisoners puzzle is an old chestnut that is somewhat similar in spirit to the second-ace puzzle discussed in Chapter 1, although it illustrates somewhat different issues.

> Of three prisoners $a$, $b$, and $c$, two are to be executed, but $a$ does not know which. He therefore says to the jailer, "Since either $b$ or $c$ is certainly going to be executed, you will give me no information about my own chances if you give me the name of one man, either $b$ or $c$, who is going to be executed." Accepting this argument, the jailer truthfully replies, "$b$ will be executed." Thereupon $a$ feels happier because before the jailer replied, his own chance of execution was 2/3, but afterward there are only two people, himself and $c$, who could be the one not executed, and so his chance of execution is 1/2.

Note that in order for $a$ to believe that his own chance of execution was 2/3 before the jailer replied, he seems to be implicitly assuming the principle of indifference. A straightforward application of the principle of indifference also seems to lead to $a$'s believing that his chances of execution goes down to 1/2 after hearing the jailer's statement. Yet it seems that the jailer did not give him any new relevant information. Is $a$ justified in believing that his chances of avoiding execution have improved? If so, it seems that $a$ would be equally justified in believing that his chances of avoiding execution would have improved if the jailer had said "$c$ will be executed." It seems that $a$'s prospects improve no matter what the jailer says! That does not seem quite right.

The principle of indifference is implicitly being applied here to a space consisting of three worlds—say $w_a$, $w_b$, and $w_c$—where in world $w_x$, prisoner $x$ is pardoned. But this representation of a world does not take into account what the jailer says. Perhaps a better representation of a possible situation is as a pair $(x, y)$, where $x$, $y \in \{a, b, c\}$. Intuitively, a pair $(x, y)$ represents a situation where $x$ is pardoned and the jailer says that $y$ will be executed in response to $a$'s question. Since the jailer answers truthfully, $x \neq y$; since the jailer will never tell $a$ directly that $a$ will be executed, $y \neq a$. Thus, the set of possible worlds is $\{(a, b), (a, c), (b, c), (c, b)\}$. The event *lives -a*—$a$ lives—corresponds to the set $\{(a, b), (a, c)\}$. Similarly, the events *lives -b* and *lives -c* correspond to the sets $\{(b, c)\}$ and $\{(c, b)\}$, respectively. Assume in accord with the principle of indifference that each prisoner is equally likely to be pardoned, so that each of these three events has probability 1/3.

The event *says-b*—the jailer says $b$—corresponds to the set $\{(a, b), (c, b)\}$; the story does not give a probability for this event. To do standard probabilistic conditioning, this set must be measurable and have a probability. The event $\{(c, b)\}$ (*lives-c*) has probability 1/3. But what is the probability of $\{(a, b)\}$? That depends on the jailer's strategy in the one case where he has a choice, namely, when $a$ lives. He gets to choose between saying $b$ and $c$ in that case. The probability of $(a, b)$ depends on the probability that he says $b$ if $a$ lives; that is, $\mu(says\text{-}b \mid lives\text{-}a)$.

If the jailer applies the principle of indifference in choosing between saying $b$ and $c$ if $a$ is pardoned, so that $\mu(says\text{-}b \mid lives\text{-}a) = 1/2$, then $\mu(\{(a, b)\}) = \mu(\{(a, c)\}) = 1/6$, and $\mu(says\text{-}b) = 1/2$. With this assumption,

$$\mu(lives\text{-}a \mid says\text{-}b) = \mu(lives\text{-}a \cap says\text{-}b)/\mu(says\text{-}b) = (1/6)/(1/2) = 1/3.$$

Thus, if $\mu(says\text{-}b) = 1/2$, the jailer's answer does not affect $a$'s probability.

Suppose more generally that $\mu_\alpha$, $0 \le \alpha \le 1$, is the probability measure such that $\mu_\alpha(lives\text{-}a) = \mu_\alpha(lives\text{-}b) = \mu_\alpha(lives\text{-}c) = 1/3$ and $\mu_\alpha(says\text{-}b \mid lives\text{-}a) = \alpha$. Then straightforward computations show that

$$\mu_\alpha(\{(a, b)\}) = \mu_\alpha(lives\text{-}a) \times \mu_\alpha(says\text{-}b \mid lives\text{-}a) = \alpha/3,$$

$$\mu_\alpha(says\text{-}b) = \mu_\alpha(\{(a, b)\}) + \mu_\alpha(\{(c, b)\}) = (\alpha + 1)/3, \text{ and}$$

$$\mu_\alpha(lives\text{-}a \mid says\text{-}b) = \frac{\alpha/3}{(\alpha + 1)/3} = \alpha/(\alpha + 1).$$

Thus, $\mu_{1/2} = \mu$. Moreover, if $\alpha \ne 1/2$ (i.e., if the jailer had a particular preference for answering either $b$ or $c$ when $a$ was the one pardoned), then $a$'s probability of being executed would change, depending on the answer. For example, if $\alpha = 0$, then if $a$ is pardoned, the jailer will definitely say $c$. Thus, if the jailer actually says $b$, then $a$ knows that he is definitely not pardoned, that is, $\mu_0(lives\text{-}a \mid says\text{-}b) = 0$. Similarly, if $\alpha = 1$, then $a$ knows that if either he or $c$ is pardoned, then the jailer will say $b$, while if $b$ is pardoned the jailer will say $c$. Given that the jailer says $b$, from $a$'s point of view the one pardoned is equally likely to be him or $c$; thus, $\mu_1(lives\text{-}a \mid says\text{-}b) = 1/2$. In fact, it is easy to see that if $\mathcal{P}_J = \{\mu_\alpha : \alpha \in [0, 1]\}$, then $(\mathcal{P}_J \mid says\text{-}b)_*(lives\text{-}a) = 0$ and $(\mathcal{P}_J \mid says\text{-}b)^*(lives\text{-}a) = 1/2$.

To summarize, the intuitive answer—that the jailer's answer gives $a$ no information—is correct if the jailer applies the principle of indifference in the one case where he has a choice in what to say, namely, when $a$ is actually the one to live. If the jailer does not apply the principle of indifference in this case, then $a$ may gain information. On the other hand, if $a$ does not know what strategy the jailer is using to answer (and is not willing to place a probability on these strategies), then his prior point probability of 1/3 "diffuses" to an interval. ∎

## 3.4   Evidence

While the three-prisoner puzzle (and many other examples) show that this approach to conditioning on sets of probabilities often behaves in a reasonable way, it does not always seem to capture all the information learned, as the following example shows:

**Example 3.4.1**   Suppose that a coin is tossed twice and the first coin toss is observed to land heads. What is the likelihood that the second coin toss lands heads? In this situation, the sample space consists of four worlds: $hh, ht, th$, and $tt$. Let $H^1 = \{hh, ht\}$ be the event that the first coin toss lands heads. There are analogous events $H^2$, $T^1$, and $T^2$. As in Example 2.4.6, all that is known about the coin is that its bias is either 1/3 or 2/3. The most obvious way to represent this seems to be with a set of probability measures $\mathcal{P} = \{\mu_{1/3}, \mu_{2/3}\}$. Further suppose that the coin tosses are independent. Intuitively, this means that the outcome of the first coin toss has no affect on the probabilities of the outcomes of the second coin toss. Independence is considered in more depth in Chapter 4; for now, all I need is for independence to imply that $\mu_\alpha(hh) = \mu_\alpha(H^1)\mu_\alpha(H^2) = \alpha^2$ and that $\mu_\alpha(ht) = \mu_\alpha(H^1)\mu_\alpha(T^2) = \alpha - \alpha^2$.

Using the definitions, it is immediate that $\mathcal{P}|H^1(H^2) = \{1/3, 2/3\} = \mathcal{P}(H^2)$. At first blush, this seems reasonable. Since the coin tosses are independent, observing heads on the first toss does not affect the likelihood of heads on the second toss; it is either 1/3 or 2/3, depending on what the actual bias of the coin is. However, intuitively, observing heads on the first toss should also give information about the coin being used: it is more likely to be the coin with bias 2/3. This point perhaps comes out more clearly if the coin is tossed 100 times and 66 heads are observed in the first 99 tosses. What is the probability of heads on the hundredth toss? Formally, using the obvious notation, the question now is what $\mathcal{P}|(H^1 \cap \ldots \cap H^{99})(H^{100})$ should be. According to the definitions, it is again $\{1/3, 2/3\}$: the probability is still either 1/3 or 2/3, depending on the coin used. But the fact that 66 of 99 tosses landed heads provides extremely strong evidence that the coin has bias 2/3 rather than 1/3. This evidence should make it more likely that the probability that the last coin will land heads is 2/3 rather than 1/3. The conditioning process does not capture this evidence at all.

Interestingly, if the bias of the coin is either 0 or 1 (i.e., the coin is either double-tailed or double-headed), then the evidence is taken into account. In this case, after seeing heads, $\mu_0$ is eliminated, so $\mathcal{P}|H^1(H^2) = 1$ (or, more precisely, $\{1\}$), not $\{0, 1\}$. On the other hand, if the bias is almost 0 or almost 1, say .005 or .995, then $\mathcal{P}|H^1(H^2) = \{.005, .995\}$. Thus, although the evidence is taken into account in the extreme case, where the probability of heads is either 0 or 1, it is not taken into account if the probability of heads is either slightly greater than 0 or slightly less than 1.

Notice that if there is a probability on the possible biases of the coin, then all these difficulties disappear. In this case, the sample space must represent the possible biases of the coin. For example, if the coin has bias either $\alpha$ or $\beta$, with $\alpha > \beta$, and the coin is tossed twice, then the sample space has eight worlds: $(\alpha, hh), (\beta, hh), (\alpha, ht), (\beta, ht),$ .... Moreover, if the probability that it has bias $\alpha$ is $a$ (so that the probability that it has bias $\beta$ is $1 - a$), then the uncertainty is captured by a single probability measure $\mu$ such that $\mu(\alpha, hh) = a\alpha^2$, $\mu(\beta, hh) = (1 - a)\alpha^2$, and so on. With a little calculus, it is not hard to show that $\mu(H^1) = \mu(H^2) = a\alpha + (1 - a)\beta$ and $\mu(H^1 \cap H^2) = a\alpha^2 + (1 - a)\beta^2$, so $\mu(H^2 \mid H^1) = (a\alpha^2 + (1 - a)\beta^2)/(a\alpha + (1 - a)\beta) \geq \mu(H^2)$, no matter what $\alpha$ and $\beta$ are, with equality holding iff $a = 0$ or $a = 1$ (Exercise 3.5). Seeing $H^1$ makes $H^2$ more likely than it was before, despite the fact the coin tosses are independent, because seeing $H^2$ makes the coin of greater bias $\beta$ more likely to be the actual coin. This intuition can be formalized in a straightforward way. Let $C_\alpha$ be the event that the coin has bias $\alpha$ (so that $C_\alpha$ consists of the four worlds of the form $(\alpha, \ldots)$). Then $\mu(C_\alpha) = a$, by assumption, while $\mu(C_\alpha \mid H^1) = a\alpha/(a\alpha + (1 - a)\beta) > a$, since $\alpha > \beta$ (Exercise 3.6).  ∎

What the example shows is that the problem here is not the use of probability or conditioning per se, but that conditioning does not quite capture the evidence when the uncertainty is represented by a *set* of probability measures with more than one element. Is there any way to represent the evidence?

Actually, this issue of evidence has arisen a number of times already. In Example 3.2.8, Bob testing positive is certainly *evidence* that he has AIDS, even though the actual probability that he has AIDS also depends on the prior probability of AIDS. Similarly, in Example 3.2.9, seeing 10 heads in a row is strong evidence that the coin is double-headed even though, again, the actual probability that he has double-headed given that 10 heads in a row are observed depends on the prior probability that a double-headed coin is chosen.

The literature contains a great deal of discussion on how to represent evidence. Most of this discussion has been in the context of probability, trying to make sense of the evidence provided by seeing 10 heads in a row in Example 3.2.9. Here I consider a notion of evidence that applies even when there is a set of probability measures, rather than just a single measure. There are interesting connections between this notion and the notion of evidence in the Dempster-Shafer theory of evidence (see Section 2.4, particularly Examples 2.4.5 and 2.4.6).

For the purposes of this discussion, I assume that there is a finite space $\mathcal{H}$ consisting of *basic hypotheses* and another set $\mathcal{O}$ of *basic observations* (also typically finite, although that is not crucial). In the spirit of the approach discussed at the beginning of

Section 2.3, the set of possible worlds is now $\mathcal{H} \times \mathcal{O}$; that is, a possible world consists of a (hypothesis, observation) pair. In Example 3.4.1, there are two hypotheses, $BH$ (the coin is biased toward heads—the probability that it lands heads is 2/3) and $BT$ (the coin is biased toward tails—the probability that it lands tails is 2/3). If the coin is tossed twice, then there are four possible observations: $hh$, $ht$, $th$, and $tt$. Thus, there are eight possible worlds. (This is precisely the sample space that was used in the last paragraph of Example 3.4.1.) Similarly, in Example 3.2.8, there are two hypotheses, $A$ (Bob has AIDS) and $\overline{A}$ (he doesn't), and two possible observations, $P$ (Bob tests positive) and $\overline{P}$ (Bob tests negative). In Example 3.2.9 there are also two hypotheses: the coin is double-headed or it is fair.

In general, I do not assume that there is a probability measure on the full space $W = \mathcal{H} \times \mathcal{O}$, since the probability of each hypothesis may be unknown. However, for each $h \in \mathcal{H}$, I do assume that there is a probability measure $\mu_h$ on $W_h = \{(h, o) \in W : o \in \mathcal{O}\}$, that is, the set of worlds associated with hypothesis $h$. For example, in the space $W_{BH}$ of Example 3.4.1, the probability of $(BH, hh)$ is 4/9. That is, the probability of tossing two heads, given that the coin with bias 2/3 is used, is 4/9. This is precisely the approach considered in Section 2.3: the set $W$ of possible worlds is partitioned into a number of subsets, with a probability measure on each subset.

For each observation $o$ such that $\mu_{h'}(o) > 0$ for some $h' \in \mathcal{H}$, let $\mu_o$ be the probability measure defined on $\mathcal{H}$ by $\mu_o(h) = \mu_h(o)/(\sum_{h' \in \mathcal{H}} \mu_{h'}(o))$. That is, $\mu_o(h)$ is essentially the probability of observing $o$, given hypothesis $h$. The denominator acts as a normalization constant; this choice guarantees that $\sum_{h' \in \mathcal{H}} \mu_o(h') = 1$. (The assumption that $\mathcal{H}$ is finite guarantees that this is a finite sum.) Clearly, $\mu_o$ is a probability measure on $\mathcal{H}$. It compares the likelihood of two different hypotheses given observation $o$ by comparing the likelihood of observing $o$, given each of these hypotheses. Thus, it does capture the intuition of evidence at some level.

Up to now I have not assumed that there is a probability measure on the whole space $\mathcal{H} \times \mathcal{O}$. But suppose that $\mu$ is a measure on $\mathcal{H} \times \mathcal{O}$. What is the connection between $\mu(h|o)$ and $\mu_o(h)$? In general, of course, there is no connection, since there is no connection between $\mu$ and $\mu_h$. A more interesting question is what happens if $\mu_h(o) = \mu(o \mid h)$.

**Definition 3.4.2**    A probability measure $\mu$ on $\mathcal{H} \times \mathcal{O}$ is *compatible with* $\{\mu_h : h \in \mathcal{H}\}$ if $\mu(o \mid h) = \mu_h(o)$ for all $(h, o) \in \mathcal{H} \times \mathcal{O}$ such that $\mu(h) > 0$.   ∎

Note that, even if $\mu$ is compatible with $\{\mu_h : h \in \mathcal{H}\}$, it does not follow that $\mu_o(h) = \mu(h \mid o)$. In Example 3.2.8,

$$\mu_P(A) = \frac{\mu_A(P)}{\mu_A(P) + \mu_{\overline{A}}(P)} = \frac{.99}{.99 + .01} = .99.$$

By definition, $\mu_P(A)$ depends only on $\mu_A(P)$ and $\mu_{\overline{A}}(P)$; equivalently, if $\mu$ is compatible with $\{\mu_A, \mu_{\overline{A}}\}$, $\mu_P(A)$ depends only on $\mu(P \mid A)$ and $\mu(P \mid \overline{A})$. On the other hand, as the calculations in Example 3.2.8 show, $\mu(A \mid P)$ depends on $\mu(P \mid A)$, $\mu(A)$, and $\mu(P)$, which can be calculated from $\mu(P \mid A)$, $\mu(P \mid \overline{A})$, *and* $\mu(A)$. Changing $\mu(A)$ affects $\mu(A \mid P)$ but not $\mu_P(A)$.

Similarly, in Example 3.2.9, suppose the coin is tossed $N$ times. Let $F$ and $DH$ stand for the hypotheses that the coin is fair and double-headed, respectively. Let $N$-*heads* be the observation that all $N$ coin tosses result in heads. Then it is easy to check that $\mu_{N\text{-}heads}(DH) = 2^N/(2^N + 1)$. This seems reasonable: the more heads are observed, the closer the likelihood of $DH$ gets to 1. Of course, if tails is observed at least once in $o$, then $\mu_o(DH) = 0$. Again, I stress that if there is a probability on the whole space then, in general, $\mu_{N\text{-}heads}(DH) \neq \mu(DH \mid N\text{-}heads)$. The conditional probability depends in part on $\mu(DH)$, the prior probability of the coin being double-headed.

Although $\mu_o(h) \neq \mu(h \mid o)$, it seems that there should be a connection between the two quantities. Indeed there is; it is provided by Dempster's Rule of Combination. Before going on, I should point out a notational subtlety. In the expression $\mu_o(h)$, the $h$ represents the singleton set $\{h\}$. On the other hand, in the expression $\mu(h \mid o)$, the $h$ really represents the event $\{h\} \times \mathcal{O}$, since $\mu$ is defined on subsets of $W = \mathcal{H} \times \mathcal{O}$. Similarly, $o$ is being identified with the event $\mathcal{H} \times \{o\} \subseteq W$. While in general I make these identifications without comment, it is sometimes necessary to be more careful. In particular, in Proposition 3.4.3, Dempster's Rule of Combination is applied to two probability measures. (This makes sense, since probability measures are belief functions.) Both probability measures need to be defined on the same space ($\mathcal{H}$, in the proposition) for Dempster's Rule to apply. Thus, given $\mu$ defined on $\mathcal{H} \times \mathcal{O}$, let $\mu_{\mathcal{H}}$ be the measure on $\mathcal{H}$ obtained by *projecting* $\mu$ onto $\mathcal{H}$; that is, $\mu_{\mathcal{H}}(h) = \mu(h \times \mathcal{O})$.

**Proposition 3.4.3** *If $\mu$ is compatible with $\{\mu_h : h \in \mathcal{H}\}$ and $\mu(o) \neq 0$, then $\mu_{\mathcal{H}} \oplus \mu_o$ is defined and $\mu(h \mid o) = (\mu_{\mathcal{H}} \oplus \mu_o)(h)$.*

**Proof** See Exercise 3.7. ∎

Proposition 3.4.3 says that if the prior on $\mathcal{H}$ is combined with the evidence given by the observation $o$ (encoded as $\mu_o$) by using Dempster's Rule of Combination, the result is the posterior $\mu(\cdot \mid o)$. Even more can be said. Suppose that two observations are made. Then the space of observations has the form $\mathcal{O} \times \mathcal{O}'$. Further assume that $\mu_h((o, o')) = \mu_h(o) \times \mu_h(o')$, for all $h \in \mathcal{H}$. (Intuitively, this assumption encodes the fact that the observations are independent; see Section 4.1 for more discussion of independence.) Then the evidence represented by the joint observation $(o, o')$ is the result of combining the individual observations.

**Proposition 3.4.4**   $\mu_{(o,o')} = \mu_o \oplus \mu_{o'}$.

**Proof**    See Exercise 3.8.   ∎

Thus, for example, in Example 3.2.9, $\mu_{(k+m)\text{-}heads} = \mu_{k\text{-}heads} \oplus \mu_{m\text{-}heads}$: the evidence corresponding to observing $k + m$ heads is the result of combining the evidence corresponding to observing $k$ and then observing $m$ heads. Similar results hold for other observations.

The belief functions used to represent the evidence given by the observations in Example 2.4.6 also exhibit this type of behavior. More precisely, in that example, it was shown that the more heads are observed, the greater the evidence for $BH$ and the stronger the agent's belief in $BH$. Consider the following special case of the belief function used in Example 2.4.6. Given an observation $o$, for $H \subseteq \mathcal{H}$, define

$$\text{Bel}_o(H) = 1 - (\max_{h \in \overline{H}} \mu_h(o)/ \max_{h \in \mathcal{H}} \mu_h(o)).$$

I leave it to the reader to check that this is in fact a belief function having the property that there is a constant $c > 0$ such that $\text{Plaus}_o(h) = c\mu_h(o)$ for all $h \in \mathcal{H}$ (see Exercise 3.9). I mention the latter property because analogues of Propositions 3.4.3 and 3.4.4 hold for any representation of evidence that has this property. (It is easy to see that $\mu_o(h) = c\mu_h(o)$ for all $h \in \mathcal{H}$, where $c = \sum_{h' \in \mathcal{H}} m\mu_{h'}(o)$.)

To make this precise, say that a belief function Bel *captures the evidence* $o \in \mathcal{O}$ if, for all probability measures $\mu$ compatible with $\{\mu_h : h \in \mathcal{H}\}$, it is the case that $\mu(h \mid o) = (\mu_{\mathcal{H}} \oplus \text{Bel})(h)$. Proposition 3.4.3 says that $\mu_o$ captures the evidence $o$. The following two results generalize Propositions 3.4.3 and 3.4.4:

**Theorem 3.4.5**    *Fix* $o \in \mathcal{O}$. *Suppose that* Bel *is a belief function on* $\mathcal{H}$ *whose corresponding plausibility function* Plaus *has the property that* $\text{Plaus}(h) = c\mu_h(o)$ *for some constant* $c > 0$ *and all* $h \in \mathcal{H}$. *Then* Bel *captures the evidence* $o$.

**Proof**    See Exercise 3.10.   ∎

**Theorem 3.4.6**    *Fix* $(o, o') \in \mathcal{O} \times \mathcal{O}'$. *If* $\mu_h(o, o') = \mu_h(o) \times \mu_h(o')$ *for all* $h \in \mathcal{H}$, Bel *captures the evidence* $o$, *and* Bel' *captures the evidence* $o'$, *then* Bel $\oplus$ Bel' *captures the evidence* $(o, o')$.

**Proof**    See Exercise 3.11.   ∎

Interestingly, the converse to Theorem 3.4.5 also holds. If Bel captures the evidence $o$, then $\text{Plaus}(h) = c\mu_h(o)$ for some constant $c > 0$ and all $h \in \mathcal{H}$ (Exercise 3.12).

So what does all this say about the problem raised at the beginning of this section, regarding the representation of evidence when uncertainty is represented by a set of probability measures? Recall from the discussion in Section 2.3 that a set of probability measures $\mathcal{P}$ on a space $W$ can be represented by a space $\mathcal{P} \times W$. In this representation, $\mathcal{P}$ can be viewed as the set of hypotheses and $W$ as the set of observations. Actually, it may even be better to consider the space $\mathcal{P} \times 2^W$, so that the observations become subsets of $W$. Suppose that $\mathcal{P}$ is finite. Given an observation $U \subseteq W$, let $p_U^*$ denote the encoding of this observation as a probability measure, as suggested earlier; that is, $p_U^*(\mu) = \mu(U)/(\sum_{\mu' \in \mathcal{P}} \mu'(U))$. It seems perhaps more reasonable to represent the result of conditioning $\mathcal{P}$ on $U$ not just by the set $\{\mu|U : \mu \in \mathcal{P}, \mu(U) > 0\}$, but by the set $\{(\mu|U, p_U^*(\mu)) : \mu \in \mathcal{P}, \mu(U) > 0\}$. That is, the conditional probability $\mu|U$ is tagged by the "likelihood" of the hypothesis $\mu$. Denote this set $\mathcal{P}||U$. For example, in Example 3.4.1, $\mathcal{P}||H^1$ is $\{(\mu_{1/3}|H^1, 1/3), (\mu_{2/3}|H^1, 2/3)\}$. Thus, $\mathcal{P}||H^1(H^2) = \{(1/3, 1/3), (2/3, 2/3)\}$. This captures the intuition that observing $H^1$ makes $BH$ more likely than $BT$. There has been no work done on this representation of conditioning (to the best of my knowledge), but it seems worth pursuing further.

## 3.5   Conditioning Inner and Outer Measures

How should conditioning be done for inner and outer measures? More precisely, suppose that $\mu$ is a probability measure defined on a subalgebra $\mathcal{F}'$ of $\mathcal{F}$. What should $\mu_*(V \mid U)$ and $\mu^*(V \mid U)$ be if $U, V \in \mathcal{F}$? The first thought might be to take the obvious analogue of the definitions of $\mu_*(V)$ and $\mu^*(V)$, and define, for example, $\mu^*(V \mid U)$ to be $\min\{\mu(V'|U') : U' \supseteq U, V' \supseteq V, U', V' \in \mathcal{F}'\}$. However, this definition is easily seen to be quite *unreasonable*. For example, if $U$ and $V$ are in $\mathcal{F}'$, it may not give $\mu(V \mid U)$. For example, suppose that $V \subseteq U$, $U, V \in \mathcal{F}'$, and $\mu(V) < \mu(U) < 1$. Taking $V' = V$ and $U' = W$, it follows from this definition that $\mu^*(V \mid U) \le \mu(V)$. Since $\mu(V) < \mu(V \mid U)$, this means that $\mu^*(V \mid U) < \mu(V \mid U)$. This certainly doesn't seem reasonable.

One way of fixing this might be to take $U'$ to be a subset of $U$ in the definition of $\mu^*$, that is, taking $\mu^*(V \mid U)$ to be $\min\{\mu(V'|U') : U' \subseteq U, V' \supseteq V, U', V' \in \mathcal{F}'\}$. But this choice also has problems. For example, if $V \subseteq U$, $U, V \in \mathcal{F}'$, and $\mu(U - V) > 0$, then according to this definition, $\mu^*(V \mid U) \le \mu(V \mid U - V) = 0$. Again, this does not seem right.

The actual definition is motivated by Theorem 2.3.3. Given a measure $\mu$ on $\mathcal{F}'$, let $\mathcal{P}_\mu$ consist of all the extensions of $\mu$ to $\mathcal{F}$. Then for $U, V \in \mathcal{F}$ such that $\mu^*(U) > 0$, define

$$\mu_*(V \mid U) = (\mathcal{P}_\mu|U)_*(V) \text{ and}$$

$$\mu^*(V \mid U) = (\mathcal{P}_\mu|U)^*(V).$$

Are there expressions for $\mu_*(V \mid U)$ and $\mu^*(V \mid U)$ in terms of expressions such as $\mu_*(V \cap U)$, $\mu^*(U)$, analogous to the standard expression when all sets are measurable? One might guess that $\mu_*(V \mid U) = \mu_*(V \cap U)/\mu^*(U)$, taking the best approximation from below for the numerator and the best approximation from above for the denominator. This does not quite work. For suppose that $\mu_*(U) < \mu^*(U)$. Then $\mu_*(U)/\mu^*(U) < 1$, while it is immediate that $\mu_*(U \mid U) = 1$.

Although this choice gives inappropriate answers, something similar does much better. The idea for $\mu_*(V \mid U)$ is to have $\mu_*(V \cap U)$ in the numerator, as expected. For the denominator, instead of using $\mu^*(U)$, the set $U$ is partitioned into $V \cap U$ and $\overline{V} \cap U$. For $V \cap U$, the inner measure is used, since this is the choice made in the numerator. It is only for $\overline{V} \cap U$ that the outer measure is used.

**Theorem 3.5.1**  *Suppose that* $\mu^*(U) > 0$. *Then*

$$\mu_*(V \mid U) = \begin{cases} \dfrac{\mu_*(V \cap U)}{\mu_*(V \cap U) + \mu^*(\overline{V} \cap U)} & \text{if } \mu^*(\overline{V} \cap U) > 0, \\ 1 & \text{if } \mu^*(\overline{V} \cap U) = 0; \end{cases} \quad (3.4)$$

$$\mu^*(V \mid U) = \begin{cases} \dfrac{\mu^*(V \cap U)}{\mu^*(V \cap U) + \mu_*(\overline{V} \cap U)} & \text{if } \mu^*(V \cap U) > 0, \\ 0 & \text{if } \mu^*(V \cap U) = 0. \end{cases} \quad (3.5)$$

**Proof**  I consider $\mu_*(V \mid U)$ here. The argument for $\mu^*(V \mid U)$ is almost identical and is left to the reader (Exercise 3.13). First, suppose that $\mu^*(\overline{V} \cap U) = 0$. Then it should be clear that $\mu'(\overline{V} \cap U) = 0$, and so $\mu'(U) = \mu'(V \cap U)$, for all $\mu' \in \mathcal{P}_\mu$. Thus $\mu'(V \mid U) = 1$ for all $\mu' \in \mathcal{P}_\mu$ with $\mu'(U) > 0$, and so $\mu_*(V \mid U) = 1$. (This is true even if $\mu_*(V \cap U) = 0$.)

To show that (3.4) works if $\mu^*(\overline{V} \cap U) > 0$, I first show that if $\mu'$ is an extension of $\mu$ to $\mathcal{F}$ such that $\mu(U) > 0$, then

$$\frac{\mu_*(V \cap U)}{\mu_*(V \cap U) + \mu^*(\overline{V} \cap U)} \leq \mu'(V \mid U).$$

By Theorem 2.3.3, $\mu_*(V \cap U) \leq \mu'(V \cap U)$ and $\mu'(\overline{V} \cap U) \leq \mu^*(\overline{V} \cap U)$. By additivity, it follows that

$$\mu'(U) = \mu'(V \cap U) + \mu'(\overline{V} \cap U) \leq \mu'(V \cap U) + \mu^*(\overline{V} \cap U).$$

In general, if $x + y > 0$, $y \geq 0$, and $x \leq x'$, then $x/(x+y) \leq x'/(x'+y)$ (Exercise 3.13). Thus,

$$\frac{\mu_*(V \cap U)}{\mu_*(V \cap U) + \mu^*(\overline{V} \cap U)} \leq \frac{\mu'(V \cap U)}{\mu'(V \cap U) + \mu^*(\overline{V} \cap U)}$$

$$\leq \frac{\mu'(V \cap U)}{\mu'(V \cap U) + \mu'(\overline{V} \cap U)}$$

$$= \frac{\mu'(V \cap U)}{\mu'(U)}$$

$$= \mu'(V \mid U).$$

It remains to show that this bound is tight, that is, that there exists an extension $\mu_1$ such that $\mu_1(V \mid U) = \frac{\mu_*(V \cap U)}{\mu_*(V \cap U) + \mu^*(\overline{V} \cap U)}$. This is also left as an exercise (Exercise 3.13). ∎

It is immediate from Theorem 3.5.1 that $\mu_*(U \mid U) = \mu^*(U \mid U) = 1$, as expected. Perhaps more interesting is the observation that if $U$ is measurable, then $\mu_*(V \mid U) = \mu_*(V \cap U)/\mu(U)$ and $\mu^*(V \mid U) = \mu^*(V \cap U)/\mu(U)$. This follows easily from the fact that

$$\mu_*(V \cap U) + \mu^*(\overline{V} \cap U) = \mu^*(V \cap U) + \mu_*(\overline{V} \cap U) = \mu(U)$$

(Exercise 3.14). The following example shows that the formulas for inner and outer measure also give intuitively reasonable answers in concrete examples:

**Example 3.5.2** What happens if the three-prisoners puzzle is represented using non-measurable sets to capture the unknown probability that the jailer will say $b$ given that $a$ is pardoned? Let $\mathcal{F}'$ consist of all the sets that can be formed by taking unions of *lives -a*, *lives -b*, and *lives -c* (where $\emptyset$ is considered to be the empty union); that is, *lives -a*, *lives -b*, and *lives -c* form a basis for $\mathcal{F}'$. Since neither of the singleton sets $\{(a, b)\}$ and $\{(a, c)\}$ is in $\mathcal{F}'$, no probability must be assigned to the event that the jailer will say $b$ (resp., $c$) if $a$ is pardoned. Note that all the measures in $\mathcal{P}_J$ agree on the sets in $\mathcal{F}'$. Let $\mu_J$ be the measure on $\mathcal{F}'$ that agrees with each of the measures in $\mathcal{P}_J$. An easy computation shows that

- $(\mu_J)_*(lives\text{-}a \cap says\text{-}b) = (\mu_J)_*(\{(a, b)\}) = 0$ (since the only element of $\mathcal{F}'$ contained in $\{(a, b)\}$ is the empty set);

- $(\mu_J)^*(lives\text{-}a \cap says\text{-}b) = (\mu_J)^*(\{(a, b)\}) = 1/3$; and

- $(\mu_J)_*(\overline{lives\text{-}a} \cap says\text{-}b) = (\mu_J)^*(\overline{lives\text{-}a} \cap says\text{-}b) = \mu(\{(c, b)\}) = 1/3.$

It follows from the arguments in Example 3.3.1 that

$$(\mu_J)_*(lives\text{-}a \mid says\text{-}b) = \frac{(\mu_J)_*(lives\text{-}a \cap says\text{-}b)}{(\mu_J)_*(lives\text{-}a \cap says\text{-}b) + (\mu_J)^*(\overline{lives\text{-}a} \cap says\text{-}b)} = 0,$$

$$(\mu_J)^*(lives\text{-}a \mid says\text{-}b) = \frac{(\mu_J)^*(lives\text{-}a \cap says\text{-}b)}{(\mu_J)^*(lives\text{-}a \cap says\text{-}b) + (\mu_J)_*(\overline{lives\text{-}a} \cap says\text{-}b)}$$

$$= 1/2.$$

Just as Theorem 3.5.1 says, these equations give the lower and upper conditional probabilities of the set $\mathcal{P}_J$ conditioned on the jailer saying $b$. ∎

## 3.6   Conditioning Belief Functions

The appropriate way to condition a belief function depends on how it is interpreted. If it is viewed as a lower probability, then the ideas of Section 3.3 apply. On the other hand, if it is viewed as a way of measuring the evidence that supports an event, a different approach to conditioning is appropriate.

Recall from Theorem 2.4.1 that given a belief function Bel, the set $\mathcal{P}_{Bel} = \{\mu : \mu(U) \geq Bel(U)$ for all $U \subseteq W\}$ of probability measures is such that $Bel = (\mathcal{P}_{Bel})_*$ and $Plaus = (\mathcal{P}_{Bel})^*$ The association of Bel with $\mathcal{P}_{Bel}$ can be used to define a notion of conditional belief in terms of conditioning on sets of probability measures.

**Definition 3.6.1**   Given a belief function Bel defined on $W$ and a set $U$ such that $Plaus(U) > 0$, define functions $Bel|U : 2^W \to [0, 1]$ and $Plaus|U : 2^W \to [0, 1]$ as follows:

$$Bel|U(V) = (\mathcal{P}_{Bel}|U)_*(V),$$
$$Plaus|U(V) = (\mathcal{P}_{Bel}|U)^*(V).$$

If $Plaus(U) = 0$, then $Bel|U$ and $Plaus|U$ are undefined. I typically write $Bel(V \mid U)$ and $Plaus(V \mid U)$ rather than $Bel|U(V)$ and $Plaus|U(V)$. ∎

Given the close relationship between beliefs and inner measures, the following analogue of Theorem 3.5.1 should not come as a great surprise.

**Theorem 3.6.2**   *Suppose that* $\text{Plaus}(U) > 0$. *Then*

$$\text{Bel}(V \mid U) = \begin{cases} \dfrac{\text{Bel}(V \cap U)}{\text{Bel}(V \cap U) + \text{Plaus}(\overline{V} \cap U)} & \text{if } \text{Plaus}(\overline{V} \cap U) > 0, \\ 1 & \text{if } \text{Plaus}(\overline{V} \cap U) = 0; \end{cases}$$

$$\text{Plaus}(V \mid U) = \begin{cases} \dfrac{\text{Plaus}(V \cap U)}{\text{Plaus}(V \cap U) + \text{Bel}(\overline{V} \cap U)} & \text{if } \text{Plaus}(V \cap U) > 0, \\ 0 & \text{if } \text{Plaus}(V \cap U) = 0. \end{cases}$$

**Proof**   See Exercise 3.15.   ∎

By definition, a conditional probability measure is a probability measure. If $\text{Bel}|U$ is to be viewed as the result of conditioning the belief function Bel on $V$, an obvious question to ask is whether $\text{Bel}|U$ is in fact a belief function. It is far from clear that it is. Recall that the lower probability of an arbitrary set of probability measures is not in general a belief function, since lower probabilities do not necessarily satisfy B3 (Exercise 2.14). Fortunately, as the next result shows, $\text{Bel}|U$ is indeed a belief function, and $\text{Plaus}|U$ is the corresponding plausibility function.

**Theorem 3.6.3**   *Let* Bel *be a belief function on* $W$ *and* Plaus *the corresponding plausibility function. Suppose that* $U \subseteq W$ *and* $\text{Plaus}(U) > 0$. *Then* $\text{Bel}|U$ *is a belief function and* $\text{Plaus}|U$ *is the corresponding plausibility function.*

**Proof**   The proof that $\text{Plaus}(V \mid U) = 1 - \text{Bel}(\overline{V} \mid U)$ is straightforward and left to the reader (Exercise 3.16). Thus, provided that $\text{Bel}|U$ is a belief function, then $\text{Plaus}|U$ is the corresponding plausibility function. Clearly $\text{Bel}|U$ satisfies B1 and B2. The proof that $\text{Bel}|U$ satisfies B3 proceeds by induction on $n$; it is somewhat difficult and beyond the scope of this book.   ∎

This approach to defining conditional belief reduces a belief function Bel to a set of probability measures whose lower probability is Bel, namely $\mathcal{P}_{\text{Bel}}$. But, as observed in Chapter 2 (see Exercise 2.24), there are in general a number of sets of probability measures all of whose lower probabilities are Bel. While Theorem 3.6.2 holds for $\mathcal{P}_{\text{Bel}}$ (i.e., taking $\text{Bel}|U = (\mathcal{P}_{\text{Bel}}|U)_*$), it does not hold for an arbitrary set $\mathcal{P}$ such that $\mathcal{P}_* = \text{Bel}$; that is, even if $\mathcal{P}_* = \text{Bel}$, it is not the case that $(\mathcal{P}|U)_* = (\mathcal{P}_{\text{Bel}}|U)$, so $(\mathcal{P}|U)_*$ is not necessarily $\text{Bel}|U$ (Exercise 3.17). This is a minor annoyance. Theorem 3.6.2 can be taken as the definition of $\text{Bel}|U$. This has the advantage of being a definition of $\text{Bel}|U$ that is given completely in terms of Bel, not in terms of an associated set of probability measures. The fact that this definition agrees with conditioning on $\mathcal{P}_{\text{Bel}}$ can then be taken as evidence of the reasonableness of this approach.

Another notion of conditioning belief functions, arguably more appropriate if a belief function is viewed as a way of representing the evidence supporting an event, can be defined using the Rule of Combination. In this approach, the information $U$ is represented by the mass function $m_U$ that gives $U$ mass 1 and all other sets mass 0. Note that the belief function $\text{Bel}_U$ based on $m_U$ is such that $\text{Bel}_U(V) = 1$ if $U \subseteq V$ and $\text{Bel}_U(V) = 0$ otherwise.

**Definition 3.6.4**   Given a belief function Bel based on mass function $m$, let $\text{Bel}\|U$ be the belief function based on the mass function $m \oplus m_U$. ∎

**Proposition 3.6.5**   $\text{Bel}\|U$ *is defined exactly if* $\text{Plaus}(U) > 0$, *in which case*

$$\text{Bel}\|U(V) = \frac{\text{Bel}(V \cup \overline{U}) - \text{Bel}(\overline{U})}{1 - \text{Bel}(\overline{U})}.$$

*The corresponding plausibility function* $\text{Plaus}\|U$ *is defined as*

$$\text{Plaus}\|U(V) = \frac{\text{Plaus}(V \cap U)}{\text{Plaus}(U)}.$$

**Proof**   See Exercise 3.18. ∎

I typically write $\text{Bel}(V \parallel U)$ and $\text{Plaus}(V \parallel U)$ rather than $\text{Bel}\|U(V)$ and $\text{Plaus}\|U(V)$; I call this *DS conditioning*. Note that $\text{Plaus}(V \parallel U)$ looks just like probabilistic conditioning, using Plaus instead of $\mu$. It is immediate from Proposition 3.6.5 that an analogue of Bayes' Rule holds for $\text{Plaus}\|U$. There is no obvious analogue that holds in the case of $\text{Bel}\|U$, $\text{Bel}|U$, or $\text{Plaus}|U$.

If Bel is in fact a probability measure (so that $\text{Bel}(V) = \text{Plaus}(V)$ for all $V \subseteq W$), then $\text{Bel}(V \mid U) = \text{Bel}(V \parallel U)$; both definitions agree with the standard definition of conditional probability (Exercise 3.19). In general, however, $\text{Bel}(V \mid U)$ and $\text{Bel}(V \parallel U)$ are different. However, it can be shown that $[\text{Bel}(V \parallel U), \text{Plaus}(V \parallel U)]$ is a subinterval of $[\text{Bel}(V \mid U), \text{Plaus}(V \mid U)]$.

**Theorem 3.6.6**   *If* $\text{Plaus}(U) > 0$, *then*

$$\text{Bel}(V \mid U) \leq \text{Bel}(V \parallel U) \leq \text{Plaus}(V \parallel U) \leq \text{Plaus}(V \mid U).$$

**Proof**   Because $\text{Bel}(V \mid U) = 1 - \text{Plaus}(\overline{V} \mid U)$ and $\text{Bel}(V \parallel U) = 1 - \text{Plaus}(\overline{V} \parallel U)$, it suffices to prove that $\text{Plaus}(V \parallel U) \leq \text{Plaus}(V \mid U)$. If $\text{Plaus}(V \cap U) = 0$, then it is immediate from Theorem 3.6.2 and Proposition 3.6.5 that $\text{Plaus}(V \parallel U) =$

Plaus$(V \mid U) = 0$. If Plaus$(V \cap U) > 0$, it clearly suffices to show that Plaus$(U) \geq$ Plaus$(V \cap U) + \text{Bel}(\overline{V} \cap U)$. This is left to the reader (Exercise 3.20). ∎

As the following example shows, in general, [Bel$(V \parallel U)$, Plaus$(V \parallel U)$] is a strict subinterval of [Bel$(V \mid U)$, Plaus$(V \mid U)$]:

**Example 3.6.7**  Consider the result of applying the two definitions of conditional belief to analyzing the three-prisoners puzzle. Using the same notation as in Example 3.3.1, let $m$ be the mass function that assigns probability 1/3 to each of the three disjoint sets *lives -a*, *lives -b*, and *lives -c*, and let Bel and Plaus be the belief function and plausibility functions respectively, corresponding to $m$. Using Proposition 3.6.5, it follows that Bel(*lives -a* $\parallel$ *says-b*) = Plaus(*lives -a* $\parallel$ *says-b*) = 1/2. Thus, for DS conditioning, the range reduces to the single point 1/2 (intuitively, the "wrong" answer). By way of contrast, it follows from Definition 3.6.1 and Example 3.3.1 that Bel(*lives -a* $\mid$ *says-b*) = 0 while Plaus(*lives -a* $\mid$ *says-b*) = 1/2. ∎

Example 3.6.7 shows that DS conditioning can give counterintuitive answers. Intuitively, this is because the lower probability interpretation of belief functions seems more appropriate in this example. While Example 2.4.6 and results such as Theorems 3.4.5 and 3.4.6 show that Dempster's Rule of Combination can give quite reasonable results, an extra argument needs to be made regarding when it is appropriate to represent the evidence $U$ by the belief function Bel$_U$. Such arguments have been made; see the notes to this chapter for more details and references. Nevertheless, these examples do point out the need to be exceedingly careful about the underlying interpretation of a belief function when trying to condition on new information.

## 3.7  Conditioning Possibility Measures

There are two approaches given in the literature for defining conditional possibility measures. The first takes the view of a possibility measure as a special case of a plausibility function and applies DS conditioning. Recall that Plaus$(V \parallel U) =$ Plaus$(V \cap U)/$Plaus$(V)$; similarly, define Poss$(V \parallel U) = $ Poss$(V \cap U)/$Poss$(U)$. It is easy to check that Poss$(\cdot \parallel U)$ defined in this way is indeed a possibility measure (Exercise 3.21).

This definition, however, is not the one usually considered in the literature. The more common definition of conditional possibility takes as its point of departure the fact that min should play the same role in the context of possibility as multiplication does for probability. In the case of probability, this role is characterized by CP3. With this in mind, I take a *conditional possibility measure* Poss to be a function mapping a Popper algebra $2^W \times \mathcal{F}'$ to $[0, 1]$, satisfying the following four properties:

CPoss1. $\text{Poss}(\emptyset \mid U) = 0$ if $U \in \mathcal{F}'$.

CPoss2. $\text{Poss}(U \mid U) = 1$ in $U \in \mathcal{F}'$.

CPoss3. $\text{Poss}(V_1 \cup V_2 \mid U) = \max(\text{Poss}(V_1 \mid U), \text{Poss}(V_2 \mid U))$ if $V_1 \cap V_2 = \emptyset$, $V_1, V_2 \in \mathcal{F}$, and $U \in \mathcal{F}'$.

CPoss4. $\text{Poss}(U_1 \cap U_2 \mid U_3) = \min(\text{Poss}(U_1 \mid U_2 \cap U_3), \text{Poss}(U_2 \mid U_3))$   if $U_2 \cap U_3 \in \mathcal{F}'$, and $U_1 \in \mathcal{F}$.

CPoss4 is just the result of replacing $\mu$ by Poss and $\times$ by min in CP3.

Proposition 3.2.1 (and some of the subsequent discussion) shows that, given an unconditional probability measure $\mu$ defined on an algebra $\mathcal{F}$, the conditional probability measure $\mu^c$ defined by taking $\mu^c(V \mid U) = \mu(V \cap U)/\mu(U)$ is the unique conditional probability measure defined on $\mathcal{F} \times \mathcal{F}'$, where $\mathcal{F}' = \{U : \mu(U) > 0\}$, satisfying CP1–3. The analogue of this observation does not hold for possibility. For example, consider the unconditional possibility measure Poss on $W = \{w_1, w_2, w_3\}$ such that $\text{Poss}(w_1) = 2/3$, $\text{Poss}(w_2) = 1/2$, and $\text{Poss}(w_3) = 1$. Let $U = \{w_1, w_2\}$ and $V = \{w_1\}$. Then, for all $\alpha \in [2/3, 1]$, there is a conditional possibility measure $\text{Poss}_\alpha$ on $W$ that is an extension of Poss (i.e., $\text{Poss}_\alpha \mid W = \text{Poss}$) and satisfies CPoss1–4 such that $\text{Poss}(V \mid U) = \alpha$ (Exercise 3.22).

One approach that has been taken in the literature to defining a canonical conditional possibility measure determined by an unconditional possibility measure is to make things "as possible as possible." That is, given an unconditional possibility measure Poss, the largest conditional possibility measure Poss' consistent with CPoss1–4 that is an extension of Poss is considered. This leads to the following definition in the case that $\text{Poss}(U) > 0$:

$$\text{Poss}|U(V) = \begin{cases} \text{Poss}(V \cap U) & \text{if } \text{Poss}(V \cap U) < \text{Poss}(U), \\ 1 & \text{if } \text{Poss}(V \cap U) = \text{Poss}(U). \end{cases} \quad (3.6)$$

I leave it to the reader to check that the conditional possibility measure defined in this way satisfies CPoss1–4 and, in fact, it is in a precise sense the largest conditional possibility measure that is an extension of Poss and CPoss1–4 (Exercise 3.23). With this definition, there is no direct analogue to Bayes' Rule; $\text{Poss}(V \mid U)$ is not determined by $\text{Poss}(U \mid V)$, $\text{Poss}(U)$, and $\text{Poss}(V)$ (Exercise 3.24). However, it is immediate from CPoss4 that there is still a close relationship among $\text{Poss}(V \mid U)$, $\text{Poss}(U \mid V)$, $\text{Poss}(U)$, and $\text{Poss}(V)$ that is somewhat akin to Bayes' Rule, namely,

$$\min(\text{Poss}(V \mid U), \text{Poss}(U)) = \min(\text{Poss}(U \mid V), \text{Poss}(V)) = \text{Poss}(V \cap U).$$

## 3.8   Conditioning Ranking Functions

Defining conditional ranking is straightforward, using an analogue of the properties CP1–3 that were used to characterize probabilistic conditioning. A *conditional ranking function* $\kappa$ is a function mapping a Popper algebra $2^W \times \mathcal{F}'$ to $\mathbb{N}^*$ satisfying the following properties:

CRk1.  $\kappa(\emptyset \mid U) = \infty$ if $U \in \mathcal{F}'$.

CRk2.  $\kappa(U \mid U) = 0$ if $U \in \mathcal{F}'$.

CRk3.  $\kappa(V_1 \cup V_2 \mid U) = \min(\kappa(V_1 \mid U), \kappa(V_2 \mid U))$ if $V_1 \cap V_2 = \emptyset$, $V_1$, $V_2 \in \mathcal{F}$, and $U \in \mathcal{F}'$.

CRk4.  $\kappa(U_1 \cap U_2 \mid U_3) = \kappa(U_1 \mid U_2 \cap U_3) + \kappa(U_2 \mid U_3)$ if $U_2 \cap U_3 \in \mathcal{F}'$ and $U_1 \in \mathcal{F}$.

Note that $+$ is the analogue for ranking functions to $\times$ in probability (and min in possibility). I motivate this shortly.

Given an unconditional ranking function $\kappa$, the unique conditional ranking function with these properties with domain $2^W \times \mathcal{F}'$, where $\mathcal{F}' = \{U : \kappa(U) \neq \infty\}$, is defined via

$$\kappa(V \mid U) = \kappa(V \cap U) - \kappa(U) \tag{3.7}$$

(Exercise 3.25). This definition of conditioning is consistent with the order-of-magnitude probabilistic interpretation of ranking functions. If $\mu(U \cap V)$ is roughly $\epsilon^k$ and $\mu(U)$ is roughly $\epsilon^m$, then $\mu(V \mid U)$ is roughly $\epsilon^{k-m}$. This, indeed, is the motivation for choosing $+$ as the replacement for $\times$ in CRk4.

Notice that there is an obvious analogue of Bayes' Rule for ranking functions:

$$\kappa(U \mid V) = \kappa(V \mid U) + \kappa(U) - \kappa(V).$$

## 3.9   Conditioning Plausibility Measures

How should conditioning be defined in the case of plausibility measures? Proceeding in a manner similar in spirit to that for probability, define a *conditional plausibility space* (cps) to be a tuple $(W, \mathcal{F}, \mathcal{F}', \text{Pl})$, where $\mathcal{F} \times \mathcal{F}'$ is a Popper algebra over $W$, $\text{Pl} : \mathcal{F} \times \mathcal{F}' \rightarrow D$, $D$ is a partially ordered set of plausibility values, and Pl is a *conditional plausibility measure* (cpm) that satisfies the following conditions:

CPl1.  $\text{Pl}(\emptyset \mid U) = \perp$.

CPl2.  $\text{Pl}(U \mid U) = \top$.

CPl3.  If $V \subseteq V'$, then $\text{Pl}(V \mid U) \leq \text{Pl}(V' \mid U)$.

CPl4.  $\text{Pl}(V \mid U) = \text{Pl}(V \cap U \mid U)$.


CPl1–3 just say that Pl1–3 hold for $\text{Pl}(\cdot \mid U)$, so that $\text{Pl}(\cdot \mid U)$ is a plausibility measure for each fixed $U \in \mathcal{F}'$. CPl4 is the obvious analogue of CP4 . Since there is no notion of multiplication (yet!) for plausibility measures, it is not possible to give an analogue of CP3 for conditional plausibility.

   $(W, \mathcal{F}, \mathcal{F}', \text{Pl})$ is *acceptable* if $U \in \mathcal{F}'$ and $\text{Pl}(V \mid U) \neq \perp$ implies that $V \cap U \in \mathcal{F}'$. Acceptability is a generalization of the observation that if $\mu(V) \neq 0$, then conditioning on $V$ should be defined. It says that if $\text{Pl}(V \mid U) \neq \perp$, then conditioning on $V \cap U$ should be defined. All the constructions that were used for defining conditional likelihood measures result in acceptable cps's. On the other hand, acceptability is not required in the definition of conditional probability space (Definition 3.2.3).

   CPl1–4 are rather minimal requirements. Should there be others? The following coherence condition, which relates conditioning on two different sets, seems quite natural:


CPl5.  If $U \cap U' \in \mathcal{F}'$, $U, U', V, V' \in \mathcal{F}$, and $\text{Pl}(U \mid U') \neq \perp$, then $\text{Pl}(V \mid U \cap U')$
          $\leq \text{Pl}(V' \mid U \cap U')$ iff $\text{Pl}(V \cap U \mid U') \leq \text{Pl}(V' \cap U \mid U')$.


It can be shown that CPl5 implies CPl4 if $\mathcal{F}'$ has the property that characterizes acceptable cps's—that is, if $U \in \mathcal{F}'$ and $\text{Pl}(V \mid U) > \perp$, then $V \cap U \in \mathcal{F}'$ (Exercise 3.26). While CPl5 seems quite natural, and it holds for all conditional probability measures, conditional possibility measures constructed as in Section 3.7 from unconditional possibility measures (both $\text{Poss}(\cdot \mid U)$ and $\text{Poss}(\cdot \parallel U)$), and conditional ranking functions as constructed in Section 3.8 from unconditional ranking functions, it does not hold in general for $\mathcal{P}_*(\cdot \mid U)$, $\text{Bel}(\cdot \mid U)$, or $\text{Bel}(\cdot \parallel U)$ (Exercise 3.27). For example, in the case of $\mathcal{P}_*$, the problem is that just because $\mu \in \mathcal{P}$ gives the minimum value for $\mu(U \cap V)$ does not mean it also gives the minimum value for $\mu(V \mid U)$. The minimization operation does not "commute" with conditioning. Without this commutativity, the "natural" coherence condition CPl5 no longer holds.

### 3.9.1   Constructing Conditional Plausibility Measures

Given an unconditional plausibility measure Pl, is it possible to construct a conditional plausibility measure extending Pl? It turns out that there is. Perhaps the easiest way of understanding it is to consider first the problem of getting a conditional plausibility measure extending the representation $\text{Pl}_{\mathcal{P}}$ of a set $\mathcal{P}$ of probability measures.

Assume that all the probability measures in $\mathcal{P}$ are defined on some algebra $\mathcal{F}$ over $W$. Recall that in the unconditional case, the domain of $\text{Pl}_{\mathcal{P}}$ is also $\mathcal{F}$ and its range is $D_{\mathcal{P}}$, the set of functions from $\mathcal{P}$ to $[0, 1]$. In particular, $\text{Pl}_{\mathcal{P}}(U)(\mu) = \mu(U)$, for $U \in \mathcal{F}$. The plan now is to define $\text{Pl}_{\mathcal{P}}(V \mid U)$ to be that function $f_{V|U}$ from $\mathcal{P}$ to values in $[0, 1]$ such that $\text{Pl}_{\mathcal{P}}(V \mid U)(\mu) = \mu(V \mid U)$. The only question is what the domain of $\text{Pl}_{\mathcal{P}}$ ought to be; that is, on what Popper algebra $\mathcal{F} \times \mathcal{F}'$ should $\text{Pl}_{\mathcal{P}}$ be defined? This issue also arose in the context of defining $\mathcal{P}_*(V \mid U)$. One approach would be to take $\mathcal{F}'$ to consist of all $U \in \mathcal{F}$ such that $\mu(U) > 0$ for all $\mu \in \mathcal{P}$. This would result in a cps that, in general, is not acceptable (Exercise 3.28). As in the case of $\mathcal{P}_*$, conditioning would not be defined for many cases of interest. Instead (again, just as in the case of $\mathcal{P}_*$), I take $\mathcal{F}'$ to consist of all $V$ such that $\mu(V) > 0$ for some $\mu \in \mathcal{P}$. But then what should $f_{V|U}(\mu)$ be if $\mu(U) = 0$? To deal with this, I add a value "undefined," denoted $*$, to the domain.

Formally, extend $D_{\mathcal{P}}$ by allowing functions that have value $*$. More precisely, let $D'_{\mathcal{P}}$ consist of all functions $f$ from $\mathcal{P}$ to $[0, 1] \cup \{*\}$ such that $f(\mu) \neq *$ for at least one $\mu \in \mathcal{P}$. The idea is to define $\text{Pl}_{\mathcal{P}}(V \mid U) = f_{V|U}$, where $f_{V|U}(\mu) = \mu(V \mid U)$ if $\mu(U) > 0$ and $*$ otherwise. (Note that this agrees with the previous definition, which applies only to the case where $\mu(U) > 0$ for all $\mu \in \mathcal{P}$.) There is a problem though. CPl1 says that $f_{\emptyset|U}$ must be $\bot$ for all $U$. Thus, it must be the case that $f_{\emptyset|U_1} = f_{\emptyset|U_2}$ for all $U_1, U_2 \subseteq W$. But if $\mu \in \mathcal{P}$ and $U_1, U_2 \subseteq W$ are such that $\mu(U_1) > 0$ and $\mu(U_2) = 0$, then $f_{\emptyset|U_1}(\mu) = 0$ and $f_{\emptyset|U_2}(\mu) = *$, so $f_{\emptyset|U_1} \neq f_{\emptyset|U_2}$. A similar problem arises with CPl2.

To deal with this problem, $D'_{\mathcal{P}}$ must be slightly modified. Say that $f \in D'_{\mathcal{P}}$ is *equivalent to* $\bot_{D^*_{\mathcal{P}}}$ if $f(\mu)$ is either 0 or $*$ for all $\mu \in \mathcal{P}$; similarly, *$f$ is equivalent to* $\top_{D^*_{\mathcal{P}}}$ if $f(\mu)$ is either 1 or $*$ for all $\mu \in \mathcal{P}$. (Since, by definition of $D'_{\mathcal{P}}$, $f(\mu) \neq *$ for at least one $\mu \in \mathcal{P}$, an element in $D'_{\mathcal{P}}$ cannot be equivalent to both $\top_{D^*_{\mathcal{P}}}$ and $\bot_{D^*_{\mathcal{P}}}$.) Let $D^*_{\mathcal{P}}$ be the same as $D'_{\mathcal{P}}$ except that all elements equivalent to $\bot_{D^*_{\mathcal{P}}}$ are identified (and viewed as one element) and all elements equivalent to $\top_{D^*_{\mathcal{P}}}$ are identified. More precisely, let $D^*_{\mathcal{P}} = \{\bot_{D^*_{\mathcal{P}}}, \top_{D^*_{\mathcal{P}}}\} \cup \{f \in D' : f \text{ is not equivalent to } \top_{D^*_{\mathcal{P}}} \text{ or } \bot_{D^*_{\mathcal{P}}}\}$. Define the order $\leq_{D^*_{\mathcal{P}}}$ on $D^*_{\mathcal{P}}$ by taking $f \leq_{D^*_{\mathcal{P}}} g$ if one of the following three conditions holds:

- $f = \perp_{D_{\mathcal{P}}^*}$,

- $g = \top_{D_{\mathcal{P}}^*}$,

- neither $f$ nor $g$ is $\perp_{D_{\mathcal{P}}^*}$ or $\top_{D_{\mathcal{P}}^*}$ and, for all $\mu \in \mathcal{P}$, either $f(\mu) = g(\mu) = *$ or $f(\mu) \neq *$, $g(\mu) \neq *$, and $f(\mu) \leq g(\mu)$.

Now define

$$\mathrm{Pl}_{\mathcal{P}}(V \mid U) = \begin{cases} \perp_{D_{\mathcal{P}}^*} & \text{if } \mu(U) \neq 0 \text{ for some } \mu \in \mathcal{P} \\ & \text{and } \mu(U) \neq 0 \text{ implies } \mu(V \mid U) = 0 \text{ for all } \mu \in \mathcal{P}, \\ \top_{D_{\mathcal{P}}^*} & \text{if } \mu(U) \neq 0 \text{ for some } \mu \in \mathcal{P} \\ & \text{and } \mu(U) \neq 0 \text{ implies } \mu(V \mid U) = 1 \text{ for all } \mu \in \mathcal{P}, \\ f_{V \mid U} & \text{if } \mu(U) \neq 0, \mu(V \mid U) \neq 0, 1 \\ & \text{for some } \mu \in \mathcal{P}, \\ \text{undefined} & \text{if } \mu(U) = 0 \text{ for all } \mu \in \mathcal{P}. \end{cases}$$

It is easy to check that this construction results in an acceptable cps that satisfies CPl5 and is an extension of $\mathrm{Pl}_{\mathcal{P}}$ (Exercise 3.29).

This construction can be used, with essentially no change, if $\mathcal{P}$ is a set of arbitrary plausibility measures; in that case, it gives a single cpm that represents $\mathcal{P}$. More interestingly, a similar construction can be used to construct a conditional plausibility measure from an arbitrary unconditional plausibility measure Pl defined on an algebra $\mathcal{F}$. The idea is quite straightforward. Given an unconditional plausibility measure Pl with range $D$, for each set $U \in \mathcal{F}$, start by defining a new plausibility measure $\mathrm{Pl}_U$ with range $D_U = \{d \in D : d \leq \mathrm{Pl}(U)\}$ by taking $\mathrm{Pl}_U(V) = \mathrm{Pl}(V \cap U)$. Note that $\top_{D_U} = \mathrm{Pl}(U)$. Thus, defining $\mathrm{Pl}(V \mid U)$ as $\mathrm{Pl}_U(V)$ will not quite work, because then CPl2 is not satisfied; in general, $\mathrm{Pl}_U(W) \neq \mathrm{Pl}_V(W)$.

To get a cps, let $D' = \{(d, V) : V \subseteq W, \ d \leq \mathrm{Pl}(V), \ \mathrm{Pl}(V) > \perp_D\}$. Say that $(d, V)$ is *equivalent to* $\perp_{D^*}$ if $d = \perp_D$; say that $(d, V)$ is *equivalent to* $\top_{D^*}$ if $d = \mathrm{Pl}(V)$. Now let $D^* = \{\perp_{D^*}, \top_{D^*}\} \cup \{(d, V) \in D' : (d, V) \text{ is not equivalent to } \top_{D^*} \text{ or } \perp_{D^*}\}$. Then define $d \leq_{D^*} d'$ for $d, d' \in D^*$ iff $d = \perp_{D^*}$, $d' = \top_{D^*}$, or there is some $V \subseteq W$ such that $d = (d_1, V)$, $d' = (d_2, V)$, and $d_1 \leq_D d_2$. Finally, for $U, V \in \mathcal{F}$, define

$$\mathrm{Pl}(V \mid U) = \begin{cases} (\mathrm{Pl}(U \cap V), U) & \text{if } \perp_D < \mathrm{Pl}(U \cap V) < \mathrm{Pl}(U), \\ \top_{D^*} & \text{if } \mathrm{Pl}(U \cap V) = \mathrm{Pl}(U) > \perp_D, \\ \perp_{D^*} & \text{if } \mathrm{Pl}(U \cap V) = \perp_D, \mathrm{Pl}(U) > \perp_D, \\ \text{undefined} & \text{if } \mathrm{Pl}(U) = \perp_D. \end{cases}$$

I leave it to the reader to check that this gives an acceptable cps that satisfies CPl5 and is an extension of Pl, if $d \in D$ is identified with $(d, W) \in D^*$ (Exercise 3.30). It is important that $\text{Pl}(V \mid U)$ is undefined if $\text{Pl}(U) = \perp_D$; if $\text{Pl}(V \mid U)$ were instead defined as $\perp_{D*}$, then $\top_{D*}$ would be equal to $\perp_{D*}$, and the whole construction would trivialize. In particular, the resulting cpm would not extend Pl.

### 3.9.2   Algebraic Conditional Plausibility Spaces

The definitions of conditional possibility and conditional ranking were motivated in part by considering analogues for possibility and ranking of addition and multiplication in probability. We saw in Section 2.8 that an analogue $\oplus$ of addition could be added to plausibility. Yet more structure emerges if, in addition, there is an analogue to multiplication.

**Definition 3.9.1**   A cps $(W, \mathcal{F}, \mathcal{F}', \text{Pl})$ where Pl has range $D$ is *algebraic* if it is acceptable and there are functions $\oplus$ and $\otimes$ mapping $D \times D$ to $D$ such that the following conditions hold:

Alg1.   Pl is additive with respect to $\oplus$; that is, $\text{Pl}(V \cup V' \mid U) = \text{Pl}(V \mid U) \oplus \text{Pl}(V' \mid U)$ if $V, V' \in \mathcal{F}$ are disjoint and $U \in \mathcal{F}'$.

Alg2.   $\text{Pl}(U_1 \cap U_2 \mid U_3) = \text{Pl}(U_1 \mid U_2 \cap U_3) \otimes \text{Pl}(U_2 \mid U_3)$ if $U_2 \cap U_3 \in \mathcal{F}'$, $U_1, U_2, U_3 \in \mathcal{F}$.

Alg3.   $\otimes$ distributes over $\oplus$; more precisely, $a \otimes (b_1 \oplus \cdots \oplus b_n) = (a \otimes b_1) \oplus \cdots \oplus (a \otimes b_n)$ if $(a, b_1), \ldots, (a, b_n), (a, b_1 \oplus \cdots \oplus b_n) \in \text{Dom}(\otimes)$ and $(b_1, \ldots, b_n), (a \otimes b_1, \ldots, a \otimes b_n) \in \text{Dom}(\oplus)$, where $\text{Dom}(\oplus) = \{(\text{Pl}(V_1 \mid U), \ldots, \text{Pl}(V_n \mid U)) : V_1, \ldots, V_n \in \mathcal{F}$ are pairwise disjoint and $U \in \mathcal{F}'\}$ and $\text{Dom}(\otimes) = \{(\text{Pl}(U_1 \mid U_2 \cap U_3), \text{Pl}(U_2 \mid U_3)) : U_2 \cap U_3 \in F', U_1, U_2, U_3 \in \mathcal{F}\}$. (The reason that this property is required only for tuples in $\text{Dom}(\oplus)$ and $\text{Dom}(\otimes)$ is discussed shortly. Note that parentheses are not required in the expression $b_1 \oplus \cdots \oplus b_n$ although, in general, $\oplus$ need not be associative. This is because it follows immediately from Alg1 that $\oplus$ is associative and commutative on tuples in $\text{Dom}(\oplus)$.)

Alg4.   If $(a, c), (b, c) \in \text{Dom}(\otimes)$, $a \otimes c \leq b \otimes c$, and $c \neq \perp$, then $a \leq b$.

If $(W, \mathcal{F}, \mathcal{F}', \text{Pl})$ is an algebraic cps, then Pl is called an *algebraic cpm*.   ∎

Alg1 and Alg2 are clearly analogues of CP2 and CP3. The restrictions in Alg3 and Alg4 to tuples in $\text{Dom}(\oplus)$ and $\text{Dom}(\otimes)$ make these conditions a little more awkward to state. It may seem more natural to consider a stronger version of, say, Alg4 that applies to all pairs in $D \times D$, such as

Alg4′. If $a \otimes c = b \otimes c$ and $c \neq \perp$, then $a = b$.

However, as Proposition 3.9.2 shows, by requiring that Alg3 and Alg4 hold only for tuples in $\mathrm{Dom}(\oplus)$ and $\mathrm{Dom}(\otimes)$ rather than on all tuples in $D \times D$, some cps's of interest become algebraic that would otherwise not be. Since $\oplus$ and $\otimes$ are significant mainly to the extent that Alg1 and Alg2 hold, and Alg1 and Alg2 apply to tuples in $\mathrm{Dom}(\oplus)$ and $\mathrm{Dom}(\otimes)$, respectively, it does not seem unreasonable that properties like Alg3 and Alg4 be required to hold only for these tuples.

**Proposition 3.9.2**   *The constructions for extending an unconditional probability measure, ranking function, possibility measure (using either* $\mathrm{Poss}(\cdot|U)$ *or* $\mathrm{Poss}(\cdot||U)$*), and the plausibility measure* $\mathrm{Pl}_{\mathcal{P}}$ *defined by a set* $\mathcal{P}$ *of probability measures to a cps result in algebraic cps's.*

**Proof**   It is easy to see that in each case the cps is acceptable. It is also easy to find appropriate notions of $\otimes$ and $\oplus$ in the case of probability measures, ranking functions, and possibility measures using $\mathrm{Poss}(V \mid U)$. For probability, clearly $\oplus$ and $\otimes$ are essentially $+$ and $\times$; however, since the range of probability is $[0, 1]$, $a \oplus b$ must be defined as $\max(1, a + b)$, and Alg3 holds only for $\mathrm{Dom}(\oplus) = \{(a_1, \ldots, a_k) : a_1 + \cdots + a_k \leq 1\}$. For ranking, $\oplus$ and $\otimes$ are min and $+$; there are no constraints on $\mathrm{Dom}(\oplus)$ and $\mathrm{Dom}(\otimes)$. For $\mathrm{Poss}(V||U)$, $\oplus$ is max and $\otimes$ is $\times$; again, there are no constraints on $\mathrm{Dom}(\max)$ and $\mathrm{Dom}(\times)$. I leave it to the reader to check that Alg1–4 hold in all these cases (Exercise 3.31).

For $\mathrm{Poss}(V \mid U)$, $\oplus$ is again max and $\otimes$ is min. There are no constraints on $\mathrm{Dom}(\max)$; however, note that $(a, b) \in \mathrm{Dom}(\min)$ iff either $a < b$ or $a = 1$. For suppose that $(a, b) = (\mathrm{Pl}(U_1|U_2 \cap U_3), \mathrm{Pl}(U_2|U_3))$, where $U_2 \cap U_3 \in \mathcal{F}'$, $U_1, U_2, U_3 \in \mathcal{F}$. If $\mathrm{Poss}(U_1 \cap U_2 \cap U_3) = \mathrm{Poss}(U_2 \cap U_3)$ then $a = \mathrm{Poss}(U_1 \cap U_2|U_3) = 1$; otherwise, $\mathrm{Poss}(U_1 \cap U_2 \cap U_3) < \mathrm{Poss}(U_2 \cap U_3)$, in which case $a = \mathrm{Poss}(U_1 \cap U_2 \cap U_3) < \mathrm{Poss}(U_2 \cap U_3) \leq \mathrm{Poss}(U_2|U_3) = b$. It is easy to check that Alg1–3 hold (Exercise 3.32). While min does not satisfy Alg4′—certainly $\min(a, c) = \min(b, c)$ does not in general imply that $a = b$—Alg4 does hold. For if $\min(a, c) = \min(b, c)$ and $a = 1$, then clearly $b = 1$. On the other hand, if $a < c$, then $\min(a, c) = a$ and the only way that $a = \min(b, c)$, given that $b < c$ or $b = 1$, is if $a = b$.

Finally, for $\mathrm{Pl}_{\mathcal{P}}$, $\oplus$ and $\otimes$ are essentially pointwise addition and multiplication. But there are a few subtleties. As in the case of probability, $\mathrm{Dom}(\oplus)$ essentially consists of sequences that sum to at most 1 for each index $i$. However, care must be taken in dealing with $\perp_{D_{\mathcal{P}}^*}$ and $\top_{D_{\mathcal{P}}^*}$. To be precise, $\mathrm{Dom}(\oplus)$ consists of all tuples $(f_1, \ldots, f_n)$ such that either

1. For all $j, k \in \{1, \ldots, n\}$ and $\mu \in \mathcal{P}$,

    (a) $f_j \neq \top_{D_\mathcal{P}^*}$;

    (b) if $f_j, f_k \neq \bot_{D_\mathcal{P}^*}$, then $f_j(\mu) = *$ iff $f_k(\mu) = *$; and

    (c) $\sum_{\{h : f_h \neq \bot_{D_\mathcal{P}^*}, f_h(\mu) \neq *\}} f_h(\mu) \leq 1$;

    or

2. there exists $j$ such that $f_j = \top_{D_\mathcal{P}^*}$ and $f_k = \bot_{D_\mathcal{P}^*}$ for all $k \neq j$.

Dom$(\otimes)$ consists of pairs $(f, g)$ such that either (a) one of $f$ or $g$ is in $\{\bot_{D_\mathcal{P}^*}, \top_{D_\mathcal{P}^*}\}$ or (b) neither $f$ nor $g$ is in $\{\bot_{D_\mathcal{P}^*}, \top_{D_\mathcal{P}^*}\}$ and $g(\mu) \in \{0, *\}$ iff $f(\mu) = *$.

The definition of $\oplus$ is relatively straightforward. Define $f \oplus \top_{D_\mathcal{P}^*} = \top_{D_\mathcal{P}^*} \oplus f = \top_{D_\mathcal{P}^*}$ and $f \oplus \bot_{D_\mathcal{P}^*} = \bot_{D_\mathcal{P}^*} \oplus f = f$. If $\{f, g\} \cap \{\bot_{D_\mathcal{P}^*}, \top_{D_\mathcal{P}^*}\} = \emptyset$, then $f \oplus g = h$, where $h(\mu) = \min(1, f(\mu) + g(\mu))$ (taking $a + * = * + a = *$ and $\min(1, *) = *$). In a similar spirit, define $f \otimes \top_{D_\mathcal{P}^*} = \top_{D_\mathcal{P}^*} \otimes f = f$ and $f \otimes \bot_{D_\mathcal{P}^*} = \bot_{D_\mathcal{P}^*} \otimes f = \bot_{D_\mathcal{P}^*}$; if $\{f, g\} \cap \{\bot_{D_\mathcal{P}^*}, \top_{D_\mathcal{P}^*}\} = \emptyset$, then $f \otimes g = h$, where $h(\mu) = f(\mu) \times g(\mu)$ (taking $* \times a = a \times * = *$ if $a \neq 0$ and $* \times 0 = 0 \times * = 0$). It is important that $* \times 0 = 0$ and $* \times * = *$, since otherwise Alg3 may not hold. For example, suppose $\mathcal{P} = \{\mu_1, \mu_2, \mu_3\}$ and a function $f \in D_\mathcal{P}'$ is identified with the tuple $(f(\mu_1), f(\mu_2), f(\mu_3))$. Then, according to Alg3, $((1/2, *, 1/2) \otimes (a, 0, b)) \oplus ((1/2, *, 1/2)) \otimes (a, 0, b)) = (1/2, *, 1/2) \oplus (1/2, *, 1/2)) \otimes (a, 0, b) = (a, 0, b)$ (since $(1/2, *, 1/2) \oplus (1/2, *, 1/2) = \top_{D_\mathcal{P}^*}$) and, similarly, $((1/2, *, 1/2) \otimes (a, *, b)) \oplus ((1/2, *, 1/2)) \otimes (a, *, b)) = (a, *, b)$. Since $* \times 0 = 0$ and $* \times * = *$, these equalities hold. I leave it to the reader to check that, with these definitions, Alg1–4 hold (Exercise 3.33).  ∎

As observed in Section 2.8, there is no analogue to $\oplus$ for belief functions and lower probabilities. Thus, these representations of uncertainty are not algebraic.

Many of the properties that are associated with (conditional) probability hold more generally for algebraic cps's. I consider three of them here that will prove useful in Section 4.5. The first two say that $\bot$ and $\top$ act like 0 and 1 with respect to addition and multiplication. Let $Range(\text{Pl}) = \{d : \text{Pl}(V \mid U) = d$ for some $(V, U) \in \mathcal{F} \times \mathcal{F}'\}$.

**Lemma 3.9.3**   *If $(W, \mathcal{F}, \mathcal{F}', \text{Pl})$ is an algebraic cps, then $d \oplus \bot = \bot \oplus d = d$ for all $d \in Range(\text{Pl})$.*

**Proof**   See Exercise 3.34.  ∎

**Lemma 3.9.4**   *If $(W, \mathcal{F}, \mathcal{F}', \text{Pl})$ is an algebraic cps then, for all $d \in Range(\text{Pl})$,*

(a) $d \otimes \top = d$;

(b) if $d \neq \bot$, then $\top \otimes d = d$;

(c) if $d \neq \bot$, then $\bot \otimes d = \bot$;

(d) if $(d, \bot) \in \text{Dom}(\otimes)$, then $\top \otimes \bot = d \otimes \bot = \bot \otimes \bot = \bot$.

**Proof**   See Exercise 3.35.   ∎

The third property is an analogue of a standard property for probability that shows how $\text{Pl}(V \mid U)$ can be computed by partitioning it into subsets.

**Lemma 3.9.5**   *Suppose that* $(W, \mathcal{F}, \mathcal{F}', \text{Pl})$ *is an algebraic cps,* $A_1, \ldots, A_n$ *is a partition of* $W$, $A_1, \ldots, A_n \in \mathcal{F}$, *and* $U \in \mathcal{F}'$. *Then*

$$\text{Pl}(V \mid U) = \oplus_{\{i : A_i \cap U \in \mathcal{F}'\}} \text{Pl}(V \mid A_i \cap U) \otimes \text{Pl}(A_i \mid U).$$

**Proof**   See Exercise 3.36.   ∎

Notice that if $A_i \cap U \in \mathcal{F}'$, then $\text{Pl}(V | A_i \cap U) \otimes \text{Pl}(A_i | U) = \text{Pl}(V \cap A_i | U)$ by Alg2. Thus, the terms arising on the right-hand side of the equation in Lemma 3.9.5 are in $\text{Dom}(\oplus)$. As I observed earlier, this means that there is no need to put in parentheses; $\oplus$ is associative on terms in $\text{Dom}(\oplus)$.

I conclude this section by abstracting a property that holds for all the constructions of cps's from unconditional plausibility measures (i.e., the constructions given in the case of Poss, ranking functions, probability, $\text{Pl}_{\mathcal{P}}$, and plausibility). A cps $(W, \mathcal{F}, \mathcal{F}', \text{Pl})$ is *standard* if $\mathcal{F}' = \{U : \text{Pl}(U) \neq \bot\}$. Note that all the constructions of cps's from unconditional plausibility measures that have been considered result in standard cps's. This follows from a more general observation. $(W, \mathcal{F}, \mathcal{F}', \text{Pl})$ is *determined by unconditional plausibility* if there is a function $g$ such that $\text{Pl}(V \mid U) = g(\text{Pl}(V \cap U | W), \text{Pl}(U | W))$ for all $(V, U) \in \mathcal{F} \times \mathcal{F}'$. It is almost immediate from the definitions that all the constructions of cps's constructed from unconditional plausibilities result in cps's that are determined by unconditional plausibility. If an acceptable cps is determined by unconditional plausibility, then it must be standard.

**Lemma 3.9.6**   *If* $(W, \mathcal{F}, \mathcal{F}', \text{Pl})$ *is an acceptable cps determined by unconditional plausibility such that* $\text{Pl}(W) \neq \text{Pl}(\emptyset)$, *then* $(W, \mathcal{F}, \mathcal{F}', \text{Pl})$ *is a standard cps.*

**Proof**   See Exercise 3.38.   ∎

## 3.10   Jeffrey's Rule

Up to now, I have assumed that the information received is of the form "the actual world is in $U$." But information does not always come in such nice packages.

**Example 3.10.1**   Suppose that an object is either red, blue, green, or yellow. An agent initially ascribes probability 1/5 to each of *red*, *blue*, and *green*, and probability 2/5 to *yellow*. Then the agent gets a quick glimpse of the object in a dimly lit room. As a result of this glimpse, he believes that the object is probably a darker color, although he is not sure. He thus ascribes probability .7 to it being green or blue and probability .3 to it being red or yellow. How should he update his initial probability measure based on this observation?   ∎

Note that if the agent had definitely observed that the object was either blue or green, he would update his belief by conditioning on *{blue, green}*. If the agent had definitely observed that the object was either red or yellow, he would condition on *{red, yellow}*. However, the agent's observation was not good enough to confirm that the object was definitely blue or green, nor that it was red or yellow. Rather, it can be represented as .7*{blue, green}*; .3*{red, yellow}*. This suggests that an appropriate way of updating the agent's initial probability measure $\mu$ is to consider the linear combination $\mu' = .7\mu|\{blue, green\} + .3\mu|\{red, yellow\}$. As expected, $\mu'(\{blue, green\}) = .7$ and $\mu'(\{red, yellow\}) = .3$. Moreover, $\mu'(red) = .1$, $\mu'(yellow) = .2$, and $\mu'(blue) = \mu'(green) = .35$. Thus, $\mu'$ gives the two sets about which the agent has information—*{blue, green}* and *{red, yellow}*—the expected probabilities. Within each of these sets, the relative probability of the outcomes remains the same as before conditioning.

More generally, suppose that $U_1, \ldots, U_n$ is a partition of $W$ (i.e., $\bigcup_{i=1}^n U_i = W$ and $U_i \cap U_j = \emptyset$ for $i \neq j$) and the agent observes $\alpha_1 U_1; \ldots; \alpha_n U_n$, where $\alpha_1 + \cdots + \alpha_n = 1$. This is to be interpreted as an observation that leads the agent to believe $U_j$ with probability $\alpha_j$, for $j = 1, \ldots, n$. In Example 3.10.1, the partition consists of two sets $U_1 = \{blue, green\}$ and $U_2 = \{red, yellow\}$, with $\alpha_1 = .7$ and $\alpha_2 = .3$. How should the agent update his beliefs, given this observation? It certainly seems reasonable that after making this observation, $U_j$ should get probability $\alpha_j$, $j = 1, \ldots, n$. Moreover, since the observation does not give any extra information regarding subsets of $U_j$, the relative likelihood of worlds in $U_j$ should remain unchanged. This suggests that $\mu|(\alpha_1 U_1; \ldots; \alpha_n U_n)$, the probability measure resulting from the update, should have the following property for $j = 1, \ldots, n$:

J.     $\mu|(\alpha_1 U_1; \ldots; \alpha_n U_n)(V) = \alpha_j \frac{\mu(V)}{\mu(U_j)}$ if $V \subseteq U_j$ and $\mu(U_j) > 0$.

Taking $V = U_j$ in J, it follows that

J1. $\quad \mu|(\alpha_1 U_1; \ldots; \alpha_n U_n)(U_j) = \alpha_j$ if $\mu(U_j) > 0$.

Moreover, if $\alpha_j > 0$, the following analogue of (3.2) is a consequence of J (and J1):

J2. $\quad \dfrac{\mu(V)}{\mu(U_j)} = \dfrac{\mu|(\alpha_1 U_1; \ldots; \alpha_n U_n)(V)}{\mu|(\alpha_1 U_1; \ldots; \alpha_n U_n)(U_j)}$ if $V \subseteq U_j$ and $\mu(U_j) > 0$

(Exercise 3.39).

Property J uniquely determines what is known as *Jeffrey's Rule* of conditioning (since it was defined by Richard Jeffrey). Define

$$\mu|(\alpha_1 U_1; \ldots; \alpha_n U_n)(V) = \alpha_1 \mu(V \mid U_1) + \cdots + \alpha_n \mu(V \mid U_n). \qquad (3.8)$$

(I take $\alpha_j \mu(V \mid U_j)$ to be 0 here if $\alpha_j = 0$, even if $\mu(U_j) = 0$.) Jeffrey's Rule is defined as long as the observation is *consistent* with the initial probability (Exercise 3.40); formally this means that if $\alpha_j > 0$ then $\mu(U_j) > 0$. Intuitively, an observation is consistent if it does not give positive probability to a set that was initially thought to have probability 0. Moreover, if the observation is consistent, then Jeffrey's Rule gives the unique probability measure satisfying property J (Exercise 3.40).

Note that $\mu|U = \mu|(1U; 0\overline{U})$, so the usual notion of probabilistic conditioning is just a special case of Jeffrey's Rule. However, probabilistic conditioning has one attractive feature that is not maintained in the more general setting of Jeffrey's Rule. Suppose that the agent makes two observations, $U_1$ and $U_2$. It is easy to see that if $\mu(U_1 \cap U_2) \neq 0$, then

$$(\mu|U_1)|U_2 = (\mu|U_2)|U_1 = \mu|(U_1 \cap U_2)$$

(Exercise 3.41). That is, the following three procedures give the same result: (a) condition on $U_1$ and then $U_2$, (b) condition on $U_2$ and then $U_1$, and (c) condition on $U_1 \cap U_2$ (which can be viewed as conditioning simultaneously on $U_1$ and $U_2$). The analogous result does not hold for Jeffrey's Rule. For example, suppose that the agent in Example 3.10.1 starts with some measure $\mu$, observes $O_1 = .7\{blue, green\}$; $.3\{red, yellow\}$, and then observes $O_2 = .3\{blue, green\}$; $.7\{red, yellow\}$. Clearly, $(\mu|O_1)|O_2 \neq (\mu|O_2)|O_1$. For example, $(\mu|O_1)|O_2$ ($\{blue, green\}) = .3$, while $(\mu|O_2)|O_1(\{blue, green\}) = .7$. The definition of Jeffrey's Rule guarantees that the last observation determines the probability of $\{blue, green\}$, so the order of observation matters. This is quite different from Dempster's Rule, which is commutative. The importance of commutativity, of course, depends on the application.

There are straightforward analogues of Jeffrey's Rule for sets of probabilities, belief functions, possibility measures, and ranking functions.

- For sets of probabilities, Jeffrey's Rule can just be applied to each element of the set (throwing out those elements to which it cannot be applied). It is then possible to take upper and lower probabilities of the resulting set. Alternatively, an analogue to the construction of $\text{Pl}_{\mathcal{P}}$ can be applied.

- For belief functions, there is an obvious analogue of Jeffrey's Rule such that

$$\text{Bel}|(\alpha_1 U_1; \ldots; \alpha_n U_n) = \alpha_1 \text{Bel}|U_1 + \cdots + \alpha_n \text{Bel}|U_n$$

(and similarly with | replaced by ||). It is easy to check that this in fact is a belief function (provided that $\text{Plaus}(U_j) > 0$ if $\alpha_j > 0$, and $\alpha_j \text{Bel}|U_j$ is taken to be 0 if $\alpha_j = 0$, just as in the case of probabilities). It is also possible to apply Dempster's Rule in this context, but this would in general give a different answer (Exercise 3.42).

- For possibility measures, the analogue is based on the observation that $+$ and $\times$ for probability becomes max and min for possibility. Thus, for an observation of the form $\alpha_1 U_1; \ldots; \alpha_n U_n$, where $\alpha_i \in [0, 1]$ for $i = 1, \ldots, n$ and $\max(\alpha_1, \ldots, \alpha_n) = 1$,

$$\text{Poss}|(\alpha_1 U_1; \ldots; \alpha_n U_n)(V)$$
$$= \max(\min(\alpha_1, \text{Poss}(V \mid U_1)), \ldots, \min(\alpha_n, \text{Poss}(V \mid U_n))).$$

- For ranking functions, $+$ becomes min and the role of 1 is played by 0. Thus, for an observation of the form $\alpha_1 U_1; \ldots; \alpha_n U_n$, where $\alpha_i \in \mathbb{N}^*$, $i = 1, \ldots, n$ and $\min(\alpha_1, \ldots, \alpha_n) = 0$,

$$\kappa|(\alpha_1 U_1; \ldots; \alpha_n U_n)(V) = \min(\alpha_1 + \kappa(V \mid U_1), \ldots, \alpha_n + \kappa(V \mid U_n)).$$

## 3.11   Relative Entropy

Jeffrey's Rule deals only with the special case of observations that lead to degrees of support for some partition of $W$. What about the more general case, where there is less information? For example, what if the observation says that $\mu(\{blue, green\})$ is at least .7, rather than exactly .7? And what if there is information regarding overlapping sets, not just disjoint sets? For example, suppose that an observation leads an agent to believe that $\mu(\{blue, green\}) = .7$ and $\mu(\{green, yellow\}) = .4$. What then? (Note that Dempster's Rule of Combination can deal with the latter observation, but not the former.)

The standard intuition here is that if an agent's initial uncertainty is characterized by a probability measure $\mu$ and the agent makes an observation that is characterized by some constraints (such as $\mu(\{blue, green\}) \geq .7$), then the agent should make the "minimal change" to his beliefs required to accommodate the observation. One way of capturing the notion of minimal change is to have the agent's updated measure of belief be that probability measure $\mu'$ that is "closest" to $\mu$ and satisfies the constraints. Of course, the choice of $\mu'$ will then depend on how "closeness" is defined.

One measure of distance is called the *variation distance*. Define $V(\mu, \mu')$, the *variation distance from $\mu$ to $\mu'$*, to be $\sup_{U \subseteq W} |\mu(U) - \mu'(U)|$. That is, the variation distance is the largest amount of disagreement between $\mu$ and $\mu'$ on the probability of some set. It can be shown that $V(\mu, \mu') = \frac{1}{2} \sum_{w \in W} |\mu(w) - \mu'(w)|$ (Exercise 3.43). (I am assuming in this section that $W$ is finite; if $W$ is infinite, then the summation needs to be replaced by integration.) The variation distance is what mathematicians call a *metric*—it has the properties that are normally associated with a measure of distance. In particular, $V(\mu, \mu') \geq 0$, $V(\mu, \mu') = 0$ iff $\mu = \mu'$, and $V(\mu, \mu') = V(\mu', \mu)$, so that distances are nonnegative, $\mu$ is the unique closest measure to itself, and the distance from $\mu$ to $\mu'$ is the same as the distance from $\mu'$ to $\mu$.

Given some constraints $C$ and a measure $\mu$, consider the probability measure $\mu'$ that is closest to $\mu$ in terms of variation distance and satisfies the constraints. There is a precise sense in which Jeffrey's Rule (and standard conditioning, which is an instance of it) can be viewed as a special case of minimizing variation distance. That is, $\mu | \alpha_1 U_1; \ldots ; \alpha_n U_n$ is one of the probability measures closest to $\mu$ among all measures $\mu'$ such that $\mu'(U_i) = \alpha_i$, for $i = 1, \ldots, n$.

**Proposition 3.11.1**   *Suppose that $U_1, \ldots, U_n$ is a partition of $W$ and $\alpha_1 + \cdots + \alpha_n = 1$. Let $C = \{\mu' : \mu'(U_i) = \alpha_i, i = 1, \ldots, n\}$. If $\alpha_1 U_1; \ldots ; \alpha_n U_n$ is consistent with $\mu$, then $V(\mu, \mu'') \geq V(\mu, \mu \mid (\alpha_1 U_1; \ldots ; \alpha_n U_n))$ for all $\mu'' \in C$.*

**Proof**   See Exercise 3.44.   ∎

Although the variation distance does support the use of Jeffrey's Rule and conditioning, it does not uniquely pick them out. There are in fact many functions that minimize the variation distance other than the one that results from the use of Jeffrey's Rule (Exercise 3.44).

Another notion of "closeness" is given by relative entropy. The *relative entropy between $\mu'$ and $\mu$*, denoted $D(\mu', \mu)$, is defined as

$$D(\mu', \mu) = \sum_{w \in W} \mu'(w) \log \left( \frac{\mu'(w)}{\mu(w)} \right).$$

(The logarithm here is taken to the base 2; if $\mu'(w) = 0$ then $\mu'(w) \log(\mu'(w)/\mu(w))$ is taken to be 0. This is reasonable since $\lim_{x \to 0} x \log(x/c) = 0$ if $c > 0$.) The relative entropy is defined provided that $\mu'$ is *consistent with* $\mu$. Analogously to the case of Jeffrey's Rule, this means that if $\mu(w) = 0$ then $\mu'(w) = 0$, for all $w \in W$. Using elementary calculus, it can be shown that $D(\mu', \mu) \geq 0$, with equality exactly if $\mu' = \mu$ (Exercise 3.45). Unfortunately, relative entropy does not quite act as a metric. For example, it is not hard to show that $D(\mu, \mu') \neq D(\mu', \mu)$ in general (Exercise 3.46). Nevertheless, relative entropy has many attractive properties. One of them is that it generalizes Jeffrey's Rule. Moreover, unlike variation distance, it picks out Jeffrey's Rule uniquely; the relative entropy between $\mu|\alpha_1 U_1; \ldots; \alpha_n U_n$ and $\mu$ is minimum among all measures $\mu'$ such that $\mu'(U_i) = \alpha_i$, $i = 1, \ldots, n$.

**Proposition 3.11.2**   *Suppose that $U_1, \ldots, U_n$ is a partition of W and $\alpha_1 + \cdots + \alpha_n = 1$. Let $C = \{\mu' : \mu'(U_i) = \alpha_i, i = 1, \ldots, n\}$. If $\alpha_1 U_1; \ldots; \alpha_n U_n$ is consistent with $\mu$, then $D(\mu, \mu'') \geq D(\mu, \mu|(\alpha_1 U_1; \ldots; \alpha_n U_n))$ for all $\mu'' \in C$. Moreover, equality holds only if $\mu'' = \mu|(\alpha_1 U_1; \ldots; \alpha_n U_n)$.*

The justification for relative entropy is closely related to the justification for the entropy function, which was first defined by Claude Shannon in the context of information theory. Given a probability measure $\mu$, define $H(\mu)$, the *entropy* of $\mu$, as follows:

$$H(\mu) = - \sum_{w \in W} \mu(w) \log(\mu(w))$$

(where $0 \log(0)$ is taken to be 0). If $\mu$ is the *uniform* probability measure on a space $W$ with $n$ elements (so that $\mu(w) = 1/n$ for all $w \in W$), then from standard properties of the log function, it follows that

$$D(\mu', \mu) = \sum_{w \in W} \mu'(w)(\log(\mu'(w)) + \log(n)) = \log(n) - H(\mu').$$

Thus, minimizing the relative entropy between $\mu'$ and the uniform distribution is the same as maximizing the entropy of $\mu'$.

$H(\mu)$ can be viewed as a measure of the degree of "uncertainty" in $\mu$. For example, if $\mu(w) = 1$ for some $w \in W$, then $H(\mu) = 0$; the agent is not at all uncertain if he knows that the probability of some world is 1. Uncertainty is maximized if all worlds are equally likely, since there is no information that allows an agent to prefer one world to another. More precisely, of all the probability measures on $W$, the one whose entropy is maximum is the uniform probability measure (Exercise 3.47). Even in the presence of constraints $C$, the measure that maximizes entropy is (very roughly) the measure that makes things "as equal as possible" subject to the constraints in $C$. Thus, for example, if $C$ consists of the constraints $\mu'(\{blue, green\}) = .8$ and $\mu'(\{red, yellow\}) = .2$, then the measure $\mu^{me}$ that maximizes entropy is the one such that $\mu^{me}(blue) = \mu^{me}(green) = .4$ and $\mu^{me}(red) = \mu^{me}(yellow) = .1$ (Exercise 3.48).

Just as entropy of $\mu$ can be thought of as a measure of the information in $\mu$, the relative entropy between $\mu'$ and $\mu$ can be thought of as a measure of the amount of extra information in $\mu'$ relative to the information already in $\mu$. There are axiomatic characterizations of maximum entropy and relative entropy that attempt to make this intuition precise, although it is beyond the scope of this book to describe them. Given this intuition, it is perhaps not surprising that there are proponents of maximum entropy and relative entropy who recommend that if an agent's information can be characterized by a set $C$ of constraints, then the agent should act "as if" the probability is determined by the measure that maximizes entropy relative to $C$ (i.e., the measure that has the highest entropy of all the measures in $C$). Similarly, if the agent starts with a particular measure $\mu$ and gets new information characterized by $C$, he should update to the measure $\mu'$ that satisfies $C$ such that the relative entropy between $\mu'$ and $\mu$ is a minimum.

Maximum entropy and relative entropy have proved quite successful in a number of applications, from physics to natural-language modeling. Unfortunately, they also exhibit some counterintuitive behavior on certain applications. Although they are valuable tools, they should be used with care.

Variation distance has an immediate analogue for all the other quantitative notions of uncertainty considered here (belief functions, inner measures, possibility measures, and ranking functions). I leave it to the reader to explore the use of variation distance with these notions (see, e.g., Exercise 3.49). Maximum entropy and relative entropy seem to be more closely bound up with probability, although analogues have in fact been proposed both for Dempster-Shafer belief functions and for possibility measures. More work needs to be done to determine what good notions of "closest" are for arbitrary plausibility measures. Different notions may well be appropriate for different applications.

## Exercises

**3.1**    Show that both CP4 and CP5 follow from CP3 (and CP1 in the case of CP4); in addition, CP3 follows immediately from CP4 and CP5.

**3.2**    Show that $\mu^s$ as defined in Section 3.2 satisfies CP1–3.

**3.3**    Fill in the missing details in the proof of Theorem 3.2.5.

**\* 3.4**    Prove Theorem 3.2.6.

**3.5**    Show that $(a\alpha^2 + (1-a)\beta^2)/(a\alpha + (1-a)\beta) \geq a\alpha + (1-a)\beta$, with equality holding iff $\alpha = \beta$, $a = 1$, or $a = 1$. (Hint: This amounts to showing that $(a\alpha^2 + (1-a)\beta^2) \geq (a\alpha + (1-a)\beta)^2$. Let $f(a) = a\alpha^2 + (1-a)\beta^2) - (a\alpha + (1-a)\beta)^2$. Clearly, $f(0) = f(1) = 0$. Show, using calculus, that $f(a) > 0$ for $0 < a < 1$.)

**3.6**    In Example 3.4.1, prove that $\mu(C_\alpha \mid H^1) > a$, using the fact that $\alpha > \beta$.

**3.7**    Prove Proposition 3.4.3.

**3.8**    Prove Proposition 3.4.4.

**3.9**    Show that $\text{Bel}_o$ is a belief function and it has the property that $\text{Plaus}_o(h) = c\mu_h(o)$ for some constant $c > 0$.

**\* 3.10**    Prove Theorem 3.4.5.

**\* 3.11**    Prove Theorem 3.4.6.

**\* 3.12**    Prove the converse of Theorem 3.4.5. That is, show that if Bel captures the evidence $o$, then $\text{Plaus}(h) = c\mu_h(o)$ for some constant $c > 0$ and all $h \in \mathcal{H}$.

**3.13**    Fill in the following missing details in the proof of Theorem 3.5.1.

    (a) Show that if $x + y > 0$, $y \geq 0$, and $x \leq x'$, then $x/(x+y) \leq x'/(x'+y)$.

    (b) Show that there exists an extension $\mu_1$ of $\mu$ such that $\mu_1(V \mid U) = \dfrac{\mu_*(V \cap U)}{\mu_*(V \cap U) + \mu^*(\overline{V} \cap U)}$.

    (c) Do the argument for $\mu^*(V \mid U)$.

**3.14**    Show that if $U$ is measurable, then

$$\mu_*(V \cap U) + \mu^*(\overline{V} \cap U) = \mu^*(V \cap U) + \mu_*(\overline{V} \cap U) = \mu(U).$$

**3.15**    Prove Theorem 3.6.2. You may use results from previous exercises.

**3.16**    Show that $\text{Plaus}(V \mid U) = 1 - \text{Bel}(\overline{V} \mid U)$.

**3.17**    Construct a belief function Bel on $W = \{a, b, c\}$ and a set $\mathcal{P} \neq \mathcal{P}_{\text{Bel}}$ of probability measures such that $\text{Bel} = \mathcal{P}_*$ and $\text{Plaus} = \mathcal{P}^*$ (as in Exercise 2.24) but $\text{Bel}|\{a, b\} \neq (\mathcal{P}|\{a, b\})_*$.

**3.18**    Prove Proposition 3.6.5.

**3.19**   Show that if Bel is a probability measure $\mu$, then $\text{Bel}(V \mid U) = \text{Bel}(V \| U) = \mu(V \mid U)$; that is, both notions of conditioning belief functions agree with conditioning for probability.

\* **3.20**   Show that $\text{Plaus}(U) \geq \text{Plaus}(V \cap U) + \text{Bel}(\overline{V} \cap U)$. (Hint: Use Theorem 2.4.1 and observe that $\mu'(U) \geq \mu'(V \cap U) + \text{Bel}(\overline{V} \cap U)$ if $\mu' \in \mathcal{P}_{\text{Bel}}$.)

**3.21**   If $\text{Poss}(U) > 0$, show that $\text{Poss}(\cdot \| U)$ is a possibility measure.

**3.22**   Show that if Poss is a possibility measure on $W = \{w_1, w_2, w_3\}$ such that $\text{Poss}(w_1) = 2/3$, $\text{Poss}(w_2) = 1/2$, and $\text{Poss}(w_3) = 1$, $U = \{w_1, w_2\}$, and $V = \{w_1\}$, then, for all $\alpha \in [2/3, 1]$, there is a conditional possibility measure $\text{Poss}_\alpha$ on $W$ that is an extension of Poss (i.e., $\text{Poss}_\alpha \mid W = \text{Poss}$) and satisfies CPoss1–4 such that $\text{Poss}(V \mid U) = \alpha$.

**3.23**   Given an unconditional possibility measure Poss, show that the conditional possibility measure defined by (3.6) satisfies CPoss1–4. Moreover, show that among conditional possibility measures defined on $2^W \times \mathcal{F}'$, where $\mathcal{F}' = \{U : \text{Poss}(U) > 0\}$, it is the largest standard conditional possibility measure extending Poss that satisfies CPoss1–4. That is, show that if Poss$'$ is another conditional possibility measure defined on $2^W \times \mathcal{F}'$ that satisfies CPoss1–4, and $\text{Poss}'(\cdot \mid W) = \text{Poss}$, then $\text{Poss}(V \mid U) \geq \text{Poss}'(V \mid U)$ for all sets $V$.

**3.24**   Show that $\text{Poss}(V \mid U)$ is not determined by $\text{Poss}(U \mid V), \text{Poss}(U)$, and $\text{Poss}(V)$. That is, show that there are two possibility measures Poss and Poss$'$ on a space $W$ such that $\text{Poss}(U \mid V) = \text{Poss}'(U \mid V), \text{Poss}(U) = \text{Poss}'(U), \text{Poss}(V) = \text{Poss}'(V)$, but $\text{Poss}(V \mid U) \neq \text{Poss}'(V \mid U)$.

**3.25**   Show that the unique conditional ranking function extending an unconditional ranking function $\kappa$ defined on $2^W \times \mathcal{F}'$, where $\mathcal{F}' = \{U : \kappa(U) \neq \infty\}$, and satisfying CRk1–4 is given by (3.7).

**3.26**   Show that if $(W, \mathcal{F}, \mathcal{F}', \text{Pl})$ is such that (a) $\mathcal{F} \times \mathcal{F}'$ is a Popper algebra of subsets of $W \times W$, (b) $\text{Pl} : \mathcal{F} \times \mathcal{F}' \to D$ for some partially ordered $D$ of values and satisfies CPl1, CPl2, CPl3, and CPl5, and (c) $U \in \mathcal{F}'$ and $\text{Pl}(V \mid U) > \bot$ implies that $V \cap U \in \mathcal{F}$, then Pl satisfies CPl4.

**3.27**   Show that all conditional probability measures satisfy CPl5, as do the conditional possibility measures (both $\text{Poss}(\cdot \mid U)$ and $\text{Poss}(\cdot \| U)$) and conditional ranking functions obtained by the constructions in Section 3.7 and Section 3.8, respectively. However, show that $\mathcal{P}_*(\cdot \mid U)$, $\text{Bel}(\cdot \mid U)$, and $\text{Bel}(\cdot \| U)$ do not in general satisfy CPl5.

**3.28**    Given a set $\mathcal{P}$ of probability measures defined on an algebra $\mathcal{F}$, let $\mathcal{F}' = \{U : \mu(U) \neq 0 \text{ for all } \mu \in \mathcal{P}\}$. Extend $\text{Pl}_\mathcal{P}$ to $\mathcal{F} \times \mathcal{F}'$ by defining $\text{Pl}_\mathcal{P}(V \mid U) = f_{V|U}$ where $f_{V|U}(\mu) = \mu(V \mid U)$. Show that $\text{Pl}_\mathcal{P}$ so defined gives a cps satisfying CPl5, but one that is not in general acceptable.

**3.29**    Show that the construction of a conditional plausibility measure starting from the unconditional plausibility measure $\text{Pl}_\mathcal{P}$ representing a set $\mathcal{P}$ of probability measures results in an acceptable cps satisfying CPl5 that is an extension of $\text{Pl}_\mathcal{P}$.

**3.30**    Show that the construction of a conditional plausibility measure starting from an unconditional plausibility measure $\text{Pl}$ results in an acceptable cps satisfying CPl5 that is an extension of $\text{Pl}$.

**3.31**    Show that Alg1–4 hold for probability (with $+$ and $\times$ for $\oplus$ and $\otimes$), as well as for $\text{Poss}(V\|U)$, with max and $\times$ for $\oplus$ and $\otimes$, and $\kappa(V \mid U)$, with min and $+$ for $\oplus$ and $\otimes$.

**3.32**    Show that Alg1–3 hold for $\text{Poss}(V \mid U)$.

**3.33**    Show that the cps defined from $\text{Pl}_\mathcal{P}$ satisfies Alg1–4.

**3.34**    Prove Lemma 3.9.3.

**3.35**    Prove Lemma 3.9.4.

**3.36**    Prove Lemma 3.9.5.

**3.37**    Given an algebraic cps, say that $\otimes$ is *monotonic* if $d \leq d'$ and $e \leq e'$ implies $d \otimes e \leq d' \otimes e'$.

  (a)  Show that all the constructions that give algebraic cps's discussed in Section 3.9 actually give monotonic cps's.

  (b)  Show that a cps that is standard, algebraic, and monotonic satisfies CPl5.

**3.38**    Prove Lemma 3.9.6.

**3.39**    Show that property J2 of Jeffrey conditioning is a consequence of property J.

**3.40**    Show that $\mu|(\alpha_1 U_1; \ldots ; \alpha_n U_n)$ is defined as long as $\mu(U_j) > 0$ if $\alpha_j > 0$ and is the unique probability measure satisfying property J if it is defined.

**3.41**    Show that if $\mu(U_1 \cap U_2) \neq 0$, then

$$(\mu|U_1)|U_2 = (\mu|U_2)|U_1 = \mu|(U_1 \cap U_2).$$

**3.42**   Show that $\mathrm{Bel}|(\alpha_1 U_1; \ldots; \alpha_n U_n)$ and $\mathrm{Bel}||(\alpha_1 U_1; \ldots; \alpha_n U_n)$ are belief functions (provided that $\mathrm{Plaus}(U_j) > 0$ if $\alpha_j > 0$). Show, however, that neither gives the same result as Dempster's Rule of Combination, in general. More precisely, given a belief function $\mathrm{Bel}$ and an observation $\alpha_1 U_1; \ldots; \alpha_n U_n$, let $\mathrm{Bel}_{\alpha_1 U_1; \ldots; \alpha_n U_n}$ be the belief function whose mass function puts mass $\alpha_j$ on the set $U_j$ (and puts mass 0 on any set $V \notin \{U_1, \ldots, U_n\}$). Show by means of a counterexample that, in general, $\mathrm{Bel} \oplus \mathrm{Bel}_{\alpha_1 U_1; \ldots; \alpha_n U_n}$ is different from both $\mathrm{Bel}|(\alpha_1 U_1; \ldots; \alpha_n U_n)$ and $\mathrm{Bel}||(\alpha_1 U_1; \ldots; \alpha_n U_n)$.

**3.43**   Show that $V(\mu, \mu') = \frac{1}{2} \sum_{w \in W} |\mu(w) - \mu'(w)|$. (Hint: Consider the set $U = \{w : \mu(w) \geq \mu'(w)\}$ and show that $\sum_{w \in U} \mu(w) - \mu'(w) = \sum_{w \in \overline{U}} \mu'(w) - \mu(w)$.)

*__3.44__   Suppose that $U_1, \ldots, U_n$ is a partition of $W$ and $\alpha_1 + \cdots + \alpha_n = 1$. Let $C = \{\mu' : \mu'(U_i) = \alpha_i, i = 1, \ldots, n\}$. Suppose that $\mu''$ is a probability measure such that

  • $\mu'' \in C$,

  • if $\mu''(U_i) < \mu(U_i)$ then $\mu''(w) < \mu(w)$ for all $w \in U_i$, $i = 1, \ldots, n$,

  • if $\mu''(U_i) = \mu(U_i)$ then $\mu''(w) = \mu(w)$ for all $w \in U_i$, $i = 1, \ldots, n$,

  • if $\mu''(U_i) > \mu(U_i)$ then $\mu''(w) > \mu(w)$ for all $w \in U_i$, $i = 1, \ldots, n$.

Show that $V(\mu, \mu'') = \inf\{V(\mu, \mu') : \mu' \in C\}$.

Since $\mu|(\alpha_1 U_1; \ldots; \alpha_n U_n)$ clearly satisfies these four conditions, it has the minimum variation distance to $\mu$ among all the measures in $C$. However, it is clearly not the unique measure with this property.

*__3.45__   (This exercise requires calculus.) Show that $D(\mu', \mu) \geq 0$ (if it is defined), with equality coming only if $\mu' = \mu$. (Hint: First show that $x \log(x) - x/\log_e(2) + 1/\log_e(2) \geq 0$ if $x \geq 0$, with equality iff $x = 1$. Then note that

$$D(\mu', \mu) = \sum_{w \in W} \mu(w)\left(\frac{\mu'(w)}{\mu(w)} \log \frac{\mu'(w)}{\mu(w)} - \frac{\mu'(w)}{\log_e(2)\mu(w)} + \frac{1}{\log_e(2)}\right).$$

The result easily follows.)

**3.46**   Show by means of a counterexample that $D(\mu, \mu') \neq D(\mu', \mu)$ in general.

*__3.47__   (This exercise requires calculus.) Show that of all probability measures on a finite space $W$, the one that has the highest entropy is the uniform probability measure. (Hint: Prove by induction on $k$ the stronger result that for all $c > 0$, if $x_i \geq 0$ for $i = 1, \ldots, k$ and $\sum_{i=1}^{k} x_i = c$, then $-\sum_{i=1}^{k} x_i \log(x_i)$ is maximized if $x_i = c/k$.)

**3.48** (This exercise requires calculus.) Show that if $C$ consists of the constraints $\mu'(\{blue, green\}) = .8$ and $\mu'(\{red, yellow\}) = .2$, then the measure $\mu^{me}$ that maximizes entropy is the one such that $\mu^{me}(blue) = \mu^{me}(green) = .4$ and $\mu^{me}(red) = \mu^{me}(yellow) = .1$.

**3.49** Formulate an analogue of variation distance for possibility measures, and then prove an analogue of Proposition 3.11.1. Repeat this for ranking functions.

**∗ 3.50** Yet another representation of uncertainty is a *lexicographic probability space* (LPS). An LPS $(W, \mathcal{F}, \vec{\mu})$ consists of a set of worlds $W$, an algebra $\mathcal{F}$ over $W$, and a tuple $\vec{\mu} = (\mu_1, \ldots, \mu_n)$ of probability measures all defined on $\mathcal{F}$, for some $n \geq 1$. (For the purposes of this exercise, assume that $n$ is finite, although the definition makes sense even if the length of the LPS is infinite.) Define $\vec{\mu}(U) = (\mu_1(U), \ldots, \mu_n(U))$. An LPS acts much like a set $\mathcal{P}$ of probability measures with one difference. Consider the *lexicographic order* on tuples in $[0, 1]^n$ defined by taking $(a_1, \ldots, a_n) <_{LPS} (b_1, \ldots, b_n)$ iff there is some $j \leq n$ such that $a_i = b_i$ for $i < j$ and $a_j < b_j$. Define $(\mu_1, \ldots, \mu_n)(U) <_{LPS} (\mu_1, \ldots, \mu_n)(V)$ if $(\mu_1(U), \ldots, \mu_n(U)) <_{LPS} (\mu_1(V), \ldots, \mu_n(V))$. Thus, the relative likelihood of $U$ and $V$ according to $(\mu_1, \ldots, \mu_n)$ is determined by looking at the first probability measure in the sequence that gives $U$ and $V$ different probabilities. The measures in the sequence $(\mu_1, \ldots, \mu_n)$ can be viewed as listed *lexicographically*, with $\mu_1$ more significant than $\mu_2$, $\mu_2$ more significant than $\mu_3$, and so on.

Conditioning in LPSs is defined as follows. Given $\vec{\mu}$ and $U \in \mathcal{F}$ such that $\mu_i(U) > 0$ for some index $i$, let $\vec{\mu}|U = (\mu_{k_0}(\cdot|U), \ldots, \mu_{k_m}(\cdot|U))$, where $(k_0, \ldots, k_m)$ is the subsequence of all indices $j$ such that $\mu_j(U) > 0$. Notice that the length of the LPS $\vec{\mu}|U$ depends on $U$.

(a) Find a set $D$ and an ordering on $D$ such that if $(W, \mathcal{F}, \vec{\mu})$ is an LPS, then $\vec{\mu}(V \mid U) \in D$ for all $U$ such that $\vec{\mu}(U) \neq \vec{0}$. Moreover, show that with this choice of $D$, $(W, \mathcal{F}, \mathcal{F}', \vec{\mu})$ is a cps that satisfies CPl1–5.

(b) Show that $(W, \mathcal{F}, \mathcal{F}', \vec{\mu})$ is actually an algebraic cps, by defining appropriate notions of $\oplus$ and $\otimes$.

**3.51** This exercise further examines lexicographic probability systems. The definition of conditioning in an LPS given in the previous exercise does not result in a cps in general, since $(\mu_1, \ldots, \mu_n)(W|W)$ is not equal to $(\mu_1, \ldots, \mu_n)(U \mid U)$ if, for example, $\mu_1(U) = 0$ and $\mu_2(U) \neq 0$. Show how to modify this definition, along that lines used for $\text{Pl}_{\mathcal{P}}$, so as to give an algebraic cps. Carefully define $\text{Dom}(\otimes)$ and $\text{Dom}(\oplus)$.

# Notes

All standard texts on probability discuss conditioning and Bayes' Rule in detail. The betting justification for conditional probability goes back to Teller [1973] (who credits David Lewis with the idea); the version of the argument given in Section 3.2.1 is based on one given by Paris [1994] (which in turn is based on work by Kemeny [1955] and Shimony [1955]). In particular, Paris [1994] provides a proof of Theorem 3.2.5.

Another defense of conditioning, given by van Fraassen [1984], is based on what he calls the *Reflection Principle*. If $\mu$ denotes the agent's current probability and $\mu_t$ denotes his probability at time $t$, the Reflection Principle says that if, upon reflection, an agent realizes that his degree of belief at time $t$ that $U$ is true will be $\alpha$, then his current degree of belief should also be $\alpha$. That is, $\mu(U|\mu_t(U) = \alpha)$ should be $\alpha$. Van Fraassen then shows that if a rational agent's beliefs obey the Reflection Principle, then he must update his beliefs by conditioning. (The Reflection Principle is sometimes called *Miller's Principle,* since it was first mentioned by Miller [1966].) Gaifman [1986] and Samet [1997; 1998b] present some more recent work connecting conditioning and reflection.

The Reflection Principle is closely related to another issue discussed in the text: the difference between an agent's current beliefs regarding $V$ if $U$ were to occur and how the agent would change his beliefs regarding $V$ if $U$ actually did occur. This issue has been discussed at length in the literature, going back to Ramsey's [1931b] seminal paper. Walley [1991, Section 6.1] and Howson and Urbach [1989, Chapter 6] both have a careful discussion of the issue and give further pointers to the literature.

Van Fraassen [1987] provides yet another defense of conditioning. He shows that any updating process that satisfies two simple properties (essentially, that updating by $U$ results in $U$ having probability 1, and that the update procedure is *representation independent* in a certain sense) must be conditioning.

Bacchus, Kyburg, and Thalos [1990] present a relatively recent collection of arguments against various defenses of probabilistic conditioning.

The problem of dealing with conditioning on sets of probability 0 is an old one. Walley [1991, Section 6.10] gives a careful discussion of the issue as well as further references. As pointed out in the text, conditional probability measures are one attempt to deal with the issue. (It is worth stressing that, even if conditioning on sets of probability 0 is not a concern, there are still compelling philosophical reasons to take conditional probability as primitive; beliefs are always relative to—that is, conditional on—the evidence at hand. With this intuition, it may not always be appropriate to assume that $\mathcal{F}'$, the set of events that can be conditioned on, is a subset of $\mathcal{F}$. An agent may not be willing to assign a probability to the event of getting certain evidence and still be willing to assign a probability to other events, conditional on having that evidence.) In any case, Popper [1968] was the first to consider formally conditional probability as the basic notion. De Finetti [1936] also did some early work, apparently independently, taking conditional probabilities as primitive. Indeed, as Rényi [1964] points out, the idea of taking conditional probabilities as primitive seems to go back as far as Keynes [1921]. CP1–3 are essentially due to Rényi [1955]. Conditional probability measures are sometimes called *Popper functions*. Van Fraassen [1976] calls an acceptable conditional probability measure a *Popper measure*. The relationship between nonstandard probability measures and conditional probability measures is considered in [Halpern 2001b; McGee 1994].

[Grove and Halpern 1998] provides a characterization of the approach to updating sets of probabilities considered here (i.e., conditioning each probability measure $\mu$ in the set individually, as long as the new information is compatible with $\mu$) in the spirit of van Fraassen's [1987] characterization. Other approaches to updating sets of probabilities are certainly also possible, even among approaches that throw out some probability measures and condition the rest. Gilboa and Schmeidler [1993] focus on one such rule. Roughly speaking, they take $\mathcal{P}||U = \{\mu|U : \mu \in \mathcal{P}, \ \mu(U) = \sup_{\mu' \in \mathcal{P}} \mu'(U)\}$. They show that if $\mathcal{P}$ is a closed, convex set of probability measures, this update rule acts like DS conditioning (hence my choice of notation). (A set of probability measures is *closed* if it contains its limits. That is, a set $\mathcal{P}$ of probability measures on $W$ is closed if for all sequences $\mu_1, \mu_2, \ldots$ of probability measures in $\mathcal{P}$, if $\mu_n \to \mu$ in the sense that $\mu_n(U) \to \mu(U)$ for all measurable $U \subseteq W$, then $\mu \in \mathcal{P}$. Thus, for example, if $W = \{0, 1\}$ and $\mu_n$ assigns probability $1/n$ to 0 and $(n-1)/n$ to 1, then $\mu_n \to \mu$, where $\mu(0) = 0$ and $\mu(1) = 1$.)

The three-prisoners puzzle is old. It is discussed, for example, in [Bar-Hillel and Falk 1982; Gardner 1961; Mosteller 1965]. The description of the story given here is taken from [Diaconis 1978], and much of the discussion is based on that given in [Fagin and Halpern 1991a], which in turn is based on that in [Diaconis 1978; Diaconis and Zabell 1986].

The fact that conditioning on sets of probability measures loses valuable information, in the sense discussed in Example 3.4.1, seems to be well known, although I am not aware of any explicit discussion of it. Peter Walley was the one who convinced me to consider it seriously. The representation of evidence using belief functions was first considered by Shafer [1976], who proved Theorems 3.4.5 and 3.4.6 (see [Shafer 1976, Theorems 9.7, 9.8]). Shafer also defined $\text{Bel}_o$. The representation $\mu_o$ is taken from [Halpern and Fagin 1992] and [Walley 1987], as is the general formulation of the results in terms of the space $\mathcal{H} \times \mathcal{O}$.

There has been a great deal of work in the literature on representing evidence in a purely probabilistic framework. Much of the work goes under the rubric *confirmation* or *weight of evidence*. In the literature evidence is typically represented as a number in the range $[-\infty, \infty]$, with 0 meaning "no evidence one way or another," $\infty$ meaning "overwhelming evidence in favor of the hypothesis," and $-\infty$ means "overwhelming evidence against the hypothesis." See, for example, [Good 1960; Milne 1996] for typical papers in this (quite vast) literature. The representation $\mathcal{P}||U$ has, to the best of my knowledge, not been considered before.

Theorem 3.5.1 was proved independently by numerous authors [Campos, Lamata, and Moral 1990; Fagin and Halpern 1991a; Smets and Kennes 1989; Walley 1981]. Indeed, it even appears (lost in a welter of notation) as Equation 4.8 in Dempster's original paper on belief functions [Dempster 1967].

Theorems 3.6.2 and 3.6.3 are proved in [Fagin and Halpern 1991a]; Theorem 3.6.3 was proved independently by Jaffray [1992]. Several characterizations of $\mathrm{Bel}(V||U)$ are also provided in [Fagin and Halpern 1991a], including a charaacterization as a lower probability of a set of probability measures (although not the set $\mathcal{P}_{\mathrm{Bel}}|U$). Gilboa and Schmeidler [1993] provide an axiomatic defense for DS conditioning.

The approach discussed here for conditioning with possibility measures is due to Hisdal [1978]. Although this is the most commonly used approach in finite spaces, Dubois and Prade [1998, p. 206] suggest that in infinite spaces, for technical reasons, it may be more appropriate to use $\mathrm{Poss}(\cdot||U)$ rather than $\mathrm{Poss}(\cdot|U)$ as the notion of conditioning. They also argue that $\mathrm{Poss}(V \mid U)$ is appropriate for a qualitative, nonnumeric representation of uncertainty, while $\mathrm{Poss}(V||U)$ is more appropriate for a numeric representation. A number of other approaches to conditioning have been considered for possibility measures; see [Dubois and Prade 1998; Fonck 1994]. The definition of conditioning for ranking functions is due to Spohn [1988].

The discussion of conditional plausibility spaces in Section 3.9, as well as the definition of an algebraic cps, is taken from [Halpern 2001a]; it is based on earlier definitions given in [Friedman and Halpern 1995]. The idea of putting an algebraic structure on likelihood measures also appears in [Darwiche 1992; Darwiche and Ginsberg 1992; Weydert 1994].

Jeffrey's Rule was first discussed and motivated by Jeffrey [1968], using an example much like Example 3.10.1. Diaconis and Zabell [1982] discuss a number of approaches to updating subjective probability, including Jeffrey's Rule, variation distance, and relative entropy. Proposition 3.11.1 was proved by May [1976].

Entropy and maximum entropy were introduced by Shannon in his classic book with Weaver [Shannon and Weaver 1949]; Shannon also characterized entropy as the unique function satisfying certain natural conditions. Jaynes [1957] was the first to argue that maximum entropy should be used as an inference procedure. That is, given a set $C$ of constraints, an agent should act "as if" the probability is determined by the measure that maximizes entropy relative to $C$. This can be viewed as a combination of relative entropy together with the principle of indifference. See Chapter 11 for more on maximum entropy and the principle of indifference.

Relative entropy was introduced by Kullback and Leibler [1951]. An axiomatic defense of maximum entropy and relative entropy was given by Shore and Johnson [1980]; a recent detailed discussion of the reasonableness of this defense is given by Uffink [1995]. See [Cover and Thomas 1991] for a good introduction to the topic.

Maximum entropy and relative entropy are widely used in many applications today, ranging from speech recognition [Jelinek 1997] to modeling queuing behavior [Kouvatsos 1994]. Analogues of maximum entropy were proposed for belief functions by Yager [1983] and for possibility measures by Klir and his colleagues [Hagashi and Klir 1983; Klir and Mariano 1987]. An example of the counterintuitive behavior of relative entropy is given by van Fraassen's *Judy Benjamin* problem [1981]; see [Grove and Halpern 1997] for further discussion of this problem.

The lexicographic probability spaces discussed in Exercises 3.50 and 3.51 were introduced by Blume, Brandenburger, and Dekel [1991a; 1991b], who showed that they could be used to model a weaker version of Savage's [1954] postulates of rationality, discussed in the notes to Chapter 2. A number of papers have discussed the connection among conditional probability spaces, nonstandard probability measures, and sequences of probability measures [Halpern 2001b; Hammond 1994; Rényi 1956; van Fraassen 1976; McGee 1994].

# Chapter 4

# Independence and Bayesian Networks

*Mad*, *adj.: Affected with a high degree of intellectual independence.*

—Ambrose Bierce, *The Devil's Dictionary*

In this chapter I examine a notion that has been studied in depth in the context of probability—independence—and then consider how it can be captured in some of the other notions of uncertainty that we have been considering. In the process, I also discuss *Bayesian networks,* an important tool for describing likelihood measures succinctly and working with them.

## 4.1  Probabilistic Independence

What exactly does it mean that two events are *independent*? Intuitively, it means that they have nothing to do with each other—they are totally unrelated; the occurrence of one has no influence on the other. Suppose that two different coins are tossed. Most people would view the outcomes as independent. The fact that the first coin lands heads should not affect the outcome of the second coin (although it is certainly possible to imagine a complicated setup whereby they are not independent). What about tossing the same coin twice? Is the second toss independent of the first? Most people would agree that it is (although see Example 4.2.1). (Having said that, in practice, after a run of nine heads of a fair coin, many people also believe that the coin is "due" to land tails, although this is incompatible with the coin tosses being independent. If they were independent, then the outcome of the first nine coin tosses would have no effect on the tenth toss.)

In any case, whatever it may mean that two events are "independent," it should be clear that none of the representations of uncertainty considered so far can express the notion of unrelatedness directly. The best they can hope to do is to capture the "footprint" of independence, in a sense that will be made more precise. In the section, I consider this issue in the context of probability. In Section 4.3 I discuss independence for other representations of uncertainty.

Certainly if $U$ and $V$ are independent or unrelated, then learning $U$ should not affect the probability of $V$ and learning $V$ should not affect the probability of $U$. This suggests that the fact that $U$ and $V$ are probabilistically independent (with respect to probability measure $\mu$) can be expressed as $\mu(U \mid V) = \mu(U)$ and $\mu(V \mid U) = \mu(V)$. There is a technical problem with this definition. What happens if $\mu(V) = 0$? In that case $\mu(U \mid V)$ is undefined. Similarly, if $\mu(U) = 0$, then $\mu(V \mid U)$ is undefined. (This problem can be avoided by using conditional probability measures. I return to this point later but, for now, I assume that $\mu$ is an unconditional probability measure.) It is conventional to say that, in this case, $U$ and $V$ are still independent. This leads to the following formal definition:

**Definition 4.1.1**   $U$ and $V$ are *probabilistically independent (with respect to probability measure $\mu$)* if $\mu(V) \neq 0$ implies $\mu(U \mid V) = \mu(U)$ and $\mu(U) \neq 0$ implies $\mu(V \mid U) = \mu(V)$.  ∎

Definition 4.1.1 is not the definition of independence that one usually sees in textbooks, which is that $U$ and $V$ are independent if $\mu(U \cap V) = \mu(U)\mu(V)$, but it turns out to be equivalent to the more standard definition.

**Proposition 4.1.2**   *The following are equivalent:*

   (a) $\mu(U) \neq 0$ *implies* $\mu(V \mid U) = \mu(V)$,

   (b) $\mu(U \cap V) = \mu(U)\mu(V)$,

   (c) $\mu(V) \neq 0$ *implies* $\mu(U \mid V) = \mu(U)$.

**Proof**   I show that (a) and (b) are equivalent. First, suppose that (a) holds. If $\mu(U) = 0$, then clearly $\mu(U \cap V) = 0$ and $\mu(U)\mu(V) = 0$, so $\mu(U \cap V) = \mu(U)\mu(V)$. If $\mu(U) \neq 0$, then $\mu(V \mid U) = \mu(U \cap V)/\mu(U)$, so if $\mu(V \mid U) = \mu(V)$, simple algebraic manipulation shows that $\mu(V \mid U) = \mu(U)\mu(V)$. For the converse, if $\mu(U \cap V) = \mu(U)\mu(V)$ and $\mu(U) \neq 0$, then $\mu(V) = \mu(U \cap V)/\mu(U) = \mu(V \mid U)$. This shows that (a) and (b) are equivalent. A symmetric argument shows that (b) and (c) are equivalent.  ∎

Note that Proposition 4.1.2 shows that I could have simplified Definition 4.1.1 by just using one of the clauses, say, $\mu(U) \neq 0$ implies $\mu(V \mid U) = \mu(V)$, and omitting the other one. While it is true that one clause could be omitted in the definition of *probabilistic* independence, this will not necessarily be true for independence with respect to other notions of uncertainty; thus I stick to the more redundant definition.

The conventional treatment of defining $U$ and $V$ to be independent if either $\mu(U) = 0$ or $\mu(V) = 0$ results in some counterintuitive conclusions if $\mu(U)$ is in fact 0. For example, if $\mu(U) = 0$, then $U$ is independent of itself. But $U$ is certainly not unrelated to itself. This shows that the definition of probabilistic independence does not completely correspond to the informal intuition of independence as unrelatedness.

To some extent it may appear that this problem can be avoided using conditional probability measures. In that case, the problem of conditioning on a set of probability 0 does not arise. Thus, Definition 4.1.1 can be simplified for conditional probability measures as follows:

**Definition 4.1.3**   $U$ and $V$ are *probabilistically independent (with respect to conditional probability space $(W, \mathcal{F}, \mathcal{F}', \mu)$)* if $V \in \mathcal{F}'$ implies $\mu(U \mid V) = \mu(U)$ and $U \in \mathcal{F}'$ implies $\mu(V \mid U) = \mu(V)$.  ∎

Note that Proposition 4.1.2 continues to hold for conditional probability measures (Exercise 4.1). It follows immediately that if both $\mu(U) \neq 0$ and $\mu(V) \neq 0$, then $U$ and $V$ are independent iff $\mu(U \cap V) = \mu(U)\mu(V)$ (Exercise 4.2). Even if $\mu(U) = 0$ or $\mu(V) = 0$, the independence of $U$ and $V$ with respect to the conditional probability measure $\mu$ implies that $\mu(U \cap V) = \mu(U)\mu(V)$ (Exercise 4.2), but the converse does not necessarily hold, as the following example shows:

**Example 4.1.4**   Consider the conditional probability measure $\mu_0^s$ defined in Example 3.2.4. Let $U = \{w_1, w_3\}$ and $V = \{w_2, w_3\}$. Recall that $w_1$ is much more likely than $w_2$, which in turn is much more likely than $w_3$. It is not hard to check that $\mu_0^s(U \mid V) = 0$ and $\mu_0^s(U) = 1$, so $U$ and $V$ are not independent according to Definition 4.1.3. On the other hand, $\mu_0^s(U)\mu_0^s(V) = \mu_0^s(U \cap V) = 0$. Moreover, $\mu_0^s(V) = \mu_0^s(V \mid U) = 0$, which shows that both conjuncts of Definition 4.1.3 are necessary; in general, omitting either one results in a different definition of independence.  ∎

Essentially, conditional probability measures can be viewed as ignoring information about "negligible" small sets when it is not significant. With this viewpoint, the fact that $\mu_0^s(U)\mu_0^s(V) = \mu_0^s(U \cap V)$ and $\mu_0^s(V \mid U) = \mu_0^s(V)$ can be understood as saying that the difference between $\mu_0^s(U)\mu_0^s(V)$ and $\mu_0^s(U \cap V)$ is negligible, as is the difference between $\mu_0^s(V \mid U)$ and $\mu_0^s(V)$. However, it does not follow that the difference between

$\mu_0^s(U \mid V)$ and $\mu^s(U)$ is negligible; indeed, this difference is as large as possible. This interpretation can be made precise by considering the nonstandard probability measure $\mu_0^{ns}$ from which $\mu_0^s$ is derived (see Example 3.2.4). Recall that $\mu_0^{ns}(w_1) = 1 - \epsilon - \epsilon^2$, $\mu_0^{ns}(w_2) = \epsilon$, and $\mu_0^{ns}(w_3) = \epsilon^2$. Thus, $\mu_0^{ns}(V \mid U) = \epsilon^2/(1 - \epsilon)$ and $\mu_0^{ns}(V) = \epsilon + \epsilon^2$. The closest real to both $\epsilon^2/(1 - \epsilon)$ and $\epsilon + \epsilon^2$ is 0 (they are both infinitesimals, since $\epsilon^2/(1 - \epsilon) < 2\epsilon^2$), which is why $\mu_0^s(V \mid U) = \mu_0^s(V) = 0$. Nevertheless, $\mu_0^{ns}(V \mid U)$ is much smaller than $\mu_0^{ns}(V)$. This information is ignored by $\mu_0^s$; it treats the difference as negligible, so $\mu_0^s(V \mid U) = \mu_0^s(V)$.

## 4.2    Probabilistic Conditional Independence

In practice, the notion of unconditional independence considered in Definition 4.1.1 is often not general enough. Consider the following example:

**Example 4.2.1**    Suppose that Alice has a coin that she knows is either fair or double-headed. Either possibility seems equally likely, so she assigns each of them probability 1/2. She then tosses the coin twice. Is the event that the first coin toss lands heads independent of the event that the second coin toss lands heads? Coin tosses are typically viewed as being independent but, in this case, that intuition is slightly misleading. There is another intuition at work here. If the first coin toss lands heads, it is more likely that the coin is double-headed, so the probability that the second coin toss lands heads is higher. This is perhaps even clearer if "heads" is replaced by "tails." Learning that the first coin toss lands tails shows that the coin must be fair, and thus makes the probability that the second coin toss lands tails 1/2. A priori, the probability that the second coin toss lands heads is only 1/4 (half of the probability 1/2 that the coin is fair).

This can be formalized using a space much like the one used in Example 3.2.2. There is one possible world corresponding to the double-headed coin, where the coin lands heads twice. This world has probability 1/2, since that is the probability of the coin being double-headed. There are four possible worlds corresponding to the fair coin, one for each of the four possible sequences of two coin tosses; each of them has probability 1/8. The probability of the first toss landing heads is 3/4: it happens in the world corresponding to the double-headed coin and two of the four worlds corresponding to the fair coin. Similarly, the probability of the second toss landing heads is 3/4, and the probability of both coins landing heads is 5/8. Thus, the conditional probability of two heads given that the first coin toss is heads is $(5/8)/(3/4) = 5/6$, which is not $3/4 \times 3/4$.

The coin tosses *are* independent conditional on the bias of the coin. That is, given that the coin is fair, then the probability of two heads given that the coin is fair is the product of the probability that the first toss lands heads given that the coin is fair and the probability that the second toss lands heads given that the coin is fair. Similarly, the coin tosses are independent conditional on the coin being double-headed. ∎

The formal definition of probabilistic conditional independence is a straightforward generalization of the definition of probabilistic independence.

**Definition 4.2.2**  *U* and *V* are *probabilistically independent given (or conditional on) V' (with respect to probability measure $\mu$),* written $I_\mu(U, V \mid V')$, if $\mu(V \cap V') \neq 0$ implies $\mu(U \mid V \cap V') = \mu(U \mid V')$ and $\mu(U \cap V') \neq 0$ implies $\mu(V \mid U \cap V') = \mu(V \mid V')$. ∎

It is immediate that *U* and *V* are (probabilistically) independent iff they are independent conditional on *W*. Thus, the definition of conditional independence generalizes that of (unconditional) independence.

The following result generalizes Proposition 4.1.2.

**Proposition 4.2.3**  *The following are equivalent if $\mu(V') \neq 0$:*

(a) $\mu(U \cap V') \neq 0$ *implies* $\mu(V \mid U \cap V') = \mu(V \mid V')$,

(b) $\mu(U \cap V \mid V') = \mu(U \mid V')\mu(V \mid V')$,

(c) $\mu(V \cap V') \neq 0$ *implies* $\mu(U \mid V \cap V') = \mu(U \mid V')$.

**Proof**  See Exercise 4.3. ∎

Just as in the case of unconditional probability, Proposition 4.2.3 shows that Definition 4.2.2 could have been simplified by using just one of the clauses. And, just as in the case of unconditional probability, I did not simplify the definition because then the generalization would become less transparent.

In general, independent events can become dependent in the presence of additional information, as the following example shows:

**Example 4.2.4**  A fair coin is tossed twice. The event that it lands heads on the first toss is independent of the event that it lands heads on the second toss. But these events are no longer independent conditional on the event *U* that exactly one coin toss lands heads. Conditional on *U*, the probability that the first coin lands heads is 1/2, the probability that the second coin lands heads is 1/2, but the probability that they both land heads is 0.  ∎

The following theorem collects some properties of conditional independence:

**Theorem 4.2.5**    *For all probability measures $\mu$ on $W$, the following properties hold for all subsets $U$, $V$, and $V'$ of $W$:*

CI1[$\mu$].  *If $I_\mu(U, V \mid V')$ then $I_\mu(V, U \mid V')$.*

CI2[$\mu$].  $I_\mu(U, W \mid V')$.

CI3[$\mu$].  *If $I_\mu(U, V \mid V')$ then $I_\mu(U, \overline{V} \mid V')$.*

CI4[$\mu$].  *If $V_1 \cap V_2 = \emptyset$, $I_\mu(U, V_1 \mid V')$, and $I_\mu(U, V_2 \mid V')$, then $I_\mu(U, V_1 \cup V_2 \mid V')$.*

CI5[$\mu$].  $I_\mu(U, V \mid V')$ *iff* $I_\mu(U, V \cap V' \mid V')$.

**Proof**    See Exercise 4.4.  ∎

I omit the parenthetical $\mu$ in CI1–5 when it is clear from context or plays no significant role. CI1 says that conditional independence is symmetric; this is almost immediate from the definition. CI2 says that the whole space $W$ is independent of every other set, conditional on any set. This seems reasonable—no matter what is learned, the probability of the whole space is still 1. CI3 says that if $U$ is conditionally independent of $V$, then it is also conditionally independent of the complement of $V$— if $V$ is unrelated to $U$ given $V'$, then so is $\overline{V}$. CI4 says that if each of two disjoint sets $V_1$ and $V_2$ is independent of $U$ given $V'$, then so is their union. Finally, CI5 says that when determining independence conditional on $V'$, all that matters is the relativization of all events to $V'$. Each of these properties is purely qualitative; no mention is made of numbers.

## 4.3    Independence for Plausibility Measures

Definition 4.2.2 can be easily adapted to each of the notions of conditioning discussed in Chapter 3. It is perhaps easiest to study independence generally by considering it in the context of plausibility—all the other notions are just special cases.

**Definition 4.3.1**   Given a cps $(W, \mathcal{F}, \mathcal{F}', \text{Pl})$, $U, V \in \mathcal{F}$ are *plausibilistically independent given $V'$ (with respect to Pl)*, written $I_{\text{Pl}}(U, V \mid V')$, if $V \cap V' \in \mathcal{F}'$ implies $\text{Pl}(U \mid V \cap V') = \text{Pl}(U \mid V')$ and $U \cap V' \in \mathcal{F}'$ implies $\text{Pl}(V \mid U \cap V') = \text{Pl}(V \mid V')$.   ∎

Given this definition of conditional independence for plausibility, it is then possible to ask whether the obvious analogues of CI1$[\mu]$–CI5$[\mu]$ hold. Let CI$n$[Pl] be the result of replacing the probability measure $\mu$ by the plausibility measure Pl in CI$n[\mu]$. CI1[Pl], CI2[Pl], and CI5[Pl] are easily seen to hold for all cpms Pl (Exercise 4.6), but CI3[Pl] and CI4[Pl] do not hold in general. CI3 and CI4 do hold for conditional ranking and for $\text{Pl}_{\mathcal{P}}$, but it is easy to see that they do not hold for conditional possibility or for conditional belief, no matter which definition of conditioning is used (Exercise 4.7).

How critical is this? Consider CI3. If $U$ is independent of $V$, should it necessarily also be independent of $\overline{V}$? Put another way, if $U$ is unrelated to $V$, should it necessarily be unrelated to $\overline{V}$ as well? My own intuitions regarding relatedness are not strong enough to say definitively. In any case, if this seems like an important component of the notion of independence, then the definition can easily be modified to enforce it, just as the current definition enforces symmetry.

Other notions of independence have been studied in the literature for specific representations of uncertainty. There is a general approach called *noninteractivity,* which takes as its point of departure the observation that $\mu(U \cap V) = \mu(U) \times \mu(V)$ if $U$ and $V$ are independent with respect to the probability measure $\mu$ (cf. Proposition 4.1.2). While noninteractivity was originally defined in the context of possibility measures, it makes sense for any algebraic cpm.

**Definition 4.3.2**   $U$ and $V$ *do not interact given $V'$ (with respect to the algebraic cpm Pl)*, denoted $NI_{\text{Pl}}(U, V \mid V')$, if $V' \in \mathcal{F}'$ implies that $\text{Pl}(U \cap V \mid V') = \text{Pl}(U \mid V') \otimes \text{Pl}(V \mid V')$.   ∎

Proposition 4.2.3 shows that, for conditional probability defined from unconditional probability, noninteractivity and independence coincide. However, they do not coincide in general (indeed, Example 4.1.4 shows that they do not coincide in general even for conditional probability spaces). In general, independence implies noninteractivity for algebraic cps's.

**Lemma 4.3.3**   *If $(W, \mathcal{F}, \mathcal{F}', \text{Pl})$ is an algebraic cps, then $I_{\text{Pl}}(U, V \mid U')$ implies $NI_{\text{Pl}}(U, V \mid U')$.*

**Proof**   See Exercise 4.8.   ∎

Noninteractivity and independence do not necessarily coincide in algebraic cps's, as the following example shows:

**Example 4.3.4**    Suppose $W = \{w_1, w_2, w_3, w_4\}$, $\mathrm{Poss}(w_1) = \mathrm{Poss}(w_2) = \mathrm{Poss}(w_3) = 1/2$, and $\mathrm{Poss}(w_4) = 1$. Let $U = \{w_1, w_2\}$ and $V = \{w_2, w_3\}$. Then $NI_{\mathrm{Poss}}(U, V \mid W)$, since $\mathrm{Poss}(U \mid W) = 1/2$, $\mathrm{Poss}(V \mid W) = 1/2$, and $\mathrm{Poss}(U \cap V \mid W) = 1/2$ (recall that $\otimes$ is min for possibility measures). But $\mathrm{Poss}(V \mid U) = 1 \neq \mathrm{Poss}(V)$, so it is not the case that $I_{\mathrm{Poss}}(U, V \mid W)$.   ∎

So what is required for noninteractivity to imply independence? It turns out that Alg4' (as defined in Section 3.9) suffices for *standard* algebraic cps's. (Recall that a cps $(W, \mathcal{F}, \mathcal{F}', \mathrm{Pl})$ is standard if $\mathcal{F}' = \{U : \{\mathrm{Pl}(U) \neq \bot\}\}$.)

**Lemma 4.3.5**    *If* $(W, \mathcal{F}, \mathcal{F}', \mathrm{Pl})$ *is a standard algebraic cps that satisfies Alg4', then* $NI_{\mathrm{Pl}}(U, V \mid U')$ *implies* $I_{\mathrm{Pl}}(U, V \mid U')$.

**Proof**    See Exercise 4.9.   ∎

It is easy to see that the assumption of standardness is necessary in Lemma 4.3.5 (Exercise 4.10). For a concrete instance of this phenomenon, consider the cps implicitly defined in Example 3.2.4. This cps is algebraic (Exercise 4.11) but nonstandard, since conditioning on $\{w_2\}$ is allowed although $\mu^s(w_2) = 0$. Example 4.1.4 shows that, in this cps, noninteractivity does not imply independence for $U = \{w_1, w_3\}$ and $V = \{w_2, w_3\}$.

The fact that noninteractivity and conditional independence coincide for the conditional plausibility spaces constructed from unconditional probability measures and ranking functions now follows from Lemmas 4.3.3 and 4.3.5. Since neither $\mathrm{Poss}(U \mid V)$ nor $\mathrm{Pl}_{\mathcal{P}}$ satisfy Alg4', it is perhaps not surprising that in neither case does noninteractivity imply conditional independence. Example 4.3.4 shows that is the case for $\mathrm{Poss}(V \mid U)$. The following example shows this for $\mathrm{Pl}_{\mathcal{P}}$:

**Example 4.3.6**    Suppose that a coin is known to be either double-headed or double-tailed and is tossed twice. This can be represented by $\mathcal{P} = \{\mu_0, \mu_1\}$, where $\mu_0(hh) = 1$ and $\mu_0(ht) = \mu_0(th) = \mu_0(tt) = 0$, while $\mu_1(tt) = 1$ and $\mu_1(ht) = \mu_1(th) = \mu_1(hh) = 0$. Let $H^1 = \{hh, ht\}$ be the event that the first coin toss lands heads, and let $H^2 = \{hh, th\}$ be the event that the second coin toss lands heads. Clearly there is a functional dependence between $H^1$ and $H^2$. Intuitively, they are related and not independent. On the other hand, it is easy to check that $H^1$ and $H^2$ are independent with respect to both $\mu_0$ and $\mu_1$ (since $\mu_0(H^1) = \mu_0(H^2) = \mu_0(H^1 \cap H^2) = 1$ and $\mu_1(H^1) = \mu_1(H^2) =$

$\mu_1(H^1 \cap H^2) = 0$). It thus follows that $H^1$ and $H^2$ do not interact: $NI_{Pl_{\mathcal{P}}}(H^1, H^2)$ holds, since $Pl_{\mathcal{P}}(H^1 \cap H^2) = Pl_{\mathcal{P}}(H^1) = Pl_{\mathcal{P}}(H^2) = (1, 0)$. On the other hand, $I_{Pl_{\mathcal{P}}}(H^1, H^2)$ does not hold. For example, $f_{H^1}(\mu_1) = 0$ while $f_{H^1|H^2}(\mu_1) = *$. (See the notes to this chapter for more discussion of this example.) ∎

Yet other notions of independence, besides analogues of Definition 4.3.1 and noninteractivity, have been studied in the literature, particularly in the context of possibility measures and sets of probability measures (see the notes for references). While it is beyond the scope of this book to go into details, it is worth comparing the notion of independence for $Pl_{\mathcal{P}}$ with what is perhaps the most obvious definition of independence with respect to a set $\mathcal{P}$ of probability measures—namely, that $U$ and $V$ are independent if $U$ and $V$ are independent with respect to each $\mu \in \mathcal{P}$. It is easy to check that $I_{Pl_{\mathcal{P}}}(U, V \mid V')$ implies $I_{\mu}(U, V \mid V')$ for all $\mu \in \mathcal{P}$ (Exercise 4.13), but the converse does not hold in general, as Example 4.3.6 shows.

This discussion illustrates an important advantage of thinking in terms of notions of uncertainty other than probability. It forces us to clarify our intuitions regarding important notions such as independence.

## 4.4   Random Variables

Suppose that a coin is tossed five times. What is the total number of heads? This quantity is what has traditionally been called a *random variable*. Intuitively, it is a variable because its value varies, depending on the actual sequence of coin tosses; the adjective "random" is intended to emphasize the fact that its value is (in a certain sense) unpredictable. Formally, however, a random variable is neither random nor a variable.

**Definition 4.4.1**   A *random variable* $X$ on a sample space (set of possible worlds) $W$ is a function from $W$ to some range. A *gamble* is a random variable whose range is the reals. ∎

**Example 4.4.2**   If a coin is tossed five times, the set of possible worlds can be identified with the set of $2^5$ sequences of five coin tosses. Let $NH$ be the gamble that corresponds to the number of heads in the sequence. In the world *httth*, where the first and last coin tosses land heads and the middle three land tails, $NH(httth) = 2$: there are two heads. Similarly, $NH(ththt) = 2$ and $NH(ttttt) = 0$. ∎

What is the probability of getting three heads in a sequence of five coin tosses? That is, what is the probability that $NH = 3$? Typically this is denoted $\mu(NH = 3)$.

But probability is defined on events (i.e., sets of worlds), not on possible values of random variables. $NH = 3$ can be viewed as shorthand for a set of worlds, namely, the set of worlds where the random variable $NH$ has value 3; that is, $NH = 3$ is shorthand for $\{w : NH(w) = 3\}$. More generally, if $X$ is a random variable on $W$ one of whose possible values is $x$, then $X = x$ is shorthand for $\{w : X(w) = x\}$ and $\mu(X = x)$ can be viewed as the probability that $X$ takes on value $x$.

So why are random variables of interest? For many reasons. One is that they play a key role in the definition of expectation; see Chapter 5. Another, which is the focus of this chapter, is that they provide a tool for structuring worlds. The key point here is that a world can often be completely characterized by the values taken on by a number of random variables. If a coin is tossed five times, then a possible world can be characterized by a 5-tuple describing the outcome of each of the coin tosses. There are five random variables in this case, say $X_1, \ldots, X_5$, where $X_i$ describes the outcome of the $i$th coin tosses.

This way of describing a world becomes particularly useful when one more ingredient is added: the idea of talking about independence for random variables. Two random variables $X$ and $Y$ are independent if learning the value of one gives no information about the value of the other. For example, if a fair coin is tossed ten times, the number of heads in the first five tosses is independent of the number of heads in the second five tosses.

**Definition 4.4.3**    Let $\mathcal{V}(X)$ denote the set of possible values (i.e., the range) of the random variable $X$. Random variables $X$ and $Y$ are *(probabilistically) conditionally independent given* $Z$ (with respect to probability measure $\mu$) if, for all $x \in \mathcal{V}(X)$, $y \in \mathcal{V}(Y)$, and $z \in \mathcal{V}(Z)$, the event $X = x$ is conditionally independent of $Y = y$ given $Z = z$. More generally, if $\mathbf{X} = \{X_1, \ldots, X_n\}$, $\mathbf{Y} = \{Y_1, \ldots, Y_m\}$, and $\mathbf{Z} = \{Z_1, \ldots, Z_k\}$ are sets of random variables, then $\mathbf{X}$ and $\mathbf{Y}$ are conditionally independent given $\mathbf{Z}$ (with respect to $\mu$), written $I_\mu^{rv}(\mathbf{X}, \mathbf{Y} \mid \mathbf{Z})$, if $X_1 = x_1 \cap \ldots \cap X_n = x_n$ is conditionally independent of $Y_1 = y_1 \cap \ldots \cap Y_m = y_m$ given $Z_1 = z_1 \cap \ldots \cap Z_k = z_k$ for all $x_i \in \mathcal{V}(X_i)$, $i = 1, \ldots, n$, $y_j \in \mathcal{V}(Y_j)$, $j = 1, \ldots, m$, and $z_h \in \mathcal{V}(Z_h)$, $h = 1, \ldots, k$. (If $\mathbf{Z} = \emptyset$, then $I_\mu^{rv}(\mathbf{X}, \mathbf{Y} \mid \mathbf{Z})$ if $\mathbf{X}$ and $\mathbf{Y}$ are unconditionally independent, that is, if $I_\mu^{rv}(\mathbf{X} = \mathbf{x}, \mathbf{Y} = \mathbf{x} \mid W)$ for all $\mathbf{x}$, $\mathbf{y}$. If either $\mathbf{X} = \emptyset$ or $\mathbf{Y} = \emptyset$, then $I_\mu^{rv}(\mathbf{X}, \mathbf{Y} \mid \mathbf{Z})$ is taken to be vacuously true.)    ∎

I stress that, in this definition, $X = x$, $Y = y$, and $Z = z$ represent events (i.e., subsets of $W$, the set of possible worlds), so it makes sense to intersect them.

The following result collects some properties of conditional independence for random variables:

**Theorem 4.4.4**   *For all probability measures $\mu$ on $W$, the following properties hold for all sets $\mathbf{X}$, $\mathbf{Y}$, $\mathbf{Y}'$, and $\mathbf{Z}$ of random variables on $W$ :*

CIRV1[$\mu$].   *If $I_\mu^{rv}(\mathbf{X}, \mathbf{Y} \mid \mathbf{Z})$, then $I_\mu^{rv}(\mathbf{Y}, \mathbf{X} \mid \mathbf{Z})$.*

CIRV2[$\mu$].   *If $I_\mu^{rv}(\mathbf{X}, \mathbf{Y} \cup \mathbf{Y}' \mid \mathbf{Z})$, then $I_\mu^{rv}(\mathbf{X}, \mathbf{Y} \mid \mathbf{Z})$.*

CIRV3[$\mu$].   *If $I_\mu^{rv}(\mathbf{X}, \mathbf{Y} \cup \mathbf{Y}' \mid \mathbf{Z})$, then $I_\mu^{rv}(\mathbf{X}, \mathbf{Y} \mid \mathbf{Y}' \cup \mathbf{Z})$.*

CIRV4[$\mu$].   *If $I_\mu^{rv}(\mathbf{X}, \mathbf{Y} \mid \mathbf{Z})$ and $I_\mu^{rv}(\mathbf{X}, \mathbf{Y}' \mid \mathbf{Y} \cup \mathbf{Z})$, then $I_\mu^{rv}(\mathbf{X}, \mathbf{Y} \cup \mathbf{Y}' \mid \mathbf{Z})$.*

CIRV5[$\mu$].   *$I_\mu^{rv}(\mathbf{X}, \mathbf{Z} \mid \mathbf{Z})$.*

**Proof**   See Exercise 4.14.   ∎

Again, I omit the parenthetical $\mu$ when it is clear from context or plays no significant role. Clearly, CIRV1 is the analogue of the symmetry property CI1. Properties CIRV2–5 have no analogue among CI1–5. They make heavy use of the fact that independence between random variables means independence of the events that result from every possible setting of the random variables. CIRV2 says that if, for every setting of the values of the random variables in $\mathbf{Z}$, the values of the variables in $\mathbf{X}$ are unrelated to the values of the variables in $\mathbf{Y} \cup \mathbf{Y}'$, then surely they are also unrelated to the values of the variables in $\mathbf{Y}$. CIRV3 says that if $\mathbf{X}$ and $\mathbf{Y} \cup \mathbf{Y}'$ are independent given $\mathbf{Z}$—which implies, by CIRV2, that $\mathbf{X}$ and $\mathbf{Y}$ are independent given $\mathbf{Z}$—then $\mathbf{X}$ and $\mathbf{Y}$ remain independent given $\mathbf{Z}$ and the (intuitively irrelevant) information in $\mathbf{Y}'$. CIRV4 says that if $\mathbf{X}$ and $\mathbf{Y}$ are independent given $\mathbf{Z}$, and $\mathbf{X}$ and $\mathbf{Y}'$ are independent given $\mathbf{Z}$ and $\mathbf{Y}$, then $\mathbf{X}$ must have been independent of $\mathbf{Y} \cup \mathbf{Y}'$ (given $\mathbf{Z}$) all along. Finally, CIRV5 is equivalent to the collection of statements $I_\mu(X = x, Z = z \mid Z = z')$, for all $x \in \mathcal{V}(X)$ and $z, z' \in \mathcal{V}(Z)$, each of which can easily be shown to follow from CI2, CI3, and CI5.

CIRV1–5 are purely qualitative properties of conditional independence for random variables, just as CI1–5 are qualitative properties of conditional independence for events. It is easy to define notions of conditional independence for random variables with respect to the other notions of uncertainty considered in this book. Just as with CI1–5, it then seems reasonable to examine whether CIRV1–5 hold for these definitions (and to use them as guides in constructing the definitions). It is immediate from the symmetry imposed by the definition of conditional independence that CIRV1[Pl] for all conditional plausibility measures Pl. It is also easy to show that CIRV5[Pl] holds for all cpms Pl (Exercise 4.15). On the other hand, it is not hard to find counterexamples showing that CIRV2–4 do not hold in general (see Exercises 4.16 and 4.17). However,

CIRV1–5 do hold for all *algebraic* cps's. Thus, the following result generalizes Theorem 4.4.4 and makes it clear that what is really needed for CIRV1–5 are the algebraic properties Alg1–4.

**Theorem 4.4.5**  *If* $(W, \mathcal{F}, \mathcal{F}', \text{Pl})$ *is an algebraic cps, then* CIRV1[Pl]–CIRV5[Pl] *hold.*

**Proof**   See Exercise 4.19.  ∎

It is immediate from Proposition 3.9.2 and Theorem 4.4.5 that CIRV1–5 holds for ranking functions, possibility measures (with both notions of conditioning), and sets $\mathcal{P}$ of probability measures represented by the plausibility measure $\text{Pl}_{\mathcal{P}}$.

## 4.5   Bayesian Networks

Suppose that $W$ is a set of possible worlds characterized by $n$ binary random variables $\mathcal{X} = \{X_1, \ldots, X_n\}$. That is, a world $w \in W$ is a tuple $(x_1, \ldots, x_n)$, where $x_i \in \{0, 1\}$ is the value of $X_i$. That means that there are $2^n$ worlds in $W$, say $w_1, \ldots, w_{2^n}$. A naive description of a probability measure on $W$ requires $2^n - 1$ numbers, $\alpha_1, \ldots, \alpha_{2^n-1}$, where $\alpha_i$ is the probability of world $w_i$. (Of course, the probability of $w_{2^n}$ is determined by the other probabilities, since they must sum to 1.)

If $n$ is relatively small, describing a probability measure in this naive way is not so unreasonable, but if $n$ is, say, 1,000 (certainly not unreasonable in many practical applications), then it is completely infeasible. Bayesian networks provide a tool that makes describing and working with probability measures far more feasible.

### 4.5.1   Qualitative Bayesian Networks

A (qualitative) *Bayesian network* (sometimes called a *belief network*) is a *dag*, that is, a directed acyclic graph, whose nodes are labeled by random variables. (For readers not familiar with graph theory, a *directed graph* consists of a collection of *nodes* or *vertices* joined by directed edges. Formally, a directed edge is just an ordered pair of nodes; the edge $(u, v)$ can be drawn by joining $u$ and $v$ by a line with an arrow pointing from $u$ to $v$. A directed graph is *acyclic* if there is no *cycle;* that is, there does not exist a sequence of vertices $v_0, \ldots, v_k$ such that $v_0 = v_k$, and there is an edge from $v_i$ to $v_{i+1}$ for $i = 0, \ldots, k - 1$.) Informally, the edges in a Bayesian network can be thought of as representing causal influence.

For example, a Bayesian network for reasoning about the relationship between smoking and cancer might include binary random variables such as $C$ for "has cancer,"

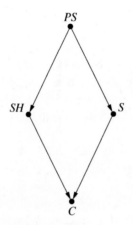

Figure 4.1   A Bayesian network $G_s$ that represents the relationship between smoking and cancer.

$SH$ for "exposed to secondhand smoke," $PS$ for "at least one parent smokes," and $S$ for "smokes." The Bayesian network $G_s$ in Figure 4.1 represents what seem to be reasonable causal relationships. Intuitively, $G_s$ says that whether or not a patient has cancer is directly influenced by whether he is exposed to secondhand smoke and whether he smokes. Both of these random variables, in turn, are influenced by whether his parents smoke. Whether or not his parents smoke also clearly influences whether or not he has cancer, but this influence is mediated through the random variables $SH$ and $S$. Once whether he smokes and was exposed to secondhand smoke is known, finding out whether his parents smoke gives no additional information. That is, $C$ is independent of $PS$ given $SH$ and $S$.

More generally, given a Bayesian network $G$ and a node $X$ in $G$, think of the *ancestors* of $X$ in the graph as those random variables that have a potential influence on $X$. (Formally, $Y$ is an ancestor of $X$ in $G$ if there is a directed path from $Y$ to $X$ in $G$—i.e., a sequence $(Y_1, \ldots, Y_k)$ of nodes—such that $Y_1 = Y$, $Y_k = X$, and there is a directed edge from $Y_i$ to $Y_{i+1}$ for $i = 1, \ldots, k - 1$.) This influence is mediated through the *parents* of $X$, those ancestors of $X$ directly connected to $X$. That means that $X$ should be conditionally independent of its ancestors, given its parents. The formal definition requires, in fact, that $X$ be independent not only of its ancestors, but of its *nondescendants*, given its parents, where the nondescendants of $X$ are those nodes $Y$ such that $X$ is not the ancestor of $Y$.

**Definition 4.5.1**   Given a qualitative Bayesian network $G$, let $\text{Par}_G(X)$ denote the parents of the random variable $X$ in $G$; let $\text{Des}_G(X)$ denote the *descendants* of $X$, that is, $X$ and all those nodes $Y$ such that $X$ is an ancestor of $Y$; let $\text{NonDes}_G(X)$ denote the nondescendants of $X$ in $G$, that is, $\mathcal{X} - \text{Des}_G(X)$. Note that all ancestors of $X$ are nondescendants of $X$. The Bayesian network $G$ *(qualitatively) represents,* or is *compatible with,* the probability measure $\mu$ if $I_\mu^{rv}(X, \text{NonDes}_G(X) \mid \text{Par}(X))$, that is, $X$ is conditionally independent of its nondescendants given its parents, for all $X \in \mathcal{X}$.   ∎

Definition 4.5.1 says that $G$ represents $\mu$ if, in a certain sense, it captures the conditional independence relations in $\mu$. But what makes this notion of representation at all interesting? In particular, why focus on conditional independencies of the form $I_\mu^{rv}(X, \text{NonDes}_G(X) \mid \text{Par}(X))$? To explain this, I digress briefly to discuss what is called the *chain rule* for probability. Given arbitrary sets $U_1, \ldots, U_n$, it is immediate from the definition of conditional probability that

$$\mu(U_1 \cap \ldots \cap U_n) = \mu(U_n \mid U_1 \cap \ldots \cap U_{n-1}) \times \mu(U_1 \cap \ldots \cap U_{n-1}).$$

(Assume for now all the relevant probabilities are positive, so that the conditional probabilities are well defined.) Applying this observation inductively gives the chain rule:

$$
\begin{aligned}
&\mu(U_1 \cap \ldots \cap U_n) \\
&= \mu(U_n \mid U_1 \cap \ldots \cap U_{n-1}) \\
&\quad \times \mu(U_{n-1} \mid U_1 \cap \ldots \cap U_{n-2}) \times \cdots \times \mu(U_2 \mid U_1) \times \mu(U_1).
\end{aligned}
\tag{4.1}
$$

As a special instance of the chain rule, take $U_i$ to be the event $X_i = x_i$. Plugging this into (4.1) gives

$$
\begin{aligned}
&\mu(X_1 = x_1 \cap \ldots \cap X_n = x_n) \\
&= \mu(X_n = x_n \mid X_1 = x_1 \cap \ldots \cap X_{n-1} = x_{n-1}) \\
&\quad \times \mu(X_{n-1} = x_{n-1} \mid X_1 = x_1 \cap \ldots \cap X_{n-2} = x_{n-2}) \\
&\quad \times \ldots \times \mu(X_2 = x_2 \mid X_1 = x_1) \times \mu(X_1 = x_1).
\end{aligned}
\tag{4.2}
$$

Now suppose without loss of generality that $\langle X_1, \ldots, X_n \rangle$ is a *topological sort* of (the nodes in) $G$; that is, if $X_i$ is a parent of $X_j$, then $i < j$. It easily follows that $\{X_1, \ldots, X_{k-1}\} \subseteq \text{NonDes}_G(X_k)$, for $k = 1, \ldots, n$ (Exercise 4.20); all the descendants of $X_k$ must have subscripts greater than $k$. Thus, all the nodes in $\{X_1, \ldots, X_{k-1}\}$ are independent of $X_k$ given $\text{Par}_G(X_k)$. It follows that

$$\mu(X_k = x_k | X_{k-1} = x_{k-1} \cap \ldots \cap X_1 = x_1) = \mu(X_k = x_k | \cap_{X_i \in \text{Par}(X_k)} X_i = x_i).$$

Thus, if $G$ represents $\mu$, then (4.2) reduces to

$$\begin{aligned}
\mu(X_1 = x_1 \cap &\ldots \cap X_n = x_n) \\
&= \mu(X_n = x_n \mid \cap_{X_i \in \text{Par}(X_n)} X_i = x_i) \\
&\times \mu(X_{n-1} = x_{n-1} \mid \cap_{X_i \in \text{Par}(X_{n-1})} X_i = x_i) \\
&\times \cdots \times \mu(X_1 = x_1).
\end{aligned} \tag{4.3}$$

Equation (4.3) shows that, if $G$ represents $\mu$, then $\mu$ is completely determined by conditional probabilities of the form

$$\mu(X_{n-1} = x_{n-1} \mid \cap_{X_i \in \text{Par}(X_{n-1})} X_i = x_i).$$

The consequences of this observation are explored in the next section.

## 4.5.2 Quantitative Bayesian Networks

A qualitative Bayesian network $G$ gives qualitative information about dependence and independence, but does not actually give the values of the conditional probabilities. A quantitative Bayesian network provides more quantitative information, by associating with each node $X$ in $G$ a *conditional probability table* (cpt) that quantifies the effects of the parents of $X$ on $X$. For example, if $X$'s parents in $G$ are $Y$ and $Z$, then the cpt for $X$ would have an entry denoted $d_{Y=j, Z=k}$ for all $(j, k) \in \{0, 1\}^2$. As the notation is meant to suggest, $d_{Y=j \cap Z=k} = \mu(X = 1 \mid Y = j \cap Z = k)$ for the probability measure $\mu$ represented by $G$. (Of course, there is no need to have an entry for $\mu(X = 0 \mid Y = j \cap Z = k)$, since this is just $1 - \mu(X = 1 \mid Y = j \cap Z = k)$.) Formally, a *quantitative Bayesian network* is a pair $(G, f)$ consisting of a qualitative Bayesian network $G$ and a function $f$ that associates with each node $X$ in $G$ a cpt, where there is an entry in the interval $[0, 1]$ in the cpt for each possible setting of the parents of $X$. If $X$ is a root of $G$, then the cpt for $X$ can be thought of as giving the unconditional probability that $X = 1$.

**Example 4.5.2** Consider the Bayesian network $G_s$ for smoking described in Figure 4.1. Let $f_s$ be the function that associates with the nodes $C$, $S$, $SH$, and $PS$ the cpts shown in Figure 4.2.

| S | SH | C |
|---|----|---|
| 1 | 1 | .6 |
| 1 | 0 | .4 |
| 0 | 1 | .1 |
| 0 | 0 | .01 |

| PS | S |
|----|---|
| 1 | .4 |
| 0 | .2 |

| PS | SH |
|----|----|
| 1 | .8 |
| 0 | .3 |

| PS |
|----|
| .3 |

Figure 4.2    Cpts for the smoking example.

The first line in the cpt for $C$ describes the conditional probability that $C = 1$ given $S = 1 \cap SH = 1$; the second line describes the conditional probability that $C = 1$ given $S = 1 \cap SH = 0$; and so on. Note that the probability that $C = 0$ given $S = 1 \cap SH = 1$ is .4 $(1 - .6)$; similarly, the probability that $C = 0$ conditional on each setting of $S$ and $SH$ can be calculated from the cpt. Finally, note that the .3 in the cpt for $PS$ is the unconditional probability of $PS$. ∎

**Definition 4.5.3**    A quantitative Bayesian network $(G, f)$ *(quantitatively) represents,* or *is compatible with,* the probability measure $\mu$ if $G$ qualitatively represents $\mu$ and the cpts agree with $\mu$ in that, for each random variable $X$, the entry in the cpt for $X$ given some setting $Y_1 = y_1, \ldots, Y_k = y_k$ of its parents is $\mu(X = 1 \mid Y_1 = y_1 \cap \ldots \cap Y_k = y_k)$ if $\mu(Y_1 = y_1 \cap \ldots \cap Y_k = y_k) \neq 0$. (It does not matter what the cpt entry for $Y_1 = y_1, \ldots, Y_k = y_k$ is if $\mu(Y_1 = y_1 \cap \ldots \cap Y_k = y_k) = 0$.) ∎

It follows immediately from (4.3) that if $(G, f)$ quantitatively represents $\mu$, then $\mu$ can be completely reconstructed from $(G, f)$. More precisely, (4.3) shows that the $2^n$ values $\mu(X_1 = x_1 \cap \ldots \cap X_n = x_n)$ can be computed from $(G, f)$; from these values, $\mu(U)$ can be computed for all $U \subseteq W$.

**Proposition 4.5.4**    *A quantitative Bayesian network $(G, f)$ always quantitatively represents a unique probability measure, the one determined by using (4.3).*

**Proof**    See Exercise 4.22. ∎

It is easy to calculate that for the unique probability measure $\mu$ represented by the quantitative Bayesian network $(G_s, f_s)$ in Example 4.5.2,

$$\mu(PS = 0 \cap S = 0 \cap SH = 1 \cap C = 1)$$
$$= \mu(C = 1 \mid S = 0 \cap SH = 1) \times \mu(S = 0 \mid PS = 0) \times \mu(SH = 1 \mid PS = 0)$$
$$\times \mu(PS = 0)$$
$$= .1 \times .8 \times .3 \times .7$$
$$= .0168.$$

(These numbers have been made up purely for this example and bear no necessary relationship to reality!)

Proposition 4.5.4, while straightforward, is important because it shows that there is no choice of numbers in a cpt that can be inconsistent with probability. Whatever the numbers are in the cpts for $(G, f)$, (as long as they are in the interval [0, 1]) there is always a probability measure that is compatible with $(G, f)$.

What about the converse? Can every probability measure on $W$ be represented by a quantitative Bayesian network? It can, and in general there are many ways of doing so.

**Construction 4.5.5** *Given $\mu$, let $Y_1, \ldots, Y_n$ be any permutation of the random variables in $\mathfrak{X}$. (Think of $Y_1, \ldots, Y_n$ as describing an ordering of the variables in $\mathfrak{X}$.) Construct a qualitative Bayesian network as follows. For each $k$, find a minimal subset of $\{Y_1, \ldots, Y_{k-1}\}$, call it $\mathbf{P}_k$, such that $I_\mu^{rv}(\{Y_1, \ldots, Y_{k-1}\}, Y_k \mid \mathbf{P}_k)$. (Clearly there is a subset with this property, namely, $\{Y_1, \ldots, Y_{k-1}\}$ itself. It follows that there must be a minimal subset with this property.) Then add edges from each of the nodes in $\mathbf{P}_k$ to $Y_k$. Call the resulting graph $G$.*

**Theorem 4.5.6** *The Bayesian network $G$ obtained by applying Construction 4.5.5 to the probability measure $\mu$ qualitatively represents $\mu$.*

**Proof** Note that $\langle Y_1, \ldots, Y_k \rangle$ represents a topological sort of $G$; edges always go from nodes in $\{Y_1, \ldots, Y_{k-1}\}$ to $Y_k$. It follows that $G$ is acyclic; that is, it is a dag. The construction guarantees that $\mathbf{P}_k = \text{Par}_G(Y_k)$ and that $I_\mu^{rv}(\{Y_1, \ldots, Y_{k-1}\}, Y_k \mid \text{Par}_G(Y_k))$. Using CIRV1-5, it can be shown that $I_\mu^{rv}(\text{NonDes}_G(Y_k), Y_k \mid \text{Par}_G(Y_k))$ (Exercise 4.23). Thus, $G$ qualitatively represents $\mu$. ∎

Of course, given $G$ and $\mu$, it is then easy to construct a quantitative Bayesian network $(G, f)$ that quantitatively represents $\mu$ by consulting $\mu$.

How much does this buy us? That depends on how sparse the graph is, that is, on how many parents each node has. If a node has $k$ parents, then its conditional probability table has $2^k$ entries. For example, there are nine entries altogether in the cpts in the Bayesian network $(G_s, f_s)$ in Example 4.5.2: the cpt for $C$ has four entries, the cpts for $SH$ and

$S$ each have two entries, and the one for $PS$ has only one entry. On the other hand, a naive description of the probability measure would require fifteen numbers. In general, if each node in a Bayesian network has at most $k$ parents, then there are at most $n2^k$ entries in all the cpts. If $k$ is small, then $n2^k$ can be much smaller than $2^n - 1$, the number of numbers needed for a naive description of the probability measure. (The numbers $2^k$ and $2^n - 1$ arise because I have considered only binary random variables. If the random variables can have $m$ values, say $0, 1, \ldots, m - 1$, the conditional probability table for a random variable $X$ with $k$ parents would have to describe the probability that $X = j$, for $j = 1, \ldots, m - 1$, for each of the $m^k$ possible settings of its parents, so would involve $(m - 1)m^k$ entries.)

Not only does a well-designed Bayesian network (I discuss what "well-designed" means in the next paragraph) typically require far fewer numbers to represent a probability measure, the numbers are typically easier to obtain. For example, for $(G_s, f_s)$, it is typically easier to obtain entries in the cpt like $\mu(C = 1 \mid S = 1 \cap SH = 0)$—the probability that someone gets cancer given that they smoke and are not exposed to secondhand smoke—than it is to obtain $\mu(C = 1 \cap S = 1 \cap SH = 0 \cap PS = 0)$.

Note that the Bayesian network constructed in Theorem 4.5.6 depends on the ordering of the random variables. For example, the first element in the ordering is guaranteed to be a root of the Bayesian network. Thus, there are many Bayesian networks that represent a given probability measure. But not all orderings lead to equally useful Bayesian networks. In a well-designed Bayesian network, the nodes are ordered so that if $X$ has a causal influence on $Y$, then $X$ precedes $Y$ in the ordering. This typically leads both to simpler Bayesian networks (in the sense of having fewer edges) and to conditional probabilities that are easier to obtain in practice. For example, it is possible to construct a Bayesian network that represents the same probability measure as $(G_s, f_s)$ but has $S$ as the root, by applying Theorem 4.5.6 with the ordering $S, C, PS, SH$ (Exercise 4.24). However, not only does this network have more edges, the conditional probability tables require entries that are harder to elicit in practice. It is easier to elicit from medical experts the probability that someone will smoke given that at least one of his parents smokes ($\mu(S = 1 \mid PS = 1)$) than the probability that at least one of a smoker's parents also smokes ($\mu(PS = 1 \mid S = 1)$).

One of the main criticisms of the use of probability in applications such as expert systems used to be that probability measures were too hard to work with. Bayesian networks deal with part of the criticism by providing a (potentially) compact representation of probability measures, one that experience has shown can be effectively constructed in realistic domains. For example, they have been used by PATHFINDER, a diagnostic expert system for lymph node diseases. The first step in the use of Bayesian networks for PATHFINDER was for experts to decide what the relevant random variables were. At one stage in the design, they used 60 binary random variables to represent diseases (did the agent have the disease or not) and over 100 random variables for findings (symptoms and test results). Deciding on the appropriate vocabulary took 8 hours, constructing the appropriate qualitative Bayesian network took 35 hours, and making the assessments to fill in the cpts took another 40 hours. This is considered a perfectly acceptable length of time to spend in constructing a significant expert system.

But, of course, constructing the Bayesian network is only part of the problem. Once a probability measure has been represented using a Bayesian network, it is important to be able to draw inferences from it. For example, a doctor using the PATHFINDER system will typically want to know the probability of a given disease given certain findings. Even if the disease is a child of the symptom, computing the probability of the disease given the symptom requires some effort. For example, consider the problem of computing $\mu_s(C = 1 \mid SH = 1)$ for the unique probability measure $\mu_s$ compatible with $(G_s, f_s)$. The cpt says that $\mu_s(C = 1 \mid SH = 1 \cap S = 1) = .6$ and that $\mu(C = 1 \mid SH = 1 \cap S = 0) = .1$. $\mu_s(C = 1 \mid SH = 1)$ can be computed using the identity

$$\mu_s(C = 1 \mid SH = 1) = \mu_s(C = 1 \mid SH = 1 \cap S = 1) \times \mu_s(S = 1)$$
$$+ \mu_s(C = 1 \mid SH = 1 \cap S = 0) \times \mu_s(S = 0).$$

That means that $\mu_s(S = 1)$ and $\mu_s(S = 0)$ must be computed. Efficient algorithms for such computations have been developed (and continue to be improved), which take advantage of the dag structure of a Bayesian network. It would take us too far afield here to go into the details; see the notes to this chapter for references.

### 4.5.3 Independencies in Bayesian Networks

By definition, a node (i.e., a random variable) in a Bayesian network $G$ that qualitatively represents a probability measure $\mu$ is independent of its nonancestors, given its parents with respect to $\mu$. What other conditional independencies hold for the probability measures represented by a Bayesian network? These can easily be computed. There is a notion of *d-separation*, which I am about to define, with the property that **X** is conditionally independent of **Y** given **Z** if the nodes in **Z** d-separate every node in **X** from every node in **Y**.

Now for the formal definition. A node $X$ is *d-separated* (the d is for *directed*) from a node $Y$ by a set of nodes **Z** in the dag $G$, written $d\text{-}sep_G(\mathbf{X}, \mathbf{Y} \mid \mathbf{Z})$, if, for every *undirected path* from $X$ to $Y$ (an undirected path is a path that ignores the arrows; e.g., $(SH, PS, S)$ is an undirected path from $SH$ to $S$ in $G_s$), there is a node $Z'$ on the path such that either

(a) $Z' \in \mathbf{Z}$ and there is an arrow on the path leading in to $Z'$ and an arrow leading out from $Z'$;

(b) $Z' \in \mathbf{Z}$ and has both path arrows leading out; or

(c) $Z'$ has both path arrows leading in, and neither $Z'$ nor any of its descendants are in $\mathbf{Z}$.

$\mathbf{X}$ is d-separated from $\mathbf{Y}$ by $\mathbf{Z}$ if every node $X$ in $\mathbf{X}$ is d-separated from every node $Y$ in $\mathbf{Y}$ by $\mathbf{Z}$. Consider the graph $G_s$. The set $\{SH, S\}$ d-separates $PS$ from $C$. One path from $PS$ to $C$ is blocked by $SH$ and the other by $S$, according to clause (a), since both $S$ and $SH$ have an arrow leading in and one leading out. Similarly, $\{PS\}$ d-separates $SH$ from $S$. The (undirected) path $(SH, PS, S)$ is blocked by $PS$ according to clause (b), and the undirected path $(SH, C, S)$ is blocked by $C \notin \{PS\}$ according to clause (c). On the other hand, $\{PS, C\}$ does *not* d-separate $SH$ from $S$, since there is no node on the path $(SH, C, S)$ that satisfies any of (a), (b), or (c).

These examples may also help explain the intuition behind each of the clauses of the definition. Clause (a) is quite straightforward. Clearly if there is a directed path from $PS$ to $C$, then $PS$ can influence $C$, so $PS$ and $C$ are not independent. However, conditioning on $\{SH, S\}$ blocks all paths from $PS$ to $C$, so $C$ is conditionally independent of $PS$ given $\{SH, S\}$. The situation in clause (b) is exemplified by the edges leading out from $PS$ to $SH$ and $S$. Intuitively, smoking ($S$) and being exposed to secondhand smoke ($SH$) are not independent because they have a common cause, a parent smoking ($PS$). Finding out that $S = 1$ increases the likelihood that $PS = 1$, which in turn increases the likelihood that $SH = 1$. However, $S$ and $SH$ are conditionally independent given $PS$.

Clause (c) in the definition of d-separation is perhaps the most puzzling. Why should the *absence* of a node in $\mathbf{Z}$ cause $X$ and $Y$ to be d-separated? Again, this can be understood in terms of the graph $G_s$. Finding out that $C = 1$ makes $S$ and $SH$ become negatively correlated. Since they are both potential causes of $C = 1$, finding out that one holds decreases the likelihood that the other holds: finding out that $S = 0$ increases the likelihood that $SH = 1$; finding out that $S = 1$ decreases the likelihood that $S = 0$.

To understand the role of descendants in clause (c), suppose that a node $D$ (for "early death") is added to $G_s$ with an edge from $C$ to $D$. Finding out that $D = 1$ makes it more likely that $C = 1$ and thus also makes $S$ and $SH$ negatively correlated.

The following theorem says that d-separation completely characterizes conditional independence in Bayesian networks:

**Theorem 4.5.7** *If* **X** *is d-separated from* **Y** *by* **Z** *in the Bayesian network G, then* $I^{rv}_{\mu}(\mathbf{X}, \mathbf{Y} \mid \mathbf{Z})$ *holds for all probability measures μ compatible with G. Conversely, if* **X** *is* not *d-separated from* **Y** *by* **Z***, then there is a probability measure μ compatible with G such that* $I^{rv}_{\mu}(\mathbf{X}, \mathbf{Y} \mid \mathbf{Z})$ *does not hold.*

The first half says that d-separation really does imply conditional independence in Bayesian networks. For future reference, it is worth noting that it can be proved using only properties CIRV1–5 and the fact that, by definition, $I^{rv}_{\mu}(\mathrm{NonDes}_G(X), X \mid \mathrm{Par}_G(X))$ holds for every μ compatible with G. The second half says that, in a precise sense, d-separation completely captures conditional independence in qualitative Bayesian networks.

### 4.5.4   Plausibilistic Bayesian Networks

It should be clear that Bayesian networks can be used with other representations of uncertainty. Certainly nothing in the definition of qualitative Bayesian networks really depends on the use of probability—all the definitions are given in terms of conditional independence of random variables, which makes sense for all the notions of uncertainty we have considered. To what extent do results like Proposition 4.5.4 and Theorems 4.5.6 and 4.5.7 depend on the use of probability? Plausibility measures provide a useful tool with which to examine this question.

As far as qualitative representation goes, note that Definition 4.5.1 makes perfect sense if the probability measure μ is replaced by a plausibility measure Pl everywhere. The proof of Theorem 4.5.6 uses only CIRV1–5; by Theorem 4.4.5, CIRV1–5 hold for all algebraic cps's. The following corollary is immediate:

**Corollary 4.5.8**   *A Bayesian network G obtained by applying (the analogue of) Construction 4.5.5 to the algebraic cpm* Pl *qualitatively represents* Pl.

In light of Corollary 4.5.8, for the remainder of this section I restrict to algebraic cps's.

The notion of a Bayesian network quantitatively representing a plausibility measure makes sense for arbitrary plausibility measures, with one minor caveat. Now a cpt for X must have entries of the form $d_{X=i \mid Y=j \cap Z=k}$, for both $i = 0$ and $i = 1$, since the conditional plausibility of $X = 0$ can no longer necessarily be determined from that of $X = 1$. (Of course, in general, if X is not a binary random variable, then there must be an entry for each possible value of X.) With this minor change, the definition of representation is the obvious analogue of Definition 4.5.3.

**Definition 4.5.9**   A quantitative Bayesian network $(G, f)$ *represents* a cpm Pl if $G$ is compatible with Pl and the cpts agree with Pl, in the sense that, for each random variable $X$, the entry $d_{X=i \mid Y_1=j_1,\ldots,Y_k=j_k}$ in the cpt is

$$\text{Pl}(X = i \mid Y_1 = j_1 \cap \ldots \cap Y_k = j_k),$$

if $Y_1 = j_1 \cap \ldots \cap Y_k = j_k \in \mathcal{F}'$. (It does not matter what $d_{X=i \mid Y_1=j_1,\ldots,Y_k=j_k}$ is if $Y_1 = j_1 \cap \ldots \cap Y_k = j_k \notin \mathcal{F}'$.) ∎

Given a cpm Pl, it is easy to construct a quantitative Bayesian network $(G, f)$ that represents Pl: simply construct $G$ so that it is compatible with Pl as in Corollary 4.5.8 and define $f$ appropriately, using Pl. The more interesting question is whether there is a unique algebraic cpm determined by a quantitative Bayesian network. As stated, this question is somewhat undetermined. The numbers in a quantitative network do not say what $\oplus$ and $\otimes$ ought to be for the algebraic cpm.

A reasonable way to make the question more interesting is the following. Recall that, for the purposes of this section, I have taken $W$ to consist of the $2^n$ worlds characterized by the $n$ binary random variables in $\mathcal{X}$. Let $\mathcal{PL}_{D,\oplus,\otimes}$ consist of all standard cps's of the form $(W, \mathcal{F}, \mathcal{F}', \text{Pl})$, where $\mathcal{F} = 2^W$, so that all subsets of $W$ are measurable, the range of Pl is $D$, and Pl is algebraic with respect to $\oplus$ and $\otimes$. Thus, for example, $\mathcal{PL}_{\mathbb{N}^*,\min,+}$ consists of all conditional ranking functions on $W$ defined from unconditional ranking functions by the construction in Section 3.8. Since a cps $(W, \mathcal{F}, \mathcal{F}', \text{Pl}) \in \mathcal{PL}_{D,\oplus,\otimes}$ is determined by Pl, I abuse notation and write $\text{Pl} \in \mathcal{PL}_{D,\oplus,\otimes}$.

With this notation, the question becomes whether a quantitative Bayesian network $(G, f)$ such that the entries in the cpts are in $D$ determines a unique element in $\mathcal{PL}_{D,\oplus,\otimes}$. The answer is yes, provided $(D, \oplus, \otimes)$ satisfies enough conditions. I do not go through all the conditions here; some of them are technical, and not much insight is gained from writing them all out carefully. They include, for example, conditions saying that $\oplus$ and $\otimes$ are commutative and associative and that $\otimes$ distributes over $\oplus$. It is worth noting that these conditions are satisfied by the definitions of $\oplus$ and $\otimes$ given in the proof of Proposition 3.9.2 for probability measures, ranking function, possibility measure (using either $\text{Poss}(\cdot \mid U)$ or $\text{Poss}(\cdot \parallel U)$), and the plausibility measure $\text{Pl}_{\mathcal{P}}$ defined by a set $\mathcal{P}$ of probability measures to a cps. Thus, it follows that, in all these cases, a quantitative Bayesian network represents a unique element in $\text{Pl} \in \mathcal{PL}_{D,\oplus,\otimes}$.

What about the analogue to Theorem 4.5.7? The first half is immediate for all algebraic cps's.

**Corollary 4.5.10**   *If* $\mathbf{X}$ *is d-separated from* $\mathbf{Y}$ *by* $\mathbf{Z}$ *in the Bayesian network* $G$, *then* $I_{\text{Pl}}^{rv}(\mathbf{X}, \mathbf{Y} \mid \mathbf{Z})$ *holds for all cpms* $\text{Pl} \in \mathcal{PL}_{D,\oplus,\otimes}$ *compatible with* $G$.

**Proof** As I observed after the statement of Theorem 4.5.7, the result depends only on CIRV1–5. Since, by Theorem 3.9.2, CIRV1–5 hold for all algebraic plausibility measures, the result follows. ∎

Getting an analogue to the second half of Theorem 4.5.7 requires a little more work. Notice that to prove such an analogue, it suffices to show that if $X$ is not d-separated from $Y$ by $\mathbf{Z}$ in $G$, then there is a plausibility measure $Pl \in \mathcal{PL}_{D,\oplus,\otimes}$ such that $I_{Pl}^{rv}(X, Y \mid \mathbf{Z})$ does not hold. Again, this result holds with enough conditions on $(D, \oplus, \otimes)$—essentially the same conditions required to get a quantitative Bayesian network to determine a unique plausibility measure in $\mathcal{PL}_{D,\oplus,\otimes}$, together with a richness condition to ensure that there are "enough" plausibility measures in $\mathcal{PL}_{D,\oplus,\otimes}$ to guarantee that if d-separation does not hold, then there is a plausibility measure that does not make the appropriate random (conditionally) independent. And again, these conditions hold for all the measures of uncertainty constructed in Proposition 3.9.2.

As these results show, the technology of Bayesian networks can be applied rather widely.

## Exercises

**4.1** Show that Proposition 4.1.2 holds for all conditional probability measures, using only CP1–3.

**4.2** Suppose that $\mu$ is a conditional probability measure.

 (a) Show that if $U$ and $V$ are independent with respect to $\mu$, then $\mu(U \cap V) = \mu(U)\mu(V)$.

 (b) Show that if $\mu(U) \neq 0$, $\mu(V) \neq 0$, and $\mu(U \cap V) = \mu(U)\mu(V)$, then $U$ and $V$ are independent with respect to $\mu$.

**4.3** Prove Proposition 4.2.3.

**4.4** Prove Theorem 4.2.5.

**4.5** Show that $I_\mu(U, V \mid V)$ follows from CI1$[\mu]$–CI5$[\mu]$.

**4.6** Show that CI1$[Pl]$, CI2$[Pl]$, and CI5$[Pl]$ hold for all cpms Pl.

**4.7** This exercise examines the extent to which various notions of conditioning satisfy CI3 and CI4.

(a) Show that ranking functions and the representation $Pl_{\mathcal{P}}$ of a set $\mathcal{P}$ of probability measures by a plausibility measure both satisfy CI3 and CI4.

(b) Show by means of counterexamples that none of $Poss(V \mid U)$, $Poss(V \parallel U)$, $Bel(V \mid U)$, or $Bel(V \parallel U)$ satisfy CI3 or CI4.

**4.8**    Prove Lemma 4.3.3.

**4.9**    Prove Lemma 4.3.5.

**4.10**   Show that the assumption of standardness is necessary in Lemma 4.3.5. More precisely, suppose that $(W, \mathcal{F}, \mathcal{F}', Pl)$ is an arbitrary nonstandard algebraic cps for which $\top \neq \bot$. Show that there must exist some $U \in \mathcal{F}'$ such that $I_{Pl}(U, U \mid W)$ does not hold although $NI_{Pl}(U, U \mid W)$ does.

**4.11**   Show that the cps implicitly defined in Example 3.2.4 is algebraic.

**4.12**   This exercise shows that a set of probabilities and its convex hull are not equivalent insofar as determination of independencies goes. Suppose that a coin with an unknown probability of heads is tossed twice, and the tosses are known to be independent. A reasonable representation of this situation is given by the set $\mathcal{P}_0$ consisting of all measures $\mu_\alpha$, where $\mu_\alpha(hh) = \alpha^2$, $\mu_\alpha(ht) = \mu_\alpha(th) = \alpha(1 - \alpha)$, $\mu_\alpha(tt) = (1 - \alpha)^2$.

(a) Show that the coin tosses are independent with respect to $Pl_{\mathcal{P}_0}$.

(b) Show that $\mathcal{P}_0$ is not convex (i.e., there exist $\mu_1, \mu_2 \in \mathcal{P}_0$ such that $a\mu_1 + b\mu_2 \notin \mathcal{P}_0$, where $a, b \in [0, 1]$ and $a + b = 1$).

(c) Show that the convex hull of $\mathcal{P}_0$ (i.e., the least convex set containing $\mathcal{P}_0$) includes measures for which the coin tosses are not independent.

**4.13**   Show that if $\mathcal{P}$ is a set of probability measures, then $I_{Pl_{\mathcal{P}}}(U, V \mid V')$ implies $I_\mu(U, V \mid V')$ for all $\mu \in \mathcal{P}$.

$*$**4.14**   Prove Theorem 4.4.4.

**4.15**   Show that CIRV5[Pl] holds for all cpms Pl.

**4.16**   Construct a cps for which none of CIRV2–4 holds.

**4.17**   Show that CIRV2 does not hold for belief functions, with conditioning defined as $Bel(V \mid U)$, nor for $\mathcal{P}_*$. (Hint: Construct a belief function Bel such that $Bel(X = i) = Bel(Y = j \cap Y' = k) = 0$ for all $i, j, k \in \{0, 1\}$, but $Bel(Y = 0) = Bel(Y = 1) = 1/2$.

Show, as a consequence, that $I_{\text{Bel}}^{rv}(X, \{Y, Y'\})$ holds, but $I_{\text{Bel}}^{rv}(X, Y)$ does not. A similar counterexample can be constructed for $\mathcal{P}_*$.)

**4.18**   Show using CIRV1-5 that $I_{\mu}^{rv}(\mathbf{X}, \mathbf{Y} \mid \mathbf{Z})$ iff $I_{\mu}^{rv}(\mathbf{X} - \mathbf{Z}, \mathbf{Y} - \mathbf{Z} \mid \mathbf{Z})$. Thus it is possible to assume without loss of generality that $\mathbf{Z}$ is disjoint from $\mathbf{X}$ and $\mathbf{Y}$.

*** 4.19**   Prove Theorem 4.4.5.

**4.20**   Show that if $\langle X_1, \ldots, X_n \rangle$ is a topological sort of $G$, then $\{X_1, \ldots, X_{i-1}\} \subseteq \text{NonDes}_G(X_i)$.

*** 4.21**   Consider the following property of conditional independence for random variables.

   CIRV6$[\mu]$. If $I_{\mu}^{rv}(\mathbf{X}, \mathbf{Y} \mid \mathbf{Y}' \cup \mathbf{Z})$ and $I_{\mu}^{rv}(\mathbf{X}, \mathbf{Y}' \mid \mathbf{Y} \cup \mathbf{Z})$, then $I_{\mu}^{rv}(\mathbf{X}, \mathbf{Y} \cup \mathbf{Y}' \mid \mathbf{Z})$.
CIRV6 can be viewed as a partial converse to CIRV3.

   (a)   Show by means of a counterexample that CIRV6 does not hold if $\mathbf{Y} = \mathbf{Y}'$.

   (b)   Show by means of a counterexample that CIRV6 does not hold even if $\mathbf{X}, \mathbf{Y}, \mathbf{Y}'$, $\mathbf{Z}$ are pairwise disjoint (i.e., if none of the random variables in $\mathbf{X}$ is in $\mathbf{Y} \cup \mathbf{Y}' \cup \mathbf{Z}$, none of the random variables in $\mathbf{Y}$ is in $\mathbf{X} \cup \mathbf{Y}' \cup \mathbf{Z}$, and so on).

   (c)   Show that CIRV6$[\mu]$ holds for all probability measures $\mu$ that are *strictly positive with respect to* $X, Y, Y'$, *and* $Z$ in that if $\mathbf{X} = \{X_1, \ldots, X_n\}$, $\mathbf{Y} = \{Y_1, \ldots, Y_m\}$, $\mathbf{Z} = \{Z_1, \ldots, Z_k\}$, and $\mathbf{Y}' = \{Y_1', \ldots, Y_p'\}$, then for all $x_i \in \mathcal{V}(X_i), i = 1, \ldots, n$, $y_j \in \mathcal{V}(Y_j), j = 1, \ldots, m, y_l' \in Y_l', l = 1, \ldots, p$, and $z_h \in \mathcal{V}(Z_h), h = 1, \ldots, k$,

$$\mu(X_1 = x_1 \cap \ldots \cap X_n = x_n \cap Y_1 = y_1 \cap \ldots \cap Y_m = y_m \cap$$
$$Y_1' = y_1' \cap \ldots \cap Y_p' = y_p' \cap Z_1 = z_1 \cap \ldots \cap Z_k = z_k) > 0.$$

**4.22**   Prove Proposition 4.5.4. Note that what requires proof here is that the required independence relations hold for the probability measure $\mu$ that is determined by $(G, f)$.

**4.23**   Complete the proof of Theorem 4.5.6 by showing that, for all nodes $Y_k$,

$$I_{\mu}^{rv}(\text{NonDes}_G(Y_k), Y_k \mid \text{Par}_G(Y_k)),$$

using CIRV1-5. (Hint: Let $\mathbf{Z}_m = \text{NonDes}_G(Y_k) \cap \{Y_1, \ldots, Y_m\}$. Prove by induction on $m$ that $I_{\mu}^{rv}(\mathbf{Z}_m, Y_k \mid \text{Par}_G(Y_k))$, using CIRV1-5.)

**4.24**   Consider the quantitative Bayesian network $(G_s, f_s)$ described in Example 4.5.2.

(a) Notice that $\{S, SH\}$ blocks both paths from $PS$ to $C$. What does this say about the relationship between $PS$ and $C$ in probabilistic terms?

(b) Calculate $\mu_s(C = 1 \mid PS = 1)$ for the unique probability measure $\mu_s$ represented by $(G_s, f_s)$.

(c) Use the construction of Theorem 4.5.6 to construct two qualitative Bayesian networks representing $\mu_s$, both having $S$ as their root.

(d) Suppose that you believe that there is a gene (that can be inherited) that results in a predisposition both to smoke and to have cancer, but otherwise smoking and cancer are unrelated. Draw a Bayesian network describing these beliefs, using the variables $PG$ (at least one parent has this gene), $G$ (has this gene), $PS$ (at least one parent smokes), $S$ (smokes), and $C$ (has cancer). Explain why each edge you included is there.

## Notes

The notions of (conditional) independence and random variable are standard in probability theory, and they are discussed in all texts on probability (and, in particular, the ones cited in Chapter 2). Fine [1973] and Walley [1991] discuss qualitative properties of conditional independence such as CI1–6; Walley, in fact, includes CI3 as part of his definition of independence. Walley calls the asymmetric version of independence *irrelevance*. It is an interesting notion in its own right; see [Cozman 1998; Cozman and Walley 1999].

   The focus on conditional independence properties can be traced back to Dawid [1979] and Spohn [1980], who both discussed properties that are variants of CIRV1– 6 (CIRV6 is discussed in Exercise 4.21). Pearl [1988] discusses these properties at length. These properties have been called the *graphoid properties* in the literature, which contains extensive research on whether they completely characterize conditional independence of random variables. Very roughly, graphoid properties do not characterize conditional independence of random variables—infinitely many extra properties are required to do that—but they do provide a complete characterization for all the properties of conditional independence of the form "if $I_\mu^{rv}(\mathbf{X_1}, \mathbf{Y_1} \mid \mathbf{Z_1})$ and $I_\mu^{rv}(\mathbf{X_2}, \mathbf{Y_2} \mid \mathbf{Z_2})$ then $I_\mu^{rv}(\mathbf{X_3}, \mathbf{Y_3} \mid \mathbf{Z_3})$," that is, where two (or fewer) conditional independence assertions imply a third one. (Note that CIRV1–6 all have this form.) Studeny [1994] proves this result, discusses the issue, and provides further references.

Noninteractivity was originally defined in the context of possibility measures by Zadeh [1978]. It was studied in the context of possibility measures by Fonck [1994], who showed that it was strictly weaker than independence for possibility measures. Shenoy [1994] defines a notion similar in spirit to noninteractivity for random variables. Lemmas 4.3.3 and 4.3.5 are taken from [Halpern 2001a]. Besides noninteractivity, a number of different approaches to defining independence for possibility measures [Campos and Huete 1999a; Campos and Huete 1999b; Dubois, Fariñas del Cerro, Herzig, and Prade 1994] and for sets of probability measures [Campos and Huete 1993; Campos and Moral 1995; Cousa, Moral, and Walley 1999] have been considered. In general, CIRV1–5 do not hold for them.

As Peter Walley [private communication, 2000] points out, Example 4.3.6 is somewhat misleading in its suggestion that independence with respect to $Pl_{\mathcal{P}}$ avoids counterintuitive results with respect to functional independence. Suppose that the probabilities in the example are modified slightly so as to make them positive. For example, suppose that the coin in the example is known to land heads with probability either .99 or .01 (rather than 1 and 0, as in the example). Let $\mu_0'$ and $\mu_1'$ be the obvious modifications of $\mu_0$ and $\mu_1$ required to represent this situation, and let $\mathcal{P}' = \{\mu_0', \mu_1'\}$. Now $H^1$ and $H^2$ are "almost functionally dependent." $H^1$ and $H^2$ continue to be type-1 independent, and noninteractivity continues to hold, but now $I_{Pl_{\mathcal{P}'}}(H^1, H^2)$ also holds. The real problem here is the issue raised in Section 3.4: this representation of uncertainty does not take evidence into account.

Theorem 4.4.5 is taken from [Halpern 2001a]. Characterizations of uncertainty measures for which CIRV1–5 hold, somewhat in the spirit of Theorem 4.4.5, can also be found in [Darwiche 1992; Darwiche and Ginsberg 1992; Friedman and Halpern 1995; Wilson 1994].

The idea of using graphical representations for probabilistic information measures can be traced back to Wright [1921] (see [Goldberger 1972] for a discussion). The work of Pearl [1988] energized the area, and it is currently a very active research topic, as a glance at recent proceedings of the Conference on Uncertainty in Artificial Intelligence (UAI) [Cooper and Moral 1998; Laskey and Prade 1999; Boutilier and Goldszmidt 2000] will attest. The books by Castillo, Gutierrez, and Hadi [1997], Jensen [1996], and Neapolitan [1990] cover Bayesian networks in detail. Charniak [1991] provides a readable introduction.

Pearl [1988] introduced the notion of d-separation. The first half of Theorem 4.5.7 was proved by Verma [1986], and the second half by Geiger and Pearl [1988]; see also [Geiger, Verma, and Pearl 1990]. Construction 4.5.5 and Theorem 4.5.6 are also essentially due to Verma [1986]. Heckerman [1990] provides a good discussion of the PATHFINDER system. Numerous algorithms for performing inference in Bayesian networks are discussed by Pearl [1988] and in many of the papers in the proceedings of the UAI Conference. Plausibilistic Bayesian networks are discussed in [Halpern 2001a], from where the results of Section 4.5.4 are taken. Independence and d-separation for various approaches to representing sets of probability measures using Bayesian networks are discussed by Cozman [2000a; 2000b]. However, the technical details are quite different from the approach taken here.

# Chapter 5

# Expectation

Imagine there is a quantity about whose value Alice is uncertain, like the amount of money that she will win in the lottery. What is a fair price for Alice to pay for a lottery ticket? Of course, that depends on what is meant by "fair." One way to answer this question is to say that a fair price would be one that is equal to what Alice can expect to win if she buys the ticket. But that seems to be just replacing one undefined concept, "fairness," by another, "expectation."

Suppose that the lottery has a grand prize of $1,000,000 and a second prize of $500,000. How much can Alice expect to win? $1,000,000? That is clearly the most Alice can win, but, unless she is an incurable optimist, she does not actually *expect* to win it. Most likely, she will not win anything at all but, if she really *expects* to win nothing, then why bother buying the ticket at all?

Intuitively, the amount that Alice can expect to win depends, at least in part, on such issues as how many tickets are sold, whether or not a prize is guaranteed to be awarded, and whether she thinks the lottery is fair. (Back to fairness again . . . ) Clearly if only four tickets are sold and both the grand prize and second prize are guaranteed to be awarded, she might expect to win quite a bit of money. But how much? The notion of *expectation* is an attempt to make this precise.

## 5.1    Expectation for Probability Measures

For definiteness, suppose that 1,000 lottery tickets are sold, numbered 1 through 1,000, and both prizes are guaranteed to be awarded. A world can be characterized by three numbers $(a, b, c)$, each between 1 and 1,000, where $a$ and $b$ are the ticket numbers that are awarded first and second prize, respectively, and $c$ is Alice's ticket number. Suppose that at most one prize is awarded per ticket, so that $a \neq b$. The amount of money that Alice wins in the lottery can be viewed as a random variable on this set of possible worlds. Intuitively, the amount that Alice can expect to win is the amount she does win in each world (i.e., the value of the random variable in each world) weighted by the probability of that world. Note that this amount may not match any of the amounts that Alice actually could win. In the case of the lottery, if all tickets are equally likely to win, then the expected amount that Alice can win, according to this intuition, is $1: 999 out of 1,000 times she gets nothing, and 1 out of 1,000 times she gets $1,000. However, she never actually wins $1. It can be shown that, if she plays the lottery repeatedly, then her average winnings are $1. So, in this sense, her expected winnings say something about what she can expect to get in the long run.

The intuition that Alice's expected winnings are just the amount she wins in each world weighted by the probability of that world can be easily formalized, using the notion of the expected value of a gamble. (Recall that a gamble is a real-valued random variable.) If $W$ is finite and every set (and, in particular, every singleton set) is measurable, then the *expected value of the gamble* $X$ (or the *expectation of* $X$) with respect to a probability measure $\mu$, denoted $E_\mu(X)$, is just

$$\sum_{w \in W} \mu(w)X(w). \tag{5.1}$$

Thus, the expected value of a gamble is essentially the "average" value of the variable. More precisely, as I said earlier, it is its value in each world weighted by the probability of the world.

If singletons are not necessarily measurable, the standard assumption is that $X$ is *measurable* with respect to $\mathcal{F}$; that is, for each value $x \in \mathcal{V}(X)$, the set of worlds $X = x$ where $X$ takes on value $x$ is in $\mathcal{F}$. Then the expected value of $X$ is defined as

$$E_\mu(X) = \sum_{x \in \mathcal{V}(X)} \mu(X = x)x. \tag{5.2}$$

It is easy to check that (5.1) and (5.2) are equivalent if all singletons are measurable and $W$ is finite (Exercise 5.1). However, (5.2) is more general. It makes sense even if

$W$ is not finite, as long as $\mathcal{V}(X)$ is finite. Expectation can be defined even if $\mathcal{V}(X)$ is infinite using integration rather than summation. Since I want to avoid integration in this book, for the purposes of this chapter, all gambles are assumed to have finite range (i.e., for all gambles $X$ considered in this chapter, $\mathcal{V}(X)$ is finite).

There are a number of other expressions equivalent to (5.2). I focus on one here. Suppose that $\mathcal{V}(X) = \{x_1, \ldots, x_n\}$, and $x_1 < \ldots < x_n$. Then

$$E_\mu(X) = x_1 + \sum_{i=1}^{n-1} \mu(X > x_i)(x_{i+1} - x_i) \tag{5.3}$$

(Exercise 5.2). A variant of (5.3), which essentially starts at the top and works down, is considered in Exercise 5.3.

What is the point of considering a definition of expectation like (5.3), given that it is equivalent to (5.2)? As long as only probability is considered, there is perhaps not much point. But analogues of these expressions for other representations of uncertainty are not, in general, equivalent. I return to this point in Section 5.2.2.

I conclude this section by listing some standard properties of expectation that will be useful in comparing expectation for probability with expectation for other forms of uncertainty. If $X$ and $Y$ are gambles on $W$ and $a$ and $b$ are real numbers, define the gamble $aX + bY$ on $W$ in the obvious way: $(aX + bY)(w) = aX(w) + bY(w)$. Say that $X \leq Y$ if $X(w) \leq Y(w)$ for all $w \in W$. Let $\tilde{c}$ denote the constant function that always returns $c$; that is, $\tilde{c}(w) = c$. Let $\mu$ be a probability measure on $W$.

**Proposition 5.1.1** *The function $E_\mu$ has the following properties for all measurable gambles $X$ and $Y$.*

(a) *$E_\mu$ is additive: $E_\mu(X + Y) = E_\mu(X) + E_\mu(Y)$.*

(b) *$E_\mu$ is affinely homogeneous: $E_\mu(aX + \tilde{b}) = aE_\mu(X) + b$ for all $a, b \in \mathbb{R}$.*

(c) *$E_\mu$ is monotone: if $X \leq Y$, then $E_\mu(X) \leq E_\mu(Y)$.*

**Proof** See Exercise 5.4. ∎

The next result shows that the properties in Proposition 5.1.1 essentially characterize probabilistic expectation. (Proposition 5.1.1 is not the only possible characterization of $E_\mu$. An alternate characterization is given in Exercise 5.5.)

**Proposition 5.1.2** *Suppose that $E$ maps gambles that are measurable with respect to $\mathcal{F}$ to $\mathbb{R}$ and $E$ is additive, affinely homogeneous, and monotone. Then there is a (necessarily unique) probability measure $\mu$ on $\mathcal{F}$ such that $E = E_\mu$.*

**Proof**   The proof is quite straightforward; I go through the details here just to show where all the assumptions are used. If $U \in \mathcal{F}$, let $X_U$ denote the gamble such that $X_U(w) = 1$ if $w \in U$ and $X_U(w) = 0$ if $w \notin U$. A gamble of the form $X_U$ is traditionally called an *indicator function*. Define $\mu(U) = E(X_U)$. Note that $X_W = \tilde{1}$, so $\mu(W) = 1$, since $E$ is affinely homogeneous. Since $X_\emptyset$ is $\tilde{0}$ and $E$ is affinely homogeneous, it follows that $\mu(\emptyset) = E(X_\emptyset) = 0$. $X_\emptyset \leq X_U \leq X_W$ for all $U \subseteq W$; since $E$ is monotone, it follows that $0 = E(X_\emptyset) \leq E(X_U) = \mu(U) \leq E(X_W) = 1$. If $U$ and $V$ are disjoint, then it is easy to see that $X_{U \cup V} = X_U + X_V$. By additivity,

$$\mu(U \cup V) = E(X_{U \cup V}) = E(X_U) + E(X_V) = \mu(U) + \mu(V).$$

Thus, $\mu$ is indeed a probability measure.

To see that $E = E_\mu$, note that it is immediate from (5.2) that $\mu(U) = E_\mu(X_U)$ for $U \in \mathcal{F}$. Thus, $E_\mu$ and $E$ agree on all measurable indicator functions. Every measurable gamble $X$ can be written as a linear combination of measurable indicator functions. For each $a \in \mathcal{V}(X)$, let $U_{X,a} = \{w : X(w) = a\}$. Since $X$ is a measurable gamble, $U_{X,a}$ must be in $\mathcal{F}$. Moreover, $X = \sum_{a \in \mathcal{V}(X)} a X_{U_{X,a}}$. By additivity and affine homogeneity, $E_\mu(X) = \sum_{a \in \mathcal{V}(X)} a E(X_{U_{X,a}})$. (Here I am using the fact that gambles have finite range, so finite additivity suffices to give this result.) By Proposition 5.1.1, $E_\mu(X) = \sum_{a \in \mathcal{V}(X)} a E_\mu(X_{U_{X,a}})$. Since $E$ and $E_\mu$ agree on measurable indicator functions, it follows that $E(X) = E_\mu(X)$. Thus, $E = E_\mu$ as desired.

Clearly, if $\mu(U) \neq \mu'(U)$, then $E_\mu(X_U) \neq E_{\mu'}(X_U)$. Thus, $\mu$ is the unique probability measure on $\mathcal{F}$ such that $E = E_\mu$. ∎

If $\mu$ is countably additive and $W$ is infinite, then $E_\mu$ has a continuity property that is much in the spirit of (2.1):

> If $X_1, X_2, \ldots$ is a sequence of random variables increasing to $X$, then $\lim_{i \to \infty} E_\mu(X_i) = E_\mu(X)$          (5.4)

(Exercise 5.6). ($X_1, X_2, \ldots$ is *increasing to* $X$ if, for all $w \in W$, $X_1(w) \leq X_2(w) \leq \ldots$ and $\lim_{i \to \infty} X_i(w) = X(w)$.) This property, together with the others in Proposition 5.1.2, characterizes expectation based on a countably additive probability measure (Exercise 5.6). Moreover, because $E_\mu(-X) = -E_\mu(X)$, and $X_1, X_2, \ldots$ decreases to $X$ iff $-X_1, -X_2, \ldots$ increases to $-X$, it is immediate that the following continuity property is equivalent to (5.4):

> If $X_1, X_2, \ldots$ is a sequence of random variables decreasing to $X$, then $\lim_{i \to \infty} E_\mu(X_i) = E_\mu(X)$.          (5.5)

## 5.2   Expectation for Other Notions of Likelihood

How should expectation be defined for other representations of uncertainty? I start with sets of probability measures, since the results in this case are fairly straightforward and form the basis for other representations.

### 5.2.1   Expectation for Sets of Probability Measures

There are straightforward analogues of lower and upper probability in the context of expectation. If $\mathcal{P}$ is a set of probability measures such that $X$ is measurable with respect to each probability measure $\mu \in \mathcal{P}$, then define $E_{\mathcal{P}}(X) = \{E_{\mu}(X) : \mu \in \mathcal{P}\}$. $E_{\mathcal{P}}(X)$ is a set of numbers. Define the *lower expectation* and *upper expectation* of $X$ with respect to $\mathcal{P}$, denoted $\underline{E}_{\mathcal{P}}(X)$ and $\overline{E}_{\mathcal{P}}(X)$, as the inf and sup of the set $E_{\mathcal{P}}(X)$, respectively. Clearly $\mathcal{P}_*(U) = \underline{E}_{\mathcal{P}}(X_U)$ and $\mathcal{P}^*(U) = \overline{E}_{\mathcal{P}}(X_U)$. The properties of $\underline{E}_{\mathcal{P}}$ and $\overline{E}_{\mathcal{P}}$ are not so different from those of probabilistic expectation.

**Proposition 5.2.1**   *The functions $\overline{E}_{\mathcal{P}}$ and $\underline{E}_{\mathcal{P}}$ have the following properties, for all gambles $X$ and $Y$.*

(a) *$\overline{E}_{\mathcal{P}}$ is subadditive: $\overline{E}_{\mathcal{P}}(X + Y) \leq \overline{E}_{\mathcal{P}}(X) + \overline{E}_{\mathcal{P}}(Y)$;*
    *$\underline{E}_{\mathcal{P}}$ is superadditive: $\underline{E}_{\mathcal{P}}(X + Y) \geq \underline{E}_{\mathcal{P}}(X) + \underline{E}_{\mathcal{P}}(Y)$.*

(b) *$\overline{E}_{\mathcal{P}}$ and $\underline{E}_{\mathcal{P}}$ are both positively affinely homogeneous: $\overline{E}_{\mathcal{P}}(aX + \tilde{b}) = a\overline{E}_{\mathcal{P}}(X) + b$ and $\underline{E}_{\mathcal{P}}(aX + \tilde{b}) = a\underline{E}_{\mathcal{P}}(X) + b$ if $a, b \in \mathbb{R}, a \geq 0$.*

(c) *$\overline{E}_{\mathcal{P}}$ and $\underline{E}_{\mathcal{P}}$ are monotone.*

(d) *$\overline{E}_{\mathcal{P}}(X) = -\underline{E}_{\mathcal{P}}(-X)$.*

**Proof**   See Exercise 5.8.   ∎

Superadditivity (resp., subadditivity), positive affine homogeneity, and monotonicity in fact characterize $\underline{E}_{\mathcal{P}}$ (resp., $\overline{E}_{\mathcal{P}}$), although the proof of this fact is beyond the scope of the book.

**Theorem 5.2.2**   *Suppose that $E$ maps gambles measurable with respect to $\mathcal{F}$ to $\mathbb{R}$ and is superadditive (resp., subadditive), positively affinely homogeneous, and monotone. Then there is a set $\mathcal{P}$ of probability measures on $\mathcal{F}$ such that $E = \underline{E}_{\mathcal{P}}$ (resp., $E = \overline{E}_{\mathcal{P}}$).*

(There is another equivalent characterization of $\underline{E}_{\mathcal{P}}$; see Exercise 5.9.)

The set $\mathcal{P}$ constructed in Theorem 5.2.2 is not unique. It is not hard to construct sets $\mathcal{P}$ and $\mathcal{P}'$ such that $\mathcal{P} \neq \mathcal{P}'$ but $\underline{E}_{\mathcal{P}} = \underline{E}_{\mathcal{P}'}$ (see Exercise 5.10). However, there is a canonical largest set $\mathcal{P}$ such that $E = \underline{E}_{\mathcal{P}}$; $\mathcal{P}$ consists of all probability measures $\mu$ such that $E_{\mu}(X) \geq E(X)$ for all gambles $X$.

There is also an obvious notion of expectation corresponding to $\text{Pl}_{\mathcal{P}}$ (as defined in Section 2.8). $E_{\text{Pl}_{\mathcal{P}}}$ maps a gamble $X$ to a function $f_X$ from $\mathcal{P}$ to $\mathbb{R}$, where $f_X(\mu) = E_{\mu}(X)$. This is analogous to $\text{Pl}_{\mathcal{P}}$, which maps sets to functions from $\mathcal{P}$ to $[0, 1]$. Indeed, it should be clear that $E_{\text{Pl}_{\mathcal{P}}}(X_U) = \text{Pl}_{\mathcal{P}}(U)$, so that the relationship between $E_{\text{Pl}_{\mathcal{P}}}$ and $\text{Pl}_{\mathcal{P}}$ is essentially the same as that between $E_{\mu}$ and $\mu$. Not surprisingly, there are immediate analogues of Proposition 5.1.1 and 5.1.2.

**Proposition 5.2.3** *The function $E_{\text{Pl}_{\mathcal{P}}}$ is additive, affinely homogeneous, and monotone.*

**Proof**   See Exercise 5.13.   ∎

**Proposition 5.2.4** *Suppose that $E$ maps gambles measurable with respect to $\mathcal{F}$ to functions from $I$ to $\mathbb{R}$ and is additive, affinely homogeneous, and monotone. Then there is a (necessarily unique) set $\mathcal{P}$ of probability measures on $\mathcal{F}$ indexed by $I$ such that $E = E_{\text{Pl}_{\mathcal{P}}}$.*

**Proof**   See Exercise 5.14.   ∎

Note that if $\mathcal{P} \neq \mathcal{P}'$, then $E_{\text{Pl}_{\mathcal{P}}} \neq E_{\text{Pl}_{\mathcal{P}'}}$. As observed earlier, this is not the case with upper and lower expectation; it is possible that $\mathcal{P} \neq \mathcal{P}'$ yet $\underline{E}_{\mathcal{P}} = \underline{E}_{\mathcal{P}'}$ (and hence $\overline{E}_{\mathcal{P}} = \overline{E}_{\mathcal{P}'}$). Thus, $E_{\text{Pl}_{\mathcal{P}}}$ can be viewed as capturing more information about $\mathcal{P}$ than $\underline{E}_{\mathcal{P}}$. On the other hand, $\underline{E}_{\mathcal{P}}$ captures more information than $\mathcal{P}_*$. Since $\mathcal{P}_*(U) = \underline{E}_{\mathcal{P}}(U)$, it is immediate that if $\mathcal{P}_* \neq \mathcal{P}'_*$, then $\underline{E}_{\mathcal{P}} \neq \underline{E}_{\mathcal{P}'}$. However, as Example 5.2.10 shows, there are sets $\mathcal{P}$ and $\mathcal{P}'$ of probability measures such that $\mathcal{P}_* = \mathcal{P}'_*$ but $\underline{E}_{\mathcal{P}} \neq \underline{E}_{\mathcal{P}*}$.

As for probability, there are additional continuity properties for $\underline{E}_{\mathcal{P}}$, $\overline{E}_{\mathcal{P}}$, and $E_{\text{Pl}_{\mathcal{P}}}$ if $\mathcal{P}$ consists of countably additive measures. They are the obvious analogues of (5.4) and (5.5).

If $X_1, X_2, \ldots$ is a sequence of random variables decreasing to $X$, then $\lim_{i \to \infty} \underline{E}_{\mathcal{P}}(X_i) = \underline{E}_{\mathcal{P}}(X)$.                     (5.6)

If $X_1, X_2, \ldots$ is a sequence of random variables increasing to $X$, then $\lim_{i \to \infty} \overline{E}_{\mathcal{P}}(X_i) = \overline{E}_{\mathcal{P}}(X)$.                     (5.7)

If $X_1, X_2, \ldots$ is a sequence of random variables increasing to $X$, then $\lim_{i \to \infty} E_{\text{Pl}_{\mathcal{P}}}(X_i) = E_{\text{Pl}_{\mathcal{P}}}(X)$.                     (5.8)

(See Exercise 5.12.) Again, just as with upper and lower probability, the analogue of (5.6) does not hold for lower expectation, and the analogue of (5.7) does not hold for upper expectation. (Indeed, counterexamples for upper and lower probability can be converted to counterexamples for upper and lower expectation by taking indicator functions.) On the other hand, it is easy to see that the analogue of (5.5) does hold for $E_{\mathrm{Pl}_p}$.

Analogues of (5.4) and (5.5) hold for all the other notions of expectation I consider if the underlying representation satisfies the appropriate continuity property. To avoid repetition, I do not mention this again.

### 5.2.2 Expectation for Belief Functions

There is an obvious way to define a notion of expectation based on belief functions, using the identification of Bel with $(\mathcal{P}_{\mathrm{Bel}})_*$ (see Theorem 2.4.1). Given a belief function Bel, define $E_{\mathrm{Bel}} = \underline{E}_{\mathcal{P}_{\mathrm{Bel}}}$. Similarly, for the corresponding plausibility function Plaus, define $E_{\mathrm{Plaus}} = \overline{E}_{\mathcal{P}_{\mathrm{Bel}}}$.

This is well defined, but, as with the case of conditional belief, it seems more natural to get a notion of expectation for belief functions that is defined purely in terms of belief functions, without reverting to probability. It turns out that this can be done using the analogue of (5.3). If $\mathcal{V}(X) = \{x_1, \ldots, x_n\}$, with $x_1 < \ldots < x_n$, define

$$E'_{\mathrm{Bel}}(X) = x_1 + \sum_{i=1}^{n-1} \mathrm{Bel}(X > x_i)(x_{i+1} - x_i). \tag{5.9}$$

An analogous definition holds for plausibility:

$$E'_{\mathrm{Plaus}}(X) = x_1 + \sum_{i=1}^{n-1} \mathrm{Plaus}(X > x_i)(x_{i+1} - x_i). \tag{5.10}$$

**Proposition 5.2.5** $E_{\mathrm{Bel}} = E'_{\mathrm{Bel}}$ *and* $E_{\mathrm{Plaus}} = E'_{\mathrm{Plaus}}$.

**Proof** See Exercise 5.15. ∎

Equation (5.9) gives a way of defining expectation for belief and plausibility functions without referring to probability. (Another way of defining expectation for belief functions, using mass functions, is given in Exercise 5.16; another way of defining expected plausibility, using a different variant of (5.2), is given in Exercise 5.17.)

The analogue of (5.2) could, of course, be used to define a notion of expectation for belief functions, but it would not give a very reasonable notion. For example, suppose that $W = \{a, b\}$ and $\text{Bel}(a) = \text{Bel}(b) = 0$. (Of course, $\text{Bel}(\{a, b\}) = 1$.) Consider a gamble $X$ such that $X(a) = 1$ and $X(b) = 2$. According to the obvious analogue of (5.1) or (5.2) (which are equivalent in this case), the expected belief of $X$ is 0, since $\text{Bel}(a) = \text{Bel}(b) = 0$. However, it is easy to see that $E_{\text{Bel}}(X) = 1$ and $E_{\text{Plaus}}(X) = 2$, which seems far more reasonable. The real problem is that (5.2) is most appropriate for plausibility measures that are additive (in the sense defined in Section 2.8; i.e., there is a function $\oplus$ such that $\text{Pl}(U \cup V) = \text{Pl}(U) \oplus \text{Pl}(V)$ for disjoint sets $U$ and $V$). Indeed, the equivalence of (5.1) and (5.2) depends critically on the fact that probability is additive. As observed in Section 2.8 (see Exercise 2.56), belief functions are not additive. Thus, not surprisingly, using (5.2) does not give reasonable results.

Since $E_{\text{Bel}}$ can be viewed as a special case of the lower expectation $\underline{E}_{\mathcal{P}}$ (taking $\mathcal{P} = \mathcal{P}_{\text{Bel}}$), it is immediate from Proposition 5.2.1 that $E_{\text{Bel}}$ is superadditive, positively affinely homogeneous, and monotone. (Similar remarks hold for $E_{\text{Plaus}}$, except that it is subadditive. For ease of exposition, I focus on $E_{\text{Bel}}$ in the remainder of this section, although analogous remarks hold for $E_{\text{Plaus}}$.) But $E_{\text{Bel}}$ has additional properties. Since it is immediate from the definition that $E_{\text{Bel}}(X_U) = \text{Bel}(X_U)$, the inclusion-exclusion property B3 of belief functions can be expressed in terms of expectation (just by replacing all instances of $\text{Bel}(V)$ in B3 by $E_{\text{Bel}}(X_V)$). Moreover, it does not follow from the other properties, since it does not hold for arbitrary lower probabilities (see Exercise 2.14).

B3 seems like a rather specialized property, since it applies only to indicator functions. There is a more general version of it that also holds for $E_{\text{Bel}}$. Given gambles $X$ and $Y$, define the gambles $X \wedge Y$ and $X \vee Y$ as the minimum and maximum of $X$ and $Y$, respectively; that is, $(X \wedge Y)(w) = \min(X(w), Y(w))$ and $(X \vee Y)(w) = \max(X(w), Y(w))$. Consider the following inclusion-exclusion rule for expectation:

$$E(\vee_{i=1}^{n} X_i) \geq \sum_{i=1}^{n} \sum_{\{I \subseteq \{1,\ldots,n\}:|I|=i\}} (-1)^{i+1} E(\wedge_{j \in I} X_j). \qquad (5.11)$$

Since it is immediate that $X_{U \cup V} = X_U \vee X_V$ and $X_{U \cap V} = X_U \wedge X_V$, (5.11) generalizes B3.

There is yet another property satisfied by expectation based on belief functions. Two gambles $X$ and $Y$ are said to be *comonotonic* if it is not the case that one increases while the other decreases; that is, there do not exist worlds $w$, $w'$ such that

$X(w) < X(w')$ while $Y(w) > Y(w')$. Equivalently, there do not exist $w$ and $w'$ such that $(X(w) - X(w'))(Y(w) - Y(w')) < 0$.

**Example 5.2.6** Suppose that

- $W = \{w_1, w_2, w_3\}$;

- $X(w_1) = 1$, $X(w_2) = 3$, and $X(w_3) = 0$;

- $Y(w_1) = 2$, $Y(w_2) = 7$, and $Y(w_3) = 4$;

- $Z(w_1) = 3$, $Z(w_2) = 5$, and $Z(w_3) = 3..$

Then $X$ and $Y$ are not comonotonic. The reason is that $X$ decreases from $w_1$ to $w_3$, while $Y$ increases from $w_1$ to $w_3$. On the other hand, $X$ and $Z$ are comonotonic, as are $Y$ and $Z$.  ∎

Consider the following property of *comonotonic additivity:*

$$\text{If } X \text{ and } Y \text{ are comonotonic, then } E(X + Y) = E(X) + E(Y). \qquad (5.12)$$

**Proposition 5.2.7** *The function $E_{\text{Bel}}$ is superadditive, positively affinely homogeneous, and monotone, and it satisfies (5.11) and (5.12).*

**Proof** The fact that $E_{\text{Bel}}$ is superadditive, positively affinely homogeneous, and monotone follows immediately from Proposition 5.2.3. The fact that it satisfies (5.11) follows from B3 and Proposition 5.2.5 (Exercise 5.18). Proving that it satisfies (5.12) requires a little more work, although it is not that difficult. I leave the details to the reader (Exercise 5.19).  ∎

**Theorem 5.2.8** *Suppose that $E$ maps gambles to $\mathbb{R}$ and $E$ is positively affinely homogeneous, is monotone, and satisfies (5.11) and (5.12). Then there is a (necessarily unique) belief function $\text{Bel}$ such that $E = E_{\text{Bel}}$.*

**Proof** Define $\text{Bel}(U) = E(X_U)$. Just as in the case of probability, it follows from positive affine homogeneity and monotonicity that $\text{Bel}(\emptyset) = 0$, $\text{Bel}(W) = 1$, and $0 \le \text{Bel}(U) \le 1$ for all $U \subseteq W$. By (5.11) (specialized to indicator functions), it follows that $\text{Bel}$ satisfies B3. Thus, $\text{Bel}$ is a belief function. Now if $X$ is a gamble such that $\mathcal{V}(X) = \{x_1, \ldots, x_n\}$ and $x_1 < x_2 < \ldots < x_n$, define

$$X_j = \tilde{x}_1 + (x_2 - x_1)X_{X > x_1} + \cdots + (x_j - x_{j-1})X_{X > x_{j-1}}$$

for $j = 1, \ldots, n$. It is not hard to show that $X = X_n$ and that $X_j$ and $(x_{j+1} - x_j)X_{X > x_j}$ are comonotonic, for $j = 1, \ldots, n - 1$ (Exercise 5.20). Now applying (5.12) repeatedly, it follows that

$$E(X) = E(\tilde{x}_1) + E((x_2 - x_1)X_{X > x_1}) + \cdots + E(x_n - x_{n-1})X_{X > x_{n-1}}).$$

Now applying positive affine homogeneity, it follows that

$$E(X) = x_1 + (x_2 - x_1)E(X_{X > x_1}) + \cdots + (x_n - x_{n-1})E(X_{X > x_{n-1}})$$
$$= x_1 + (x_2 - x_1)\,\mathrm{Bel}(X > x_1) + \cdots + (x_n - x_{n-1})\,\mathrm{Bel}(X > x_{n-1})$$
$$= E_{\mathrm{Bel}}(X). \quad \blacksquare$$

Note that superadditivity was not assumed in the statement of Theorem 5.2.8. Indeed, it is a consequence of Theorem 5.2.8 that superadditivity follows from the other properties. In fact, the full strength of positive affine homogeneity is not needed either in Theorem 5.2.8. It suffices to assume that $E(\tilde{b}) = b$.

**Lemma 5.2.9**  *Suppose that $E$ is such that (a) $E(\tilde{b}) = b$, (b) $E$ is monotone, and (c) $E$ satisfies (5.12). Then $E$ satisfies positive affine homogeneity.*

**Proof**  See Exercise 5.21.  $\blacksquare$

It follows easily from these results that $E_{\mathrm{Bel}}$ is the unique function $E$ mapping gambles to $\mathbb{R}$ that is superadditive, positively affinely homogeneous, monotone, and it satisfies (5.11) and (5.12) such that $E(X_U) = \mathrm{Bel}(U)$ for all $U \subseteq W$. Proposition 5.2.7 shows that $E_{\mathrm{Bel}}$ has these properties. If $E'$ is a function from gambles to $\mathbb{R}$ that has these properties, by Theorem 5.2.8, $E' = E_{\mathrm{Bel}'}$ for some belief function $\mathrm{Bel}'$. Since $E'(X_U) = \mathrm{Bel}'(U) = \mathrm{Bel}(U)$ for all $U \subseteq W$, it follows that $\mathrm{Bel} = \mathrm{Bel}'$.

This observation says that $\mathrm{Bel}$ and $E_{\mathrm{Bel}}$ contain the same information. Thus, so do $(\mathcal{P}_{\mathrm{Bel}})^*$ and $\underline{E}_{\mathcal{P}_{\mathrm{Bel}}}$ (since $\mathrm{Bel} = (\mathcal{P}_{\mathrm{Bel}})_*$ and $E_{\mathrm{Bel}} = \underline{E}_{\mathcal{P}_{\mathrm{Bel}}}$). However, this is not true for arbitrary sets $\mathcal{P}$ of probability measures, as the following example shows:

**Example 5.2.10**  Let $W = \{1, 2, 3\}$. A probability measure $\mu$ on $W$ can be characterized by a triple $(a_1, a_2, a_3)$, where $\mu(i) = a_i$. Let $\mathcal{P}$ consist of the three probability measures $(0, 3/8, 5/8)$, $(5/8, 0, 3/8)$, and $(3/8, 5/8, 0)$. It is almost immediate that $\mathcal{P}_*$ is 0 on singleton subsets of $W$ and $\mathcal{P}_* = 3/8$ for doubleton subsets. Let $\mathcal{P}' = \mathcal{P} \cup \{\mu_4\}$, where $\mu_4 = (5/8, 3/8, 0)$. It is easy to check that $\mathcal{P}'_* = \mathcal{P}_*$. However, $\underline{E}_{\mathcal{P}} \neq \underline{E}_{\mathcal{P}'}$. In particular, let $X$ be the gamble such that $X(1) = 1$, $X(2) = 2$, and $X(3) = 3$. Then $\underline{E}_{\mathcal{P}}(X) = 13/8$, but $\underline{E}_{\mathcal{P}'}(X) = 11/8$. Thus, although $\underline{E}_{\mathcal{P}}$ and $\underline{E}_{\mathcal{P}'}$ agree on indicator functions, they do not agree on all gambles. In light of the earlier discussion, it should be no surprise that $\mathcal{P}_*$ is not a belief function (Exercise 5.23).   ∎

### 5.2.3   Inner and Outer Expectation

Up to now, I have assumed that all gambles $X$ were measurable, that is, for each $x \in \mathcal{V}(X)$, the set $\{w : X(w) = x\}$ was in the domain of whatever representation of uncertainty was being used. But what if $X$ is not measurable? In this case, it seems reasonable to consider an analogue of inner and outer measures for expectation.

The naive analogue is just to replace $\mu$ in (5.2) with the inner measure $\mu_*$ and the outer measure $\mu^*$, respectively. Let $\underline{E}^?_\mu$ and $\overline{E}^?_\mu$ denote these notions of *inner* and *outer expectation*, respectively. As the notation suggests, defining inner and outer expectation in this way can lead to intuitively unreasonable answers. In particular, these functions are not monotone, as the following example shows:

**Example 5.2.11**   Consider a space $W = \{w_1, w_2\}$ and the trivial algebra $\mathcal{F} = \{\emptyset, W\}$. Let $\mu$ be the unique (trivial) probability measure on $\mathcal{F}$. Suppose that $X_1$, $X_2$, and $X_3$ are gambles such that $X_1(w_1) = X_1(w_2) = 1$, $X_3(w_1) = X_3(w_2) = 2$, and $X_2(w_1) = 1$ and $X_2(w_2) = 2$. Clearly, $X_1 \leq X_2 \leq X_3$. Moreover, it is immediate from the definitions that $\underline{E}^?_\mu(X_1) = 1$ and $\overline{E}^?_\mu(X_3) = 2$. However, $\underline{E}^?_\mu(X_2) = 0$, since $\mu_*(w_1) = \mu_*(w_2) = 0$, and $\overline{E}^?_\mu(X_2) = 3$, since $\mu_*(w_1) = \mu_*(w_2) = 1$. Thus, neither $\underline{E}^?_\mu$ nor $\overline{E}^?_\mu$ is monotone.

Note that it is important that $\underline{E}^?_\mu$ and $\overline{E}^?_\mu$ are defined using (5.2), rather than (5.1). If (5.1) were used then, for example, $\underline{E}^?_\mu$ and $\overline{E}^?_\mu$ would be monotone. On the other hand, $\underline{E}^?_\mu(X_1)$ would be 0. Indeed, $\underline{E}^?_\mu(Y)$ would be 0 for every gamble $Y$. This certainly is not particularly reasonable either!   ∎

Since an inner measure is a belief function, the discussion of expectation for belief suggests two other ways of defining inner and outer expectation.

- The first uses sets of probabilities. As in Section 2.3, given a probability measure $\mu$ defined on an algebra $\mathcal{F}'$ that is a subalgebra of $\mathcal{F}$, let $\mathcal{P}_\mu$ consist of all the extensions of $\mu$ to $\mathcal{F}$. Recall from Theorem 2.3.3 that $\mu_*(U) = (\mathcal{P}_\mu)_*(U)$ and $\mu^*(U) = (\mathcal{P}_\mu)^*(U)$ for all $U \in \mathcal{F}$. Define $\underline{E}_\mu = \underline{E}_{\mathcal{P}_\mu}$ and $\overline{E}_\mu = \overline{E}_{\mathcal{P}_\mu}$.

- The second approach uses (5.3); define $\underline{E}'_\mu$ and $\overline{E}'_\mu$ by replacing the $\mu$ in (5.3) by $\mu_*$ and $\mu^*$, respectively.

In light of Proposition 5.2.5, the following should come as no surprise:

**Proposition 5.2.12**   $\underline{E}_\mu = \underline{E}'_\mu$ and $\overline{E}_\mu = \overline{E}'_\mu$.

**Proof**   Since it is immediate from the definitions that $\mathcal{P}_\mu$ is $\mathcal{P}_{\text{Bel}}$ for $\text{Bel} = \mu_*$, the fact that $\underline{E}_\mu = \underline{E}'_\mu$ is immediate from Proposition 5.2.5. It is immediate from Proposition 5.2.1(d) and the definition that $\overline{E}_\mu(X) = -\underline{E}_\mu(-X)$. It is easy to check that $\overline{E}'_\mu(X) = -\underline{E}'_\mu(-X)$ (Exercise 5.24). Thus, $\overline{E}_\mu = \overline{E}'_\mu$. ∎

$\underline{E}_\mu$ has much more reasonable properties than $\underline{E}^?_\mu$. (Since $\overline{E}_\mu(X) = -\underline{E}_\mu(-X)$, the rest of the discussion is given in terms of $\underline{E}_\mu$.) Indeed, since $\mu_*$ is a belief function, $\underline{E}_\mu$ is superadditive, positively affinely homogeneous, and monotone, and it satisfies (5.11) and (5.12). But $\underline{E}_\mu$ has an additional property, since it is determined by a probability measure. If $\mu$ is a measure on $\mathcal{F}$, then the lower expectation of a gamble $Y$ can be approximated by the lower expectation of random variables measurable with respect to $\mathcal{F}$.

**Lemma 5.2.13**   *If $\mu$ is a probability measure on an algebra $\mathcal{F}$, and $X$ is a gamble measurable with respect to an algebra $\mathcal{F}' \supseteq \mathcal{F}$, then $\underline{E}_\mu(X) = \sup\{\underline{E}_\mu(Y) : Y \le X, Y$ is measurable with respect to $\mathcal{F}\}$.*

**Proof**   See Exercise 5.25. ∎

To get a characterization of $\underline{E}_\mu$, it is necessary to abstract the property characterized in Lemma 5.2.13. Unfortunately, the abstraction is somewhat ugly. Say that a function $E$ on $\mathcal{F}'$-measurable gambles is *determined by* $\mathcal{F} \subseteq \mathcal{F}'$ if

1. for all $\mathcal{F}'$-measurable gambles $X$, $E(X) = \sup\{E(Y) : Y \le X, Y$ is measurable with respect to $\mathcal{F}\}$,

2. $E$ is additive for gambles measurable with respect to $\mathcal{F}$ (so that $E(X + Y) = E(X) + E(Y)$ if $X$ and $Y$ are measurable with respect to $\mathcal{F}$.

**Theorem 5.2.14**   *Suppose that $E$ maps gambles measurable with respect to $\mathcal{F}'$ to $\mathbb{R}$ and is positively affinely homogeneous, is monotone, and satisfies (5.11) and (5.12), and there is some $\mathcal{F} \subseteq \mathcal{F}'$ such that $E$ is determined by $\mathcal{F}$. Then there is a unique probability measure $\mu$ on $\mathcal{F}$ such that $E = \underline{E}_\mu$.*

**Proof**   See Exercise 5.26. ∎

### 5.2.4   Expectation for Possibility Measures and Ranking Functions

Since a possibility measure can be viewed as a plausibility function, expectation for possibility measures can be defined using (5.10). It follows immediately from Poss3 that the expectation $E_{\text{Poss}}$ defined from a possibility measure Poss in this way satisfies the *sup property:*

$$E_{\text{Poss}}(X_{U \cup V}) = \max(E_{\text{Poss}}(X_U), E_{\text{Poss}}(X_V)). \qquad (5.13)$$

**Proposition 5.2.15**   *The function $E_{\text{Poss}}$ is positively affinely homogeneous, is monotone, and satisfies (5.12) and (5.13).*

**Proof**   See Exercise 5.27.   ∎

I do not know if there is a generalization of (5.13) that can be expressed using arbitrary gambles, not just indicator functions. The obvious generalization—$E_{\text{Poss}}(X \vee Y) = \max(E_{\text{Poss}}(X), E_{\text{Poss}}(Y))$—is false (Exercise 5.28). In any case, (5.13) is the extra property needed to characterize expectation for possibility.

**Theorem 5.2.16**   *Suppose that $E$ is a function on gambles that is positively affinely homogeneous, is monotone, and satisfies (5.12) and (5.13). Then there is a (necessarily unique) possibility measure Poss such that $E = E_{\text{Poss}}$.*

**Proof**   See Exercise 5.29.   ∎

Note that, although Poss is a plausibility function, and thus satisfies the analogue of (5.11) with $\geq$ replaced by $\leq$ and $\vee$ switched with $\wedge$, there is no need to state this analogue explicitly; it follows from (5.13). Similarly, subadditivity follows from the other properties. (Since a possibility measure is a plausibility function, not a belief function, the corresponding expectation is subadditive rather than superadditive.)

While this definition of $E_{\text{Poss}}$ makes perfect sense and, as Theorem 5.2.16 shows, has an elegant characterization, it is worth noting that there is somewhat of a mismatch between the use of max in relating $\text{Poss}(U \cup V)$, $\text{Poss}(U)$, and $\text{Poss}(V)$ (i.e., using max for $\oplus$) and the use of $+$ in defining expectation. Using max instead of $+$ gives a perfectly reasonable definition of expectation for possibility measures (see Exercise 5.30). However, going one step further and using min for $\times$ (as in Section 3.7) does *not* give a very reasonable notion of expectation (Exercise 5.31).

With ranking functions, yet more conceptual issues arise. Since ranking functions can be viewed as giving order-of-magnitude values of uncertainty, it does not seem appropriate to mix real-valued gambles with integer-valued ranking functions. Rather, it seems more reasonable to restrict to nonnegative integer-valued gambles, where the integer again describes the order of magnitude of the value of the gamble. With this interpretation, the standard move of replacing $\times$ and $+$ in probability-related expressions by $+$ and min, respectively, in the context of ranking functions seems reasonable. This leads to the following definition of the expectation of a (nonnegative, integer-valued) gamble $X$ with respect to a ranking function $\kappa$:

$$E_\kappa(X) = \min_{x \in \mathcal{V}(X)} (x + \kappa(X = x)).$$

It is possible to prove analogues of Propositions 5.1.1 and 5.1.2 for $E_\kappa$ (replacing $\times$ and $+$ by $+$ and min, respectively); I omit the details here (see Exercise 5.32). Note that, with this definition, there is no notion of a negative-valued gamble, so the intuition that negative values can "cancel" positive values when computing expectation does not apply.

## 5.3   Plausibilistic Expectation

My goal in this section is to define a general notion of expectation for plausibility measures that generalizes the notions that have been considered for other representations of uncertainty. Since expectation is defined in terms of operations such as $+$ and $\times$, expectation for plausibility is more interesting if there are analogues to $+$ and $\times$, much as in the case of algebraic conditional plausibility spaces. In general, the analogues of $+$ and $\times$ used for expectation may be different from that used for plausibility; nevertheless, I still denote them using $\oplus$ and $\otimes$.

How can expectation for a random variable $X$ on $W$ be defined? To start with, a plausibility measure on $W$ is needed. Suppose that the range of the plausibility measure is $D_1$ and the range of the random variable $X$ is $D_2$. ($D_2$ may not be the reals, so $X$ is not necessarily a gamble.) To define an analogue of (5.2), what is needed is an operation $\otimes$ that maps $D_1 \times D_2$ to some *valuation domain* $D_3$, where $D_3$ extends $D_2$, and an operation $\oplus$ that maps $D_3 \times D_3$ to $D_3$. If $d_2$ is a prize, as in the example at the beginning of the chapter, then $d_1 \otimes d_2$ can be viewed as the "value" of getting $d_2$ with likelihood $d_1$. Similarly, $d_3 \oplus d_4$ can be viewed as the value of getting both $d_3$ and $d_4$. It is often the case that $D_2 = D_3$, but it is occasionally convenient to distinguish between them.

**Definition 5.3.1**   An *expectation domain* is a tuple $ED = (D_1, D_2, D_3, \oplus, \otimes)$, where

- $D_1$ is a set partially ordered by $\leq_1$;

- $D_2$ and $D_3$ are sets partially preordered by $\leq_2$ and $\leq_3$, respectively;

- there exist elements $\perp$ and $\top$ in $D_1$ such that $\perp \leq_1 d \leq_1 \top$ for all $d \in D_1$;

- $D_2 \subseteq D_3$ and $\leq_2$ is the restriction of $\leq_3$ to $D_2$;

- $\oplus : D_3 \times D_3 \to D_3$;

- $\otimes : D_1 \times D_2 \to D_3$;

- $\oplus$ is commutative and associative;

- $\top \otimes d_2 = d_2$.  ∎

The *standard expectation domain* is $([0, 1], \mathbb{R}, \mathbb{R}, +, \times)$, where $\leq_1, \leq_2$, and $\leq_3$ are all the standard order on the reals. The standard expectation domain is denoted $\overline{\overline{\mathbb{R}}}$.

Given an expectation domain $ED = (D_1, D_2, D_3, \oplus, \otimes)$, a plausibility measure Pl with range $D_1$, and a random variable $X$ with range $D_2$, one notion of expected value of $X$ with respect to Pl and $ED$, denoted $E_{\text{Pl},ED}(X)$, can be defined by obvious analogy to (5.2):

$$E_{\text{Pl},ED}(X) = \oplus_{x \in \mathcal{V}(X)} \text{Pl}(X = x) \otimes x. \tag{5.14}$$

(I include $ED$ in the subscript because the definition depends on $\oplus$ and $\otimes$; I omit $ED$ if $\otimes$ and $\oplus$ are clear from context.)

It is also possible to define an analogue of (5.3) if $D_2$ is linearly ordered and a notion of subtraction can be defined in $ED$; I don't pursue this further here and focus on (5.14) instead.

It is almost immediate from their definitions that $E_\mu$, $E_\kappa$, $E'_{\text{Poss}}$ (as defined in Exercise 5.30), and $E''_{\text{Poss}}$ (as defined in Exercise 5.31) can be viewed as instances of $E_{\text{Pl},ED}$, for the appropriate choice of $ED$. It is not hard to see that $E_{\text{Pl}_{\mathcal{P}}}$ is also an instance of $E_{\text{Pl}_{\mathcal{P}},ED}$. Since the construction will be useful in other contexts, I go through the steps here. Suppose that the probability measures in $\mathcal{P}$ are indexed by $I$. Let $ED_{D_{\mathcal{P}}} = (D_1, D_2, D_3, \otimes, \oplus)$, where

- $D_1 = D_{\mathcal{P}}$, the functions from $\mathcal{P}$ to $[0, 1]$ with the pointwise ordering (recall that this is just the range of $\text{Pl}_{\mathcal{P}}$);

- $D_2$ consists of the constant functions from $\mathcal{P}$ to $\mathbb{R}$;

- $D_3$ consists of all functions from $\mathcal{P}$ to $\mathbb{R}$, again with the pointwise ordering;

- $\oplus$ is pointwise addition; and

- $\otimes$ is pointwise multiplication.

Since the constant function $\tilde{b}$ can be identified with the real number $b$, it follows that $D_2$ can be identified with $\mathbb{R}$. It is easy to see that $E_{\text{Pl}_\mathcal{P}, ED_{D_\mathcal{P}}} = E_{\text{Pl}_\mathcal{P}}$ (Exercise 5.33).

Although $\underline{E}_\mathcal{P}$ and $\overline{E}_\mathcal{P}$ cannot be directly expressed using $E_{\text{Pl}, ED}$, the order they induce on random variables can be represented. Consider $\underline{E}_\mathcal{P}$. Let $ED'_{D_\mathcal{P}}$ be identical to $ED_{D_\mathcal{P}}$ except that the order on $D_3$ is modified so that, instead of using the pointwise ordering, $f \leq g$ iff $\inf_{\mu \in \mathcal{P}} f(\mu) \leq \inf_{\mu \in \mathcal{P}} g(\mu)$. (Note that this is actually a preorder.) It is almost immediate from the definitions that $E_{\text{Pl}_\mathcal{P}, ED'_{D_\mathcal{P}}}(X) \leq E_{\text{Pl}_\mathcal{P}, ED'_{D_\mathcal{P}}}(Y)$ iff $\underline{E}(X) \leq \underline{E}(Y)$. Similarly, the order induced by $\overline{E}_\mathcal{P}$ can be represented by simply changing the order on $D_3$ so that it uses sup rather than inf. Since $E_{\text{Bel}} = \underline{E}_{\mathcal{P}_{\text{Bel}}}$, it follows that the order on random variables induced by $E_{\text{Bel}}$ can also be represented. As discussed in the next section, what often matters in decision making is the order that expectation induces on random variables so, in a sense, this is good enough.

Note that $E_{\text{Pl}}(\tilde{b}) = b$. Properties like subadditivity, superadditivity, monotonicity, or positive affine homogeneity make sense for $E_{\text{Pl}}$. Whether they hold depends in part on the properties of $\oplus$, $\otimes$, and Pl; I do not pursue this here (but see Exercise 5.34). Rather, I consider one of the most important applications of expectation, decision making, and see to what extent plausibilistic expectation can help in understanding various approaches to making decisions.

## 5.4   Decision Theory

The aim of decision theory is to help agents make rational decisions. Consider an agent that has to choose between a number of acts, such as whether to bet on a horse race and, if so, which horse to bet on. Are there reasonable rules to help the agent decide how to make this choice?

### 5.4.1   The Basic Framework

There are a number of equivalent ways of formalizing the decision process. Intuitively, a decision situation describes the objective part of the circumstance that an agent faces (i.e., the part that is independent of the tastes and beliefs of the agent). Formally, a *decision situation* is a tuple $DS = (A, W, C)$, where

- $W$ is the set of possible worlds (or states of the world),

- $C$ is the set of *consequences*, and

- $A$ is the set of *acts* (i.e., functions from $W$ to $C$).

An act **a** is *simple* if its range is finite. That is, **a** is simple if it has only finitely many possible consequences. For simplicity, I assume here that all acts are simple. (Note that this is necessarily the case if either $W$ or $C$ is finite, although I do not require this.) The advantage of using simple acts is that the expected utility of an act can be defined using (plausibilistic) expectation.

A *decision problem* is essentially a decision situation together with information about the preferences and beliefs of the agent. These tastes and beliefs are represented using a *utility function* and a plausibility measure, respectively. A utility function maps consequences to utilities. Intuitively, if $u$ is the agent's utility function and $c$ is a consequence, then $u(c)$ measures how happy the agent would be if $c$ occurred. That is, the utility function quantifies the preferences of the agent. Consequence $c$ is at least as good as consequence $c'$ iff $u(c) \geq u(c')$. In the literature, the utility function is typically assumed to be real-valued and the plausibility measure is typically taken to be a probability measure. However, assuming that the utility function is real-valued amounts to assuming (among other things) that the agent can totally order all consequences. Moreover, there is the temptation to view a consequence with utility 6 as being "twice as good" as a consequence with utility 3. This may or may not be reasonable. In many cases, agents are uncomfortable about assigning real numbers with such a meaning to utilities. Even if an agent is willing to compare all consequences, she may be willing to use only labels such as "good," "bad," or "outstanding."

Nevertheless, in many simple settings, assuming that people have real-valued utility function and a probability measure does not seem so unreasonable. In the horse race example, the worlds could represent the order in which the horses finished the race. The plausibility measure thus represents the agent's subjective estimate of the likelihood of various orders of finish. The acts correspond to possible bets (perhaps including the act of not betting at all). The consequence of a bet of $10 on Northern Dancer depends on how Northern Dancer finishes in the world. The consequence could be purely monetary (the agent wins $50 in the worlds where Northern Dancer wins the race) but could also include feelings (the agent is dejected if Northern Dancer finishes last, and he also loses $10). Of course, if the consequence includes feelings such as dejection, then it may be more difficult to assign it a numeric utility.

Formally, a *(plausibilistic) decision problem* is a tuple $DP = (DS, ED, \text{Pl}, u)$, where $DS = (A, W, C)$ is a decision situation, $ED = (D_1, D_2, D_3, \oplus, \otimes)$ is an expectation domain, $\text{Pl}: 2^W \to D_1$ is a plausibility measure, and $u: C \to D_2$ is a utility function. It is occasionally useful to consider *nonplausibilistic decision problems,* where there is no plausibility measure. A nonplausibilistic decision problem is a tuple $DP = (DS, D, u)$ where $DS = (A, W, C)$ is a decision situation and $u: C \to D$ is a utility function.

## 5.4.2   Decision Rules

I have taken utility and probability as primitives in representing a decision problem. But decision theorists are often reluctant to take utility and probability as primitives. Rather, they take as primitive a preference order on acts, since preferences on acts are observable (by observing agents actions), while utilities and probabilities are not. However, when writing software agents that make decisions on behalf of people, it does not seem so unreasonable to somehow endow the software agent with a representation of the tastes of the human for which it is supposed to be acting. Using utilities is one way of doing this. The agent's beliefs can be represented by a probability measure (or perhaps by some other representation of uncertainty). Alternatively, the software agent can then try to learn something about the world by gathering statistics. In any case, the agent then needs a *decision rule* for using the utility and plausibility to choose among acts. Formally, a *(nonplausibilistic) decision rule* $\mathcal{DR}$ is a function mapping (nonplausibilistic) decision problems $DP$ to preference orders on the acts of $DP$. Many decision rules have been studied in the literature.

Perhaps the best-known decision rule is *expected utility maximization*. To explain it, note that corresponding to each act $\mathbf{a}$ there is a random variable $u_{\mathbf{a}}$ on worlds, where $u_{\mathbf{a}}(w) = u(\mathbf{a}(w))$. If $u$ is real-valued and the agent's uncertainty is characterized by the probability measure $\mu$, then $E_\mu(u_{\mathbf{a}})$ is the expected utility of performing act $\mathbf{a}$. The rule of expected utility maximization orders acts according to their expected utility: $\mathbf{a}$ is considered at least as good as $\mathbf{a}'$ if the expected utility of $\mathbf{a}$ is greater than or equal to that of $\mathbf{a}'$.

There have been arguments made that a "rational" agent must be an expected utility maximizer. Perhaps the best-known argument is due to Savage. Savage assumed that an agent starts with a preference order $\preceq_A$ on a rather rich set $A$ of acts: all the simple acts mapping some space $W$ to a set $C$ of consequences. He did *not* assume that the agents have either a probability on $W$ or a utility function associating with each consequence in $C$ its utility. Nevertheless, he showed that if $\preceq_A$ satisfies certain postulates, then the agent is acting as if she has a probability measure $\mu$ on $W$ and a real-valued utility function $u$ on $C$, and is maximizing expected utility; that is, $\mathbf{a} \preceq_A \mathbf{a}'$ iff $E_\mu(u_{\mathbf{a}}) \le E_\mu(u_{\mathbf{a}'})$. Moreover, $\mu$ is uniquely determined by $\preceq_A$ and $u$ is determined up to positive affine transformations. That is, if the same result holds with $u$ replaced by $u'$, then there exist real values $a > 0$ and $b$ such that $u(c) = au'(c) + b$ for all consequences $c$. (This is because $E_\mu(aX + b) = aE_\mu(X) + b$ and $x \le y$ iff $ax + b \le ay + b$.)

Of course, the real question is whether the postulates that Savage assumes for $\preceq_A$ are really ones that the preferences of all rational agents should obey. Not surprisingly, this issue has generated a lot of discussion. (See the notes for references.) Two of the postulates are analogues of RAT2 and RAT3 from Section 2.2.1: $\preceq_A$ is transitive and is total. While it seems reasonable to require that an agent's preferences on acts be transitive, in practice transitivity does not always hold (as was already observed in Section 2.2.1). And it is far from clear that it is "irrational" for an agent not to have a total order on the set of all simple acts. Suppose that $W = \{w_1, w_2, w_3\}$, and consider the following two acts, $\mathbf{a}_1$ and $\mathbf{a}_2$:

- In $w_1$, $\mathbf{a}_1$ has the consequence "live in a little pain for three years"; in $w_2$, $\mathbf{a}_1$ results in "live for four years in moderate pain"; and in $w_3$, $\mathbf{a}_1$ results in "live for two years with moderate pain."

- In $w_1$, $\mathbf{a}_2$ has the consequence "undergo a painful medical operation and live for only one day"; in $w_2$, $\mathbf{a}_2$ results in "undergo a painful operation and live a pain-free life for one year"; and in $w_3$, $\mathbf{a}_2$ results in "undergo a painful operation and live a pain-free life for five years."

These acts seem hard enough to compare. Now consider what happens if the set of worlds is extended slightly, to allow for acts that involve buying stocks. Then the worlds would also include information about whether the stock price goes up or down, and an act that results in gaining $10,000 in one world and losing $25,000 in another would have to be compared to acts involving consequences of operations. These examples all involve a relatively small set of worlds. Imagine how much harder it is to order acts when the set of possible worlds is much larger.

There are techniques for trying to elicit preferences from an agent. Such techniques are quite important in helping people decide whether or not to undergo a risky medical procedure, for example. However, the process of elicitation may itself affect the preferences. In any case, assuming that preferences can be elicited from an agent is not the same as assuming that the agent "has" preferences.

Many experiments in the psychology literature show that people systematically violate Savage's postulates. While this could be simply viewed as showing that people are irrational, other interpretations are certainly possible. A number of decision rules have been proposed as alternatives to expected utility maximization. Some of them try to model more accurately what people do; others are viewed as more normative. Just to give a flavor of the issues involved, I start by considering two well-known decision rules: *maximin* and *minimax regret*.

Maximin orders acts by their worst-case outcomes. Let $worst_u(\mathbf{a}) = \min\{u_\mathbf{a}(w) : w \in W\}$; $worst_u(\mathbf{a})$ is the utility of the worst-case consequence if $\mathbf{a}$ is chosen. Maximin prefers $\mathbf{a}$ to $\mathbf{a}'$ if $worst_u(\mathbf{a}) \geq worst_u(\mathbf{a}')$. Maximin is a "conservative" rule; the "best" act according to maximin is the one with the best worst-case outcome. The disadvantage of maximin is that it prefers an act that is guaranteed to produce a mediocre outcome to one that is virtually certain to produce an excellent outcome but has a very small chance of producing a bad outcome. Of course, "virtually certain" and "very small chance" do not make sense unless there is some way of comparing the likelihood of two sets. Maximin is a nonplausibilistic decision rule; it does not take uncertainty into account at all.

Minimax regret is based on a different philosophy. It tries to hedge an agent's bets, by doing reasonably well no matter what the actual world is. It is also a nonplausibilistic rule. As a first step to defining it, for each world $w$, let $u^*(w)$ be the sup of the outcomes in world $w$; that is, $u^*(w) = \sup_{\mathbf{a} \in A} u_\mathbf{a}(w)$. The *regret* of $\mathbf{a}$ in world $w$, denoted $regret_u(\mathbf{a}, w)$, is $u^*(w) - u_\mathbf{a}(w)$; that is, the regret of $\mathbf{a}$ in $w$ is essentially the difference between the utility of the best possible outcome in $w$ and the utility of performing $\mathbf{a}$ in $w$. Let $regret_u(\mathbf{a}) = \sup_{w \in W} regret_u(\mathbf{a}, w)$ (where $regret_u(\mathbf{a})$ is taken to be $\infty$ if there is no bound on $\{regret_u(\mathbf{a}, w) : w \in W\}$). For example, if $regret_u(\mathbf{a}) = 2$, then in each world $w$, the utility of performing $\mathbf{a}$ in $w$ is guaranteed to be within 2 of the utility of any act the agent could choose, even if she knew that the actual world was $w$. The decision rule of minimax regret orders acts by their regret and thus takes the "best" act to be the one that minimizes the maximum regret. Intuitively, this rule is trying to minimize the regret that an agent would feel if she discovered what the situation actually was: the "I wish I had done $\mathbf{a}'$ instead of $\mathbf{a}$" feeling.

As the following example shows, maximin, minimax regret, and expected utility maximization give very different recommendations in general:

**Example 5.4.1**   Suppose that $W = \{w_1, w_2\}$, $A = \{\mathbf{a}_1, \mathbf{a}_2, \mathbf{a}_3\}$, and $\mu$ is a probability measure on $W$ such that $\mu(w_1) = 1/5$ and $\mu(w_2) = 4/5$. Let the utility function be described by the following table:

|           | $w_1$ | $w_2$ |
|-----------|-------|-------|
| $\mathbf{a}_1$ | 3     | 3     |
| $\mathbf{a}_2$ | −1    | 5     |
| $\mathbf{a}_3$ | 2     | 4     |

Thus, for example, $u(\mathbf{a}_3(w_2)) = 4$. It is easy to check that $E_\mu(u_{\mathbf{a}_1}) = 3$, $E_\mu(u_{\mathbf{a}_2}) = 3.8$, and $E_\mu(u_{\mathbf{a}_3}) = 3.6$, so the expected utility maximization rule recommends $\mathbf{a}_2$. On the other hand, $worst_u(\mathbf{a}_1) = 3$, $worst_u(\mathbf{a}_2) = -1$, and $worst_u(\mathbf{a}_3) = 2$, so the maximin rule recommends $\mathbf{a}_1$. Finally, $regret_u(\mathbf{a}_1) = 2$, $regret_u(\mathbf{a}_2) = 4$, and $regret_u(\mathbf{a}_3) = 1$, so the regret minimization rule recommends $\mathbf{a}_3$.

Intuitively, maximin "worries" about the possibility that the true world may be $w_1$, even if it is not all that likely relative to $w_2$, and tries to protect against the eventuality of $w_1$ occurring. Although, a utility of $-1$ may not be so bad, if all these number are multiplied by 1,000,000—which does not affect the recommendations at all (Exercise 5.35)—it is easy to imagine an executive feeling quite uncomfortable about a loss of \$1,000,000, even if such a loss is relatively unlikely and the gain in $w_2$ is \$5,000,000. (Recall that essentially the same point came up in the discussion of RAT4 in Section 2.2.1.) On the other hand, if $-1$ is replaced by 1.99 in the original table (which can easily be seen not to affect the recommendations), expected utility maximization starts to seem more reasonable.  ∎

Even more decision rules can be generated by using representations of uncertainty other than probability. For example, consider a set $\mathcal{P}$ probability measures. Define $\succeq_{\mathcal{P}}^1$ so that $\mathbf{a} \succeq_{\mathcal{P}}^1 \mathbf{a}'$ iff $\underline{E}_{\mathcal{P}}(u_\mathbf{a}) \geq \underline{E}_{\mathcal{P}}(u_{\mathbf{a}'})$. This can be seen to some extent as a maximin rule; the best act(s) according to $\succeq_{\mathcal{P}}^1$ are those whose worst-case expectation (according to the probability measures in $\mathcal{P}$) are best. Indeed, if $\mathcal{P}_W$ consists of all probability measures on $W$, then it is easy to show that $\underline{E}_{\mathcal{P}_W}(u_\mathbf{a}) = worst_u(\mathbf{a})$; it thus follows that $\succeq_{\mathcal{P}_W}^1$ defines the same order on acts as maximin (Exercise 5.36). Thus, $\succeq_{\mathcal{P}}^1$ can be viewed as a generalization of maximin. If there is no information at all about the probability measure, then the two orders agree. However, $\succeq_{\mathcal{P}}^1$ can take advantage of partial information about the probability measure. Of course, if there is complete information about the probability measure (i.e., $\mathcal{P}$ is a singleton), then $\succeq_{\mathcal{P}}^1$ just reduces to the ordering provided by maximizing expected utility. It is also worth recalling that, as observed in Section 5.3, the ordering on acts induced by $E_{\mathrm{Bel}}$ for a belief function Bel is the same as that given by $\succeq_{\mathcal{P}_{\mathrm{Bel}}}^1$.

Other orders using $\mathcal{P}$ can be defined in a similar way:

- $\mathbf{a} \succeq_{\mathcal{P}}^2 \mathbf{a}'$ iff $\overline{E}_{\mathcal{P}}(u_\mathbf{a}) \geq \overline{E}_{\mathcal{P}}(u_{\mathbf{a}'})$;

- $\mathbf{a} \succeq_{\mathcal{P}}^3 \mathbf{a}'$ iff $\underline{E}_{\mathcal{P}}(u_\mathbf{a}) \geq \overline{E}_{\mathcal{P}}(u_{\mathbf{a}'})$;

- $\mathbf{a} \succeq_{\mathcal{P}}^4 \mathbf{a}'$ iff $E_{\mathrm{Pl}_{\mathcal{P}}}(\mathbf{a}) \geq E_{\mathrm{Pl}_{\mathcal{P}}}(\mathbf{a}')$.

The order on acts induced by $\succeq_{\mathcal{P}}^3$ is very conservative; $\mathbf{a} \succeq_{\mathcal{P}}^3 \mathbf{a}'$ iff the best expected outcome according to $\mathbf{a}$ is no better than the worst expected outcome according to $\mathbf{a}'$. The order induced by $\succeq_{\mathcal{P}}^4$ is more refined. Clearly $E_{\mathrm{Pl}_{\mathcal{P}}}(u_\mathbf{a}) \geq E_{\mathrm{Pl}_{\mathcal{P}}}(u_{\mathbf{a}'})$ iff $E_\mu(u_\mathbf{a}) \geq E_\mu(u_{\mathbf{a}'})$ for all $\mu \in \mathcal{P}$. It easily follows that if $\mathbf{a} \succeq_{\mathcal{P}}^3 \mathbf{a}'$, then $\mathbf{a} \succeq_{\mathcal{P}}^4 \mathbf{a}'$ (Exercise 5.37). The converse may not hold. For example, suppose that $\mathcal{P} = \{\mu, \mu'\}$, and acts **a** and **a'** are such that $E_\mu(u_\mathbf{a}) = 2$, $E_{\mu'}(u_\mathbf{a}) = 4$, $E_\mu(u_{\mathbf{a'}}) = 1$, and $E_{\mu'}(u_{\mathbf{a'}}) = 3$. Then $\underline{E}_\mathcal{P}(u_\mathbf{a}) = 2$, $\overline{E}_\mathcal{P}(u_\mathbf{a}) = 4$, $\underline{E}_\mathcal{P}(u_{\mathbf{a'}}) = 1$, and $\overline{E}_\mathcal{P}(u_{\mathbf{a'}}) = 3$, so **a** and **a'** are incomparable according to $\succeq_\mathcal{P}^3$, yet **a** $\succeq_\mathcal{P}^4$ **a'**.

Given this plethora of decision rules, it would be useful to have one common framework in which to make sense of them all. The machinery of expectation domains developed in the previous section helps.

### 5.4.3   Generalized Expected Utility

There is a sense in which all of the decision rules mentioned in Section 5.4.2 can be viewed as instances of generalized expected utility maximization, that is, utility maximization with respect to plausibilistic expectation, defined using (5.14) for some appropriate choice of expectation domain. The goal of this section is to investigate this claim in more depth.

Let GEU (*generalized expected utility*) be the decision rule that uses (5.14). That is, if $DP = (DS, ED, \text{Pl}, u)$, then GEU(*DP*) is the preference order $\preceq$ such that **a** $\preceq$ **a'** iff $E_{\text{Pl},ED}(u_\mathbf{a}) \leq E_{\text{Pl},ED}(u_{\mathbf{a'}})$. The following result shows that GEU can represent any preference order on acts:

**Theorem 5.4.2** *Given a decision situation $DS = (A, W, C)$ and a partial preorder $\preceq_A$ on A, there exists an expectation domain $ED = (D_1, D_2, D_3, \oplus, \otimes)$, a plausibility measure $\text{Pl} : W \to D_1$, and a utility function $u : C \to D_2$ such that GEU(DP) = $\preceq_A$, where $DP = (DS, ED, \text{Pl}, u)$ (i.e., $E_{\text{Pl},ED}(u_\mathbf{a}) \leq E_{\text{Pl},ED}(u_{\mathbf{a'}})$ iff **a** $\preceq_A$ **a'**).*

**Proof**   See Exercise 5.38.  ∎

Theorem 5.4.2 can be viewed as a generalization of Savage's result. It says that, whatever the agent's preference order on acts, the agent can be viewed as maximizing expected plausibilistic utility with respect to some plausibility measure and utility function. Unlike Savage's result, the plausibility measure and utility function are not unique in any sense.

The key idea in the proof of Theorem 5.4.2 is to construct $D_3$ so that its elements are expected utility expressions. The order $\leq_3$ on $D_3$ then mirrors the preference order $\preceq_A$ on $A$. This flexibility in defining the order somewhat undercuts the interest in Theorem 5.4.2. However, just as in the case of plausibility measures, this flexibility has some advantages. In particular, it makes it possible to understand exactly which properties of the plausibility measure and the expectation domain (in particular, $\oplus$ and

$\otimes$) are needed to capture various properties of preferences, such as those characterized by Savage's postulates. Doing this is beyond the scope of the book (but see the notes for references). Instead, I now show that GEU is actually a stronger representation tool than this theorem indicates. It turns out that GEU can represent not just orders on actions, but the decision process itself.

Theorem 5.4.2 shows that for any preference order $\preceq_A$ on the acts of $A$, there is a decision problem $DP$ whose set of acts is $A$ such that $\text{GEU}(DP) = \preceq_A$. What I want to show is that, given a decision rule $\mathcal{DR}$, GEU can represent $\mathcal{DR}$ in the sense that there exists an expectation domain (in particular, a choice of $\oplus$ and $\otimes$) such that $\text{GEU}(DP) = \mathcal{DR}(DP)$ for all decision problems $DP$. Thus, the preference order on acts given by $\mathcal{DR}$ is the same as that derived from GEU.

The actual definition of representation is a little more refined, since I want to be able to talk about a plausibilistic decision rule (like maximizing expected utility) representing a nonplausibilistic decision rule (like maximin). To make this precise, a few definitions are needed.

Two decision problems are *congruent* if they agree on the tastes and (if they are both plausibilistic decision problems) the beliefs of the agent. Formally, $DP_1$ and $DP_2$ are *congruent* if they involve the same decision situation, the same utility function, and (where applicable) the same plausibility measure. Note, in particular, that if $DP_1$ and $DP_2$ are both nonplausibilistic decision problems, then they are congruent iff they are identical. However, if they are both plausibilistic, it is possible that they use different notions of $\oplus$ and $\otimes$ in their expectation domains.

A *decision-problem transformation* $\tau$ maps decision problems to decision problems. Given two decision rules $\mathcal{DR}_1$ and $\mathcal{DR}_2$, $\mathcal{DR}_1$ *represents* $\mathcal{DR}_2$ iff there exists a decision-problem transformation $\tau$ such that, for all decision problems $DP$ in the domain of $\mathcal{DR}_2$, the decision problem $\tau(DP)$ is in the domain of $\mathcal{DR}_1$, $\tau(DP)$ is congruent to $DP$, and $\mathcal{DR}_1(\tau(DP)) = \mathcal{DR}_2(DP)$. Intuitively, this says that $\mathcal{DR}_1$ and $\mathcal{DR}_2$ order acts the same way on corresponding decision problems.

I now show that GEU can represent a number of decision rules. Consider maximin with real-valued utilities (i.e., where the domain of maximin consists of all decision problems where the utility is real-valued). Let $ED_{\max} = (\mathbb{R}, \{0, 1\}, \mathbb{R}, \min, \times)$, and let $\text{Pl}_{\max}$ be the plausibility measure such that $\text{Pl}_{\max}(U)$ is 0 if $X = \emptyset$ and 1 otherwise. For the decision problem described in Example 5.4.1,

$$E_{\text{Pl}_{\max}, ED_{\max}}(u_{a_1}) EW = \min(3 \times 1, 3 \times 1) = 3,$$

$$E_{\text{Pl}_{\max}, ED_{\max}}(u_{a_2}) = \min(-1 \times 1, 5 \times 1) = -1, \text{ and}$$

$$E_{\text{Pl}_{\max}, ED_{\max}}(u_{a_3}) = \min(2 \times 1, 4 \times 1) = 2.$$

Note that $E_{Pl_{max}, ED_{max}}(u_{\mathbf{a}}) = worst_u(\mathbf{a}_i)$, for $i = 1, 2, 3$. Of course, this is not a fluke. If $DP = (DS, \mathbb{R}, u)$, where $DS = (A, W, C)$, then it is easy to check that $E_{Pl_{max}, ED_{max}}(u_{\mathbf{a}}) = worst_u(\mathbf{a})$ for all actions $\mathbf{a} \in A$ (Exercise 5.39).

Take $\tau(DP) = (DS, ED_{max}, Pl_{max}, u)$. Clearly $DP$ and $\tau(DP)$ are congruent; the agent's tastes have not changed. Moreover, it is immediate that $GEU(\tau(DP)) = $ maximin$(DP)$. Thus, GEU represents maximin. (Although maximin is typically considered only for real-valued utility functions, it actually makes perfect sense as long as utilities are totally ordered. GEU also represents this "generalized" maximin, using essentially the same transformation $\tau$; see Exercise 5.40.)

Next, I show that GEU can represent minimax regret. For ease of exposition, I consider only decision problems $DP = ((A, W, C), \mathbb{R}, u)$ with real-valued utilities such that $M_{DP} = \sup\{u^*(w) : w \in W\} < \infty$. (If $M_{DP} = \infty$, given the restriction to simple acts, then it is not hard to show that every act has infinite regret; see Exercise 5.41.) Let $ED_{reg} = ([0, 1], \mathbb{R}, \mathbb{R}, \min, \otimes)$, where $x \otimes y = y - \log(x)$ if $x > 0$, and $x \otimes y = 0$ if $x = 0$. Note that $\bot = 0$ and $\top = 1$. Clearly, min is associative and commutative, and $\top \otimes r = r - \log(1) = r$ for all $r \in \mathbb{R}$. Thus, $ED_{reg}$ is an expectation domain.

For $\emptyset \neq U \subseteq W$, define $M_U = \sup\{u^*(w) : w \in U\}$. Note that $M_{DP} = M_W$. Since, by assumption, $M_{DP} < \infty$, it follows that $M_U < \infty$ for all $U \subseteq W$. Let $Pl_{DP}$ be the plausibility measure such that $Pl_{DP}(\emptyset) = 0$ and $Pl_M(U) = e^{M_U - M_{DP}}$ for $U \neq \emptyset$.

For the decision problem described in Example 5.4.1, $M_{DP} = 5$. An easy computation shows that, for example,

$$E_{Pl_{DP}, ED_{reg}}(u_{\mathbf{a}_3}) = \min(2 - (3 - 5), 4 - (5 - 5)) = 4 = 5 - regret_u(\mathbf{a}_3).$$

Similar computations show that $E_{Pl_{DP}, ED_{reg}}(u_{\mathbf{a}_i}) = 5 - regret_u(\mathbf{a}_i)$ for $i = 1, 2, 3$. More generally, it is easy to show that

$$E_{Pl_{DP}, ED_{reg}}(u_{\mathbf{a}}) = M_{DP} - regret_u(\mathbf{a})$$

for all acts $\mathbf{a} \in A$ (Exercise 5.42). Let $\tau$ be the decision-problem transformation such that $\tau(DP) = (DS, ED_{reg}, Pl_{DP}, u)$. Clearly, higher expected utility corresponds to lower regret, so $GEU(\tau(DP)) = $ regret$(DP)$.

Note that, unlike maximin, the plausibility measure in the transformation from $DP$ to $\tau(DP)$ for minimax regret depends on $DP$ (more precisely, it depends on $M_{DP}$). This is unavoidable; see the notes for some discussion.

Finally, given a set $\mathcal{P}$ of probability measures, consider the decision rules induced by $\succeq_{\mathcal{P}}^1$, $\succeq_{\mathcal{P}}^2$, $\succeq_{\mathcal{P}}^3$, and $\succeq_{\mathcal{P}}^4$, (Formally, these rules take as inputs plausibilistic decision problems where the plausibility measure is $Pl_{\mathcal{P}}$.) Proposition 5.4.3 shows that all these rules can be represented by GEU.

The following proposition summarizes the situation:

**Proposition 5.4.3** GEU *represents maximin, minimax regret, and the decision rules induced by* $\succeq_{\mathcal{P}}^1$, $\succeq_{\mathcal{P}}^2$, $\succeq_{\mathcal{P}}^3$, *and* $\succeq_{\mathcal{P}}^4$.

Conspicuously absent from the list in Proposition 5.4.3 is the decision rule determined by expected belief (i.e., $\mathbf{a}_1 \succeq \mathbf{a}_2$ iff $E_{Bel}(u_{\mathbf{a}_1}) \geq E_{Bel}(u_{\mathbf{a}_2})$. In fact, this rule cannot be represented by GEU. To understand why, I give a complete characterization of the rules that can be represented.

There is a trivial condition that a decision rule must satisfy in order to be represented by GEU. Say that a decision rule $\mathcal{DR}$ *respects utility* if the preference order on acts induced by $\mathcal{DR}$ agrees with the utility ordering. More precisely, $\mathcal{DR}$ respects utility if, given as input a decision problem $DP$ with utility function $u$, if two acts $\mathbf{a}_1$ and $\mathbf{a}_2$ in $DP$ induce constant utilities $d_1$ and $d_2$ (i.e., if $u_{\mathbf{a}_i}(w) = d_i$ for all $w \in W$, for $i = 1, 2$), then $d_1 \leq d_2$ iff $\mathbf{a}_1 \preceq_{\mathcal{DR}(DP)} \mathbf{a}_2$. It is easy to see that all the decision rules I have considered respect utility. In particular, it is easy to see that GEU respects utility, since the expected utility of the constant act with utility $d$ is just $d$. (This depends on the assumption that $\top \otimes d = d$.) Thus, GEU cannot possibly represent a decision rule that does not respect utility. (Note that there is no requirement of respecting utility in Theorem 5.4.2, nor does there have to be. Theorem 5.4.2 starts with a preference order, so there is no utility function in the picture. Here, I am starting with a decision rule, so it makes sense to require that it respect utility.)

While respecting utility is a necessary condition for a decision rule to be representable by GEU, it is not sufficient. It is also necessary for the decision rule to treat acts that behave in similar ways similarly. Given a decision problem $DP$, two acts $\mathbf{a}_1, \mathbf{a}_2$ in $DP$ are *indistinguishable*, denoted $\mathbf{a}_1 \sim_{DP} \mathbf{a}_2$ iff either

- $DP$ is nonplausibilistic and $u_{\mathbf{a}_1} = u_{\mathbf{a}_2}$, or

- $DP$ is plausibilistic, $\mathcal{V}(u_{\mathbf{a}_1}) = \mathcal{V}(u_{\mathbf{a}_2})$, and $Pl(u_{\mathbf{a}_1}^{-1}(d)) = Pl(u_{\mathbf{a}_2}^{-1}(d))$ for all utilities $d$ in the common range of $u_{\mathbf{a}_1}$ and $u_{\mathbf{a}_2}$, where $Pl$ is the plausibility measure in $DP$.

In the nonplausibilistic case, two acts are indistinguishable if they induce the same utility random variable; in the nonplausibilistic case, they are indistinguishable if they induce the same plausibilistic "utility lottery."

A decision rule is uniform if it respects indistinguishability. More formally, a decision rule $\mathcal{DR}$ is *uniform* iff, for all $DP$ in the domain of $\mathcal{DR}$ and all $\mathbf{a}_1, \mathbf{a}_2, \mathbf{a}_3$

in $DP$, if $\mathbf{a}_1 \sim_{DP} \mathbf{a}_2$ then

$$\mathbf{a}_1 \leq_{\mathcal{DR}(DP)} \mathbf{a}_3 \text{ iff } \mathbf{a}_2 \leq_{\mathcal{DR}(DP)} \mathbf{a}_3 \text{ and } \mathbf{a}_3 \leq_{\mathcal{DR}(DP)} \mathbf{a}_1 \text{ iff } \mathbf{a}_3 \leq_{\mathcal{DR}(DP)} \mathbf{a}_2.$$

Clearly GEU is uniform, so a decision rule that is not uniform cannot be represented by GEU. However, as the following result shows, this is the only condition other than respecting utility that a decision rule must satisfy in order to be represented by GEU:

**Theorem 5.4.4**  *If $\mathcal{DR}$ is a decision rule that respects utility, then $\mathcal{DR}$ is uniform iff $\mathcal{DR}$ can be represented by GEU.*

**Proof**   See Exercise 5.43. ∎

Most of the decision rules I have discussed are uniform. However, the decision rule induced by expected belief is not, as the following example shows:

**Example 5.4.5**   Consider the decision problem $DP = ((A, W, C), \overline{\mathbb{R}}, \text{Bel}, u)$, where

- $A = \{\mathbf{a}_1, \mathbf{a}_2\}$;
- $W = \{w_1, w_2, w_3\}$;
- $C = \{1, 2, 3\}$;
- $u(j) = j$, for $j = 1, 2, 3$;
- $\mathbf{a}_1(w_j) = j$ and $\mathbf{a}_2(w_j) = 3 - j$, for $j = 1, 2, 3$; and
- Bel is the belief function such that $\text{Bel}(\{w_1, w_2\}) = \text{Bel}(W) = 1$, and $\text{Bel}(U) = 0$ if $U$ is not a superset of $\{w_1, w_2\}$.

Clearly $\mathbf{a}_1 \sim_{DP} \mathbf{a}_2$, since $u_{\mathbf{a}_i}^{-1}(j)$ is a singleton, so $\text{Bel}(u_{\mathbf{a}_i}^{-1}(j)) = 0$ for $i = 1, 2$ and $j = 1, 2, 3$. On the other hand, by definition,

$$E_{\text{Bel}}(u_{\mathbf{a}_1}) = 1 + (2 - 1)\,\text{Bel}(\{w_2, w_3\}) + (3 - 2)\,\text{Bel}(\{w_3\}) = 1,$$

while

$$E_{\text{Bel}}(u_{\mathbf{a}_2}) = 1 + (2 - 1)\,\text{Bel}(\{w_1, w_2\}) + (3 - 2)\,\text{Bel}(\{w_1\}) = 2.$$

It follows that the decision rule that orders acts based on their expected belief is not uniform, and so cannot be represented by GEU. ∎

The alert reader may have noticed an incongruity here. By Theorem 2.4.1, $\text{Bel} = (\mathcal{P}_{\text{Bel}})_*$ and, by definition, $E_{\text{Bel}} = \underline{E}_{\mathcal{P}_{\text{Bel}}}$. Moreover, the preference order $\succeq_{\mathcal{P}}^1$ induced by

$\underline{E}_{\mathcal{P}_{Bel}}$ *can* be represented by GEU. There is no contradiction to Theorem 5.4.4 here. If $\mathcal{DR}_{BEL}$ is the decision rule induced by expected belief and *DP* is the decision problem in Example 5.4.5, then there is no decision problem $\tau(DP) = (DS, ED', Bel, u)$ such that $\text{GEU}(\tau(DP)) = \mathcal{DR}_{BEL}(DP)$. Nevertheless, $\text{GEU}((A, W, C), ED_{D_{\mathcal{P}}}, \text{Pl}_{\mathcal{P}_{Bel}}, u) = \mathcal{DR}_{BEL}(DP)$. (Recall that $ED_{D_{\mathcal{P}}}$ is defined at the end of Section 5.4.2.) $(A, W, C)$, $ED_{D_{\mathcal{P}}}$, $\text{Pl}_{\mathcal{P}_{Bel}}, u)$ and *DP* are not congruent; $\text{Pl}_{\mathcal{P}_{Bel}}$ and Bel are *not* identical representations of the agent's beliefs. They are related, of course. It is not hard to show that if $\text{Pl}_{\mathcal{P}_{Bel}}(U) \leq \text{Pl}_{\mathcal{P}_{Bel}}(V)$, then $\text{Bel}(U) \leq \text{Bel}(V)$, although the converse does not hold in general (Exercise 5.44).

For a decision rule $\mathcal{DR}_1$ to represent a decision rule $\mathcal{DR}_2$, there must be a decision-problem transformation $\tau$ such that $\tau(DP)$ and *DP* are congruent and $\mathcal{DR}_1(\tau(DP)) = \mathcal{DR}_2(DP)$ for every decision problem *DP* in the domain of $\mathcal{DR}_2$. Since $\tau(DP)$ and *DP* are congruent, they agree on the tastes and (if they are both plausibilistic) the beliefs of the agent. I now want to weaken this requirement somewhat, and consider transformations that preserve an important aspect of an agent's tastes and beliefs, while not requiring them to stay the same.

There is a long-standing debate in the decision-theory literature as to whether preferences should be taken to be *ordinal* or *cardinal*. If they are ordinal, then all that matters is their order. If they are cardinal, then it should be meaningful to talk about the *differences* between preferences, that is, how much more an agent prefers one outcome to another. Similarly, if expressions of likelihood are taken to be ordinal, then all that matters is whether one event is more likely than another.

Two utility functions $u_1$ and $u_2$ *represent the same ordinal tastes* if they are defined on the same set *C* of consequences and for all $c_1, c_2 \in C, u_1(c_1) \leq u_1(c_2)$ iff $u_2(c_1) \leq u_2(c_2)$. Similarly, two plausibility measures $\text{Pl}_1$ and $\text{Pl}_2$ *represent the same ordinal beliefs* if $\text{Pl}_1$ and $\text{Pl}_2$ are defined on the same domain *W* and $\text{Pl}_1(U) \leq \text{Pl}_1(V)$ iff $\text{Pl}_2(U) \leq \text{Pl}_2(V)$ for all $U, V \subseteq W$. Finally, two decision problems $DP_1$ and $DP_2$ are *similar* iff they involve the same decision situations, their utility functions represent the same ordinal tastes, and their plausibility measures represent the same ordinal beliefs. Note that two congruent decision problems are similar, but the converse may not be true.

Decision rule $\mathcal{DR}_1$ *ordinally represents* decision rule $\mathcal{DR}_2$ iff there exists a decision-problem transformation $\tau$ such that, for all decision problems *DP* in the domain of $\mathcal{DR}_2$, the decision problem $\tau(DP)$ is in the domain of $\mathcal{DR}_1$, *DP* is similar to $\tau(DP)$, and $\mathcal{DR}_1(\tau(DP)) = \mathcal{DR}_2(DP)$. Thus, the definition of emulation is just like that of representation, except that $\tau(DP)$ is now required only to be similar to *DP*, not congruent.

I now want to show that GEU can ordinally represent essentially all decision rules. Doing so involves one more subtlety. Up to now, I have assumed that the range of a plausibility measure is partially ordered. To get the result, I need to allow it to be partially *preordered*. That allows two sets that have equivalent plausibility to act differently when combined using $\oplus$ and $\otimes$ in the computation of expected utility. So, for this result, I assume that the relation $\leq$ on the range of a plausibility measure is reflexive and transitive, but not necessarily antisymmetric. With this assumption, GEU ordinally represents $\mathcal{DR}_{\mathrm{BEL}}$ (Exericse 5.45). In fact, an even more general result holds.

**Theorem 5.4.6** *If* $\mathcal{DR}$ *is a decision rule that respects utility, then* GEU *ordinally represents* $\mathcal{DR}$.

**Proof** See Exercise 5.46. ∎

Theorem 5.4.6 shows that GEU ordinally represents essentially all decision rules. Thus, there is a sense in which GEU can be viewed as a universal decision rule.

Thinking of decision rules as instances of expected utility maximization gives a new perspective on them. The relationship between various properties of an expectation domain and properties of decision rules can then be studied. To date, there has been no work on this topic, but it seems like a promising line of inquiry.

## 5.5　Conditional Expectation

Just as it makes sense to update beliefs in light of new information, it makes sense to update expectations in light of new information. In the case of probability, there is an obvious definition of expectation on $U$ if $\mu(U) > 0$:

$$E_\mu(X \mid U) = E_{\mu|U}(X).$$

That is, to update the expected value of $X$ with respect to $\mu$ given the new information $U$, just compute the expected value of $X$ with respect to $\mu|U$.

It is easy to check that $E_\mu(X_V \mid U) = \mu(V \mid U)$ (Exercise 5.47), so conditional expectation with respect to a probability measure can be viewed as a generalization of conditional probability.

For sets of probability measures, the obvious definition of conditional lower expectation is just

$$\underline{E}_{\mathcal{P}}(X \mid U) = \underline{E}_{\mathcal{P}|U}(X) = \inf\{\underline{E}_\mu(X \mid U) : \mu \in \mathcal{P}, \ \mu(U) > 0\},$$

where $\underline{E}_{\mathcal{P}}(X \mid U)$ is undefined if $\mathcal{P}|U$ is, that is, if $\mathcal{P}^*(U) = 0$ (i.e., if $\mu(U) = 0$ for all $\mu \in \mathcal{P}$). An analogous definition applies to upper expectation.

By identifying $E_{Bel}$ with $\underline{E}_{\mathcal{P}_{Bel}}$, this approach immediately gives a definition of $E_{Bel}(\cdot | U)$. Moreover, it is easy to check that $E_{Bel}(X | U) = E_{Bel | U}(X)$ (Exercise 5.48).

These examples suggest an obvious definition for conditional expectation with respect to an arbitrary plausibility measure. Given a cps $(W, \mathcal{F}, \mathcal{F}', Pl)$ and an expectation domain $ED$, define $E_{Pl,ED}(X | U) = E_{Pl | U, ED}(X)$ for $U \in \mathcal{F}'$.

There is another approach to defining conditional expectation, which takes as its point of departure the following characterization of conditional expectation in the case of probability:

**Lemma 5.5.1** *If $\mu(U) > 0$, then $E_\mu(X | U) = \alpha$ iff $E_\mu(X \times X_U - \alpha X_U) = 0$ (where $X \times X_U - \alpha X_U$ is the gamble $Y$ such that $Y(w) = X(w) \times X_U(w) - \alpha X_U(w)$).*

**Proof** See Exercise 5.50. ∎

Lemma 5.5.1 says that conditional expectation can be viewed as satisfying a generalization of Bayes' Rule. In the special case that $X = X_V$, using the fact that $X_V \times X_U = X_{U \cap V}$ and $E_\mu(X_V | U) = \mu(V | U)$, as well as the linearity of expectation, Lemma 5.5.1 says that $E_\mu(X_{U \cap V}) = \alpha E(X_U)$, that is, $\mu(U \cap V) = \mu(V | U) \times \mu(U)$, so this really is a generalization of Bayes' Rule.

A characterization similar to that of Lemma 5.5.1 also holds in the case of sets of probability measures.

**Lemma 5.5.2** *If $\mathcal{P}^*(U) > 0$, then $\underline{E}_\mathcal{P}(X | U) = \alpha$ iff $\underline{E}_\mathcal{P}(X \times X_U - \alpha X_U) = 0$.*

**Proof** See Exercise 5.51. ∎

Analogues of this characterization of conditional expected utility for other notions of expectation have not been considered; it may be interesting to do so.

## Exercises

**5.1**    Show that the two definitions of expectation for probability measures, (5.1) and (5.2), coincide if all sets are measurable.

**5.2**    Prove (5.3) (under the assumption that $X = x_i$ is measurable for $i = 1, \ldots, n$).

**5.3**    Prove that

$$E_\mu(X) = x_n + \sum_{i=1}^{n-1} \mu(X \le x_i)(x_i - x_{i+1})$$

and that

$$E_{\mu}(X) = x_n - \sum_{i=1}^{n-1} \mu(X \le x_i)(x_{i+1} - x_i). \tag{5.15}$$

**5.4**    Prove Proposition 5.1.1.

\***5.5**    Show that $E$ is (a) additive, (b) affinely homogeneous, and (c) monotone iff $E$ is (a') additive, (b') positive (in the sense that if $X \ge 0$ then $E(X) \ge 0$), and (c') $E(\tilde{1}) = 1$. Thus, in light of Proposition 5.1.1, (a'), (b'), and (c') together give an alternate characterization of $E_{\mu}$.

\***5.6**    Show that if $\mu$ is a countably additive probability measure, then (5.4) holds. Moreover, show that if $E$ maps gambles that are measurable with respect to a $\sigma$-algebra $\mathcal{F}$ to $\mathbb{R}$, and $E$ is additive, affinely homogeneous, and monotone and satisfies (5.4), then $E = E_{\mu}$ for a unique countably additive probability measure $\mu$ on $\mathcal{F}$.

\***5.7**    Up to now I have focused on finite sets of worlds. This means that expectation can be expressed as a finite sum. With infinitely many worlds, new subtleties arise because infinite sums are involved. As long as the random variable is always positive, the problems are minor (although it is possible that the expected value of the variable may be infinite). If the random variable is negative on some worlds, then the expectation may not be well defined. This is a well-known problem when dealing with infinite sums, and has nothing to do with expectation per se. For example, consider the finite sum $1 - 1 + 1 - 1 + \cdots$. If this is grouped as $(1 - 1) + (1 - 1) + \cdots$, then the sum is 0. However, if it is grouped as $1 - (1 - 1) - (1 - 1) + \cdots$, then the sum is 1. Having negative numbers in the sum does not always cause problems, but, when it does, the infinite sum is taken to be undefined.

To see how this issue can affect expectation, consider the following *two-envelope* puzzle. Suppose that there are two envelopes, $A$ and $B$. You are told that one envelope has twice as much money as the other and that you can keep whatever amount is in the envelope you choose. You choose envelope $A$. Before opening it, you are asked if you want to switch to envelope $B$ and take the money in envelope $B$ instead. You reason as follows. Suppose that envelope $A$ has \$$n$. Then with probability 1/2, envelope $B$ has $2n$, and with probability 1/2, envelope $B$ has \$$n/2$. Clearly you will gain \$$n$ if you stick with envelope $A$. If you choose envelope $B$, with probability 1/2, you will get \$$2n$, and with probability 1/2, you will get \$$n/2$. Thus, your expected gain is \$$(n + n/4)$, which is clearly greater than \$$n$. Thus, it seems that if your goal is to maximize your expected gain, you should switch. But a symmetric argument shows that if you had originally chosen envelope $B$ and were offered a chance to switch, then you should also do so.

That seems very strange. No matter what envelope you choose, you want to switch! To make matters even worse, there is yet another argument showing that you should *not* switch. Suppose that envelope $B$ has $\$n$. Then, $A$ has either $\$2n$ or $\$n/2$, each with probability $1/2$. With this representation, the expected gain of switching is $\$n$ and the expected gain of sticking with $A$ is $\$5n/4$.

The two-envelope puzzle, while on the surface quite similar to the Monty Hall problem discussed in Chapter 1 (which will be analyzed formally in Chapter 6), is actually quite different. The first step in a more careful analysis is to construct a formal model. One thing that is missing in this story is the prior probability. For definiteness, suppose that there are infinitely many slips of paper, $p_0, p_1, p_2, \ldots$. On slip $p_i$ is written the pair of numbers $(2^i, 2^{i+1})$ (so that $p_0$ has $(1,2)$, $p_1$ has $(2,4)$, etc.). Then $p_i$ is chosen with probability $\alpha_i$ and the slip is cut in half; one number is put in envelope $A$, the other in envelope $B$, with equal probability. Clearly at this point—whatever the choice of $\alpha_i$— the probabilities match those in the story. It really is true that one envelope has twice as much as the other. However, the earlier analysis does not apply. Suppose that you open envelope $A$ and find a slip of paper saying $\$32$. Certainly envelope $B$ has either $\$16$ or $\$64$, but are both of these possibilities equally likely?

(a) Show that it is equally likely that envelope $B$ has $\$16$ or $\$64$, given that envelope $A$ has $\$32$, if and only if $\alpha_4 = \alpha_5$.

(b) Similarly, show that, if envelope $A$ contains $2^k$ for some $k \geq 1$, then envelope is equally likely to contain $2^{k-1}$ and $2^{k+1}$ iff $\alpha_{k-1} = \alpha_k$. (Of course, if envelope $A$ has $\$1$, then envelope $B$ must have $\$2$.)

It must be the case that $\sum_{i=0}^{\infty} \alpha_i = 1$ (since, with probability 1, some slip is chosen). It follows that the $\alpha_i$s cannot all be equal. Nevertheless, there is still a great deal of scope in choosing them. The problem becomes most interesting if $\alpha_{i+1}/\alpha_i > 1/2$. For definiteness, suppose that $\alpha_i = 1/3(2/3)^i$. This means $\alpha_{i+1}/\alpha_i = 2/3$.

(c) Show that $\sum_{i=0}^{\infty} \alpha_i = 1$, so this is a legitimate choice of probabilities.

(d) Describe carefully a set of possible worlds and a probability measure $\mu$ on them that corresponds to this instance of the story.

(e) Show that, for this choice of probability measure $\mu$, if $k \geq 2$, then

$$\mu(B \text{ has } 2^{i+1} \mid A \text{ has } 2^i) = 2/5 \text{ and } \mu(B \text{ has } 2^{i-1} \mid A \text{ has } 2^i) = 3/5.$$

(f) Show that, as a consequence, no matter what envelope $A$ has, the expected gain of switching is greater than 0. (A similar argument shows that, no matter what envelope $B$ has, the expected gain of switching is greater.)

This seems paradoxical. If you choose envelope $A$, no matter what you see, you want to switch. This seems to suggest that, even without looking at the envelopes, if you choose envelope $A$, you want to have envelope $B$. Similarly, if you choose envelope $B$, you want to have envelope $A$. But that seems absurd. Clearly, your expected winnings with both $A$ and $B$ are the same. Indeed, suppose the game were played over and over again. Consider one person who always chose $A$ and kept it, compared to another who always chose $A$ and then switched to $B$. Shouldn't they expect to win the same amount? The next part of the exercise examines this a little more carefully.

(g) Suppose that you are given envelope $A$ and have two choices. You can either keep envelope $A$ (and get whatever amount is on the slip in envelope $A$) or switch to envelope $B$ (and get whatever amount is on the slip in envelope $B$). Compute the expected winnings of each of the two choices. That is, if $X_{keep}$ is the random variable that describes the amount you gain if you keep envelope $A$ and $X_{switch}$ is the random variable that describes the amount you win if you switch to envelope $B$, compute $E_\mu(X_{keep})$ and $E_\mu(X_{switch})$.

(h) What is $E_\mu(X_{switch} - X_{keep})$?

If you did part (h) right, you should see that $E_\mu(X_{switch} - X_{keep})$ is undefined. There are two ways of grouping the infinite sum that give different answers. In fact, one way gives an answer of 0 (corresponding to the intuition that it doesn't matter whether you keep $A$ or switch to $B$; either way your expected winnings are the same) while another gives a positive answer (corresponding to the intuition that you're always better off switching). Part (g) helps explain the paradox. Your expected winnings are infinite either way (and, when dealing with infinite sums, $\infty + a = \infty$ for any finite $a$).

**5.8**    Prove Proposition 5.2.1. Show that the restriction to *positive* affine homogeneity is necessary; in general, $\underline{E}_\mu(aX) \neq a\underline{E}_\mu(X)$ and $\overline{E}_\mu(aX) \neq a\overline{E}_\mu(X)$ if $a < 0$.

**\* 5.9**    Show that a function mapping gambles to $\mathbb{R}$ is superadditive, positively affinely homogeneous, and monotone iff $E$ is superadditive, $E(cX) = cE(X)$, and $E(X) \geq \inf\{X(w) : w \in W\}$. In light of Theorem 5.2.2, the latter three properties provide an alternate characterization of $\leq_{\mathcal{P}}$.

**5.10**    Show that if the smallest closed convex set of probability measures containing $\mathcal{P}$ and $\mathcal{P}'$ is the same, then $\underline{E}_{\mathcal{P}} = \underline{E}_{\mathcal{P}'}$. (The notes to Chapters 2 and 3 have the definitions of convex and closed, respectively.) It follows, for example, that if $W = \{0, 1\}$ and $\mu_\alpha$ is the probability measure on $W$ such that $\mu(0) = \alpha$, $\mathcal{P} = \{\mu_{\alpha_0}, \mu_{\alpha_1}\}$, and $\mathcal{P}' = \{\mu_\alpha : \alpha_0 \leq \alpha \leq \alpha_1\}$, then $\leq_{\mathcal{P}} = \leq_{\mathcal{P}'}$.

**5.11** Some of the properties in Proposition 5.2.1 follow from others. Show in particular that all the properties of $\overline{E}_\mathcal{P}$ given in parts (a)–(c) of Lemma 5.2.1 follow from the corresponding property of $\underline{E}_\mathcal{P}$ and part (d) (i.e., the fact that $\overline{E}_\mathcal{P}(X) = -\underline{E}_\mathcal{P}(-X)$). Moreover, show that it follows from these properties that

$$\underline{E}_\mathcal{P}(X + Y) \le \underline{E}_\mathcal{P}(X) + \overline{E}_\mathcal{P}(Y) \le \overline{E}_\mathcal{P}(X + Y).$$

**5.12** Show that (5.6), (5.7), and (5.8) hold if $\mathcal{P}$ consists of countably additive measures.

**5.13** Prove Proposition 5.2.3.

**5.14** Prove Proposition 5.2.4.

**\*5.15** Prove Proposition 5.2.5.

**\*5.16** Show that expectation for belief functions can be defined in terms of mass functions as follows. Given a belief function Bel with corresponding mass function $m$ on a set $W$ and a random variable $X$, let $x_U = \min_{w \in U} X(w)$. Show that

$$\underline{E}_{\mathrm{Bel}}(X) = \sum_{U \subseteq W} m(U) x_U.$$

**5.17** Show that

$$E_{\mathrm{Plaus}}(X) = x_n + \sum_{i=1}^{n-1} \mathrm{Bel}(X \le x_i)(x_i - x_{i+1}).$$

Thus, the expression (5.15) for probabilistic expectation discussed in Exercise 5.3 can be used to define expectation for plausibility functions, using belief instead of probability. Since $E_{\mathrm{Bel}}(X) \ne E_{\mathrm{Plaus}}(X)$ in general, it follows that although (5.3) and (5.15) define equivalent expressions for probabilistic expectation, for other representations of uncertainty, they are not equivalent.

**\*5.18** Show that $E_{\mathrm{Bel}}$ satisfies (5.11). (Hint: Observe that if $X$ and $Y$ are random variables, then $(X \vee Y > x) = (X > x) \cup (Y > x)$ and $(X \wedge Y > x) = (X > x) \cap (Y > x)$, and apply Proposition 5.2.5.)

**\*5.19** Show that $E_{\mathrm{Bel}}$ satisfies (5.12). (Hint: Observe that if $X$ and $Y$ are comonotonic, then it is possible to write $X$ as $a_1 X_{U_1} + \cdots + a_n X_{U_n}$ and $Y$ as $b_1 X_{U_1} + \cdots + b_n X_{U_n}$, where the $U_i$s are pairwise disjoint, $a_i \le a_j$ iff $i \le j$, and $b_i \le b_j$ iff $i \le j$. The result then follows easily from Proposition 5.2.5.)

**5.20**   Show that if $X$ is a gamble such that $\mathcal{V}(X) = \{x_1, \ldots, x_n\}$ and $x_1 < x_2 < \ldots < x_n$, and

$$X_j = \tilde{x}_1 + (x_2 - x_1)X_{X > x_1} + \cdots + (x_j - x_{j-1})X_{X > x_{j-1}}$$

for $j = 1, \ldots, n$, then (a) $X = X_n$ and (b) $X_j$ and $(x_{j+1} - x_j)X_{X > x_j}$ are comonotonic, for $j = 1, \ldots, n - 1$.

**5.21**   Prove Lemma 5.2.9. (Hint: First show that $E(aX) = aE(X)$ for $a$ a positive natural number, by induction, using the fact that $E$ satisfies comonotonic additivity. Then show it for $a$ a rational number. Finally, show it for $a$ a real number, using the fact that $E$ is monotone.)

**5.22**   Show $E_{\text{Bel}}$ is the unique function $E$ mapping gambles to $\mathbb{R}$ that is superadditive, positively affinely homogeneous, and monotone and that satisfies (5.11) and (5.12) such that $E(X_U) = \text{Bel}(U)$ for all $U \subseteq W$.

**5.23**   Show explicitly that, for the set $\mathcal{P}$ of probability measures constructed in Example 5.2.10, $\mathcal{P}_*$ is not a belief function.

**5.24**   Show that $\overline{E}'_\mu(X) = -\underline{E}'_\mu(-X)$.

*__5.25__   Prove Lemma 5.2.13.

**5.26**   Prove Theorem 5.2.14. (You may assume Lemma 5.2.13.)

**5.27**   Prove Proposition 5.2.15.

**5.28**   Find gambles $X$ and $Y$ and a possibility measure Poss for which $E_{\text{Poss}}(X \vee Y) \neq \max(E_{\text{Poss}}(X), E_{\text{Poss}}(Y))$.

**5.29**   Prove Proposition 5.2.16.

**5.30**   Let $E'_{\text{Poss}}(X) = \max_{x \in \mathcal{V}(X)} Poss(X = x)x$. Show that $E'_{\text{Poss}}$ satisfies monotonicity, the sup property, and the following three properties:

$$E(a_1 X_{U_1} + \cdots + a_n X_{U_n}) = \max(E(a_1 X_{U_1}), \ldots, E(a_n X_{U_n})) \tag{5.16}$$
$$\text{if } U_1, \ldots, U_n \text{ are pairwise disjoint.}$$

$$E(aX) = aE(X) \text{ if } a \geq 0. \tag{5.17}$$

$$E(\tilde{b}) = b. \tag{5.18}$$

Moreover, show that if $E$ maps gambles to $\mathbb{R}$ and satisfies monotonicity, the sup property, (5.16), (5.17), and (5.18), then there is a possibility measure Poss such that $E = E'_{\text{Poss}}$.

**5.31**   Let

$$E''_{\text{Poss}}(X) = \max_{x \in \mathcal{V}(X)} (\min(Poss(X = x), x)).$$

Show that $E''_{\text{Poss}}(\tilde{b}) = 1$ for all $b \geq 1$. This suggests that $E''_{\text{Poss}}$ is not a reasonable definition of expectation for possibility measures.

**5.32**   Prove analogues of Propositions 5.1.1 and 5.1.2 for $E_\kappa$ (replacing $\times$ and $+$ by $+$ and min, respectively).

**5.33**   Verify that $E_{\text{Pl}_\mathcal{P}, ED_{D_\mathcal{P}}} = E_{\text{Pl}_\mathcal{P}}$.

**\*5.34**   Show that $E_{\text{Pl}}(\tilde{b}) = b$. Then define natural sufficient conditions on $\oplus$, $\otimes$, and Pl that guarantee that $E_{\text{Pl}}$ is (a) monotone, (b) superadditive, (c) additive, and (d) positively affinely homogeneous.

**5.35**   Given a utility function $u$ on $C$ and real numbers $a > 0$ and $b$, let the utility function $u_{a,b} = au + b$. That is, $u_{a,b}(c) = au(c) + b$ for all $c \in C$. Show that the order on acts is the same for $u$ and $u_{a,b}$ according to (a) the expected utility maximization rule, (b) the maximin rule, and (c) the minimax regret rule. This result shows that these three decision rules are unaffected by positive affine transformations of the utilities.

**5.36**   Show that if $\mathcal{P}_W$ is the set of all probability measures on $W$, then $\underline{E}_{\mathcal{P}_W}(u_{\mathbf{a}}) = worst_u(\mathbf{a})$. Thus, $\mathbf{a} \succeq \mathbf{a}'$ iff $worst_u(\mathbf{a}) \geq worst_u(\mathbf{a}')$.

**5.37**   Show that if $\mathbf{a} \succeq_\mathcal{P}^3 \mathbf{a}'$, then $\mathbf{a} \succeq_\mathcal{P}^4 \mathbf{a}'$.

**5.38**   Prove Theorem 5.4.2. (Hint: Given $DS = (A, W, C)$, let the expectation domain $ED = (D_1, D_2, D_3, \oplus, \otimes)$ be defined as follows:

- $D_1 = 2^W$, partially ordered by $\subseteq$.

- $D_2 = C$, and $c_1 \leq_2 c_2$ if $\mathbf{a}_{c_1} \preceq_A \mathbf{a}_{c_2}$, where $\mathbf{a}_{c_i}$ is the constant act that returns $c_i$ in all worlds in $W$.

- $D_3$ consist of all subsets of $W \times C$. (Note that since a function can be identified with a set of ordered pairs, acts in $A$ can be viewed as elements of $D_3$.)

- $x \oplus y = x \cup y$ for $x, y \in D_3$; for $U \in D_1$ and $c \in D_2$, define $U \otimes c = U \times \{c\}$.

- The preorder $\leq_3$ on $D_3$ is defined by taking $x \leq y$ iff $x = y$ or $x = \mathbf{a}$ and $y = \mathbf{a}'$ for some acts $\mathbf{a}, \mathbf{a}' \in A$ such that $\mathbf{a} \preceq_A \mathbf{a}'$.

Note that $D_2$ can be viewed as a subset of $D_3$ by identifying $c \in D_2$ with $W \times \{c\}$. With this identification, $\leq_2$ is easily seen to be the restriction of $\leq_3$ to $D_2$. Define $\text{Pl}(U) = U$ for all $U \subseteq W$. Show that $E_{\text{Pl}, ED}(u_{\mathbf{a}}) = \mathbf{a}$.)

**5.39**   Fill in the details showing that GEU can represent maximin. In particular, show that $E_{\text{Pl}_{\max}, ED_{\max}}(u_{\mathbf{a}}) = worst_u(\mathbf{a})$ for all actions $\mathbf{a} \in A$.

**5.40**   This exercise shows that GEU can represent a generalized version of maximin, where the range of the utility function is an arbitrary totally ordered set. If $DP = (DS, D, u)$, where $D$ is totally preordered by $\leq_D$, then let $\tau(DP) = (DS, ED_{\max, D}, \text{Pl}_{\max, D}, u)$, where $ED_{\max, D} = (\{0, 1\}, D, D, \min, \otimes)$, $0 \otimes x = 1 \otimes x = x$ for all $x \in D$, and $\text{Pl}_{\max, D}$ is defined as in the real-valued case; that is, $\text{Pl}_{\max, D}(U)$ is 1 if $U \neq \emptyset$ and 0 if $U = \emptyset$. Show that $ED_{\max, D}$ is an expectation domain and that $\text{GEU}(\tau(DP)) = \text{maximin}(DP)$.

**5.41**   Show that if $M_{DP} = \infty$, then all acts have infinite regret.

**5.42**   Show that $E_{\text{Pl}_{DP}, ED_{reg}}(u_{\mathbf{a}}) = M_{DP} - regret_u(\mathbf{a})$ for all acts $\mathbf{a} \in A$.

*$\,$**5.43**   Prove Theorem 5.4.4. (Hint: Use a construction much like that used in Exercise 5.38 to prove Theorem 5.4.2.)

**5.44**   Show that if $\text{Pl}_{\mathcal{P}_{\text{Bel}}}(U) \leq \text{Pl}_{\mathcal{P}_{\text{Bel}}}(V)$ then $\text{Bel}(U) \leq \text{Bel}(V)$, but the converse does not hold in general.

*$\,$**5.45**   This exercise shows that GEU ordinally represents $\mathcal{DR}_{\text{BEL}}$.

(a) Define a partial preorder $\leq$ on $D_{\mathcal{P}} \times 2^W$ by taking $(f, U) \leq (g, V)$ iff $\inf_{i \in I} f(i) \leq \inf_{i \in I} g(i)$. Show that $\leq$ is a partial preorder, although not a partial order.

(b) Given a belief function Bel, define $\text{Pl}'_{\mathcal{P}_{\text{Bel}}}$ by taking $\text{Pl}'_{\mathcal{P}_{\text{Bel}}}(U) = (\text{Pl}_{\mathcal{P}_{\text{Bel}}}(U), U)$. Show that $\text{Pl}'_{\mathcal{P}_{\text{Bel}}}$ is a plausibility measure that represents the same ordinal tastes as Bel. (Note that for the purposes of this exercise, the range of a plausibility measure can be partially preordered.)

(c) Define an expectation domain $ED'_{D_{\mathcal{P}}}$ such that

$$\text{GEU}(DS, ED'_{D_{\mathcal{P}}}, \text{Pl}'_{\mathcal{P}_{\text{Bel}}}, u) = \mathcal{DR}_{\text{BEL}}(DS, \overline{\mathbb{R}}, \text{Bel}, u).$$

*$\,$**5.46**   Prove Theorem 5.4.6. (Hint: Combine ideas from Exercises 5.38 and 5.45.)

**5.47**   Show that $E_\mu(X_V \mid U) = \mu(V \mid U)$.

**5.48**  Show that $E_{\text{Bel}}(X \mid U) = E_{\text{Bel} \mid U}(X)$.

**5.49**  Show that conditional expectation can be used as a tool to calculate unconditional expectation. More precisely, show that if $V_1, \ldots, V_n$ is a partition of $W$ and $X$ is a random variable over $W$, then

$$E_{\mu}(X) = \mu(V_1)E_{\mu}(X \mid V_1) + \cdots + \mu(V_n)E_{\mu}(X \mid V_n).$$

(Compare this result with Lemma 3.9.5.)

**5.50**  Prove Lemma 5.5.1.

**5.51**  Prove Lemma 5.5.2.

## Notes

Expectation is a standard notion in the context of probability and is discussed in all standard texts on probability. Proposition 5.1.1 is proved in all of the standard texts. Proposition 5.1.2 is also well known. Walley [1991] gives a proof; he also gives the characterization of Exercise 5.5.

Huber [1981] discusses upper and lower expectation and proves Proposition 5.2.1, Theorem 5.2.2, and a number of other related results. The characterization of lower expectation given in Exercise 5.9 is due to Walley [1991]. Choquet [1953] used (5.9) to define expectation for capacities. (Recall from the notes to Chapter 2 that a belief function is an infinitely monotone capacity.)

Walley's notion of lower and upper previsions, mentioned in the notes to Chapter 2, are essentially lower and upper expectations of sets of probability measures. (Technically, lower and upper expectations are what Walley calls *coherent* lower and upper previsions, respectively.) Thus, lower and upper previsions are really expectations (and associate numbers with random variables, not events). There is a close connection between sets of probability measures and lower and upper expectations. Proposition 5.2.1 and Theorem 5.2.2 show that lower and upper expectations can be obtained from sets of probability measures and vice versa. In fact, the connection is even stronger than that. Theorem 5.2.2 actually provides a one-to-one mapping from closed convex sets of probability measures to lower and upper expectations. That is, if $\mathcal{P}$ is a closed convex set, then $\mathcal{P}$ is the largest set $\mathcal{P}'$ of probability measures such that $\underline{E}_{\mathcal{P}} = \underline{E}_{\mathcal{P}'}$. Thus, lower and upper expectations (and coherent lower and upper previsions) can be identified with closed convex sets of probability measures. It then follows from Example 5.2.10 and Exercise 5.10 that lower and upper previsions are strictly more expressive than lower and upper probability, but less expressive than $\text{Pl}_{\mathcal{P}}$.

As discussed in the notes to Chapter 2, sets of probabilities are often taken to be convex (and, in fact, closed as well). Moreover, there are cases where there is no loss of generality in assuming that a set $\mathcal{P}$ is closed and convex (or, equivalently, in replacing a set $\mathcal{P}$ by the least closed convex set that contains it). On the other hand, as observed in the notes to Chapter 2, there are cases where it does not seem appropriate to represent uncertainty using a convex set. Exercise 4.12 shows that a set of probabilities and its convex hull act differently with respect to determination of independencies.

Walley [1991] discusses both the philosophical and technical issues involved in using lower and upper previsions as a way of representing uncertainty in great detail. His book is perhaps the most thorough account of an alternative approach to reasoning about uncertainty that can be viewed as generalizing both probability measures and belief functions.

Dempster [1967] discusses expectation for belief functions. The fact that expected belief satisfies comonotonic additivity was shown by Dellacherie [1970]; Proposition 5.2.5 and Theorem 5.2.8 are due to Schmeidler [1986].

Inner and outer expectations do not appear to have been studied in the literature. Lemma 5.2.13 was observed by Dieter Denneberg [personal communication, 2002].

Dubois and Prade [1987] discuss expectation for possibility measures, using the same approach as considered here for belief functions, namely, $E_{\text{Poss}}$. Other approaches to defining expectation for possibility measures have been discussed. Some involve using functions $\oplus$ and $\otimes$ (defined on $\mathbb{R}$), somewhat in the spirit of the notion of expected plausibility defined here; see, for example, [Benvenuti and Mesiar 2000]. Results essentially like Theorem 5.2.16 are also proved by Benvenuti and Mesiar [2000]. Luce [1990; 2000] also considers general additive-like operations applied to utilities.

Decision theory is also a well-established research area; some book-length treatments include [Jeffrey 1983; Kreps 1988; Luce and Raiffa 1957; Resnik 1987; Savage 1954]. Savage's [1954] result is the standard defense for identifying utility maximization with rationality. (As discussed in the notes to Chapter 2, it is also viewed as a defense of probability.) Of course, there has been a great deal of criticism of Savage's assumptions; see, for example, [Shafer 1986] for a discussion and critique, as well as related references. Moreover, there are many empirical observations that indicate that humans do not act in accord with Savage's postulates; perhaps the best-known examples of violations are those of Allais [1953] and Ellsberg [1961]. Camerer and Weber [1992] and Kagel and Roth [1995] discuss the experimental evidence.

In the economics literature, Knight [1921] already drew a distinction between decision making under *risk* (roughly speaking, where there is an "objective" probability measure that quantifies the uncertainty) and decision making under *uncertainty* (where there is not). Prior to Savage's work, many decision rules that did not involve probability were discussed; maximin and minimax regret are perhaps the best-known. The maximin rule was promoted by Wald [1950]; minimax regret was introduced (independently) by Niehans [1948] and Savage [1951]. The decision rule $\succeq_{\mathcal{P}}^1$ corresponding to lower expectation has a long history. It was discussed by Wald [1950], examined carefully by Gärdenfors and Sahlin [1982] (who also discussed how the set of probability measures might be chosen), and axiomatized by Gilboa and Schmeidler [1989]. Borodin and El Yaniv [1998, Chapter 15] give a number of examples of other rules, with extensive pointers to the literature.

Savage's work on expected utility was so influential that it shifted the focus to probability and expected utility maximization for many years. More recently, there have been attempts to get decision rules that are more descriptively accurate, either by using a different representation of uncertainty or using a decision rule other than maximizing expected utility. These include decision rules based on belief functions (also called *nonadditive probabilities* and *Choquet capacities*) [Schmeidler 1989], rules based on nonstandard reals [Lehmann 1996; Lehmann 2001], *prospect theory* [Kahneman and Tversky 1979], and *rank-dependent expected utility* [Quiggin 1993].

There has been a great deal of effort put into finding techniques for utility elicitation and probability elicitation. Utility elicitation can, for example, play an important role in giving doctors the information they need to help patients make appropriate decisions regarding medical care. (Should I have the operation or not?) Farquhar [1984] gives a good theoretical survey of utility elicitation techniques; the first few chapters of [Yates 1990] give a gentle introduction to probability elicitation.

All the material in Section 5.4.3 is taken from [Chu and Halpern 2003a; Chu and Halpern 2003b], where GEU and the notion of one decision rule representing another are introduced. A more refined notion of uniformity is also defined. The decision-problem transformation $\tau$ that takes nonplausibilistic decision problems to plausibilistic decision problems is *uniform* if the plausibility measure in $\tau(DP)$ depends only on the set of worlds in $DP$. That is, if $DP_i = ((A_i, W_i, C_i), D_i, u_i)$, $i = 1, 2$, and $W_1 = W_2$, then the plausibility measure in $\tau(DP_1)$ is the same as that in $\tau(DP_2)$. The plausibility measure must depend on the set of worlds (since it is a function from subsets of worlds to plausibility values); uniformity requires that it depends only on the set of worlds (and not on other features of the decision problem, such as the set of acts). The decision problem transformation used to show that regret minimization can be represented by GEU is not uniform. There is a characterization in the spirit of Theorem 5.4.4 of when GEU can uniformly represent a decision rule (see [Chu and Halpern 2003b]). It follows from the characterization that GEU cannot uniformly represent regret minimization. Roughly speaking, this is because the preference order induced by regret minimization can be affected by irrelevant acts. Suppose that $DP_1$ and $DP_2$ are decision problems that differ only in that $DP_2$ involves an act **a** that is not among the acts in $DP_1$. The presence of **a** can affect the preference order induced by regret minimization among the remaining acts. This does not happen with the other decision rules I have considered here, such as maximin and expected utility maximization.

This general framework has yet another advantage. Theorem 5.4.2 shows that any partial preorder on acts can be reprsented by GEU. Savage considers orders on acts that satisfy certain postulates. Each of Savage's constraints can be shown to correspond to a constraint on expectation domains, utility functions, and plausibility measures. This gives an understanding of what properties the underlying expectation domain must have to guarantee that each of Savage's postulates hold. See [Chu and Halpern 2003a] for details.

Besides the additive notion of regret that I have considered here, there is a multiplicative notion, where $regret_u(\mathbf{a}, w)$ is defined to be $u(w, \mathbf{a}_w)/u(w, \mathbf{a})$. With this definition, if $regret_u(\mathbf{a}) = k$, then **a** is within a multiplicative factor $k$ of the best act the agent could perform, even if she knew exactly what the state was. This notion of regret (unlike additive regret) is affected by linear transformations of the utility (in the sense of Exercise 5.35). Moreover, it makes sense only if all utilities are positive. Nevertheless, it has been the focus of significant recent attention in the computer science community, under the rubric of *online algorithms;* [Borodin and El-Yaniv 1998] is a book-length treatment of the subject.

*Influence diagrams* [Howard and Matheson 1981; Shachter 1986] combine the graphical representation of probability used in Bayesian networks with a representation of utilities, and thus they are a very useful tool in decision analysis. There have also been attempts to define analogues of independence and conditional independence for utilities, in the hope of getting representations for utility in the spirit of Bayesian networks; see [Bacchus and Grove 1995; Keeney and Raiffa 1976; La Mura and Shoham 1999]. To date, relatively little progress has been made toward this goal.

The two-envelope puzzle discussed in Exercise 5.7 is well known. The earliest appearance in the literature that I am aware of is in Kraitchik's [1953] book of mathematical puzzles, although it is probably older. Nalebuff [1989] presents an interesting introduction to the problem as well as references to its historical antecedents. In the mid-1990s a spate of papers discussing various aspects of the puzzle appeared in the philosophy journals *Analysis* and *Theory and Decision;* see [Arntzenius and McCarthy 1997; McGrew, Shier, and Silverstein 1997; Rawlings 1994; Scott and Scott 1997; Sobel 1994] for a sampling of these papers as well as pointers to some of the others.

Walley [1991] discusses carefully the notion of conditional expectation. Denneberg [2002] gives a recent discussion of updating and conditioning expectation.

# Chapter 6

# Multi-Agent Systems

*Synergy means behavior of whole systems unpredicted by the behavior of their parts.*

—R. Buckminster Fuller, *What I Have Learned*

Up to now, I have made two (quite standard) simplifying assumptions in presenting models: I have focused on a single agent and I have modeled only static situations. Although these assumptions are reasonable in many cases, they certainly do not always hold. We often want to model interactive situations, for example, when agents are bargaining, playing a game, or performing a distributed computation. In an interactive situation, an agent must reason about other agents (who are in turn reasoning about her). And clearly for situations that evolve over time, it useful to model time explicitly.

In this chapter, I present one framework that models time and multiple agents in a natural way. It has one important added benefit. For the most part, worlds have been black boxes, with no structure. The one exception was in Section 4.4, where a world was viewed as being characterized by a collection of random variables. In the multi-agent systems framework presented here, worlds have additional structure. This structure is useful for, among other things, characterizing what worlds an agent considers possible. While the framework presented here is certainly not the only way of describing multi-agent systems, it is quite useful, as I shall try to demonstrate by example. Before describing the approach, I describe the way multiple agents have traditionally been handled in the literature.

## 6.1    Epistemic Frames

Before dealing with many agents, consider the single-agent case again. Starting with Section 2.1, an agent's uncertainty has been represented by a single set $W$ of possible worlds. In general, however, the set of worlds an agent considers possible depends on the actual world. To take a trivial example, the set of worlds the agent considers possible when it is raining is clearly different from the set of worlds the agent considers possible when it is sunny.

The dependence of the set of possible worlds on the actual world can be modeled using *(epistemic) frames*. ("Epistemic" means "of or pertaining to knowledge or the conditions for acquiring it.") An epistemic frame $F$ is a pair $(W, \mathcal{K})$, where, as before, $W$ is a set of possible worlds. The new feature here is the $\mathcal{K}$. $\mathcal{K}$ is a *binary relation* on $W$ (sometimes called a *possibility relation* or *accessibility relation*), that is, a subset of $W \times W$. Intuitively, $(w, w') \in \mathcal{K}$ if the agent considers $w'$ a possible world in world $w$. Define $\mathcal{K}(w) = \{w' : (w, w') \in \mathcal{K}\}$; $\mathcal{K}(w)$ is the set of worlds that the agent considers possible in world $w$. Although taking $\mathcal{K}$ to be a binary relation is more standard in the literature, viewing $\mathcal{K}$ as a function from worlds to sets of worlds will often turn out to be more convenient.

Now the question of whether an agent considers an event possible or knows an event depends on the world. An agent considers $U$ possible at world $w$ (in an epistemic frame $F$) if $U \cap \mathcal{K}(w) \neq \emptyset$; the agent knows $U$ at world $w$ if $\mathcal{K}(w) \subseteq U$. Put another way, the agent knows $U$ if every world she considers possible is in $U$.

There are various natural constraints that can be placed on the $\mathcal{K}$ relation; these constraints capture some standard assumptions about the agent's possibility relation. For example, if the agent always considers the actual world possible, then $(w, w) \in \mathcal{K}$ for all $w \in W$, that is, $\mathcal{K}$ is *reflexive*. Similarly, it may be appropriate to assume that if $(u, v)$ and $(v, w)$ are both in $\mathcal{K}$ (so that $v$ is considered possible in world $u$, and $w$ is considered possible in $v$) then $(u, w) \in \mathcal{K}$ (so that $w$ is considered possible in $u$). This just says that $\mathcal{K}$ is *transitive*. There are many other constraints that could be placed on $\mathcal{K}$. I mention some other standard ones here.

- $\mathcal{K}$ is *Euclidean* if $(u, v), (u, w) \in \mathcal{K}$ implies $(v, w) \in \mathcal{K}$, for all $u, v, w \in W$.

- $\mathcal{K}$ is *symmetric* if $(u, v) \in \mathcal{K}$ implies that $(v, u) \in \mathcal{K}$ for all $u, v, \in W$.

- $\mathcal{K}$ is *serial* if for all $w \in W$, there is some $w' \in W$ such that $(w, w') \in \mathcal{K}$. This just says that the agent always considers some world possible.

- $\mathcal{K}$ is an *equivalence relation* if it is reflexive, symmetric, and transitive. It is easy to see that this is equivalent to $\mathcal{K}$ being reflexive, Euclidean, and transitive (Exercise 6.1).

Note that these constraints have natural interpretations if $\mathcal{K}$ is viewed as a function from worlds to sets of worlds. In particular, $\mathcal{K}$ is reflexive iff $w \in \mathcal{K}(w)$ for all worlds $w$; $\mathcal{K}$ is transitive iff, for all worlds $w$ and $w'$, if $w' \in \mathcal{K}(w)$ then $\mathcal{K}(w') \subseteq \mathcal{K}(w)$; and $\mathcal{K}$ is Euclidean iff, for all worlds $w$, $w'$, if $w' \in \mathcal{K}(w)$, then $\mathcal{K}(w') \supseteq \mathcal{K}(w)$ (Exercise 6.2). It follows that if $\mathcal{K}$ is Euclidean and transitive, then $\mathcal{K}(w') = \mathcal{K}(w)$ for all $w' \in \mathcal{K}(w)$; the set of worlds that the agent considers possible is then the same in all worlds that she considers possible (and thus can be viewed as being independent of the actual world). Reflexivity is the property taken to distinguish *knowledge* from *belief;* I discuss belief in Section 8.1 and Chapter 9. In many applications, the $\mathcal{K}$ relation is naturally viewed as being an equivalence relation, which makes it reflexive, Euclidean, and transitive.

Epistemic frames can easily be generalized to accommodate many agents. There is then one possibility relation for each agent. Formally, *an epistemic frame F for n agents* is a tuple $(W, \mathcal{K}_1, \ldots, \mathcal{K}_n)$, where each $\mathcal{K}_i$ is a binary relation on $W$. $\mathcal{K}_i(w)$ should be thought of as the set of worlds that agent $i$ considers possible at world $w$. In general, $\mathcal{K}_i(w)$ will be different from $\mathcal{K}_j(w)$ if $i \neq j$. Different agents will consider different worlds possible.

One of the advantages of an epistemic frame is that it can be viewed as a labeled graph, that is, a set of labeled nodes connected by directed, labeled edges. The nodes are the worlds in $W$, and there is an edge from $w$ to $w'$ labeled $i$ exactly if $(w, w') \in \mathcal{K}_i$. The graphical viewpoint makes it easier to see the connection between worlds. Consider the following example:

**Example 6.1.1** Suppose that a deck consists of three cards labeled $A$, $B$, and $C$. Agents 1 and 2 each get one of these cards; the third card is left face down. A possible world is characterized by describing the cards held by each agent. For example, in the world $(A, B)$, agent 1 holds card $A$ and agent 2 holds card $B$ (while card $C$ is face down). There are clearly six possible worlds: $(A, B)$, $(A, C)$, $(B, A)$, $(B, C)$, $(C, A)$, and $(C, B)$. In the world $(A, B)$, agent 1 thinks two worlds are possible: $(A, B)$ itself and $(A, C)$. Agent 1 knows that he has card $A$ but considers it possible that agent 2 could hold either card $B$ or card $C$. Similarly, in world $(A, B)$, agent 2 also considers two worlds: $(A, B)$ and $(C, B)$. In general, in a world $(x, y)$, agent 1 considers $(x, y)$ and $(x, z)$ possible, while agent 2 considers $(x, y)$ and $(z, y)$ possible, where $z$ is different from both $x$ and $y$.

From this description, the $\mathcal{K}_1$ and $\mathcal{K}_2$ relations can easily be constructed. It is easy to check that they are equivalence relations. This is because an agent's knowledge is determined by the information he has, namely, the card he is holding. (Considerations similar to these lead to the use of equivalence relations in many examples involving knowledge.) The frame is described in Figure 6.1, where, since the relations are equivalence relations, I omit the self loops and the arrows on edges for simplicity (if

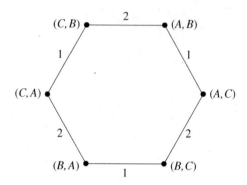

Figure 6.1    An epistemic frame describing a simple card game.

there is an edge labeled $i$ from state $w$ to state $w'$, there has to be an edge labeled $i$ from $w'$ to $w$ as well by symmetry).

Notice how important it is to include in the frame worlds that both agents know to be impossible. For example, in the world $(A, B)$, both agents know perfectly well that the world $(B, A)$ cannot be the case (after all, agent 1 knows that his own card is $A$, not $B$, and agent 2 knows that her card is $B$, not $A$). Nevertheless, because agent 1 considers it possible that agent 2 considers it possible that agent 1 considers it possible that $(B, A)$ is the case, $(B, A)$ must be included in the frame. The fact that both agents consider $(B, A)$ impossible in situation $(A, B)$ is captured in the frame by the fact that there is no edge from $(A, B)$ to $(B, A)$; the fact that agent 1 considers it possible that agent 2 considers it possible that agent 1 considers it possible that $(B, A)$ is the case is captured by the path from $(A, B)$ to $(B, A)$ consisting of three edges, labeled 1, 2, and 1, respectively.

Notice that, in this frame, in the world $(A, B)$, agent 1 knows that agent 2 holds either the $B$ or $C$ (since agent 1 considers two worlds possible, $(A, B)$ and $(A, C)$, and in both of them, agent 2 holds either the $B$ or the $C$). At world $(A, B)$, agent 1 also knows that agent 2 does not know that agent 1 has card $A$. That is because in each of the two worlds that agent 1 considers possible, agent 2 does not know that agent 1 has card $A$. In world $(A, B)$, agent 2 considers it possible that agent 1 has card $C$ (since agent 2 considers world $(C, B)$ possible), and in world $(A, C)$, agent 2 considers it possible that agent 1 has card $B$.  ∎

At least in this simple setting, the formal definition of knowledge seems to capture some of the intuitions usually associated with the word "knowledge." The examples in the rest of this chapter provide further justification, as does the axiomatic characterization of knowledge given in Section 7.2.3.

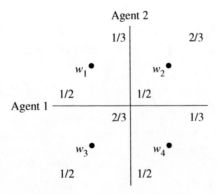

Figure 6.2    A probability frame.

## 6.2   Probability Frames

The analogue of an epistemic frame in the case where uncertainty is represented using probability is a *probability frame*. It has the form $(W, \mathcal{PR}_1, \ldots, \mathcal{PR}_n)$, where, as before, $W$ is a set of worlds, and $\mathcal{PR}_i$ is a *probability assignment*, a function that associates with each world $w$ a probability space $(W_{w,i}, \mathcal{F}_{w,i}, \mu_{w,i})$. Although it is possible to take $W_{w,i} = W$ (by extending $\mu_{w,i}$ so that it is 0 on all sets in $W - W_{w,i}$), it is often more convenient to think of $\mu_{w,i}$ as being defined on only a subset of $W$, as the examples in this chapter show. The special case where $n = 1$ and $\mathcal{PR}_1(w) = (W, \mathcal{F}, \mu)$ for all $w \in W$ can be identified with a standard probability space; this is called a *simple probability frame*.

**Example 6.2.1**   Consider the frame $F$ described in Figure 6.2.

There are four worlds in this frame, $w_1, \ldots, w_4$. $\mathcal{PR}_1$ and $\mathcal{PR}_2$ are defined as follows:

- $\mathcal{PR}_1(w_1) = \mathcal{PR}_1(w_2) = (\{w_1, w_2\}, \mu_1)$, where $\mu_1$ gives each world probability 1/2;

- $\mathcal{PR}_1(w_3) = \mathcal{PR}_1(w_4) = (\{w_3, w_4\}, \mu_2)$, where $\mu_2$ gives each world probability 1/2;

- $\mathcal{PR}_2(w_1) = \mathcal{PR}_1(w_3) = (\{w_1, w_3\}, \mu_3)$, where $\mu_3(w_1) = 1/3$ and $\mu_3(w_3) = 2/3$;

- $\mathcal{PR}_2(w_2) = \mathcal{PR}_1(w_4) = (\{w_2, w_4\}, \mu_4)$, where $\mu_4(w_2) = 2/3$ and $\mu_4(w_4) = 1/3$. ∎

In epistemic frames, conditions are typically placed on the accessibility relations. Analogously, in probability frames, it is often reasonable to consider probability assignments that satisfy certain natural constraints. One such constraint is called *uniformity*:

UNIF. For all $i$, $v$, and $w$, if $\mathcal{PR}_i(w) = (W_{w,i}, \mathcal{F}_{w,i}, \mu_{w,i})$ and $v \in W_{w,i}$, then $\mathcal{PR}_i(v) = \mathcal{PR}_i(w)$.

Recall that the Euclidean and transitive property together imply that if $v \in \mathcal{K}_i(w)$, then $\mathcal{K}_i(w) = \mathcal{K}_i(v)$; uniformity is the analogue of these properties in the context of probability frames.

Other natural constraints can be imposed if both knowledge and probability are represented. An *epistemic probability frame* has the form $M = (W, \mathcal{K}_1, \ldots, \mathcal{K}_n, \mathcal{PR}_1, \ldots, \mathcal{PR}_n)$. Now it is possible to consider constraints on the relationship between $\mathcal{K}_i$ and $\mathcal{PR}_i$. The standard assumption, particularly in the economics literature (which typically assumes that the $\mathcal{K}_i$s are equivalence relations) are that (1) an agent's probability assignment is the same at all worlds that she considers possible and (2) the agent assigns probability only to worlds that she considers possible. The first assumption is called SDP (*state-determined probability*). It is formalized as follows:

SDP.   For all $i$, $v$, and $w$, if $v \in \mathcal{K}_i(w)$, then $\mathcal{PR}_i(v) = \mathcal{PR}_i(w)$.

The reason for this name will become clearer later in this chapter, after I have presented a framework in which it makes sense to talk about an agent's state. SDP then says exactly that the agent's state determines her probability assignment. The second assumption can be viewed as a consistency assumption, so it is abbreviated as CONS.

CONS. For all $i$ and $w$, if $\mathcal{PR}_i(w) = (W_{w,i}, \mathcal{F}_{w,i}, \mu_{w,i})$, then $W_{w,i} \subseteq \mathcal{K}_i(w)$.

In the presence of CONS (which I will always assume), SDP clearly implies UNIF, but the converse is not necessarily true. Examples later in this chapter show that there are times when UNIF is a more reasonable assumption than SDP.

One last assumption, which is particularly prevalent in the economics literature, is the *common prior* (CP) assumption. This assumption asserts that the agents have a common prior probability on the set of all worlds and each agent's probability assignment at world $w$ is induced from this common prior by conditioning on his set of possible worlds. Thus, CP implies SDP and CONS (and hence UNIF), since it requires that $\mathcal{K}_i(w) = W_{w,i}$. There is one subtlety involved in making CP precise, which is to specify what happens if the agent's set of possible worlds has probability 0. One way to deal with this is just to insist that this does not happen. An alternative way (which is actually more common in the literature) is to make no requirements if the agent's set of possible worlds has probability 0; that is what I do here. However, I do make one technical requirement. Say that a world $w'$ is *reachable* from $w$ if there exist worlds $w_0, \dots, w_m$ with $w_0 = w$ and $w_m = w'$ and agents $i_1, \dots, i_m$ such that $w_j \in \mathcal{K}_{i_j}(w_{j-1})$ for $j = 1, \dots, m$. Intuitively, $w'$ is reachable from $w$ if, in world $w$, some agent considers it possible that some agent considers it possible that $\dots w'$ is the case. Let $C(w)$ denote the worlds reachable from $w$. I require that $C(w)$ have positive prior probability for all worlds $w \in W$. The reason for this technical requirement will become clearer in Section 7.6.

CP.   There exists a probability space $(W, \mathcal{F}_W, \mu_W)$ such that $\mathcal{K}_i(w)$, $C(w) \in \mathcal{F}_W$, $\mu_W(C(w)) > 0$, and $\mathcal{PR}_i(w) = (\mathcal{K}_i(w), \mathcal{F}_W | \mathcal{K}_i(w), \mu_{w,i})$ for all agents $i$ and worlds $w \in W$, where $\mathcal{F}_W | \mathcal{K}_i(w)$ consists of all sets of the form $U \cap \mathcal{K}_i(w)$ for $U \in \mathcal{F}_W$, and $\mu_{w,i} = \mu_W | \mathcal{K}_i(w)$ if $\mu_W(\mathcal{K}_i(w)) > 0$. (There are no constraints on $\mu_{w,i}$ if $\mu_W(\mathcal{K}_i(w)) = 0$.)

Until quite recently, the common prior assumption was almost an article of faith among economists. It says that differences in beliefs among agents can be completely explained by differences in information. Essentially, the picture is that agents start out with identical prior beliefs (the common prior) and then condition on the information that they later receive. If their later beliefs differ, it must thus be due to the fact that they have received different information.

   CP is a nontrivial requirement. For example, consider an epistemic probability frame $F = (\{w_1, w_2\}, \mathcal{K}_1, \mathcal{K}_2, \mathcal{PR}_1, \mathcal{PR}_2)$ where both agents consider both worlds possible, that is, $\mathcal{K}_1(w_1) = \mathcal{K}_1(w_2) = \mathcal{K}_2(w_1) = \mathcal{K}_2(w_2) = \{w_1, w_2\}$. It is easy to see that the only way that this frame can be consistent with CP is if $\mathcal{PR}_1(w_1) = \mathcal{PR}_2(w_1) = \mathcal{PR}_1(w_2) = \mathcal{PR}_2(w_2)$ (Exercise 6.3). But there are less trivial constraints placed by CP, as the following example shows:

**Example 6.2.2**   Extend the probability frame $F$ from Example 6.2.1 to an epistemic probability frame by taking $\mathcal{K}_1(w_1) = \mathcal{K}_1(w_2) = \{w_1, w_2\}$, $\mathcal{K}_1(w_3) = \mathcal{K}_1(w_4) = \{w_3, w_4\}$, $\mathcal{K}_2(w_1) = \mathcal{K}_1(w_3) = \{w_1, w_3\}$, and $\mathcal{K}_2(w_2) = \mathcal{K}_1(w_4) = \{w_2, w_4\}$. It is not hard to show that this frame does not satisfy CP (Exercise 6.4).  ∎

   The assumptions CONS, SDP, UNIF, and CP can be characterized axiomatically. I defer this discussion to Section 7.6.

## 6.3   Multi-Agent Systems

Frames as presented in the previous two sections are static. In this section, I introduce
*multi-agent systems,* which incorporate time and give worlds more structure. I interpret the phrase "multi-agent system" rather loosely. Players in a poker game, agents
conducting a bargaining session, robots interacting to clean a house, and processes performing a distributed computation can all be viewed as multi-agent systems. The only
assumption I make here about a system is that, at all times, each of the agents in the
system can be viewed as being in some *local* or *internal* state. Intuitively, the local state
encapsulates all the relevant information to which the agent has access. For example,
in a poker game, a player's state might consist of the cards he currently holds, the bets
made by the other players, any other cards he has seen, and any information he may
have about the strategies of the other players (e.g., Bob may know that Alice likes to
bluff, while Charlie tends to bet conservatively). These states could have further structure (and typically will in most applications of interest). In particular, they can often be
characterized by a set of random variables.

It is also useful to view the system as a whole as being in a state. The first thought
might be to make the system's state be a tuple of the form $(s_1, \ldots, s_n)$, where $s_i$ is
agent $i$'s state. But, in general, more than just the local states of the agents may be
relevant to an analysis of the system. In a message-passing system where agents send
messages back and forth along communication lines, the messages in transit and the
status of each communication line (whether it is up or down) may also be relevant. In
a system of sensors observing some terrain, features of the terrain may certainly be
relevant. Thus, the system is conceptually divided into two components: the agents and
the *environment,* where the environment can be thought of as "everything else that is
relevant." In many ways the environment can be viewed as just another agent. A *global
state* of a system with $n$ agents is an $(n + 1)$-tuple of the form $(s_e, s_1, \ldots, s_n)$, where
$s_e$ is the state of the environment and $s_i$ is the local state of agent $i$.

A global state describes the system at a given point in time. But a system is not a
static entity. It is constantly changing over time. A *run* captures the dynamic aspects
of a system. Intuitively, a run is a complete description of one possible way in which
the system's state can evolve over time. Formally, a run is a function from time to
global states. For definiteness, I take time to range over the natural numbers. Thus, $r(0)$
describes the initial global state of the system in a possible execution, $r(1)$ describes the
next global state, and so on. A pair $(r, m)$ consisting of a run $r$ and time $m$ is called a
*point.* If $r(m) = (s_e, s_1, \ldots, s_n)$, then define $r_e(m) = s_e$ and $r_i(m) = s_i, i = 1, \ldots, n$;
thus, $r_i(m)$ is agent $i$'s local state at the point $(r, m)$ and $r_e(m)$ is the environment's
state at $(r, m)$.

Typically global states change as a result of actions. *Round m* takes place between time $m - 1$ and $m$. I think of actions in a run $r$ as being performed during a round. The point $(r, m - 1)$ describes the situation just before the action at round $m$ is performed, and the point $(r, m)$ describes the situation just after the action has been performed.

In general, there are many possible executions of a system: there could be a number of possible initial states and many things that could happen from each initial state. For example, in a draw poker game, the initial global states could describe the possible deals of the hand by having player $i$'s local state describe the cards held by player $i$. For each fixed deal of the cards, there may still be many possible betting sequences, and thus many runs. Formally, a *system* is a nonempty set of runs. Intuitively, these runs describe all the possible sequences of events that could occur in the system. Thus, I am essentially identifying a system with its possible behaviors.

Although a run is an infinite object, there is no problem representing a finite process (e.g., a finite protocol or finite game) using a system. For example, there could be a special global state denoting that the protocol/game has ended, or the final state could be repeated infinitely often. These are typically minor modeling issues.

A system (set of runs) $\mathcal{R}$ can be identified with an epistemic frame $F_{\mathcal{R}} = (W, \mathcal{K}_1, \ldots, \mathcal{K}_n)$, where the $\mathcal{K}_i$s are equivalence relations. The worlds in $F_{\mathcal{R}}$ are the points in $\mathcal{R}$, that is, the pairs $(r, m)$ such that $r \in \mathcal{R}$. If $s = (s_e, s_1, \ldots, s_n)$ and $s' = (s'_e, s'_1, \ldots, s'_n)$ are two global states in $\mathcal{R}$, then $s$ and $s'$ are *indistinguishable to agent i*, written $s \sim_i s'$, if $i$ has the same state in both $s$ and $s'$, that is, if $s_i = s'_i$. The indistinguishability relation $\sim_i$ can be extended to points. Two points $(r, m)$ and $(r', m')$ are *indistinguishable to i*, written $(r, m) \sim_i (r', m')$, if $r(m) \sim_i r'(m')$ (or, equivalently, if $r_i(m) = r'_i(m')$). Clearly $\sim_i$ is an equivalence relation on points; take the equivalence relation $\mathcal{K}_i$ of $F_{\mathcal{R}}$ to be $\sim_i$. Thus, $\mathcal{K}_i(r, m) = \{(r', m') : r_i(m) = r'_i(m')\}$, the set of points indistinguishable by $i$ from $(r, m)$.

To model a situation as a multi-agent system requires deciding how to model the local states. The same issues arise as those discussed in Section 2.1: what is relevant and what can be omitted. This, if anything, is an even harder task in a multi-agent situation than it is in the single-agent situation, because now the uncertainty includes what agents are thinking about one another. This task is somewhat alleviated by being able to separate the problem into considering the local state of each agent and the state of the environment. Still, it is by no means trivial. The following simple example illustrates some of the subtleties that arise:

**Example 6.3.1**   Suppose that Alice tosses two coins and sees how the coins land. Bob learns how the first coin landed after the second coin is tossed, but does not learn the outcome of the second coin toss. How should this be represented as a multi-agent system? The first step is to decide what the local states look like. There is no "right" way of modeling the local states. What I am about to describe is one reasonable way of doing it, but clearly there are others.

The environment state will be used to model what actually happens. At time 0, it is $\langle\,\rangle$, the empty sequence, indicating that nothing has yet happened. At time 1, it is either $\langle H \rangle$ or $\langle T \rangle$, depending on the outcome of the first coin toss. At time 2, it is either $\langle H, H \rangle$, $\langle H, T \rangle$, $\langle T, H \rangle$, or $\langle T, T \rangle$, depending on the outcome of both coin tosses. Note that the environment state is characterized by two random variables, describing the outcome of each coin toss. Since Alice knows the outcome of the coin tosses, I take Alice's local state to be the same as the environment state at all times.

What about Bob's local state? After the first coin is tossed, Bob still knows nothing; he learns the outcome of the first coin toss after the second coin is tossed. The first thought might then be to take his local states to have the form $\langle\,\rangle$ at time 0 and time 1 (since he does not know the outcome of the first coin toss at time 1) and either $\langle H \rangle$ or $\langle T \rangle$ at time 2. This would be all right if Bob cannot distinguish between time 0 and time 1; that is, if he cannot tell when Alice tosses the first coin. But if Bob is aware of the passage of time, then it may be important to keep track of the time in his local state. (The time can still be ignored if it is deemed irrelevant to the analysis. Recall that I said that the local state encapsulates all the *relevant* information to which the agent has access. Bob has all sorts of other information that I have chosen not to model: his sister's name, his age, the color of his car, and so on. It is up to the modeler to decide what is relevant here.) In any case, if the time is deemed to be relevant, then at time 1, Bob's state must somehow encode the fact that the time is 1. I do this by taking Bob's state at time 1 to be $\langle tick \rangle$, to denote that one time tick has passed. (Other ways of encoding the time are, of course, also possible.) Note that the time is already implicitly encoded in Alice's state: the time is 1 if and only if her state is either $\langle H \rangle$ or $\langle T \rangle$.

Under this representation of global states, there are seven possible global states:

- $(\langle\,\rangle, \langle\,\rangle, \langle\,\rangle)$, the initial state,

- two time-1 states of the form $(\langle X_1 \rangle, \langle X_1 \rangle, \langle tick \rangle)$, for $X_1 \in \{H, T\}$,

- four time-2 states of the form $(\langle X_1, X_2 \rangle, \langle X_1, X_2 \rangle, \langle tick, X_1 \rangle)$, for $X_1, X_2 \in \{H, T\}$.

In this simple case, the environment state determines the global state (and is identical to Alice's state), but this is not always so.

The system describing this situation has four runs, $r^1, \ldots, r^4$, one for each of the time-2 global states. The runs are perhaps best thought of as being the branches of the *computation tree* described in Figure 6.3.  ∎

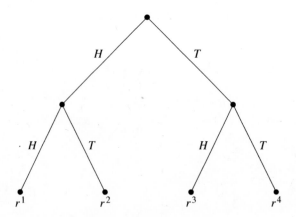

Figure 6.3    Tossing two coins.

Example 6.3.1 carefully avoided discussion of probabilities. There is, of course, no problem adding probability (or any other representation of uncertainty) to the framework. I focus on probability in most of the chapter and briefly discuss the few issues that arise when using nonprobabilistic representations of uncertainty in Section 6.10. A *probability system* is a tuple $(\mathcal{R}, \mathcal{PR}_1, \ldots, \mathcal{PR}_n)$, where $\mathcal{R}$ is a system and $\mathcal{PR}_1, \ldots, \mathcal{PR}_n$ are probability assignments; just as in the case of probability frames, the probability assignment $\mathcal{PR}_i$ associates with each point $(r, m)$ a probability space $\mathcal{PR}_i(r, m) = (W_{r,m,i}, \mathcal{F}_{r,m,i}, \mu_{r,m,i})$.

In the multi-agent systems framework, it is clear where the $\mathcal{K}_i$ relations that define knowledge are coming from; they are determined by the agents' local states. Where should the probability assignments come from? It is reasonable to expect, for example, that $\mathcal{PR}_i(r, m + 1)$ would somehow incorporate whatever agent $i$ learned at $(r, m + 1)$ but otherwise involve minimal changes from $\mathcal{PR}_i(r, m)$. This suggests the use of conditioning—and, indeed, conditioning will essentially be used—but there are some subtleties involved. It may well be that $W_{r,m,i}$ and $W_{r,m+1,i}$ are disjoint sets. In that case, clearly $\mu_{r,m+1,i}$ cannot be the result of conditioning $\mu_{r,m,i}$ on some event. Nevertheless, there is a way of viewing $\mu_{r,m+1,i}$ as arising from $\mu_{r,m,i}$ by conditioning. The idea is to think in terms of a probability on runs, not points. The following example illustrates the main ideas:

**Example 6.3.2**   Consider the situation described in Example 6.3.1, but now suppose that the first coin has bias 2/3, the second coin is fair, and the coin tosses are independent, as shown in Figure 6.4. Note that, in Figure 6.4, the edges coming out of each

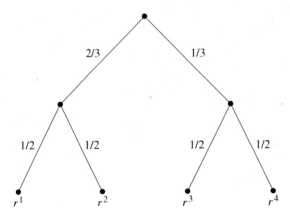

Figure 6.4   Tossing two coins, with probabilities.

node are labeled with a probability, which is intuitively the probability of taking that transition. Of course, the probabilities labeling the edges coming out of any fixed node must sum to 1, since some transition must be taken. For example, the edges coming out of the root have probability 2/3 and 1/3. Since the transitions in this case (i.e., the coin tosses) are assumed to be independent, it is easy to compute the probability of each run. For example, the probability of run $r^1$ is $2/3 \times 1/2 = 1/3$; this represents the probability of getting two heads.

The probability on runs can then be used to determine probability assignments. Note that in a probability assignment, the probability is put on *points,* not on runs. Suppose that $\mathcal{PR}_i(r^j, m) = (W_{r^j,m,i}, 2^{W_{r^j,m,i}}, \mu_{r^j,m,i})$. An obvious choice for $W_{r^j,m,i}$ is $\mathcal{K}_i(r^j, m)$; the agents ascribe probability to the worlds they consider possible. Moreover, the relative probability of the points is determined by the probability of the runs. For example, $W_{r^1,0,A} = \mathcal{K}_A(r^1, 0) = \{(r^1, 0), (r^2, 0), (r^3, 0), (r^4, 0)\}$, and $\mu_{r^1,0,A}$ assigns probability $\mu_{r^1,0,A}(r^1, 0) = 1/3$; similarly, $W_{r^1,2,B} = \mathcal{K}_B(r^1, 2) = \{(r^1, 2), (r^2, 2)\}$ and $\mu_{r^1,2,B}(r^1, 2) = 1/2$. Note that to compute $\mu_{r^1,2,B}(r^1, 2)$, Bob essentially takes the initial probability on the runs, and he conditions on the two runs he considers possible at time 2, namely, $r^1$ and $r^2$. It is easy to check that this probability assignment satisfies SDP and CONS. Indeed, as shown in the next section, this is a general property of the construction.  ∎

As long as there is some way of placing a probability on the set of runs, the ideas in this example generalize. This is formalized in the following section.

## 6.4   From Probability on Runs to Probability Assignments

In this section, I assume for simplicity that each agent starts with a probability on the set of runs. From that, I provide one natural way of deriving the probability assignments. The basic idea is simple. Roughly speaking, the probability of a point $(r', m')$ according to the probability assignment at $(r, m)$ is the probability of $r'$, conditioned on the set of runs that the agent considers possible at $(r, m)$.

It is easy to see how this works in Example 6.3.2. At the point $(r^1, 1)$, Alice considers two points possible: $(r^1, 1)$ and $(r^2, 1)$. She ascribes these points each probability $1/2$. She considers two runs possible, namely $r^1$ and $r^2$. The probability of $(r^1, 1)$ is just the conditional probability of $r^1$ given $\{r^1, r^2\}$, and similarly for $(r^2, 1)$. At $(r^1, 1)$, Bob considers four points possible: $(r^1, 1)$, $(r^2, 1)$, $(r^3, 1)$, and $(r^4, 1)$. He ascribes these points probability $1/3$, $1/3$, $1/6$, and $1/6$, respectively, since this is the probability of the runs that they are on (conditional on the set of all runs).

To make this precise, it is helpful to have some notation that relates sets of runs to sets of points. If $\mathcal{S}$ is a set of runs and $U$ is a set of points, let $\mathcal{S}(U)$ be the set of runs in $\mathcal{S}$ going through some point in $U$ and let $U(\mathcal{S})$ be the set of points in $U$ that lie on some run in $\mathcal{S}$. That is,

$$\mathcal{S}(U) = \{r \in \mathcal{S} : (r, m) \in U \text{ for some } m\} \text{ and}$$
$$U(\mathcal{S}) = \{(r, m) \in U : r \in \mathcal{S}\}.$$

The condition that the agents' probability assignments in the probability system $(\mathcal{R}, \mathcal{PR}_1, \dots, \mathcal{PR}_m)$ are determined by a (prior) probability on runs can now be formalized as follows:

PRIOR. For each agent $i$, there exists a probability space $(\mathcal{R}, \mathcal{F}_{\mathcal{R},i}, \mu_{\mathcal{R},i})$ such that $\mathcal{R}(\mathcal{K}_i(r, m)) \in \mathcal{F}_{\mathcal{R},i}$ and $\mu_{\mathcal{R},i}(\mathcal{R}(\mathcal{K}_i(r, m))) > 0$ for all $r, m, i$ (i.e., the set of runs that agent $i$ considers possible at any point has positive probability) and $\mathcal{PR}_i(r, m) = (W_{r,m,i}, \mathcal{F}_{r,m,i}, \mu_{r,m,i})$, where

- $W_{r,m,i} = \mathcal{K}_i(r, m)$;

- $\mathcal{F}_{r,m,i} = \{\mathcal{K}_i(r, m)(\mathcal{S}) : \mathcal{S} \in \mathcal{F}_{\mathcal{R},i}\}$;

- $\mu_{r,m,i}(U) = \mu_{\mathcal{R},i}(\mathcal{R}(U) \mid \mathcal{R}(\mathcal{K}_i(r, m)))$, for $U \in \mathcal{F}_{r,m,i}$.

If a system satisfies PRIOR, a set $U$ of points is measurable if it consists of all the points that lie on the runs in some measurable subset of runs; the probability of $U$ (according to $\mu_{r,m,i}$) is just the probability of the set of runs going through $U$ (according to $\mu_{\mathcal{R},i}$) conditioned on the set of runs going through $\mathcal{K}_i(r, m)$.

It is easy to see that the probability assignments defined this way satisfy CONS and SDP. (Indeed, as promised, agent $i$'s probability assignment at the point $(r, m)$ is determined by $\mathcal{K}_i(r, m)$, and hence by agent $i$'s local state at $(r, m)$.) Moreover, if the agents have a common prior on runs (i.e., if $\mathcal{F}_{\mathcal{R},i} = \mathcal{F}_{\mathcal{R},j}$ and $\mu_{\mathcal{R},i} = \mu_{\mathcal{R},j}$ for all $i$ and $j$), then CP holds as well (Exercise 6.5). An *SDP system* is one where PRIOR holds and the agents have a common prior on runs.

What is the connection between $\mathcal{PR}_i(r, m)$ and $\mathcal{PR}_i(r, m + 1)$ in systems satisfying PRIOR? Since $\mathcal{PR}_i(r, m)$ and $\mathcal{PR}_i(r, m + 1)$ are each obtained by conditioning the prior probability on agent $i$'s current information, it seems that $\mathcal{PR}_i(r, m + 1)$ should be, roughly speaking, the result of conditioning $\mathcal{PR}_i(r, m)$ on $\mathcal{K}_i(r, m + 1)$. In general, this is not true.

**Example 6.4.1**    Consider the system described in Example 6.3.2, where Alice tosses two coins, with one modification. Assume that although Alice knows the outcome of the first coin toss after she has tossed it, she forgets it after she tosses the second coin. Thus, Alice's state has the form $(i, o)$, where $i \in \{0, 1, 2\}$ is the time and $o \in \{\langle\,\rangle, \textit{heads}, \textit{tails}\}$ describes the outcome of the coin toss in the previous round ($o = \langle\,\rangle$ at time 0, since no coin was tossed in the previous round). Suppose that, in fact, Alice tosses two heads (so that run $r^1$ occurs). In this case, $\mu_{r^1,1,A}(r^1, 1) = 1/2$. This seems reasonable; at time 1, after observing heads, Alice assigns probability $1/2$ to the point $(r^1, 1)$, where the coin will land heads in the next round. After all, given her information, $r^1$ is just as likely as $r^2$. If she is using conditioning, after observing heads in the next round, Alice should assign the point $(r^1, 2)$ probability 1. However, $\mu_{r^1,2,A}(r^1, 2) = 2/3$ since Alice forgets the outcome of the first coin toss at time 2. Thus, at time 2, Alice considers both $r^1$ and $r^3$ possible, even though at time 1 she knew that $r^3$ was impossible.    ∎

As Example 6.4.1 suggests, a necessary condition for conditioning to be applicable is that agents do not forget, in a sense I now make precise. This observation is closely related to the observation made back in Section 3.1 that conditioning is appropriate only if the agents have perfect recall.

Modeling perfect recall in the systems framework is not too difficult, although it requires a little care. In this framework, an agent's knowledge is determined by his local state. Intuitively, an agent has perfect recall if his local state is always "growing," by adding the new information he acquires over time. This is essentially how the local states were modeled in Example 6.3.1. In general, local states are not required to grow in this sense, quite intentionally. It is quite possible that information encoded in $r_i(m)$—$i$'s local state at time $m$ in run $r$—no longer appears in $r_i(m + 1)$. Intuitively, this means that agent $i$ has lost or "forgotten" this information. There is a good reason not to make this requirement. There are often scenarios of interest where it is important to model the fact that certain information is discarded. In practice, for example, an agent may simply not have enough memory capacity to remember everything he has learned.

Nevertheless, there are many instances where it is natural to model agents as if they do not forget. This means, intuitively, that an agent's local state encodes everything that has happened (from that agent's point of view) thus far in the run. That is, an agent with perfect recall should, essentially, be able to reconstruct his complete local history from his current local state. This observation motivates the following definition.

Let *agent i's local-state sequence at the point* $(r, m)$ be the sequence of local states that she has gone through in run $r$ up to time $m$, without consecutive repetitions. Thus, if from time 0 through time 4 in run $r$ agent $i$ has gone through the sequence $\langle s_i, s_i, s_i', s_i, s_i \rangle$ of local states, where $s_i \neq s_i'$, then her local-state sequence at $(r, 4)$ is $\langle s_i, s_i', s_i \rangle$. Agent $i$'s local-state sequence at a point $(r, m)$ essentially describes what has happened in the run up to time $m$, from $i$'s point of view. Omitting consecutive repetitions is intended to capture the fact that agent $i$ is not aware of time passing, so she cannot distinguish a run where she stays in a given state $s$ for three rounds from one where she stays in $s$ for only one round.

An agent has perfect recall if her current local state encodes her whole local-state sequence. More formally, *agent i has perfect recall in system* $\mathcal{R}$ if at all points $(r, m)$ and $(r', m')$ in $\mathcal{R}$, if $(r, m) \sim_i (r', m')$, then agent $i$ has the same local-state sequence at both $(r, m)$ and $(r', m')$. Thus, agent $i$ has perfect recall if she "remembers" her local-state sequence at all times. In a system with perfect recall, $r_i(m)$ encodes $i$'s local-state sequence in that, at all points where $i$'s local state is $r_i(m)$, she has the same local-state sequence. A system where agent $i$ has perfect recall is shown in Figure 6.5, where the vertical lines denote runs (with time 0 at the top) and all points that $i$ cannot distinguish are enclosed in the same region.

How reasonable is the assumption of perfect recall? That, of course, depends on the application. It is easy to see that perfect recall requires every agent to have a number of local states at least as large as the number of distinct local-state sequences she can have in the system. In systems where agents change state rather infrequently, this may not be too unreasonable. On the other hand, in systems where there are frequent state changes or in long-lived systems, perfect recall may require a rather large (possibly unbounded) number of states. This typically makes perfect recall an unreasonable assumption over long periods of time, although it is often a convenient idealization and may be quite reasonable over short time periods.

In any case, perfect recall gives the desired property: $\mu_{r,m+1,i}$ is essentially the result of conditioning $\mu_{r,m,i}$ on the set of points that lie on runs going through points in $\mathcal{K}_i(r, m + 1)$. To make this precise, given a set $U$ of points, let $U_{r,m,i}$ be the set of

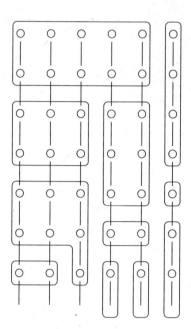

Figure 6.5    A system where agent $i$ has perfect recall.

points in $\mathcal{K}_i(r, m)$ that are on the same runs as points in $U$; that is, $U_{r,m,i} = \{(r', m') \in \mathcal{K}_i(r, m) : (r', m'') \in U$ for some $m''\}$.

**Proposition 6.4.2**   *If $(\mathcal{R}, \mathcal{PR}_1, \ldots, \mathcal{PR}_n)$ is a probability system satisfying PRIOR where agents have perfect recall, then for all points $(r, m)$ and agents $i$, if $U \in \mathcal{F}_{r,m+1,i}$, then $U_{r,m,i} \in \mathcal{F}_{r,m,i}$ and*

$$\mu_{r,m+1,i}(U) = \mu_{r,m,i}(U_{r,m,i} \mid \mathcal{K}_i(r, m + 1)_{r,m,i}).$$

**Proof**    See Exercise 6.6.    ∎

The assumption of perfect recall is crucial in Proposition 6.4.2; it does not hold in general without it (Exercise 6.7).

The sets $U_{r,m,i}$ have a particularly elegant form if one additional assumption is made, namely, that agents know the time. This assumption already arose in the discussion of Example 6.3.1, when I assumed that Bob knew at time 1 that it was time 1, and thus knew that Alice had chosen a number; it is also implicit in all the other examples I have considered so far. Perhaps more significant, game theorists (almost always) assume that agents know the time when analyzing games, as do linguists when analyzing a conversation. The assumption is not quite as common in computer science; *asynchronous systems,* where agents do not necessarily have any idea of how much time has passed between successive moves, are often considered. Nevertheless, even in the computer science literature, protocols that proceed in "phases" or rounds, where no agent starts phase $m + 1$ before all agents finish phase $m$, are often considered.

The assumption that agents know the time is easily captured in the systems framework. $\mathcal{R}$ is *synchronous for agent i* if for all points points $(r, m)$ and $(r', m')$ in $\mathcal{R}$, if $(r, m) \sim_i (r', m')$, then $m = m'$. Thus, if $\mathcal{R}$ is synchronous for agent $i$, then at time $m$, agent $i$ knows that it is time $m$, because it is time $m$ at all the points he considers possible. $\mathcal{R}$ is *synchronous* if it is synchronous for all agents.

It is easy to see that the system of Example 6.3.1 is synchronous, precisely because Bob's local state at time 1 is *tick*. If Bob's state at both time 0 and time 1 were $\langle \rangle$, then the resulting system would not have been synchronous for Bob.

Given a set $U$ of points, let $U^- = \{(r, m) : (r, m + 1) \in U\}$; that is, $U^-$ consists of all the points preceding points in $U$.

**Proposition 6.4.3**   *If $\mathcal{R}$ is synchronous for agent $i$ and agent $i$ has perfect recall in $\mathcal{R}$, then $U_{r,m,i} = U^-$.*

**Proof**   See Exercise 6.8.   ∎

That means that if $\mathcal{R}$ is synchronous for agent $i$ and agent $i$ has perfect recall in $\mathcal{R}$, then the sets $U_{r,m,i}$ and $(\mathcal{K}_i(r, m + 1))_{r,m,i}$ in the statement of Proposition 6.4.2 can be replaced by $U^-$ and $\mathcal{K}_i(r, m + 1)^-$, respectively. Thus, the following corollary holds:

**Corollary 6.4.4**   *If $(\mathcal{R}, \mathcal{PR}_1, \ldots, \mathcal{PR}_n)$ is a synchronous probability system satisfying PRIOR where agents have perfect recall, then for all points $(r, m)$ and agents $i$, if $U \in \mathcal{F}_{r,m+1,i}$, then $U_{r,m,i} \in \mathcal{F}_{r,m,i}$ and*

$$\mu_{r,m+1,i}(U) = \mu_{r,m,i}(U^- \mid \mathcal{K}_i(r, m + 1)^-).$$

## 6.5   Markovian Systems

Although assuming a prior probability over runs helps explain where the probability measure at each point is coming from, runs are still infinite objects and a system may have infinitely many of them. Indeed, even in systems where there are only two global states, there may be uncountably many runs. (Consider a system where a coin is tossed infinitely often and the global state describes the outcome of the last coin toss.) Where is the probability on runs coming from? Is there a compact way of describing and representing it?

In many cases it is possible to assign a probability to the transition from one state to another. Consider the two-coin example described in Figure 6.4. Because the first coin has a probability 2/3 of landing heads, the transition from the initial state to the state where it lands heads has probability 2/3; this is denoted by labeling the left edge coming from the root by 2/3 in Figure 6.4. Similarly, the right edge is labeled by 1/3 to denote that the probability of making the transition to the state where the coin lands heads is 1/3. All the other edges are labeled by 1/2, since the probability of each transition resulting from tossing the second (fair) coin is 1/2. Because the coin tosses are assumed independent and there is a single initial state, the probability of a run in this system can be calculated by multiplying the probabilities labeling its edges.

This type of calculation is quite standard and is abstracted in the notion of a *Markovian system*. In Markovian systems, appropriate independence assumptions are made that allow the prior probability on runs to be generated from a probability on state transitions.

To make this precise, let $\mathcal{R}$ be a system whose global states come from a set $\Sigma$. For $m = 0, 1, 2, \ldots$, let $G_m$ be a random variable on $\mathcal{R}$ such that $G_m(r) = r(m)$—that is, $G_m$ maps $r$ to the global state in $r$ at time $m$. A *time-m event* is a Boolean combination of events of the form $G_i = g$ for $i \leq m$. Of particular interest are time-$m$ events of the form $(G_0 = g_0) \cap \cdots \cap (G_m = g_m)$, which is abbreviated as $[g_0, \ldots, g_m]$; this is the set of all runs in $\mathcal{R}$ with initial prefix $g_0, \ldots, g_m$. Such an event is called an *m-prefix*. As the name suggests, this is the event consisting of all runs whose first $m + 1$ global states are $g_0, \ldots, g_m$. It is easy to show that every time-$m$ event $U$ is a union of $m$-prefixes; moreover, the set $\mathcal{F}_{pref}$, which consists of the time-$m$ events for all $m$, is an algebra (Exercise 6.9).

**Definition 6.5.1**   A probability measure $\mu$ on the algebra $\mathcal{F}_{pref}$ is *Markovian* if, for all $m, m' \geq 0$,

- $\mu(G_{m+1} = g' \mid G_m = g) = \mu(G_{m'+1} = g' \mid G_{m'} = g)$; and

- $\mu(G_{m+1} = g' \mid U \cap G_m = g) = \mu(G_{m+1} = g' \mid G_m = g)$, where $U$ is a time-$m$ event in $\mathcal{R}$.   ∎

The first requirement essentially says that, for each pair $(g, g')$ of global states, there is a well-defined *transition probability*—the probability of making the transition from $g$ to $g'$—that does not depend on the time of the transition. The second requirement says the probability that the $(m + 1)$st global state in a run $g'$ is independent of preceding global states given the value of the $m$th global state. Put another way, the probability of making a transition from global state $g$ at time $m$ to $g'$ at time $m + 1$ is independent of *how* the system reached global state $g$.

The main interest in Markovian probability measures on systems is not that they admit well-defined transition probabilities, but that, starting with the transition probabilities and a prior on initial states, a unique Markovian probability measure on runs can be defined. Define a *transition probability function* $\tau$ to be a mapping from pairs of global state $g$, $g'$ to $[0, 1]$ such that $\sum_{g' \in \Sigma} \tau(g, g') = 1$ for each $g \in \Sigma$. The requirement that the transition probabilities from a fixed $g$ must sum to 1 just says that the sum of the probabilities over all possible transitions from $g$ must be 1.

**Proposition 6.5.2** *Given a transition probability function $\tau$ and a prior $\mu_0$ on 0-prefixes, there is a unique Markovian probability measure $\mu$ on $\mathcal{F}_{pref}$ such that $\mu(G_{n+1} = g' \mid G_n = g) = \tau(g, g')$ and $\mu([g_0]) = \mu_0([g_0])$.*

**Proof** Since $\mathcal{F}_{pref}$ consists of time-$m$ events (for all $m$) and, by Exercise 6.9(a), every time-$m$ event can be written as the disjoint union of $m$-prefixes, it suffices to show that $\mu$ is uniquely defined on $m$-prefixes. This is done by induction on $m$. If $m = 0$, then clearly $\mu([g_0]) = \mu_0([g_0])$. For the inductive step, assume that $m > 0$ and that $\mu$ has been defined on all $(m - 1)$-prefixes. Then

$$\mu([g_0, \ldots, g_m])$$
$$= \mu(G_m = g_m \mid [g_0, \ldots, g_{m-1}]) \times \mu([g_0, \ldots, g_{m-1}]))$$
$$= \tau(g_{m-1}, g_m) \times \mu([g_0, \ldots, g_{m-1}]).$$

Thus, $\mu$ is uniquely defined on $m$-prefixes. Moreover, an easy induction argument now shows that

$$\mu([g_0, \ldots, g_m]) = \mu([g_0]) \times \tau(g_0, g_1) \times \cdots \times \tau(g_{m-1}, g_m).$$

It is easy to check that $\mu$ is in fact Markovian and is the unique probability measure on $\mathcal{F}_{pref}$ such that $\mu(G_{n+1} = g' \mid G_n = g) = \tau(g, g')$ and $\mu([g_0]) = \mu_0([g_0])$ (Exercise 6.10). ∎

## 6.6 Protocols

Systems provide a useful way of representing situations. But where does the system come from? Changes often occur as a result of *actions*. These actions, in turn, are often performed as a result of agents using a *protocol* or *strategy*.

Actions change the global state. Typical actions include tossing heads, going left at an intersection, and sending a message. A protocol for agent $i$ is a description of what actions $i$ may take as a function of her local state. For simplicity, I assume here that all actions are deterministic, although protocols may be nondeterministic or probabilistic. Thus, for example, Alice's protocol may involve tossing a coin in some round. I view "coin tossing" as consisting of two deterministic actions—tossing heads and tossing tails (denoted *toss-heads* and *toss-tails,* respectively).

This can be formalized as follows. Fix a set $L_i$ of local states for agent $i$ (intuitively, these are the local states that arise in some system) and a set $ACT_i$ of possible actions that agent $i$ can take. A *protocol* $P_i$ *for agent* $i$ is a function that associates with every local state in $L_i$ a nonempty subset of actions in $ACT_i$. Intuitively, $P_i(\ell)$ is the set of actions that agent $i$ may perform in local state $\ell$. The fact that $P_i$ is a function of the local state of agent $i$, and not of the global state, is meant to capture the intuition that an agent's actions can be a function only of the agent's information.

If $P_i$ is *deterministic,* then $P_i$ prescribes a unique action for $i$ at each local state; that is, $|P_i(\ell)| = 1$ for each local state in $\ell \in L_i$. For protocols that are not deterministic, rather than just describing what actions agent $i$ may take at a local state, it is often useful to associate a measure of likelihood, such as probability, possibility, or plausibility, with each action. A *probabilistic protocol for* $i$ is a protocol where each local state is associated with a probability measure over a subset of actions in $ACT_i$. Thus, if $P$ is a probabilistic protocol that involves tossing a fair coin at some local state $\ell$, then $P(\ell) = \{toss\text{-}heads, toss\text{-}tails\}$, where each of these actions is performed with probability $1/2$.

Just like the agents, the environment has a protocol $P_e$, which is a map from $L_e$, the set of possible environment states, to nonempty subsets of $ACT_e$, the set of possible environment actions. The environment's protocol models those features that are beyond the control of the agents, such as when messages get delivered in a distributed system, what the weather will be like, or the type of opponent a player will face in a game.

In general, agents do not run their protocols in isolation. A *joint protocol* $(P_e, P_1, \ldots, P_n)$, consisting of a protocol for the environment and a protocol for each of the agents, associates with each global state a subset of possible *joint actions,* that is, a subset of $ACT = ACT_e \times ACT_1 \times \cdots \times ACT_n$. If each of the "local" protocols that make up the joint protocol is probabilistic, then a probability on the joint actions can be obtained by treating each of the local protocols as independent. Thus, for example, if Alice and Bob each toss a coin simultaneously, then taking the coin tosses to be independent leads to an obvious measure on $\{toss\text{-}heads, toss\text{-}tails\} \times \{toss\text{-}heads, toss\text{-}tails\}$. (In most of the examples given here, I ignore the environment protocol and the environment state. In general, however, it plays an important role.)

There is a minor technical point worth observing here. Although I am taking the local protocols to be independent, this does not mean that there cannot be correlated actions. Rather, it says that if there are, there must be something in the local state that allows this correlation. For example, suppose that Alice and Bob each have two coins, one of bias 2/3 and one of bias 1/3. Charlie has a fair coin. Alice and Bob observe Charlie's coin toss, and then use the coin of bias 2/3 if Charlie tosses heads and the coin of bias 1/3 if Charlie tosses tails. Alice and Bob's protocols are still independent. Nevertheless, Alice getting heads is correlated with Bob getting heads. The correlation is due to a correlation in their local states, which reflect the outcome of Charlie's coin toss.

Joint actions transform global states. To capture their effect, associate with every joint action a function from global states to global states. For example, the joint action consisting of Alice choosing 1 and Bob doing nothing maps the initial global state $(\langle \rangle, \langle \rangle, \langle \rangle)$ to the global state $(\langle 1 \rangle, \langle 1 \rangle, \langle tick \rangle)$. Given a joint protocol and a set of initial global states, it is possible to generate a system in a straightforward way. Intuitively, the system consists of all the runs that are obtained by running the joint protocol from one of the initial global states. More formally, say that run $r$ is *consistent with protocol* $P$ if it could have been generated by $P$, that is, for all $m$, $r(m + 1)$ is the result of applying a joint action $\mathbf{a}$ that could have been performed according to protocol $P$ to $r(m)$. (More precisely, there exists a joint action $\mathbf{a} = (\mathbf{a}_1, \ldots, \mathbf{a}_n)$ such that $\mathbf{a}_i \in P_i(r_i(m))$ and $r(m + 1) = \mathbf{a}(r(m))$.) Given a set *Init* of global states, the system $\mathcal{R}(P, Init)$ consists of all the runs consistent with $P$ that start at some initial global state in *Init*. The system $\mathcal{R}$ *represents* $P$ if $\mathcal{R} = \mathcal{R}(P, Init)$ for some set *Init* of global states.

If $P$ is a probabilistic joint protocol (i.e., if each component is probabilistic), $\mathcal{R}$ represents $P$, and there is a probability on the initial global states in $\mathcal{R}$, then there is a straightforward way of putting a probability of $\mathcal{R}$ by viewing $\mathcal{R}$ as Markovian. The probability of a time-$m$ event is just the probability of the initial state multiplied by the probabilities of the joint actions that generated it. This probability on runs can then be used to generate an SDP system, as discussed earlier.

**Example 6.6.1** If on sunny days Alice tosses a coin with bias 2/3, on cloudy days Alice tosses a coin with bias 1/4, and sunny days happen with probability 3/4 (these numbers do not necessarily correspond to reality!), the resulting system consists of four runs, in two computation trees, as shown in Figure 6.6. Now the probability of $r^1$, for example, is $3/4 \times 2/3 = 1/2$. The probability of the other runs can be computed in a similar way. ∎

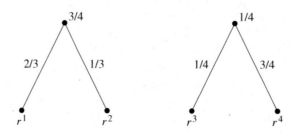

Figure 6.6    Tossing a coin whose bias depends on the initial state.

This discussion assumes that the protocol was probabilistic and that there was a probability on the initial states. Although these assumptions are often reasonable, and they have always been made in the models used in game theory, situations where they do not hold turn out to be rather common in the distributed computing literature. I defer a more detailed look at this issue to Section 6.9.

## 6.7    Using Protocols to Specify Situations

The use of protocols helps clarify what is going on in many examples. In this section, I illustrate this point with three examples, two of which were introduced in Chapter 1—the second-ace puzzle and the Monty Hall puzzle. The first (admittedly somewhat contrived) example formalizes some of the discussion in Chapter 3 regarding when conditioning is applicable.

### 6.7.1    A Listener-Teller Protocol

Suppose that the world is characterized by $n$ binary random variables, $X_1, \ldots, X_n$. Thus, a world $w$ can be characterized by an $n$-tuple of 0s and 1s, $(x_1, \ldots, x_n)$, where $x_i \in \{0, 1\}$ is the value of $X_i$ at world $w$. There are two agents, a *Teller,* who knows what the true values of the random variables are, and a *Listener,* who initially has no idea what they are. In each round, the Teller gives the Listener very limited information: she describes (truthfully) one world that is not the true world. For example, if $n = 4$, the Teller can say "not $(1, 0, 0, 1)$" to indicate that the true world is not $(1, 0, 0, 1)$.

How can this situation be modeled as a system? This depends on what the local states are and what protocol the Teller is following. Since the Teller is presumed to know the actual situation, her state should include (a description of) the actual world. What else should it include? That depends on what the Teller remembers. If she remembers everything, then her local state would have to encode the sequence of facts that she has told the Listener. If she does not remember everything, it might include only some of the facts that she has told the Listener—perhaps even none of them—or only partial information about these facts, such as the fact that all of the worlds mentioned had a 0 in the first component. The form of the local state affects what protocol the Teller could be using. For example, the Teller cannot use a protocol that says "Tell the Listener something new in each round" unless she remembers what she has told the Listener before.

For definiteness, I assume that the Teller remembers everything she has said and that the local state includes nothing else. Thus, the Teller's local state has the form $(w_0, \langle w_1, \ldots, w_m \rangle)$, where $w_0$ and, for $i \geq 1$, $w_i$ is the world that the Teller said was not the actual world in round $i$. (Of course, since the Teller is being truthful, $w_i \neq w_0$ for $i \geq 1$.) For simplicity, I take the environment's state to be identical to the Teller's state, so that the environment is also keeping track of what the actual world is like and what the Teller said. (I could also take the environment state to be empty, since everything relevant to the system is already recorded in the Teller's state.)

What about the Listener? What does he remember? I consider just three possibilities here.

1. The Listener remembers everything that he was told by the Teller.

2. The Listener remembers only the last thing that the Teller said.

3. The Listener remembers only the last two things that the Teller said.

If the Teller's local state is $(w_0, \langle w_1, \ldots, w_m \rangle)$ then, in the first case, the Listener's local state would be $\langle w_1, \ldots, w_m \rangle$; in the second case, it would be just $w_m$ (and $\langle \rangle$ if $m = 0$); in the third case, it would be $(w_{m-1}, w_m)$ (and $\langle \rangle$ if $m = 0$, and $\langle w_1 \rangle$ if $m = 1$). Since the environment state and the Teller's state are the same in all global states, I denote a global state as $(\cdot, (w_0, \langle w_1, \ldots, w_m \rangle), \ldots)$ rather than $((w_0, \langle w_1, \ldots, w_m \rangle), (w_0, \langle w_1, \ldots, w_m \rangle), \ldots)$, where exactly what goes into the ellipsis depends on the form of the Listener's state.

Just specifying the form of the global states is not enough; there are also constraints on the allowable sequences of global states. In the first case, a run $r$ has the following form:

- $r(0) = (\cdot, (w_0, \langle \rangle), \langle \rangle)$,

- if $r(m) = (\cdot, (w_0, \langle w_1, \ldots, w_m \rangle), \langle w_1, \ldots, w_m \rangle)$, then $r(m+1) = (\cdot, (w_0, \langle w_1, \ldots, w_m, w_{m+1} \rangle), \langle w_1, \ldots, w_m, w_{m+1} \rangle)$ for some world $w_{m+1}$.

The first component of the Teller's (and environment's) state, the actual world, remains unchanged throughout the run; this implicitly encodes the assumption that the external world is unchanging. The second component, the sequence of worlds that the Teller has told the listener are not the actual world, grows by one in each round; this implicitly encodes the assumption that the Teller tells the Listener something in every round. Neither of these are necessary assumptions; I have just made them here for definiteness. Analogous constraints on runs hold if the Listener remembers only the last thing or the last two things that the Teller says.

I have now specified the form of the runs, but this still does not characterize the system. That depends on the Teller's protocol. Consider the following two protocols:

- The first is probabilistic. In round $m < 2^n$, the Teller chooses a world $w'$ uniformly at random among the $2^n - m$ world different from the actual world and the $(m - 1)$ worlds that the Listener has already been told about, and the Teller tells the Listener "not $w'$." After round $2^n$, the Teller says nothing.

- The second protocol is deterministic. Order the $2^n$ worlds from $(0, \ldots, 0)$ to $(1, \ldots, 1)$ in the obvious way. Let $w_k$ be the $k$th world in this ordering. In round $m < 2^n$, the Teller tells the Listener "not $w_m$" if the actual world is not among the first $m$ worlds; otherwise, the Teller tells the Listener "not $w_{m+1}$." Again, after round $2^n$, the Teller says nothing.

If the Listener considers all the initial global states to be equally likely, then it is easy to construct probabilistic systems representing each of these two protocols, for each of the three assumptions made about the Listener's local state. (Note that these constructions implicitly assume that the Teller's protocol is common knowledge: the Listener knows what the protocol is, the Teller knows that the Listener knows, the Listener knows that the Teller knows that the Listener knows, and so on. The construction does not allow for uncertainty about the Teller's protocol, although the framework can certainly model such uncertainty.) Call the resulting systems $\mathcal{R}_{ij}$, $i \in \{1, 2\}$, $j \in \{1, 2, 3\}$ (where $i$ determines which of the two protocols is used and $j$ determines which of the three ways the Listener's state is being modeled). It is easy to see that (1) $\mathcal{R}_{11}$, $\mathcal{R}_{13}$, $\mathcal{R}_{21}$, and $\mathcal{R}_{23}$ are synchronous, (2) the Teller has perfect recall in all the systems, and (3) the Listener has perfect recall only in $\mathcal{R}_{11}$ and $\mathcal{R}_{21}$ (Exercise 6.11).

In the system $\mathcal{R}_{11}$, where the Teller is using the probabilistic protocol and the Listener has perfect recall, the Listener can be viewed as using conditioning at the level of worlds. That is, if the Listener is told "not $w$" in the $m$th round, then the set of worlds he considers possible consists of all the worlds he considered possible at time

$m - 1$, other than $w$. Moreover, the Listener considers each of these worlds equally likely (Exercise 6.12).

In both $\mathcal{R}_{12}$ and $\mathcal{R}_{13}$, conditioning on worlds is not appropriate. Because the Listener forgets everything he has been told (except for the very last thing), the Listener considers possible all worlds other than the one he was just told was impossible. Thus, if $w'$ is not the world he heard about in the $m$th round, then he ascribes $w'$ probability $1/(2^n - 1)$. Note, nevertheless, that conditioning at the level of runs is still used to construct the Listener's probability space in $\mathcal{R}_{13}$. Equivalently, the Listener's probability at time $m$ is obtained by conditioning the Listener's initial probability (all the $2^n$ worlds are equally likely) on what he knows at time $m$ (which is just the last thing the Teller told him).

In $\mathcal{R}_{21}$, even though the Listener has perfect recall, conditioning on worlds is also not appropriate. That is, if the Listener is told "not $w$" in the $m$th round, then the set of worlds he considers possible at time $m$ does not necessarily consist of all the worlds he considered possible at time $m - 1$ other than $w$. In particular, if $w = w_{m+1}$, then the Listener will know that the actual world is $w_m$. Since he has perfect recall, he will also know it from then on.

By way of contrast, in $\mathcal{R}_{22}$, because the Listener has forgotten everything he has heard, he is in the same position as in $\mathcal{R}_{12}$ and $\mathcal{R}_{13}$. After hearing "not $w$," he considers possible all $2^n - 1$ worlds not other $w$, and he considers them all equally likely. On the other hand, in $\mathcal{R}_{23}$, because he remembers the last two things that the Teller said, if the Listener hears "not $w_{m+1}$" at time $m$ in run $r$ (rather than "not $w_m$"), then he knows, at the point $(r, m)$, that the actual world is $w_m$. However, he forgets this by time $m + 1$.

While this example is quite contrived, it does show that, in general, if an agent starts with a set of possible worlds and learns something about the actual world in each round, then in order for conditioning to be appropriate, not only must perfect recall be assumed, but also that agents learn nothing from what is said beyond the fact that it is true.

## 6.7.2   The Second-Ace Puzzle

Thinking in terms of protocols also helps in understanding what is going on in the second-ace puzzle from Chapter 1. Recall that in this story, Alice is dealt two cards from a deck of four cards, consisting of the ace and deuce of spades and the ace and deuce of hearts. Alice tells Bob that she has an ace and then tells him that she has the ace of spades. What should the probability be, according to Bob, that Alice has both aces? The calculation done in Chapter 1 gives the answer 1/3. The trouble is that it seems that the probability would also be 1/3 if Alice had said that she had the ace of hearts. It seems unreasonable that Bob's probability that Alice has two aces increases from 1/5 after round 1 to 1/3 after round 2, no matter what ace Alice says she has in round 2.

The first step in analyzing this puzzle in the systems framework is to specify the global states and the exact protocol being used. One reasonable model is to take Alice's local state to consist of the two cards that she was dealt together with the sequence of things she has said and Bob's local state to consist of the sequence things he has heard. (The environment state plays no role here; it can be taken to be the same as Alice's state, just as in the Listener-Teller protocol.)

What about the protocol? One protocol that is consistent with the story is that, initially, Alice is dealt two cards. In the first round, Alice tells Bob whether or not she has an ace. Formally, this means that in a local state where she has an ace, she performs the action of saying "I have an ace"; in a local state where she does not have an ace, she says "I do not have an ace." Then, in round 2, Alice tells Bob she has the ace of spades if she has it and otherwise says she hasn't got it. This protocol is deterministic. There are six possible pairs of cards that Alice could have been dealt, and each one determines a unique run. Since the deal is supposed to be fair, each of these runs has probability 1/6. I leave it to the reader to specify this system formally (Exercise 6.15(a)).

In this system, the analysis of Chapter 1 is perfectly correct. When Alice tells Bob that she has an ace in the first round, then at all time-1 points, Bob can eliminate the run where Alice was not dealt an ace, and his conditional probability that Alice has two aces is indeed 1/5, as suggested in Chapter 1. At time 2, Bob can eliminate two more runs (the runs where Alice does not have the ace of spades), and he assesses the probability that Alice has both aces as 1/3 (Exercise 6.15(b)). Notice, however, that the concern as to what happens if Alice had told Bob that she has the ace of hearts does not arise. This cannot happen, according to the protocol. All that Alice can say is whether or not she has the ace of spades.

Now consider a different protocol (although still one consistent with the story). Again, in round 1, Alice tells Bob whether or not she has an ace. However, now, in round 2, Alice tells Bob which ace she has if she has an ace (and says nothing if she has no ace). This still does not completely specify the protocol. What does Alice tell Bob in round 2 if she has both aces? One possible response is for her to say "I have the ace of hearts" and "I have the ace of spades" with equal probability. This protocol is almost deterministic. The only probabilistic choice occurs if Alice has both aces. With this protocol there are seven runs. Each of the six possible pairs of cards that Alice could have been dealt determines a unique run with the exception of the case where Alice is dealt two aces, for which there are two possible runs (depending on which ace Alice tells Bob she has). Each run has probability 1/6 except for the two runs where Alice

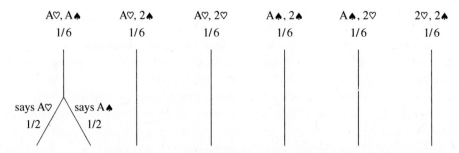

Figure 6.7   A probabilistic protocol for Alice.

was dealt two aces, which each have probability 1/12. Again, I leave it to the reader to model the resulting system formally (Exercise 6.16(a)); it is sketched in Figure 6.7.

It is still the case that at all time-1 points in this system, Bob's conditional probability that Alice has two aces is 1/5. What is the situation at time 2, after Alice says she has the ace of spades? In this case Bob considers three points possible, those in the two runs where Alice has the ace of spades and a deuce, and the point in the run where Alice has both aces and tells Bob she has the ace of spades. Notice, however, that after conditioning, the probability of the point on the run where Alice has both aces is 1/5, while the probability of each of the other two points is 2/5! This is because the probability of the run where Alice holds both aces and tells Bob she has the ace of spades is 1/12, half the probability of the runs where Alice holds only one ace. Thus, Bob's probability that Alice holds both aces at time 2 is 1/5, not 1/3, if this is the protocol. The fact that Alice says she has the ace of spades does not change Bob's assessment of the probability that she has two aces. Similarly, if Alice says that she has the ace of hearts in round 2, the probability that she has two aces remains at 1/5.

The 1/5 here is not the result of Bob conditioning his probability on the initial deal by the information that Alice has the ace of spades (which would result in 1/3, as in the naive analysis in Chapter 1). Naive conditioning is not appropriate here; see the discussion in Section 6.8 and, in particular, Theorem 6.8.1, for a discussion of why this is so.

Now suppose that Alice's protocol is modified so that, if she has both aces, the probability that she says she has the ace of spades is $\alpha$. Again, there are seven runs. Each of the runs where Alice does not have two aces has probability 1/6. Of the two runs where Alice has both aces, the one where Alice says she has the ace of spades in round 2 has probability $\alpha/6$; the one where Alice says she the ace of hearts has probability $(1 - \alpha)/6$. In this case, a similar analysis shows that Bob's probability that Alice holds both aces at time 2 is $\alpha/(\alpha + 2)$ (Exercise 6.16(b)). In the original analysis, $\alpha = 1/2$, so $\alpha/(\alpha + 2)$ reduces to 1/5. If $\alpha = 0$, then Alice never says "I have the ace of spades" if she has both aces. In this case, when Bob hears Alice say "I have the ace of spades" in round 2, his probability that Alice has both aces is 0, as expected. If $\alpha = 1$, which corresponds to Alice saying "I have the ace of spades" either if she has only the ace of spades or if she has both aces, Bob's probability that Alice has both aces is 1/3.

What if Alice does not choose which ace to say probabilistically but uses some deterministic protocol which Bob does not know? In this case, all Bob can say is that the probability that Alice holds both aces is either 0 or 1/3, depending on which protocol Alice is following.

### 6.7.3    The Monty Hall Puzzle

Last but not least, consider the Monty Hall puzzle. As I observed in Chapter 1, a case can be made that there is no advantage to switching. After all, conditioning says that the car is equally likely to be behind one of the two remaining closed doors. However, another argument says that you ought to switch. You lose by switching if the goat is behind the door you've picked; otherwise, you gain. Since the goat is behind the door you pick initially with probability 2/3 and the car is behind the door with probability 1/3, the probability of gaining by switching is 2/3. Is this argument reasonable? It depends. I'll just sketch the analysis here, since it's so similar to that of the second-ace puzzle.

What protocol describes the situation? Assume that, initially, Monty places a car behind one door and a goat behind the other two. For simplicity, let's assume that the car is equally likely to be placed behind any door. In round 1, you choose a door. In round 2, Monty opens a door (one with a goat behind it other than the one you chose). Finally, in round 3, you must decide if you'll take what's behind your door or what's behind the other unopened door. Again, to completely specify the protocol, it is necessary to say what Monty does if the door you choose has a car behind it (since then he can open either of the other two doors). Suppose that the probability of his opening door $j$ if you choose door $i$ and it has a car behind it is $\alpha_{ij}$ (where $\alpha_{ii}$ is 0: Monty never opens the door you've chosen). Computations similar to those used for the second-ace puzzle show that, if you initially take door $i$ and Monty then opens door $j$, the probability of your gaining by switching is $1/(\alpha_{ij} + 1)$ (Exercise 6.17). If $\alpha_{ij} = 1/2$—that is, if Monty is equally likely to open either of the two remaining doors if you choose the door with the car behind it—then the probability of winning if you switch is 2/3, just as in the second argument. If $\alpha_{ij} = 0$, then you are certain that the car cannot be behind the door you opened once Monty opens door $j$. Not surprisingly, in this case, you certainly should switch; you are certain to win. On the other hand, if $\alpha_{ij} = 1$, you are just as likely to win by switching as by not. Since, with any choice of $\alpha_{ij}$, you are at least as likely to win by switching as by not switching, it seems that you ought to switch.

Is that all there is to it? Actually, it's not quite that simple. This analysis was carried out under the assumption that, in round 2, Monty *must* open another door. Is this really Monty's protocol? It certainly does not have to be. Suppose that Monty's protocol is such that he opens another door only if the door that you choose has a car behind it (in order to tempt you away from the "good" door). Clearly in this case you should not switch! If Monty opens the door, then you become certain that the door you chose has the car behind it. A more careful analysis of this puzzle must thus consider carefully what Monty's protocol is for opening a door.

The analysis of the three-prisoners puzzle from Example 3.3.1 is, not surprisingly, quite similar to that of the second-ace puzzle and the Monty Hall puzzle. I leave this to the reader (Exercise 6.18).

## 6.8   When Conditioning Is Appropriate

Why is it that in the system $\mathcal{R}_{11}$ in Section 6.7.1, the Listener can condition (at the level of worlds) when he hears "not $w_m$," while in $\mathcal{R}_{23}$ this is not the case? The pat answer is that the Listener gets extra information in $\mathcal{R}_{23}$ because he knows the Teller's protocol. But what is it about the Teller's protocol in $\mathcal{R}_{23}$ that makes it possible for the Listener to get extra information? A good answer to this question should also explain why, in Example 3.1.2, Bob gets extra information from being told that Alice saw the book in the room. It should also help explain why naive conditioning does not work in the second-ace puzzle and the Monty Hall puzzle.

In all of these cases, roughly speaking, there is a *naive* space and a *sophisticated* space. For example, in both $\mathcal{R}_{11}$ and $\mathcal{R}_{23}$, the naive space consists of the $2^n$ possible worlds; the sophisticated spaces are $\mathcal{R}_{11}$ and $\mathcal{R}_{23}$. In the second-ace puzzle, the naive space consists of the six possible pairs of cards that Alice could have. The sophisticated space is the system generated by Alice's protocol; various examples of sophisticated spaces are discussed in Section 6.7.2. Similarly, in the Monty Hall puzzle the naive space consists of three worlds (one for each possible location of the car), and the sophisticated space again depends on Monty's protocol. Implicitly, I have been assuming that conditioning in the sophisticated space always gives the right answer; the question is when conditioning in the naive space gives the same answer.

The naive space is typically smaller and easier to work with than the sophisticated space. Indeed, it is not always obvious what the sophisticated space should be. For example, in the second-ace puzzle, the story does not say what protocol Alice is using, so it does not determine a unique sophisticated space. On the other hand, as these examples show, working in the naive space can often give incorrect answers. Thus, it is important to understand when it is "safe" to condition in the naive space.

Consider the systems $\mathcal{R}_{11}$ and $\mathcal{R}_{23}$ again. It turns out that the reason that conditioning in the naive space is not safe in $\mathcal{R}_{23}$ is that, in $\mathcal{R}_{23}$, the probability of Bob hearing "not $w_m$" is not the same at all worlds that Bob considers possible at time $m - 1$. At world $w_m$ it is 1; at all other worlds Bob considers possible it is 0. On the other hand, in $\mathcal{R}_{11}$, Bob is equally likely to hear "not $w_m$" at all worlds where he could in principle hear "not $w_m$" (i.e., all worlds other than $w_m$ that have not already been eliminated). Similarly, in Example 3.1.2, Bob is more likely to hear that the book is in the room when the light is on than when the light is off. I now make this precise.

Fix a system $\mathcal{R}$ and a probability $\mu$ on $\mathcal{R}$. Suppose that there is a set $W$ of worlds and a map $\sigma$ from the runs in $\mathcal{R}$ to $W$. $W$ is the naive space here, and $\sigma$ associates with each run a world in the naive space. (Implicitly, I am assuming here that the "world" does not change over time.) In the Listener-Teller example, $W$ consists of the $2^n$ worlds and $\sigma(r)$ is the true world in run $r$. (It is important that the actual world remain unchanged; otherwise, the map $\sigma$ would not be well defined in this case.) Of course, it is possible that more than one run will be associated with the same world. I focus on agent 1's beliefs about what the world the actual world is. In the Listener-Teller example, the Listener is agent 1. Suppose that at time $m$ in a run of $\mathcal{R}$, agent 1's local state has the form $\langle o_1, \ldots, o_m \rangle$, where $o_i$ is the agent's $i$th observation. Taking agent 1's local state to have this form ensures that the system is synchronous for agent 1 and that agent 1 has perfect recall.

For the remainder of this section, assume that the observations $o_i$ are subsets of $W$ and that they are *accurate,* in that if agent 1 observes $U$ at the point $(r, m)$, then $\sigma(r) \in U$. Thus, at every round of every run of $\mathcal{R}$, agent 1 correctly observes or learns that ($\sigma$ of) the actual run is in some subset $U$ of $W$.

This is exactly the setup in the Listener-Teller example (where the sets $U$ have the form $W - \{w\}$ for some $w \in W$). It also applies to Example 3.1.2, the second-ace puzzle, the Monty Hall puzzle, and the three-prisoners puzzle from Example 3.3.1. For example, in the Monty Hall Puzzle, if $W = \{w_1, w_2, w_3\}$, where $w_i$ is the worlds where the car is behind door $i$, then when Monty opens door 3, the agent essentially observes $\{w_1, w_2\}$ (i.e., the car is behind either door 1 or door 2).

Let $(\mathcal{R}, \mathcal{PR}_1, \ldots)$ be the unique probability system generated from $\mathcal{R}$ and $\mu$ that satisfies PRIOR. Note that, at each point $(r, m)$, agent 1's probability $\mu_{r,m,1}$ on the points in $\mathcal{K}_1(r, m)$ induces an obvious probability $\mu^W_{r,m,1}$ on $W$: $\mu^W_{r,m,1}(V) = \mu_{r,i,1}(\{(r', m) \in \mathcal{K}_1(r, m) : \sigma(r') \in V\})$. The question of whether conditioning is appropriate now becomes whether, on observing $U$, agent 1 should update his probability on $W$ by conditioning on $U$. That is, if agent 1's $(m + 1)$st observation in $r$ is $U$ (i.e., if $r_1(m + 1) = r_1(m) \cdot U$), then is it the case that $\mu^W_{r,m+1,1} = \mu^W_{r,m,1}(\cdot \mid U)$? (For the purposes of this discussion, assume that all sets that are conditioned on are measurable and have positive probability.)

In Section 3.1, I discussed three conditions for conditioning to be appropriate. The assumptions I have made guarantee that the first two hold: agent 1 does not forget and what agent 1 learns/observes is true. That leaves the third condition, that the agent learns nothing from what she observes beyond the fact that it is true. To make this precise, it is helpful to have some notation. Given a local state $\ell = \langle U_1, \ldots, U_m \rangle$ and $U \subseteq W$, let $\mathcal{R}[\ell]$ consist of all runs $r$ where $r_1(m) = \ell$, let $\mathcal{R}[U]$ consist of all runs $r$ such that $\sigma(r) \in U$, and let $\ell \cdot U$ be the result of appending $U$ to the sequence $\ell$. If $w \in W$, I abuse notation and write $\mathcal{R}[w]$ rather than $\mathcal{R}[\{w\}]$. To simplify the exposition, assume that if $\ell \cdot U$ is a local state in $\mathcal{R}$, then $\mathcal{R}[U]$ and $\mathcal{R}[\ell]$ are measurable sets and $\mu(\mathcal{R}[U] \cap \mathcal{R}[\ell]) > 0$, for each set $U \subseteq W$ and local state $\ell$ in $\mathcal{R}$. (Note that this assumption implies that $\mu(\mathcal{R}[\ell]) > 0$ for each local state $\ell$ that arises in $\mathcal{R}$.) The fact that learning $U$ in local state $\ell$ gives no more information (about $W$) than the fact that $U$ is true then corresponds to the condition that

$$\mu(\mathcal{R}[V] \mid \mathcal{R}[\ell] \cap \mathcal{R}[U]) = \mu(\mathcal{R}[V] \mid \mathcal{R}[\ell \cdot U]), \text{ for all } V \subseteq W. \qquad (6.1)$$

Intuitively, (6.1) says that in local state $\ell$, observing $U$ (which results in local state $\ell \cdot U$) has the same effect as discovering that $U$ is true, at least as far as the probabilities of subsets of $W$ is concerned.

The following theorem makes precise that (6.1) is exactly what is needed for conditioning to be appropriate:

**Theorem 6.8.1**   *Suppose that $r_1(m + 1) = r_1(m) \cdot U$ for $r \in \mathcal{R}$. The following conditions are equivalent:*

(a) *if $\mu^W_{r,m,1}(U) > 0$, then $\mu^W_{r,m+1,1} = \mu^W_{r,m,1}(\cdot \mid U)$;*

(b) *if $\mu(\mathcal{R}[r_1(m) \cdot U]) > 0$, then*

$$\mu(\mathcal{R}[V] \mid \mathcal{R}[r_1(m)] \cap \mathcal{R}[U]) = \mu(\mathcal{R}[V] \mid \mathcal{R}[r_1(m) \cdot U])$$

*for all $V \subseteq W$;*

(c) *for all $w_1, w_2 \in U$, if $\mu(\mathcal{R}[r_1(m)] \cap \mathcal{R}[w_i]) > 0$ for $i = 1, 2$, then*

$$\mu(\mathcal{R}[r_1(m)] \cdot U] \mid \mathcal{R}[r_1(m)] \cap \mathcal{R}[w_1]) = \mu(\mathcal{R}[r_1(m)] \cdot U] \mid \mathcal{R}[r_1(m)] \cap \mathcal{R}[w_2]).$$

*(d) for all $w \in U$ such that $\mu(\mathcal{R}[r_1(m)] \cap \mathcal{R}[w]) > 0$,*

$$\mu(\mathcal{R}[r_1(m)] \cdot U] \mid \mathcal{R}[r_1(m)] \cap \mathcal{R}[w]) = \mu(\mathcal{R}[r_1(m)] \cdot U] \mid \mathcal{R}[r_1(m)] \cap \mathcal{R}[U]).$$

*(e) The event $\mathcal{R}[w]$ is independent of the event $\mathcal{R}[r_1(m)] \cdot U]$, given $\mathcal{R}[r_1(m)] \cap \mathcal{R}[U]$.*

**Proof**   See Exercise 6.13.   ∎

Part (a) of Theorem 6.8.1 says that conditioning in the naive space agrees with conditioning in the sophisticated space. Part (b) is just (6.1). Part (c) makes precise the statement that the probability of learning/observing $U$ is the same at all worlds compatible with $U$ that the agent considers possible. The condition that the worlds be compatible with $U$ is enforced by requiring that $w_1$, $w_2 \in U$; the condition that the agent consider these worlds possible is enforced by requiring that $\mu(\mathcal{R}[r_1(m)] \cap \mathcal{R}[w_i]) > 0$ for $i = 1, 2$.

Part (c) of Theorem 6.8.1 gives a relatively straightforward way of checking whether conditioning is appropriate. Notice that in $\mathcal{R}_{11}$, the probability of the Teller saying "not $w$" is the same at all worlds in $\mathcal{K}_L(r, m)$ other than $w$ (i.e., it is the same at all worlds in $\mathcal{K}_L(r, m)$ compatible with what the Listener learns), namely, $1/(2^n - m)$. This is not the case in $\mathcal{R}_{22}$. If the Listener has not yet figured out what the world is at $(r, m)$, the probability of the Teller saying "not $w_m$" is the same (namely, 1) at all points in $\mathcal{K}_L(r, m)$ where the actual world is not $w_m$. On the other hand, the probability of the Teller saying "not $w_{m_1}$" is not the same at all points in $\mathcal{K}_L(r, m)$ where the actual world is not $w_{m+1}$. It is 0 at all points in $\mathcal{K}_L(r, m)$ where the actual world is not $w_m$, but it is 1 at points where the actual world is $w_m$. Thus, conditioning is appropriate in $\mathcal{R}_{11}$ in all cases; it is also appropriate in $\mathcal{R}_{21}$ at the point $(r, m)$ if the Listener hears "not $w_m$," but not if the Listener hears "not $w_{m+1}$."

Theorem 6.8.1 explains why naive conditioning does not work in the second-ace puzzle and the Monty Hall puzzle. In the second-ace puzzle, if Alice tosses a coin to decide what to say if she has both aces, then she is *not* equally likely to say "I have the ace of spades" at all the worlds that Bob considers possible at time 1 where she in fact has the ace of spades. She is twice as likely to say it if she has the ace of spades and one of the twos as she is if she has both aces. Similarly, if Monty chooses which door to open with equal likelihood if the goat is behind door 1, then he is not equally likely to show door 2 in all cases where the goat is not behind door 2. He is twice is likely to show door 2 if the goat is behind door 3 as he is if the goat is behind door 1.

The question of when conditioning is appropriate goes far beyond these puzzles. It turns out that to be highly relevant in the statistical areas of *selectively reported data* and *missing data.* For example, consider a questionnaire where some people answer only some questions. Suppose that, of 1,000 questionnaires returned, question 6 is answered "yes" in 300, "no" in 600, and omitted in the remaining 100. Assuming people answer truthfully (clearly not always an appropriate assumption!), is it reasonable to assume that in the general population, 1/3 would answer "yes" to question 6 and 2/3 would answer "no"? This is reasonable if the data is "missing at random," so that people who would have said "yes" are equally likely not to answer the question as people who would have said "no." However, consider a question such as "Have you ever shoplifted?" Are shoplifters really just as likely to answer that question as nonshoplifters?

This issue becomes particularly significant when interpreting census data. Some people are invariably missed in gathering census data. Are these people "missing at random"? Almost certainly not. For example, homeless people and people without telephones are far more likely to be underrepresented, and this underrepresentation may skew the data in significant ways.

## 6.9   Non-SDP Systems

SDP seems like such a natural requirement. Indeed, $\mathcal{K}_i(w)$ seems by far the most natural choice for $W_{w,i}$, and taking $\mu_{w',i} = \mu_{w,i}$ for $w' \in \mathcal{K}_i(w)$ seems like almost a logical necessity, given the intuition behind $\mathcal{K}_i(w)$. If agent $i$ has the same information at all the worlds in $\mathcal{K}_i(w)$ (an intuition that is enforced by the multi-agent systems framework), then how could agent $i$ use a different probability measure at worlds that he cannot distinguish? The following example shows that all is not as obvious as it may first appear:

**Example 6.9.1**   Alice chooses a number, either 0 or 1, and writes it down. She then tosses a fair coin. If the outcome of the coin toss agrees with the number chosen (i.e., if the number chosen is 1 and the coin lands heads, or if the number chosen is 0 and the coin lands tails), then she performs an action **a**; otherwise, she does not. Suppose that Bob does not know Alice's choice. What is the probability, according to Bob, that Alice performs action **a**? What is the probability according to Alice? (For definiteness, assume that both of these probabilities are to be assessed at time 1, after Alice has chosen the number but before the coin is tossed.)

The story can be represented in terms of the computation tree shown in Figure 6.8.

It seems reasonable to say that, according to Alice, who knows the number chosen, the probability (before she tosses the coin) that she performs action **a** is 1/2. There is also a reasonable argument to show that, even according to Bob (who does not know the

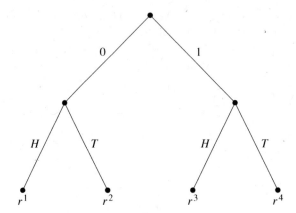

Figure 6.8   Choosing a number, then tossing a coin.

number chosen), the probability is 1/2. Clearly from Bob's viewpoint, if Alice chose 0, then the probability that Alice performs action **a** is 1/2 (since the probability of the coin landing heads is 1/2); similarly, if Alice chose 1, then the probability of her performing action **a** is 1/2. Since, no matter what number Alice chose, the probability according to Bob that Alice performs action **a** is 1/2, it seems reasonable to say that Bob *knows* that the probability of Alice's performing action **a** is 1/2.

Note that this argument does not assume a probability for the event that Alice chose 0. This is a good thing. No probability is provided by the problem statement, so none should be assumed.  ∎

Clearly this example involves reasoning about knowledge and probability, so it should be possible to model it using an epistemic probability frame. (It does not add any insight at this point to use a multi-agent system although, of course, it can be represented using a multi-agent system too.) I consider three frames for modeling it, which differ only in Bob's probability assignment $\mathcal{PR}_B$. Let $F^i = (W, \mathcal{K}_A, \mathcal{K}_B, \mathcal{PR}_A, \mathcal{PR}^i_B)$, $i = 1, 2, 3$. Most of the components of $F^i$ are defined in (what I hope by now is) the obvious way.

- $W = \{(0, H), (0, T), (1, H), (1, T)\}$: Alice chose 0 and the coin lands heads, Alice chose 0 and the coin lands tails, and so on. The worlds correspond to the runs in the computation tree.

- Bob cannot distinguish any of these worlds; in any one of them, he considers all four possible. Thus, $\mathcal{K}_B(w) = W$ for all $w \in W$.

- Alice knows the number she chose. Thus, in a world of the form $(0, x)$, Alice considers only worlds of the form $(0, y)$ possible; similarly, in a world of the form $(1, x)$, Alice considers only worlds of the form $(1, y)$ possible. Alice's probability assignment $\mathcal{PR}_A$ is the obvious one: $W_{w,A} = \mathcal{K}_A(w) = \{(0, H), (0, T)\}$ and $\mu_{w,A}(0, H) = \mu_{w,A}(0, T) = 1/2$ for $w \in \{(0, H), (0, T)\}$, and similarly for $w \in \{(1, H), (1, T)\}$.

It remains to define $\mathcal{PR}_B^i$, $i = 1, 2, 3$. If Bob could assign some probability $\alpha$ to Alice's choosing 0, there would be no problem: in all worlds $w$, it seems reasonable to take $W_{w,B} = W$ and define $\mu_{w,B}$ so that both $(0, H)$ and $(0, T)$ get probability $\alpha/2$, while both $(1, H)$ and $(1, T)$ get probability $(1 - \alpha)/2$. This gives a set of probability measures on $W$, parameterized by $\alpha$.

It is not hard to show that the event $U = \{(0, T), (1, H)\}$ that Alice performs action **a** has probability $1/2$, for any choice of $\alpha$. A Bayesian (i.e., someone who subscribes to the subjective viewpoint of probability) might feel that each agent should choose *some* $\alpha$ and work with that. Since the probability of $U$ is $1/2$, independent of the $\alpha$ chosen, this may seem reasonable. There are, however, two arguments against this viewpoint. The first argument is pragmatic. Since the problem statement does not give $\alpha$, any particular choice may lead to conclusions beyond those justified by the problem. In this particular example, the choice of $\alpha$ may not matter but, in general, it will. It certainly seems unreasonable to depend on conclusions drawn on the basis of a particular $\alpha$. The second argument is more philosophical: adding a probability seems unnecessary here. After all, the earlier informal argument did not seem to need the assumption that there was some probability of Alice choosing 0. And since the argument did not seem to need it, it seems reasonable to hope to model the argument without using it.

What alternatives are there to assuming a fixed probability $\alpha$ on Alice choosing 0? This situation is reminiscent of the situations considered at the beginning of Section 2.3. Three different approaches were discussed there; in principle, they can all be applied in this example. For example, it is possible to use an *epistemic lower probability frame*, so that there are sets of probabilities rather than a single probability. The set could then consist of a probability measure for each choice of $\alpha$. While something like this would work, it still does not address the second point, that the argument did not depend on having a probability at all.

Another possibility is using nonmeasurable sets, making the event that Alice chooses 0 nonmeasurable. Unfortunately, this has some unpleasant consequences. Define $\mathcal{PR}_B^1$ so that $\mathcal{PR}_B^1(w) = (W, \mathcal{F}^1, \mu^1)$ for all $w \in W$, where $\mathcal{F}^1$ is the algebra with basis $\{(0, H), (1, H)\}$ and $\{(0, T), (1, T)\}$ and where $\mu^1(\{(0, H), (1, H)\}) =$

$\mu^1(\{(0, T), (1, T)\}) = 1/2$. That is, in $F^1$, the only events to which Bob assigns a probability are those for which the problem statement gives a probability: the event of the coin landing heads and the event of the coin landing tails. Of course, both these events are assigned probability $1/2$.

The problem with this approach is that the event $U$ of interest is not in $\mathcal{F}^1$. Thus, it is not true that Bob believes that Alice performs action **a** with probability $1/2$. The event that Alice performs action **a** is not assigned a probability at all according to this approach!

A better approach is the first approach considered in Section 2.3: partitioning Bob's possible worlds into two subspaces, depending on whether Alice chooses 0 or 1. Bob's probability space when Alice chooses 0 consists of the two worlds where 0 is chosen, and similarly when Alice chooses 1. In this probability space, all worlds are measurable and have the obvious probability. This can be easily represented using probability assignments. Let $\mathcal{PR}_B^2(w) = \mathcal{PR}_A(w)$ for all $w \in W$; Bob's probability assignment is the same as Alice's.

Frame $F^2$ supports the reasoning in the example. In fact, in $F^2$, the probability that Alice performs action **a** is $1/2$ in every world $w$. More precisely, $\mu_{w,B}(U) = 1/2$ for all $w$. To see this, consider, for example, the world $(0, T)$. Since $W_{(0,T),B} = \{(0, T), (0, H)\}$, it follows that $U \cap W_{(0,T),B} = \{(0, T)\}$. By definition, $\mu_{(0,T),B}((0, T)) = 1/2$, as desired. Similar arguments apply for all the other worlds. It follows that Bob *knows* that the probability that Alice performs action **a** is $1/2$. Similarly, in this frame, Bob knows that the probability that the coin lands heads is $1/2$ and that the probability that the coin lands tails is $1/2$.

What is the probability that 0 was chosen, according to Bob? In the worlds where 0 is actually chosen—that is, $(0, H)$ and $(0, T)$—it is 1; in the other two worlds, it is 0. So Bob knows that the probability that 0 was chosen is either 0 or 1.

Of course, once the door is open to partitioning Bob's set of possible worlds into separate subspaces, there is nothing to stop us from considering other possible partitions. In particular, consider frame $F^3$, where $\mathcal{PR}_B^3(w) = (\{w\}, \mathcal{F}_w, \mu_w)$ for each world $w \in W$. $\mathcal{F}_w$ and $\mu_w$ are completely determined in this case, because the set of possible worlds is a singleton: $\mathcal{F}_w$ consists of $\{w\}$ and $\emptyset$, and $\mu_w$ assigns probability 1 and 0, respectively, to these sets. Now there are four hypotheses: "Alice chose 0 and her coin lands heads," "Alice chose 0 and her coin lands tails," and so on. $F^3$ does not support the reasoning of the example; it is easy to check that at each world in $F^3$, the probability of $U$ is either 0 or 1 (Exercise 6.19). Bob knows that the probability that Alice chooses action **a** is either 0 or 1, but Bob does not know which.

To summarize, in $F^1$, the probability of Alice choosing **a** (according to Bob) is undefined; it corresponds to a nonmeasurable set. In $F^2$, the probability is $1/2$. Finally, in $F^3$, the probability is either 0 or 1, but Bob does not know which. Note that each of $F^1$, $F^2$, and $F^3$ satisfies CONS and UNIF, but only $F^1$ (which arguably is the least satisfactory model) satisfies SDP. While $F^2$ corresponds perhaps most closely to the way Example 6.9.1 was presented, is there anything intrinsically wrong with the frame $F^3$? I would argue that there isn't.

The question of the acceptability of $F^3$ is actually an instance of a larger question: Are there any reasonable constraints on how the subspaces can be chosen? Recall that a natural approach to doing the partitioning was discussed in Section 3.4. There, the subspaces were determined by the possible hypotheses. The "hypotheses" in $F^2$ are "Alice chose 0" and "Alice chose 1." In $F^3$, there are four hypotheses: "Alice chose 0 and her coin lands heads," "Alice chose 0 and her coin lands tails," and so on. To see that such hypotheses are not so unnatural, consider the one-coin problem from Chapter 1 again.

**Example 6.9.2**   This time Alice just tosses a fair coin and looks at the outcome. What is the probability of heads according to Bob? (I am now interested in the probability *after* the coin toss.) Clearly before the coin was tossed, the probability of heads according to Bob was 1/2. Recall that there seem to be two competing intuitions regarding the probability of heads after the coin is tossed. One says the probability is still 1/2. After all, Bob has not learned anything about the outcome of the coin toss, so why should he change his valuation of the probability? On the other hand, runs the counterargument, once the coin has been tossed, does it really make sense to talk about the probability of heads? It has either landed heads or tails, so at best, Bob can say that the probability is either 0 or 1, but he doesn't know which.  ∎

How can this example be modeled? There are two reasonable candidate frames, which again differ only in Bob's probability assignment. Let $F^i = (\{H, T\}, \mathcal{K}_A, \mathcal{K}_B, \mathcal{PR}_A, \mathcal{PR}^i_B)$, $i = 4, 5$, where

- $\mathcal{K}_A(w) = \{w\}$, for $w \in \{H, T\}$ (Alice knows the outcome of the coin toss);

- $\mathcal{K}_B(w) = \{H, T\}$ (Bob does not know the outcome); and

- $\mathcal{PR}_A(w) = (\{w\}, \mathcal{F}_w, \mu_w)$ (Alice puts the obvious probability on her set of possible worlds, which is a singleton, just as in $\mathcal{PR}^3_B$).

It remains to define $\mathcal{PR}^4_B$ and $\mathcal{PR}^5_B$. $\mathcal{PR}^4_B$ is the probability assignment corresponding to the answer 1/2; $\mathcal{PR}^4_B(w) = (\{H, T\}, 2^{\{H,T\}}, \mu)$, where $\mu(H) = \mu(T) = 1/2$, for both $w = H$ and $w = T$. That is, according to $\mathcal{PR}^4_B$, Bob uses the same probability space in both of the worlds he considers possible; in this probability space, he assigns both heads and tails probability 1/2. $\mathcal{PR}_B^5$ is quite different; $\mathcal{PR}_B^5(w) = \mathcal{PR}_A(w) = (\{w\}, \mathcal{F}_w, \mu_w)$. It is easy to see that in each world in $F^4$, Bob assigns probability 1/2 to heads. On the other hand, in each world in $F^5$, Bob assigns either probability 0 or probability 1 to heads. Thus, Bob knows that the probability of heads is either 0 or 1, but he does not know which (Exercise 6.20). Note that $F^4$ is similar in spirit to $F^2$, while $F^5$ is similar to $F^3$. Moreover, $F^4$ and $F^5$ give the two answers for the probability of heads discussed in Chapter 1: "it is 1/2" vs. "it is either 0 or 1, but Bob does not know which."

In $\mathcal{F}^5$, the components of the partition can be thought of as corresponding to the hypotheses "the coin landed heads" and "the coin landed tails." While this is reasonable, besides thinking in terms of possible hypotheses, another way to think about the partitioning is in terms of betting games or, more accurately, the knowledge of the person one is betting against. Consider Example 6.9.2 again. Imagine that besides Bob, Charlie is also watching Alice toss the coin. Before the coin is tossed, Bob may be willing to accept an offer from either Alice or Charlie to bet $1 for a payoff of $2 if the coin lands heads. Half the time the coin will land heads and Bob will be $1 ahead, and half the time the coin will land tails and Bob will lose $1. On average, he will break even. On the other hand, Bob should clearly not be willing to accept such an offer from Alice after the coin is tossed (since Alice saw the outcome of the coin toss), although he might still be willing to accept such an offer from Charlie. Roughly speaking, when playing against Charlie, it is appropriate for Bob to act as if the probability of heads is 1/2, whereas while playing against Alice, he should act is if it is either 0 or 1, but he does not know which. Similarly, under this interpretation, the frame $F^5$ in Example 6.9.2 amounts to betting against an adversary who knows the outcome of the coin toss, while $F^4$ amounts to betting against an adversary that does not know the outcome. This intuition regarding betting games can be generalized, although that is beyond the scope of the book. (See the notes for references.)

Example 6.9.1, where there are nonprobabilistic choices as well as probabilistic choices, may seem artificial. But, in fact, such situations are quite common, as the following example shows:

**Example 6.9.3**    Consider the problem of testing whether a number $n$ is prime. There is a well-known deterministic algorithm for testing primality, often taught in elementary school: test each number between 1 and $n$ to see if it divides $n$ evenly. If one of them does, then $n$ is composite; otherwise, it is prime.

This algorithm can clearly be improved. For example, there is no need to check *all* the numbers up to $n - 1$. Testing up to $\sqrt{n}$ suffices: if $n$ is composite, its smaller factor is bound to be at most $\sqrt{n}$. Moreover, there is no need to check any even number besides 2. Even with these improvements, if $n$ is represented in binary (as a string of

0s and 1s), then there are still exponentially many numbers to check in the worst case as a function of the length of $n$. For example, if $n$ is a 100-digit number, the square root of $n$ is a 50-digit number, so there will still be roughly $2^{50}$ numbers to check to see if $n$ is prime. This is infeasible on current computers (and likely to remain so for a while). Until recently, no polynomial-time algorithm for testing primality was known. Now there is one. Nevertheless, by far the fastest primality-testing algorithm currently available is probabilistic.

Before discussing the algorithm, it is worth noting that the problem of testing whether a number is prime is not just of academic interest. The well-known RSA algorithm for *public-key cryptography* depends on finding composite numbers that are the product of two large primes. Generating these primes requires an efficient primality-testing algorithm. (Theorems of number theory assure us that there are roughly $n/\log n$ primes less than $n$ and that these are well distributed. Thus, it is easy to find a prime quickly by simply testing many 100-digit numbers generated at random for primality, provided that the primality test itself is fast.)

The probabilistic primality-testing algorithm is based on the existence of a predicate $P$ that takes two arguments, $n$ and $a$ (think of $n$ as the number whose primality we are trying to test and $a$ as an arbitrary number between 1 and $n$), and has the following properties:

1. $P(n, a)$ is either 1 (true) or 0 (false); computing which it is can be done very rapidly (technically, in time polynomial in the length of $n$ and $a$).

2. If $n$ is composite, then $P(n, a)$ is true for at least $n/2$ possible choices of $a$ in $\{1, \ldots, n - 1\}$.

3. If $n$ is prime, then $P(n, a)$ is false for all $a$.

The existence of such a predicate $P$ can be proved using number-theoretic arguments. Given $P$, there is a straightforward Choose, say, 100 different values for $a$, all less than $n$, at random. Then compute $P(n, a)$ for each of these choices of $a$. If $P(n, a)$ is false for any of these choices of $a$, then the algorithm outputs "composite"; otherwise, it outputs "prime." This algorithm runs very quickly even on small computers. Property (1) guarantees that this algorithm is very efficient. Property (3) guarantees that if the algorithm outputs "composite," then $n$ is definitely composite. If the algorithm outputs "prime," then there is a chance that $n$ is not prime, but property (2) guarantees that this is very rarely the case: if $n$ is indeed composite, then with high probability (probability at least $1 - (1/2)^{100}$) the algorithm outputs "composite."

Corresponding to this algorithm is a set of runs. The first round in these runs is nonprobabilistic: an input $n$ is given (or chosen somehow). The correctness of the algorithm should not depend on how it is chosen. Moreover, in proving the correctness of this algorithm, it seems inappropriate to assume that there is a probability measure on the inputs. The algorithm should be correct for *all* inputs. But what does "correct" even mean? The preceding arguments show that if the algorithm outputs "composite," then it is correct in the sense that $n$ is really composite. On the other hand, if the algorithm outputs "prime," then $n$ may not be prime. It might seem natural to say that $n$ is then prime with high probability, but that is not quite right. The input $n$ is either prime or it is not; it does not make sense to say that it is prime with high probability. But it does make sense to say that the algorithm gives the correct answer with high probability. (Moreover, if the algorithm says that $n$ is prime, then it seems reasonable for an agent to ascribe a high subjective degree of belief to the proposition "$n$ is prime.")

The natural way to make this statement precise is to partition the runs of the algorithm into a collection of subsystems, one for each possible input, and to prove that the algorithm gives the right answer with high probability in each of these subsystems, where the probability on the runs in each subsystem is generated by the random choices for $a$. While for a fixed composite input $n$ there may be a few runs where the algorithm incorrectly outputs "prime," in almost all runs it will give the correct output. The spirit of this argument is identical to that used in Example 6.9.1 to argue that the probability that Alice performs action **a** is $1/2$, because she performs **a** with probability $1/2$ whichever number she chooses in the first round.  ∎

**Example 6.9.4** The *coordinated attack* problem is well-known in the distributed systems literature. Two generals, $A$ and $B$, want to coordinate an attack on the enemy village. If they attack together, they will win the battle. However, if either attacks alone, his division will be wiped out. Thus, neither general wants to attack unless he is certain that the other will also attack. Unfortunately, the only way they have of communicating is by means of a messenger, who may get lost or captured. As is well known, no amount of communication suffices to guarantee coordination. But suppose it is known that each messenger sent will, with probability .5, deliver his message within an hour; otherwise, the messenger will get lost or captured, and never arrive. Moreover, messengers are independent. In that case, there is a trivial algorithm for coordination with high probability. If General $A$ wants to attack on a particular day, $A$ sends $n$ messengers with messages saying "Attack at dawn" over an hour before dawn, then attacks at dawn. General $B$ attacks at dawn iff he receives a message from $A$ instructing him to do so. It is easy to see that if $A$ attacks, then with probability $1 - (1/2)^n$, $B$ does too, and if $A$ does not attack, then $B$ definitely does not attack. Thus, the probability of coordination is high, whether or not $A$ attacks.

Consider the question of whether there is an attack on a particular day $d$. The multi-agent system representing this situation can be partitioned into two sets of runs, one corresponding to the runs where $A$ wants to attack on day $d$, and the other corresponding to the run where $A$ does not want to attack on day $d$. The runs where $A$ wants to attack differ in terms of which of the messengers actually manages to deliver his message. It is easy to describe a probability measure on each of these two sets of runs separately, but there is no probability measure on the whole set, since the problem statement does not give the probability that $A$ wants to attack. Nevertheless, by partitioning the runs, depending on $A$'s choice, it is possible to conclude that both $A$ and $B$ know (indeed, it is common knowledge among them) that, with high probability, they will coordinate, no matter what $A$ chooses to do. ∎

In Examples 6.3.1, 6.9.3, and 6.9.4, only the first choice is nonprobabilistic. (In the coordinated attack example, the nonprobabilistic choice is whether or not $A$ wants to attack; this can be viewed as an initial nondeterministic choice made by the environment.) However, in general, nonprobabilistic choices or moves may be interleaved with probabilistic moves. In this case though, it is possible to represent what happens in such a way that all nonprobabilistic choices happen in the first round. The following example should help make this clear:

**Example 6.9.5**   Suppose that Alice has a fair coin and Bob has a biased coin, which lands heads with probability $2/3$. There will be three coin tosses; Charlie gets to choose who tosses each time. That is, in rounds 1, 3, and 5, Charlie chooses who will toss a coin in the next round; in rounds 2, 4, and 6, the person Charlie chose in the previous round tosses his or her coin. Notice that, in this example, the probabilistic rounds—the coin tosses—alternate with the nonprobabilistic rounds—Charlie's choices.

One way of representing this situation is by taking the environment state at a point $(r, m)$ to represent what happened up to that point: who Charlie chose and what the outcome of his or her coin toss was. Since what happens is public, the local states of Alice, Bob, and Charlie can be taken to be identical to that of the environment. It is easy to see that, with this representation, there are 64 ($= 2^6$) runs in the system, since there are two possibilities in each round. In one run, for example, Charlie chooses Alice, who tosses her coin and gets heads, then Charlie chooses Bob, who gets heads, and then Charlie chooses Alice again, who gets tails.

What is the probability of getting heads in all three coin tosses? That depends, of course, on who Charlie chose in each round; the story does not give probabilities for these choices. Intuitively, however, it should be somewhere between $1/8$ (if Alice was chosen all the time) and 8/27 (if Bob was chosen all the time). Can the set of runs be partitioned as in Example 6.3.1 to make this precise?

When the only nonprobabilistic choice occurs at the beginning, it is straightforward to partition the runs according to the outcome of the nonprobabilistic choice. (The possible choices can be taken to be the "hypotheses.") However, because the nonprobabilistic choices here are interspersed with the probabilistic moves, it is not so obvious how to do the partitioning. One approach to dealing with this problem is to convert this situation to one where there is only one nonprobabilistic choice, which happens at the beginning. The trick is to ask what Charlie's strategy or protocol is for deciding who goes next. Charlie may have a very simple strategy like "pick Alice in every round" or "pick Alice, then Bob, then Alice again." However, in general, Charlie's strategy may depend on what has happened thus far in the run (in this case, the outcome of the coin tosses), as encoded in his local state. (I am implicitly assuming that Charlie sees the outcome of each coin toss here. If not, then Charlie's local state would not include the outcome, and hence his strategy cannot depend on it.) For example, Charlie's strategy may be the following: "First pick Alice. If she tosses tails, pick Alice again; otherwise, pick Bob. If whoever was picked the second time tosses tails, then pick him/her again; otherwise, pick the other person." Note that both this strategy and the strategy "pick Alice, then Bob, then Alice again" are consistent with the run described earlier. In general, more than one strategy is consistent with observed behavior.

In any case, notice that once Charlie chooses a strategy, then all his other choices are determined. Fixing a strategy factors out all the nondeterminism. The story in this example can then be captured by a multi-agent system where, in the first round, Charlie chooses a strategy and from then on picks Alice and Bob according to the strategy. In more detail, Charlie's local state now would include his choice of strategy together with what has happened thus far, while, as before, the local state of Alice, Bob, and the environment just describe the observable events (who Charlie chose up to the current time and the outcome of the coin tosses).

It can be shown that Charlie has $2^{21}$ possible strategies (although many of these can be identified; see Exercise 6.21(a)), and for each of these strategies, there are eight runs, corresponding to the possible outcomes of the coin tosses. Thus, this representation leads to a system with $2^{21} \cdot 8 = 2^{24}$ runs. These runs can be partitioned according to the initial choice of strategy; there is a natural probability measure on the eight runs that arise from any fixed strategy (Exercise 6.21(b)). With this representation, it is indeed the case that the probability of getting three heads is somewhere between 1/8 and 8/27, since in the probability space corresponding to each strategy, the probability of the run with three heads is between 1/8 and 8/27.

Each of the 64 runs in the original representation corresponds to $2^{18}$ runs in this representation (Exercise 6.21(c)). Although, in some sense, the new representation can be viewed as "inefficient," it has the advantage of partitioning the system cleanly into subsystems, each of which gives rise to a natural probability space.   ∎

As this example shows, in systems where there is possibly an initial nonprobabilistic choice, and from then on actions are chosen probabilistically (or deterministically) as a function of the local state, the system can be partitioned into subsystems according to the initial choice, and each subsystem can be viewed as a probability space in a natural way. The key point is that, once an agent can partition the set of runs in the system and place a probability on each subspace of the partition, the techniques of Section 6.4 can be applied with no change to get a probability assignment. These probability assignments satisfy UNIF and CONS, but not necessarily SDP. If agent $i$ partitions the set of runs into subspaces $\mathcal{R}_1, \ldots, \mathcal{R}_m$, then $\mathcal{K}_i(r, m)$ is then partitioned into $\mathcal{K}_i(r, m)(\mathcal{R}_j)$, $j = 1, \ldots, m$. If $(r', m') \in \mathcal{K}_i(r, m)$, then $W_{r',m',i}$ is the unique set $\mathcal{K}_i(r, m)(\mathcal{R}_j)$ that includes $(r', m')$.

Each of the three systems $F^1$, $F^2$, and $F^3$ in Example 6.9.1 can be thought of as arising from this construction applied to the four runs illustrated in Figure 6.8. If Bob does not partition these runs at all, but takes the only nontrivial measurable sets to be $\{r_1, r_3\}$ and $\{r_2, r_4\}$, the resulting frame is $F^1$. Frame $F^1$ satisfies SDP precisely because the original set of runs is not partitioned into separate subspaces. If Bob partitions the runs into two subspaces $\{r_1, r_2\}$ and $\{r_3, r_4\}$, then the resulting frame is $F^2$. Finally, if the four runs are partitioned into four separate subspaces, the resulting frame is $F^3$. Since $F^2$ is the frame that best seems to capture the informal argument, what all this shows is that, although SDP may seem like an unavoidable assumption initially, in fact, there are many cases where it is too strong an assumption, and UNIF may be more appropriate.

## 6.10   Plausibility Systems

The discussion in Sections 6.2–6.9 was carried out in terms of probability. However, probability did not play a particularly special role in the discussion; everything I said carries over without change to other representations of uncertainty. I briefly touch on some of the issues in the context of plausibility; all the other representations are just special cases.

As expected, a *plausibility system* is a tuple $(\mathcal{R}, \mathcal{PL}_1, \ldots, \mathcal{PL}_n)$, where $\mathcal{R}$ is a system and $\mathcal{PL}_1, \ldots, \mathcal{PL}_n$ are plausibility assignments. CONS makes sense without change for plausibility systems; SDP, UNIF, PRIOR, and CP have obvious analogues (just replacing "probability" with "plausibility" everywhere in the definitions). However, for PRIOR and CP to make sense, there must be a *conditional* plausibility measure on the set of runs, so that conditioning can be applied. Furthermore, the sets $\mathcal{R}(\mathcal{K}_i(r, m))$ must be in $\mathcal{F}'$, so that it makes sense to condition on them. (Recall that in Section 6.4 I assumed that $\mu_{r,i}(\mathcal{R}(\mathcal{K}_i(r, m))) > 0$ to ensure that conditioning on $\mathcal{R}(\mathcal{K}_i(r, m))$ is always possible in the case of probability.) I assume that in the case of plausibility, these assumptions are part of PRIOR.

It also makes sense to talk about a Markovian conditional plausibility measure, defined by the obvious analogue of Definition 6.5.1. However, Markovian probability measures are mainly of interest because of Proposition 6.5.2. For the analogue of this proposition to hold for plausibility measures, there must be analogues of $+$ and $\times$. Thus, Markovian plausibility measures are mainly of interest in algebraic cps's (see Definition 3.9.1).

## Exercises

**6.1**    Show that a binary relation is reflexive, symmetric, and transitive if and only if it is reflexive, Euclidean, and transitive.

**6.2**    Show that $\mathcal{K}$ is reflexive iff $w \in \mathcal{K}(w)$ for all worlds $w$; $\mathcal{K}$ is transitive iff, for all worlds $w$ and $w'$, if $w' \in \mathcal{K}(w)$ then $\mathcal{K}(w') \subseteq \mathcal{K}(w)$; and $\mathcal{K}$ is Euclidean iff, for all worlds $w$, $w'$, if $w' \in \mathcal{K}(w)$, then $\mathcal{K}(w') \supseteq \mathcal{K}(w)$.

**6.3**    Given the definition of $W$, $\mathcal{K}_1$, and $\mathcal{K}_2$, show that the only way the frame $F$ described just before Example 6.2.2 can be consistent with CP is if $\mathcal{PR}_1(w_1) = \mathcal{PR}_2(w_1) = \mathcal{PR}_2(w_1) = \mathcal{PR}_2(w_2)$.

**6.4**    Show that the frame $F$ in Example 6.2.2 does not satisfy CP. (This is not quite as easy as it seems. It is necessary to deal with the case that some sets have measure 0.)

**6.5**    Show that the construction of probability assignments given in Section 6.4 satisfies CONS and SDP. Moreover, show that CP holds if the agents have a common prior on runs.

**6.6**    Prove Proposition 6.4.2.

**6.7** Show that the analogue of Proposition 6.4.2 does not hold in general in systems where agents do not have perfect recall.

**6.8** Prove Proposition 6.4.3.

**6.9** This exercise takes a closer look at time-$m$ events and $m$-prefixes.

  (a) Show that every time-$m$ event in a system is the disjoint union of $m$-prefixes.

  (b) Show that if $m < m'$, then an $m'$-prefix is a union of $m$-prefixes.

  (c) Show that if $m < m'$, then the union of a time-$m$ event and a time-$m'$ event is a time-$m'$ event.

  (d) Show that $\mathcal{F}_{pref}$ is an algebra; that is, it is closed under union and complementation.

**6.10** Complete the proof of Proposition 6.5.2 by showing that the probability measure $\mu$ defined in the proof is in fact Markovian and is the unique probability measure on $\mathcal{F}_{pref}$ such that $\mu(G_{n+1} = g' \mid G_n = g) = \tau(g, g')$ and $\mu([g_0]) = \mu_0([g_0])$.

**6.11** For the systems constructed in Section 6.7.1, show that

  (a) $\mathcal{R}_{11}$, $\mathcal{R}_{13}$, $\mathcal{R}_{21}$, and $\mathcal{R}_{23}$ are synchronous, while $\mathcal{R}_{21}$ and $\mathcal{R}_{22}$ are not;

  (b) the Teller has perfect recall in all six systems; and

  (c) the Listener has perfect recall in $\mathcal{R}_{11}$ and $\mathcal{R}_{21}$ but not in the other four systems.

**6.12** Show that in the system $\mathcal{R}_{11}$ constructed in Section 6.7.1, if $r$ is a run in which the Listener is told "not $w$" in the $m$th round, then the set of worlds he considers possible consists of all the worlds he considered possible at time $m - 1$, other than $w$. Moreover, the Listener considers each of these worlds equally likely.

\* **6.13** Prove Theorem 6.8.1.

**6.14** Describe a simple system that captures Example 3.1.2, where Alice is about to look for a book in a room where the light may or may not be on. Explain in terms of Theorem 6.8.1 under what conditions conditioning is appropriate.

**6.15** Consider Alice's first protocol for the second-ace puzzle, where in the second round, she tells Bob whether or not she has the ace of spades.

  (a) Specify the resulting system formally.

  (b) Show that in the runs of this system where Alice has the ace of spades, at time 2, Bob knows that the probability that Alice has both aces is $1/3$.

**6.16**   Consider Alice's second protocol for the second-ace puzzle, where in the second round, she tells Bob which ace she has. Suppose that if she has both aces, she says that she has the ace of spades with probability $\alpha$.

(a) Specify the resulting system formally.

(b) Show that in the runs of this system where Alice has the ace of spades, at time 2, Bob knows that the probability that Alice has both aces is $\alpha/(\alpha + 2)$.

**6.17**   Consider the Monty Hall puzzle, under the assumption that Monty must open a door in the second round. Suppose that the probability of his opening door $j$, if you choose door $i$ and it has a car behind it, is $\alpha_{ij}$.

(a) Specify the resulting system formally (under the assumption that you know the probabilities $\alpha_{ij}$).

(b) Show that in this system, the probability of gaining by switching is $1/(\alpha_{ij} + 1)$.

**6.18**   Analyze the three-prisoners puzzle from Example 3.3.1 under the assumption that the probability that the jailer says $b$ given that $a$ lives is $\alpha$. That is, describe the jailer's protocol carefully, construct the set of runs in the system, and compute the probability that $a$ lives given that the jailer actually says $b$. Explain in terms of Theorem 6.8.1 when conditioning gives the correct answer and why it gives the incorrect answer in general.

**6.19**   Show that in $F^3$, Bob knows that the probability of $U$ is either 0 or 1, but he does not know which.

**6.20**   Show that in $F^5$, Bob knows that the probability of heads is either 0 or 1, but he does not know which.

**6.21**   This exercise refers to the second system constructed in Example 6.9.5.

(a) Show that there are $2^{21}$ strategies possible for Charlie. (Hint: Recall that a strategy is a function from what Charlie observes, regarding who tosses a coin and the outcome of his or her coin tosses, to actions (in this case, the decision as to who goes next). Show that there are 21 different sequences of observations that describe what Charlie has seen just before he must move. Since there are two possible actions he can take, this gives the desired result.)

(b) Show that these strategies can be partitioned into $2^6$ sets of $2^{15}$ strategies each, where each of the strategy in a given set leads to precisely the same outcomes (who tossed the coin at each step and how the coin lands). Note that each of these sets corresponds to one run in the original representation.

(c) Describe the probability on the set of runs corresponding to a fixed strategy for Charlie.

## Notes

Some of the material in Section 6.1 is taken from *Reasoning About Knowledge* [Fagin, Halpern, Moses, and Vardi 1995]. This book explores the topic of reasoning about knowledge, and its applications to artificial intelligence, distributed systems, and game theory, in much more detail. Frames were introduced by Lemmon and Scott [Lemmon 1977], who called them "world systems"; the term "frame" is due to Segerberg [1968]. (Epistemic frames are called *Aumann structures* in [Fagin, Halpern, Moses, and Vardi 1995], in honor of Robert Aumann, an economist who introduced epistemic reasoning to the economics/game theory literature.)

The notions of CONS, SDP, and UNIF were formalized in [Fagin and Halpern 1994], where epistemic probability frames were first considered. There is related work in the economics literature by Monderer and Samet [1989]. The common prior assumption and its implications have been well studied in the economics literature; some significant references include [Aumann 1976; Harsanyi 1968; Morris 1995].

The general framework presented here for ascribing knowledge in multi-agent systems first used in [Halpern and Moses 1990] and [Rosenschein 1985]. Slight variants of this framework were introduced in a number of other papers [Fischer and Immerman 1986; Halpern and Fagin 1989; Parikh and Ramanujam 1985; Rosenschein and Kaelbling 1986]. The presentation here is based on that of [Fagin, Halpern, Moses, and Vardi 1995, Chapter 4], which in turn is based on [Halpern and Fagin 1989]. The reader is encouraged to consult [Fagin, Halpern, Moses, and Vardi 1995] for further references and a much more detailed discussion of this approach, examples of its use, and a discussion of alternative approaches to representing multi-agent systems.

*Markov chains* (which is essentially what Markovian systems are) are of great practical and theoretical interest and have been studied in depth; a good introduction to the field is the book by Kemeny and Snell [1960]. An extension of Markov chains allows an agent to take an action in each round. The transition probabilities then depend on the action $\mathbf{a}$ as well as the states involved and thus have the form $\tau(g, \mathbf{a}, g')$. Intuitively, $\tau(g, \mathbf{a}, g')$ is the probability of making the transition from $g$ to $g'$ if action $\mathbf{a}$ is taken. With each action is associated a *reward* or utility. The problem is then to find an optimal *policy* or strategy, that is, an optimal choice of action at each state (under various definitions of optimality). This model is called a *Markov decision process* (MDP); see [Puterman 1994] for an introduction to MDPs.

The approach for getting a probability assignment from a probability on runs was first discussed in [Halpern and Tuttle 1993]. The formal definition of synchronous systems and of systems where agents have perfect recall is taken from [Halpern and Vardi 1989]. For a discussion of perfect recall in the context of game theory, see [Fudenberg and Tirole 1991]. The definition of perfect recall given here is actually not quite the same as that used in game theory; see [Halpern 1997b] for a discussion of the differences.

The Listener-Teller protocol discussed in Section 6.7.1 is based on a nonprobabilistic version of the protocol discussed in [Fagin, Halpern, Moses, and Vardi 1995]. The importance of the role of the protocol in analyzing the second-ace puzzle was already stressed by Shafer [1985]. Morgan et al. [1991] seem to have been the first to observe in print that the standard analysis of the Monty Hall puzzle (e.g., that given by vos Savant [1990]) depends crucially on the assumption that Monty Hall must open a door in the second round. The analysis of the second-ace puzzle and the Monty Hall puzzle presented here is essentially taken from [Halpern 1998b].

As I mentioned earlier, the question of when conditioning is appropriate is highly relevant in the statistical areas of *selectively reported data* and *missing data*. Originally studied within these contexts [Rubin 1976; Dawid and Dickey 1977], it was later found to also play a fundamental role in the statistical work on *survival analysis* [Kleinbaum 1999]. Building on previous approaches, Heitjan and Rubin [1991] presented a necessary and sufficient condition for when conditioning in the "naive space" is appropriate. Nowadays this so-called *CAR (Coarsening at Random)* condition is an established tool in survival analysis. (See [Gill, van der Laan, and Robins 1997; Nielsen 1998] for overviews.) Theorem 6.8.1 is a slight restatement of the CAR condition. See [Grünwald and Halpern 2002] for further discussion of when conditioning is appropriate.

The deterministic polynomial-time algorithm for testing primality is due to Agrawal, Keyal, and Saxena [2002]. The probabilistic primality-testing algorithms were developed by Rabin [1980] and Solovay and Strassen [1977]. The RSA algorithm was developed by Rivest, Shamir, and Adleman [1978]; their article also gives a brief introduction to public-key cryptography.

The need to go beyond SDP systems was first discussed in [Fagin and Halpern 1994]. The notion that different choices of probability assignment correspond to betting against adversaries with different information is discussed in [Halpern and Tuttle 1993], where the betting interpretation discussed after Example 6.9.2 is developed.

The coordinated attack problem was introduced by Gray [1978]. It has become part of the folklore of distributed systems; a formal proof of its impossibility (by induction on the number of messages) is given by Yemini and Cohen [1979]. The problem is discussed in detail in [Fagin, Halpern, Moses, and Vardi 1995; Halpern and Moses 1990].

The idea of factoring out all the nonprobabilistic choices in a system and viewing them as being under the control of some adversary is standard in the distributed computing and theoretical computer science literature (see, e.g., [Rabin 1982; Vardi 1985]); it was first formalized in the context of reasoning about knowledge and probability by Fischer and Zuck [1988].

# Chapter 7

# Logics for Reasoning about Uncertainty

*Proof*, n. Evidence having a shade more of plausibility than of unlikelihood. The testimony of two credible witnesses as opposed to that of only one.

—Ambrose Bierce, *The Devil's Dictionary*

The previous chapters considered various issues regarding the representation of uncertainty. This chapter considers formal logics for reasoning about uncertainty. These logics provide tools for carefully representing arguments involving uncertainty, as well as methods for characterizing the underlying notion of uncertainty. Note that I said "logics," not "logic." I consider a number of logics. The choice of logic depends in part on (1) the underlying representation of uncertainty (e.g., is it a probability measure or a ranking function?), (2) the degree to which quantitative reasoning is significant (is it enough to say that $U$ is more likely than $V$, or is it important to be able to talk about the probability of $U$?), and (3) the notions being reasoned about (e.g., likelihood or expectation). In this chapter, I consider how each of these questions affects the choice of logic.

As I said in Chapter 1, a formal logic consists of an appropriate syntax (i.e., a language) and semantics, essentially, models that are used for deciding if formulas in the language are true and false. Quite often logics are also characterized *axiomatically:* a collection of *axioms* and *inference rules* is provided from which (hopefully all) *valid* formulas (i.e., formulas that are true in all semantic models) can be derived.

The various types of frames that were discussed in Chapter 6 (epistemic frames, probability frames, etc.) provide the basis for the semantic models used in this chapter. Thus, not much work needs to be done on the semantic front in this chapter. Instead, I focus is on issues of language and, to a lesser extent, on axiomatizations.

Perhaps the simplest logic considered in the literature, and the one that most students encounter initially, is *propositional logic* (sometimes called *sentential logic*). It is intended to capture features of arguments such as the following:

> Borogroves are mimsy whenever it is brillig. It is now brillig and this thing is a borogrove. Hence this thing is mimsy.

While propositional logic is useful for reasoning about conjunctions, negations, and implications, it is not so useful when it comes to dealing with notions like knowledge or likelihood. For example, notions like "Alice *knows* it is mimsy" or "it is more likely to be mimsy than not" cannot be expressed in propositional logic. Such statements are crucial for reasoning about uncertainty. Knowledge is an example of what philosophers have called a *propositional attitude*. Propositional attitudes can be expressed using *modal logic*.

Since not all readers will have studied formal logic before, I start in this chapter with a self-contained (but short!) introduction to propositional logic. (Even readers familiar with propositional logic may want to scan the next section, just to get comfortable with the notation I use.) I go on to consider *epistemic logic,* a modal logic suitable for reasoning about knowledge, and then consider logics for reasoning about more quantitative notions of uncertainty, reasoning about independence, and reasoning about expectation. The following chapters consider yet other logics; for example, Chapter 8 considers logics for reasoning about defaults and counterfactuals, and Chapter 9 considers logics for reasoning about belief revision. All the logics considered in the next three chapters are *propositional;* they cannot express quantified statements like "there exists someone in this room who is very likely to be a millionaire within five years" nor can they express structure such as "Alice is a graduate student and Bob is not." *First-order logic* can express such structure; it is considered in Chapter 10.

## 7.1   Propositional Logic

The formal syntax for propositional logic is quite straightforward. Fix a *vocabulary*— a nonempty set $\Phi$ of *primitive propositions,* which I typically label by letters such as $p$ and $q$ (perhaps with a prime or subscript). These primitive propositions can be thought of as representing statements such as "it is brillig" or "this thing is mimsy." Intuitively, these statements describe the basic facts of the situation. More complicated formulas are formed by closing off under conjunction and negation, so that if $\phi$ and $\psi$ are formulas, then so are $\neg\phi$ and $\phi \wedge \psi$ (read "not $\phi$" and "$\phi$ and $\psi$," respectively). Thus, if $p$ stands for "it is brillig" and $q$ stands for "this thing is mimsy," then $\neg p$ says "it is not brillig" while $p \wedge q$ says "it is brillig and this thing is mimsy." The set $\mathcal{L}^{Prop}(\Phi)$ of formulas consists of all the formulas that can be formed in this way.

There are some other standard connectives that can easily be defined in terms of conjunction and negation:

- $\phi \vee \psi$ (read "$\phi$ or $\psi$") is an abbreviation for $\neg(\neg\phi \wedge \neg\psi)$;

- $\phi \Rightarrow \psi$ (read "$\phi$ implies $\psi$" or "if $\phi$ then $\psi$") is an abbreviation for $\neg\phi \vee \psi$;

- $\phi \Leftrightarrow \psi$ (read "$\phi$ if and only if $\psi$") is an abbreviation for $(\phi \Rightarrow \psi) \wedge (\psi \Rightarrow \phi)$;

- *true* is an abbreviation for $p \vee \neg p$ (where $p$ is a fixed primitive proposition in $\Phi$);

- *false* is an abbreviation for $\neg true$.

If $p$ and $q$ stand for "it is brillig" and "this thing is mimsy," as before, and $r$ stands "this thing is a borogrove," then the informal English argument at the beginning of the chapter can be readily expressed in propositional logic. "Borogroves are mimsy whenever it is brillig" can be restated as "if it is brillig then [if this thing is a borogrove, then it is mimsy]." (Check that these two English statements really are saying the same thing!) Thus, this becomes $p \Rightarrow (r \Rightarrow q)$. "It is now brillig and this thing is a borogrove" becomes $p \wedge r$. It seems reasonable to conclude $q$: "this thing is mimsy." Can this conclusion be justified?

So far, I have defined a formal language, along with an intended reading of formulas in the language. The intended reading is supposed to correspond to intuitions that we have regarding words like "and," "or," and "not." These intuitions are captured by providing a *semantics* for the formulas in the language, that is, a method for deciding whether a given formula is true or false.

The key component of the semantics for propositional logic is a *truth assignment* $v$, a function that maps the primitive propositions in $\Phi$ to a *truth value*, that is, an element of the set {**true, false**}. The form of the truth assignment guarantees that each primitive proposition has exactly one truth value. It is either true or false; it cannot be both true and false, or neither true nor false. This commitment, which leads to *classical* or *two-valued* logic, has been subject to criticism; some alternative approaches are mentioned in the notes to this chapter.

A truth assignment determines which primitive propositions are true and which are false. There are standard rules for then determining whether an arbitrary formula $\phi$ is *true under truth assignment* $v$, or *satisfied by truth assignment* $v$, written $v \models \phi$. Formally, the $\models$ relation is defined by induction on the structure of $\phi$. That is, it is first defined for the simplest formulas, namely, the primitive propositions, and then extended to more complicated formulas of the form $\neg\phi$ or $\phi \wedge \psi$ under the assumption that the truth under $v$ of each constituent has already been determined. For a primitive proposition $p$,

$$v \models p \text{ iff } v(p) = \textbf{true}.$$

Thus, a primitive proposition is true under truth assignment $v$ if and only if $v$ assigns it truth value **true**.

Intuitively, $\neg\phi$ is true if and only if $\phi$ is false. This intuition is captured as follows:

$$v \models \neg\phi \text{ iff } v \not\models \phi.$$

It is also easy to formalize the intuition that $\phi \wedge \psi$ is true if and only if both $\phi$ and $\psi$ are true:

$$v \models \phi \wedge \psi \text{ iff } v \models \phi \text{ and } v \models \psi.$$

What about the other connectives that were defined in terms of $\wedge$ and $\neg$? It seems reasonable to expect that $\phi \vee \psi$ is true if and only if one of $\phi$ or $\psi$ is true. It is not immediately obvious that defining $\phi \vee \psi$ as an abbreviation for $\neg(\neg\phi \wedge \neg\psi)$ enforces this intuition. As the following lemma shows, it does. The other definitions have the appropriate meaning as well.

**Lemma 7.1.1**   *For every truth assignment $v$,*

*(a) $v \models \phi \vee \psi$ iff $v \models \phi$ or $v \models \psi$;*

*(b) if $v \models \phi \Rightarrow \psi$, then if $v \models \phi$ then $v \models \psi$;*

*(c) $v \models \phi \Leftrightarrow \psi$ iff either $v \models \phi$ and $v \models \psi$ or $v \models \neg\phi$ and $v \models \neg\psi$;*

*(d) $v \models true$;*

*(e) $v \not\models false$.*

**Proof**   I prove part (a), leaving the remaining parts as an exercise for the reader (Exercise 7.1). Suppose that $v \models \phi \vee \psi$. This is the case iff $v \models \neg(\neg\phi \wedge \neg\psi)$. This, in turn, is the case iff $v \not\models \neg\phi \wedge \neg\psi$. The definition of $\models$ guarantees that $v$ does not satisfy a conjunction iff it does not satisfy one of the conjuncts: that is, iff $v \not\models \neg\phi$ or $v \not\models \neg\psi$. But this last situation holds iff $v \models \phi$ or $v \models \psi$. This completes the proof of part (a).   ∎

Lemma 7.1.1 says, among other things, that the formula *true* is always true and *false* is always false. This is certainly the intent! Similarly, it says that $\phi \Leftrightarrow \psi$ is true exactly if $\phi$ and $\psi$ have the same truth value: either they must both be true, or they must both be false. It also says that if $\phi \Rightarrow \psi$ is true, then if $\phi$ is true, then $\psi$ is true. Put another way, it says that the truth of $\phi$ implies the truth of $\psi$. Again, this seems consistent with the interpretation of implication. However, notice that viewing $\phi \Rightarrow \psi$ as an abbreviation for $\neg\phi \vee \psi$ guarantees that $\phi \Rightarrow \psi$ will automatically be true if $\phi$ is false. This may seem counterintuitive. There has been a great deal of discussion regarding the reasonableness of this definition of $\Rightarrow$; alternative logics have been proposed that attempt to retain the intuition that $\phi \Rightarrow \psi$ is true if the truth of $\phi$ implies the truth of $\psi$ without automatically making $\phi \Rightarrow \psi$ true if $\phi$ is false. I use the standard definition in this book because it has proved so useful; references for alternative approaches are provided in the notes to this chapter. One important thing to remember (perhaps the most important thing, as far as the proofs in this book are concerned) is that when trying to show that $v \models \phi \Rightarrow \psi$, it suffices to assume that $v \models \phi$, and then try to show that $v \models \psi$ under this assumption; for if $v \models \neg\phi$, then $v \models \phi \Rightarrow \psi$ is vacuously true.

A formula such as *true* is true under every truth assignment. A formula that is true under every truth assignment is said to be a *tautology*, or to be *valid*. Other valid formulas include $(p \wedge q) \Leftrightarrow (q \wedge p)$, and $p \Leftrightarrow \neg\neg p$. The first one says that the truth value of a conjunction is independent of the order in which the conjuncts are taken; the second says that two negations cancel each other out. A formula that is true under some truth assignment is said to be *satisfiable*. It is easy to see that $\phi$ is valid if and only if $\neg\phi$ is not satisfiable (Exercise 7.2).

To make precise the sense in which the argument about mimsy borogroves at the beginning of the chapter is legitimate, I need one more definition. A set $\Sigma$ of formulas *entails* a formula $\phi$ if every truth assignment that makes all the formulas in $\Sigma$ true also makes $\phi$ true. Note that a formula $\phi$ is valid iff Ø (the empty set of formulas) entails $\phi$. The argument at the beginning of the chapter is legitimate precisely because $\{p \Rightarrow (r \Rightarrow q),\ p \wedge r\}$ entails $q$ (Exercise 7.3).

## 7.2   Modal Epistemic Logic

I now move beyond propositional logic to a logic that allows reasoning about uncertainty within the logic. Perhaps the simplest kind of reasoning about uncertainty involves reasoning about whether certain situations are possible or impossible. I start with a logic of knowledge that allows just this kind of reasoning.

## 7.2.1   Syntax and Semantics

The syntax of propositional *epistemic* logic is just a slight extension of that for propositional logic. As an example, consider a propositional modal logic for reasoning about the knowledge of $n$ agents. As in the case of propositional logic, we start with a nonempty set $\Phi$ of primitive propositions, but now there are also *modal* operators $K_1, \ldots, K_n$, one for each agent. Formulas are formed by starting with primitive propositions and closing off under negation and conjunction (as in propositional logic) and the application of modal operators, so that if $\phi$ is a formula, so is $K_i\phi$. Although $K_i\phi$ is typically read "agent $i$ knows $\phi$," in some contexts it may be more appropriate to read it as "agent $i$ believes $\phi$." Let $\mathcal{L}_n^K(\Phi)$ be the language consisting of all formulas that can be built up this way; for notational convenience, I often suppress the $\Phi$. The subscript $n$ denotes that there are $n$ agents; I typically omit the subscript if $n = 1$. I also make use of abbreviations such as $\vee$, $\Rightarrow$, and $\Leftrightarrow$, just as in propositional logic.

Quite complicated statements can be expressed in a straightforward way in this language. For example, the formula

$$K_1 K_2 p \wedge \neg K_2 K_1 K_2 p$$

says that agent 1 knows that agent 2 knows $p$, but agent 2 does not know that agent 1 knows that agent 2 knows $p$. More colloquially, if I am agent 1 and you are agent 2, this can be read as "I know that you know $p$, but you don't know that I know that you know it."

Notice that possibility is the dual of knowledge. Agent $i$ considers $\phi$ possible exactly if he does not know $\neg\phi$. This situation can be described by the formula $\neg K_i \neg \phi$. A statement such as "Alice does not know whether it is sunny in San Francisco" means that Alice considers possible both that it is sunny in San Francisco and that it is not sunny in San Francisco. This can be expressed by formula $\neg K_A \neg p \wedge \neg K_A \neg(\neg p)$, if $p$ stands for "it is sunny in San Francisco."

When is a formula in modal logic true? Truth will be defined relative to a possible world in an epistemic frame. The truth conditions for conjunction and negation are the same as in propositional logic. The interesting case is a formula of the form $K_i\phi$. Recall that an agent is said to know an event $U$ in an epistemic frame if every world that the agent considers possible is in $U$. This intuition is also used to define the truth of $K_i\phi$. The idea is to associate an event $[\![\phi]\!]$ with the formula $\phi$—the event consisting of the set of worlds where $\phi$ is true. Then $K_i\phi$ is true at a world $w$ if $\mathcal{K}_i(w) \subseteq [\![\phi]\!]$. Roughly speaking, this says that $K_i\phi$ is true if $\phi$ is true at every world that agent $i$ considers possible.

To get this definition off the ground, there must be some way of deciding at which worlds the primitive propositions are true. This is done by adding one more component to an epistemic frame. An *epistemic structure* (sometimes called a *Kripke structure*) for $n$ agents is a tuple $(W, \mathcal{K}_1, \ldots, \mathcal{K}_n, \pi)$, where $(W, \mathcal{K}_1, \ldots, \mathcal{K}_n)$ is an epistemic frame, and $\pi$ is an *interpretation*, a function that associates with each world in $W$ a truth assignment to the primitive propositions. That is, $\pi(w)(p) \in \{\textbf{true}, \textbf{false}\}$ for each primitive proposition $p \in \Phi$ and world $w \in W$. There may be two worlds associated with the same truth assignment; that is, it is possible that $\pi(w) = \pi(w')$ for $w \neq w'$. This amounts to saying that there may be more to a world than what can be described by the primitive propositions.

In propositional logic, a formula is true or false given a truth assignment. In modal logic, of which this is an example, the truth of a formula depends on the world. A primitive proposition such as $p$ may be true in one world and false in another. I now define under what circumstances a formula $\phi$ is true at world $w$ in structure $M = (W, \mathcal{K}_1, \ldots, \mathcal{K}_n, \pi)$, written $(M, w) \models \phi$. The definition proceeds by induction on the structure of formulas.

$(M, w) \models p$ (for a primitive proposition $p \in \Phi$) iff $\pi(w)(p) = \textbf{true}$;

$(M, w) \models \phi \wedge \phi'$ iff $(M, w) \models \phi$ and $(M, w) \models \phi'$;

$(M, w) \models \neg\phi$ iff $(M, w) \not\models \phi$;

$(M, w) \models K_i\phi$ iff $(M, w') \models \phi$ for all $w' \in \mathcal{K}_i(w)$.

The first three clauses are the same as the corresponding clauses for propositional logic; the last clause captures the intuition that agent $i$ knows $\phi$ if $\phi$ is true in all the worlds that $i$ considers possible.

Recall that a system can be viewed as an epistemic frame. To reason about knowledge in a system using epistemic logic, an interpretation is needed. A pair $\mathcal{I} = (\mathcal{R}, \pi)$ consisting of a system $\mathcal{R}$ and an interpretation $\pi$ is called an *interpreted system*. Just as a system can be viewed as an epistemic frame, an interpreted system can be viewed as an epistemic structure. Satisfiability ($\models$) can then be defined in interpreted systems in the obvious way. In particular,

$(\mathcal{I}, r, m) \models \phi$ iff $(\mathcal{I}, r', m') \models \phi$ for all $(r', m')$ such that $r'_i(m') = r_i(m)$.

## 7.2.2 Properties of Knowledge

One way to assess the reasonableness of the semantics for knowledge given in Section 7.2.1 is to try to characterize its properties. A formula $\phi$ is *valid in an epistemic structure* $M$, denoted $M \models \phi$, if $(M, w) \models \phi$ for all $w$ in $M$. (Of course, a world $w$ is in $M = (W, \ldots)$ if $w \in W$.) A formula $\phi$ is *satisfiable in* $M$ if $(M, w) \models \phi$ for some world $w$ in $M$. If $\mathcal{N}$ is a class of structures (e.g., the class of all epistemic structures, or the class of all epistemic structures where the $\mathcal{K}_i$ relations are equivalence relations), then $\phi$ is *valid in* (or *with respect to*) $\mathcal{N}$, denoted $\mathcal{N} \models \phi$, if $\phi$ is valid in every structure in $\mathcal{N}$.

One important property of the definition of knowledge is that each agent knows all the logical consequences of his knowledge. If an agent knows $\varphi$ and knows that $\varphi$ implies $\psi$, then both $\varphi$ and $\varphi \Rightarrow \psi$ are true at all worlds he considers possible. Thus $\psi$ must be true at all worlds that the agent considers possible, so he must also know $\psi$. It follows that

$$(K_i\varphi \wedge K_i(\varphi \Rightarrow \psi)) \Rightarrow K_i\psi$$

is valid in epistemic structures. This property is called the *Distribution Axiom* since it allows the $K_i$ operator to distribute over implication. It suggests that the definition of $K_i$ assumes that agents are quite powerful reasoners.

Further evidence of this comes from the fact that agents know all the formulas that are valid in a given structure. If $\varphi$ is true at all the possible worlds of structure $M$, then $\varphi$ must be true at all the worlds that an agent considers possible in any given world in $M$, so it must be the case that $K_i\phi$ is true at all possible worlds of $M$. More formally, the following *Rule of Knowledge Generalization* holds:

For all epistemic structures $M$, if $M \models \varphi$ then $M \models K_i\varphi$.

Note that from this it follows that if $\phi$ is valid, then so is $K_i\phi$. This rule is very different from the formula $\varphi \Rightarrow K_i\varphi$, which says that if $\varphi$ is true then agent $i$ knows it. An agent does not necessarily know all things that are true. In Example 6.1.1, agent 1 may hold card $A$ without agent 2 knowing it. However, agents do know all valid formulas. Intuitively, these are the formulas that are *necessarily* true, as opposed to the formulas that just happen to be true at a given world. It requires a rather powerful reasoner to know all necessarily true facts.

Additional properties of knowledge hold if the $\mathcal{K}_i$ relations satisfy additional properties. For example, if the $\mathcal{K}_i$ relation is transitive, then

$$K_i\varphi \Rightarrow K_iK_i\varphi$$

turns out to be valid, while if the $\mathcal{K}_i$ relation is Euclidean, then

$$\neg K_i\varphi \Rightarrow K_i\neg K_i\varphi$$

is valid. Imagine that an agent has the collection of all facts that he knows written in a database. Then the first of these properties, called the *Positive Introspection Axiom*, says that the agent can look at this database and see what facts are written there, so that if he knows $\varphi$, then he knows that he knows it (and thus the fact that he knows $\varphi$ is also written in his database). The second property, called the *Negative Introspection Axiom*, says that he can also look over his database to see what he doesn't know. Thus, if he doesn't know $\phi$, so that $\phi$ is not written in his database, he knows that $\phi$ is not written there, so that he knows that he doesn't know $\phi$.

It is possible for $K_i false$ to hold at a world $w$ in an epistemic structure, but only if it holds vacuously because $\mathcal{K}_i(w)$ is empty; that is, agent $i$ does not consider any worlds possible at world $w$. If $\mathcal{K}_i$ is *serial* (so that $\mathcal{K}_i(w)$ is nonempty for all $w$), then $\neg K_i false$ is valid.

If $\mathcal{K}_i$ is reflexive (which certainly implies that it is serial), then an even stronger property holds: what an agent knows to be true is in fact true; more precisely, $K_i\phi \Rightarrow \phi$ is valid in reliable structures. This property, occasionally called the *Knowledge Axiom* or the *veridicality* property (since "veridical" means "truthful"), has been taken by philosophers to be the major one distinguishing knowledge from *belief*. Although you may have false beliefs, you cannot know something that is false.

This discussion is summarized in the following theorem:

**Theorem 7.2.1**  *Suppose that $M = (W, \mathcal{K}_1, \ldots, \mathcal{K}_n, \pi)$ is an epistemic structure. Then for all agents $i$,*

(a)  $M \models (K_i\varphi \wedge K_i(\varphi \Rightarrow \psi)) \Rightarrow K_i\psi$;

(b)  *if* $M \models \varphi$ *then* $M \models K_i\varphi$;

(c)  *if* $\mathcal{K}_i$ *is transitive, then* $M \models K_i\varphi \Rightarrow K_i K_i\varphi$;

(d)  *if* $\mathcal{K}_i$ *is Euclidean, then* $M \models \neg K_i\varphi \Rightarrow K_i\neg K_i\varphi$;

(e)  *if* $\mathcal{K}_i$ *is serial, then* $M \models \neg K_i false$;

(f)  *if* $\mathcal{K}_i$ *is reflexive, then* $M \models K_i\phi \Rightarrow \phi$.

**Proof**

(a)  If $(M, w) \models K_i\varphi \wedge K_i(\varphi \Rightarrow \psi)$, then $(M, w') \models \varphi$ and $(M, w') \models \varphi \Rightarrow \psi$ for all worlds $w' \in \mathcal{K}_i(w)$. It follows from the definition of $\models$ that $(M, w') \models \psi$ for all $w' \in \mathcal{K}_i(w)$. Therefore, $(M, w) \models K_i\psi$. Thus, $(M, w) \models (K_i\phi \wedge K_i(\phi \Rightarrow \psi)) \Rightarrow K_i\psi$. Since this is true for all $w \in W$, it follows that $M \models (K_i\phi \wedge K_i(\phi \Rightarrow \psi)) \Rightarrow K_i\psi$. (I omit the analogue of these last two sentences in parts (c), (d), and (f) and in all future proofs.)

(b) If $M \models \varphi$ then $(M, w') \models \varphi$ for all worlds $w' \in W$. It immediately follows that $(M, w) \models K_i \phi$ for all $w \in W$ (since $\mathcal{K}_i(w) \subseteq W$).

(c) Suppose that $(M, w) \models K_i \varphi$. Then $(M, w') \models \phi$ for all $w' \in \mathcal{K}_i(w)$. Let $w' \in \mathcal{K}_i(w)$. Since $\mathcal{K}_i$ is transitive, it follows that $\mathcal{K}_i(w') \subseteq \mathcal{K}_i(w)$. Thus, $(M, w'') \models \phi$ for all $w'' \in \mathcal{K}_i(w')$, and so $(M, w') \models K_i \phi$. Since this is true for all $w' \in \mathcal{K}_i(w)$, it follows that $(M, w) \models K_i K_i \phi$.

(d) Suppose that $(M, w) \models \neg K_i \varphi$. Then $(M, w'') \models \neg \phi$ for some $w'' \in \mathcal{K}_i(w)$. Let $w' \in \mathcal{K}_i(w)$. Since $\mathcal{K}_i$ is Euclidean, it follows that $w'' \in \mathcal{K}_i(w')$. Thus, $(M, w') \models \neg K_i \phi$. Since this is true for all $w' \in \mathcal{K}_i(w)$, it follows that $(M, w) \models K_i \neg K_i \phi$.

(e) Choose $w \in W$. Since $\mathcal{K}_i$ is serial, there is some world $w' \in \mathcal{K}_i(w)$. Clearly, $(M, w') \models \neg false$. Thus, $(M, w) \models \neg K_i false$.

(f) If $(M, w) \models K_i \varphi$, then $(M, w') \models \varphi$ for all $w' \in \mathcal{K}_i(w)$. Since $\mathcal{K}_i$ is reflexive, $w \in \mathcal{K}_i(w)$. Thus, $(M, w) \models \phi$.  ∎

Notice that the proof of part (a) did not start by assuming $M \models K_i \phi \wedge K_i(\phi \Rightarrow \psi)$ and then go on to show that $M \models K_i \psi$. $M \models K_i \phi$ means that $(M, w) \models K_i \phi$ for all $w \in W$; this cannot be assumed in the proof of part (a). Showing that $M \models (K_i \phi \wedge K_i(\phi \Rightarrow \psi)) \Rightarrow K_i \psi$ requires showing that $(M, w) \models (K_i \phi \wedge K_i(\phi \Rightarrow \psi)) \Rightarrow K_i \psi$ for all $w \in W$. This means that only $(M, w) \models K_i \phi \wedge K_i(\phi \Rightarrow \psi)$ can be assumed. By way of contrast, note that the proof of part (b) shows that if $M \models \phi$, then $M \models K_i \phi$. It does *not* follow that $M \models \phi \Rightarrow K_i \phi$. Just because $\phi$ is true, the agent does not necessarily know it!

Theorem 7.2.1 makes it clear how certain properties of knowledge are related to properties of the possibility relation. However, note that there are two properties that follow from the possible worlds approach, no matter what assumptions are made about the possibility relation: the Distribution Axiom and the Rule of Knowledge Generalization. To the extent that knowledge is viewed as something acquired by agents through some reasoning process, these properties suggest that this notion of knowledge is appropriate only for idealized agents who can do perfect reasoning. Clearly, this is not always reasonable. In the multi-agent systems model introduced in Section 6.3, knowledge is ascribed to agents in a multi-agent system based on their current information, as encoded in their local state. This notion of knowledge explicitly does not take computation into account. While it is useful in many contexts, not surprisingly, it is not adequate for modeling agents who must compute what they know.

### 7.2.3 Axiomatizing Knowledge

Are there other important properties of the possible-worlds definition of knowledge that I have not yet mentioned? In a precise sense, the answer is no. All the properties of knowledge (at least, in the propositional case) follow from those already discussed. This can be formalized using the notions of *provability* and *sound and complete axiomatization*.

An *axiom system AX* consists of a collection of *axioms* and *inference rules*. An axiom is just a formula, while a rule of inference has the form "from $\phi_1, \ldots, \phi_k$ infer $\psi$," where $\phi_1, \ldots, \phi_k, \psi$ are formulas. An inference rule can be viewed as a method for inferring new formulas from old ones. A *proof* in $AX$ consists of a sequence of steps, each of which is either an instance of an axiom in $AX$, or follows from previous steps by an application of an inference rule. More precisely, if "from $\phi_1, \ldots, \phi_k$ infer $\psi$" is an inference rule, and the formulas $\phi_1, \ldots, \phi_k$ have appeared earlier in the proof, then $\psi$ follows by an application of this inference rule. A proof is a *proof of the formula* $\phi$ if the last step of the proof is $\phi$. A formula $\phi$ is *provable in AX*, denoted $AX \vdash \phi$, if there is a proof of $\phi$ in $AX$.

Suppose that $\mathcal{N}$ is a class of structures and $\mathcal{L}$ is a language such that a notion of validity is defined for the formulas in $\mathcal{L}$ with respect to the structures in $\mathcal{N}$. For example, if $\mathcal{L} = \mathcal{L}^{Prop}$, then $\mathcal{N}$ could consist of all truth assignments; if $\mathcal{L} = \mathcal{L}_n^K$, then $\mathcal{N}$ could be the class of epistemic structures. An axiom system $AX$ is *sound* for $\mathcal{L}$ with respect to $\mathcal{N}$ if every formula of $\mathcal{L}$ that is provable in $AX$ is valid in every structure in $\mathcal{N}$. $AX$ is *complete* for $\mathcal{L}$ with respect to $\mathcal{N}$ if every formula in $\mathcal{L}$ that is valid in every structure in $\mathcal{N}$ is provable in $AX$. $AX$ can be viewed as characterizing the class $\mathcal{N}$ if it provides a sound and complete axiomatization of that class; notationally, this amounts to saying that $AX \vdash \phi$ iff $\mathcal{N} \models \phi$ for all formulas $\phi$. Soundness and completeness provide a connection between the *syntactic* notion of provability and the *semantic* notion of validity.

There are well-known sound and complete axiomatizations for propositional logic (see the notes to this chapter). Here I want to focus on axioms for knowledge, so I just take for granted that all the tautologies of propositional logic are available. Consider the following collection of axioms and inference rules:

Prop. All substitution instances of tautologies of propositional logic.

K1. $(K_i\varphi \wedge K_i(\varphi \Rightarrow \psi)) \Rightarrow K_i\psi$ (Distribution Axiom).

K2. $K_i\phi \Rightarrow \phi$ (Knowledge Axiom).

K3. $\neg K_i \, false$ (Consistency Axiom).

K4.    $K_i\phi \Rightarrow K_i K_i \phi$ (Positive Introspection Axiom).

K5.    $\neg K_i\phi \Rightarrow K_i \neg K_i\phi$ (Negative Introspection Axiom).

MP.    From $\varphi$ and $\varphi \Rightarrow \psi$ infer $\psi$ (Modus Ponens).

Gen.   From $\varphi$ infer $K_i\varphi$ (Knowledge Generalization).

Technically, Prop and K1–5 are axiom schemes, rather than single axioms. K1, for example, holds for all formulas $\phi$ and $\psi$ and all agents $i = 1, \ldots, n$. Prop gives access to all propositional tautologies "for free." Prop could be replaced by the axioms for propositional logic given in the notes to this chapter. Note that a formula such as $K_1 q \vee \neg K_1 q$ is an instance of Prop (since it is a substitution instance of the propositional tautology $p \vee \neg p$, obtained by substituting $K_1 q$ for $p$).

Historically, axiom K1 has been called **K**, K2 has been called **T**, K3 has been called **D**, K4 has been called **4**, and K5 has been called **5**. Different modal logics can be obtained by considering various subsets of these axioms. One approach to naming these logics is to name them after the significant axioms used. In the case of one agent, the system with axioms and rules Prop, **K** (i.e., K1), MP, and Gen has been called K. The axiom system KD45 is the result of combining the axioms **K**, **D**, **4**, and **5** with Prop, MP, and Gen; KT4 is the result of combining the axioms **K**, **T**, and **4** with Prop, MP, and Gen. Some of the axiom systems are commonly called by other names as well. The K is quite often omitted, so that KT becomes T, KD becomes D, and so on; KT4 has traditionally been called S4 and KT45 has been called S5. I stick with the traditional names here for those logics that have them, since they are in common usage, except that I use the subscript $n$ to emphasize the fact that these are systems with $n$ agents rather than only one agent. I occasionally omit the subscript if $n = 1$, in line with more traditional notation. In this book I focus mainly on $S5_n$ and $KD45_n$.

Philosophers have spent years arguing which of these axioms, if any, best captures the knowledge of an agent. I do not believe that there is one "true" notion of knowledge; rather, the appropriate notion depends on the application. For many applications, the axioms of S5 seem most appropriate (see Chapter 6), although philosophers have argued quite vociferously against them, particularly axiom K5. Rather than justify these axioms further, I focus here on the relationship between these axioms and the properties of the $\mathcal{K}_i$ relation.

Theorem 7.2.1 suggests that there is a connection between K4 and transitivity of $\mathcal{K}_i$, K5 and the Euclidean property, K3 and seriality, and K2 and reflexivity. This connection is a rather close one. To formalize it, let $\mathcal{M}_n$ consist of all structures for $n$ agents, and let $\mathcal{M}_n^r$ (resp., $\mathcal{M}_n^{rt}$; $\mathcal{M}_n^{rst}$; $\mathcal{M}_n^{elt}$; $\mathcal{M}_n^{et}$) be the class of all structures for $n$ agents where the possibility relations are reflexive (resp., reflexive and transitive; reflexive, symmetric, and transitive; Euclidean, serial, and transitive; Euclidean and transitive).

**Theorem 7.2.2**  *For the language $\mathcal{L}^K$,*

*(a)* $K_n$ *is a sound and complete axiomatization with respect to* $\mathcal{M}_n$;

*(b)* $T_n$ *is a sound and complete axiomatization with respect to* $\mathcal{M}_n^r$;

*(c)* $S4_n$ *is a sound and complete axiomatization with respect to* $\mathcal{M}_n^{rt}$;

*(d)* $K45_n$ *is a sound and complete axiomatization with respect to* $\mathcal{M}_n^{et}$;

*(e)* $KD45_n$ *is a sound and complete axiomatization with respect to* $\mathcal{M}_n^{elt}$;

*(f)* $S5_n$ *is a sound and complete axiomatization with respect to* $\mathcal{M}_n^{rst}$.

**Proof**  Soundness follows immediately from Theorem 7.2.1. The proof of completeness is beyond the scope of this book. (See the notes to this chapter for references.) ∎

This theorem says, for example, that the axiom system $S5_n$ completely characterizes propositional modal reasoning in $\mathcal{M}_n^{rst}$. There are no "extra" properties (beyond those that can be proved from $S5_n$) that are valid in structures in $\mathcal{M}_n^{rst}$.

## 7.2.4  A Digression: The Role of Syntax

I have presented logic here using the standard logician's approach (which is also common in the philosophy and AI communities): starting with a language and assigning formulas in the language truth values in a semantic structure. In other communities (such as the statistics and economics communities), it is more standard to dispense with language and work directly with what can be viewed as frames. For example, as I already observed in Section 6.2, a probability space can be viewed as a simple probability frame. Economists quite often use epistemic frames, where the $\mathcal{K}_i$s are equivalence relations or even epistemic probability frames (typically satisfying SDP).

It is not possible to give formulas a truth value in an epistemic frame. There is no interpretation $\pi$ to even give a truth value to primitive propositions. Nevertheless, economists still want to talk about knowledge. To do this, they use a knowledge operator that works directly on sets of possible worlds. To understand how this is done, it is best to start with the propositional operators, $\wedge$ and $\neg$. Each of these can be associated with an operation on sets of worlds. The operator corresponding to $\wedge$ is intersection, and the operator corresponding to $\neg$ is complementation. The correspondence is easy to explain. Given an epistemic structure $M = (W, \mathcal{K}_1, \ldots, \mathcal{K}_n, \pi)$, let $[\![\phi]\!]_M = \{w : (M, w) \models \phi\}$. Thus, $[\![\phi]\!]_M$, called the *intension* of $\phi$, is the event corresponding to $\phi$, namely, the set of worlds where $\phi$ is true. Then it is easy to see that $[\![\phi \wedge \psi]\!]_M = [\![\phi]\!]_M \cap [\![\psi]\!]_M$—that is, the event corresponding to $\phi \wedge \psi$ is the intersection of the events corresponding to $\phi$ and to $\psi$. Similarly, $[\![\neg\phi]\!]_M = \overline{[\![\phi]\!]_M}$. The semantic analogue of $K_i$ turns out to be the operator $\mathsf{K}_i$ on sets, which is defined so that $\mathsf{K}_i(U) = \{w : \mathcal{K}_i(w) \subseteq U\}$. I was essentially thinking in terms of the $\mathsf{K}_i$ operator when I defined knowledge in Section 6.1. The following proposition makes precise the sense in which $\mathsf{K}_i$ is the analogue of $\mathcal{K}_i$:

**Proposition 7.2.3**   *For all formulas $\phi$ and $\psi$,*

(a) $[\![\phi \wedge \psi]\!]_M = [\![\phi]\!]_M \cap [\![\psi]\!]_M$,

(b) $[\![\neg\phi]\!]_M = \overline{[\![\phi]\!]_M}$,

(c) $[\![K_i\phi]\!]_M = \mathsf{K}_i([\![\phi]\!]_M)$.

**Proof**   See Exercise 7.5.  ∎

Not surprisingly, $\mathsf{K}_i$ satisfies many properties analogous to $K_i$.

**Proposition 7.2.4**   *For all epistemic frames $F = (W, \mathcal{K}_1, \ldots, \mathcal{K}_n)$, the following properties hold for all $U, V \subseteq W$ and all agents $i$:*

(a) $\mathsf{K}_i(U \cap V) = \mathsf{K}_i(U) \cap \mathsf{K}_i(V)$,

(b) *if $\mathcal{K}_i$ is reflexive, then $\mathsf{K}_i(U) \subseteq U$,*

(c) *if $\mathcal{K}_i$ is transitive, then $\mathsf{K}_i(U) \subseteq \mathsf{K}_i(\mathsf{K}_i(U))$,*

(d) *if $\mathcal{K}_i$ is Euclidean, then $\overline{\mathsf{K}_i(U)} \subseteq \mathsf{K}_i(\overline{\mathsf{K}_i(U)})$.*

**Proof**   See Exercise 7.6.  ∎

Part (a) is the semantic analogue of $K_i(\phi \wedge \psi) \Leftrightarrow (K_i\phi \wedge K_i\psi)$, which is easily seen to be valid in all epistemic structures (Exercise 7.7). Parts (b), (c), and (d) are the semantic analogues of axioms K2, K4, and K5, respectively.

For reasoning about a fixed situation, there is certainly an advantage in working with a frame rather than a structure. There is no need to define an interpretation $\pi$ and a satisfiability relation $\models$; it is easier to work directly with sets (events) rather than formulas.

So why bother with the overhead of syntax? Having a language has a number of advantages; I discuss three of them here.

- There are times when it is useful to distinguish logically equivalent formulas. For example, in any given structure, it is not hard to check that the events corresponding to the formulas $K_i true$ and $K_i((p \Rightarrow q) \vee (q \Rightarrow p))$ are logically equivalent, since $(p \Rightarrow q) \vee (q \Rightarrow p)$ is a tautology. However, a computationally bounded agent may not recognize that $(p \Rightarrow q) \vee (q \Rightarrow p)$ is a tautology, and thus may not know it. Although all the semantics for modal logic that I consider in this book have the property that they do not distinguish logically equivalent formulas, it is possible to give semantics where such formulas are distinguished. (See the notes to this chapter for some pointers to the literature.) This clearly would not be possible with a set-based approach.

- The structure of the syntax provides ways to reason and carry out proofs. For example, many technical results proceed by induction on the structure of formulas. Similarly, formal axiomatic reasoning typically takes advantage of the syntactic structure of formulas.

- Using formulas allows certain notions to be formulated in a structure-independent way. For example, economists are interested in notions of rationality and would like to express rationality in terms of knowledge and belief. Rationality is a complicated notion, and there is certainly no agreement on exactly how it should be defined. Suppose for now though that the definition of what it means to be rational is a formula involving knowledge (and perhaps other operators; see the references in the notes for some discussion). The formula can then be used to identify corresponding events (such as "agent 1 is rational") in two different structures.

Similarly, formulas can be used to compare two or more structures that, intuitively, are "about" the same basic phenomena. For a simple example, consider the following two epistemic structures. In $M_1$, both agents know the true situation. There are two worlds in $M_1$: in one, $p$ is true, both agents know it, know that they know it, and so on; in the other, $p$ is false, both agents know it, know that they know it, and so on. In $M_2$, agent 1 knows the true situation, although agent 2 does not. There are also two worlds in $M_2$: in one, $p$ is true and agent 1 knows it; in the other, $p$ is false and agent 1 knows that it is false; agent 2 cannot distinguish these two worlds. Figure 7.1 (where self-loops are omitted) illustrates the situation:

Notice that $K_1 p \vee K_1 \neg p$ holds in every state of both $M_1$ and $M_2$, while $K_2 p \vee K_2 \neg p$ holds in both states of $M_1$, but not in both states of $M_2$. Using formulas makes

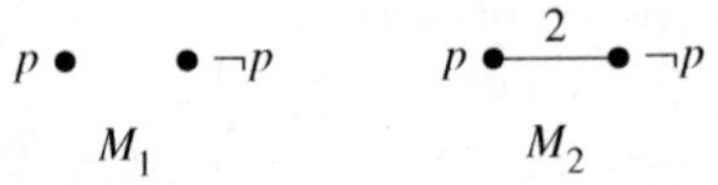

$$p \bullet \qquad \bullet \neg p \qquad \qquad p \bullet \overset{2}{\rule{2cm}{0.4pt}} \bullet \neg p$$

$$M_1 \qquad \qquad \qquad \qquad M_2$$

Figure 7.1   Two related epistemic structures.

it possible to relate $M_1$ and $M_2$ in a way that cannot be done using events. Formulas such as $p$ and $K_1 p$ are represented by totally different sets in $M_1$ and $M_2$. That is, the set of worlds where $p$ is true in $M_1$ bears no relationship to the set of worlds where $p$ is true in $M_2$, and similarly for $K_1 p$. Nevertheless, it seems reasonable to say that these sets correspond in some way. There is no obvious way to do that without invoking a language.

## 7.3   Reasoning about Probability: The Measurable Case

Reasoning about probability can be formalized along lines similar to those used for reasoning about knowledge. An interpretation $\pi$ can be added to a probability frame to obtain a probability structure. This gives the appropriate semantic model. Let $\mathcal{M}_n^{prob}$ be the class of probability structures. An important special case is a structure where, at each point, all sets are measurable (i.e., $\mathcal{F}_{w,i} = 2^{W_{w,i}}$ for all worlds $w$ and agents $i$). Let $\mathcal{M}_n^{meas}$ be the class of all measurable probability structures. It is convenient occasionally to be able to talk about *simple probability structures*. These are the obvious analogues of simple probability frames and have the form $(W, \mathcal{F}, \mu, \pi)$: that is, a probability space with an associated interpretation.

   This takes care of the semantics. What about the syntax? I consider a language with *likelihood terms* of the form $\ell_i(\phi)$. The $\ell$ stands for *likelihood*. For this section, $\ell_i(\phi)$ should be interpreted as "the probability of $\phi$ according to agent $i$." In later sections, the $\ell$ is interpreted as "belief" or "plausibility" or "possibility," depending on the notion of likelihood being considered. For this section, I allow linear combinations of likelihood terms, such as $2\ell(\phi) + 3\ell(\psi)$. This makes sense for probability (and possibility), where $\ell(\phi)$ and $\ell(\psi)$ are real numbers that can be added, but not for plausibility measures. I later consider a language that allows only comparison of likelihoods and makes sense for all the representation methods.  Using the addition operator, it is possible to say, for example, that the probability of the union of two disjoint sets is the sum of their individual probabilities. Linear combinations make it possible to express expectation, for example.

The formal syntax is quite straightforward. Formulas are formed by starting with a set $\Phi$ of primitive propositions and closing off under conjunction, negation, and the formation of *(linear) likelihood formulas;* a likelihood formula has the form $a_1 \ell_{i_1}(\phi_1) + \cdots + a_k \ell_{i_k}(\phi_k) > b$, where $a_1, \ldots, a_k, b$ are real numbers, $i_1, \ldots, i_k$ are (not necessarily distinct) agents, and $\phi_1, \ldots, \phi_k$ are formulas. Thus, a linear likelihood formula talks about a linear combination of likelihood terms of the form $\ell_i(\phi)$. For example, $2\ell_1(p_1 \wedge p_2) + 7\ell_1(p_1 \vee \neg p_3) \geq 3$ is a likelihood formula. Since nesting is allowed, so is $\ell_1(\ell_2(p) = 1/2) = 1/2$. $\mathcal{L}_n^{QU}(\Phi)$ (the *QU* stands for *quantitative uncertainty*) is the language that results from starting with $\Phi$ and closing off under conjunction, negation, and the formation of likelihood formulas for $n$ agents (i.e., using $\ell_1, \ldots, \ell_n$).

$\mathcal{L}_n^{QU}$ (as usual, I suppress $\Phi$) is rich enough to express many notions of interest. For example, I use obvious abbreviations such as

- $\ell_i(\phi) - \ell_i(\psi) > b$ for $\ell_i(\phi) + (-1)\ell_i(\psi) > b$,

- $\ell_i(\phi) > \ell_i(\psi)$ for $\ell_i(\phi) - \ell_i(\psi) > 0$,

- $\ell_i(\phi) < \ell_i(\psi)$ for $\ell_i(\psi) - \ell_i(\phi) > 0$,

- $\ell_i(\phi) \leq b$ for $\neg(\ell_i(\phi) > b)$,

- $\ell_i(\phi) \geq b$ for $-\ell_i(\phi) \leq -b$,

- $\ell_i(\phi) = b$ for $(\ell_i(\phi) \geq b) \wedge (\ell_i(\phi) \leq b)$.

Simple conditional probabilities such as $\ell_i(\phi \mid \psi) \geq 2/3$ can also be expressed in $\mathcal{L}_n^{QU}$. Since $\ell_i(\phi \mid \psi) = \ell_i(\phi \wedge \psi)/\ell_i(\psi)$, after clearing the denominator, this becomes $3\ell_i(\phi \wedge \psi) \geq 2\ell_i(\psi)$.

As I mentioned earlier, the expected value of a random variable can also be expressed in $\mathcal{L}_n^{QU}$, provided that the worlds in which the random variable takes on a particular value can be characterized by formulas. For example, suppose that you win \$2 if a coin lands heads and lose \$3 if it lands tails. Then your expected winnings are $2\ell(heads) - 3\ell(tails)$. The formula $2\ell(heads) - 3\ell(tails) \geq 1$ says that your expected winnings are at least \$1.

Although $\mathcal{L}_n^{QU}$ is a very expressive language, it cannot express some important notions. One example is independence. Informally, (after expanding and clearing the denominators) the fact that $\phi$ is independent of $\psi$ according to agent $i$ corresponds to the formula $\ell_i(\phi \wedge \psi) = \ell_i(\phi) \times \ell_i(\psi)$. There is no difficulty giving to semantics such formulas in the semantic framework I am about to describe. However, this formula is not in the language, since I have not allowed multiplication of likelihood terms in linear likelihood formulas. I return to this issue in Section 7.7.

So why not include such formulas in the language? There is a tradeoff here: added expressive power comes at a price. Richer languages are typically harder to axiomatize, and it is typically harder to determine the validity of formulas in a richer language. (See the notes to this chapter for further discussion of this issue and references.) Thus, I stick to the simpler language in this book, for purposes of illustration.

Formulas in $\mathcal{L}_n^{QU}$ are either true or false at a world in a probability structure; they do not get "probabilistic" truth values. A logic for reasoning about probability can still be two-valued! In this section, I focus on measurable probability structures; this makes life simpler. In a measurable probability structure $M$, the term $\ell_i(\phi)$ is interpreted as the probability (according to agent $i$) of the set $[\![\phi]\!]_M$. But if this set is not measurable, it does not make sense to talk about its probability. As long as all sets are measurable, this problem does not arise. (I consider the case where sets are not necessarily measurable in Section 7.4.)

Defining the truth of formulas in a measurable probability structure $M = (W, \mathcal{PR}_1, \ldots, \mathcal{PR}_n, \pi)$ is straightforward. The definition in the case of primitive propositions, conjunctions, and negations is identical to that for propositional logic. For likelihood formulas,

$$(M, w) \models a_1\ell_{i_1}(\phi_1) + \cdots + a_k\ell_{i_k}(\phi_k) \geq b$$
$$\text{iff } a_1\mu_{w,i_1}([\![\phi_1]\!]_M \cap W_{w,i_1}) + \cdots + a_k\mu_{w,i_k}([\![\phi_k]\!]_M \cap W_{w,i_k}) \geq b,$$

where $\mathcal{PR}_{i_j}(w) = (W_{w,i_j}, \mu_{w,i_j})$.

**Example 7.3.1** Suppose that $M_1 = (W, 2^W, \mu, \pi)$ is a simple probability structure, where

- $W = \{w_1, w_2, w_3, w_4\}$;

- $\mu(w_1) = \mu(w_2) = .25$, $\mu(w_3) = .3$, $\mu(w_4) = .2$; and

- $\pi$ is such that $(M_1, w_1) \models p \wedge q$, $(M_1, w_2) \models p \wedge \neg q$, $(M_1, w_3) \models \neg p \wedge q$, and $(M_1, w_4) \models \neg p \wedge \neg q$.

Thus, the worlds in $W$ correspond to the four possible truth assignments to $p$ and $q$. The structure $M_1$ is described in Figure 7.2.

It is straightforward to check that, for example,

$$(M_1, w_1) \models p \wedge q \wedge (\ell_1(\neg p \wedge q) > \ell_1(p \wedge q)).$$

Even though $p \wedge q$ is true at $w_1$, the agent considers $\neg p \wedge q$ to be more probable than $p \wedge q$. In addition,

$$M_1 \models \ell_1(q \mid \neg p) = .6;$$

equivalently, sticking closer to the syntax of $\mathcal{L}_1^{QU}$,

$$M_1 \models \ell_1(\neg p \wedge q) - .6\ell_1(\neg p) = 0. \quad \blacksquare$$

**Example 7.3.2**  Let $M_2 = (W, \mathcal{PR}_1, \mathcal{PR}_2, \pi)$, where $W$, $\pi$, and $\mathcal{PR}_1$ are as in the structure $M_1$ in Example 7.3.1, and $\mathcal{PR}_2(w_1) = \mathcal{PR}_2(w_2) = (\{w_1, w_2\}, \mu_1')$, where $\mu_1'(w_1) = .6$ and $\mu_1'(w_2) = .4$, and $\mathcal{PR}_2(w_3) = \mathcal{PR}_2(w_4) = (\{w_3, w_4\}, \mu_2')$, where $\mu_2'(w_3) = \mu_2'(w_4) = .5$. The structure $M_2$ is described in Figure 7.3.

It is straightforward to check that, for example,

$$(M_2, w_1) \models p \wedge q \wedge (\ell_1(p) = .5) \wedge (\ell_2(p) = 1) \wedge (\ell_1(\ell_2(p) = 1) = .5) \wedge$$
$$(\ell_2(\ell_1(p) = .5) = 1) \wedge (\ell_1(\ell_2(p) = 1 \vee \ell_2(p) = 0) = 1).$$

At world $w_1$, agent 1 thinks that $p$ and $\neg p$ are equally likely, while agent 2 is certain that $p$ is true. Moreover, agent 2 is certain that agent 1 thinks that $p$ and $\neg p$ are equally likely, while agent 1 is certain that agent 2 ascribes $p$ either probability 0 or probability 1.  $\blacksquare$

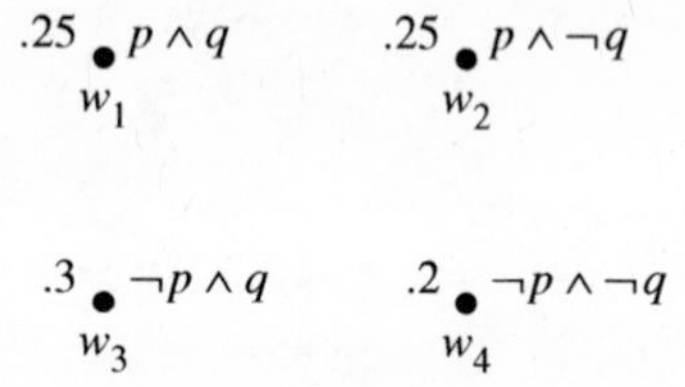

.25 $\bullet \ p \wedge q$      .25 $\bullet \ p \wedge \neg q$
$w_1$            $w_2$

.3 $\bullet \ \neg p \wedge q$      .2 $\bullet \ \neg p \wedge \neg q$
$w_3$            $w_4$

Figure 7.2   The simple probability structure $M_1$.

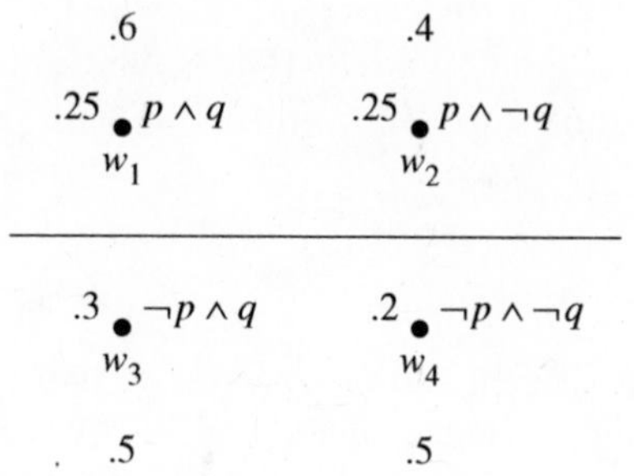

.6                .4

.25 $\bullet \ p \wedge q$      .25 $\bullet \ p \wedge \neg q$
$w_1$            $w_2$

_____

.3 $\bullet \ \neg p \wedge q$      .2 $\bullet \ \neg p \wedge \neg q$
$w_3$            $w_4$

.5                .5

Figure 7.3   The probability structure $M_2$.

I next present a complete axiomatization for reasoning about probability. The system, called $AX_n^{prob}$, divides nicely into three parts, which deal respectively with propositional reasoning, reasoning about linear inequalities, and reasoning about probability. It consists of the following axioms and inference rules, which hold for $i = 1, \ldots, n$:

Propositional reasoning:

Prop.   All substitution instances of tautologies of propositional logic.

MP.   From $\varphi$ and $\varphi \Rightarrow \psi$ infer $\psi$ (Modus Ponens).

Reasoning about probability:

QU1.   $\ell_i(\phi) \geq 0$.

QU2.   $\ell_i(true) = 1$.

QU3.   $\ell_i(\phi \wedge \psi) + \ell_i(\phi \wedge \neg\psi) = \ell_i(\phi)$.

QUGen.   From $\varphi \Leftrightarrow \psi$ infer $\ell_i(\varphi) = \ell_i(\psi)$.

Reasoning about linear inequalities:

Ineq.   All substitution instances of valid linear inequality formulas. (*Linear inequality formulas* are discussed shortly.)

Prop and MP should be familiar from the systems $K_n$ in Section 7.2.3. However, note that Prop represents a different collection of axioms in each system, since the underlying language is different in each case. For example, $\neg(\ell_1(p) > 0 \wedge \neg(\ell_1(p) > 0))$ is an instance of Prop in $AX_n^{prob}$, obtained by substituting formulas in the language $\mathcal{L}_n^{QU}$ into the propositional tautology $\neg(p \wedge \neg p)$. It is not an instance of Prop in $K_n$, since this formula is not even in the language $\mathcal{L}_n^K$. Axioms QU1–3 correspond to the properties of probability: every set gets nonnegative probability (QU1), the probability of the whole space is 1 (QU2), and finite additivity (QU3). The rule of inference QUGen is an analogue to the generalization rule Gen from Section 7.2. The most obvious analogue is perhaps

QUGen'.   From $\phi$ infer $\ell_i(\phi) = 1$.

QUGen' is provable from QUGen and QU2, but is actually weaker than QUGen and does not seem strong enough to give completeness. For example, it is almost immediate that $\ell_1(p) = 1/3 \Rightarrow \ell_1(p \wedge p) = 1/3$ is provable using QUGen, but it does not seem to be provable using QUGen'.

The axiom Ineq consists of "all substitution instances of valid linear inequality formulas." To make this precise, let $\mathcal{X}$ be a fixed infinite set of *variables*. A *(linear) inequality term* (over $\mathcal{X}$) is an expression of the form $a_1 x_1 + \cdots + a_k x_k$, where $a_1, \ldots, a_k$ are real numbers, $x_1, \ldots, x_k$ are variables in $\mathcal{X}$, and $k \geq 1$. A *basic (linear) inequality formula* is a statement of the form $t \geq b$, where $t$ is an inequality term and $b$ is a real number. For example, $2x_3 + 7x_2 \geq 3$ is a basic inequality formula. A *(linear) inequality formula* is a Boolean combination of basic inequality formulas. I use $f$ and $g$ to refer to inequality formulas. An *assignment to variables* is a function $A$ that assigns a real number to every variable. It is straightforward to define the truth of inequality formulas with respect to an assignment $A$ to variables. For a basic inequality formula,

$$A \models a_1 x_1 + \cdots + a_k x_k \geq b \text{ iff } a_1 A(x_1) + \cdots + a_k A(x_k) \geq b.$$

The extension to arbitrary inequality formulas, which are just Boolean combinations of basic inequality formulas, is immediate:

$$A \models \neg f \text{ iff } A \not\models f; \text{ and}$$
$$A \models f \wedge g \text{ iff } A \models f \text{ and } A \models g.$$

As usual, an inequality formula $f$ is *valid* if $A \models f$ for all assignments $A$ to variables.

A typical valid inequality formula is

$$
\begin{aligned}
&(a_1 x_1 + \cdots + a_k x_k \geq b) \wedge (a_1' x_1 + \cdots + a_k' x_k \geq b') \\
&\Rightarrow (a_1 + a_1') x_1 + \cdots + (a_k + a_k') x_k \geq (b + b').
\end{aligned}
\tag{7.1}
$$

To get an instance of Ineq, simply replace each variable $x_j$ that occurs in a valid formula about linear inequalities with a likelihood term $\ell_{i_j}(\phi_j)$. (Of course, each occurrence of the variable $x_j$ must be replaced by the same primitive likelihood term $\ell_{i_j}(\phi_j)$.) Thus, the following likelihood formula, which results from replacing each occurrence of $x_j$ in (7.1) by $\ell_{i_j}(\phi_j)$, is an instance of Ineq:

$$
\begin{aligned}
&(a_1 \ell_{i_1}(\phi_1) + \cdots + a_k \ell_{i_k}(\phi_k) \geq b) \wedge (a_1' \ell_{i_1}(\phi_1) + \cdots + a_k' \ell_{i_k}(\phi_k) \geq b') \\
&\Rightarrow (a_1 + a_1') \ell_{i_1}(\phi_1) + \cdots + (a_k + a_k') \ell_{i_k}(\phi_k) \geq (b + b').
\end{aligned}
\tag{7.2}
$$

There is an elegant sound and complete axiomatization for Boolean combinations of linear inequalities; however, describing it is beyond the scope of this book (see the notes for a reference). The axiom Ineq gives a proof access to all the valid formulas of this logic, just as Prop gives a proof access to all valid propositional formulas.

The following result says that $AX_n^{prob}$ completely captures probabilistic reasoning, to the extent that it is expressible in the language $\mathcal{L}_n^{QU}$.

**Theorem 7.3.3** $AX_n^{prob}$ *is a sound and complete axiomatization with respect to* $\mathcal{M}_n^{meas}$ *for the language* $\mathcal{L}_n^{QU}$.

**Proof**   Soundness is straightforward (Exercise 7.8). The completeness proof is beyond the scope of this book.   ∎

What happens in the case of countably additive probability measures? Actually, nothing changes. Let $\mathcal{M}_n^{meas,c}$ be the class of all measurable probability structures where the probability measures are countably additive. $AX_n^{prob}$ is also a sound and complete axiomatization with respect to $\mathcal{M}_n^{meas,c}$ for the language $\mathcal{L}_n^{QU}$. Intuitively, this is because the language $\mathcal{L}_n^{QU}$ cannot distinguish between finite and infinite structures. It can be shown that if a formula in $\mathcal{L}_n^{QU}$ is satisfiable at all, then it is satisfiable in a finite structure. Of course, in finite structure, countable additivity and finite additivity coincide. Thus, no additional axioms are needed to capture countable additivity. For similar reasons, there is no need to attempt to axiomatize continuity properties for the other representations of uncertainty considered in this chapter.

## 7.4   Reasoning about Other Quantitative Representations of Likelihood

The language $\mathcal{L}_n^{QU}$ is appropriate not just for reasoning about probability, but also for reasoning about lower probability, inner measure, belief, and possibility. That is, formulas in this language can be interpreted perfectly well in a number of different types of structures. All that changes is the class of structures considered and the interpretation of $\ell$. Again, at the risk of boring the reader, I summarize the details here.

Much like the case of probability, *lower probability structures, belief structures,* and *possibility structures* have the form $(W, \mathcal{X}_1, \ldots, \mathcal{X}_n, \pi)$, where $\mathcal{X}_i(w) = (W_{w,i}, \mathcal{F}_{w,i}, X_{w,i})$. As expected, for lower probability, $X_{w,i}$ is a set of probability measures on $\mathcal{F}_{w,i}$; for belief structures, $X_{w,i}$ is a belief function on all subsets of $W_{w,i}$; and for possibility structures, $X_{w,i}$ is a possibility measure on all subsets of $W_{w,i}$. (Recall that for belief functions and possibility measures, I assumed that all sets were measurable.) Let $\mathcal{M}_n^{lp}$, $\mathcal{M}_n^{bel}$, and $\mathcal{M}_n^{poss}$ denote the denote the class of all lower probability structures, belief structures, and possibility structures, respectively, for $n$ agents.

It is straightforward to define a notion of satisfaction for formulas in $\mathcal{L}_n^{QU}$ for all these structures as well as for $\mathcal{M}_n^{prob}$, the set of arbitrary probability structures (where not all sets are necessarily measurable). In the latter case, $\ell_i$ is interpreted as "inner measure," rather than "probability."

- In a lower probability structure $M = (W, \mathcal{LP}_1, \ldots, \mathcal{LP}_n, \pi)$,

$$(M, w) \models a_1 \ell_{i_1}(\phi_1) + \cdots + a_k \ell_{i_k}(\phi_k) \geq b$$
$$\text{iff } a_1(\mathcal{P}_{w,i_1})_*([\![\phi_1]\!]_M \cap W_{w,i_1}) + \cdots + a_k(\mathcal{P}_{w,i_k})_*([\![\phi_k]\!]_M \cap W_{w,i_k}) \geq b,$$

  where $\mathcal{LP}_i(w) = (W_{w,i}, \mathcal{P}_{w,i})$ for $i = 1, \ldots, n$. Thus, $\ell$ is now being interpreted as a lower probability. It could equally well have been interpreted as an upper probability; since lower probability is definable from upper probability, and vice versa (Equation 2.11), the choice is essentially a matter of taste.

- In a belief structure $M = (W, \mathcal{BEL}_1, \ldots, \mathcal{BEL}_n, \pi)$,

$$(M, w) \models a_1 \ell_{i_1}(\phi_1) + \cdots + a_k \ell_{i_k}(\phi_k) \geq b$$
$$\text{iff } a_1 \text{Bel}_{w,i_1}([\![\phi_1]\!]_M \cap W_{w,i_1}) + \cdots + a_k \text{Bel}_{w,i_k}([\![\phi_k]\!]_M \cap W_{w,i_k}) \geq b,$$

  where $\mathcal{BEL}_i(w) = (W_{w,i}, \text{Bel}_{w,i})$ for $i = 1, \ldots, n$.

- In a probability structure $M = (W, \mathcal{PR}_1, \ldots, \mathcal{PR}_n)$ where not all sets are necessarily measurable, $\ell$ is interpreted as an inner measure, so

$$(M, w) \models a_1 \ell_{i_1}(\phi_1) + \cdots + a_k \ell_{i_k}(\phi_k) \geq b$$
$$\text{iff } a_1(\mu_{w,i_1})_*([\![\phi_1]\!]_M \cap W_{w,i_1}) + \cdots + a_k(\mu_{w,i_k})_*([\![\phi_k]\!]_M \cap W_{w,i_k}) \geq b,$$

  where $\mathcal{PR}_i(w) = (W_{w,i}, \mathcal{F}_{w,i}, \mu_{w,i})$ for $i = 1, \ldots, n$. This is a generalization of the measurable case; if all sets are in fact measurable, then the inner measure agrees with the measure. Again, it is possible to use outer measure here instead of inner measure; no new difficulties arise.

- Finally, in a possibility structure $M = (W, \mathcal{POSS}_1, \ldots, \mathcal{POSS}_n, \pi)$, $\ell$ is interpreted as a possibility measure, so

$$(M, w) \models a_1 \ell_{i_1}(\phi_1) + \cdots + a_k \ell_{i_k}(\phi_k) \geq b$$
$$\text{iff } a_1 \text{Poss}_{w,i_1}([\![\phi_1]\!]_M \cap W_{w,i_1}) + \cdots + a_k \text{Poss}_{w,i_k}([\![\phi_k]\!]_M \cap W_{w,i_k}) \geq b,$$

  where $\mathcal{POSS}_i(w) = (W_{w,i}, \text{Poss}_{w,i})$ for $i = 1, \ldots, n$.

Can these notions of uncertainty be characterized axiomatically? Clearly all the axioms and inference rules other than QU3 (finite additivity) are still valid in $\mathcal{M}_n^{lp}$, $\mathcal{M}_n^{bel}$, and $\mathcal{M}_n^{prob}$. In the case of $\mathcal{M}_n^{bel}$, there is an obvious replacement for QU3: the analogues of B1 and B3.

QU5.  $\ell_i(false) = 0$.

QU6.  $\ell_i(\bigvee_{j=1}^n \phi_j) \geq \sum_{j=1}^n \sum_{\{I \subseteq \{1,\dots,n\}:|I|=j\}} (-1)^{j+1} \ell_i(\wedge_{k \in I} \phi_k)$.

It turns out that QU1, QU2, QU5, QU6, together with Prop, MP, QUGen, and Ineq, give a sound and complete axiomatization for reasoning about belief functions. This is not so surprising, since the key axioms just capture the properties of belief functions in an obvious way. What is perhaps more surprising is that these axioms also capture reasoning about inner measures. As I observed in Section 2.4, every inner measure is a belief function, but not every belief function is an inner measure. This suggests that, although inner measures satisfy the analogue of B3 (namely, (2.8)), they may satisfy additional properties. In a precise sense, the following theorem shows they do not. Let $AX_n^{bel}$ consist of QU1, QU2, QU5, QU6, QUGen, Prop, MP, and Ineq.

**Theorem 7.4.1**   $AX_n^{bel}$ *is a sound and complete axiomatization with respect to both* $\mathcal{M}_n^{bel}$ *and* $\mathcal{M}_n^{prob}$ *for the language* $\mathcal{L}_n^{QU}$.

**Proof**   Soundness is again straightforward (Exercise 7.9), and completeness is beyond the scope of this book. However, Exercises 7.10 and 7.11 explain why the same axioms characterize belief structures and probability structures, even though not every belief function is an inner measure. Roughly speaking, these exercises show that a formula is satisfiable in a belief structure if and only if it is satisfiable in a probability structure. Since every probability measure is a belief function, one direction is almost immediate. For the opposite direction, the key step is to show that, given a belief function Bel on $W$, it is possible to embed $W$ in a larger space $W'$ and to define a measure $\mu$ on $W'$ such that $\mu_*$ and Bel agree on the sets definable by formulas; see Exercise 7.11 for details. ∎

For possibility structures, QU6 must be replaced by the key axiom that characterizes possibility, namely, that the possibility of a union of two disjoint sets is the max of their individual possibilities. The following axiom does the job:

QU7.  $(\ell_i(\phi \wedge \psi) \geq \ell_i(\phi \wedge \neg\psi)) \Rightarrow \ell_i(\phi) = \ell_i(\phi \wedge \psi)$.

Let $AX_n^{poss}$ consist of QU1, QU2, QU5, QU7, QUGen, Prop, MP, and Ineq.

**Theorem 7.4.2** $AX_n^{poss}$ *is a sound and complete axiomatization with respect to* $\mathcal{M}_n^{poss}$ *for the language* $\mathcal{L}_n^{QU}$.

What about lower probability? As was observed earlier (Exercise 2.14), lower probabilities do not satisfy the analogue of B3. It follows that QU6 is not valid in $\mathcal{M}_n^{lp}$. All the other axioms in $AX_n^{bel}$ are valid though (Exercise 7.12). Since lower probabilities are superadditive (Exercise 2.14), the following axiom is also valid in $\mathcal{M}_n^{lp}$:

$$\ell_i(\phi \wedge \psi) + \ell_i(\phi \wedge \neg \psi) \leq \ell_i(\phi).$$

However, this does not give a complete axiomatization. Recall from Section 2.3 that the following property holds for inner and outer measures:

$$\mathcal{P}_*(U \cup V) \geq \mathcal{P}_*(U) + \mathcal{P}_*(V) + \mathcal{P}_*(\overline{U \cap V}) - 1.$$

Moreover (Exercise 2.15), this property does not follow from the superadditivity of lower probabilities. Thus, the axiom corresponding to this property is valid in $\mathcal{M}_n^{lp}$ and does not follow from the other axioms. There is a property given by (2.13) in Chapter 2 that characterizes lower probabilities. Consider the following axiom:

QU8.  $\ell_i(\phi_1) + \cdots + \ell_i(\phi_k) - n\ell_i(\phi) \leq m$ if $\phi \Leftrightarrow \bigvee_{J \subseteq \{1,\ldots,k\}, |J|=m+n} \bigwedge_{j \in J} \phi_j$
and $\neg \phi \Leftrightarrow \bigvee_{J \subseteq \{1,\ldots,k\}, |J|=m} \bigwedge_{j \in J} \phi_j$ are propositional tautologies.

Note that if $\phi \Leftrightarrow \bigvee_{J \subseteq \{1,\ldots,k\}, |J|=m+n} \bigwedge_{j \in J} \phi_j$ and $\neg \phi \Leftrightarrow \bigvee_{J \subseteq \{1,\ldots,k\}, |J|=m} \bigwedge_{j \in J} \phi_j$ are propositional tautologies, then in any structure $M = (W, \mathcal{PR}_1, \ldots, \mathcal{PR}_n)$, the sets $[\![\phi_1]\!]_M, \ldots, [\![\phi_m]\!]_M$ must cover $[\![\phi]\!]_M$ exactly $m + n$ times and must cover $[\![\neg \phi]\!]_M$ exactly $m$ times. The soundness of QU8 in $\mathcal{M}_n^{lp}$ now easily follows from (2.13) (Exercise 7.13). Moreover, QU8 is just what is needed to get completeness. Let $AX_n^{lp}$ consist of QU1, QU2, QU5, QU8, QUGen, Prop, MP, and Ineq. (That is, $AX_n^{lp}$ is the result of replacing QU7 in $AX_n^{poss}$ by QU8.)

**Theorem 7.4.3** $AX_n^{lp}$ *is a sound and complete axiomatization with respect to* $\mathcal{M}_n^{lp}$ *for the language* $\mathcal{L}_n^{QU}$.

## 7.5   Reasoning about Relative Likelihood

The language $\mathcal{L}_n^{QU}$ is not appropriate for reasoning about representations of likelihood whose range is not the reals. For example, it is clearly inappropriate for reasoning about plausibility measures, since a formula like $\ell_i(\phi) = 1/2$ does not make sense for an arbitrary plausibility measure; plausibility values may not be real numbers. But even in the case of ranking functions, a formula such as that is not so interesting. Since ranks are nonnegative integers, it is impossible to have $\ell_i(\phi) = 1/2$ if $\ell_i$ represents a ranking function.

To reason about ranking functions, it seems more appropriate to consider a variant of $\mathcal{L}_n^{QU}$ that restricts the coefficients in likelihood formulas to $\mathbb{N}^*$. There is no difficulty in obtaining a complete axiomatization for this language with respect to ranking structures. It is very similar to that for possibility structures, except that QU2 and QU5 needs to be changed to reflect the fact that for ranking structures, 0 and $\infty$ play the same role as 1 and 0 do in possibility structures, and QU7 needs to be modified to use min rather than max. Rather than belaboring the details here, I instead consider a more restricted sublanguage of $\mathcal{L}_n^{QU}$ that is appropriate not just for ranking, but also for reasoning about relative likelihood as discussed in Section 2.7. In this sublanguage, denoted $\mathcal{L}_n^{RL}$, linear combinations of likelihood terms are not allowed. All that is allowed is the comparison of likelihood between two formulas. That is, $\mathcal{L}_n^{RL}$ is the sublanguage of $\mathcal{L}_n^{QU}$ that is formed by starting with primitive propositions and closing off under conjunction, negation, and restricted likelihood formulas of the form $\ell_i(\phi) > \ell_i(\psi)$.

$\mathcal{L}_n^{RL}$ can be interpreted in a straightforward way in *preferential structures,* that is, structures where there is a partial preorder $\succeq$ on worlds that can be lifted to an ordering on sets as discussed in Section 2.7. Recall that in Section 2.7 I actually considered two different ways of defining a preorder on sets based on $\succeq$; one was denoted $\succeq^e$ and the other $\succeq^s$. Thus, there are two possible semantics that can be defined for formulas in $\mathcal{L}_n^{RL}$, depending on whether $\succeq^e$ or $\succeq^s$ is used as the underlying preorder on sets.

Formally, a *preferential structure* is a tuple $M = (W, \mathcal{O}_1, \ldots, \mathcal{O}_n, \pi)$, where for each world $w \in W$, $\mathcal{O}_i(w)$ is a pair $(W_{w,i}, \succeq_{w,i})$, where $W_{w,i} \subseteq W$ and $\succeq_{w,i}$ is a partial preorder on $W_{w,i}$. Let $\mathcal{M}_n^{pref}$ denote the class of all preferential structures for $n$ agents; let $\mathcal{M}_n^{tot}$ be the subset of $\mathcal{M}_n^{pref}$ consisting of all total structures, that is, structures where $\succeq_{w,i}$ is a total preorder for each world $w$ and agent $i$. If $M$ is a preferential structure, then

$$(M, w) \models^e \ell_i(\phi) \geq \ell_i(\psi) \text{ iff } W_{w,i} \cap [\![\phi]\!]_M \succeq^e_{w,i} W_{w,i} \cap [\![\psi]\!]_M,$$

where $\succeq^e_{w,i}$ is the partial order on $2^{W_{w,i}}$ determined by $\succeq_{w,i}$. The superscript $e$ in $\models^e$ is meant to emphasize the fact that $\geq$ is interpreted using $\succeq^e$. Another semantics can be obtained using $\succeq^s$ in the obvious way:

$$(M, w) \models^s \ell_i(\phi) \geq \ell_i(\psi) \text{ iff } W_{w,i} \cap [\![\phi]\!]_M \succeq^s_{w,i} W_{w,i} \cap [\![\psi]\!]_M.$$

Note that in preferential structures, $(M, w) \models^x (\ell_i(\neg\phi) = \ell_i(false))$ exactly if $[\![\neg\phi]\!]_M \cap W_{w,i} = \emptyset$, both if $x = e$ and if $x = s$. This, in turn, is true exactly if $W_{w,i} \subseteq [\![\phi]\!]_M$. That is, $(M, w) \models^x \ell_i(\neg\phi) = \ell_i(false)$ if and only if $W_{w,i} \subseteq [\![\phi]\!]_M$. Thus, $\ell_i(\neg\phi) = \ell_i(false)$ can be viewed as a way of expressing $K_i\phi$ in $\mathcal{L}_n^{RL}$. From here on, I take $K_i\phi$ to be an abbreviation for $\ell_i(\neg\phi) = \ell_i(false)$ when working in the language $\mathcal{L}_n^{RL}$.

Let $AX^{RLe}$ consist of the following axioms and inference rules:

**Prop.**   All substitution instances of tautologies of propositional logic.

**RL1.**   $\ell_i(\phi) \geq \ell_i(\phi)$.

**RL2.**   $[(\ell_i(\phi_1) \geq \ell_i(\phi_2)) \wedge (\ell_i(\phi_2) \geq \ell_i(\phi_3))] \Rightarrow (\ell_i(\phi_1) \geq \ell_i(\phi_3))$.

**RL3.**   $K_i(\phi \Rightarrow \psi) \Rightarrow (\ell_i(\psi) \geq \ell_i(\phi))$.

**RL4.**   $[(\ell_i(\phi_1) \geq \ell_i(\phi_2)) \wedge (\ell_i(\phi_1) \geq \ell_i(\phi_3))] \Rightarrow (\ell_i(\phi_1) \geq \ell_i(\phi_2 \vee \phi_3))$.

**MP.**   From $\varphi$ and $\varphi \Rightarrow \psi$ infer $\psi$ (Modus Ponens).

**Gen.**   From $\varphi$ infer $K_i\varphi$ (Knowledge Generalization).

In the context of preferential structures, these axioms express the properties of relative likelihood discussed in Section 2.7. In particular, RL1 and RL2 say that $\succeq^e$ is reflexive and transitive (and thus a preorder), RL3 says that it respects subsets, and RL4 says that it satisfies the finite union property.

Let $AX^{RLTe}$ consist of $AX^{RLe}$ together with the following axiom, which says that $\succeq^e$ is total:

**RL5.**   $(\ell_i(\phi) \geq \ell_i(\psi)) \vee (\ell_i(\psi) \geq \ell_i(\phi))$.

Finally, let $AX^{RLs}$ and $AX^{RLTs}$ be the result of adding the following axiom, which characterizes the qualitative property, to $AX^{RLe}$ and $AX^{RLTe}$, respectively.

**RL6.**   $(K_i(\neg(\phi_1 \wedge \phi_2)) \wedge K_i(\neg(\phi_2 \wedge \phi_3)) \wedge K_i(\neg(\phi_1 \wedge \phi_3)))$
$\Rightarrow ((\ell_i(\phi_1 \vee \phi_2) > \ell_i(\phi_3)) \wedge (\ell_i(\phi_1 \vee \phi_3) > \ell_i(\phi_2))$
$\Rightarrow (\ell_i(\phi_1) > \ell_i(\phi_2 \vee \phi_3)))$.

Note that if $(M, w) \models K_i(\neg(\phi \wedge \psi))$, then $[\![\phi]\!]_M \cap W_{w,i}$ and $[\![\psi]\!]_M \cap W_{w,i}$ are disjoint. Thus, the antecedent in RL5 is really saying that (the intensions of) the formulas $\phi_1$, $\phi_2$, and $\phi_3$ are pairwise disjoint. It should be clear that the rest of the axiom characterizes the qualitative property.

**Theorem 7.5.1**   *For the language* $\mathcal{L}_n^{RL}$:

(a) $AX^{RLe}$ *is a sound and complete axiomatization for the* $\models^e$ *semantics with respect to* $\mathcal{M}_n^{pref}$;

(b) $AX^{RLTe}$ *is a sound and complete axiomatization for the* $\models^e$ *semantics with respect to* $\mathcal{M}_n^{tot}$;

(c) $AX^{RLs}$ *is a sound and complete axiomatization for the* $\models^s$ *semantics with respect to* $\mathcal{M}_n^{pref}$;

(d) $AX^{RLTs}$ *is a sound and complete axiomatization for the* $\models^s$ *semantics with respect to* $\mathcal{M}_n^{tot}$.

**Proof**   The soundness of these axioms follows almost immediately from Theorems 2.7.1 and 2.7.5, which characterize the properties of $\succeq^e$ and $\succeq^s$ semantically. I leave the formal details to the reader (Exercise 7.14). The completeness proof for $AX^{RLs}$ uses Theorem 2.7.6, although the details are beyond the scope of this book. One subtlety is worth noting. Two properties used in Theorem 2.7.6 have no corresponding axiom: the fact that $\succeq^s$ is conservative and that it is determined by singletons.   ∎

What happens if formulas in $\mathcal{L}_n^{RL}$ are interpreted with respect to arbitrary plausibility measures? A *plausibility structure* has the form $(W, \mathcal{PL}_1, \ldots, \mathcal{PL}_n, \pi)$, where $\mathcal{PL}_i$ is a plausibility assignment; a *measurable plausibility structure* is one where $\mathcal{F}_{w,i} = 2^{W_{w,i}}$. Let $\mathcal{M}_n^{plaus}$ and $\mathcal{M}_n^{plaus,meas}$ denote the class of plausibility structures and measurable plausibility structures, respectively. Formulas in $\mathcal{L}_n^{RL}$ are interpreted in measurable plausibility structures in the natural way. (Later I will also talk about $\mathcal{M}_n^{rank}$, the class of all ranking structures. I omit the obvious definitions here.)

It is easy to see that RL1–3 are sound for arbitrary measurable plausibility structures, since $\geq$ is still a preorder, and Pl3 guarantees RL3. These axioms, together with Prop, Gen, and MP, provide a sound and complete axiomatization for the language $\mathcal{L}_n^{RL}$ with respect to measurable plausibility structures. Let $AX_n^{ord}$ consist of Prop, RL1–3, MP, and Gen.

**Theorem 7.5.2**   $AX_n^{ord}$ *is a sound and complete axiomatization with respect to* $\mathcal{M}_n^{plaus,meas}$ *for the language* $\mathcal{L}_n^{RL}$.

**Proof**   Again, soundness is straightforward and completeness is beyond the scope of the book.   ∎

Of course, additional axioms arise for particular subclasses of plausibility structures. Interestingly, as far as reasoning about relative likelihood goes, possibility structures and ranking structures are characterized by precisely the same axioms. Moreover, these are the axioms that characterize $\succeq^e$ in totally preordered relative likelihood, that is, the axiom system $AX^{RLTe}$. The extra structure of the real numbers (in the case of possibility measures) or $\mathbb{N}^*$ (in the case of ranking functions) plays no role when reasoning about statements of relative likelihood.

**Theorem 7.5.3** *$AX^{RLTe}$ is a sound and complete axiomatization for the language $\mathcal{L}_n^{RL}$ with respect to $\mathcal{M}_n^{rank}$ and $\mathcal{M}_n^{poss}$.*

**Proof**   It is not hard to show that the same formulas in the language $\mathcal{L}_n^{RL}$ are valid in each of $\mathcal{M}_n^{rank}$, $\mathcal{M}_n^{poss}$, and $\mathcal{M}_n^{tot}$ (using the $\models^e$ semantics) (Exercise 7.16). Thus, it follows from Theorem 7.5.1 that $AX^{RLTe}$ is sound and complete with respect to all three classes of structures. ∎

What about $\mathcal{M}_n^{meas}$, $\mathcal{M}_n^{prob}$, $\mathcal{M}_n^{bel}$, and $\mathcal{M}_n^{lp}$? Clearly all the axioms of $AX_n^{ord}$ hold in these subclasses. In addition, since the plausibility ordering is total in all these subclasses, RL5 holds as well. (It does not hold in general in $\mathcal{M}_n^{plaus,meas}$, since the domain of plausibility values may be partially ordered.) It is easy to check that none of the other axioms in $AX^{RLTs}$ is sound. However, $AX_n^{ord} \cup \{RL5\}$ is *not* a complete axiomatization with respect to $\mathcal{M}_n^{meas}$, $\mathcal{M}_n^{prob}$, $\mathcal{M}_n^{bel}$, or $\mathcal{M}_n^{lp}$ for the language $\mathcal{L}_n^{RL}$. For example, a formula such as $\ell_i(p) > \ell_i(\neg p)$ is true at a world $w$ in a structure $M \in \mathcal{M}_n^{meas}$ iff $\mu_{w,i}(\llbracket p \rrbracket_M) > 1/2$. Thus, the following formula is valid in $\mathcal{M}_n^{meas}$:

$$(\ell_i(p) > \ell_i(\neg p) \wedge \ell_i(q) > \ell_i(\neg q)) \Rightarrow \ell_i(p) > \ell_i(\neg q).$$

However, this formula is not provable in $AX^{RLTs}$, let alone $AX_n^{ord} \cup \{RL5\}$ (Exercise 7.17). This example suggests that it will be difficult to find an elegant collection of axioms that is complete for $\mathcal{M}_n^{meas}$ with respect to $\mathcal{L}_n^{RL}$. Even though this simple language does not have facilities for numeric reasoning, it can still express some non-trivial consequences of numeric properties. Other examples can be used to show that there are formulas valid in $\mathcal{M}_n^{prob}$, $\mathcal{M}_n^{bel}$, and $\mathcal{M}_n^{lp}$ that are not provable in $AX^{RLTs}$ (Exercise 7.18). Finding a complete axiomatization for $\mathcal{L}_n^{RL}$ with respect to any of $\mathcal{M}_n^{meas}$, $\mathcal{M}_n^{prob}$, $\mathcal{M}_n^{bel}$, and $\mathcal{M}_n^{lp}$ remains an open problem.

## 7.6   Reasoning about Knowledge and Probability

Although up to now I have considered modalities in isolation, it is often of interest to reason about combinations of modalities. For example, in (interpreted) systems, where time is represented explicitly, it is often useful to reason about both knowledge and time. In probabilistic interpreted systems, it is useful to reason about knowledge, probability, and time. In Chapter 8, I consider reasoning about knowledge and belief and about probability and counterfactuals.

In all these cases, there is no difficulty getting an appropriate syntax and semantics. The interest typically lies in the interaction between the accessibility relations for the various modalities. In this section, I focus on one type of multimodal reasoning— reasoning about knowledge and probability, with the intention of characterizing the properties CONS, SDP, UNIF, and CP considered in Chapter 6.

Constructing the syntax for a combined logic of knowledge and probability is straightforward. Let $\mathcal{L}_n^{KQU}$ be the result of combining the syntaxes of $\mathcal{L}_n^K$ and $\mathcal{L}_n^{QU}$ in the obvious way. $\mathcal{L}_n^{KQU}$ allows statements such as $K_1(\ell_2(\phi) = 1/3)$—agent 1 knows that, according to agent 2, the probability of $\phi$ is 1/3. It also has facilities for asserting uncertainty regarding probability. For example,

$$K_1(\ell_1(\phi) = 1/2 \vee \ell_1(\phi) = 2/3) \wedge \neg K_1(\ell_1(\phi) = 1/2) \wedge \neg K_1(\ell_1(\phi) = 2/3)$$

says that agent 1 knows that the probability of $\phi$ is either 1/2 or 2/3, but he does not know which. It may seem unnecessary to have subscripts on both $K$ and $\ell$ here. Would it not be possible to get rid of the subscript in $\ell$, and write something like $K_1(\ell(\phi) = 1/2)$? Doing this results in a significant loss of expressive power. For example, it seems perfectly reasonable for a formula such as $K_1(\ell_1(\phi) = 1/2) \wedge K_2(\ell_2(\phi) = 2/3)$ to hold. Because of differences in information, agents 1 and 2 assign different (subjective) probabilities to $\phi$. Replacing $\ell_1$ and $\ell_2$ by $\ell$ would result in a formula that is inconsistent with the Knowledge Axiom (K2).

The semantics of $\mathcal{L}_n^{KQU}$ can be given using *epistemic probability structures,* formed by adding an interpretation to an epistemic probability frame. Let $\mathcal{M}_n^{K,prob}$ consist of all epistemic probability structures for $n$ agents, and let $\mathcal{M}_n^{K,meas}$ consist of all the epistemic probability structures for $n$ agents where all sets are measurable. Let $AX_n^{K,prob}$ consist of the axioms and inference rules of S5$_n$ for knowledge together with the axioms and inference rules of $AX_n^{prob}$ for probability. Let $AX_n^{K,bel}$ consist of the axioms and inference rules of S5$_n$ and $AX_n^{bel}$.

**Theorem 7.6.1**  $AX_n^{K,prob}$ *(resp., $AX_n^{K,bel}$) is a sound and complete axiomatization with respect to $\mathcal{M}_n^{K,meas}$ (resp., $\mathcal{M}_n^{K,prob}$) for the language $\mathcal{L}_n^{KQU}$.*

**Proof**  Soundness is immediate from the soundness of $S5_n$ and $AX_n^{prob}$; completeness is beyond the scope of the book.  ∎

Now what happens in the presence of conditions like CONS or SDP? There are axioms that characterize each of CONS, SDP, and UNIF. Recall from Section 7.3 that an *i-likelihood formula* is one of the form $a_1\ell_i(\phi_1) + \cdots + a_k\ell_i(\phi_k) \geq b$. That is, it is a formula where the outermost likelihood terms involve only agent $i$. Consider the following three axioms:

KP1.  $K_i\phi \Rightarrow (\ell_i(\phi) = 1)$.

KP2.  $\phi \Rightarrow K_i\phi$ if $\phi$ is an $i$-likelihood formula.

KP3.  $\phi \Rightarrow (\ell_i(\phi) = 1)$ if $\phi$ is an $i$-likelihood formula or the negation of an $i$-likelihood formula.

In a precise sense, KP1 captures CONS, KP2 captures SDP, and KP3 captures UNIF. KP1 essentially says that the set of worlds that agent $i$ considers possible has probability 1 (according to agent $i$). It is easy to see that KP1 is sound in structures satisfying CONS. Since SDP says that agent $i$ knows his probability space (in that it is the same for all worlds in $\mathcal{K}_i(w)$), it is easy to see that SDP implies that in a given world, agent $i$ knows all $i$-likelihood formulas that are true in that world. Thus, KP2 is sound in structures satisfying SDP. Finally, since a given $i$-likelihood formula has the same truth value at all worlds where agent $i$'s probability assignment is the same, the soundness of KP3 in structures satisfying UNIF is easy to verify.

As stated, KP3 applies to both $i$-likelihood formulas and their negations, while KP2 as stated applies to only $i$-likelihood formulas. It is straightforward to show, using the axioms of $S5_n$, that KP2 also applies to negated $i$-likelihood formulas (Exercise 7.19). With this observation, it is almost immediate that KP1 and KP2 together imply KP3, which is reasonable since CONS and SDP together imply UNIF (Exercise 7.20).

The next theorem makes the correspondence between various properties and axioms precise.

**Theorem 7.6.2**  *Let $\mathcal{A}$ be a subset of {CONS,SDP,UNIF} and let A be the corresponding subset of {KP1,KP2,KP3}. Then $AX_n^{K,prob} \cup A$ (resp., $AX_n^{K,bel} \cup A$) is a sound and* complete axiomatization for the language $\mathcal{L}_n^{KQU}$ with respect to structures in $\mathcal{M}_n^{K,meas}$ (resp., $\mathcal{M}_n^{K,prob}$) satisfying $\mathcal{A}$.

**Proof**  As usual, soundness is straightforward (Exercise 7.21) and completeness is beyond the scope of this book. ∎

Despite the fact that CP puts some nontrivial constraints on structures, it turns out that CP adds no new properties in the language $\mathcal{L}_n^{KQU}$ beyond those already implied by CONS and SDP.

**Theorem 7.6.3**  $AX_n^{K,prob} \cup \{KP1, KP2\}$ is a sound and complete axiomatization for the language $\mathcal{L}_n^{KQU}$ with respect to structures in $\mathcal{M}_n^{K,meas}$ satisfying CP.

Although CP does not lead to any new axioms in the language $\mathcal{L}_n^{KQU}$, things change significantly if *common knowledge* is added to the language. Common knowledge of $\phi$ holds if everyone knows $\phi$, everyone knows that everyone knows $\phi$, everyone knows that everyone knows that everyone knows, and so on. It is straightforward to extend the logic of knowledge introduced in Section 7.2 to capture common knowledge. Add the modal operator $C$ (for common knowledge) to the language $\mathcal{L}_n^{KQU}$ to get the language $\mathcal{L}_n^{KQUC}$. Let $E^1\phi$ be an abbreviation for $K_1\phi \wedge \ldots \wedge K_n\phi$, and let $E^{m+1}\phi$ be an abbreviation $E^1(E^m\phi)$. Thus, $E\phi$ is true if all the agents in $\{1, \ldots, n\}$ know $\phi$, while $E^3\phi$, for example, is true if everyone knows that everyone knows that everyone knows $\phi$. Given a structure $M \in \mathcal{M}_n^{K,prob}$, define

$$(M, w) \models C\phi \text{ iff } (M, w) \models E^k\phi \text{ for all } k \geq 1.$$

In the language $\mathcal{L}_n^{KQUC}$, CP does result in interesting new axioms. In particular, in the presence of CP, agents cannot disagree on the expected value of random variables. For example, if Alice and Bob have a common prior, then it cannot be common knowledge that the expected value of a random variable $X$ is 1/2 according to Alice and 2/3 according to Bob (Exercise 7.22). On the other hand, without a common prior, this can easily happen. For a simple example, suppose that there are two possible worlds, $w_1$ and $w_2$, and it is common knowledge that Alice assigns them equal probability while Bob assigns probability 2/3 to $w_1$ and 1/3 to $w_2$. (Such an assignment of probabilities is easily seen to be impossible with a common prior.) If $X$ is the random variable such that $X(w_1) = 1$ and $X(w_2) = 0$, then it is common knowledge that the expected value of $X$ is 1/2 according to Alice and 2/3 according to Bob.

The fact that two agents cannot disagree on the expected value of a random variable can essentially be expressed in the language $\mathcal{L}_2^{KQUC}$. Consider the following axiom:

CP$_2$.   If $\phi_1, \ldots, \phi_m$ are pairwise *mutually exclusive* formulas (i.e., if $\neg(\phi_i \wedge \phi_j)$ is an instance of a propositional tautology for $i \neq j$), then

$$\neg C(a_1 \ell_1(\phi_1) + \cdots + a_m \ell_1(\phi_m) > 0 \wedge a_1 \ell_2(\phi_1) + \cdots + a_m \ell_2(\phi_m) < 0).$$

Notice that $a_1 \ell_1(\phi_1) + \cdots + a_m \ell_1(\phi_m)$ is the expected value according to agent 1 of a random variable that takes on the value $a_i$ in the worlds where $\phi_i$ is true, while $a_1 \ell_2(\phi_1) + \cdots + a_m \ell_2(\phi_m)$ is the expected value of the same random variable according to agent 2. Thus, CP$_2$ says that it cannot be common knowledge that the expected value of this random variable according to agent 1 is positive while the expected value according to agent 2 is negative.

It can be shown that CP$_2$ is valid in structures in $\mathcal{M}_2^{K,meas}$ satisfying CP; moreover, there is a natural generalization CP$_n$ that is valid in structures $\mathcal{M}_n^{K,meas}$ satisfying CP (Exercise 7.23). It is worth noting that the validity depends on the assumption that $\mu_W(C(w)) > 0$ for all $w \in W$; that is, the prior probability of the set of worlds reachable from any given world is positive. To see why, consider an arbitrary structure $M = (W, \ldots)$. Now construct a new structure $M'$ by adding one more world $w^*$ such that $\mathcal{K}_i(w^*) = \{w^*\}$ for $i = 1, \ldots, n$. It is easy to see that $C(w^*) = \{w^*\}$, and for each world $w \in W$, the set of worlds reachable from $w$ in $M$ is the same as the set of worlds reachable from $w$ in $M'$. Without the requirement that $C(w)$ must have positive prior probability, then it is possible that, in $M'$, all the worlds in $W$ have probability 0. But then CP can hold in $M'$, although $\mu_{w,i}$ can be arbitrary for each $w \in W$ and agent $i$; CP$_2$ need not hold in this case (Exercise 7.24).

What about completeness? It turns out that CP$_n$ (together with standard axioms for reasoning about knowledge and common knowledge) is still not quite enough to get completeness. A slight strengthening of CP$_n$ is needed, although the details are beyond the scope of this book.

## 7.7   Reasoning about Independence

As was observed earlier, the language $\mathcal{L}_n^{QU}$ cannot express independence. A fortiori, neither can $\mathcal{L}_n^{RL}$. What is the best way of extending the language to allow reasoning about independence? I discuss three possible approaches below. I focus on probabilistic independence, but my remarks apply to all other representations of likelihood as well.

One approach, which I mentioned earlier, is to extend linear likelihood formulas to polynomial likelihood formulas, which allow multiplication of terms as well as addition. Thus, a typical polynomial likelihood formula is $a_1 \ell_{i_1}(\phi_1) \ell_{i_2}(\phi_2)^2 - a_3 \ell_{i_3}(\phi_3) > b$.

Let $\mathcal{L}_n^{QU,\times}$ be the language that extends $\mathcal{L}_n^{QU}$ by using polynomial likelihood formulas rather than just linear likelihood formulas. The fact that $\phi$ and $\psi$ are independent (according to agent $i$) can be expressed in $\mathcal{L}_n^{QU,\times}$ as $\ell_i(\phi \wedge \psi) = \ell_i(\phi) \times \ell_i(\psi)$.

An advantage of using $\mathcal{L}_n^{QU,\times}$ to express independence is that it admits an elegant complete axiomatization with respect to $\mathcal{M}_n^{meas}$. In fact, the axiomatization is just $AX_n^{prob}$, with one small change—Ineq is replaced by the following axiom:

Ineq$^+$. All instances of valid formulas about polynomial inequalities.

Allowing polynomial inequalities rather than just linear inequalities in the language makes it necessary to reason about polynomial inequalities. Interestingly, all the necessary reasoning can be bundled up into Ineq$^+$. The axioms for reasoning about probability are unaffected. Let $AX_n^{prob,\times}$ be the result of replacing Ineq by Ineq$^+$ in $AX_n^{prob}$.

**Theorem 7.7.1** $AX_n^{prob,\times}$ *is a sound and complete axiomatization with respect to* $\mathcal{M}_n^{meas}$ *for the language* $\mathcal{L}_n^{QU,\times}$.

There is a price to be paid for using $\mathcal{L}_n^{QU,\times}$ though, as I hinted earlier: it seems to be harder to determine if formulas in this richer language are valid. There is another problem with using $\mathcal{L}_n^{QU,\times}$ as an approach for capturing reasoning about independence. It does not extend so readily to other notions of uncertainty. As I argued in Chapter 4, it is perhaps better to think of the independence of $U$ and $V$ being captured by the equation $\mu(U \mid V) = \mu(U)$ and $\mu(V \mid U) = \mu(V)$ rather than by the equation $\mu(U \cap V) = \mu(U) \times \mu(V)$. It is the former definition that generalizes more directly to other approaches.

This approach can be captured directly by extending $\mathcal{L}_n^{QU}$ in a different way, by allowing conditional likelihood terms of the form $\ell_i(\phi \mid \psi)$ and linear combinations of such terms. Of course, in this extended language, the fact that $\phi$ and $\psi$ are independent (according to agent $i$) can be expressed as $(\ell_i(\phi \mid \psi) = \ell_i(\phi)) \wedge (\ell_i(\psi \mid \phi) = \ell_i(\psi))$.

There is, however, a slight technical difficulty with this approach. Consider a probability structure $M$. What is the truth value of a formula such as $\ell_i(\phi \mid \psi) > b$ at a world $w$ in a probability structure $M$ if $\mu_{w,i}([\![\psi]\!]_M) = 0$? To some extent this problem can be dealt with by taking $\mu_{w,i}$ to be a conditional probability measure, as defined in Section 4.1. But even if $\mu_{w,i}$ is a conditional probability measure, there are still some difficulties if $[\![\phi]\!]_M = \emptyset$ (or, more generally, if $[\![\phi]\!]_M \notin \mathcal{F}'$, i.e., if it does not make sense to condition on $\phi$). Besides this technical problem, it is not clear how to axiomatize this extension of $\mathcal{L}_n^{QU}$ without allowing polynomial terms. In particular, it is not clear how to capture the fact that $\ell_i(\phi \mid \psi) \times \ell_i(\psi) = \ell_i(\phi \wedge \psi)$ without allowing expressions of the form $\ell_i(\phi \mid \psi) \times \ell_i(\psi)$ in the language. On the other hand, if multiplicative terms are allowed, then the language $\mathcal{L}_n^{QU,\times}$ can express independence without having to deal with the technical problem of giving semantics to formulas with terms of the form $\ell_i(\phi \mid \psi)$ if $\mu([\![\psi]\!]_M) = 0$.

A third approach to reasoning about independence is just to add formulas directly to the language that talk about independence. That is, using the notation of Chapter 4, formulas of the form $I(\psi_1, \psi_2 \mid \phi)$ or $I^{rv}(\psi_1, \psi_2 \mid \phi)$ can be added to the language, with the obvious interpretation. When viewed as a random variable, a formula has only two possible values—true or false—so $I^{rv}(\psi_1, \psi_2 \mid \phi)$ is equivalent to $I(\psi_1, \psi_2 \mid \phi) \wedge I(\psi_1, \psi_2 \mid \neg\phi)$. Of course, the notation can be extended as in Chapter 4 to allow sets of formulas as arguments of $I^{rv}$.

$I$ and $I^{rv}$ inherit all the properties of the corresponding operators on events and random variables, respectively, considered in Chapter 4. In addition, if the language contains both facilities for talking about independence (via $I$ or $I^{rv}$) and for talking about probability in terms of $\ell$, there will in general be some interaction between the two. For example, $(\ell_i(p) = 1/2) \wedge (\ell_i(q) = 1/2) \wedge I(p, q \mid true) \Rightarrow \ell_i(p \wedge q) = 1/4$ is certainly valid. No work has been done to date on getting axioms for such a combined language.

## 7.8   Reasoning about Expectation

The basic ingredients for reasoning about expectation are quite similar to those for reasoning about likelihood. The syntax and semantics follow similar lines, and using the characterizations of expectation functions from Chapter 5, it is possible to get elegant complete axiomatizations.

### 7.8.1   Syntax and Semantics

What is a reasonable logic for reasoning about expectation? Note that, given a simple probability structure $M = (W, \mathcal{F}, \mu, \pi)$, a formula $\phi$ can be viewed as a gamble on $W$, which is 1 in worlds where $\phi$ is true and 0 in other worlds. That is, $\phi$ can be identified with the indicator function $X_{[\![\phi]\!]_M}$. A *linear propositional gamble* of the form $a_1\phi_1 + \cdots + a_n\phi_n$ can then also be viewed as a random variable in the obvious way. Moreover, if $W$ is finite and every basic measurable set in $\mathcal{F}$ is of the form $[\![\phi]\!]_M$ for some formula $\phi$, then every gamble on $W$ is equivalent to one of the form $a_1\phi_1 + \cdots + a_m\phi_m$. These observations motivate the definition of the language $\mathcal{L}_n^E$ for reasoning about expectation. $\mathcal{L}_n^E(\Phi)$ is much like $\mathcal{L}_n^{QU}$, except that instead of likelihood terms $\ell_i(\phi)$, it has *expectation terms* of the form $e_i(\gamma)$, where $\gamma$ is a linear propositional gamble.

Formally, $\mathcal{L}_n^E(\Phi)$ is the result of starting off with $\Phi$ and closing off under conjunction, negation, and *basic expectation formulas* of the form

$$b_1 e_{i_1}(\gamma_1) + \cdots + b_k e_{i_k}(\gamma_k) > c,$$

where $\gamma_1, \ldots, \gamma_k$ are linear propositional gambles, and $b_1, \ldots, b_k$, $c$ are real numbers.

A formula such as $e_i(a_1\phi_1 + \cdots + a_m\phi_m) > c$ is interpreted as saying that the expectation (according to agent $i$) of the gamble $a_1\phi_1 + \cdots + a_m\phi_m$ is at least $c$. More precisely, given a propositional linear gamble $\gamma = a_1\phi_1 + \cdots + a_k\phi_k$ and a structure $M$, there is an obvious random variable associated with $\gamma$, namely, $X_\gamma^M = a_1 X_{[\![\phi_1]\!]_M} + \cdots + a_m X_{[\![\phi_n]\!]_M}$. Then $e_i(\gamma)$ is interpreted in structure $M$ as the expectation of $X_\gamma^M$. The notion of "expectation" depends, of course, on the representation of uncertainty being considered.

For example, for a probability structure $M = (W, \mathcal{PR}_1, \ldots, \mathcal{PR}_n, \pi) \in \mathcal{M}_n^{meas}$, not surprisingly,

$$(M, w) \models e_i(\gamma) \text{ iff } E_{\mu_{w,i}}(X_\gamma^M) > c,$$

where $\mu_{w,i}$ is the probability measure in $\mathcal{PR}_i(w)$. Linear combinations of expectation terms are dealt with in the obvious way.

Just as in the case of the $\ell_i$ operator for likelihood, it is also possible to interpret $e_i$ in lower probability structures, belief structures, arbitrary probability structures, and possibility structures. It then becomes lower expectation, expected belief, inner expectation, and expected possibility. I leave the obvious details of the semantics to the reader.

## 7.8.2   Expressive Power

As long as $\nu$ is a measure of uncertainty such that $E_\nu(X_U) = \nu(U)$ (which is the case for all representations of uncertainty considered in Chapter 5), then $\mathcal{L}_n^E$ is at least as expressive as $\mathcal{L}_n^{QU}$, since the likelihood term $\ell_i(\phi)$ is equivalent to the expectation term $e_i(\phi)$. More precisely, by replacing each likelihood term $\ell_i(\phi)$ by the expectation term $e_i(\phi)$, it immediately follows that, for every formula $\psi \in \mathcal{L}_n^{QU}$, there is a formula $\psi^T \in \mathcal{L}_n^E$ such that, for any structure in $\mathcal{M}_n^{meas}$, $\mathcal{M}_n^{prob}$, $\mathcal{M}_n^{bel}$, or $\mathcal{M}_n^{poss}$, $\psi$ is equivalent to $\psi^T$.

What about the converse? Given a formula in $\mathcal{L}_n^{QU}$, is it always possible to find an equivalent formula in $\mathcal{L}_n^E$? That depends on the underlying semantics. It is easy to see that, when interpreted over measurable probability structures, it is. Note that the expectation term $e_i(a_1\phi_1 + \cdots + a_m\phi_m)$ is equivalent to the likelihood term $a_1\ell_i(\phi_1) + \cdots + a_m\ell_i(\phi_m)$, when interpreted over (measurable) probability structures. The equivalence holds because $E_\mu$ is additive and affinely homogeneous.

Interestingly, $\mathcal{L}_n^{QU}$ continues to be just as expressive as $\mathcal{L}_n^E$ when interpreted over belief structures, possibility structures, and general probability structures (where $\ell_i$ is interpreted as inner measure and $e_i$ is interpreted as inner expectation). The argument is essentially the same in all cases. Given a formula $f \in \mathcal{L}_n^E$, (5.12) can be used to give a formula $f' \in \mathcal{L}_n^E$ equivalent to $f$ (in structures in $\mathcal{M}_n^{bel}$, $\mathcal{M}_n^{prob}$, and $\mathcal{M}_n^{poss}$) such that $e$ is applied only to propositional formulas in $f'$ (Exercise 7.25). It is then easy to find a formula $f^T \in \mathcal{L}_n^{QU}$ equivalent to $f'$ with respect to structures in $\mathcal{M}_n^{bel}$, $\mathcal{M}_n^{prob}$, and $\mathcal{M}_n^{poss}$. However, unlike the case of probability, the translation from $f$ to $f^T$ can cause an exponential blowup in the size of the formula.

What about lower expectation/probability? In this case, $\mathcal{L}_n^E$ is strictly more expressive than $\mathcal{L}_n^{QU}$. It is not hard to construct two structures in $\mathcal{M}_n^{lp}$ that agree on all formulas in $\mathcal{L}_n^{QU}$ but disagree on the formula $e_i(p + q) > 1/2$ (Exercise 7.26). That means that there cannot be a formula in $\mathcal{L}_n^{QU}$ equivalent to $e_i(p + q) > 1/2$.

The following theorem summarizes this discussion:

**Theorem 7.8.1** $\mathcal{L}_n^E$ *and* $\mathcal{L}_n^{QU}$ *are equivalent in expressive power with respect to* $\mathcal{M}_n^{meas}$, $\mathcal{M}_n^{prob}$, $\mathcal{M}_n^{bel}$, *and* $\mathcal{M}_n^{poss}$. $\mathcal{L}_n^E$ *is strictly more expressive than* $\mathcal{L}_n^{QU}$ *with respect to* $\mathcal{M}_n^{lp}$.

### 7.8.3 Axiomatizations

The fact that $\mathcal{L}_n^E$ is no more expressive than $\mathcal{L}_n^{QU}$ in probability structures means that a complete axiomatization for $\mathcal{L}_n^E$ can be obtained essentially by translating the axioms in $AX_n^{prob}$ to $\mathcal{L}_n^E$, as well as by giving axioms that capture the translation. The same is true for expected belief, inner expectation, and expected possibility. However, it is instructive to consider a complete axiomatization for $\mathcal{L}_n^E$ with respect to all these structures, using the characterization theorems proved in Chapter 5.

I start with the measurable probabilistic case. Just as in the case of probability, the axiomatization splits into three parts. There are axioms and inference rules for propositional reasoning, for reasoning about inequalities, and for reasoning about expectation. As before, propositional reasoning is captured by Prop and MP, and reasoning about linear inequalities is captured by Ineq. (However, Prop now consists of all instances of propositional tautologies in the language $\mathcal{L}_n^E$; Ineq is similarly relativized to $\mathcal{L}_n^E$.) The interesting new axioms capture reasoning about expectation. Consider the following axioms, where $\gamma_1$ and $\gamma_2$ represent linear propositional gambles:

EXP1. $e_i(\gamma_1 + \gamma_2) = e_i(\gamma_1) + e_i(\gamma_2)$.

EXP2. $e_i(a\phi) = ae_i(\phi)$ for $a \in \mathbb{R}$.

EXP3. $e_i(\textit{false}) = 0$.

EXP4. $e_i(\textit{true}) = 1$.

EXP5. $e_i(\gamma_1) \leq e_i(\gamma_2)$ if $\gamma_1 \leq \gamma_2$ is an instance of a valid propositional gamble inequality. (*Propositional gamble inequalities* are discussed shortly.)

EXP1 is simply additivity of expectations. EXP2, EXP3, and EXP4, in conjunction with additivity, capture affine homogeneity. EXP5 captures monotonicity. A propositional gamble inequality is a formula of the form $\gamma_1 \leq \gamma_2$, where $\gamma_1$ and $\gamma_2$ are linear propositional gambles. The inequality is valid if the random variable represented by $\gamma_1$ is less than the random variable represented by $\gamma_2$ in all structures. Examples of valid propositional gamble inequalities are $p = p \wedge q + p \wedge \neg q$, $\phi \leq \phi + \psi$, and $\phi \leq \phi \vee \psi$. As in the case of Ineq, EXP5 can be replaced by a sound and complete axiomatization for Boolean combinations of gamble inequalities, but describing it is beyond the scope of this book.

Let $\mathrm{AX}_n^{e,prob}$ consist of the axioms Prop, Ineq, and EXP1–5 and the rule of inference MP.

**Theorem 7.8.2** $\mathrm{AX}_n^{e,prob}$ *is a sound and complete axiomatization with respect to* $\mathcal{M}_n^{meas}$ *for the language* $\mathcal{L}_n^E$.

Again, as for the language $\mathcal{L}_n^{QU}$, there is no need to add extra axioms to deal with continuity if the probability measures are countably additive.

The characterization of Theorems 5.2.2 suggests a complete axiomatization for lower expectation. Consider the following axioms:

EXP6. $e_i(\gamma_1 + \gamma_2) \geq e_i(\gamma_1) + e_i(\gamma_2)$.

EXP7. $e_i(a\gamma + b\ \textit{true}) = ae_i(\gamma) + b$, where $a, b \in \mathbb{R}, a \geq 0$.

EXP8. $e_i(a\gamma + b\ \textit{false}) = ae_i(\gamma)$, where $a, b \in \mathbb{R}, a \geq 0$.

EXP6 expresses superadditivity. EXP7 and EXP8 capture positive affine homogeneity; without additivity, simpler axioms such as EXP2–4 are insufficient. Monotonicity is captured, as in the case of probability measures, by EXP5. Let $\mathrm{AX}_n^{e,lp}$ consist of the axioms Prop, Ineq, EXP5, EXP6, EXP7, and EXP8, together with the inference rule MP.

**Theorem 7.8.3**   $\mathrm{AX}_n^{e,lp}$ *is a sound and complete axiomatization with respect to* $\mathcal{M}_n^{lp}$ *for the language* $\mathcal{L}_n^E$.

Although it would seem that Theorem 7.8.3 should follow easily from Proposition 5.2.1, this is, unfortunately, not the case. Of course, it is the case that any expectation function that satisfies the constraints in the formula $f$ and also every instance of EXP6, EXP7, and EXP8 must be a lower expectation, by Theorem 5.2.2. The problem is that, a priori, there are infinitely many relevant instances of the axioms. To get completeness, it is necessary to reduce this to a finite number of instances of these axioms. It turns out that this can be done, although it is surprisingly difficult; see the notes for references.

It is also worth noting that, although $\mathcal{L}_n^E$ is a more expressive language than $\mathcal{L}_n^{QU}$ in the case of lower probability/expectation, the axiomatization for $\mathcal{L}_n^E$ is much more elegant than the corresponding axiomatization for $\mathcal{L}_n^{QU}$ given in Section 7.4. There is no need for an ugly axiom like QU8. Sometimes having a richer language leads to simpler axioms!

Next, consider reasoning about expected belief. As expected, the axioms capturing expected belief rely on the properties pointed out in Proposition 5.2.7. Dealing with the inclusion-exclusion property (5.11) requires a way to express the max and min of two propositional gambles. Fortunately, given linear propositional gambles $\gamma_1$ and $\gamma_2$, it is not difficult to construct gambles $\gamma_1 \vee \gamma_2$ and $\gamma_1 \wedge \gamma_2$ such that, in all structures $M$, $X_{\gamma_1 \vee \gamma_2}^M = X_{\gamma_1}^M \vee X_{\gamma_2}^M$, and $X_{\gamma_1 \wedge \gamma_2}^M = X_{\gamma_1}^M \wedge X_{\gamma_2}^M$ (Exercise 7.27). With this definition, the following axiom accounts for the property (5.11):

EXP9.   $e_i(\gamma_1 \vee \cdots \vee \gamma_n) = \sum_{i=1}^n \sum_{\{I \subseteq \{1,\ldots,n\}:|I|=i\}} (-1)^{i+1} e_i(\bigwedge_{j \in I} \gamma_j)$.

To deal with the comonotonic additivity property (5.12), it seems that comonotonicity must be expressed in the logic. It turns out that it suffices to capture only a restricted form of comonotonicity. Note that if $\phi_1, \ldots, \phi_m$ are pairwise mutually exclusive, $a_1 \leq \ldots \leq a_m$, and $b_1 \leq \ldots \leq b_m$, $\gamma_1 = a_1\phi_1 + \cdots + a_m\phi_m$, and $\gamma_2 = b_1\phi_1 + \cdots + b_m\phi_m$, then in all structures $M$, the gambles $X_{\gamma_1}^M$ and $X_{\gamma_2}^M$ are comonotonic (Exercise 7.28). Thus, by (5.12), it follows that $E_{\mathrm{Bel}}((X_{\gamma_1+\gamma_2}^M) = E_{\mathrm{Bel}}(X_{\gamma_1}^M) + E_{\mathrm{Bel}}(X_{\gamma_2}^M)$. The argument that $E_{\mathrm{Bel}}$ satisfies comonotonic additivity sketched in Exercise 5.19 shows that it suffices to consider only gambles of this form. These observations lead to the following axiom:

EXP10. If $\gamma_1 = a_1\phi_1 + \cdots + a_m\phi_m$, $\gamma_2 = b_1\phi_1 + \cdots + b_m\phi_m$, $a_1 \leq \ldots \leq a_m$, $b_1 \leq \ldots \leq b_m$, and $\phi_i \Rightarrow \neg\phi_j$ is a propositional tautology for all $i \neq j$, then $e_i(\gamma_1 + \gamma_2) = e_i(\gamma_1) + e_i(\gamma_2)$.

Let $\text{AX}_n^{e,bel}$ consist of the axioms Ineq, EXP5, EXP7, EXP8, EXP9, and EXP10, and the rule of inference MP. As expected, $\text{AX}_n^{e,bel}$ is a sound and complete axiomatization with respect to $\mathcal{M}_n^{bel}$. Perhaps somewhat surprisingly, just as in the case of likelihood, it is also a complete axiomatization with respect to $\mathcal{M}_n^{prob}$ (where $e_i$ is interpreted as inner expectation). Although inner expectation has an extra property over and above expected belief, expressed in Lemma 5.2.13, this extra property is not expressible in the language $\mathcal{L}_n^E$.

**Theorem 7.8.4**  $\text{AX}_n^{e,bel}$ *is a sound and complete axiomatization with respect to* $\mathcal{M}_n^{bel}$ *and* $\mathcal{M}_n^{prob}$ *for the language* $\mathcal{L}_n^E$.

Finally, consider expectation with respect to possibility. The axioms capturing the interpretation of possibilistic expectation $E_{\text{Poss}}$ rely on the properties given in Proposition 5.2.15. The following axiom accounts for the max property (5.13):

EXP11.  $(e_i(\phi_1) \geq e_i(\phi_2)) \Rightarrow (e_i(\phi_1 \vee \phi_2) = e_i(\phi_1))$.

Let $\text{AX}_n^{poss}$ consist of the axioms Prop, Ineq, EXP5, EXP7, EXP8, EXP10, and EXP11, and the inference rule MP.

**Theorem 7.8.5**  $\text{AX}_n^{poss}$ *is a sound and complete axiomatization with respect to* $\mathcal{M}_n^{poss}$ *for* $\mathcal{L}_n^E$.

## Exercises

**7.1**    Prove the remaining parts of Lemma 7.1.1.

**7.2**    Prove that a formula $\phi$ is valid iff $\neg\phi$ is not satisfiable.

**7.3**    Show that $\{p \Rightarrow (r \Rightarrow q),\, p \wedge r\}$ entails $q$.

**7.4**    Show that $M \models p \Rightarrow q$ iff $[\![p]\!]_M \subseteq [\![q]\!]_M$.

**7.5**    Prove Proposition 7.2.3.

**7.6**    Prove Proposition 7.2.4.

**7.7**    Show that $K_i(\phi \wedge \psi) \Leftrightarrow (K_i\phi \wedge K_i\psi)$ is valid in all epistemic structures.

**7.8** Show that $AX_n^{prob}$ is sound with respect to $\mathcal{M}_n^{meas}$ for the language $\mathcal{L}_n^{QU}$.

**7.9** Show that $AX_n^{bel}$ is sound with respect to both $\mathcal{M}_n^{bel}$ and $\mathcal{M}_n^{prob}$ for the language $\mathcal{L}_n^{QU}$.

**7.10** Given a (not necessarily measurable) probability structure $M = (W, \mathcal{PR}_1, \ldots, \mathcal{PR}_n, \pi)$, define a belief structure $M' = (W, \mathcal{BEL}_1, \ldots, \mathcal{BEL}_n, \pi)$ by taking $Bel_{w,i}(U) = (\mu_{w,i})_*(U)$. (Since every inner measure is a belief function, $Bel_{w,i}$ is indeed a belief function.) Show that $(M, w) \models \phi$ iff $(M', w) \models \phi$, for every formula $\phi \in \mathcal{L}_n^{QU}$ and $w \in W$. (In $M$, $\ell$ is interpreted as inner measure, as in Section 7.4.)

This shows that every formula satisfiable in a probability structure is satisfiable in a belief structure. The next exercise shows that the converse also holds. This explains why belief structures and probability structures are characterized by exactly the same axiom system.

**7.11** Given a belief structure $M = (W, \mathcal{BEL}_1, \ldots, \mathcal{BEL}_n, \pi)$, where $W$ is finite and $\mathcal{BEL}_{w,i} = (W_{w,i}, Bel_{w,i})$, this exercise shows how to construct a probability structure $M' = (W', \mathcal{PR}_1, \ldots, \mathcal{PR}_n, \pi')$ that satisfies the same formulas as $M$.

Let $W' = \{(U, u) : U \subseteq W, u \in U\}$. For $U \subseteq W$, define $U^* = \{(U, u) : u \in U\}$. Clearly $U^* \subseteq W'$.

(a) Show that if $U \neq V$, then $U^*$ and $V^*$ are disjoint.

(b) Show that $W' = \cup_{U \subseteq W} U^*$.

Define $\mathcal{PR}_i(U, u) = (W_{(U,u),i}, \mathcal{F}_{(U,u),i}, \mu_{(U,u),i})$ as follows:

- Let $W_{(U,u),i} = \{(V, v) \in W' : V \subseteq W_{u,i}\}$.

- Take the sets $V^*$ for $V \subseteq W_{u,i}$ to be a basis for $\mathcal{F}_{(U,u),i}$. (That is, the sets in $\mathcal{F}_{(U,u),i}$ consist of all possible unions of sets of the form $V^*$ for $V \subseteq W_{u,i}$.)

- Let $m_{w,i}$ be the mass function corresponding to $Bel_{w,i}$. Let $\mu_{(U,u),i}(V^*) = m_{u,i}(V)$ for $V \subseteq W_{u,i}$, and extend $\mu_{(U,u),i}$ to all the sets in $\mathcal{F}_{(U,u),i}$ by finite additivity.

Finally, define $\pi'(U, u) = \pi(u)$ for all $(U, u) \in W'$. This completes the definition of $M'$.

(c) Show that $(M, u) \models \phi$ iff $(M', (U, u)) \models \phi$ for all sets $U$ such that $u \in U$.

Note that this result essentially says that a belief function on $W$ can be viewed as the inner measure corresponding to a probability measure defined on $W'$, at least as far as sets definable by formulas are concerned. That is, $Bel_{u,i}(\llbracket\phi\rrbracket_M) = (\mu_{(U,u),i})_*(\llbracket\phi\rrbracket_{M'})$ for all formulas $\phi$.

**7.12**   Show that all the axioms in $\mathrm{AX}_n^{bel}$ other than QU6 are valid in $\mathcal{M}_n^{lp}$.

**7.13**   Show that if $\phi \Rightarrow \bigvee_{J \subseteq \{1,\dots,k\}, |J|=m+n} \bigwedge_{j \in J} \phi_j$ and $\bigvee_{J \subseteq \{1,\dots,k\}, |J|=m} \bigwedge_{j \in J} \phi_j$ are propositional tautologies, then in any structure $M = (W, \mathcal{PR}_1, \dots)$, the sets $[\![\phi_1]\!]_M, \dots, [\![\phi_m]\!]_M$ must cover $W$ $m$ times and $[\![\phi]\!]_M$ $m+n$ times. Now, using (2.13), show that QU8 is sound in $\mathcal{M}_n^{lp}$.

**7.14**   Prove the soundness of the axioms systems given in Theorem 7.5.1 with respect to the appropriate class of structures.

* **7.15**   This exercise shows that a formula in $\mathcal{L}_n^{RL}$ is satisfiable in $\mathcal{M}_n^{poss}$ iff it is satisfiable in $\mathcal{M}_n^{tot}$ with respect to the $\models^e$ semantics. A very similar argument can be used to prove the same result for $\mathcal{M}_n^{rank}$ instead of $\mathcal{M}_n^{poss}$. These results prove Theorem 7.5.3.

   (a) Show that if a formula is satisfiable in a possibility structure, it is satisfiable in one where the possibility of all worlds is positive. More precisely, given a structure $M = (W, \mathcal{POSS}_1, \dots, \mathcal{POSS}_n, \pi)$, let $M' = (W, \mathcal{POSS}'_1, \dots, \mathcal{POSS}'_n, \pi)$, where $\mathcal{POSS}'_{w,i} = (W'_{w,i}, \mathrm{Poss}'_{w,i})$, $W'_{w,i} = \{w' \in W_{w,i} : \mathrm{Poss}_{w,i}(w') > 0\}$, and $\mathrm{Poss}'_{w,i}(w') = \mathrm{Poss}_{w,i}(w')$ for $w' \in W'_{w,i}$. Show that for all formulas $\phi$ and all $w \in W$, $(M, w) \models \phi$ iff $(M', w) \models \phi$.

   (b) Given a possibility structure $M = (W, \mathcal{POSS}_1, \dots, \mathcal{POSS}_n, \pi)$ such that $\mathrm{Poss}_{w,i}(w') > 0$ for all agents $i$ and worlds $w$, $w'$ with $w' \in W_{w,i}$, construct a preferential structure $M' = (W, \mathcal{O}_1, \dots, \mathcal{O}_n, \pi) \in \mathcal{M}_n^{tot}$ by setting $\mathcal{O}_i(w, i) = (W_{w,i}, \succeq_{w,i})$, where $w' \succeq_{w,i} w''$ iff $\mathrm{Poss}_{w,i}(w') \geq \mathrm{Poss}_{w,i}(w'')$. Show that, for all subsets $U, V \subseteq W_{w,i}$, $\mathrm{Poss}_{w,i}(U) \geq \mathrm{Poss}_{w,i}(V)$ iff $U \succeq^e_{w,i} V$. (Note that this would not be true without the assumption that $\mathrm{Poss}_{w,i}(w') > 0$ for all $w' \in W_{w,i}$. For if $\mathrm{Poss}_{w,i}(w') = 0$, then $\mathrm{Poss}(\{w'\}) = \mathrm{Poss}(\emptyset)$ although $\emptyset \not\succeq^e_{w,i} \{w'\}$.) Then show that $(M, w) \models \phi$ iff $(M', w) \models \phi$ for all formulas $\phi \in \mathcal{L}_n^{RL}$. (Note that this argument works even if $W_{w,i}$ is infinite.)

   (c) This part of the exercise shows that if a formula in $\mathcal{L}_n^{RL}$ is satisfied in a preferential structure in $\mathcal{M}_n^{tot}$, it is also satisfied in some possibility structure. Given $\phi \in \mathcal{L}_n^{RL}$, let $p_1, \dots, p_n$ be the primitive propositions that appear in $\phi$. Suppose that $(M, w) \models \phi$ for some preferential structure $M = (W, \mathcal{O}_1, \dots, \mathcal{O}_n, \pi) \in \mathcal{M}_n^{tot}$. For a world $w' \in W$, define the formula $\phi_{w'}$ to be of the form $q_1 \wedge \dots \wedge q_n$, where $q_i$ is $p_i$ if $(M, w') \models p_i$ and $\neg p_i$ otherwise. Note that $(M, w') \models \phi_{w'}$. Show that there exists a possibility measure $\mathrm{Poss}_{w,i}$ on $W_{w,i}$ such that $\mathrm{Poss}_{w,i}(w') > 0$ for all $w' \in W_{w,i}$ on $\mathrm{Poss}_{w,i}(w') \geq \mathrm{Poss}_{w,i}(w'')$ iff $[\![M]\!]_{\phi_{w'}} \cap W_{w,i} \succeq^e_{w,i} [\![M]\!]_{\phi_{w''}} \cap W_{w,i}$. (The key point is that since there are only finitely many possible sets of the form $[\![M]\!]_{\phi_{w'}} \cap W_{w,i}$, the range of $\mathrm{Poss}_{w,i}$ is finite, even if $W_{w,i}$ is infinite; thus it is easy to define $\mathrm{Poss}_{w,i}$. Let $M' = (W, \mathcal{POSS}_1, \ldots, \mathcal{POSS}_n, \pi)$ be the possibility structure such that $\mathcal{POSS}_i(w) = (W_{w,i}, \mathrm{Poss}_{w,i})$. Show that $(M, w') \models \psi$ iff $(M', w') \models \psi$ for all subformulas $\psi$ of $\phi$ and worlds $w' \in W$. In particular, it follows that $(M', w) \models \phi$, so $\phi$ is satisfied in $M'$.

Since (a) and (b) together show that if a formula is satisfiable in a possibility structure, it is satisfiable in a preferential structure in $\mathcal{M}_n^{tot}$, and (c) shows that if a formula is satisfiable in a preferential structure in $\mathcal{M}_n^{tot}$, then it is satisfiable in a possibility structure. It follows that a formula is valid in possibility structures iff it is valid in totally ordered preferential structures.

**7.16** Show that the same formulas in the language $\mathcal{L}_n^{RL}$ are valid in each of $\mathcal{M}_n^{rank}$, $\mathcal{M}_n^{poss}$, and $\mathcal{M}_n^{tot}$ (using the $\models^e$ semantics).

**7.17** Show that $(\ell_i(p) > \ell_i(\neg p) \wedge \ell_i(q) > \ell_i(\neg q)) \Rightarrow \ell_i(p) > \ell_i(\neg q)$ is not provable in $\mathrm{AX}^{RLTs}$. (Hint: If it were provable in $\mathrm{AX}^{RLTs}$, it would be valid in $\mathcal{M}_n^{poss}$ and $\mathcal{M}_n^{rank}$.)

\*  **7.18** Show that there are formulas valid in $\mathcal{M}_n^{prob}$, $\mathcal{M}_n^{bel}$, and $\mathcal{M}_n^{lp}$ that are not provable in $\mathrm{AX}^{RLTs}$.

**7.19** Suppose that $\phi$ is an $i$-likelihood formula. Show that $\neg\phi \Rightarrow K_i\neg\phi$ is provable from KP2 and S5$_n$.

**7.20** Show that KP1 and KP2 (together with Prop and MP) imply KP3.

**7.21** Show that KP1, KP2, and KP3 are valid in structures in $\mathcal{M}_n^{K,meas}$ that satisfy CONS, SDP, and UNIF, respectively.

**7.22** Suppose that $X$ is a random variable that takes on only countably many values. Show that if Alice and Bob have a common prior on a (finite or) countable set of worlds, then it cannot be common knowledge that the expected value of $X$ is 1/2 according to Alice and 2/3 according to Bob.

\*  **7.23** This exercise considers the axiom CP$_2$ and a generalization of it for $n$ agents.

(a) Show that CP$_2$ is valid in structures in $\mathcal{M}_2^{K,meas}$ satisfying CP.

(b) Consider the following axiom:

CP$_n$.  If $\phi_1, \ldots, \phi_m$ are pairwise mutually exclusive formulas and $a_{ij}$, $i = 1, \ldots, n$, $j = 1, \ldots, m$, are rational numbers such that $\sum_{i=1}^n a_{ij} = 0$, for $j = 1, \ldots, m$, then

$$\neg C(a_{11}\ell_1(\phi_1) + \cdots + a_{1m}\ell_1(\phi_m) > 0 \wedge$$
$$\ldots \wedge a_{n1}\ell_n(\phi_1) + \cdots + a_{nm}\ell_n(\phi_m) > 0).$$

(i) Show that $CP_2$ is equivalent to the axiom that results from $CP_n$ when $n = 2$. (This justifies using the same name for both.)

(ii) Show that $CP_n$ is valid in structures in $\mathcal{M}_n^{K,meas}$ satisfying CP.

**7.24**   Construct a concrete example showing that $CP_2$ does not hold without the requirement that $C(w)$ have positive prior probability for each world $w \in W$.

**7.25**   Use (5.12) together with ideas similar to those of Exercise 5.20 to show that a formula $f \in \mathcal{L}_n^E$ is equivalent (in structures in $\mathcal{M}_n^{bel}$, $\mathcal{M}_n^{prob}$, and $\mathcal{M}_n^{poss}$) to a formula $f' \in \mathcal{L}_n^E$ such that, $e$ is applied only to propositional formulas in $f'$.

**7.26**   Construct two structures in $\mathcal{M}_n^{lp}$ that agree on all formulas in $\mathcal{L}_n^{QU}$ but disagree on the formula $e_i(p + q) > 1/2$.

**7.27**   Given linear propositional gambles $\gamma_1$ and $\gamma_2$, this exercise considers how to construct gambles $\gamma_1 \vee \gamma_2$ and $\gamma_1 \wedge \gamma_2$ such that $X_{\gamma_1 \vee \gamma_2}^M = X_{\gamma_1}^M \vee X_{\gamma_2}^M$, and $X_{\gamma_1 \wedge \gamma_2}^M = X_{\gamma_1}^M \wedge X_{\gamma_2}^M$ in all belief structures $M$.
Assume without loss of generality that $\gamma_1$ and $\gamma_2$ involve the same propositional formulas, say $\phi_1, \ldots, \phi_m$, so that $\gamma_1 = a_1\phi_1 + \cdots + a_m\phi_m$ and $\gamma_2 = b_1\phi_1 + \cdots + b_m\phi_m$. (It is always possible to ensure that $\gamma_1$ and $\gamma_2$ involve the same propositional formulas by adding "dummy" terms of the form $0\psi$ to each sum.) Define a family $\rho_A$ of propositional formulas indexed by $A \subseteq \{1, \ldots, m\}$ by taking $\rho_A = \bigwedge_{i \in A} \phi_i \wedge (\bigwedge_{j \notin A} \neg \phi_j)$. Thus, $\rho_A$ is true exactly if the $\phi_i$s for $i \in A$ are true and the other $\phi_j$s are false. Note that the formulas $\rho_A$ are pairwise mutually exclusive. Define the real numbers $a_A, b_A$ for $A \subseteq \{1, \ldots, n\}$ by taking $a_A = \sum_{i \in A} a_i$ and $b_A = \sum_{i \in A} b_i$. Define $\gamma_1' = \sum_{A \subseteq \{1,\ldots,n\}} a_A \rho_A$ and $\gamma_2' = \sum_{A \subseteq \{1,\ldots,n\}} b_A \rho_A$.

(a) Show that $X_{\gamma_i}^M = X_{\gamma_i'}^M$ for $i = 1, 2$, for all belief structures $M$.

(b) Define $\gamma_1 \vee \gamma_2 = \sum_{A \subseteq \{1,\ldots,n\}} \max(a_A, b_A)\rho_A$. Show that $X_{\gamma_1 \vee \gamma_2}^M = X_{\gamma_1}^M \vee X_{\gamma_2}^M$.

(c) Define $\gamma_1 \wedge \gamma_2 = \sum_{A \subseteq \{1,\ldots,n\}} \min(a_A, b_A)\rho_A$. Show that $X_{\gamma_1 \wedge \gamma_2}^M = X_{\gamma_1}^M \wedge X_{\gamma_2}^M$.

(d) Show that if $\gamma_1$ and $\gamma_2$ are the propositional formulas $\phi_1$ and $\phi_2$, respectively, then $\gamma_1 \vee \gamma_2$ is a gamble equivalent to the propositional formula $\phi_1 \vee \phi_2$, and $\gamma_1 \wedge \gamma_2$ is a gamble equivalent to the propositional formula $\phi_1 \wedge \phi_2$. This justifies the use of $\vee$ and $\wedge$ for max and min in the context of random variables.

**7.28** Show that if $\phi_1, \ldots, \phi_m$ are pairwise mutually exclusive, $a_1 \leq \ldots \leq a_m$, and $b_1 \leq \ldots \leq b_m$, $\gamma_1 = a_1\phi_1 + \cdots + a_m\phi_m$, and $\gamma_2 = b_1\phi_1 + \cdots + b_m\phi_m$, then in all structures $M$, the gambles $X^M_{\gamma_1}$ and $X^M_{\gamma_2}$ are comonotonic.

## Notes

An excellent introduction to propositional logic can be found in Enderton's text [1972], which is the source of the example about borogroves. Numerous alternatives to classical logic have been proposed over the years. Perhaps the best known include *multi-valued logics* [Rescher 1969; Rine 1984], *intuitionistic logic* [Heyting 1956], and *relevance logics* [Anderson and Belnap 1975].

A simple complete axiomatization for propositional logic with connectives $\Rightarrow$ and $\neg$ is given by the three axioms

$$\phi \Rightarrow (\psi \Rightarrow \phi)$$
$$(\phi_1 \Rightarrow (\phi_2 \Rightarrow \phi_3)) \Rightarrow ((\phi_1 \Rightarrow \phi_2) \Rightarrow (\phi_1 \Rightarrow \phi_3))$$
$$(\neg\phi \Rightarrow \psi) \Rightarrow ((\neg\phi \Rightarrow \neg\psi) \Rightarrow \phi),$$

together with the inference rule Modus Ponens. Mendelson [1997] provide a completeness proof.

Modal logic was discussed by several authors in ancient times, but the first symbolic and systematic approach to the subject appears to be the work of Lewis beginning in 1912 and culminating in his book *Symbolic Logic* with Langford [Lewis and Langford 1959]. Modal logic was originally viewed as the logic of possibility and necessity. (That is, the only modal operators considered were operators for necessity and possibility.) More recently, it has become common to view knowledge, belief, time, and so on, as modalities, and the term "modal logic" has encompassed logics for reasoning about these notions as well. Possible-worlds semantics seems to have first been suggested by Carnap [1946; 1947], and was further developed independently by many researchers, reaching its current form with Kripke [1963]. The first to consider a modal logic of knowledge was Hintikka [1962]. A thorough discussion of modal logic can be found in some of the standard texts in the area, such as [Blackburn, de Rijke, and Venema 2001; Chellas 1980; Hughes and Cresswell 1968; Popkorn 1994].

The historical names S4 and S5 are due to Lewis, and are discussed in his book with Langford. The names K and T are due to Lemmon [1977], as is the idea of naming the logic for the significant axioms used.

The presentation of Section 7.2 is largely taken from [Fagin, Halpern, Moses, and Vardi 1995]. A proof of Theorem 7.2.1 can also be found there, as well as a discussion of approaches to giving semantics to knowledge that distinguish between logically equivalent formulas (in that one of two logically equivalent formulas may be known while the other is not) and take computational issues into account. Finally, the book contains an extensive bibliography of the literature on the subject. One particularly useful reference is [Lenzen 1978], which discusses in detail the justifications of various axioms for knowledge.

See [Halpern 2001c] for a recent discussion of a definition of rationality in terms of knowledge and counterfactuals (a topic discussed in Chapter 8). This paper represents only the very tip of the iceberg as far as rationality goes; the references in the paper give some additional pointers for further reading.

The logics $\mathcal{L}^{QU}$ and $\mathcal{L}^{QU,\times}$ were introduced in [Fagin, Halpern, and Megiddo 1990] and used for reasoning about both probability and belief functions. $\mathcal{L}^{QU}$ can be viewed as a formalization of Nilsson's [1986] *probabilistic logic;* it is also a fragment of a propositional probabilistic *dynamic logic* introduced by Feldman [1984]. (Dynamic logic is a logic for reasoning about actions; see [Harel, Kozen, and Tiuryn 2000].) Theorems 7.3.3 and 7.7.1 are proved in [Fagin, Halpern, and Megiddo 1990]. (Actually, a somewhat simpler version of these theorems is proved. Only simple probability structures are considered, and the language is simplified so that in a likelihood term of the form $\ell(\phi)$, the formula $\phi$ is required to be a propositional formula. Nevertheless, the same basic proof techniques work for the more general result stated here.) In addition, a finite collection of axioms is given that characterizes Ineq. Finally, the complexity of these logics is also considered. The satisfiability problem for $\mathcal{L}^{QU}$ in simple probability structures (whether measurable or not) is shown to be *NP*-complete, no worse than that of propositional logic. The satisfiability problem for $\mathcal{L}^{QU}$ in simple belief structures and in simple lower probability structures is also *NP*-complete [Fagin and Halpern 1991b; Halpern and Pucella 2001]. It would be interesting to understand if there is some deeper reason why the complexity of the satisfiability problem for all these logics turns out to be the same.

For $\mathcal{L}^{QU,\times}$, as shown in [Fagin, Halpern, and Megiddo 1990], satisfiability in simple probability structures can be decided in polynomial space (although no lower bound other than NP is known). The satisfiability problem for $\mathcal{L}^{QU,\times}$ for other logics has not been considered, although I conjecture the PSPACE upper bound still holds.

For the more general probability structures considered here, where there are $n$ agents and the probability assignment may depend on the world, the complexity of the satisfiability problem for both $\mathcal{L}_n^{QU}$ and $\mathcal{L}_n^{QU,\times}$ is *PSPACE*-complete [Fagin and Halpern 1994]. (The lower bound holds even if $n = 1$, as long as no constraints are placed on the probability assignment.) Again, although the satisfiability problem for other logics has not been considered, I conjecture that PSPACE completeness still holds.

Theorem 7.4.1, Exercise 7.10 and Exercise 7.11 are proved in [Fagin and Halpern 1991b], using results of [Fagin, Halpern, and Megiddo 1990]. Fariñas del Cerro and

Herzig [1991] provide a complete axiomatization for $\mathcal{M}_n^{poss}$ that is similar in spirit to (although their axiomatization is not quite complete as stated; see [Halpern 1997a]).

The proof of Theorem 7.5.1 follows similar lines to the proofs of Theorems 3.1 and 3.2 in [Halpern 1997a].

The logic of probability and knowledge considered here was introduced in [Fagin and Halpern 1994]. As mentioned in the notes to Chapter 6, this is also where the notions CONS, SDP, and UNIF were introduced; Theorems 7.6.1 and 7.6.2 are taken from there. Although this was the first paper to consider a combined logic of probability and knowledge, combinations of probability with other modal operators had been studied earlier. Propositional probabilistic variants of *temporal logic* (a logic for reasoning about time; see Chapter 6) were considered by Hart and Sharir [1984] and Lehmann and Shelah [1982], while probabilistic variants of dynamic logic were studied by Feldman [1984] and Kozen [1985]. Monderer and Samet [1989] also considered a semantic model that allows the combination of probability and knowledge, although they did not introduce a formal logic for reasoning about them.

The fact that CP implies no disagreement in expectation (and, in a sense, can be characterized by this property) was observed by Bonanno and Nehring [1999], Feinberg [1995; 2000], Morris [1994], and Samet [1998a]. The axiom $CP_2$ (and $CP_n$ in Exercise 7.23) is taken from [Feinberg 2000; Samet 1998a]. An axiomatization of $\mathcal{L}_n^{KQUC}$ in the presence of CP can be found in [Halpern 1998a], from where Theorem 7.6.3 is taken.

See the notes to Chapter 4 for references regarding $I$ and $I^{rv}$. Some work has been done on providing a logical characterization of $I^{rv}$ (again, see the notes to Chapter 4); I am not aware of any work on characterizing $I$.

The material in Section 7.8 on reasoning about expectation is taken from [Halpern and Pucella 2002]. More details can be found there, including an axiomatization of reasoning about propositional gamble inequalities (EXP5).

# Chapter 8

# Beliefs, Defaults, and Counterfactuals

*You are so convinced that you believe only what you believe that you believe, that you remain utterly blind to what you* really *believe without believing you believe it.*

—Orson Scott Card, *Shadow of the Hegemon*

Two types of reasoning that arise frequently in everyday life are *default reasoning* and *counterfactual reasoning*. Default reasoning involves leaping to conclusions. For example, if an agent sees a bird, she may conclude that it flies. Now flying is not a logical consequence of being a bird. Not all birds fly. Penguins and ostriches do not fly, nor do newborn birds, injured birds, dead birds, or birds made of clay. Nevertheless flying is a prototypical property of birds. Concluding that a bird flies seems reasonable, as long as the agent is willing to retract that conclusion in the face of extra information.

Counterfactual reasoning involves reaching conclusions with assumptions that may be counter to fact. In legal cases it is often important to assign blame. A lawyer might well want to argue as follows: "I admit that my client was drunk and it was raining. Nevertheless, if the car's brakes had functioned properly, the car would not have hit Mrs. McGraw's cow. The car's manufacturer is at fault at least as much as my client."

As the lawyer admits here, his client was drunk and it was raining. He is arguing though that even if the client hadn't been drunk and it weren't raining, the car would have hit the cow. This is a classic case of counterfactual reasoning: reasoning about what might have happened if things had been different from the way they actually were. (Note the use of the subjunctive clause starting with "even if"; this is the natural-language signal that a counterfactual is about to follow.)

Why am I discussing default reasoning and counterfactual reasoning at this point in the book? It should be clear that both involve reasoning about uncertainty. Moreover, it turns out that some of the representation of uncertainty that I have been

287

considered—specifically, possibility measures, ranking functions, and plausibility measures—provide good frameworks for capturing both default reasoning and counterfactual reasoning. A closer look at these notions helps to explain why. In fact, it turns out that default reasoning and counterfactual reasoning are closely related, and are best understood in terms of *belief*. Thus, I start this chapter with a closer look at belief.

## 8.1    Belief

For the purposes of this section, I use "belief" in the sense that it is used in a sentence like "I believe that Alice is at home today." If $p$ is believed, then the speaker thinks that $p$ is almost surely true. Although I have spoken loosely in previous chapters about representing an agent's beliefs using, say, a probability measure, in this section, if belief is modeled probabilistically, an event is said to be believed iff it has probability 1. Typically, it is assumed that (1) beliefs are closed under conjunction (at least, finite conjunction) so that if Bob believes $p_1, \ldots, p_n$, then Bob also believes their conjunction, $p_1 \wedge \ldots \wedge p_n$ and (2) beliefs are closed under implication, so that if Bob believes $p$, and $p$ implies $q$, then Bob believes $q$.

Many ways of representing beliefs have been proposed. Perhaps the two most common are using probability, where an event is believed if it has probability 1 (so that Alice believes formula $p$ in a probability structure $M$ if $\mu_A(\llbracket p \rrbracket_M) = 1$), and using epistemic frames, where Alice believes $U$ at world $w$ if $\mathcal{K}_A(w) \subseteq U$. Note that, in the latter case, the definition of belief is identical to that of knowledge. This is by design. The difference between knowledge and belief is captured in terms of the assumptions made on the $\mathcal{K}$ relation. For knowledge, as I said in Section 6.1, the $\mathcal{K}$ relation is taken to be reflexive. For belief it is not; however, it is usually taken to be serial. (The $\mathcal{K}$ relation is also typically assumed to be Euclidean and transitive when modeling belief, but that is not relevant to the discussion in this section.)

A yet more general model of belief uses *filters*. Given a set $W$ of possible worlds, a *filter F* is a nonempty set of subsets of $W$ that (1) is closed under supersets (so that if $U \in F$ and $U \subseteq U'$, then $U' \in F$), (2) is closed under finite intersection (so that if $U, U' \in F$, then $U \cap U' \in F$), and (3) does not contain the empty set. Given a filter $F$, an agent is said to believe $U$ iff $U \in F$. Note that the set of sets that are given probability 1 by a probability measure form a filter; the events believed by agent $i$ at world $w$ in an epistemic frame (i.e., those events $U$ such that $\mathcal{K}_i(w) \subseteq U$) are also easily seen to be a filter (Exercise 8.1). Similarly, given an epistemic frame, the events that are believed at world $w$ (i.e., those sets $U$ such that $\mathcal{K}_i(w) \subseteq U$) clearly form a filter. Conversely, if each agent's beliefs at each world are characterized by a filter, then it is easy to construct an epistemic frame representing the agent's beliefs: take $\mathcal{K}_i(w)$ to be the intersection of all the sets in agent $i$'s filter at $w$. (This will not work in general in an infinite space; see Exercise 8.2.)

The use of filters can be viewed as a descriptive approach to modeling belief; the filter describes what an agent's beliefs are by listing the events believed. The requirement that filters be closed under supersets and under intersection corresponds precisely to the requirement that beliefs be closed under implication and conjunction. (Recall from Exercise 7.4 that $M \models p \Rightarrow q$ iff $[\![p]\!]_M \subseteq [\![q]\!]_M$.) However, filters do not give any insight into where beliefs are coming from. It turns out that plausibility measures are a useful framework for getting a general understanding of belief.

Given a plausibility space $(W, \mathcal{F}, \mathrm{Pl})$, say that an agent *believes* $U \in \mathcal{F}$ if $\mathrm{Pl}(U) > \mathrm{Pl}(\overline{U})$; that is, the agent believes $U$ if $U$ is more plausible than not. It easily follows from Pl3 that this definition satisfies closure under implication: if $U \subseteq V$ and $\mathrm{Pl}(U) > \mathrm{Pl}(\overline{U})$, then $\mathrm{Pl}(V) > \mathrm{Pl}(\overline{V})$ (Exercise 8.3). However, in general, this definition does not satisfy closure under conjunction. In the case of probability, for example, this definition just says that $U$ is believed if the probability of $U$ is greater than $1/2$. What condition on a plausibility measure Pl is needed to guarantee that this definition of belief is closed under conjunction? Simple reverse engineering shows that the following restriction does the trick:

PL4″. If $\mathrm{Pl}(U_1) > \mathrm{Pl}(\overline{U_1})$ and $\mathrm{Pl}(U_2) > \mathrm{Pl}(\overline{U_2})$, then $\mathrm{Pl}(U_1 \cap U_2) > \mathrm{Pl}(\overline{U_1 \cap U_2})$.

I actually want a stronger version of this property, to deal with *conditional* beliefs. An agent believes $U$ *conditional on* $V$, if given $V$, $U$ is more plausible than $\overline{U}$, that is, if $\mathrm{Pl}(U \mid V) > \mathrm{Pl}(\overline{U} \mid V)$. In the presence of the coherency condition CPl5 from Section 3.9 (which I implicitly assume for this section), if $V \in \mathcal{F}'$, then $\mathrm{Pl}(U \mid V) > \mathrm{Pl}(\overline{U} \mid V)$ iff $\mathrm{Pl}(U \cap V) > \mathrm{Pl}(\overline{U} \cap V)$ (Exercise 8.4). In this case, conditional beliefs are closed under conjunction if the following condition holds:

PL4′. If $\mathrm{Pl}(U_1 \cap V) > \mathrm{Pl}(\overline{U_1} \cap V)$ and $\mathrm{Pl}(U_2 \cap V) > \mathrm{Pl}(\overline{U_2} \cap V)$,
then $\mathrm{Pl}(U_1 \cap U_2 \cap V) > \mathrm{Pl}(\overline{U_1 \cap U_2} \cap V)$.

Pl4′ is somewhat complicated. In the presence of Pl3, there is a much simpler property that is equivalent to Pl4′. It is a variant of a property that we have seen before in the context of partial preorders: the qualitative property (see Section 2.7).

PL4. If $U_0$, $U_1$, and $U_2$ are pairwise disjoint sets, $\mathrm{Pl}(U_0 \cup U_1) > \mathrm{Pl}(U_2)$, and $\mathrm{Pl}(U_0 \cup U_2) > \mathrm{Pl}(U_1)$, then $\mathrm{Pl}(U_0) > \mathrm{Pl}(U_1 \cup U_2)$.

In words, Pl4 says that if $U_0 \cup U_1$ is more plausible than $U_2$ and if $U_0 \cup U_2$ is more plausible than $U_1$, then $U_0$ by itself is already more plausible than $U_1 \cup U_2$.

**Proposition 8.1.1**  *A plausibility measure satisfies Pl4 if and only if it satisfies Pl4'.*

**Proof**   See Exercise 8.5.  ∎

Thus, for plausibility measures, Pl4 is necessary and sufficient to guarantee that conditional beliefs are closed under conjunction. (See Exercise 8.27 for other senses in which Pl4 is necessary and sufficient.) Proposition 8.1.1 helps explain why all the notions of belief discussed earlier are closed under conjunction. More precisely, for each notion of belief discussed earlier, it is trivial to construct a plausibility measure Pl satisfying Pl4 that captures it: Pl gives plausibility 1 to the events that are believed and plausibility 0 to the rest. Perhaps more interesting, Proposition 8.1.1 shows that it is possible to define other interesting notions of belief. In particular, it is possible to use a preference order on worlds, taking $U$ to be believed if $U \succ^s \overline{U}$. As Exercise 2.49 shows, $\succ^s$ satisfies the qualitative property, and hence Pl4. Moreover, since possibility measures and ranking functions also satisfy the qualitative property (see Exercises 2.52 and 2.53), they can also be used to define belief. For example, given a possibility measure on $W$, defining belief in $U$ as $\text{Poss}(U) > \text{Poss}(\overline{U})$ gives a notion of belief that is closed under conjunction.

Pl4 is necessary and sufficient for beliefs to be closed under finite intersection, but it does not guarantee closure under infinite intersection. This is a feature: beliefs are not always closed under infinite intersection. The classic example is the *lottery paradox*.

**Example 8.1.2**   Consider a situation with infinitely many individuals, each of whom holds a ticket to a lottery. It seems reasonable to believe that, for each $i$, individual $i$ will not win, and yet to believe that someone will win. If $U_i$ is the event that individual $i$ does not win, this amounts to believing $U_1, U_2, U_3, \ldots$ and also believing $\cup_i \overline{U_i}$ (and not believing $\cap_i U_i$). It is easy to capture this with a plausibility measure. Let $W = \{w_1, w_2, \ldots\}$, where $w_i$ is the world where individual $i$ wins (so that $U_i = W - \{w_i\}$). Let $\text{Pl}_{lot}$ be a plausibility measure that assigns plausibility 0 to the empty set, plausibility 1/2 to all finite sets, and plausibility 1 to all infinite sets. $\text{Pl}_{lot}$ satisfies Pl4 (Exercise 8.6); nevertheless, each event $U_i$ is believed according to $\text{Pl}_{lot}$, as is $\cup_i \overline{U_i}$.  ∎

The key property that guarantees that (conditional) beliefs are closed under infinite intersection is the following generalization of Pl4:

PL4*.   For any index set $I$ such that $0 \in I$ and $|I| \geq 2$, if $\{U_i : i \in I\}$ are pairwise disjoint sets, $U = \cup_{i \in I} U_i$, and $\text{Pl}(U - U_i) > \text{Pl}(U_i)$ for all $i \in I - \{0\}$, then $\text{Pl}(U_0) > \text{Pl}(U - U_0)$.

Pl4 is the special case of Pl4* where $I = \{0, 1, 2\}$. Because Pl4* does not hold for $Pl_{lot}$, it can be used to represent the lottery paradox. On the other hand, Pl4* does hold for the plausibility measure corresponding to beliefs in epistemic frames; thus, belief in epistemic frames is closed under infinite conjunction. A countable version of Pl4* holds for $\sigma$-additive probability measures, which is why probability-1 beliefs are closed under countable conjunctions (but not necessarily under arbitrary infinite conjunctions). I defer further discussion of Pl4* to Section 10.4.

## 8.2   Knowledge and Belief

The previous section focused on a semantic characterization of belief. In this section, I consider an axiomatic characterization, and also examine the relationship between knowledge and belief.

Philosophers have long discussed the relationship between knowledge and belief. To distinguish them, I use the modal operator $K$ for knowledge and $B$ for belief (or $K_i$ and $B_i$ if there are many agents). Does knowledge entail belief; that is, does $K\phi \Rightarrow B\phi$ hold? (This has been called the *entailment* property.) Do agents know their beliefs; that is, do $B\phi \Rightarrow KB\phi$ and $\neg B\phi \Rightarrow K\neg B\phi$ hold? Are agents introspective with regard to their beliefs; that is, do $B\phi \Rightarrow BB\phi$ and $\neg B\phi \Rightarrow B\neg B\phi$ hold? While it is beyond the scope of this book to go into the philosophical problems, it is interesting to see how notions like CONS, SDP, and UNIF, as defined in Section 6.2, can help illuminate them.

In this section, for definiteness, I model belief using plausibility measures satisfying Pl4. However, all the points I make could equally well be made in any of the other models of belief discussed in Section 8.1. Since I also want to talk about knowledge, I use *epistemic belief structures,* that is, epistemic plausibility structures where all the plausibility measures that arise satisfy Pl4. (See Exercise 8.7 for more on the relationship between using plausibility measures to model belief and using accessibility relations. The exercise shows that, if the set of worlds is finite, then the two approaches are equivalent. However, if the set of worlds is infinite, plausibility measures have more expressive power.)

If $M = (W, \mathcal{K}_1, \ldots, \mathcal{K}_n, \mathcal{PL}_1, \ldots, \mathcal{PL}_n, \pi)$ is a measurable epistemic belief structure, then

$$(M, w) \models B_i\phi$$
$$\text{iff } Pl_{w,i}(W_{w,i}) = \bot \text{ or } Pl_{w,i}(\llbracket\phi\rrbracket_M \cap W_{w,i}) > Pl_{w,i}(\llbracket\neg\phi\rrbracket_M \cap W_{w,i}),$$

where $\mathcal{PL}_i(w) = (W_{w,i}, Pl_{w,i})$. (In this chapter I follow the convention introduced in Chapter 2 of omitting the set of measurable sets from the description of the space when all sets are measurable.) The clause for $\mathrm{Pl}_{w,i}(W_{w,i}) = \bot$ just takes care of the vacuous case where $\bot = \top$ according to $\mathrm{Pl}_{w,i}$; in that case, everything is believed. This is the analogue of the case where $\mathcal{K}_i(w) = \emptyset$, when everything is vacuously known.

Analogues of CONS, UNIF, SDP, and CP can be defined in structures for knowledge and plausibility: simply replace $\mathcal{PR}_i$ with $\mathcal{PL}_i$ throughout. Interestingly, these properties are closely related to some of the issues regarding the relationship between knowledge and belief, as the following proposition shows:

**Proposition 8.2.1**    *Let M be an epistemic plausibility structure. Then*

(a) *if M satisfies CONS, then $M \models K_i\phi \Rightarrow B_i\phi$ for all $\phi$;*

(b) *if M satisfies SDP, then $M \models B_i\phi \Rightarrow K_i B_i\phi$ and $M \models \neg B_i\phi \Rightarrow K_i \neg B_i\phi$ for all formulas $\phi$;*

(c) *if M satisfies UNIF, then $M \models B_i\phi \Rightarrow B_i B_i\phi$ and $M \models \neg B_i\phi \Rightarrow B_i \neg B_i\phi$ for all formulas $\phi$.*

**Proof**    See Exercise 8.9.  ∎

Thus, CONS gives the entailment property; with SDP, agents know their beliefs; and with UNIF, agents are introspective regarding their beliefs.

# 8.3    Characterizing Default Reasoning

In this section, I consider an axiomatic characterization of default reasoning. To start with, consider a very simple language for representing defaults. Given a set $\Phi$ of primitive propositions, let the language $\mathcal{L}^{def}(\Phi)$ consist of all formulas of the form $\phi \to \psi$, where $\phi, \psi \in \mathcal{L}^{Prop}(\Phi)$; that is, $\phi$ and $\psi$ are propositional formulas over $\Phi$. Notice that $\mathcal{L}^{def}$ is not closed under negation or disjunction; for example, $\neg(p \to q)$ is not a formula in $\mathcal{L}^{def}$, nor is $(p \to q) \Rightarrow (p \to (q \vee q'))$ (although, of course, $\neg p \to q$ and $p \to (q \Rightarrow q')$ are in $\mathcal{L}^{def}$).

The formula $\phi \to \psi$ can be read in various ways, depending on the application. For example, it can be read as "if $\phi$ (is the case) then typically $\psi$ (is the case)," "if $\phi$, then normally $\psi$," "if $\phi$, then by default $\psi$," and "if $\phi$, then $\psi$ is very likely." Thus, the default statement "birds typically fly" is represented as $bird \to fly$. $\mathcal{L}^{def}$ can also be used for counterfactual reasoning, in which case $\phi \to \psi$ is interpreted as "if $\phi$ were true, then $\psi$ would be true."

All these readings are similar in spirit to the reading of the formula $\phi \Rightarrow \psi$ in propositional logic as "if $\phi$ then $\psi$." How do the properties of $\Rightarrow$ (often called a *material conditional* or *material implication*) and → compare? More generally, what properties should → have? That depends to some extent on how → is interpreted. We should not expect default reasoning and counterfactual reasoning to have the same properties (although, as we shall see, they do have a number of properties in common). In this section, I focus on default reasoning.

There has in fact been some disagreement in the literature as to what properties → should have. However, there seems to be some consensus on the following set of six *core* properties, which make up the axiom system **P**:

LLE.   If $\phi \Leftrightarrow \phi'$ is a propositional tautology, then from $\phi \rightarrow \psi$ infer $\phi' \rightarrow \psi$ (left logical equivalence).

RW.   If $\psi \Rightarrow \psi'$ is a propositional tautology, then from $\phi \rightarrow \psi$ infer $\phi \rightarrow \psi'$ (right weakening).

REF.   $\phi \rightarrow \phi$ (reflexivity).

AND.   From $\phi \rightarrow \psi_1$ and $\phi \rightarrow \psi_2$ infer $\phi \rightarrow \psi_1 \wedge \psi_2$.

OR.   From $\phi_1 \rightarrow \psi$ and $\phi_2 \rightarrow \psi$ infer $\phi_1 \vee \phi_2 \rightarrow \psi$.

CM.   From $\phi \rightarrow \psi_1$ and $\phi \rightarrow \psi_2$ infer $\phi \wedge \psi_2 \rightarrow \psi_1$ (cautious monotonicity).

The first three properties of **P** seem noncontroversial. If $\phi$ and $\phi'$ are logically equivalent, then surely if $\psi$ follows by default from $\phi$, then it should also follow by default from $\phi'$. Similarly, if $\psi$ follows from $\phi$ by default, and $\psi$ logically implies $\psi'$, then surely $\psi'$ should follow from $\phi$ by default as well. Finally, reflexivity just says that $\phi$ follows from itself.

The latter three properties get more into the heart of default reasoning. The AND rule says that defaults are closed under conjunction. For example, if an agent sees a bird, she may want to conclude that it flies. She may also want to conclude that it has wings. The AND rule allows her to put these two conclusions together and conclude that, by default, birds both fly and have wings.

The OR rule corresponds to reasoning by cases. If red birds typically fly (($red \wedge bird) \rightarrow fly$) and nonred birds typically fly (($\neg red \wedge bird) \rightarrow fly$), then birds typically fly, no matter what color they are. Note that the OR rule actually gives only (($red \wedge bird) \vee (\neg red \wedge bird)) \rightarrow fly$ here. The conclusion $bird \rightarrow fly$ requires LLE, using the fact that $bird \Leftrightarrow ((red \wedge bird) \vee (\neg red \wedge bird))$ is a propositional tautology.

To understand cautious monotonicity, note that one of the most important properties of the material conditional is that it is *monotonic*. Getting extra information never results in conclusions being withdrawn. For example, if $\phi \Rightarrow \psi$ is true under some truth assignment, then so is $\phi \wedge \phi' \Rightarrow \psi$, no matter what $\phi'$ is (Exercise 8.12). On the other hand, default reasoning is not always monotonic. From $bird \rightarrow fly$ it does not follow that $bird \wedge penguin \rightarrow fly$. Discovering that a bird is a penguin should cause the retraction of the conclusion that it flies.

Cautious monotonicity captures one instance when monotonicity seems reasonable. If both $\psi_1$ and $\psi_2$ follow from $\phi$ by default, then discovering $\psi_2$ should not cause the retraction of the conclusion $\psi_1$. For example, if birds typically fly and birds typically have wings, then it seems reasonable to conclude that birds that have wings typically fly.

All the properties of **P** hold if $\rightarrow$ is interpreted as $\Rightarrow$, the material conditional (Exercise 8.13). However, this interpretation leads to unwarranted conclusions, as the following example shows:

**Example 8.3.1**    Consider the following collection of defaults:

$$\Sigma_1 = \{bird \rightarrow fly, \; penguin \rightarrow \neg fly, \; penguin \rightarrow bird\}.$$

It is easy to see that if $\rightarrow$ is interpreted as $\Rightarrow$, then *penguin* must be false (Exercise 8.14). But then, for example, it is possible to conclude $penguin \rightarrow fly$; this is surely an undesirable conclusion!    ∎

In light of this example, I focus here on interpretations of $\rightarrow$ that allow some degree of nontrivial nonmonotonicity.

If $\Sigma$ is a finite set of formulas in $\mathcal{L}^{def}$, write $\Sigma \vdash_{\mathbf{P}} \phi \rightarrow \psi$ if $\phi \rightarrow \psi$ can be deduced from $\Sigma$ using the rules and axioms of **P**, that is, if there is a sequence of formulas in $\mathcal{L}^{def}$, each of which is either an instance of REF (the only axiom in **P**), a formula in $\Sigma$, or follows from previous formulas by an application of an inference rule in **P**. Roughly speaking, $\Sigma \vdash_{\mathbf{P}} \phi \rightarrow \psi$ is equivalent to $\vdash_{\mathbf{P}} \wedge \Sigma \Rightarrow (\phi \rightarrow \psi)$, where $\wedge \Sigma$ denotes the conjunction of the formulas in $\Sigma$. The problem with the latter formulation is that $\wedge \Sigma \Rightarrow (\phi \rightarrow \psi)$ is not a formula in $\mathcal{L}^{def}$, since $\mathcal{L}^{def}$ is not closed under conjunction and implication. In Section 8.6, I consider a richer language that allows such formulas.

## 8.4    Semantics for Defaults

There have been many attempts to give semantics to formulas in $\mathcal{L}^{def}$. The surprising thing is how many of them have ended up being characterized by the axiom system **P**. In this section, I describe a number of these attempts. I conclude with a semantics based on plausibility measures that helps explain why **P** characterizes so many different approaches. It turns out that Pl4 is the key property for explaining why **P** is sound.

### 8.4.1   Probabilistic Semantics

One compelling approach to giving semantics to defaults is based on the intuition that $\phi \to \psi$ should mean that when $\phi$ is the case, $\psi$ is very likely. Suppose that uncertainty is represented using a probability measure $\mu$. In that case, "when $\phi$ is the case, $\psi$ is very likely" should mean that the probability of $\psi$ given $\phi$ is high, or at least significantly higher than the probability of $\neg\psi$ given $\phi$.

But how high is high enough? Consider a simple measurable probability structure $M = (W, \mu, \pi)$. (In the next two sections I consider only simple structures, which makes it easier to focus on the basic issues of default reasoning.) The first thought might be to emulate the definition of belief and take $\phi \to \psi$ to hold in $M$ if the conditional probability of $\psi$ given $\phi$ is 1. This essentially works, but there is one subtlety that must be dealt with. What happens if the probability of $\phi$ is 0? This turns out to be a significant problem in the context of default reasoning. Consider again the set of defaults $\Sigma_1$ from Example 8.3.1. Ignoring for a moment the issue of dividing by 0, satisfying this collection of defaults requires that $\mu(\llbracket fly \rrbracket_M \mid \llbracket bird \rrbracket_M) = 1$, $\mu(\llbracket fly \rrbracket_M \mid \llbracket penguin \rrbracket_M) = 0$, and $\mu(\llbracket bird \rrbracket_M \mid \llbracket penguin \rrbracket_M) = 1$. These requirements together imply that $\mu(\llbracket penguin \rrbracket_M) = 0$ (Exercise 8.15). Thus, conditioning on sets of measure 0 is unavoidable with this approach. Taking $\phi \to \psi$ to hold vacuously if $\mu(\llbracket \phi \rrbracket) = 0$ leads to the same difficulties as interpreting $\to$ as $\Rightarrow$; for example, it then follows that *penguin* $\to$ *fly*. Some other approach must be found to deal with conditioning on sets of measure 0.

There is a simple solution to this problem: take $\mu$ to be a conditional probability measure, so that $\mu(\llbracket \psi \rrbracket_M \mid \llbracket \phi \rrbracket_M)$ can be defined even if $\mu(\llbracket \phi \rrbracket_M) = 0$. This, in fact, works. Define a *simple measurable conditional probability structure* to be one of the form $M = (W, 2^W, 2^W - \{\emptyset\}, \mu, \pi)$. The fact that $\mathcal{F}' = 2^W - \{\emptyset\}$ means that it is possible to condition on all nonempty sets. I abbreviate this as $(W, \mu, \pi)$, just as in the case of a simple measurable structure. It should be clear from context whether $\mu$ is a conditional probability measure or an unconditional probability measure. Define $M \models \phi \to \psi$ if $\mu(\llbracket \psi \rrbracket_M \mid \llbracket \phi \rrbracket_M) = 1$. Let $\mathcal{M}^{cps}$ be the class of all simple measurable conditional probability structures.

This definition of defaults in conditional probability structures satisfies all the axioms and rules of axiom system **P**. In fact, it is characterized by **P**. (That is, **P** can be viewed as a sound and complete axiomatization of default reasoning for $\mathcal{L}^{def}$ with respect to such simple conditional probability structures.) If $\Sigma$ is a finite set of default formulas, write $M \models \Sigma$ if $M \models \sigma$ for every formula $\sigma \in \Sigma$. Given a collection $\mathcal{M}$ of structures, write $\Sigma \models_{\mathcal{M}} \phi$ if, for all $M \in \mathcal{M}$, if $M \models \Sigma$ then $M \models \phi$. Thus, $\Sigma \models_{\mathcal{M}} \phi$ holds if every structure in $\mathcal{M}$ that satisfies the formulas in $\Sigma$ also satisfies $\phi$. This is a generalization of the definition of validity, since $\emptyset \models_{\mathcal{M}} \phi$ iff $\phi$ is valid in $\mathcal{M}$.

**Theorem 8.4.1**  *If $\Sigma$ is a finite set of formulas in $\mathcal{L}^{def}$, then $\Sigma \vdash_{\mathbf{P}} \phi \to \psi$ iff $\Sigma \models_{\mathcal{M}^{cps}}$ $\phi \to \psi$.*

**Proof**  I leave it to the reader to check soundness (Exercise 8.16). Soundness also follows from two results proved in Section 8.4.3: Theorem 8.4.10, a more general soundness result, which applies to many classes of structures, and Theorem 8.4.11, which shows that Theorem 8.4.10 applies in particular to $\mathcal{M}^{cps}$. Completeness follows from two other theorems proved in Section 8.4.3: Theorem 8.4.14, a more general completeness result, which applies to many classes of structures, and Theorem 8.4.15, which shows that Theorem 8.4.14 applies in particular to $\mathcal{M}^{cps}$.  ∎

Although conditional probability measures provide a model for defaults, there may be some conceptual difficulties in thinking of the probability of penguin as being 0. (There is also the question of what event *penguin* represents. Is $\mu([\![penguin]\!])$ the probability that a particular bird is a penguin? The probability that a bird chosen at random is a penguin? In the latter case, from what set is the bird being chosen? I ignore these issues for now. They are dealt with in more detail in Chapters 10 and 11.) Perhaps penguins are unlikely, but surely they do not have probability 0. Thus, there has been some interest in getting a probabilistic interpretation of defaults that does not involve 0.

One thought might be to consider a definition somewhat in the spirit of the plausibilistic definition of belief discussed in Section 8.1. Suppose that $M$ is a simple measurable probability structure and that $\phi \to \psi$ is taken to be true in $M$ if $\mu([\![\phi]\!]_M) = 0$ or $\mu([\![\psi]\!]_M \mid [\![\phi]\!]_M) > \mu([\![\neg\psi]\!]_M \mid [\![\phi]\!]_M)$. It is easy to check that, under this interpretation, $M \models \phi \to \psi$ if and only if $\mu([\![\phi]\!]_M) = 0$ or $\mu([\![\phi \wedge \psi]\!]_M) > \mu([\![\phi \wedge \neg\psi]\!]_M)$, or, equivalently, if and only if $\mu([\![\phi]\!]_M) = 0$ or $\mu([\![\psi]\!]_M \mid [\![\phi]\!]_M) > 1/2$. Moreover, this interpretation satisfies LLE, RW, and REF (Exercise 8.17). However, it does not necessarily satisfy AND, OR, or CM, as the following example shows:

**Example 8.4.2**  Consider the simple probability structure $M_1$ from Example 7.3.1. Then

- $\mu([\![\neg p \vee \neg q]\!]_{M_1}) = \mu(\{w_2, w_3, w_4\}) = .75,$

- $\mu([\![\neg p]\!]_{M_1}) = \mu(\{w_3, w_4\}) = .5,$

- $\mu([\![\neg q]\!]_{M_1}) = \mu(\{w_2, w_4\}) = .45,$ and

- $\mu([\![\neg p \wedge \neg q]\!]_{M_1}) = \mu(\{w_4\}) = .2.$

Thus, $\mu([\![\neg p]\!]_{M_1} \mid [\![\neg p \vee \neg q]\!]_{M_1}) > .5$ and $\mu([\![\neg q]\!]_{M_1} \mid [\![\neg p \vee \neg q]\!]_{M_1}) > .5$, but $\mu([\![\neg p \wedge \neg q]\!]_{M_1} \mid [\![\neg p \vee \neg q]\!]_{M_1}) < .5$. So $M_1 \models (\neg p \vee \neg q) \rightarrow \neg p$ and $M_1 \models (\neg p \vee \neg q) \rightarrow \neg q$, but $M_1 \not\models (\neg p \vee \neg q) \rightarrow (\neg p \wedge \neg q)$, violating the AND rule. More-over, $M_1 \not\models ((\neg p \vee \neg q) \wedge \neg p) \rightarrow \neg q$ (since $[\![(\neg p \vee \neg q) \wedge \neg p]\!]_{M_1} = [\![\neg p]\!]_{M_1}$ and $\mu([\![\neg q]\!]_{M_1} \mid [\![\neg p]\!]_{M_1}) < .5$). This is a violation of CM. It is also possible to construct a violation of OR in $M_1$ (Exercise 8.18).  ∎

Perhaps the problem is the choice of 1/2. Another thought might be to define $M \models \phi \rightarrow \psi$ if and only if $\mu([\![\phi]\!]_M) = 0$ or $\mu([\![\psi]\!]_M \mid [\![\phi]\!]_M) > 1 - \epsilon$, for some fixed, small $\epsilon$. This interpretation fares no better than the previous one. Again, it is easy to see that it satisfies LLE, RW, and REF, but not AND, CM, or OR (Exercise 8.19).

The problem here is that no fixed $\epsilon$ will work. For any fixed $\epsilon$, it is easy to construct counterexamples. One solution to this problem is to allow infinitesimals. That is, using the notation of Section 3.2, if $\mu^{ns}$ is a nonstandard probability measure, then $\phi \rightarrow \psi$ holds if the closest standard real number to $\mu^{ns}([\![\psi]\!] \mid [\![\phi]\!])$ is 1. It is not hard to show that this approach does indeed satisfy all the properties of **P** (Exercise 8.20), although the conceptual problem of assigning a probability that is essentially 0 to penguins still remains.

As Theorem 8.4.1 shows, using conditional probability measures works as well; there is yet another approach that uses only standard (unconditional) probability mea-sures. It sidesteps the problem of specifying an $\epsilon$ by taking, not one, but a sequence of probability measures and requiring that the probability of $\psi$ given $\phi$ go to 1 in the limit. With this approach, the probability of *penguin* is not 0, although it does get arbitrarily close. Since this approach is also related to some of the discussion in Chapter 11, I explore it in a little more detail here.

**Definition 8.4.3**  A *probability sequence* on $W$ is just a sequence $(\mu_1, \mu_2, \ldots)$ of probability measures on $W$ (where, implicitly, every subset of $W$ is measurable with respect to every probability measure in the sequence). A *(simple) PS structure* is a tuple $(W, (\mu_1, \mu_2, \ldots), \pi)$, where $(\mu_1, \mu_2, \ldots)$ is a probability sequence on $W$. Let $\mathcal{M}^{ps}$ be the class of all simple PS structures. In a simple PS structure, the truth of a formula of the form $\phi \rightarrow \psi$ is independent of the world. If $M = (W, (\mu_1, \mu_2, \ldots), \pi)$ is a simple PS structure, then

$$M \models \phi \rightarrow \psi \text{ iff } \lim_{k \to \infty} \mu_k([\![\psi]\!]_M \mid [\![\phi]\!]_M) = 1,$$

where $\mu_k([\![\psi]\!]_M \mid [\![\phi]\!]_M)$ is taken to be 1 if $\mu_k([\![\phi]\!]_M) = 0$.  ∎

This definition is also characterized by **P**.

**Theorem 8.4.4** *If $\Sigma$ is a finite set of formulas in $\mathcal{L}^{def}$, then $\Sigma \vdash_{\mathbf{P}} \phi \to \psi$ iff $\Sigma \models_{\mathcal{M}^{ps}} \phi \to \psi$.*

**Proof**    Again, soundness follows from Theorems 8.4.10 and Theorem 8.4.12. However, it can also be proved directly. For example, consider the AND rule. Suppose that $M$ is a simple PS structure such that $M \models \phi \to \psi_1$ and $M \models \phi \to \psi_2$. Then $\lim_{k\to\infty} \mu_k([\![\psi_1]\!]_M \mid [\![\phi]\!]_M) = 1$ and $\lim_{k\to\infty} \mu_k([\![\psi_2]\!]_M \mid [\![\phi]\!]_M) = 1$. By definition, for all $\epsilon$, there must be some $k$ such that $\mu_k([\![\psi_1]\!]_M \mid [\![\phi]\!]_M) \geq 1 - \epsilon$ and $\mu_k([\![\psi_2]\!]_M \mid [\![\phi]\!]_M) \geq 1 - \epsilon$. By the inclusion-exclusion rule (2.5),

$$\mu_k([\![\psi_1 \wedge \psi_2]\!]_M \mid [\![\phi]\!]_M)$$
$$= \mu_k([\![\psi_1]\!]_M \mid [\![\phi]\!]_M) + \mu_k([\![\psi_2]\!]_M \mid [\![\phi]\!]_M) - \mu_k([\![\psi_1 \vee \psi_2]\!]_M \mid [\![\phi]\!]_M)$$
$$\geq (1 - \epsilon) + (1 - \epsilon) - 1$$
$$= 1 - 2\epsilon.$$

Thus, $\lim_{k\to\infty} \mu_k([\![\psi_1 \wedge \psi_2]\!]_M \mid [\![\phi]\!]_M) = 1$, so $M \models \phi \to (\psi_1 \wedge \psi_2)$, as desired. The proof that OR and CM also hold in PS structures is equally straightforward (Exercise 8.21).

Completeness again follows from Theorem 8.4.14 and Theorem 8.4.15. ∎

While PS structures are a technically useful tool for capturing default reasoning, it is not so clear where the sequence of probabilities is coming from. Under what circumstances would an agent use a sequence of probability measures to describe her uncertainty? In Chapter 11, we shall see a context in which such sequences arise naturally.

## 8.4.2    Using Possibility Measures, Ranking Functions, and Preference Orders

Taking $\phi \to \psi$ to hold iff $\mu(\psi \mid \phi) > \mu(\neg\psi \mid \phi)$ does not work, in the sense that it does not satisfy some properties that seem important in the context of default reasoning. Belief functions and lower probabilities fare no better than probability measures; again, they satisfy LLE, RW, and REF, but not AND, OR, or CM. Indeed, since probability measures are a special case of belief functions and sets of probability measures, the counterexamples in the previous section apply without change. It is also possible to use sequences of belief functions or sequences of sets of probability measures, just as in PS structures. This in fact would result in the desired properties, although I do not go through the exercise of showing that here. More interestingly, possibility measures, ranking functions, and partial preorders have the desired properties without the need to consider sequences. The idea is to take $\phi \to \psi$ to hold if $\psi$ is believed conditional on $\phi$. The reason this works is essentially because these representations of uncertainty all satisfy Pl4.

The formal definitions are just the obvious analogue of the definitions in the case of probability.

- If $M = (W, \text{Poss}, \pi)$ is a simple possibility structure, then

$$M \models \phi \to \psi \text{ iff } \text{Poss}([\![\phi]\!]_M) = 0 \text{ or } \text{Poss}([\![\phi \wedge \psi]\!]_M) > \text{Poss}([\![\phi \wedge \neg\psi]\!]_M).$$

- If $M = (W, \kappa, \pi)$ is a simple ranking structure, then

$$M \models \phi \to \psi \text{ iff } \kappa([\![\phi]\!]_M) = \infty \text{ or } \kappa([\![\phi \wedge \psi]\!]_M) < \kappa([\![\phi \wedge \neg\psi]\!]_M).$$

- Finally, if $M = (W, \succeq, \pi)$ is a simple preferential structure, then

$$M \models \phi \to \psi \text{ iff } [\![\phi]\!]_M = \emptyset \text{ or } [\![\phi \wedge \psi]\!]_M \succ^s [\![\phi \wedge \neg\psi]\!]_M.$$

**Theorem 8.4.5**   *Let $\Sigma$ be a finite set of formulas in $\mathcal{L}^{def}$. The following are equivalent:*

(a) $\Sigma \vdash_{\mathbf{P}} \phi \to \psi$,

(b) $\Sigma \models_{\mathcal{M}^{poss}} \phi \to \psi$,

(c) $\Sigma \models_{\mathcal{M}^{rank}} \phi \to \psi$,

(d) $\Sigma \models_{\mathcal{M}^{pref}} \phi \to \psi$,

(e) $\Sigma \models_{\mathcal{M}^{tot}} \phi \to \psi$.

**Proof**   Soundness follows from Theorem 8.4.10. However, it is again straightforward to provide a direct proof. I show that the AND rule is sound for possibility measures here, and I leave the remaining parts of the soundness proof as an exercise (Exercise 8.23). Suppose that $M = (W, \text{Poss}, \pi)$ is a possibility structure, $M \models \phi \to \psi_1$, and $M \models \phi \to \psi_2$. If $\text{Poss}([\![\phi]\!]_M) = 0$, then it is immediate that $M \models \phi \to (\psi_1 \wedge \psi_2)$. So suppose that $\text{Poss}([\![\phi]\!]_M) > 0$. Let $U_j = [\![\phi \wedge \psi_j]\!]_M$ and $V_j = [\![\phi \wedge \neg\psi_j]\!]_M$ for $j = 1, 2$. Note that $U_1 \cup V_1 = U_2 \cup V_2 = [\![\phi]\!]_M$. Suppose that $\text{Poss}(U_1 \cap U_2) = \alpha$, $\text{Poss}(U_1 \cap V_2) = \beta$, $\text{Poss}(V_1 \cap U_2) = \gamma$, and $\text{Poss}(V_1 \cap V_2) = \delta$. Since $U_1 \cup V_1 = U_2 \cup V_2$, it easily follows that $(U_1 \cap U_2) \cup (U_1 \cap V_2) = U_1$ (Exercise 8.23). Thus, $\text{Poss}(U_1) = \max(\alpha, \beta)$. Similarly, $\text{Poss}(V_1) = \max(\gamma, \delta)$, $\text{Poss}(U_2) = \max(\alpha, \gamma)$, and $\text{Poss}(V_2) = \max(\beta, \delta)$. Since $\text{Poss}(U_j) > \text{Poss}(V_j)$ for $j = 1, 2$, $\max(\alpha, \beta) > \max(\gamma, \delta)$ and $\max(\alpha, \gamma) > \max(\beta, \delta)$. It easily follows that $\alpha > \max(\beta, \gamma, \delta)$ (Exercise 8.23). Thus, $\text{Poss}(U_1 \cap U_2) > \text{Poss}(V_1 \cup V_2)$, which means that

$\text{Poss}(\llbracket \phi \wedge \psi_1 \wedge \psi_2 \rrbracket_M) > \text{Poss}(\llbracket \phi \wedge \neg(\psi_1 \wedge \psi_2) \rrbracket_M)$. Thus, $M \models \phi \rightarrow (\psi_1 \wedge \psi_2)$, as desired.

Again, completeness follows from Theorems 8.4.14 and 8.4.15. ∎

Recall that one interpretation of ranking functions is that they represent order-of-magnitude reasoning. That is, given a ranking function $\kappa$, there is a probability measure $\mu_\kappa$ such that if $\kappa(U) = k$, then $\mu_\kappa(U)$ is roughly $\epsilon^k$ for some infinitesimal $\epsilon$. With this interpretation, $\kappa(\llbracket \phi \wedge \psi \rrbracket_M) < \kappa(\llbracket \phi \wedge \neg \psi \rrbracket_M)$ if $\mu(\llbracket \psi \rrbracket_M \mid \llbracket \phi \rrbracket_M) > 1 - \epsilon$. This is another way of understanding the observation made in Section 8.4.1: although giving semantics to defaults in this way using a standard $\epsilon$ does not satisfy the axioms of **P** (AND, OR, and CM all fail), this approach does work if $\epsilon$ is an infinitesimal.

Theorem 8.4.5 provides further evidence that $\mathcal{L}^{def}$ is a relatively weak language. For example, it cannot distinguish total preferential structures from arbitrary preferential structures; the same axioms (in $\mathcal{L}^{def}$) characterize both. Roughly speaking, **P** is the "footprint" of default reasoning on the language $\mathcal{L}^{def}$. Since $\mathcal{L}^{def}$ is not a very expressive language, the footprints of the various semantic approaches are indistinguishable. By way of contrast, the language $\mathcal{L}_n^{RL}$ defined in Section 7.5 can distinguish (some of) these approaches, as can the conditional logic $\mathcal{L}_n^{\rightarrow}$ that will be defined in Section 8.6. Futher distinctions can be made with first-order conditional logic; see Section 10.4.

The approaches for giving semantics to $\mathcal{L}^{def}$ that we have considered so far take the view that $\phi \rightarrow \psi$ means "if $\phi$ then $\psi$ is very likely" or, perhaps better, "$\psi$ is believed given $\phi$." However, there is another semantics that focuses more on interpreting $\phi \rightarrow \psi$ as "if $\phi$, then normally $\psi$." This is perhaps best seen in the context of preferential structures. Suppose that $\succeq$ is taken to define a normality (pre)ordering. That is, $w \succeq w'$ means that $w$ is more "normal" than $w'$. For example, a world where $bird \wedge fly$ holds might be viewed as more normal than one where $bird \wedge \neg fly$ holds. Given a simple preferential structure $M = (W, \succeq, \pi)$ and a set $U \subseteq W$, define $\text{best}_M(U)$ to be the most normal worlds in $U$ (according to the preorder $\succeq$ in $M$). Since $\succeq$ in general is a partial preorder, the formal definition is

$$\text{best}_M(U) = \{w \in U : \text{for all } w' \in U, \ w' \not\succ w\}.$$

Define a new operator $\rightarrow'$ in simple preferential structures as follows:

$$M \models \phi \rightarrow' \psi \text{ iff } \text{best}_M(\llbracket \phi \rrbracket_M) \subseteq \llbracket \psi \rrbracket_M.$$

The intuition behind this definition should be clear: $\phi \rightarrow' \psi$ holds in $M$ if, in the most normal worlds where $\phi$ is true, $\psi$ is also true. By way of contrast, notice that $M \models \phi \Rightarrow \psi$ iff $\llbracket \phi \rrbracket_M \subseteq \llbracket \psi \rrbracket_M$ (Exercise 8.24). Thus, for $\phi \Rightarrow \psi$ to be valid in $M$, $\psi$

must hold in *all* worlds where $\phi$ holds; for $\phi \to' \psi$ to be valid in $M$, $\psi$ must just hold in the most normal worlds where $\phi$ holds.

**Example 8.4.6**   Normally, a bird flies and hence is not a penguin; normally, penguins do not fly. This property holds in the simple preferential structure $M_2 = (W, \succeq, \pi)$, where $W = \{w_1, w_2, w_3, w_4\}$ and $\pi$ is such that

- $(M_2, w_1) \models bird \wedge fly \wedge \neg penguin$,
- $(M_2, w_2) \models bird \wedge \neg fly \wedge penguin$,
- $(M_2, w_3) \models bird \wedge fly \wedge penguin$,
- $(M_2, w_4) \models bird \wedge \neg fly \wedge \neg penguin$,

and $\succeq$ is such that $w_1 \succ w_2 \succ w_3$, $w_1 \succ w_4$, and $w_4$ is incomparable to both $w_2$ and $w_3$. Since $\text{best}_{M_2}(\llbracket bird \rrbracket_{M_2}) = \{w_1\} \subseteq \llbracket fly \rrbracket_{M_2}$ and $\text{best}_{M_2}(\llbracket bird \wedge penguin \rrbracket_{M_2}) = \{w_2\} \subseteq \llbracket \neg fly \rrbracket_{M_2}$, it follows that $M_2 \models bird \to' fly$ and $M_2 \models bird \wedge penguin \to' \neg fly$, as we would hope and expect.  ∎

Although $\to$ and $\to'$ may seem on the surface to be quite different, the following theorem shows that they are in fact equivalent:

**Theorem 8.4.7**   *In every simple preferential structure $M$,*

$$M \models \phi \to \psi \text{ iff } M \models \phi \to' \psi.$$

**Proof**   See Exercise 8.25.  ∎

Of course, since $\to$ and $\to'$ are equivalent, it follows that this semantics for $\to'$ is also characterized by **P**.

### 8.4.3   Using Plausibility Measures

As I said before, the key reason that all these approaches for giving semantics to defaults are characterized by axiom system **P** is because they can all be understood as plausibility measures that satisfy Pl4. It actually turns out that Pl4 is not quite enough; one more property is needed. In this section, I make this precise. This discussion gives an excellent example of how the use of plausibility measures can help explain what is going on. The lack of structure in the plausibility framework makes it possible to understand exactly what structure is needed to get the properties of **P**.

The definition of $\rightarrow$ in plausibility structures is the obvious analogue of the definitions given earlier. If $M = (W, \succeq, \text{Pl})$ is a simple measurable plausibility structure, then

$$M \models \phi \rightarrow \psi \text{ iff } \text{Pl}([\![\phi]\!]_M) = \bot \text{ or } \text{Pl}([\![\phi \wedge \psi]\!]_M) > \text{Pl}([\![\phi \wedge \neg\psi]\!]_M).$$

Note that if Pl satisfies CPl5, this is equivalent to saying that $\text{Pl}([\![\psi]\!]_M \mid [\![\phi]\!]_M) > \text{Pl}([\![\neg\psi]\!]_M \mid [\![\phi]\!]_M)$ if $[\![\phi]\!]_M \neq \bot$ (the implicit assumption here is that $[\![\phi]\!]_M \in \mathcal{F}'$ iff $[\![\phi]\!]_M \neq \bot$). Abusing notation somewhat, $\phi \rightarrow \psi$ can be understood as a statement about conditional belief, namely, $B(\psi \mid \phi)$. In particular, $B\phi$ can be viewed as an abbreviation for *true* $\rightarrow \phi$.

Just as with all the other representations of uncertainty, LLE, RW, and REF hold for this definition of uncertainty.

**Lemma 8.4.8**  *All simple measurable plausibility structures satisfy LLE, RW, and REF.*

**Proof**  See Exercise 8.26. It is worth noting that REF holds in simple measurable plausibility structures because of Pl1 (recall that Pl1 says that $\text{Pl}(\emptyset) = \bot$ and, by assumption, $\bot$ is the minimum element with respect to $\leq$) and that RW holds because of Pl3 (recall that Pl3 says that $\text{Pl}(U) \leq \text{Pl}(V)$ if $U \subseteq V$).  ∎

AND, OR, and CM do not hold in general in plausibility structures. Indeed, since probability is a special case of plausibility, the counterexample given earlier in the case of probability applies here without change. This leads to an obvious question: What properties of plausibility would force AND, OR, and CM to hold? Not surprisingly, Pl4′ (and hence Pl4) turns out to be exactly what is needed to get the AND rule. This follows immediately from Proposition 8.1.1 and the following simple lemma:

**Lemma 8.4.9**  *If $M = (W, \text{Pl}, \pi)$ is a simple measurable plausibility structure such that Pl satisfies Pl4′, then the AND rule holds in $M$.*

**Proof**  Suppose that $M \models \phi \rightarrow \psi_1$ and $M \models \phi \rightarrow \psi_2$. If $\text{Pl}([\![\phi]\!]_M) = \bot$, then, by definition, $M \models \phi \rightarrow (\psi_1 \wedge \psi_2)$. On the other hand, if $\text{Pl}([\![\phi]\!]_M) \neq \bot$, then $\text{Pl}([\![\phi \wedge \psi_1]\!]_M) > \text{Pl}([\![\phi \wedge \neg\psi_1]\!]_M)$ and $\text{Pl}([\![\phi \wedge \psi_2]\!]_M) > \text{Pl}([\![\phi \wedge \neg\psi_2]\!]_M)$. From Pl4′, it follows that

$$\text{Pl}([\![\phi \wedge \psi_1 \wedge \psi_2]\!]_M) > \text{Pl}([\![\phi \wedge \neg(\psi_1 \wedge \psi_2)]\!]_M).$$

Thus, $M \models \phi \rightarrow (\psi_1 \wedge \psi_2)$, as desired.  ∎

Somewhat surprisingly, Pl4 is also just what is needed to get CM and the nonvacuous case of OR. More precisely, suppose that $M = (W, \text{Pl}, \pi)$ is a simple measurable plausibility structure and that $M$ satisfies Pl4 (and Pl1–3, of course). By Proposition 8.1.1 and Lemma 8.4.9, $M$ satisfies the AND rule. Moreover, $M$ also satisfies CM, and if $M \models \phi_1 \to \psi$, $M \models \phi_2 \to \psi$, and either $\text{Pl}(\llbracket \phi_1 \rrbracket_M) \neq \perp$ or $\text{Pl}(\llbracket \phi_2 \rrbracket_M) \neq \perp$, then $M \models (\phi_1 \vee \phi_2) \to \psi$ (Exercise 8.28). Dealing with the vacuous case of OR (where both $\text{Pl}(\llbracket \phi_1 \rrbracket_M) = \perp$ and $\text{Pl}(\llbracket \phi_2 \rrbracket_M) = \perp$) requires one more (rather innocuous) property:

P15.   If $\text{Pl}(U) = \text{Pl}(V) = \perp$, then $\text{Pl}(U \cup V) = \perp$.

Note that Pl5 holds for many, but not all, the notions of uncertainty considered so far, when viewed as plausibility measures. For example, if Poss is a possibility measure, then certainly $\text{Poss}(U) = \text{Poss}(V) = 0$ implies $\text{Poss}(U \cup V) = 0$. The same is true for probability. On the other hand, it is not true of belief functions or inner measures. For example, it is not hard to find a belief function Bel such that $\text{Bel}(U) = \text{Bel}(V) = 0$ but $\text{Bel}(U \cup V) \neq 0$ (Exercise 8.29).

A plausibility measure is said to be *qualitative* if it satisfies Pl4 and Pl5 (as well as Pl1–3). A simple measurable plausibility structure $M = (W, \text{Pl}, \pi)$ is qualitative if Pl is. Let $\mathcal{M}^{qual}$ be the class of all simple qualitative plausibility structures.

**Theorem 8.4.10**   *If $\Sigma$ is a finite set of formulas in $\mathcal{L}^{def}$, then*

$$\Sigma \vdash_{\mathbf{P}} \phi \to \psi \text{ iff } \Sigma \models_{\mathcal{M}^{qual}} \phi \to \psi.$$

**Proof**   The soundness of LLE, RW, and CM follows from Lemma 8.4.8; the soundness of AND follows from Proposition 8.1.1 and Lemma 8.4.9. The soundness of CM and OR is left to Exercise 8.30. Again, completeness follows from Theorems 8.4.14 and 8.4.15. ∎

Exercise 2.49 and Exercise 2.52 show that simple possibility structures, ranking structures, and preferential structures can all be viewed as simple qualitative plausibility structures. Indeed, in the remainder of this chapter, I am somewhat sloppy and view $\mathcal{M}^{poss}$, $\mathcal{M}^{rank}$, $\mathcal{M}^{pref}$, and $\mathcal{M}^{tot}$ as being contained in $\mathcal{M}^{qual}$. It follows immediately from Theorem 8.4.10 that $\mathbf{P}$ is sound in $\mathcal{M}^{poss}$, $\mathcal{M}^{rank}$, $\mathcal{M}^{pref}$, and $\mathcal{M}^{tot}$, since these can all be viewed as subclasses of $\mathcal{M}^{qual}$. Properties that are valid in $\mathcal{M}^{qual}$ are bound to be valid in all of its subclasses. It is because possibility measures, ranking functions, and partial preorders can all be viewed as plausibility measures that satisfy Pl4 and Pl5 that, when used to give semantics to defaults, they satisfy all the properties in $\mathbf{P}$. By way of contrast, probability measures do not satisfy Pl4, and hence the obvious way of using them to give semantics to defaults does not satisfy all the properties of $\mathbf{P}$.

The alert reader may sense a problem here. Conditional probability measures do not satisfy Pl4 any more than unconditional probability measures. Yet conditional probability measures were used successfully to give semantics to defaults. What is going on here? There is no contradiction, of course. In fact, there is a way to view a conditional probability measure as a plausibility measure that satisfies Pl4, at least as far as the semantics of defaults is concerned. Given a simple measurable conditional probability structure $M = (W, \mu, \pi)$, define a simple plausibility structure $M_\mu = (W, \text{Pl}, \pi)$, where

$$\text{Pl}(U) \le \text{Pl}(V) \text{ if and only if } \mu(V \mid U \cup V) = 1. \tag{8.1}$$

Intuitively, $\text{Pl}(U) \le \text{Pl}(V)$ if $V$ is "almost all" of $U \cup V$. It is not hard to show that there is a plausibility measure with this property (Exercise 8.31); that is, there is a set $D$ of plausibility values and a mapping $\text{Pl} : 2^W \to D$ satisfying Pl3 and (8.1). Moreover, $M_\mu$ is qualitative and satisfies the same defaults as $M$.

**Theorem 8.4.11** *Suppose that $M \in \mathcal{M}^{cps}$. Then $M_\mu \in \mathcal{M}^{qual}$ and $M \models \phi \to \psi$ iff $M_\mu \models \phi \to \psi$.*

**Proof**   See Exercise 8.31.  ∎

What about probability sequences? A simple PS structure can also be viewed as a plausibility structure, using much the same construction as used in the case of a conditional probability measure. Given a simple PS structure $M = (W, (\mu_1, \mu_2, \ldots), \pi)$, define a simple plausibility structure $M_{PS} = (W, \text{Pl}, \pi)$ such that

$$\text{Pl}(U) \le \text{Pl}(V) \text{ if and only if } \lim_{i \to \infty} \mu_i(V \mid U \cup V) = 1. \tag{8.2}$$

Again, it is not hard to show that there is a plausibility measure with this property (Exercise 8.32) and that $M_{PS}$ is qualitative and satisfies the same defaults as $M$.

**Theorem 8.4.12** *Suppose that $M \in \mathcal{M}^{ps}$. Then $M_{PS} \in \mathcal{M}^{qual}$ and $M \models \phi \to \psi$ iff $M_{PS} \models \phi \to \psi$.*

**Proof**   See Exercise 8.32.  ∎

Thus, Theorem 8.4.10 also explains why structures in $\mathcal{M}^{ps}$ are characterized by **P**; it is because they too satisfy Pl4 and Pl5. Indeed, there is a sense in which Pl4 and Pl5 completely characterize the plausibility structures that satisfy **P**. Roughly speaking, if **P** is sound for a collection $\mathcal{M}$ of plausibility structures, then all the structures in $\mathcal{M}$ must be qualitative. (See Exercise 8.33 for details.)

For **P** to be sound for a class $\mathcal{M}$ of structures, $\mathcal{M}$ cannot have "too many" structures—in particular, no structures that are not qualitative. For **P** to be complete for $\mathcal{M}$, it is important that $\mathcal{M}$ have "enough" structures; if $\mathcal{M}$ has too few structures, there may be additional properties valid in $\mathcal{M}$. In particular, if $\Sigma \nvdash_{\mathbf{P}} \phi \to \psi$, there must be a plausibility structure $M \in \mathcal{M}$ such that $M \models \Sigma$ and yet $M \not\models \phi \to \psi$. The following weak condition suffices to ensure that $\mathcal{M}$ has enough structures in this sense:

**Definition 8.4.13**   A class $\mathcal{M}$ of simple plausibility structures is *rich* if, for every collection $\phi_1, \ldots, \phi_k$, $k > 1$, of pairwise mutually exclusive and satisfiable propositional formulas, there is a plausibility structure $M = (W, \text{Pl}, \pi) \in \mathcal{M}$ such that

$$\text{Pl}(\llbracket \phi_1 \rrbracket_M) > \text{Pl}(\llbracket \phi_2 \rrbracket_M) > \ldots > \text{Pl}(\llbracket \phi_k \rrbracket_M) = \bot \quad \blacksquare$$

The richness requirement is quite mild. It says that $\mathcal{M}$ does not place a priori constraints on the relative plausibilities of a collection of disjoint sets. In the case of probability, it just says that given any collection of disjoint sets $A_1, \ldots, A_k$, there is a probability measure $\mu$ such that $\mu(A_1) > \ldots > \mu(A_k) = 0$. Every representation method considered thus far (viewed as a collection of plausibility structures) can easily be shown to satisfy this richness condition.

**Theorem 8.4.14**   *Each of* $\mathcal{M}^{ps}$, $\mathcal{M}^{poss}$, $\mathcal{M}^{rank}$, $\mathcal{M}^{pref}$, $\mathcal{M}^{tot}$, *and* $\mathcal{M}^{qual}$ *is rich.*

**Proof**   This is almost immediate from the definitions; the details are left to Exercise 8.34. Note that I am viewing $\mathcal{M}^{ps}$, $\mathcal{M}^{poss}$, $\mathcal{M}^{rank}$, $\mathcal{M}^{pref}$, and $\mathcal{M}^{tot}$ as subsets of $\mathcal{M}^{qual}$ here, so that the richness condition as stated applies to them.   $\blacksquare$

Richness is a necessary and sufficient condition to ensure that the axiom system **P** is complete.

**Theorem 8.4.15**   *A set $\mathcal{M}$ of qualitative plausibility structures is rich if and only if* $\Sigma \models_{\mathcal{M}} \phi \to \psi$ *implies* $\Sigma \vdash_{\mathbf{P}} \phi \to \psi$ *for all finite sets $\Sigma$ of formulas in $\mathcal{L}^{def}$ and defaults* $\phi \to \psi$.

**Proof**   The proof that richness is necessary for completeness is not hard; see Exercise 8.35. The proof that richness is sufficient for completeness is sketched (with numerous hints) in Exercise 8.36.   $\blacksquare$

To summarize, the results of this section say that for representations of uncertainty that can be associated with a subclass of plausibility structures, **P** is sound as long as the representation satisfies Pl4 and Pl5. Moreover, **P** is complete if the associated class of plausibility structures is rich, a rather mild restriction.

## 8.5   Beyond System P

As I said before, the axiom system **P** has been viewed as characterizing the "conserva-tive core" of default reasoning. Is there a reasonable, principled way of going beyond System **P** to obtain inferences that do not follow from treating $\rightarrow$ as material implica-tion? The kinds of inference of most interest involve ignoring "irrelevant" information and allowing subclasses to inherit properties from superclasses. The following exam-ples give a sense of the issues involved:

**Example 8.5.1**   If birds typically fly and penguins typically do not fly (although penguins are birds), it seems reasonable to conclude that red penguins do not fly. Thus, if $\Sigma_1$ is as in Example 8.3.1, then it might seem reasonable to expect that $penguin \wedge red \rightarrow \neg fly$ follows from $\Sigma_1$. However, $\Sigma_1 \not\vdash_{\mathbf{P}} penguin \wedge red \rightarrow \neg fly$ (Ex-ercise 8.37(a)). Intuitively, this is because it is conceivable that although penguins typically do not fly, red penguins might be unusual penguins, and so might in fact fly. Much as we might like to treat redness as irrelevant, it might in fact be relevant to whether or not penguins fly. The "conservative core" does not let us conclude that red penguins do not fly because of this possibility.

Notice that $\Sigma_1$ says only that penguins are typically birds, rather than all penguins are birds. This is because universal statements cannot be expressed in $\mathcal{L}^{def}$. The point here could be made equally well if $penguin \rightarrow bird$ were replaced by $penguin \Rightarrow bird$ in $\Sigma_1$. There is no problem handling a mix of properties involving both the material conditional and the default conditional. (However, as Example 8.3.1 shows, replacing all occurrences of $\rightarrow$ by $\Rightarrow$ has significant consequences.)

Now suppose that the default "birds typically have wings" is added to $\Sigma_1$. Let

$$\Sigma_2 = \Sigma_1 \cup \{bird \rightarrow winged\}.$$

Does it follow from $\Sigma_2$ that penguins typically have wings? This property has been called *exceptional subclass inheritance* in the literature: although penguins are an ex-ceptional subclass of birds (in that they do not fly, although birds typically do), it seems reasonable for them to still inherit the property of having wings from birds. This prop-erty holds for the material conditional, since material implication is transitive. (That is, $penguin \Rightarrow winged$ follows from $penguin \Rightarrow bird$ and $bird \Rightarrow winged$.) However, it does not hold for $\rightarrow$ in general. For example, $\Sigma_2 \not\vdash_{\mathbf{P}} penguin \rightarrow winged$ (Exercise 8.37(b)). After all, if penguins are atypical birds in one respect, they may also be atypical in other respects.

But suppose that $\Sigma_3 = \Sigma_1 \cup \{yellow \rightarrow easy\text{-}to\text{-}see\}$: yellow things are easy to see. It certainly seems reasonable to expect that yellow penguins are typically easy to see.

However, $\Sigma_3 \not\vdash_\mathbf{P} (penguin \wedge yellow) \rightarrow easy\text{-}to\text{-}see$ (Exercise 8.37(c)). Note that this type of exceptional subclass inheritance is somewhat different from that exemplified by $\Sigma_2$. Whereas penguins are atypical birds, there is no reason to expect them to be atypical yellow objects. Nevertheless, it does not follow from $\mathbf{P}$ that yellow penguins inherit the property of being easy to see.

One last example: Suppose that $\Sigma_4 = \Sigma_2 \cup \{robin \rightarrow bird\}$. Does it follow from $\Sigma_4$ that robins typically have wings? Although penguins are atypical birds, as far as $\Sigma_4$ is concerned, robins are completely unexceptional birds, and birds typically have wings. Unfortunately, it is not hard to show that $\Sigma_4 \not\vdash_\mathbf{P} robin \rightarrow winged$, nor does it help to replace *robin* by *robin* $\wedge$ *bird* (Exercise 8.37(d)). ∎

In light of these examples, it is perhaps not surprising that there has been a great deal of effort devoted to finding principled methods of going beyond $\mathbf{P}$. However, it has been difficult to find one that gives all and only the "reasonable" inferences, whatever they might be. The results of the previous section point to one source of the difficulties. We might hope to find (1) an axiom system $\mathbf{P}^+$ that is stronger than $\mathbf{P}$ (in the sense that everything provable in $\mathbf{P}$ is also provable in $\mathbf{P}^+$, and $\mathbf{P}^+$ can make some additional "reasonable" inferences) and (2) a class $\mathcal{M}$ of structures with respect to which $\mathbf{P}^+$ is sound and complete. If the structures in $\mathcal{M}$ can be viewed as plausibility structures, then they must all satisfy Pl4 and Pl5 to guarantee that $\mathbf{P}$ is sound with respect to $\mathcal{M}$. However, $\mathcal{M}$ cannot be rich, for then $\mathbf{P}$ would also be complete; no additional inferences could be drawn.

Richness is not a very strong assumption and it is not easy to avoid. One way of doing so that has been taken in the literature is the following: Given a class $\mathcal{M}$ of structures, recall that $\Sigma \models_\mathcal{M} \phi$ if $M \models \Sigma$ implies $M \models \phi$ for every structure $M \in \mathcal{M}$. Rather than considering *every* structure that satisfies $\Sigma$, the idea is to consider a "preferred" structure that satisfies $\Sigma$ and to check whether $\phi$ holds in that preferred structure. Essentially, this approach takes the idea used in preferential structures of considering the most preferred worlds and lifts it to the level of structures. This gets around richness since only one structure is being considered rather than a whole collection of structures. It is clear that one structure by itself cannot in general hope to satisfy the richness condition.

Here are two examples of how this general approach works. The first uses ranking structures (which are, after all, just a special case of plausibility structures). Suppose that an agent wants to reason about some phenomena involving, say, birds, described by some fixed set $\Phi$ of primitive propositions. Let $W_\Phi$ consist of all the truth assignments to the primitive propositions in $\Phi$. Let $\mathcal{M}_\Phi^{rank}$ consist of all simple ranking structures of the form $(W_\Phi, \kappa, \pi_\Phi)$, where $\pi_\Phi(w) = w$ (this makes sense since the worlds in $W_\Phi$ are truth assignments). Define a partial order $\succeq$ on ranking functions on $W_\Phi$ by defining

$\kappa_1 \succeq \kappa_2$ if $\kappa_1(w) \leq \kappa_2(w)$ for all $w \in W_\Phi$. Thus, $\kappa_1$ is preferred to $\kappa_2$ if every world is no more surprising according to $\kappa_1$ than it is according to $\kappa_2$. The order $\succeq$ can be lifted to a partial order on ranking structures in $\mathcal{M}_\Phi^{rank}$ by defining $(W_\Phi, \kappa_1, \pi_\Phi) \succeq (W_\Phi, \kappa_2, \pi_\Phi)$ if $\kappa_1 \succeq \kappa_2$.

Given a finite set $\Sigma$ of formulas in $\mathcal{L}^{def}(\Phi)$, let $\mathcal{M}_\Sigma^{rank}$ consist of all the ranking structures in $\mathcal{M}_\Phi^{rank}$ that satisfy all the defaults in $\Sigma$. Although $\succeq$ is a partial order on ranking structures, it turns out that if $\mathcal{M}_\Sigma^{rank} \neq \emptyset$, then there is a unique structure $M_\Sigma \in \mathcal{M}_\Sigma^{rank}$ that is most preferred. That is, $M_\Sigma \succeq M$ for all $M \in \mathcal{M}_\Sigma^{rank}$ (Exercise 8.38). Intuitively, $M_\Sigma$ makes worlds as unsurprising as possible, while still satisfying the defaults in $\Sigma$. For $\phi \in \mathcal{L}^{def}$, define $\Sigma \approx^Z \phi$ if either $\mathcal{M}_\Sigma^{rank} = \emptyset$ or $M_\Sigma \models \phi$. That is, $\Sigma \approx^Z \phi$ if $\phi$ is true in the most preferred structure of all the structures satisfying $\Sigma$. (The superscript $Z$ is there because this approach has been called *System Z* in the literature.)

Since **P** is sound in ranking structures, it certainly follows that $\Sigma \approx^Z \phi$ if $\Sigma \vdash_{\mathbf{P}} \phi$. But the System Z approach has some additional desirable properties. For example, as desired, red penguins continue not to fly, that is, in the notation of Example 8.5.1, $\Sigma_1 \approx^Z$ *penguin* $\wedge$ *red* $\rightarrow$ $\neg$*fly*. More generally, System Z can ignore "irrelevant" attributes and deals well with some of the other issues raised by Example 8.5.1, as the following lemma shows:

**Lemma 8.5.2**    Let $\Sigma_a = \{\phi_1 \rightarrow \phi_2, \phi_2 \rightarrow \phi_3\}$ and let $\Sigma_b = \Sigma_a \cup \{\phi_1 \rightarrow \neg\phi_3, \phi_1 \rightarrow \phi_4\}$.

(a) $\Sigma_a \approx^Z \phi_1 \wedge \psi \rightarrow \phi_3$ if $\phi_1 \wedge \phi_2 \wedge \phi_3 \wedge \psi$ is satisfiable.

(b) $\Sigma_b \approx^Z \phi_1 \wedge \psi \rightarrow \neg\phi_3 \wedge \phi_4$ if $\phi_1 \wedge \phi_2 \wedge \neg\phi_3 \wedge \phi_4 \wedge \psi$ is satisfiable.

**Proof**    For part (a), suppose that $\phi_1 \wedge \phi_2 \wedge \phi_3 \wedge \psi$ is satisfiable. Then $\mathcal{M}_{\Sigma_a}^{rank} \neq \emptyset$, since both defaults in $\Sigma_a$ are satisfied in a structure where all worlds in which $\phi_1 \wedge \phi_2 \wedge \phi_3$ is true have rank 0 and all others have rank 1. Suppose that $M_{\Sigma_a} = (W, \kappa_1, \pi)$. In $M_{\Sigma_a}$, it is easy to see that all worlds satisfying $\phi_1 \wedge \phi_2 \wedge \phi_3$ have rank 0 and all worlds satisfying $\phi_1 \wedge \neg\phi_2$ or $\phi_2 \wedge \neg\phi_3$ have rank 1 (Exercise 8.39(a)). Since, by assumption, $\phi_1 \wedge \phi_2 \wedge \phi_3 \wedge \psi$ is satisfiable, there is a world of rank 0 satisfying this formula. Moreover, since any world satisfying $\phi_1 \wedge \neg\phi_3 \wedge \psi$ must satisfy either $\phi_1 \wedge \neg\phi_2$ or $\phi_2 \wedge \neg\phi_3$, it follows that $\kappa_1(\llbracket \phi_1 \wedge \neg\phi_3 \wedge \psi \rrbracket_{M_{\Sigma_a}}) \leq 1$. Thus, $\kappa_1(\llbracket \phi_1 \wedge \phi_3 \wedge \psi \rrbracket_{M_{\Sigma_a}}) < \kappa_1(\llbracket \phi_1 \wedge \neg\phi_3 \wedge \psi \rrbracket_{M_{\Sigma_a}})$, so $M_{\Sigma_a} \models \phi_1 \wedge \psi \rightarrow \phi_3$.

For part (b), if $\mathcal{M}_{\Sigma_b}^{rank} = \emptyset$, then the result is trivially true. Otherwise, suppose that $M_{\Sigma_b} = (W, \kappa_2, \pi)$. It can be shown that (i) all worlds in $M_{\Sigma_b}$ satisfying $\neg\phi_1 \wedge \phi_2 \wedge \phi_3$ have rank 0, (ii) there are some worlds in $M_{\Sigma_b}$ satisfying $\neg\phi_1 \wedge \phi_2 \wedge \phi_3$, (iii) all worlds satisfying $\phi_1 \wedge \phi_2 \wedge \neg\phi_3 \wedge \phi_4$ have rank 1, and (iv) all worlds satisfying $\phi_1 \wedge \phi_3$

or $\phi_1 \wedge \neg\phi_4$ have rank 2 (Exercise 8.39(b)). Since, by assumption, $\phi_1 \wedge \phi_2 \wedge \neg\phi_3 \wedge \phi_4 \wedge \psi$ is satisfiable, there is a world of rank 1 satisfying this formula. It follows that $\kappa_2(\llbracket\phi_1 \wedge \psi \wedge \neg\phi_3 \wedge \phi_4\rrbracket_{M_{\Sigma_b}}) < \kappa_2(\llbracket\phi_1 \wedge \psi \wedge (\phi_3 \vee \neg\phi_4)\rrbracket_{M_{\Sigma_b}})$, so $M_{\Sigma_b} \models \phi_1 \wedge \psi \rightarrow \neg\phi_3 \wedge \phi_4$. ∎

Part (a) says that in the System Z approach, red robins do fly (taking $\phi_1 = robin$, $\phi_2 = bird$, $\phi_3 = fly$, and $\psi = red$). Part (b) says that if penguins have wings, then red penguins have wings but do not fly (taking $\phi_1 = penguin$, $\phi_2 = bird$, $\phi_3 = fly$, $\phi_4 = winged$, and $\psi = red$). Indeed, it follows from $\Sigma_b$ (with this interpretation of the formulas) that red penguins have all the properties that penguins have. But red penguins do not necessarily inherit properties of birds, such as flying. So, for these examples, System Z does the "right" things. However, System Z does not always deliver the desired results. In particular, not only do penguins not inherit properties of birds such as flying (which, intuitively, they should not inherit), they also do not inherit properties of birds like having wings (which, intuitively, there is no reason for them not to inherit). For example, returning to Example 8.5.1, notice that it is neither the case that $\Sigma_2 \not\approx^Z (penguin \wedge bird) \rightarrow winged$ nor that $\Sigma_3 \not\approx^Z (penguin \wedge yellow) \rightarrow easy\text{-}to\text{-}see$ (Exercise 8.40). The next approach I consider has these properties.

This approach uses PS structures. Given a collection $\Sigma$ of defaults, let $\Sigma^k$ consist of the statements that result by replacing each default $\phi \rightarrow \psi$ in $\Sigma$ by the $\mathcal{L}^{QU}$ formula $\ell(\psi \mid \phi) \geq 1 - 1/k$. Let $\mathcal{P}^k$ be the set of probability measures that satisfy these formulas. More precisely, let $\mathcal{P}^k = \{\mu : (W_\Phi, \mu, \pi_\Phi) \models \Sigma^k\}$. If $\mathcal{P}^k \neq \emptyset$, let $\mu_k^{me}$ be the probability measure of maximum entropy in $\mathcal{P}^k$. (It can be shown that there is a unique probability measure of maximum entropy in this set, since it is defined by linear inequalities, but that is beyond the scope of this book.) As long as $\mathcal{P}^k \neq \emptyset$ for all $k \geq 1$, this procedure gives a probability sequence $(\mu_1^{me}, \mu_2^{me}, \ldots)$. Let $M_\Sigma^{me} = (W_\Phi, (\mu_1^{me}, \mu_2^{me}, \ldots), \pi_\Phi)$. Define the relation $\approx^{me}$ as follows: $\Sigma \approx^{me} \phi$ if either there is some $k$ such that $\mathcal{P}^k = \emptyset$ (in which case $\mathcal{P}^{k'} = \emptyset$ for all $k' \geq k$) or $M_\Sigma^{me} \models \phi$.

P is again sound for the maximum-entropy approach.

**Proposition 8.5.3**   *If $\Sigma \vdash_P \phi$ then $\Sigma \approx^{me} \phi$.*

**Proof**   Suppose that $\Sigma \vdash \phi$. It is easy to show that if $\mathcal{P}^k = \emptyset$ for some $k > 0$, then there is no structure $M \in \mathcal{M}^{ps}$ such that $M \models \Sigma$. On the other hand, if $\mathcal{P}^k \neq \emptyset$ for all $k \geq 1$, then $M_\Sigma^{me} \models \Sigma$ (Exercise 8.41). The result now follows immediately from Theorem 8.4.4. ∎

Standard properties of maximum entropy can be used to show that $\approx^{me}$ has a number of additional attractive properties. In particular, it is able to ignore irrelevant attributes

and it sanctions inheritance across exceptional subclasses, giving the desired result in
all the cases considered in Example 8.5.1.

**Lemma 8.5.4**   *Let $\Sigma_a = \{\phi_1 \rightarrow \phi_2, \phi_2 \rightarrow \phi_3\}$, $\Sigma_b = \Sigma_a \cup \{\phi_1 \rightarrow \neg\phi_3, \phi_1 \rightarrow \phi_4\}$, $\Sigma_c = \Sigma_a \cup \{\phi_1 \rightarrow \neg\phi_3, \phi_2 \rightarrow \phi_4\}$, and $\Sigma_d = \Sigma_a \cup \{\phi_1 \rightarrow \neg\phi_3, \phi_5 \rightarrow \phi_4\}$.*

*(a) $\Sigma_a \mathrel{\vert\!\approx^{me}} \phi_1 \wedge \psi \rightarrow \phi_3$ if $\phi_1 \wedge \phi_2 \wedge \phi_3 \wedge \psi$ is satisfiable.*

*(b) $\Sigma_b \mathrel{\vert\!\approx^{me}} \phi_1 \wedge \psi \rightarrow \neg\phi_3 \wedge \phi_4$ if $\phi_1 \wedge \phi_2 \wedge \neg\phi_3 \wedge \phi_4 \wedge \psi$ is satisfiable.*

*(c) $\Sigma_c \mathrel{\vert\!\approx^{me}} \phi_1 \rightarrow \phi_4$ if $\phi_1 \wedge \phi_2 \wedge \neg\phi_3 \wedge \phi_4$ is satisfiable.*

*(d) $\Sigma_d \mathrel{\vert\!\approx^{me}} \phi_1 \wedge \phi_5 \rightarrow \phi_4$ if $\phi_1 \wedge \phi_2 \wedge \neg\phi_3 \wedge \phi_4 \wedge \phi_5$ is satisfiable.*

Notice that parts (a) and (b) are just like Lemma 8.5.2. Part (c) actually follows from
part (d). (Taking $\phi_5 = \phi_2$ in part (d) shows that $\Sigma_c \mathrel{\vert\!\approx^{me}} \phi_1 \wedge \phi_2 \rightarrow \phi_4$ if $\phi_1 \wedge \phi_2 \wedge \neg\phi_3 \wedge$
$\phi_4$ is satisfiable. Part (c) then follows using the CUT rule; see Exercise 8.42.) In terms
of the examples we have been considering, part (b) says that penguins inherit properties
of birds; in particular, they have wings. Part (d) says that yellow penguins are easy to
see.

While the proof of Lemma 8.5.4 is beyond the scope of this book, I can explain
the basic intuition. It depends on the fact that maximum entropy makes things "as
independent as possible." For example, given a set of constraints of the form $\ell(\psi \mid \phi) = \alpha$ and a primitive proposition $q$ that does not appear in any of these constraints,
the structure that maximizes entropy subject to these constraints also satisfies $\ell(\psi \mid \phi \wedge q) = \alpha$. Now consider the set $\Sigma_2$ of defaults from Example 8.5.1. Interpreting these
defaults as constraints, it follows that $\mu_n^{me}(winged \mid bird) \approx 1 - 1/n$ (most birds fly) and
$\mu_n^{me}(bird \mid penguin) \approx 1 - 1/n$ (most birds are penguins). By the previous observation,
it also follows that $\mu_n^{me}(winged \mid bird \wedge penguin) \approx 1 - 1/n$. Thus,

$$\mu^{me}(winged \mid penguin)$$
$$\geq \mu^{me}(winged \wedge bird \mid penguin)$$
$$= \mu_n^{me}(winged \mid bird \wedge penguin) \times \mu_n^{me}(bird \mid penguin)$$
$$\approx (1 - 1/n)^2$$
$$\approx 1 - 2/n.$$

(In the last step, I am ignoring the $1/n^2$ term, since it is negligible compared to $1/2n$
for $n$ large.) Thus, $\Sigma_2 \mathrel{\vert\!\approx^{me}} penguin \rightarrow winged$, as desired.

The maximum-entropy approach may seem somewhat ad hoc. While it seems to have a number of attractive properties, why is it the appropriate thing to use for non-monotonic reasoning? One defense of it runs in the spirit of the usual defense of maximum entropy. If $\Sigma_n$ is viewed as a set of constraints, the probability measure $\mu_n^{me}$ is the one that satisfies the constraints and gives the least "additional information" over and above this fact. But then why consider a sequence of measures like this at all? Some further motivation for the use of such a sequence will be given in Chapter 11. There is also the problem of characterizing the properties of this maximum-entropy approach, something that has yet to be done. Besides the attractive properties described in Lemma 8.5.4, the approach may have some not-so-attractive properties, just as maximum entropy itself has unattractive properties in some contexts. Without a characterization, it is hard to feel completely comfortable using this approach.

## 8.6   Conditional Logic

$\mathcal{L}^{def}$ is a rather weak language. For example, although it can express the fact that a certain default holds, it cannot express the fact that a certain default does *not* hold, since $\mathcal{L}^{def}$ does not allow negated defaults. There is no great difficulty extending the language to allow negated and nested defaults, and many agents as well. Let $\mathcal{L}_n^{\rightarrow}$ be the language defined by starting with primitive propositions, and closing off under $\wedge$, $\neg$, and $\rightarrow_i$, $i = 1, \ldots, n$. A formula such as $\phi \rightarrow_i \psi$ should be read as "according to agent $i$, $\phi$'s are typically $\psi$'s." Formulas in $\mathcal{L}_n^{\rightarrow}$ can describe logical combination of defaults (e.g., $(p \rightarrow_1 q) \vee (p \rightarrow_1 \neg q)$), negated defaults (e.g., $\neg(p \rightarrow_1 q)$), and nested defaults (e.g., $(p \rightarrow_1 q) \rightarrow_2 r$).

There is no difficulty giving semantics to formulas in $\mathcal{L}_n^{\rightarrow}$ in $\mathcal{M}_n^{ps}$, $\mathcal{M}_n^{poss}$, $\mathcal{M}_n^{pref}$, and $\mathcal{M}_n^{qual}$ (where $\mathcal{M}_n^{ps}$ and $\mathcal{M}_n^{qual}$ are the obvious generalizations of $\mathcal{M}^{ps}$ and $\mathcal{M}^{qual}$ to $n$ agents), just by extending the definition in the single-agent case in the obvious way. For example, if $M = (W, \mathcal{POSS}, \pi) \in \mathcal{M}_n^{poss}$, then

$$(M, w) \models \phi \rightarrow_i \psi \text{ iff } \mathrm{Poss}_{w,i}(\llbracket \phi \rrbracket_M \cap W_{w,i}) = 0 \text{ or}$$
$$\mathrm{Poss}_{w,i}(\llbracket \phi \wedge \psi \rrbracket_M \cap W_{w,i}) > \mathrm{Poss}_{w,i}(\llbracket \phi \wedge \neg\psi \rrbracket_M \cap W_{w,i}),$$

where $\mathcal{POSS}_i(w) = (W_{w,i}, \mathrm{Poss}_{w,i})$. Note that, since the possibility measure may depend on the world and the agent, the world $w$ must now explicitly appear on the left-hand side of $\models$ and $\rightarrow$ must have subscripts denoting agents.

$\mathcal{L}^{\rightarrow}$ with this semantics has been called *conditional logic*. Statements of the form $\phi \rightarrow \psi$ are called *conditionals* (but not material conditionals, of course!).

It should be clear from the definitions that formulas in $\mathcal{L}_n^{\rightarrow}$ can be expressed in $\mathcal{L}_n^{RL}$.

**Proposition 8.6.1**   *For every structure M in $\mathcal{M}_n^{poss}$, $\mathcal{M}_n^{pref}$, $\mathcal{M}_n^{rank}$, and $\mathcal{M}_n^{qual}$,*

$$(M, w) \models \phi \rightarrow_i \psi \text{ iff } (M, w) \models \neg(\ell_i(\phi) > \ell_i(false)) \vee (\ell_i(\phi \wedge \psi) > \ell_i(\phi \wedge \neg\psi)).$$

**Proof**   The result is immediate from the definitions.   ∎

What about the converse? Can all formulas in $\mathcal{L}_n^{RL}$ be expressed in $\mathcal{L}_n^{\rightarrow}$? In $\mathcal{M}_n^{poss}$, $\mathcal{M}_n^{rank}$, and $\mathcal{M}_n^{pref}$, they can.

**Proposition 8.6.2**   *For every structure M in $\mathcal{M}_n^{poss}$, $\mathcal{M}_n^{rank}$, and $\mathcal{M}_n^{pref}$,*

$$(M, w) \models \ell_i(\phi) > \ell_i(\psi) \text{ iff } (M, w) \models \neg(\phi \rightarrow_i false) \wedge \neg((\phi \vee \psi) \rightarrow_i \neg\psi)).$$

**Proof**   See Exercise 8.43.   ∎

The key step in the proof of Proposition 8.6.2 involves showing that $M \models \ell_i(\phi) > \ell_i(\psi)$ iff $M \models \ell_i(\phi \wedge \neg\psi) > \ell_i(\psi)$. While this property holds for structures $M$ in $\mathcal{M}_n^{poss}$, $\mathcal{M}_n^{rank}$, and $\mathcal{M}_n^{pref}$, it does not hold in $\mathcal{M}_n^{qual}$ in general, so Proposition 8.6.2 does not extend to $\mathcal{M}_n^{qual}$. In fact, there is no formula in $\mathcal{L}_n^{\rightarrow}$ that is equivalent to $\ell_i(\phi) > \ell_i(\psi)$ in all structures in $\mathcal{M}_n^{qual}$ (Exercise 8.44). Thus, in $\mathcal{M}_n^{qual}$, the language $\mathcal{L}_n^{RL}$ is strictly more expressive than $\mathcal{L}_n^{\rightarrow}$.

Although it is possible to translate $\mathcal{L}_n^{\rightarrow}$ to $\mathcal{L}_n^{RL}$ and then use $AX_n^{ord}$ (in the case of plausibility measures and partial preorders) or $AX^{RLTe}$ (in the case of possibility measures and ranking functions, since they define total preorders) to reason about defaults, it is desirable to be able to characterize default reasoning directly in the language $\mathcal{L}_n^{\rightarrow}$. Of course, the characterization will depend to some extent on whether the underlying order is partial or total.

Let $AX^{cond}$ consist of the following axioms and inference rules:

Prop.   All substitution instances of propositional tautologies.

C1.   $\phi \rightarrow_i \phi$.

C2.   $((\phi \rightarrow_i \psi_1) \wedge (\phi \rightarrow_i \psi_2)) \Rightarrow (\phi \rightarrow_i (\psi_1 \wedge \psi_2))$.

C3.   $((\phi_1 \rightarrow_i \psi) \wedge (\phi_2 \rightarrow_i \psi)) \Rightarrow ((\phi_1 \vee \phi_2) \rightarrow_i \psi)$.

C4.   $((\phi \rightarrow_i \psi_1) \wedge (\phi \rightarrow_i \psi_2)) \Rightarrow ((\phi \wedge \psi_2) \rightarrow_i \psi_1)$.

MP.   From $\phi$ and $\phi \Rightarrow \psi$ infer $\psi$.

RC1.   From $\phi \Leftrightarrow \phi'$ infer $(\phi \rightarrow_i \psi) \Rightarrow (\phi' \rightarrow_i \psi)$.

RC2.   From $\psi \Rightarrow \psi'$ infer $(\phi \rightarrow_i \psi) \Rightarrow (\phi \rightarrow_i \psi')$.

AX$^{cond}$ can be viewed as a generalization of **P**. For example, the richer language allows the AND to be replaced with the axiom C2. Similarly, C1, C3, C4, RC1, and RC2 are the analogues of REF, OR, CM, LLE, and RW, respectively. As usual, Prop and MP are needed to deal with propositional reasoning.

**Theorem 8.6.3**  AX$_n^{cond}$ *is a sound and complete axiomatization for the language* $\mathcal{L}_n^{\rightarrow}$ *with respect to both* $\mathcal{M}_n^{pref}$ *and* $\mathcal{M}_n^{qual}$.

**Proof**  As usual, soundness is straightforward (Exercise 8.45) and completeness is beyond the scope of this book. ∎

The language $\mathcal{L}^{def}$ cannot distinguish between notions of likelihood based on partial preorders and ones based on total preorders. Conditional logic can make this distinction and others as well. Consider the following two axioms:

C5.    $(\phi \rightarrow_i \psi_1) \wedge \neg(\phi \rightarrow_i \neg\psi_2) \Rightarrow ((\phi \wedge \psi_2) \rightarrow_i \psi_1)$.

C6.    $\neg(true \rightarrow_i false)$.

C5 is almost the same as C4, except that the clause $\phi \rightarrow_i \psi_2$ in C4 is replaced by $\neg(\phi \rightarrow_i \neg\psi_2)$ in C5. C5 expresses a property called *Rational Monotonicity* in the literature. Roughly speaking, it is what distinguishes notions of uncertainty where the underlying notion of likelihood puts a total preorder on events from ones where the preorder is only partial. C5 does not hold in general in $\mathcal{M}_n^{qual}$ or $\mathcal{M}_n^{pref}$ (Exercise 8.46), but it does hold in $\mathcal{M}_n^{poss}$, $\mathcal{M}_n^{rank}$, and $\mathcal{M}_n^{tot}$. Reverse engineering shows that C5 corresponds to the following property of plausibility measures:

Pl6.    If $Pl(U \cap U') > Pl(\overline{U} \cap U')$ and $Pl(\overline{V} \cap U') \not> Pl(V \cap U')$, then $Pl(U \cap V \cap U') > Pl(\overline{U} \cap V \cap U')$.

Just as Pl4' is equivalent to the arguably more natural Pl4 (in the presence of Pl3), so too Pl6 is equivalent to arguably more natural properties in the presence of Pl3 and Pl4. The first is a property that is closely related to the assumption that disjoint sets are totally ordered; the second is closely related to the union property (see Exercises 8.47 and 8.48 for more details on these relationships).

Pl7.    If $U_1$, $U_2$, and $U_3$ are pairwise disjoint and $Pl(U_1) < Pl(U_2)$, then either $Pl(U_3) < Pl(U_2)$ or $Pl(U_1) < Pl(U_3)$ (or both).

Pl8.    If $U_1, U_2,$ and $U_3$ are pairwise disjoint and $Pl(U_1) < Pl(U_2 \cup U_3)$, then either $Pl(U_1) < Pl(U_2)$ or $Pl(U_1) < Pl(U_3)$ (or both).

**Proposition 8.6.4**   *In the presence of Pl3 and Pl4, Pl7 and Pl8 together are equivalent to Pl6.*

**Proof**   See Exercise 8.49.   ■

Since Pl7 and Pl8 clearly hold in $\mathcal{M}_n^{poss}$, $\mathcal{M}_n^{rank}$, and $\mathcal{M}_n^{tot}$ (indeed, they hold without the restriction to disjoint sets), this explains why they all satisfy C5.

C6 corresponds to a property called *normality* in the literature. It holds for a plausibility measure Pl if it satisfies the following property:

Pl9.   $\text{Pl}(W) > \bot$.

This property holds for the plausibility measures arising from ranking functions, possibility measures, and probability sequences.

Call a plausibility measure *rational* if it satisfies Pl6 (or, equivalently, Pl7 and Pl8) and *normal* if it satisfies Pl9. Ranking functions and possibility measures are both rational and normal; PS structures also give rise to normal (but not necessarily rational) plausibility measures. The following theorem shows that C5 characterizes qualitative rational structures and C6 characterizes qualitative normal structures. Moreover, these axioms suffice to characterize reasoning about $\mathcal{L}^\rightarrow$ in $\mathcal{M}_n^{ps}$, $\mathcal{M}_n^{poss}$, $\mathcal{M}_n^{rank}$, and $\mathcal{M}_n^{tot}$. Let $\mathcal{M}_n^{rat}$ (resp., $\mathcal{M}_n^{norm}$; $\mathcal{M}_n^{rat,norm}$) consist of all qualitative plausibility structures for $n$ agents whose plausibility measure satisfies Pl7 and Pl8 (resp., Pl9; Pl7–9).

**Theorem 8.6.5**

(a)  $\text{AX}_n^{cond} + \{C5\}$ *is a sound and complete axiomatization for the language* $\mathcal{L}_n^\rightarrow$ *with respect to* $\mathcal{M}_n^{rat}$.

(b)  $\text{AX}_n^{cond} + \{C6\}$ *is a sound and complete axiomatization for the language* $\mathcal{L}_n^\rightarrow$ *with respect to* $\mathcal{M}_n^{norm}$ *and* $\mathcal{M}_n^{ps}$.

(c)  $\text{AX}_n^{cond} + \{C5, C6\}$ *is a sound and complete axiomatization for the language* $\mathcal{L}_n^\rightarrow$ *with respect to* $\mathcal{M}_n^{rat,norm}$, $\mathcal{M}_n^{tot}$, $\mathcal{M}_n^{rank}$, *and* $\mathcal{M}_n^{poss}$.

## 8.7   Reasoning about Counterfactuals

The language $\mathcal{L}^\rightarrow$ can be used to reason about counterfactuals as well as defaults. Now the interpretation of a formula such as $\phi \rightarrow \psi$ is "if $\phi$ were the case, then $\psi$ would be true." In this section, $\phi \rightarrow \psi$ gets this counterfactual reading.

Under what circumstances should such a counterfactual formula be true at a world $w$? Certainly if $\phi$ is already true at $w$ (so that $\phi$ is not counter to fact) then it seems reasonable to take $\phi \to \psi$ to be true at $w$ if $\psi$ is also true at $w$. But what if $\phi$ is not true at $w$? In that case, one approach is to consider the world(s) "most like $w$" where $\phi$ is true and to see if $\psi$ is true there as well. But which worlds are "most like $w$"?

I am not going to try to characterize similarity here. Rather, I just show how the tools already developed can be used to at least *describe* when one world is similar to another; this, in turn, leads to a way of giving semantics to counterfactuals. In fact, as I now show, all the approaches discussed in Section 8.4 can be used to give semantics to counterfactuals.

Consider partial preorders. Associate with each world $w$ a partial preorder $\succeq_w$, where $w_1 \succeq_w w_2$ means that $w_1$ is at least as close to, or at least as similar to, $w$ as $w_2$. Clearly $w$ should be more like itself than any other world; that is, $w \succeq_w w'$ for all $w, w' \in W$. Note that this means simple structures cannot be used to give semantics to counterfactuals: the preorder really depends on the world.

A *counterfactual preferential structure* is a preferential structure (for one agent) $M = (W, \mathcal{O}, \pi)$ that satisfies the following condition:

Cfac$^{\succeq}$.  If $\mathcal{O}(w) = (W_w, \succeq_w)$, then $w \in W_w$ and is the maximum element with respect to $\succeq_w$ (so that $w$ is closer to itself than any other world in $W_w$); formally, $w \in W_w$ and $w \succ_w w'$ for all $w' \in W_w$ such that $w' \neq w$.

Let $\mathcal{M}_c^{pref}$ consist of all (single-agent) counterfactual preferential structures. This can be generalized to $n$ agents in the obvious way.

I have already given a definition for $\to$ in preferential structures, according to which, roughly speaking, $\phi \to \psi$ holds if $\phi \wedge \psi$ is more likely than $\phi \wedge \neg\psi$. However, this does not seem to accord with the intuition that I gave earlier for counterfactuals. Fortunately, Theorem 8.4.5 shows that another equivalent definition could have been used, one given by the operator $\to'$. Indeed, under the reinterpretation of $\succeq_w$, the operator $\to'$ has exactly the desired properties.

To make this precise, I generalize the definition of best$_M$ so that it can depend on the world. Define

$$\text{best}_{M,w}(U) = \{w' \in U \cap W_w : \text{for all } w'' \in U \cap W_w, \; w'' \not\succ_w w'\}.$$

Earlier, best$_M(U)$ was interpreted as "the most normal worlds in $U$"; now interpret it as "the worlds in $U$ closest to $w$." The formal definitions use the preorder in the same way. The proof of Theorem 8.4.5 shows that in a general preferential structure $M$ (whether or not it satisfies Cfac$^{\succeq}$)

$$(M, w) \models \phi \to \psi \text{ iff } \text{best}_{M,w}(\llbracket \phi \rrbracket_M) \subseteq \llbracket \psi \rrbracket_M.$$

That is, $\phi \rightarrow \psi$ holds at $w$ if all the worlds closest to or most like $w$ that satisfy $\phi$ also satisfy $\psi$.

Note that in a counterfactual preferential structure, $W_w$ is *not* the set of worlds the agent considers possible. $W_w$ in general includes worlds that the agent knows perfectly well to be impossible. For example, suppose that in the actual world $w$ the lawyer's client was drunk and it was raining. The lawyer wants to make the case that, even if his client hadn't been drunk and it had been sunny, the car would have hit the cow. (Actually, he may want to argue that there is a reasonable probability that the car would have hit the cow, but I defer a discussion of counterfactual probabilities to Section 8.8.) Thus, to evaluate the lawyer's claim, the worlds $w' \in W_w$ that are closest to $w$ where it is sunny and the client is sober and driving his car must be considered. But these are worlds that are currently known to be impossible. This means that the interpretation of $W_w$ in preferential structures depends on whether the structure is used for default reasoning or counterfactual reasoning.

Nevertheless, since counterfactual preferential structures are a subclass of preferential structures, all the axioms in $\text{AX}^{cond}$ are valid (when specialized to one agent). There is one additional property that corresponds to the condition Cfac$^{\succeq}$:

C7.    $\phi \Rightarrow (\psi \Leftrightarrow (\phi \rightarrow \psi))$.

C7 is in fact the property that I discussed earlier, which says that if $\phi$ is already true at $w$, then the counterfactual $\phi \rightarrow \psi$ is true at $w$ if and only if $\psi$ is true at $w$.

**Theorem 8.7.1**   $\text{AX}_n^{cond} + \{\text{C7}\}$ *is a sound and complete axiomatization for the language $\mathcal{L}^{\rightarrow}$ with respect to $\mathcal{M}_c^{pref}$.*

**Proof**   I leave it to the reader to check that C7 is valid in counterfactual preferential structures (Exercise 8.50). The validity of all the other axioms in $\text{AX}^{cond}$ follows from Theorem 8.6.3. Again, completeness is beyond the scope of the book. ∎

Of course, rather than allowing arbitrary partial preorders in counterfactual structures, it is possible to restrict to total preorders. In this case, C5 is sound.

Not surprisingly, all the other approaches that were used to give semantics to defaults can also be used to give semantics to counterfactuals. Indeed, the likelihood interpretation also makes sense for counterfactuals. A statement such as "if $\phi$ were true, then $\psi$ would be true" can still be interpreted as "the likelihood of $\psi$ given $\phi$ is much higher than that of $\neg\psi$ given $\phi$." However, "$\psi$ given $\phi$" cannot be interpreted in terms of conditional probability, since the probability of $\phi$ may well be 0 (in fact, the antecedent $\phi$ in a counterfactual is typically a formula that the agent knows to be false);

however, there is no problem using possibility, ranking, or plausibility here. All that is needed is an analogue to the condition Cfac$^\geq$. The analogues are not hard to come up with. For example, for ranking structures, the analogue is

Cfac$^\kappa$. If $\mathcal{RANK}(w) = (W_w, \kappa_w)$, then $w \in W_w$ and $\kappa_w(w) < \kappa_w(W_w - \{w'\})$.

Similarly, for plausibility structures, the analogue is

Cfac$^{\text{Pl}}$. If $\mathcal{PL}(w) = (W_w, \text{Pl}_w)$, then $w \in W_w$ and $\text{Pl}_w(w) > \text{Pl}_w(W_w - \{w\})$.

I leave it to the reader to check that counterfactual ranking structures and counterfactual plausibility structures satisfy C7, and to come up with the appropriate analogue to Cfac$^\geq$ in the case of probability sequences and possibility measures (Exercises 8.51 and 8.52).

## 8.8   Combining Probability and Counterfactuals

Subtleties similar in spirit to those discussed in Sections 6.2 and 8.2 that arise when combining knowledge and probability or knowledge and belief arise when combining other modalities. The combination of modalities brings into sharp focus the question of what "possible worlds" really are, and what their role is in the reasoning process. I conclude this chapter with a brief discussion of one more example—combining counterfactuals and probability.

To reason about both counterfactuals and probability requires that an agent have two different sets of possible worlds at a world $w$, say, $W_w^p$ and $W_w^c$, where $W_w^p$ is used when doing probabilistic reasoning and $W_w^c$ is used for doing counterfactual reasoning. How are these sets related?

It seems reasonable to require that $W_w^p$ be a subset of $W_w^c$—the worlds considered possible for probabilistic reasoning should certainly all be considered possible for counterfactual reasoning—but the converse may not hold. It might also seem reasonable to require, if a partial preorder is used to model similarity to $w$, that worlds in $W_w^p$ be closer to $w$ than worlds not in $W_w^p$. That is, it may seem that worlds that are ascribed positive probability should be considered closer than worlds that are considered impossible. However, some thought shows that this may not be so. For example, suppose that there are three primitive propositions, $p$, $q$, and $r$, and the agent knows that $p$ is true if and only if exactly one of $q$ or $r$ is true. Originally, the agent considers two worlds possible, $w_1$ and $w_2$, and assigns each of them probability 1/2; the formula $p \wedge q$ is true in $w_1$, while $p \wedge \neg q$ is true in $w_2$. Now what is the closest world to $w_1$ where $q$ is false? Is it necessarily $w_2$? That depends. Suppose that, intuitively, $w_1$ is a world where

$p$'s truth value is determined by $q$'s truth value (so that $p$ is true if $q$ is true and $p$ is false if $q$ is false) and, in addition, $q$ happens to be true, making $p$ true as well. The agent may well say that, even though he considers it quite possible that the actual world is $w_2$, where $\neg q$ is true, *if* the actual world were $w_1$, then the closest world to $w_1$ where $q$ is not true is the world $w_3$ where $\neg p \wedge \neg q$ is true. It may be reasonable to take the closest world to $w_1$ to be one that preserves the property that $p$ and $q$ have the same truth value, even though this world is considered impossible.

I leave it to the reader to consider other possible connections between $W_w^p$ and $W_w^c$. The real moral of this discussion is simply that these issues are subtle. However, I stress that, given a structure for probability and counterfactuals, there is no difficulty giving semantics to formulas involving probability and counterfactuals.

## Exercises

**8.1**   Show that $\{U : \mathcal{K}_i(w) \subseteq U\}$ is a filter. Also show that, given a probability measure $\mu$ on $W$, the set $\{U \subseteq W : \mu(U) = 1\}$ is a filter.

**8.2**   This exercise examines the connection between filters and epistemic frames. Suppose that $W$ is a set of worlds and $\mathcal{G}$ associates with every world in $W$ a filter.

  (a) If $W$ is finite, show that there exists a (unique) binary relation $\mathcal{K}$ on $W$ such that $\mathcal{G}(w) = \{U : \mathcal{K}(w) \subseteq U\}$.

  (b) (b) What conditions on $\mathcal{G}$ guarantee that $\mathcal{K}$ is (i) reflexive, (ii) transitive, and (iii) Euclidean?

  (c) (c) Show that if $W$ is infinite, there is a function $\mathcal{G}$ such that for no binary relation $\mathcal{K}$ on $W$ is it the case that $\mathcal{G}(w) = \{U : \mathcal{K}_i(w) \subseteq U\}$.

**8.3**   Show that if $U \subseteq V$ and $\mathrm{Pl}(U) > \mathrm{Pl}(\overline{U})$, then $\mathrm{Pl}(V) > \mathrm{Pl}(\overline{V})$.

**8.4**   Show that if $\mathrm{Pl}$ is a cpm satisfying CPl5, then $\mathrm{Pl}(U \mid V) > \mathrm{Pl}(\overline{U} \mid V)$ iff $\mathrm{Pl}(U \cap V) > \mathrm{Pl}(\overline{U} \cap V)$.

**8.5**   Prove Proposition 8.1.1.

**8.6**   Show that the plausibility measure $\mathrm{Pl}_{lot}$ defined in Example 8.1.2 satisfies Pl4.

**\*8.7**   This exercise compares the expressive power of the belief operator defined in terms of an accessibility relation and the belief operator defined in terms of plausibility measures that satisfy Pl4. An *epistemic belief structure* is one of the form $M = (W, \mathcal{K}_1, \ldots, \mathcal{K}_n, \mathcal{B}_1, \ldots, \mathcal{B}_n, \pi)$, where $\mathcal{K}_1, \ldots, \mathcal{K}_n$ are accessibility relations used to capture knowledge and $\mathcal{B}_1, \ldots, \mathcal{B}_n$ are accessibility relations used to capture belief. Let $\mathcal{L}_n^{KB}$ be the language with modal operators $K_1, \ldots, K_n$ for knowledge and $B_1, \ldots, B_n$ for belief. As expected, the semantics for $B_i\phi$ is

$$(M, w) \models B_i\phi \text{ iff } (M, w') \models \phi \text{ for all } w' \in \mathcal{B}_i(w).$$

(The semantics of knowledge remains unchanged: $(M, w) \models K_i\phi$ iff $(M, w') \models \phi$ for all $w' \in \mathcal{K}_i(w)$.)

(a) Given an epistemic belief' structure $M = (W, \mathcal{K}_1, \ldots, \mathcal{K}_n, \mathcal{B}_1, \ldots, \mathcal{B}_n, \pi)$, define plausibility assignments $\mathcal{PL}_1, \ldots, \mathcal{PL}_n$ by taking $\mathcal{PL}_i(w) = (\mathcal{B}_i(w), \text{Pl}_{w,i})$, where, for $U \subseteq \mathcal{B}_i(w)$,

$$\text{Pl}_{w,i}(U) = \begin{cases} 1 & \text{if } U = \mathcal{B}_i(w) \neq \emptyset, \\ 1/2 & \text{if } U \neq \emptyset, U \neq \mathcal{B}_i(w), \\ 0 & \text{if } U = \emptyset. \end{cases}$$

Let $M' = (W, \mathcal{K}_1, \ldots, \mathcal{K}_n, \mathcal{PL}_1, \ldots, \mathcal{PL}_n, \pi)$. Show that $M'$ is an epistemic belief structure (i.e., show that all the plausibility measures that arise satisfy Pl4) and that $M$ and $M'$ agree on all formulas in $\mathcal{L}^{KB}$, that is, if $\phi \in \mathcal{L}_n^{KB}$, then, for all $w \in W$,

$$(M, w) \models \phi \text{ iff } (M', w) \models \phi.$$

(b) Given an epistemic belief structure $M = (W, \mathcal{K}_1, \ldots, \mathcal{K}_n, \mathcal{PL}_1, \ldots, \mathcal{PL}_n, \pi)$, where $W$ is finite, define a binary relation $\mathcal{B}_i$ by setting $\mathcal{B}_i(w) = \cap\{U : \text{Pl}_{w,i}(U \cap W_{w,i}) > \text{Pl}_{w,i}(\overline{U} \cap W_{w,i})\}$ if $\text{Pl}(W_{w,i}) > \bot$, and setting $\mathcal{B}_i(w) = \emptyset$ if $\text{Pl}(W_{w,i}) = \bot$. Let $M' = (W, \mathcal{K}_1, \ldots, \mathcal{K}_n, \mathcal{B}_1, \ldots, \mathcal{B}_n, \pi)$. Show that $M$ and $M'$ agree on all formulas in $\mathcal{L}^{KB}$, that is, if $\phi \in \mathcal{L}_n^{KB}$, then, for all $w \in W$,

$$(M, w) \models \phi \text{ iff } (M', w) \models \phi.$$

(Hint: If your proof does not use the fact that $W$ is finite and invoke Pl4', then it is probably not completely correct.)

(c) Show that the construction in part (b) does not work if $W$ is infinite, by constructing a structure $M$ for knowledge and qualitative plausibility for which the set $W$ of possible worlds is infinite and the corresponding structure $M'$ for knowledge and belief does not agree with $M$ on all formulas in $\mathcal{L}^{KB}$.

**8.8** Consider a simple measurable plausibility structure $M = (W, \text{Pl}, \pi)$, where Pl satisfies Pl4. Define $B$, as in Section 8.2, in terms of plausibility. Show that this definition satisfies the axioms of KD45. (It can actually be shown that KD45 is a sound and complete axiomatization with respect to this semantics, but that is beyond the scope of this book.)

**8.9**    Prove Proposition 8.2.1.

**8.10**    State analogues of CONS, SDP, and UNIF in the case where a binary relation $\mathcal{B}_i$ is used to model belief, and prove an analogue of Proposition 8.2.1 for your definition.

**8.11**    Another property of interest relating knowledge and belief is called *certainty*. It is characterized by the following two axioms:

$$B\phi \Rightarrow BK\phi \qquad \text{(positive certainty); and}$$

$$\neg B\phi \Rightarrow B\neg K\phi \qquad \text{(negative certainty).}$$

(a) Show that if $B$ satisfies the axioms of KD45 and the entailment property holds, then $B$ satisfies negative certainty as well.

(b) Show that if $B$ satisfies the axioms of KD45, $K$ satisfies the axioms of S5, the entailment property holds, and positive certainty for $B$ holds, then $B$ is equivalent to $K$; that is, $B\phi \Leftrightarrow K\phi$ is provable. Thus, under these assumptions, an agent cannot hold false beliefs: $\neg\phi \wedge B\phi$ is not satisfiable. (This result holds even if $B$ does not satisfy the introspection axioms K4 and K5.)

**8.12**    Show that if $\phi \Rightarrow \psi$ is true under a truth assignment $v$, then so is $\phi \wedge \phi' \Rightarrow \psi$, no matter what $\phi'$ is.

**8.13**    Show that all the properties of **P** hold if $\rightarrow$ is interpreted as $\Rightarrow$, the material conditional.

**8.14**    Show that, in Example 8.3.1, if $\rightarrow$ is interpreted as $\Rightarrow$, then *penguin* must be false.

**8.15**    Show that, if $\mu([\![fly]\!]_M \mid [\![bird]\!]_M) = 1$, $\mu([\![fly]\!]_M \mid [\![penguin]\!]_M) = 0$, and $\mu([\![bird]\!]_M \mid [\![penguin]\!]_M) = 1$, then $\mu([\![penguin]\!]_M) = 0$.

**8.16**    Show that soundness holds in Theorem 8.4.1. That is, show that if $\Sigma \vdash_{\mathbf{P}} \phi \rightarrow \psi$ then $\Sigma \models_{\mathcal{M}^{cps}} \phi \rightarrow \psi$.

**8.17**    Suppose that $M \in \mathcal{M}^{meas}$. For this exercise, use the definition of $\rightarrow$ in terms of probability: $M \models \phi \rightarrow \psi$ if $\mu([\![\phi]\!]_M) = 0$ or $\mu([\![\psi]\!]_M \mid [\![\phi]\!]_M) > \mu([\![\neg\psi]\!]_M \mid [\![\phi]\!]_M)$. Show that the following are equivalent:

(a) $M \models \phi \rightarrow \psi$;

(b) $\mu([\![\phi]\!]_M) = 0$ or $\mu([\![\phi \wedge \psi]\!]_M) > \mu([\![\phi \wedge \neg\psi]\!]_M)$;

(c) $\mu([\![\phi]\!]_M) = 0$ or $\mu([\![\psi]\!]_M \mid [\![\phi]\!]_M) > 1/2$.

Moreover, show that this interpretation satisfies LLE, RW, and REF.

**8.18** Show that the OR rule is violated in the structure $M_1$ of Example 8.4.2.

**8.19** Fix $\epsilon > 0$. For this exercise, if $M \in \mathcal{M}^{meas}$, say that $M \models \phi \to \psi$ if $\mu([\![\phi]\!]_M) = 0$ or $\mu([\![\psi]\!]_M \mid [\![\phi]\!]_M) > 1 - \epsilon$. Show that this interpretation satisfies LLE, RW, and REF, but not AND, CM, or OR.

**8.20** Given a simple nonstandard probability structure $M = (W, \mu^{ns}, \pi)$ (which is just like a simple probability structure, except that now $\mu^{ns}$ is a nonstandard probability measure on $W$), say $M \models \phi \to \psi$ if either $\mu^{ns}([\![\phi]\!]_M) = 0$ or the closest standard real number to $\mu^{ns}([\![\psi]\!]_M \mid [\![\phi]\!]_M)$ is 1. Show this approach satisfies all the properties of **P**. (In fact, it follows from Theorem 8.4.15 that **P** is a sound and complete axiomatization of default reasoning with respect to nonstandard probability structures.)

**8.21** Show directly that OR and CM hold in simple PS structures (i.e., without using Theorems 8.4.10 and 8.4.12).

*__8.22__ Show that $\{p \wedge q \to r, p \to \neg r\} \vdash_{\mathbf{P}} p \to \neg q$.

**8.23** Show directly that OR and CM hold in possibility structures (i.e., without using Theorems 8.4.10 and 8.4.12). In addition, complete the proof of the soundness of the AND rule given in Theorem 8.4.5 by showing that $(U_1 \cap U_2) \cup (U_1 \cap V_2) = U_1$ and that if $\max(\alpha, \beta) > \max(\gamma, \delta)$ and $\max(\alpha, \gamma) > \max(\beta, \delta)$, then $\alpha > \max(\beta, \gamma, \delta)$.

**8.24** Show that $M \models \phi \Rightarrow \psi$ iff $[\![\phi]\!]_M \subseteq [\![\psi]\!]_M$ for every structure $M$.

**8.25** Prove Theorem 8.4.7.

**8.26** Prove Lemma 8.4.8.

**8.27** Proposition 8.1.1 gives a sense in which Pl4 is necessary and sufficient for conditional beliefs to be closed under conjunction. The AND rule can also be viewed as saying that conditional beliefs are closed under conjunction (viewing $\phi \to \psi$ as $B(\psi \mid \phi)$). This exercise shows that Pl4 is necessary for the AND rule in three (related) senses.

(a) Suppose that $(W, Pl)$ is a plausibility space that does not satisfy Pl4. Show that there exists an interpretation $\pi$ such that the simple measurable plausibility structure $(W, Pl, \pi)$ does not satisfy the AND rule.

(b) Suppose that $M = (W, \text{Pl}, \pi)$ is a plausibility structure such that $\pi(w) \neq \pi(w')$ if $w \neq w'$ and Pl does not satisfy Pl4. Again, show that $M$ does not satisfy the AND rule.

(c) Suppose that $M = (W, \text{Pl}, \pi)$ is a simple plausibility structure such that Pl does not satisfy Pl4 when restricted to sets definable by formulas. That is, there exist formulas $\phi_1, \phi_2,$ and $\phi_3$ such that $[\![\phi_1]\!]_M, [\![\phi_2]\!]_M,$ and $[\![\phi_3]\!]_M$ are pairwise disjoint, $\text{Pl}([\![\phi_1 \vee \phi_2]\!]_M) > \text{Pl}([\![\phi_3]\!]_M)$, $\text{Pl}([\![\phi_1 \vee \phi_3]\!]_M) > \text{Pl}([\![\phi_2]\!]_M)$, and $\text{Pl}([\![\phi_1]\!]_M) \not\succ \text{Pl}([\![\phi_2 \vee \phi_3]\!]_M)$. Again, show that $M$ does not satisfy the AND rule.

Show that the requirement in part (b) that $\pi(w) \neq \pi(w')$ if $w \neq w'$ is necessary by demonstrating a plausibility structure that does not satisfy Pl4 and yet satisfies the AND rule. (Of course, for this plausibility structure, it must be the case that there are two distinct worlds that satisfy the same truth assignment.)

**8.28**   Show that if $M = (W, \text{Pl}, \pi)$ is a simple measurable plausibility structure where Pl satisfies Pl4, then $M$ satisfies CM, and if $M \models \phi_1 \rightarrow \psi$, $M \models \phi_2 \rightarrow \psi$, and either $\text{Pl}([\![\phi_1]\!]_M) \neq \bot$ or $\text{Pl}([\![\phi_2]\!]_M) \neq \bot$, then $M \models (\phi_1 \vee \phi_2) \rightarrow \psi$.

**8.29**   Find a belief function Bel such that $\text{Bel}(U) = \text{Bel}(V) = 0$ but $\text{Bel}(U \cup V) \neq 0$.

**8.30**   Show that CM and OR are sound in $\mathcal{M}^{qual}$.

*   **8.31**   This exercise gives the proof of Theorem 8.4.11. Fix a simple measure conditional probability structure $M = (W, \mu, \pi)$.

(a) Define a partial preorder $\succeq'$ on subsets of $W$ such that $U \succeq' V$ if $\mu(U \mid U \cup V) = 1$. Show that $\succeq'$ is reflexive and transitive.

(b) Show by means of a counterexample that $\succeq'$ is not necessarily antisymmetric.

(c) Define a relation $\sim$ on subsets of $W$ by defining $U \sim V$ if $U \succeq' V$ and $V \succeq' U$. Show that $\sim$ is reflexive, symmetric, and transitive.

(d) Define $[U] = \{V : V \sim U\}$. Since $\sim$ is an equivalence relation, show that for all $U, U' \subseteq W$, either $[U] = [U']$ or $[U] \cap [U'] = \emptyset$. Let $W/\!\!\sim = \{[U] : U \subseteq W\}$.

(e) Define a relation $\succeq$ on $W/\!\!\sim$ by defining $[U] \succeq [V]$ iff there exist some $U \in [U]$ and $V \in [V]$ such that $U \succeq V$. Show that $\succeq$ is a partial order (i.e., reflexive, antisymmetric, and transitive).

(f) Show that $[\emptyset] = \{\emptyset\}$ and that $[\emptyset]$ is the element $\bot$ in $W/\!\!\sim$.

(g) Define a plausibility measure Pl on $W$ by taking $\text{Pl}(U) = [U]$ for $U \subseteq W$. Show that Pl satisfies Pl1–5.

(h) Let $M_\mu = (W, \text{Pl}, \pi)$. By part (g), $M_\mu \in \mathcal{M}^{qual}$. Show that $M \models \phi \rightarrow \psi$ iff $M_\mu \models \phi \rightarrow \psi$.

*8.32   This exercise fills in the details of the proof of Theorem 8.4.12. The general lines are similar to those of Exercise 8.31. Fix a PS structure $M = (W, (\mu_1, \mu_2, \ldots), \pi)$.

(a) Define a partial preorder $\succeq'$ on subsets of $W$ such that $U \succeq' V$ if $\lim_{i \to \infty} \mu_i(U \mid U \cup V) = 1$. Show that $\succeq'$ is reflexive and transitive.

(b) Show by example that $\succeq'$ is not necessarily antisymmetric. This problem can be dealt with just as in Exercise 8.32. Define $\sim$ on subsets of $W$ so that $U \sim V$ if $U \succeq' V$ and $V \succeq' U$, let $[U] = \{V : V \sim U\}$, and define a relation $\succeq$ on $W/\sim$ by defining $[U] \succeq [V]$ iff there exist some $U \in [U]$ and $V \in [V]$ such that $U \succeq V$. Show that $\succeq$ is a partial order (i.e., reflexive, antisymmetric, and transitive).

(c) Show that $[\emptyset]$ consists of all sets $U$ such that there exists some $N$ such that $\mu_n(U) = 0$ for all $n > N$ and that $[\emptyset]$ is the element $\perp$ in the partially ordered domain $W/\sim$.

(d) Define a plausibility measure Pl on $W$ by taking $\text{Pl}(U) = [U]$, for $U \subseteq W$. Show that Pl satisfies Pl1–5.

(e) Let $M_{PS} = (W, \text{Pl}, \pi)$. By part (d), $M_{PS} \in \mathcal{M}^{qual}$. Show that $M \models \phi \rightarrow \psi$ iff $M_{PS} \models \phi \rightarrow \psi$.

8.33   Show that Pl4 and Pl5 completely characterize the plausibility structures that satisfy **P** in the following sense. Let $\mathcal{M}$ be a collection of simple plausibility structures such that for each structure $M = (W, \text{Pl}, \pi) \in \mathcal{M}$, if $w \neq w' \in W$, then $\pi(w) \neq \pi(w')$. Show that if there is a structure in $\mathcal{M}$ that does not satisfy Pl4 or Pl5, then **P** is not sound in $\mathcal{M}$. (Note that the argument in the case of Pl4 is just part (b) of Exercise 8.27; a similar argument works for Pl5. In fact, variants of this results corresponding to parts (a) and (c) of Exercise 8.27 can also be proved.)

8.34   Prove Theorem 8.4.14.

*8.35   This exercise provides a proof of the first half of Theorem 8.4.15, namely, that richness is necessary for completeness.

(a) Let $\phi_1, \ldots, \phi_n$ be a collection of mutually exclusive and satisfiable propositional formulas. Let $\Sigma$ consist of the default $\phi_n \rightarrow false$ and the defaults $\phi_i \vee \phi_j \rightarrow \phi_i$

for all $1 \leq i < j \leq n$. Show that $(W, \mathrm{Pl}, \pi) \models \Sigma$ if and only if there is some $j$ with $1 \leq j \leq n$ such that

$$\mathrm{Pl}(\llbracket \phi_1 \rrbracket_M) > \mathrm{Pl}(\llbracket \phi_2 \rrbracket_M) > \cdots > \mathrm{Pl}(\llbracket \phi_j \rrbracket_M) = \cdots = \mathrm{Pl}(\llbracket \phi_n \rrbracket_M) = \perp.$$

(b) Suppose $\mathcal{M}$ is not rich. Let $\phi_1, \ldots, \phi_n$ be the formulas that provide a counterexample to richness and let $\Sigma$ be the set of defaults defined in part (a). Show that if $(W, \mathrm{Pl}, \pi) \in \mathcal{M}$ satisfies the defaults in $\Sigma$, then $\mathrm{Pl}(\llbracket \phi_{n-1} \rrbracket_M) = \perp$.

(c) Using part (b), show that $\Sigma \models_{\mathcal{M}} \phi_{n-1} \rightarrow \mathit{false}$.

(d) Show that $\Sigma \not\vdash_{\mathbf{P}} \phi_{n-1} \rightarrow \mathit{false}$. (Hint: Show that there exists a qualitative plausibility structure satisfying all the defaults in $\Sigma$ but not $\phi_{n-1} \rightarrow \mathit{false}$, and then use the fact that $\mathbf{P}$ is sound with respect to $\mathcal{M}^{qual}$.)

This shows that if $\mathcal{M}$ is not rich, then $\mathbf{P}$ is not complete with respect to $\mathcal{M}$. Although $\Sigma \models_{\mathcal{M}} \phi_{n-1} \rightarrow \mathit{false}$, the default $\phi_{n-1} \rightarrow \mathit{false}$ is not provable from $\Sigma$ in $\mathbf{P}$.

**8.36** This exercise provides a proof of the second half of Theorem 8.4.15, namely, that richness is sufficient for completeness. Suppose that there is some $\Sigma$ and $\phi \rightarrow \psi$ such that $\Sigma \models_{\mathcal{M}} \phi \rightarrow \psi$ but $\Sigma \not\vdash_{\mathbf{P}} \phi \rightarrow \psi$. Show that $\mathcal{M}$ is not rich as follows.

(a) Let $\Phi$ consist of all the primitive propositions that appear in $\Sigma$, $\phi$, or $\psi$. Show that there is a preferential structure structure $M = (W, \succeq, \pi)$ such that

(i) if $w \neq w'$, then either $w \succ w'$ or $w' \succ w$ (so that $\succeq$ is a total order);

(ii) if $w \neq w'$, then $(\pi(w))(p) \neq (\pi(w_j))(p)$ for some $p \in \Phi$ if $i \neq j$ (so that the truth assignments in all worlds are different);

(iii) $M \models \Sigma$;

(iv) $M \not\models \phi \rightarrow \psi$.

(Note that this result essentially proves the completeness of $\mathbf{P}$ for $\mathcal{M}^{tot}$.)

(b) Suppose that $\Phi = \{p_1, \ldots, p_m\}$. Define an *atom* over $\Phi$ to be a conjunction of the form $q_1 \wedge \ldots \wedge q_m$, where $q_i$ is either $p_i$ or $\neg p_i$. Thus, an atom over $\Phi$ can be identified with a truth assignment to the primitive propositions in $\Phi$. Let $\phi_i$ be the atom over $\Phi$ that characterizes the truth assignment to $w_i$, $i = 1, \ldots, n$, and let $\phi_{n+1} = \neg(\phi_1 \vee \ldots \vee \phi_n)$. Show that $\phi_1, \ldots, \phi_{n+1}$ are mutually exclusive.

(c) Show that if $M' = (W', \mathrm{Pl}', \pi')$ is a simple plausibility structure such that $\mathrm{Pl}'(\llbracket \phi_1 \rrbracket_{M'}) > \cdots > \mathrm{Pl}'(\llbracket \phi_{n+1} \rrbracket_{M'}) = \perp$, then $M'$ satisfies the defaults in $\Sigma$ but not $\phi \rightarrow \psi$.

(d) Show that $\mathcal{M}$ is not rich. (Hint: If $\mathcal{M}$ were rich, it would contain a structure like that in part (c). But that would contradict the assumption that $\Sigma \not\vdash_{\mathbf{P}} \phi \to \psi$.)

**8.37** This exercise refers to Example 8.5.1. Show that

(a) $\Sigma_1 \not\vdash_{\mathbf{P}} (penguin \wedge red) \to \neg fly$;

(b) $\Sigma_2 \not\vdash_{\mathbf{P}} penguin \to winged$ and $\Sigma_2 \not\vdash_{\mathbf{P}} (penguin \wedge bird) \to winged$;

(c) $\Sigma_3 \not\vdash_{\mathbf{P}} (penguin \wedge yellow) \to easy\text{-}to\text{-}see$;

(d) $\Sigma_4 \not\vdash_{\mathbf{P}} robin \to winged$ and $\Sigma_4 \not\vdash_{\mathbf{P}} (robin \wedge bird) \to winged$.

(Hint: For part (a), by Theorem 8.4.5, it suffices to find a preferential structure—or a possibility structure or a ranking structure—satisfying all the formulas in $\Sigma_1$, but not $penguin \wedge red \to \neg fly$. A similar approach works for parts (b), (c), and (d).)

**\*8.38** Show that if $\mathcal{M}_\Sigma^{rank} \neq \emptyset$, then there is a unique structure $M_\Sigma \in \mathcal{M}_\Sigma^{rank}$ that is most preferred, in that $M_\Sigma \succeq M$ for all $M \in \mathcal{M}_\Sigma^{rank}$.

**8.39** Complete the proof of Lemma 8.5.2, by showing that

(a) in $M_{\Sigma_a}$, all worlds satisfying $\phi_1 \wedge \phi_2 \wedge \phi_3$ have rank 0 and all worlds satisfying $\phi_1 \wedge \neg\phi_2$ or $\phi_2 \wedge \neg\phi_3$ have rank 1; and

(b) in $M_{\Sigma_b}$, (i) all worlds satisfying $\neg\phi_1 \wedge \phi_2 \wedge \phi_3$ have rank 0, (ii) there are some worlds satisfying $\neg\phi_1 \wedge \phi_2 \wedge \phi_3$, (iii) all worlds satisfying $\phi_1 \wedge \phi_2 \wedge \neg\phi_3 \wedge \phi_4$ have rank 1, and (iv) all worlds satisfying $\phi_1 \wedge \phi_3$ or $\phi_1 \wedge \neg\phi_4$ have rank 2.

**8.40** Show that $\Sigma_2 \not\approx^Z (penguin \wedge bird) \to winged$ and $\Sigma_3 \not\approx^Z (penguin \wedge yellow) \to easy\text{-}to\text{-}see$.

**8.41** Complete the proof of Proposition 8.5.3 by showing that

(a) if $\mathcal{P}^k = \emptyset$ for some $k > 0$, then there is no structure $M \in \mathcal{M}^{ps}$ such that $M \models \Sigma$,

(b) if $\mathcal{P}^k \neq \emptyset$ for all $k \geq 1$, then $M_\Sigma^{me} \models \Sigma$.

**\*8.42** The CUT rule is the following:

CUT. From $\phi \to \psi_1$ and $\phi \wedge \psi_1 \to \psi_2$ infer $\phi \to \psi_2$.

The CUT rule is essentially the converse of CM. It says that if $\psi_2$ follows (by default) from $\phi \wedge \psi_1$ and $\psi_1$ follows by default from $\phi$, then $\psi_2$ follows from $\phi$ alone. Show that CUT is provable in **P**. (Hint: First show that both $\phi \wedge \psi_1 \to \neg\psi_1 \vee \psi_2$ and $\phi \wedge \neg\psi_1 \to \neg\psi_1 \vee \psi_2$ are provable from $\phi \wedge \psi_1 \to \psi_2$.)

**8.43** Prove Proposition 8.6.2.

**8.44**  Let $W = \{a, b, c\}$. Define two plausibility measures, $Pl_1$ and $Pl_2$, on $W$. Each of these plausibility measures assigns to each subset of $W$ a triple of integers. Define a straightforward ordering on triples: $(i, j, k) \leq (i', j', k')$ if $i \leq i'$, $j \leq j'$, and $k \leq k'$; $(i, j, k) < (i', j', k')$ if $(i, j, k) \leq (i', j', k')$ and $(i', j', k') \not\leq (i, j, k)$. $Pl_1$ is defined so that $Pl_1(\emptyset) = (0, 0, 0)$, $Pl_1(a) = (1, 0, 0)$, $Pl_1(b) = (0, 1, 0)$, $Pl_1(c) = (0, 0, 1)$, $Pl_1(\{a, b\}) = (1, 1, 1)$, $Pl_1(\{a, c\}) = (2, 0, 1)$, $Pl_1(\{b, c\}) = (0, 2, 1)$, and $Pl_1(\{a, b, c\}) = (2, 2, 2)$. $Pl_2$ is identical to $Pl_1$ except that $Pl_2(\{a, b\}) = (2, 2, 1)$. Let $\Phi = \{p_a, p_b, p_c\}$ and define $\pi$ so that $\pi(d)(p_e) = \textbf{true}$ iff $d = e$ (so that $p_a$ is true only at world $a$, $p_b$ is true only at world $b$, and $p_c$ is true only at world $c$). Let $M_j = (W, \mathcal{PL}_1^j, \pi)$, where $\mathcal{PL}_1^j(w) = (W, Pl_j)$, for $j = 1, 2$.

(a) Show that both $M_1$ and $M_2$ are in $\mathcal{M}^{qual}$; that is, show that $Pl_1$ and $Pl_2$ satisfy Pl4 and Pl5.

(b) Show that if $U$ and $V$ are disjoint subsets of $W$, then $Pl_1(U) > Pl_1(V)$ iff $Pl_2(U) > Pl_2(V)$.

(c) Show as a consequence that $(M_1, w) \models \phi$ iff $(M_2, w) \models \phi$ for all formulas $\phi \in \mathcal{L}_1^{\rightarrow}$ and all $w \in W$.

(d) Note, however, that $(M_1, w) \models \neg(\ell_1(p_a \vee p_b) > \ell_1(p_b \vee p_c))$ while $(M_2, w) \models \ell_1(p_a \vee p_b) > \ell_1(p_b \vee p_c)$.

This exercise shows that $\ell_1(p_a \vee p_b) > \ell_1(p_b \vee p_c)$ is not equivalent to any formula in $\mathcal{L}_1^{\rightarrow}$. For if it were equivalent to some formula $\phi$, then by part (d), it would follow that $(M_1, a) \models \neg\phi$ and $(M_2, a) \models \phi$. However, part (c) shows that this cannot happen.

**8.45**  Prove that system $AX_n^{cond}$ is a sound axiomatization of $\mathcal{L}_n^{\rightarrow}$ with respect to both $\mathcal{M}_n^{pref}$ and $\mathcal{M}_n^{qual}$.

**8.46**  Show that C5 does not hold in general in $\mathcal{M}_n^{qual}$ or $\mathcal{M}_n^{pref}$, by providing a counterexample.

**8.47**  Show that Pl6 holds if Pl is a total preorder when restricted to disjoint sets. Conversely, show that if Pl satisfies Pl6, then there is a total order $\preceq$ on disjoint sets such that $U_1 \prec U_2$ iff $Pl(U_1) < Pl(U_2)$ for disjoint sets $U_1$ and $U_2$.

**8.48**  Show that the following are equivalent:

(a) $Pl(U_1) < Pl(U_3)$ and $Pl(U_2) < Pl(U_3)$ implies that $Pl(U_1 \cup U_2) < Pl(U_3)$. (This is the union property.)

(b) $Pl(U_1 \cup U_2) = \max(Pl(U_1), Pl(U_2))$.

(c) If $\mathrm{Pl}(U_1) < \mathrm{Pl}(U_2 \cup U_3)$, then either $\mathrm{Pl}(U_1) < \mathrm{Pl}(U_2)$ or $\mathrm{Pl}(U_1) < \mathrm{Pl}(U_3)$. (This is Pl8, without the restriction to disjoint sets.)

(Hint: It is probably easiest to prove that both (a) and (c) are equivalent to (b).)

**\*8.49**   Prove Proposition 8.6.4.

**8.50**   Show that C7 is valid in counterfactual preferential structures.

**8.51**   Show that counterfactual ranking structures (i.e., ranking structures satisfying $\mathrm{Cfac}^\kappa$) and counterfactual plausibility structures (i.e., plausibility structures satisfying $\mathrm{Cfac}^{\mathrm{Pl}}$) satisfy C7.

**8.52**   Construct conditions analogous to $\mathrm{Cfac}^\succeq$ appropriate for possibility structures and PS structures, and show that the resulting classes of structures satisfy C7.

**8.53**   In counterfactual preferential structures, there may in general be more than one world closest to $w$ satisfying $\phi$. In this exercise I consider counterfactual preferential structures where, for each formula $\phi$ and world $w$, there is always a unique closest world to $w$ satisfying $\phi$.

(a) $M = (W, \mathcal{O}, \pi)$, where $\mathcal{O}(w) = (W_w, \succeq_w)$, is a *totally ordered (counterfactual) structure* if, for all $w \in W$, $\succeq_w$ is a *total order*—that is, for all $w', w'' \in W$ such that $w' \neq w''$, either $w' \succ_w w''$ or $w'' \succ_w w'$. Show that in totally ordered structures, there is always a unique closest world to $w$ satisfying $\phi$ for each world $w$ and formula $\phi$.

(b) Show that in totally ordered counterfactual structures, the following axiom is valid:

C8.   $(\phi \to \psi) \vee (\phi \to \neg\psi)$.

In fact, it can be shown that C8 characterizes totally ordered counterfactual structures (although doing so is beyond the scope of this book).

(c) Show that C5 follows from C8 and all the other axioms and inference rules in $\mathrm{AX}^{cond}$.

# Notes

Defining belief as "holds with probability 1" is common in the economics/game theory literature (see, e.g., [Brandenburger and Dekel 1987]). As I mentioned in Chapter 7, interpreting belief as "truth in all worlds considered possible," just like knowledge, is standard in the modal logic literature. Typically, the Knowledge Axiom ($K_i\phi \Rightarrow \phi$) is taken to hold for knowledge, but not belief. Brandenburger [1999] uses filters to model beliefs.

There has been a great deal of work on logics of knowledge and belief; see, for example, [Halpern 1996; Hoek 1993; Kraus and Lehmann 1988; Lamarre and Shoham 1994; Lenzen 1978; Lenzen 1979; Moses and Shoham 1993; Voorbraak 1991]. The use of plausibility to model belief is discussed in [Friedman and Halpern 1997], from where Proposition 8.2.1 and Exercise 8.7 are taken. The observation in Exercise 8.11 is due to Lenzen [1978; 1979]; see [Halpern 1996] for further discussion of this issue.

There has been a great deal of discussion in the philosophical literature about *conditional statements*. These are statements of the form "if $\phi$ then $\psi$," and include counterfactuals as a special case. Stalnaker [1992] provides a short and readable survey of the philosophical issues involved.

Many approaches to giving semantics to defaults have been considered in the literature. Much of the work goes under the rubric *nonmonotonic logic*; see Marek and Truszczyński's book [1993] and Reiter's overview paper [1987a] for a general discussion of the issues. Some of the early and most influential approaches include Reiter's *default logic* [1980], McCarthy's *circumscription* [1980], McDermott and Doyle's *nonmonotonic logic* [1980], and Moore's *autoepistemic logic* [1985].

The approach discussed in this chapter, characterized by axiom system **P**, was introduced by Kraus, Lehmann, and Magidor [1990] (indeed, the axioms and rules of **P** are often called the *KLM properties* in the literature) and Makinson [1989], based on ideas that go back to Gabbay [1985]. Kraus, Lehmann, and Magidor and Makinson gave semantics to default formulas using preferential structures. Pearl [1989] gave probabilistic semantics to default formulas using what he called *epsilon semantics*, an approach that actually was used independently and earlier by Adams [1975] to give semantics to conditionals. The formulation given here using PS structures was introduced by Goldszmidt, Morris, and Pearl [1993], and was shown by them to be equivalent to Pearl's original notion of epsilon semantics. Geffner [1992b] showed that this approach is also characterized by **P**.

Dubois and Prade [1991] were the first to use possibility measures for giving semantics to defaults; they showed that **P** characterized reasoning about defaults using this semantics. Goldszmidt and Pearl [1992] did the same for ranking functions. Friedman and I used plausibility measures to explain why all these different approaches are characterized by **P**. Theorems 8.4.10, 8.4.12, 8.4.14, and 8.4.15, and Proposition 8.6.4 are from [Friedman and Halpern 2001].

There has been a great deal of effort applied to going beyond axiom system **P**. The issue was briefly discussed by Kraus, Lehmann, and Magidor [1990], where the property of Rational Monotonicity was first discussed. This property is considered in greater detail by Lehmann and Magidor [1992]. The basic observation that many of the approaches to nonmonotonic reasoning (in particular, ones that go beyond **P**) can be understood in terms of choosing a preferred structure that satisfies some defaults is due to Shoham [1987]. Delgrande [1988] presented an approach to nonmonotonic reasoning that tried to incorporate default notions of irrelevance, although his semantic basis was somewhat different from those considered here. (See [Lehmann and Magidor 1992] for a discussion of the differences.) The System Z approach discussed in Section 8.5 was introduced by Pearl [1990] (see also [Goldszmidt and Pearl 1992]). The conclusions obtained by System Z are precisely those obtained by considering what Lehmann and Magidor [Lehmann 1989; Lehmann and Magidor 1992] call the *rational closure* of a knowledge base. Lehmann and Magidor give a formulation of rational closure essentially equivalent to System Z, using total preferential structures (i.e., using $\mathcal{M}^{tot}$ rather than $\mathcal{M}^{rank}$). They also give a formulation using nonstandard probabilities, as in Exercise 8.20. Goldszmidt, Morris, and Pearl [1993] introduce the maximum-entropy approach discussed in Section 8.5. Two other approaches that have many of the properties of the maximum-entropy approach are due to Geffner [1992a] and Bacchus et al. [1996]; the latter appxroach is discussed further in Chapter 11.

The language $\mathcal{L}^{\rightarrow}$ was introduced by Lewis [1973]. Lewis first proved the connection between $\rightarrow$ and $\rightarrow'$ given in Theorem 8.4.7; he also showed that $>$ could be captured by $\rightarrow$ in partial preorders, as described in Proposition 8.6.2. (Lewis assumed that the preorder was in fact total; the fact that the same connection holds even if the order is partial was observed in [Halpern 1997a].) The soundness and completeness of $AX^{cond}$ for preferential structures (Theorem 8.6.3) was proved by Burgess [1981]; the result for measurable plausibility structures is proved in [Friedman and Halpern 2001].

Stalnaker [1968] first gave semantics to counterfactuals using what he called *selection functions*. A selection function $f$ takes as arguments a world $w$ and a formula $\phi$; $f(w, \phi)$ is taken to be the world closest to $w$ satisfying $\phi$. (Notice that this means that there is a unique closest world, as in Exercise 8.53.) Stalnaker and Thomason [1970] provided a complete axiomatization for counterfactuals using this semantics. The semantics for counterfactuals using preorders presented here is due to Lewis [1973].

Balke and Pearl [1994] provide a model for reasoning about probability and counterfactuals, but it does not use a possible-worlds approach. It would be interesting to relate their approach carefully to the possible-worlds approach.

# Chapter 9

# Belief Revision

*I was always puzzled by the fact that people have a great deal of trouble and pain when and if they are forced or feel forced to change a belief or circumstance which they hold dear. I found what I believe is the answer when I read that a Canadian neurosurgeon discovered some truths about the human mind which revealed the intensity of this problem. He conducted some experiments which proved that when a person is forced to change a basic belief or viewpoint, the brain undergoes a series of nervous sensations equivalent to the most agonizing torture.*

—Sidney Madwed

Suppose that an agent believes $\phi_1, \ldots, \phi_n$ ("belief" here is taken in the sense of Section 8.1) and then learns or observes $\psi$. How should she revise her beliefs? If $\psi$ is consistent with $\phi_1 \wedge \ldots \wedge \phi_n$, then it seems reasonable for her to just add $\psi$ to her stock of beliefs. This is just the situation considered in Section 3.1. But what if $\psi$ is, say, $\neg \phi_1$? It does not seem reasonable to just add $\neg \phi_1$ to her stock of beliefs, for then her beliefs become inconsistent. Nor is it just a simple matter of discarding $\phi_1$ and adding $\neg \phi_1$. Discarding $\phi_1$ may not be enough, for (at least) two reasons:

1. Suppose that $\phi_1$ is $\phi_2 \wedge \phi_3$. If the agent's beliefs are closed under implication (as I will be assuming they are), then both $\phi_2$ and $\phi_3$ must be in her stock of beliefs. Discarding $\phi_1$ and adding $\neg \phi_1$ still leaves an inconsistent set. At least one of $\phi_2$ or $\phi_3$ will also have to be discarded to regain consistency, but which one?

2. Even if the result of discarding $\phi_1$ and adding $\neg \phi_1$ is consistent, it may not be an appropriate belief set. For example, suppose that $\phi_4$ is $\phi_1 \vee p$. Since $\phi_4$ is a logical consequence of $\phi_1$, it seems reasonable to assume that $\phi_4$ is in the agent's belief set (before learning $\neg \phi_1$). But suppose that the only reason that

331

the agent believed $\phi_4$ originally was that she believed $\phi_1$. Discarding $\phi_1$ removes the justification for $\phi_4$. Shouldn't it be removed too? Note that if $\phi_4$ remains among the agent's beliefs, then the fact that both $\neg\phi_1$ and $\phi_4$ are included in the agent's beliefs suggests that $p$ should be too. But there is nothing special about $p$ here; it could be any formula. It certainly does not seem reasonable to have a procedure that allows an arbitrary formula to be among the agent's beliefs after learning $\neg\phi_1$.

Chapter 3 has a great deal of discussion as to how an agent's beliefs should be updated in the light of new information. Surely some of that discussion should be relevant here. In fact, it is highly relevant. Characterizing an agent's beliefs in terms of formulas (which is the standard approach in the literature) obscures what is really going on here. I argue in this chapter that belief revision can be completely understood in terms of conditioning. Using an (unconditional) probability measure as a representation of belief (where belief is taken to mean "probability 1") will not quite work, since the main issue here is what happens if an event that previously was not believed is observed. This amounts to conditioning on an event of probability 0. However, if beliefs are represented using a qualitative plausibility measure (i.e., using any of the representations discussed in Chapter 8, including using a conditional probability measure), then the appropriate notion of conditioning for that representation does indeed capture the standard properties of belief revision. Different decisions as to how to revise turn out to correspond to different prior plausibilities.

Most of the effort in this chapter involves showing that the standard approaches to belief revision in the literature can be understood in terms of conditioning, and that doing so leads to further insights into the belief revision process. Making the connection also brings into sharper focus some of the issues discussed in Sections 3.1 and 6.7.1, such as the need to assume perfect recall and that the way that an agent obtains new information does not itself give information.

## 9.1    The Circuit-Diagnosis Problem

The *circuit-diagnosis problem* provides a good test bed for understanding the issues involved in belief revision. A *circuit* consists of a number of components (AND, OR, NOT, and XOR gates) and lines. For example, the circuit of Figure 9.1 contains five components, $X_1$, $X_2$, $A_1$, $A_2$, $O_1$ and eight lines, $l_1, \ldots, l_8$. Inputs (which are either 0 or 1) come in along lines $l_1$, $l_2$, and $l_3$. $A_1$ and $A_2$ are AND gates; the output of an AND gate is 1 if both of its inputs are 1, otherwise it is 0. $O_1$ is an OR gate; its output is 1 if

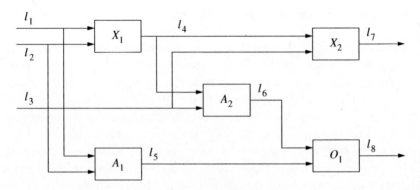

Figure 9.1    A typical circuit.

either of its inputs is 1, otherwise it is 0. Finally, $X_1$ and $X_2$ are XOR gates; the output of a XOR gate is 1 iff exactly one of its inputs is 1.

The circuit-diagnosis problem involves identifying which components in a circuit are faulty. An agent is given a circuit diagram as in Figure 9.1; she can set the values of input lines of the circuit and observe the output values. By comparing the actual output values with the expected output values, the agent can attempt to locate faulty components.

The agent's knowledge about a circuit can be modeled using an epistemic structure $M_{diag}^K = (W_{diag}, \mathcal{K}_{diag}, \pi_{diag})$. Each possible world $w \in W_{diag}$ is composed of two parts: $fault(w)$, the *failure set,* that is, the set of faulty components in $w$, and $value(w)$, the value of all the lines in the circuit. Formally, $value(w)$ is a set of pairs of the form $(l, i)$, where $l$ is a line in the circuit and $i$ is either 0 or 1. Components that are not in the failure sets perform as expected. Thus, for the circuit in Figure 9.1, if $w \in W_{diag}$ and $A_1 \notin fault(w)$, then $(l_5, 1)$ is in $value(w)$ iff both $(l_1, 1)$ and $(l_2, 1)$ are in $value(w)$. Faulty components may act in arbitrary ways (and are not necessarily required to exhibit faulty behavior on all inputs, or to always act the same way when given the same inputs).

What language should be used to reason about faults in circuits? Since an agent needs to be able to reason about which components are faulty and the values of various lines, it seems reasonable to take

$$\Phi_{diag} = \{faulty(c_1), \dots, faulty(c_n), hi(l_1), \dots, hi(l_k)\},$$

where $faulty(c_i)$ denotes that component $c_i$ is faulty and $hi(l_i)$ denotes that line $l_i$ in a "high" state (i.e., has value 1). Define the interpretation $\pi_{diag}$ in the obvious way:

$\pi_{diag}(w)(faulty(c_i)) = $ **true** if $c_i \in fault(w)$, and $\pi_{diag}(w)(hi(l_i)) = $ **true** if $(l_i, 1) \in value(w)$.

The agent knows which tests she has performed and the results that she observed. Let $obs(w) \subseteq value(w)$ consist of the values of those lines that the agent sets or observes. (For the purposes of this discussion, I assume that the agent sets the value of a line only once.) I assume that the agent's local state consists of her observations, so that $(w, w') \in \mathcal{K}_{diag}$ if $obs(w) = obs(w')$. For example, suppose that the agent observes $hi(l_1) \wedge hi(l_2) \wedge hi(l_3) \wedge hi(l_7) \wedge hi(l_8)$. The agent then considers possible all worlds where lines $l_1, l_2, l_3, l_7$ and $l_8$ have value 1. Since these observations are consistent with the circuit being correct, one of these worlds has an empty failure set. However, other worlds are possible. For example, it might be that the AND gate $A_2$ is faulty. This would not affect the outputs in this case, since if $A_1$ is nonfaulty, then its output is "high," and thus, $O_1$'s output is "high" regardless of $A_2$'s output.

Now suppose that the agent observes $hi(l_1) \wedge \neg hi(l_2) \wedge hi(l_3) \wedge hi(l_7) \wedge \neg hi(l_8)$. These observations imply that the circuit is faulty. (If $l_1$ and $l_3$ are "high" and $l_2$ is "low," then the correct values for $l_7$ and $l_8$ should be "low" and "high," respectively.) In this case there are several failure sets consistent with the observations, including $\{X_1\}$, $\{X_2, O_1\}$, and $\{X_2, A_2\}$.

In general, there is more than one explanation for the observed faulty behavior. Thus, the agent cannot *know* exactly which components are faulty, but she may have *beliefs* on that score. The beliefs depend on her plausibility measure on runs. One way of constructing a reasonable family of plausibility measures on runs is to start with a plausibility measure over possible failures of the circuit. I actually construct two plausibility measures over failures, each capturing slightly different assumptions. Both plausibility measures embody the assumptions that (1) failures are unlikely and (2) failures of individual components are independent of one another. It follows that the failure of two components is much more unlikely than the failure of any one of them. The plausibility measures differ in what they assume about the relative likelihood of the failure of different components.

The first plausibility measure embodies the assumption that the likelihood of each component failing is the same. This leads to an obvious order of failure sets: if $f_1$ and $f_2$ are two failure sets, then $f_1 \succeq_1 f_2$ if (and only if) $|f_1| \leq |f_2|$, that is, if $f_1$ consists of fewer faulty components than $f_2$. The order on failure sets, in turn, leads to a total order on worlds: $w_1 \succeq_1 w_2$ iff $fault(w_1) \succeq_1 fault(w_2)$. Using the construction of Section 2.7, this ordering on worlds can be lifted to a total order $\succeq_1^s$ on sets of sets of worlds. Moreover, by Theorem 2.7.5 and Exercise 2.49, $\succ_1^s$ can be viewed as a qualitative plausibility measure. Call this plausibility measure $Pl_1$.

$\text{Pl}_1$ can also be constructed by using probability sequences. Let $\mu_m$ be the probability measure that takes the probability of a component failing to be $1/m$ and takes component failures to be independent. Then for a circuit with $n$ components,

$$\mu_m(w) = \left(\frac{1}{m}\right)^{|fault(w)|} \left(\frac{m-1}{m}\right)^{n-|fault(w)|}.$$

It is now easy to check that $\text{Pl}_1$ is just the plausibility measure obtained from the probability sequence $(\mu_1, \mu_2, \mu_3, \ldots)$ using the construction preceding Theorem 8.4.12 (Exercise 9.1(a)). Note that the probability of a component being faulty tends to 0 as the subscript increases. However, at each measure in the sequence, each component is equally likely to fail and the failures are independent.

In some situations it might be unreasonable to assume that all components have equal failure probability. Moreover, the relative probability of failure for various components might be unknown. Without assumptions on failure probabilities, it is not possible to compare failure sets unless one is a subset of the other. This intuition leads to a different order on failure sets. Define $f \succeq_2 f'$ iff $f \subseteq f'$. Again this leads to an ordering on worlds by taking $w_1 \succeq_2 w_2$ iff $fault(w_1) \succeq_2 fault(w_2)$ and, again, $\succeq_2^s$ determines a plausibility measure $\text{Pl}_2$ on $W_{diag}$. It is not hard to find a probability sequence that gives the same plausibility measure (Exercise 9.1(b)).

$\text{Pl}_1$ and $\text{Pl}_2$ determine structures $M_1$ and $M_2$, respectively, for knowledge and plausibility: $M_i = (W_{diag}, \mathcal{K}_{diag}, \mathcal{PL}_{diag,i}, \pi_{diag})$, where $\mathcal{PL}_{diag,i}(w) = (\mathcal{K}_{diag}(w), \text{Pl}^i_w)$ and $\text{Pl}^i_w(U) = \text{Pl}_i(\mathcal{K}_{diag}(w) \cap U)$, for $i = 1, 2$.

Suppose that the agent makes some observations $o$. In both $M_1$ and $M_2$, if there is a world $w$ compatible with the observations $o$ and $fault(w) = \emptyset$, then the agent believes that the circuit is fault-free. That is, the agent believes the circuit is fault-free as long as her observations are compatible with this hypothesis. If not, then the agent looks for a *minimal explanation* of her observations, where the notion of minimality differs in the two structures. More precisely, if $f$ is a failure set, let $\text{Diag}(f)$ be the formula that says that exactly the failures in $f$ occur, so that $(M, w) \models \text{Diag}(f)$ if and only if $fault(w) = f$. For example, if $f = \{c_1, c_2\}$, then $\text{Diag}(f) = faulty(c_1) \wedge faulty(c_2) \wedge \neg faulty(c_3) \wedge \ldots \wedge \neg faulty(c_n)$. The agent believes that $f$ is a *possible diagnosis* (i.e., an explanation of her observations) in world $w$ of structure $M_i$ if $(M_i, w) \models \neg B \neg \text{Diag}(f)$. The set of diagnoses the agent considers possible is $\text{DIAG}(M, w) = \{f : (M, w) \models \neg B \neg \text{Diag}(f)\}$. A failure set $f$ is *consistent* with an observation $o$ if it is possible to observe $o$ when $f$ occurs, that is, if there is a world $w$ in $W$ such that $fault(w) = f$ and $obs(w) = o$.

**Proposition 9.1.1**

(a) DIAG($M_1$, $w$) contains all failure sets $f$ that are consistent with $obs(w)$ such that there is no failure set $f'$ with $|f'| < |f|$ that is consistent with $obs(w)$.

(b) DIAG($M_2$, $w$) contains all failure sets $f$ that are consistent with $obs(w)$ such that there is no failure set $f'$ with $f' \subset f$ that is consistent with $obs(w)$. (Recall that $\subset$ denotes strict subset.)

**Proof**  See Exercise 9.2.  ∎

Thus, both DIAG($M_1$, $w$) and DIAG($M_2$, $w$) consist of minimal sets of failure sets consistent with $obs(w)$, but for different notions of minimality. In the case of $M_1$, "minimality" means "of minimal cardinality," while in the case of $M_2$, it means "minimal in terms of set containment." More concretely, in the circuit of Figure 9.1, if the agent observes $hi(l_1) \wedge \neg\, hi(l_2) \wedge hi(l_3) \wedge hi(l_7) \wedge \neg\, hi(l_8)$, then in $M_1$ she would believe that $X_1$ is faulty, since $\{X_1\}$ is the only diagnosis with cardinality one. On the other hand, in $M_2$ she would believe that one of the three minimal diagnoses occurred: $\{X_1\}$, $\{X_2, O_1\}$, or $\{X_2, A_2\}$.

The structures $M_i$, $i = 1, 2$, model a static situation. They describe the agent's beliefs given some observations, but do not describe the *process* of belief revision—how those beliefs change in the light of new observations. One way to model the process is to add time to the picture and model the agent and the circuit as part of an interpreted plausibility system. This can be done using a straightforward modification of what was done in the static case.

The first step is to describe the agent's set of local states and the set of environment states. In the spirit of the static model, I assume that the agent sets the value of some lines in the circuit and observes the value of others. Let $o_{(r,m)}$ be a description of what the agent has set/observed in round $m$ of run $r$, where $o_{(r,m)}$ is a conjunction of formulas of the form $hi(l_j)$ and their negations. The form of the agent's local states depends on the answers to some of the same questions that arose in the Listener-Teller protocol of Section 6.7.1. Does the agent remember her observations? If not, what does she remember of them? For simplicity here, I assume that the agent remembers all her observations and makes an additional observation at each round. Given these assumptions, it seems reasonable to model the agent's local state at a point $(r, m)$ as the sequence $\langle o_{(r,1)}, \ldots, o_{(r,m)} \rangle$. Thus, the agent's initial state at $(r, 0)$ is $\langle \, \rangle$, since she has not made any observations; after each round in $r$, a new observation is added.

The environment states play the role of the worlds in the static models; they describe the faulty components of the circuit and the values of all the lines. Thus, I assume that the environment's state at $(r, m)$ is a pair $(fault(r, m), value(r, m))$, where $fault(r, m)$ describes the failure set at the point $(r, m)$ and $value(r, m)$ describes the values of the lines at $(r, m)$. Of course, $o_{(r,m)}$ must be compatible with $value(r, m)$: the values of the lines that the agent observes/sets at $(r, m)$ must be the actual values. (Intuitively, this says that the agents observations are correct and when the agent sets a line's value, it actually has that value.) Moreover, $fault(r, m)$ must be compatible with $value(r, m)$, in the sense discussed earlier: if a component $c$ is not in $fault(r, m)$, then it outputs values according to its specification, while if $c$ is in $fault(r, m)$, then it exhibits its faultiness by not obeying its specification for all inputs. I further assume that the set of faulty components does not change over time; this is captured by assuming $fault(r, m) = fault(r, 0)$ for all $r$ and $m$. On the other hand, I do not assume that the values on the lines are constant over time since, by assumption, the agent can set certain values. Let $\mathcal{R}_{diag}$ consist of all runs $r$ satisfying these requirements.

There are obvious analogues to $Pl_1$ and $Pl_2$ defined on runs; I abuse notation and continue to call these $Pl_1$ and $Pl_2$. For example, to get $Pl_1$, first define a total order $\succeq_1$ on the runs in $\mathcal{R}_{diag}$ by taking $r_1 \succeq_1 r_2$ iff $fault(r_1, 0)) \succeq_1 fault(r_2, 0)$; then $\succeq_1^s$ gives a total order on sets of runs, which can be viewed as a plausibility measure on runs. Similarly, the plausibility measure $Pl_2$ on $\mathcal{R}_{diag}$ is the obvious analogue to $Pl_2$ defined earlier on $W_{diag}$.

$Pl_1$ and $Pl_2$ determine two interpreted plausibility systems whose set of runs in $\mathcal{R}_{diag}$; call them $\mathcal{I}_1$ and $\mathcal{I}_2$. Since $Pl_1$ and $Pl_2$ put plausibility on all of $\mathcal{R}_{diag}$, $\mathcal{I}_1$ and $\mathcal{I}_2$ are actually SDP systems (see Section 6.4). In each system, the agent believes that the failure set is one of the ones that provides a minimal explanation for her observations, where the notion of minimal depends on the plausibility measure. As the agent performs more tests, her knowledge increases and her beliefs might change.

Let $DIAG(\mathcal{I}, r, m)$ be the set of failure sets (i.e., diagnoses) that the agent considers possible at the point $(r, m)$ in the system $\mathcal{I}$. Belief change in $\mathcal{I}_1$ is characterized by the following proposition, similar in spirit to Proposition 9.1.1:

**Proposition 9.1.2**  *If there is some $f \in DIAG(\mathcal{I}_1, r, m)$ that is consistent with the new observation $o_{(r,m+1)}$, then $DIAG(\mathcal{I}_1, r, m + 1)$ consists of all the failure sets in $DIAG(\mathcal{I}_1, r, m)$ that are consistent with $o_{(r,m+1)}$. If all $f \in Bel(\mathcal{I}_1, r, m)$ are inconsistent with $o_{(r,m+1)}$, then $Bel(\mathcal{I}_1, r, m + 1)$ consists of all failure sets of cardinality $j$ that are consistent with $o_{(r,m+1)}$, where $j$ is the least cardinality for which there is at least one failure set consistent with $o_{(r,m+1)}$.*

**Proof**  See Exercise 9.3.  ∎

Thus, in $\mathfrak{I}_1$, if an observation is consistent with the pre-observation set of most likely explanations, then the post-observation set of most likely explanations is a subset of the pre-observation set of most likely explanations (the subset consisting of those explanations that are consistent with the new observation). On the other hand, a surprising observation (one inconsistent with the current set of most likely explanations) has a rather drastic effect. It easily follows from Proposition 9.1.2 that if $o_{(r,m+1)}$ is surprising, then $\text{DIAG}(\mathfrak{I}_1, r, m) \cap \text{DIAG}(\mathfrak{I}_1, r, m + 1) = \emptyset$, so the agent discards all her pre-observation explanations. Moreover, an easy induction on $m$ shows that if $\text{DIAG}(\mathfrak{I}_1, r, m) \cap \text{DIAG}(\mathfrak{I}_1, r, m + 1) = \emptyset$, then the cardinality of the failure sets in $\text{DIAG}(\mathfrak{I}_1, r, m + 1)$ is greater than the cardinality of the failure sets in $\text{DIAG}(\mathfrak{I}_1, r, m)$. Thus, in this case, the explanations in $\text{DIAG}(\mathfrak{I}_1, r, m + 1)$ are more "complicated" than those in $\text{Bel}(\mathfrak{I}_1, r, m)$, in the sense that they involve more failures.

Belief change in $\mathfrak{I}_2$ is quite different, as the following proposition shows. Roughly speaking, it says that after making an observation, the agent believes possible all minimal extensions of the diagnoses she believed possible before making the observation.

**Proposition 9.1.3**   $\text{DIAG}(\mathfrak{I}_2, r, m + 1)$ consists of the minimal (according to $\subseteq$) failure sets in $\{ f' : f' \supseteq f$ for some $f \in \text{DIAG}(\mathfrak{I}_2, r, m)\}$ that are consistent with $o_{(r,m+1)}$.

**Proof**   See Exercise 9.4.   ∎

As with $\mathfrak{I}_1$, diagnoses that are consistent with the new observation are retained. However, unlike $\mathfrak{I}_1$, diagnoses that are discarded are replaced by more complicated diagnoses even if some of the diagnoses considered at $(r, m)$ are consistent with the new observation. Moreover, while new diagnoses in $\text{DIAG}(\mathfrak{I}_1, r, m + 1)$ can be unrelated to the diagnoses in $\text{DIAG}(\mathfrak{I}_1, r, m)$, in $\mathfrak{I}_2$ the new diagnoses must be extensions of some discarded diagnoses. Thus, in $\mathfrak{I}_1$ the agent does not consider new diagnoses as long as the observation is not surprising. On the other hand, in $\mathfrak{I}_2$ the agent has to examine new candidates after each test.

This point is perhaps best understood by example.

**Example 9.1.4**   Suppose that in the circuit of Figure 9.1, the agent initially sets $l_1 = 1$ and $l_2 = l_3 = 0$. If there were no failures, then $l_4$ and $l_7$ would be 1, while, $l_5, l_6$, and $l_8$ would be 0. But if the agent observes that $l_8$ is 1, then in both systems the agent would believe that exactly one of $X_1, A_1, A_2$, or $O_1$ was faulty; that would be the minimal explanation of the problem, under both notions of minimality. Now suppose that the agent later observes that $l_7 = 0$ while all the other settings remain the same. In that case, the only possible diagnosis according to $\text{Pl}_1$ is that $X_1$ is faulty. This is also a possible diagnosis according to $\text{Pl}_2$, but there are three others, formed by taking $X_2$

and one of $A_1$, $A_2$, or $O_1$. Thus, even though a diagnosis considered possible after the first observation—that $X_1$ is faulty—is consistent with the second observation, some new diagnoses (all extensions of the diagnoses considered after the first observation) are also considered.  ∎

## 9.2   Belief-Change Systems

It will be convenient for the remainder of this chapter to focus on a class of interpreted plausibility systems called *belief-change systems,* or just BCSs. BCSs will make it easier to relate the view of belief revision as conditioning with the more traditional view in the literature, where belief revision is characterized by postulates on beliefs as represented by sets of formulas. In BCSs, an agent makes observations about an external environment. As in the analysis of circuit-diagnosis problem, I assume that these observations are described by formulas in some logical language, since this is the traditional approach. I further assume that the agent does not forget, so that her local state can be characterized by the sequence of observations she has made. (This is in the spirit of one of the ways taken to model the Listener-Teller protocol in Section 6.7.1. Recall that when this is not done, conditioning is not appropriate.) Finally, I assume that the agent starts with a prior plausibility on runs, so that the techniques of Section 6.4 can be used to construct a plausibility assignment. This means that the agent's plausibility at a given point can essentially be obtained by conditioning the prior plausibility on her information at that point. These assumptions are formalized by conditions BCS1 and BCS2, described later.

   To state these conditions, I need some notation and a definition. The notation that I need is much in the spirit of that introduced in Section 6.8. Let $\mathcal{I} = (\mathcal{R}, \mathcal{PL}, \pi)$ be an interpreted plausibility system and let $\Phi$ be the set of primitive propositions whose truth values are determined by $\pi$. Given a formula $\phi \in \mathcal{L}^{Prop}(\Phi)$, let $\mathcal{R}[\phi]$ consist of all runs $r \in \mathcal{R}$ where $\phi$ is true initially; given a local state $\ell = \langle o_1, \ldots, o_k \rangle$, let $\mathcal{R}[\ell]$ consist of all runs $r$ where the agent is in local state $\ell$ at some point in $r$. Formally,

$$\mathcal{R}[\phi] = \{r \in \mathcal{I} : (\mathcal{I}, r, 0) \models \phi\} \text{ and}$$
$$\mathcal{R}[\ell] = \{r \in \mathcal{I} : r_a(k) = \ell \text{ for some } k \geq 0\}.$$

   A primitive proposition $p$ *depends only on the environment state* in $\mathcal{I}$ if $\pi(r, m)(p) = $ **true** iff $\pi(r', m')(p) = $ **true** for all points $(r', m')$ such that $r_e(m) = r'_e(m')$. Note that in the case of the interpretations used to capture the circuit-diagnosis problem, all the primitive propositions in $\Phi_{diag}$ depend only on the environment in both $\mathcal{I}_1$ and $\mathcal{I}_2$.

$\mathcal{J}$ is a *belief-change system* if the following two conditions hold:

BCS1. There exists a set $\Phi_e \subseteq \Phi$ of primitive propositions that depend only on the environment state such that for all $r \in R$ and for all $m$, the agent's local state is $r_a(m) = \langle o_{(r,1)}, \ldots, o_{(r,m)} \rangle$, where $o_{(r,k)} \in \mathcal{L}_e = \mathcal{L}^{Prop}(\Phi_e)$ for $1 \leq k \leq m$. (I have used $r_a$ to denote the agent's local state rather than $r_1$, to stress that there is a single agent.)

BCS2. $\mathcal{J}$ is an interpreted SDP system. Recall that means that there is a prior conditional plausibility measure $\text{Pl}_a$ on the runs in $\mathcal{J}$ and that the agent's plausibility space at each point is generated by conditioning, using the techniques described in Section 6.4. Moreover, the prior conditional plausibility space $(\mathcal{R}, \mathcal{F}, \mathcal{F}', \text{Pl}_a)$ has the following properties:

- $\text{Pl}_a$ satisfies CPl5, Pl4, and Pl5 (i.e., $\text{Pl}_a$ satisfies CPl5 and for all sets $U$ of runs in $\mathcal{F}'$, $\text{Pl}_a(\cdot \mid U)$ satisfies Pl4 and Pl5);

- $\mathcal{R}[\ell] \in \mathcal{F}'$ for all local states $\ell$ such that $\mathcal{R}[\ell] \neq \emptyset$;

- $\mathcal{R}[\phi] \in \mathcal{F}$ for all $\phi \in \mathcal{L}_e$;

- if $U \in \mathcal{F}'$ and $\text{Pl}_a(V \mid U) > \perp$, then $V \cap U \in \mathcal{F}'$.

BCS1 says that the agent's observations are formulas in $\mathcal{L}_e$ and that her local state consists of the sequence of observations she has made. Since BCS1 requires that the agent has made $m$ observations by time $m$, it follows that her local state effectively encodes the time. Thus, a BCS is a synchronous system where the agent has perfect recall. This is quite a strong assumption. The perfect recall is needed for conditioning to be appropriate (see the discussion in Sections 3.1 and 6.8). The assumption that the system is synchronous is not so critical; it is made mainly for convenience. The fact that the agent's observations can all be described by formulas in $\mathcal{L}_e$ says that $\mathcal{L}_e$ may have to be a rather expressive language or that the observations are rather restricted. In the case of an agent observing a circuit, $\Phi_e = \Phi_{diag}$, so I implicitly assumed the latter; the only observations were the values of various lines. However, in the case of agents observing people, the observations can include obvious features such as eye color and skin color, as well as more subtle features like facial expressions. Even getting a language rich enough to describe all the gradations of eye and skin color is nontrivial; things become much harder when facial expressions are added to the mix. In any case, $\mathcal{L}_e$ must be expressive enough to describe whatever can be observed. This assumption is not just an artifact of using formulas to express observations. No matter how the observations are expressed, the environment state must be rich enough to distinguish the observations.

BCS2 says that the agent starts with a single prior plausibility on all runs. This makes the system an SDP system. It would also be possible to consider systems where the set of runs was partitioned, with a separate plausibility measure on each set in the partition, as in Section 6.9, but that would complicate the analysis. The fact that the prior satisfies Pl4 and Pl5 means that belief in $\mathsf{J}$ behaves in a reasonable way; the fact that it also satisfies CPl5 means that certain natural coherence properties hold between various conditional plausibility measures. The assumption that $\mathcal{R}[\ell] \in \mathcal{F}'$ is the analogue of the assumption made in Section 6.4 that $\mu_{\mathcal{R},i}(\mathcal{R}_{r,m,i}) > 0$; it makes it possible to define the agent's plausibility measure at a point $(r, m)$ to be the result of conditioning her prior on her information at $(r, m)$.

Just as in the case of probability (see Exercise 6.5), in an (interpreted) SDP plausibility system, the agent's plausibility space at each point satisfies the SDP property. Moreover, if the prior satisfies Pl4 and Pl5, so does the plausibility space at each point (Exercise 9.5). It follows from Proposition 8.2.1(b) that the agent's beliefs depend only on the agent's local state. That is, at any two points where the agent has the same local state, she has the same beliefs. I use the notation $(\mathsf{J}, s_a) \models B\phi$ as shorthand for $(\mathsf{J}, r, m) \models B\phi$ for some (and hence for all) $(r, m)$ such that $r_a(m) = s_a$. The agent's *belief set* at $s_a$ is the set of formulas that the agent believes at $s_a$, that is,

$$\text{Bel}(\mathsf{J}, s_a) = \{\phi \in \Phi_e : (\mathsf{J}, s_a) \models B\phi\}.$$

Since the agent's state is a sequence of observations, the agent's state after observing $\phi$ is simply $s_a \cdot \phi$, where $\cdot$ is the append operation. Thus, $\text{Bel}(\mathsf{J}, s_a \cdot \phi)$ is the belief set after observing $\phi$. I adopt the convention that if there is no point where the agent has local state $s_a$ in system $\mathsf{J}$, then $\text{Bel}(\mathsf{J}, s_a)$ consists of all the propositional formulas over $\Phi_e$. With these definitions, the agent's belief set before and after observing $\phi$— that is, $\text{Bel}(\mathsf{J}, s_a)$ and $\text{Bel}(\mathsf{J}, s_a \cdot \phi)$—can be compared. Thus, a BCS can conveniently express (properties of) belief change in terms of formulas. The agent's state encodes observations, which are formulas in the language, and there are formulas that talk about what the agent believes and how the agent's beliefs change over time.

There is one other requirement that is standard in many approaches to belief change considered in the literature: that observations are "accepted," so that after the agent observes $\phi$, she believes $\phi$. This requirement is enforced by the next assumption, BCS3. BCS3 says that observations are reliable, so that the agent observes $\phi$ only if the current state of the environment satisfies $\phi$.

BCS3. $(\mathsf{J}, r, m) \models o_{(r,m)}$ for all runs $r$ and times $m$.

Note that BCS3 implies that the agent never observes *false*. Moreover, it implies that after observing $\phi$, the agent knows that $\phi$ is true. A system that satisfies BCS1–3 is said to be a *reliable BCS*.

It is easy to check that $\mathfrak{I}_1$ and $\mathfrak{I}_2$ are both reliable BCSs.

## 9.3   Belief Revision

The most common approach to studying belief change in the literature has been the ax-iomatic approach. This has typically involved starting with a collection of postulates, arguing that they are reasonable, and proving some consequences of these postulates. Perhaps the most-studied postulates are the *AGM postulates,* named after the researchers who introduced them: Alchourrón, Gärdenfors, and Makinson. These axioms are in-tended to characterize a particular type of belief change, called *belief revision*.

As I have suggested, in this approach, the agent's beliefs are represented by a set of formulas and what the agent observes is represented by a formula. More precisely, the AGM approach assumes that an agent's epistemic state is represented by a *belief set,* that is, a set $K$ of formulas in a logical language $\mathcal{L}$, describing the subject matter about which the agent holds beliefs. For simplicity here, I assume that $\mathcal{L}$ is propositional (which is consistent with most of the discussions of the postulates). In the background, there are also assumed to be some axioms $\mathrm{AX}_{\mathcal{L}}$ characterizing the situation. For example, for the circuit-diagnosis example of Figure 9.1, $\mathcal{L}$ could be $\mathcal{L}^{Prop}(\Phi_{diag})$. There would then be an axiom in $\mathrm{AX}_{\mathcal{L}}$ saying that if $A_1$ is not faulty, then $l_5$ is 1 iff both $l_1$ and $l_2$ are:

$$\neg\, faulty(A_1) \Rightarrow (hi(l_5) \Leftrightarrow (hi(l_1) \wedge hi(l_2))).$$

Similar axioms would be used to characterize all the other components.

Let $\vdash_{\mathcal{L}}$ denote the *consequence relation* that characterizes provability from $\mathrm{AX}_{\mathcal{L}}$; $\Sigma \vdash_{\mathcal{L}} \phi$ holds iff $\phi$ is provable from $\Sigma$ and the axioms in $\mathrm{AX}_{\mathcal{L}}$, using propositional reasoning (Prop and MP). $\mathrm{Cl}(\Sigma)$ denotes the logical closure of the set $\Sigma$ under $\mathrm{AX}_{\mathcal{L}}$; that is, $\mathrm{Cl}(\Sigma) = \{\phi : \Sigma \vdash_{\mathcal{L}} \phi\}$. I assume, in keeping with most of the literature on belief change, that belief sets are closed under logical consequence, so that if $K$ is a belief set, then $\mathrm{Cl}(K) = K$. This assumption can be viewed as saying that agents are being treated as perfect reasoners who can compute all logical consequences of their beliefs. But even if agents are perfect reasoners, there may be good reason to separate the core of an agent's beliefs from those beliefs that are derived from the core. Consider the second example discussed at the beginning of the chapter, where the agent initially believes $\phi_1$ and thus also believes $\phi_1 \vee p$. If he later learns that $\phi_1$ is false, it may be useful to somehow encode that the only reason he originally believed $\phi_1 \vee p$ is because of his belief in $\phi_1$. This information may certainly affect how his beliefs change. Although I do not pursue this issue further here, it is currently an active area of research.

What the agent learns is assumed to be characterized by some formula $\phi$, also in $\mathcal{L}$; $K \circ \phi$ describes the belief set of an agent who starts with belief set $K$ and learns $\phi$. Two subtle but important assumptions are implicit in this notation:

- The functional form of $\circ$ suggests that all that matters regarding how an agent revises her beliefs is the belief set and what is learned. In any two situations where the agent has the same beliefs, she will revise her beliefs in the same way.

- The notation also suggests that the second argument of $\circ$ can be an arbitrary formula in $\mathcal{L}$ and the first can be an arbitrary belief set.

These are nontrivial assumptions. With regard to the first one, it is quite possible for two different plausibility measures to result in the same belief sets and yet behave differently under conditioning, leading to different belief sets after revision. With regard to the second one, at a minimum, it is not clear what it would mean to observe *false*. (It is perfectly reasonable to observe something inconsistent with one's current beliefs, but that is quite different from observing *false*, which is a contradictory formula.) Similarly, it is not clear how reasonable it is to consider an agent whose belief set is Cl(*false*), the trivial belief set consisting of all formulas. But even putting this issue aside, it may not be desirable to allow every consistent formula to be observed in every circumstance. For example, in the circuit-diagnosis problem, the agent does not observe the behavior of a component directly; she can only infer it by setting the values of some lines and observing the values of others. While some observations are essentially equivalent to observing that a particular component is faulty (e.g., if setting $l_1$ to 1 and $l_2$ to 1 results in $l_5$ being 0 in the circuit of Figure 9.1, then $A_1$ must be faulty), no observations can definitively rule out a component being faulty (the faulty behavior may display itself only sporadically).

Indeed, in general, what is observable may depend on the belief set itself. Consider a situation where an agent can reliably observe colors. After observing that a coat is blue (and thus, having this fact in her belief set), it may not be possible for her to observe that the same coat is red.

The impact of these assumptions will be apparent shortly. For now, I simply state the eight postulates used by Alchourrón, Gärdenfors, and Makinson to characterize belief revision.

R1.     $K \circ \phi$ is a belief set.

R2.     $\phi \in K \circ \phi$.

R3.    $K \circ \phi \subseteq Cl(K \cup \{\phi\})$.

R4.    If $\neg\phi \notin K$, then $Cl(K \cup \{\phi\}) \subseteq K \circ \phi$.

R5.    $K \circ \phi = Cl(false)$ iff $\vdash_{\mathcal{L}} \neg\phi$.

R6.    If $\vdash_{\mathcal{L}} \phi \Leftrightarrow \psi$, then $K \circ \phi = K \circ \psi$.

R7.    $K \circ (\phi \wedge \psi) \subseteq Cl(K \circ \phi \cup \{\psi\})$.

R8.    If $\neg\psi \notin K \circ \phi$, then $Cl(K \circ \phi \cup \{\psi\}) \subseteq K \circ (\phi \wedge \psi)$.

Where do these postulates come from and why are they reasonable? It is hard to do them justice in just a few paragraphs, but the following comments may help:

- R1 says that ∘ maps a belief set and a formula to a belief set. As I said earlier, it implicitly assumes that the first argument of ∘ can be an arbitrary belief set and the second argument can be an arbitrary formula.

- R2 says that the belief set that results after revising by $\phi$ includes $\phi$. Now it is certainly not true in general that when an agent observes $\phi$ she necessarily believes $\phi$. After all, if $\phi$ represents a somewhat surprising observation, then she may think that her observation was unreliable. This certainly happens in science; experiments are often repeated to confirm the results. This suggests that perhaps these postulates are appropriate only when revising by formulas that have been accepted in some sense, that is, formulas that the agent surely wants to include in her belief set. Under this interpretation, R2 should certainly hold.

- R3 and R4 together say that if $\phi$ is consistent with the agent's current beliefs, then the revision should not remove any of the old beliefs or add any new beliefs except these implied by the combination of the old beliefs with the new belief. This property certainly holds for the simple notion of conditioning knowledge by intersecting the old set of possible worlds with the set of worlds characterizing the formula observed, along the lines discussed in Section 3.1. It also is easily seen to hold if belief is interpreted as "holds with probability 1" and revision proceeds by conditioning. The formulas that hold with probability 1 after conditioning on $\phi$ are precisely those that follow from $\phi$ together with the formulas that held before. Should this hold for all notions of belief? As the later discussion shows, not necessarily. Note that R3 and R4 are vacuous if $\neg\phi \in K$ (in the case of R3, this is because, in that case, $Cl(K \cup \{\phi\})$ consists of all formulas). Moreover, note that in the presence of R1 and R2, R4 can be simplified to just $K \subseteq K \circ \phi$, since

R2 already guarantees that $\phi \in K \circ \phi$, and R1 guarantees that $K \circ \phi$ is a belief set, hence a closed set of beliefs.

- Postulate R5 discusses situations that I believe, in fact, should not even be considered. As I hinted at earlier, I am not sure that it is even appropriate to consider the trivial belief set Cl(*false*), nor is it appropriate to revise by *false* (or any formula logically equivalent to it; i.e., a formula $\phi$ such that $\vdash_{\mathcal{L}} \neg\phi$). If the trivial belief and revising by contradictory formulas were disallowed, then R5 would really be saying nothing more than R1. If revising by contradictory formulas is allowed, then taking $K \circ \phi = $ Cl(*false*) does seem reasonable if $\phi$ is contradictory, but it is less clear what Cl(*false*) $\circ \phi$ should be if $\phi$ is not contradictory. R5 requires that it be a consistent belief set, but why should this be so? It seems just as reasonable that, if an agent ever has incoherent beliefs, then she should continue to have them no matter what she observes.

- R6 states that the syntactic form of the new belief does not affect the revision process; it is much in the spirit of the rule LLE in system **P** from Section 8.3. Although this property holds for all the notions of belief change I consider here, it is worth stressing that this postulate is surely not descriptively accurate. People do react differently to equivalent formulas (especially since it is hard for them to tell that they are equivalent; this is a problem that is, in general, co-NP complete).

- Postulates R7 and R8 can be viewed as analogues of R3 and R4 for iterated revision. Note that, by R3 and R4, if $\psi$ is consistent with $K \circ \phi$ (i.e., if $\neg\psi \notin K \circ \phi$), then $(K \circ \phi) \circ \psi = $ Cl($K \circ \phi \cup \{\psi\}$). Thus, R7 and R8 are saying that if $\psi$ is consistent with $K \circ \phi$, then $K \circ (\phi \wedge \psi) = (K \circ \phi) \circ \psi$. As we have seen, this is a property satisfied by probabilistic conditioning: if $\mu(U_1 \cap U_2) \neq 0$, then $(\mu|U_1)|U_2 = (\mu|U_2)|U_1 = \mu|(U_1 \cap U_2)$.

As the following example shows, conditional probability measures provide a model for the AGM postulates:

**Example 9.3.1**  Fix a finite set $\Phi$ of primitive propositions. Let $\vdash_{\mathcal{L}}$ be a consequence relation for the language $\mathcal{L}^{Prop}(\Phi)$. Since $\Phi$ is finite, $\vdash_{\mathcal{L}}$ can be characterized by a single formula $\sigma \in \mathcal{L}^{Prop}(\Phi)$; that is, $\vdash_{\mathcal{L}} \phi$ iff $\sigma \Rightarrow \phi$ is a propositional tautology (Exercise 9.7(a)). Let $M = (W, 2^W, 2^W - \emptyset, \mu, \pi)$ be a simple conditional probability structure, where $\pi$ is such that (a) $(M, w) \models \sigma$ for all $w \in W$ and (b) if $\sigma \wedge \psi$ is satisfiable, then there is some world $w \in W$ such that $(M, w) \models \psi$. Let $K$ consist of all the formulas to which the agent assigns unconditional probability 1; that is, $K = \{\psi : \mu(\llbracket \psi \rrbracket_M) = 1\}$. If $\llbracket \phi \rrbracket_M \neq \emptyset$, define $K \circ \phi = \{\psi : \mu(\llbracket \psi \rrbracket_M \mid \llbracket \phi \rrbracket_M) = 1\}$.

That is, the belief set obtained after revising by $\phi$ consists of just those formulas whose conditional probability is 1; if $[\![\phi]\!]_M = \emptyset$, define $K \circ \phi = Cl(false)$. It can be checked that this definition of revision satisfies R1–8 (Exercise 9.7(b)). Moreover, disregarding the case where $K = Cl(false)$ (a case I would argue should never arise, since an agent should also have consistent beliefs), then every belief revision operator can in a precise sense be captured this way (Exercise 9.7(c)). ∎

The fact that the AGM postulates can be captured by using conditional probability, treating revision as conditioning, lends support to the general view of revision as conditioning. However, conditional probability is just one of the methods considered in Section 8.3 for giving semantics to defaults as conditional beliefs. Can all the other approaches considered in that section also serve as models for the AGM postulates? It turns out that ranking functions and possibility measures can, but arbitrary preferential orders cannot. My goal now is to understand what properties of conditional probability make it an appropriate model for the AGM postulates. As a first step, I relate AGM revision to BCSs. More precisely, the plan is to find some additional conditions (REV1–3) on BCSs that ensure that belief change in a BCS satisfies R1–8. Doing this will help bring out the assumptions implicit in the AGM approach.

The first assumption is that, although the agent's beliefs may change, the propositions about which the agent has beliefs do not change during the revision process. The original motivation for belief revision came from the study of scientists' beliefs about laws of nature. These laws were taken to be unvarying, although experimental evidence might cause scientists to change their beliefs about the laws.

This assumption underlies R3 and R4. If $\phi$ is consistent with $K$, then according to R3 and R4, observing $\phi$ should result in the agent adding $\phi$ to her stock of beliefs and then closing off under implication. In particular, this means that all her old beliefs are retained. But if the world can change, then there is no reason for the agent to retain her old beliefs. Consider the systems $\mathfrak{I}_1$ and $\mathfrak{I}_2$ used to model the diagnosis problem. In these systems, the values on the line could change at each step. If $l_1 = 1$ before observing $l_2 = 1$, then why should $l_1 = 1$ after the observation, even if it is consistent with the observation that $l_2 = 1$? Perhaps if $l_1$ is not set to 1, its value goes to 0.

In any case, it is easy to capture the assumption that the propositions observed do not change their truth value. That is the role of REV1.

REV1.  $\pi(r, m)(p) = \pi(r, 0)(p)$ for all $p \in \Phi_e$ and points $(r, m)$.

Note that REV1 does not say that all propositions are time invariant, nor that the environment state does not change over time. It simply says that the propositions in $\Phi_e$ do not change their truth value over time. Since the formulas being observed are, by assumption, in $\mathcal{L}_e$, and so are Boolean combinations of the primitive propositions in $\Phi_e$, their truth values also do not change over time. In the model in Example 9.3.1, there is no need to state REV1 explicitly, since there is only one time step. Considering only one time step simplifies things, but the simplification sometimes disguises the subtleties.

In the BCSs $\mathfrak{I}_1$ and $\mathfrak{I}_2$, propositions of the form *faulty(c)* do not change their truth value over time, by assumption; however, propositions of the form *hi(l)* do. There is a slight modification of these systems that does satisfy REV1. The idea is to take $\mathcal{L}_e$ to consist only of Boolean combinations of formulas of the form *faulty(c)* and then convert the agent's observations to formulas in $\mathcal{L}_e$. Note that to every observation $o$ made by the agent regarding the value of the lines, there corresponds a formula in $\mathcal{L}_e$ that characterizes all the fault sets that are consistent with $o$. For example, the observation $hi(l_1) \wedge hi(l_2) \wedge hi(l_4)$ corresponds to the conjunction of the formulas characterizing all fault sets that include $X_1$ (which is equivalent to the formula *faulty(X_1)*). For every observation $\phi$ about the value of lines, let $\phi^\dagger \in \mathcal{L}_e$ be the corresponding observation regarding fault sets. Given a run $r \in \mathfrak{I}_i$, $i = 1, 2$, let $r^\dagger$ be the run where each observation $\phi$ is replaced by $\phi^\dagger$. Let $\mathfrak{I}_i^\dagger$ be the BCS consisting of all the runs $r^\dagger$ corresponding to the runs in $\mathfrak{I}_i$. The plausibility assignments in $\mathfrak{I}_i^\dagger$ and $\mathfrak{I}_i$ correspond in the obvious way. That means that the agent has the same beliefs about formulas in $\mathcal{L}_e$ at corresponding points in the two systems. More precisely, if $\phi \in \mathcal{L}_e$, then $(\mathfrak{I}_i^\dagger, r^\dagger, m) \models \phi$ if and only if $(\mathfrak{I}_i, r, m) \models \phi$ for all points $(r, m)$ in $\mathfrak{I}_i$. Hence, $(\mathfrak{I}_i^\dagger, r^\dagger, m) \models B\phi$ if and only if $(\mathfrak{I}_i, r, m) \models B\phi$. By construction, $\mathfrak{I}_i^\dagger$, $i = 1, 2$, are BCSs that satisfy REV1.

Belief change in $\mathfrak{I}_1^\dagger$ can be shown to satisfy all of R1–8 in a precise sense (see Theorem 9.3.5 and Exercise 9.11); however, $\mathfrak{I}_2^\dagger$ does not satisfy either R4 or R8, as the following example shows:

**Example 9.3.2**   Consider Example 9.1.4 again. Initially (before making any observations) that agent believes that no components are faulty. Recall that the agent sets $l_1 = l$ and $l_2 = l_3 = 0$, then observes that $l_8$ is 1. That is, the agent observes $\phi = \neg\, hi(l_1) \wedge \neg\, hi(l_2) \wedge hi(l_3)$. It is easy to see that $\phi^\dagger$ is *faulty(X_1)* $\vee$ *faulty(A_1)* $\vee$ *faulty(A_2)* $\vee$ *faulty(O_1)*. Since the agent prefers minimal explanations, $Bel(\mathfrak{I}_2^\dagger, \langle \phi^\dagger \rangle)$ includes the belief that exactly one of $X_1$, $A_1$, $A_2$, or $O_1$ is faulty. Let $K = Bel(\mathfrak{I}_2^\dagger, \langle\, \rangle)$. Think of $Bel(\mathfrak{I}_2^\dagger, \langle \phi^\dagger \rangle)$ as $K \circ \phi^\dagger$. Suppose that the agent then observes $l_7$ is 0, that is, the agent observes $\psi = \neg\, hi(l_7))$. Now $\psi^\dagger$ says that the fault set contains $X_1$ or contains both $X_2$ and one of $A_1$, $A_2$, or $O_1$. Notice that $\psi^\dagger$ implies $\phi^\dagger$. Thus, $Bel(\mathfrak{I}_2^\dagger, \langle \phi^\dagger, \psi^\dagger \rangle) = Bel(\mathfrak{I}_2^\dagger, \langle \phi^\dagger \wedge \psi^\dagger \rangle) = Bel(\mathfrak{I}_2^\dagger, \langle \psi^\dagger \rangle)$. That means that $(K \circ \phi^\dagger) \circ \psi^\dagger = \mathcal{K} \circ (\phi^\dagger \wedge \psi^\dagger)$, and this belief set consists of the belief that the fault set is exactly one of $X_1$, $\{X_2, A_1\}$, $\{X_2, A_2\}$, and $\{X_2, O_1\}$, and all of the consequences of this belief. On the other hand, it is a consequence of $K \circ \phi^\dagger \cup \{\psi^\dagger\}$ that $X_1$ is the only fault. Thus,

$$K \circ \phi^\dagger \cup \{\psi^\dagger\} \not\subseteq (K \circ \phi^\dagger) \circ \psi^\dagger = \mathcal{K} \circ (\phi^\dagger \wedge \psi^\dagger),$$

showing that neither R4 nor R8 holds in $\mathcal{I}_2^\dagger$.  ∎

Why do R4 and R8 hold in $\mathcal{I}_1^\dagger$ and not in $\mathcal{I}_2^\dagger$? It turns out that the key reason is that the plausibility measure in $\mathcal{I}_1^\dagger$ is totally ordered; in $\mathcal{I}_2^\dagger$ it is only partially ordered. In fact, I show shortly that R4 and R8 are just Rational Monotonicity in disguise. (Recall that Rational Monotonicity is axiom C5 in Section 8.6, the axiom that essentially captures the fact that the plausibility measure is totally ordered.) REV2 strengthens BCS2 to ensure that Rational Monotonicity holds for $\rightarrow$.

REV2.  The conditional plausibility measure $\text{Pl}_a$ on runs that is guaranteed to exist by BCS2 satisfies Pl6 (or, equivalently, Pl7 and Pl8; see Section 8.6); more precisely, $\text{Pl}(\cdot \mid U)$ satisfies Pl6 for all sets $U$ of runs in $\mathcal{F}'$.

Another condition on BCSs required to make belief change satisfy R1–8 makes precise the intuition that observing $\phi$ does not give any information beyond $\phi$. As Example 3.1.2 and the discussion in Section 6.8 show, without this assumption, conditioning is not appropriate. To see the need for this assumption in the context of belief revision, consider the following example:

**Example 9.3.3**  Suppose that $\mathcal{I}$ is a BCS such that $\text{Bel}(\mathcal{I}, \langle \rangle) = \text{Cl}(p)$. Moreover, in $\mathcal{I}$, the agent observes $q$ at time 0 only if $p$ is false and both $p'$ and $q$ are true. It is easy to construct a BCS satisfying REV1 and REV2 that also satisfies this requirement (Exercise 9.8). Thus, after observing $q$, the agent believes $\neg p \wedge p' \wedge q$. It follows that neither R3 nor R4 hold in $\mathcal{I}$. Indeed, taking $K = \text{Cl}(p)$, the fact that $p' \in K \circ q$ means that $K \circ q \not\subseteq \text{Cl}(K \cup \{q\})$, violating R3, and the fact that $\neg p \in K \circ q$ means that $K \not\subseteq K \circ q$ (for otherwise $K \circ q$ would be inconsistent, and all belief sets in a BCS are consistent), violating R4. With a little more effort, it is possible to construct a BCS that satisfies REV1 and REV2 and violates R7 and R8 (Exercise 9.8)  ∎

The assumption that observations do not give additional information is captured by REV3 in much the same way as was done in the probabilistic case in Section 6.8.

REV3.  If $s_a \cdot \phi$ is a local state in $\mathcal{I}$ and $\psi \in \mathcal{L}^{Prop}(\Phi_e)$, then $\mathcal{R}[s_a] \cap \mathcal{R}[\phi] \in \mathcal{F}'$ and $\text{Pl}_a(\mathcal{R}[\psi] \mid \mathcal{R}[s_a \cdot \phi]) = \text{Pl}_a(\mathcal{R}[\psi] \mid \mathcal{R}[s_a] \cap \mathcal{R}[\phi])$.

(The requirement that $\mathcal{R}[s_a] \cap \mathcal{R}[\phi] \in \mathcal{F}'$ in fact follows from BCS1–3; see Exercise 9.9.) The need for REV3 is obscured if no distinction is made between $\phi$ being true and the agent observing $\phi$. This distinction is quite explicit in the BCS framework. Note that REV3 does not require that $\mathrm{Pl}_{a'}(\cdot \mid \mathcal{R}[s_a \cdot \phi]) = \mathrm{Pl}_a(\cdot \mid \mathcal{R}[s_a] \cap \mathcal{R}[\phi])$. It makes the somewhat weaker requirement that $\mathrm{Pl}_a(\mathcal{R}' \mid \mathcal{R}[s_a \cdot \phi]) = \mathrm{Pl}_a(\mathcal{R}' \mid \mathcal{R}[s_a] \cap \mathcal{R}[\phi])$ only if $\mathcal{R}'$ is a set of runs of the form $\mathcal{R}[\psi]$ for some formula $\psi \in \mathcal{L}^{Prop}(\Phi_e)$.

It is not hard to see that REV3 fails in the BCS $\mathcal{J}$ constructed in Example 9.3.3. For suppose that $\mathrm{Pl}_a$ is the prior plausibility in $\mathcal{J}$. By assumption, in $\mathcal{J}$, after observing $p_1$, the agent believes $p_2$ and $q$, but after observing $p_1 \wedge p_2$, the agent believes $\neg q$. Thus,

$$\mathrm{Pl}_a(\mathcal{R}[p_2 \wedge q] \mid \mathcal{R}[\langle p_1 \rangle]) > \mathrm{Pl}_a(\mathcal{R}[\neg(p_2 \wedge q)] \mid \mathcal{R}[\langle p_1 \rangle]) \tag{9.1}$$

and

$$\mathrm{Pl}_a(\mathcal{R}[\neg q] \mid \mathcal{R}[\langle p_1 \wedge p_2 \rangle]) > \mathrm{Pl}_a(\mathcal{R}[q] \mid \mathcal{R}[\langle p_1 \wedge p_2 \rangle]). \tag{9.2}$$

If REV3 held, then (9.1) and (9.2) would imply

$$\mathrm{Pl}_a(\mathcal{R}[p_2 \wedge q] \mid \mathcal{R}[p_1]) > \mathrm{Pl}_a(\mathcal{R}[\neg(p_2 \wedge q)] \mid \mathcal{R}[p_1]) \tag{9.3}$$

and

$$\mathrm{Pl}_a(\mathcal{R}[\neg q] \mid \mathcal{R}[p_1 \wedge p_2]) > \mathrm{Pl}_a(\mathcal{R}[q] \mid \mathcal{R}[p_1 \wedge p_2]). \tag{9.4}$$

From (9.3), it follows that $\mathrm{Pl}_a(\mathcal{R}[p_2] \mid \mathcal{R}[p_1]) > \mathrm{Pl}_a(\mathcal{R}[p_2 \wedge q] \mid \mathcal{R}[p_1]) > \bot$, so by CPl5 (which holds in $\mathcal{J}$ by BCS2) applied to (9.4), it follows that

$$\mathrm{Pl}_a(\mathcal{R}[p_2 \wedge \neg q] \mid \mathcal{R}[p_1]) > \mathrm{Pl}_a(\mathcal{R}[p_2 \wedge q] \mid \mathcal{R}[p_1]). \tag{9.5}$$

Since $\mathcal{R}[\neg(p_2 \wedge q)] \supseteq \mathcal{R}[\neg q \wedge p_2]$, it follows from CPl3 and (9.3) that

$$\mathrm{Pl}_a(\mathcal{R}[p_2 \wedge q] \mid \mathcal{R}[p_1]) > \mathrm{Pl}_a(\mathcal{R}[\neg q \wedge p_2] \mid \mathcal{R}[p_1]),$$

contradicting (9.5). Thus, REV3 does not hold in $\mathcal{J}$.

Among other things, REV3 says that the syntactic form of the observation does not matter. That is, suppose that $\phi$ and $\phi'$ are equivalent formulas, and the agent observes $\phi$. It is possible that the observation is encoded as $\phi'$. Should this matter? A priori, it could. REV3 says that it does not, as the following lemma shows:

**Lemma 9.3.4**  *If $\phi$ and $\phi'$ are equivalent formulas (i.e., $\vdash_{\mathcal{L}} \phi \Leftrightarrow \phi'$), and $s_a \cdot \phi$ and $s_a \cdot \phi'$ are both states in $\mathcal{J}$, then $\mathrm{Pl}_a(\mathcal{R}[\psi] \mid \mathcal{R}[s_a \cdot \phi]) = \mathrm{Pl}_a(\mathcal{R}[\psi] \mid \mathcal{R}[s_a \cdot \phi']).$*

**Proof**  See Exercise 9.10.  ∎

Let $\mathcal{REV}$ consist of all reliable BCSs satisfying REV1–3. It is easy to see that $\mathfrak{I}_1^\dagger \in \mathcal{REV}$ (Exercise 9.11). The next result shows that, in a precise sense, every BCS in $\mathcal{REV}$ satisfies R1–8.

**Theorem 9.3.5** *Suppose that $\mathfrak{I} \in \mathcal{REV}$ and $s_a$ is a local state of the agent at some point in $\mathfrak{I}$. Then there is a belief revision operator $\circ_{s_a}$ satisfying R1–8 such that for all $\phi \in \mathcal{L}_e$ such that the observation $\phi$ can be made in $s_a$ (i.e., for all $\phi$ such that $s_a \cdot \phi$ is a local state at some point in $\mathfrak{I}$) $\mathrm{Bel}(\mathfrak{I}, s_a) \circ_{s_a} \phi = \mathrm{Bel}(\mathfrak{I}, s_a \cdot \phi)$.*

**Proof**   Fix $s_a$. If $K = \mathrm{Bel}(\mathfrak{I}, s_a)$ and $s_a \cdot \phi$ is a local state in $\mathfrak{I}$, then define $K \circ_{s,a} \phi = \mathrm{Bel}(\mathfrak{I}, s_a \cdot \phi)$. (This is clearly the only definition that will satisfy the theorem.) Recall for future reference that this means that

$$\psi \in K \circ_{s,a} \phi \text{ iff } \mathrm{Pl}_a(\mathcal{R}[\phi \wedge \psi] \mid \mathcal{R}[s_a \cdot \phi]) > \mathrm{Pl}_a(\mathcal{R}[\phi \wedge \neg\psi] \mid \mathcal{R}[s_a \cdot \phi]). \ (9.6)$$

There is also a straightforward definition for $K' \circ_{s,a} \phi$ if $K' \neq K$ that suffices for the theorem. If $\neg\phi \notin K'$, then $K' \circ_{s,a} \phi = \mathrm{Cl}(K \cup \{\phi\})$; if $\neg\phi \in K'$, then $K' \circ_{s,a} \phi = \mathrm{Cl}(\{\phi\})$.

The hard part is to define $K \circ_{s,a} \phi$ if $s_a \cdot \phi$ is not a local state in $\mathfrak{I}$. The idea is to use (9.6) as much as possible. The definition splits into a number of cases:

- There exists some formula $\phi'$ such that $s_a \cdot \phi'$ is a local state in $\mathfrak{I}$ and $\vdash_{\mathcal{L}} \phi' \Rightarrow \phi$. By REV3, $\mathcal{R}[s_a] \cap \mathcal{R}[\phi'] \in \mathcal{F}'$. Since $\mathcal{F}'$ is closed under supersets, it follows that $\mathcal{R}[s_a] \cap \mathcal{R}[\phi] \in \mathcal{F}'$. Define

$$K \circ_{s,a} \phi = \{\psi : \mathrm{Pl}_a(\mathcal{R}[\psi] \mid \mathcal{R}[s_a] \cap \mathcal{R}[\phi]) > \mathrm{Pl}_a(\mathcal{R}[\neg\psi] \mid \mathcal{R}[s_a] \cap \mathcal{R}[\phi]). \ (9.7)$$

By REV3, this would be equivalent to (9.6) if $s_a \cdot \phi$ were a state. Note that the definition is independent of $\phi'$; the fact that there exists $\phi'$ such that $\vdash_{\mathcal{L}} \phi' \Rightarrow \phi$ is used only to ensure that $\mathcal{R}[s_a] \cap \mathcal{R}[\phi] \in \mathcal{F}'$.

- There exists some formula $\phi'$ such that $s_a \cdot \phi'$ is a local state in $\mathfrak{I}$, $\vdash_{\mathcal{L}} \phi \Rightarrow \phi'$, and $\neg\phi \notin \mathrm{Bel}(\mathfrak{I}, s_a \cdot \phi')$. Since $\neg\phi \notin \mathrm{Bel}(\mathfrak{I}, s_a \cdot \phi')$, it follows that $\mathrm{Pl}_a(\mathcal{R}[\phi] \mid \mathcal{R}[s_a \cdot \phi']) > \bot$. By REV3, $\mathcal{R}[s_a] \cap \mathcal{R}[\phi'] \in \mathcal{F}'$ and $\mathrm{Pl}_a(\mathcal{R}[\phi] \mid \mathcal{R}[s_a \cdot \phi']) = \mathrm{Pl}_a(\mathcal{R}[\phi] \mid \mathcal{R}[s_a] \cap \mathcal{R}[\phi']) > \bot$. By BCS2, $\mathcal{R}[s_a] \cap \mathcal{R}[\phi'] \cap \mathcal{R}[\phi] = \mathcal{R}[s_a] \cap \mathcal{R}[\phi] \in \mathcal{F}'$. That means $K \circ_{s,a} \phi$ can again be defined using (9.7).

- If $s_a \cdot \phi'$ is not a state in $\mathfrak{I}$ for any formula $\phi'$ such that $\vdash_{\mathcal{L}} \phi' \Rightarrow \phi$ or $\vdash_{\mathcal{L}} \phi \Rightarrow \phi'$, then define $K \circ_{s,a} \phi$ in the same way as $K' \circ_{s,a} \phi$ for $K' \neq K$. If $\neg\phi \notin K$, then $K \circ_{s,a} \phi = \mathrm{Cl}(K \cup \{\phi\})$; if $\neg\phi \in K$, the $K \circ_{s,a} \phi = \mathrm{Cl}(\{\phi\})$.

It remains to show that this definition satisfies R1–8. I leave it to the reader to check that this is the case if $K \neq \mathrm{Bel}(\mathcal{I}, s_a)$ or $s_a \cdot \phi$ is not a local state in $\mathcal{I}$ (Exercise 9.12), and I focus here on the case that $K = \mathrm{Bel}(\mathcal{I}, s_a)$, just to make it clear why REV1–3, BCS2, and BCS3 are needed for the argument.

- R1 is immediate from the definition.

- R2 follows from BCS3.

- For R3, it suffices to show that if $\psi \in \mathrm{Bel}(\mathcal{I}, s_a \cdot \phi)$ then $\psi \vee \neg\phi \in \mathrm{Bel}(\mathcal{I}, s_a)$, for then $\psi \in \mathrm{Cl}(K \cup \{\phi\})$, by simple propositional reasoning. If $\psi \in \mathrm{Bel}(\mathcal{I}, s_a \cdot \phi)$, then $\mathrm{Pl}_a(\mathcal{R}[\psi] \mid \mathcal{R}[s_a \cdot \phi]) > \mathrm{Pl}_a(\mathcal{R}[\neg\psi] \mid \mathcal{R}[s_a \cdot \phi])$. It follows from REV3 that $\mathrm{Pl}_a(\mathcal{R}[\psi] \mid \mathcal{R}[s_a] \cap \mathcal{R}[\phi]) > \mathrm{Pl}_a(\mathcal{R}[\neg\psi] \mid \mathcal{R}[s_a] \cap \mathcal{R}[\phi])$. Now there are two cases. If $\mathrm{Pl}(\mathcal{R}[\phi] \mid \mathcal{R}[s_a]) > \perp$, then by CPl5, it immediately follows that

$$\mathrm{Pl}_a(\mathcal{R}[\psi \wedge \phi] \mid \mathcal{R}[s_a]) > \mathrm{Pl}_a(\mathcal{R}[\neg\psi \wedge \phi] \mid \mathcal{R}[s_a]).$$

Now CPl3 gives

$$\mathrm{Pl}_a(\mathcal{R}[\psi \vee \neg\phi] \mid \mathcal{R}[s_a]) > \mathrm{Pl}_a(\mathcal{R}[\neg\psi \wedge \phi] \mid \mathcal{R}[s_a]),$$

and it follows that $\psi \vee \neg\phi \in K$. On the other hand, if $\mathrm{Pl}(\mathcal{R}[\phi] \mid \mathcal{R}[s_a]) = \perp$, then by Pl5 (which holds in $\mathcal{I}$, by BCS2) and CPl2, it follows that $\mathrm{Pl}(\mathcal{R}[\neg\phi] \mid \mathcal{R}[s_a]) > \perp$. (For if $\mathrm{Pl}(\mathcal{R}[\neg\phi] \mid \mathcal{R}[s_a]) = \perp$, then Pl5 implies that $\mathrm{Pl}(\mathcal{R}[\neg\phi] \cup \mathcal{R}[\phi] \mid \mathcal{R}[s_a]) = \mathrm{Pl}(\mathcal{R} \mid \mathcal{R}[s_a]) = \perp$, contradicting CPl2.) Thus,

$$\mathrm{Pl}_a(\mathcal{R}[\psi \vee \neg\phi] \mid \mathcal{R}[s_a]) \geq \mathrm{Pl}(\mathcal{R}[\neg\phi] \mid \mathcal{R}[s_a]) > \mathrm{Pl}_a(\mathcal{R}[\neg\psi \wedge \phi] \mid \mathcal{R}[s_a]) = \perp,$$

so again, $\psi \vee \neg\phi \in K$.

- For R4, REV2 comes into play. Suppose that $\neg\phi \notin K$. To show that $\mathrm{Cl}(K \cup \{\phi\}) \subseteq K \circ_{s,a} \phi$, it clearly suffices to show that $K \subseteq K \circ_{s,a} \phi$, since by R2, $\phi \in K \circ_{s,a} \phi$, and by R1, $K \circ_{s,a} \phi$ is closed. Thus, suppose that $\psi \in K = \mathrm{Bel}(\mathcal{I}, s_a)$. Thus, $\mathrm{Pl}_a(\mathcal{R}[\psi] \mid \mathcal{R}[s_a]) > \mathrm{Pl}_a(\mathcal{R}[\neg\psi] \mid \mathcal{R}[s_a])$. By Pl6, $\mathrm{Pl}_a(\mathcal{R}[\psi \wedge \phi] \mid \mathcal{R}[s_a]) > \mathrm{Pl}_a(\mathcal{R}[\neg\psi \wedge \phi] \mid \mathcal{R}[s_a])$. Since $\neg\phi \notin K$, it must be the case that $\mathrm{Pl}_a(\mathcal{R}[\phi] \mid \mathcal{R}[s_a]) > \perp$, so by CPl5, it follows that $\mathrm{Pl}_a(\mathcal{R}[\psi] \mid \mathcal{R}[s_a] \cap \mathcal{R}[\phi]) > \mathrm{Pl}_a(\mathcal{R}[\neg\psi] \mid \mathcal{R}[s_a] \cap \mathcal{R}[\phi])$. Now REV3 gives

$$\mathrm{Pl}_a(\mathcal{R}[\psi] \mid \mathcal{R}[s_a \cdot \phi]) > \mathrm{Pl}_a(\mathcal{R}[\neg\psi] \mid \mathcal{R}[s_a \cdot \phi]),$$

so $\psi \in K \circ_{s,a} \phi$, as desired.

- For R5, note that if $s_a \cdot \phi$ is a local state in $\mathfrak{I}$, by BCS3, $\phi$ is consistent (i.e., it cannot be the case that $\vdash_{\mathcal{L}} \neg\phi$), and so is $K \circ_{s,a} \phi$.

- R6 is immediate from the definition and Lemma 9.3.4.

- The arguments for R7 and R8 are similar in spirit to those for R3 and R4; I leave the details to the reader (Exercise 9.12). Note that there is a subtlety here, since it is possible that $s \cdot \phi$ is a local state in $\mathfrak{I}$ while $s \cdot (\phi \wedge \psi)$ is not, or vice versa. Nevertheless, the definitions still ensure that everything works out.   ∎

Theorem 9.3.5 is interesting not just for what it shows, but for what it does *not* show. Theorem 9.3.5 considers a fixed local state $s_a$ in $\mathfrak{I}$ and shows that there is a belief revision operator $\circ_{s_a}$ characterizing belief change from $s_a$. It does not show that there is a single belief revision operator characterizing belief change in all of $\mathfrak{I}$. That is, it does not say that there is a belief revision operator $\circ_{\mathfrak{I}}$ such that $\mathrm{Bel}(\mathfrak{I}, s_a) \circ_{\mathfrak{I}} \phi = \mathrm{Bel}(\mathfrak{I}, s_a \cdot \phi)$, for all local states $s_a$ in $\mathfrak{I}$. This stronger result is, in general, false. That is because there is more to a local state than the beliefs that are true at that state. The following example illustrates this point:

**Example 9.3.6**   Consider a BCS $\mathfrak{I} = (\mathcal{R}, \mathcal{PL}, \pi)$ such that the following hold:

- $\mathcal{R} = \{r_1, r_2, r_3, r_4\}$.

- $\pi$ is such that $p_1 \wedge p_2$ is true throughout $r_1$, $\neg p_1 \wedge \neg p_2$ is true throughout $r_2$; and $p_1 \wedge \neg p_2$ is true throughout $r_3$ and $r_4$.

- In $r_1$, the agent observes $p_1$ and then $p_2$; in $r_2$, the agent observes $\neg p_2$ and then $\neg p_1$; in $r_3$, agent observes $p_1$ and then $\neg p_2$; and in $r_4$, the agent observes $\neg p_2$ and then $p_1$.

- $\mathcal{PL}$ is determined by a prior $\mathrm{Pl}_a$ on runs, where

$$\mathrm{Pl}_a(r_1) > \mathrm{Pl}_a(r_2) > \mathrm{Pl}_a(r_3) = \mathrm{Pl}_a(r_4).$$

It is easy to check that $\mathfrak{I} \in \mathcal{REV}$ (Exercise 9.13). Note that $\mathrm{Bel}(\mathfrak{I}, \langle\rangle) = \mathrm{Bel}(\mathfrak{I}, \langle p_1 \rangle) = \mathrm{Cl}(p_1 \wedge p_2)$, since $p_1 \wedge p_2$ is true in the unique most plausible run, $r_1$, and in $r_1$, the agent initially observes $p_1$. Similarly, $\mathrm{Bel}(\mathfrak{I}, \langle \neg p_2 \rangle) = \mathrm{Cl}(\neg p_1 \wedge p_2)$, since $r_2$ is the unique most plausible run where the agent observes $\neg p_2$ first, and $\mathrm{Bel}(\mathfrak{I}, \langle p_1, \neg p_2 \rangle) = \mathrm{Cl}(\neg p_1 \wedge \neg p_2)$. Suppose that there were a revision operator $\circ$ such that $\mathrm{Bel}(\mathfrak{I}, s_a) \circ \phi = \mathrm{Bel}(\mathfrak{I}, s_a \cdot \phi)$ for all local states $s_a$. It would then follow that $\mathrm{Bel}(\mathfrak{I}, \langle \neg p_2 \rangle) = \mathrm{Bel}(\mathfrak{I}, \langle p_1, \neg p_2 \rangle)$. But this is clearly false, since $\neg p_1 \in \mathrm{Bel}(\mathfrak{I}, \langle \neg p_2 \rangle)$ and $\neg p_1 \notin \mathrm{Bel}(\mathfrak{I}, \langle p_1, \neg p_2 \rangle)$.   ∎

Example 9.3.6 illustrates a problem with the assumption implicit in AGM belief revision, that all that matters regarding how an agent revises her beliefs is her belief set and what is learned. I return to this problem in the next section.

Theorem 9.3.5 shows that for every BCS $\mathcal{J} \in \mathcal{REV}$ and local state $s_a$, there is a revision operator characterizing belief change at $s_a$. The next result is essentially a converse.

**Theorem 9.3.7**   *Let $\circ$ be a belief revision operator satisfying R1–8 and let $K \subseteq \mathcal{L}_e$ be a consistent belief set. Then there is a BCS $\mathcal{J}_K$ in $\mathcal{REV}$ such that $\mathrm{Bel}(\mathcal{J}_K, \langle\,\rangle) = K$ and*

$$K \circ \phi = \mathrm{Bel}(\mathcal{J}_K, \langle\phi\rangle)$$

*for all $\phi \in \mathcal{L}_e$.*

**Proof**   See Exercise 9.14.   ∎

Notice that Theorem 9.3.7 considers only *consistent* belief sets $K$. The requirement that $K$ be consistent is necessary in Theorem 9.3.7. The AGM postulates allow the agent to "escape" from an inconsistent belief set, so that $K \circ \phi$ may be consistent even if $K$ is inconsistent. Indeed, R5 *requires* that it be possible to escape from an inconsistent belief set. On the other hand, if *false* $\in \mathrm{Bel}(\mathcal{J}_K, s_a)$ for some state $s_a$ and $r_a(m) = s_a$, then $\mathrm{Pl}_{(r,m)}(W_{(r,m)}) = \bot$. Since updating is done by conditioning, $\mathrm{Pl}_{(r,m+1)}(W_{(r,m+1)}) = \bot$, so the agent's belief set will remain inconsistent no matter what she learns. Thus, BCSs do not allow an agent to escape from an inconsistent belief set. This is a consequence of the use of conditioning to update.

Although it would be possible to modify the definition of BCSs to handle updates of inconsistent belief sets differently (and thus to allow the agent to escape from an inconsistent belief set), this does not seem so reasonable to me. Once an agent has learned *false*, why should learning something else suddenly make everything consistent again? Part of the issue here is exactly what it would mean for an agent to learn or discover *false*. (Note that this is very different from, say, learning $p$ and then learning $\neg p$.) Rather than modifying BCSs, I believe that it would in fact be more appropriate to reformulate R5 so that it does not require escape from an inconsistent belief set. Consider the following postulate:

R5*.   $K \circ \phi = Cl(false)$ iff $\vdash_{\mathcal{L}} \neg\phi$ or *false* $\in K$.

If R5 is replaced by R5*, then Theorem 9.3.7 holds even if $K$ is inconsistent (for trivial reasons, since in that case $K \circ \phi = K$ for all $\phi$). Alternatively, as I suggested earlier, it might also be reasonable to restrict belief sets to being consistent, in which case R5 is totally unnecessary.

## 9.4    Belief Revision and Conditional Logic

It is perhaps not surprising that there should be a connection between belief revision and the conditional logic considered in Section 8.6, given that both use plausibility measures as a basis for their semantics. Indeed, one approach to belief revision, called the *Ramsey test* (named after Frank Ramsey, who first proposed it; this is the same Ramsey who provided the first justification of the subjectivist view of probability, as mentioned in the notes to Chapter 2), basically defines belief revision in terms of conditional logic. The idea is that an agent should believe $\psi$ after observing or learning $\phi$ iff he currently believes that $\psi$ would be true if $\phi$ were true (i.e., if he currently believes $\phi \to \psi$). As the following theorem shows, this connection holds in reliable BCSs that satisfy REV1 and REV3:

**Theorem 9.4.1**    *Suppose that $\Im$ is a reliable BCS that satisfies REV1 and REV3. If $r$ is a run in $\Im$ such that $o_{(r,m+1)} = \phi$, then $(\Im, r, m) \models \phi \to \psi$ iff $(\Im, r, m+1) \models B\psi$. Equivalently, if $s_a \cdot \phi$ is a local state in $\Im$, then*

$$(\Im, s_a) \models \phi \to \psi \text{ iff } (\Im, s_a \cdot \phi) \models B\psi.$$

**Proof**    See Exercise 9.15.  ∎

A priori, it could be the case that Theorem 9.4.1 is an artifact of the semantics of BCSs. The next result, Theorem 9.4.2, shows that there is an even deeper connection between the AGM postulates and conditional logic, which goes beyond the use of BCSs to model belief revision. Roughly speaking, the theorem shows that a system satisfies the AGM postulates iff it satisfies all the properties of **P** as well as Rational Monotonicity. Theorem 9.4.2 can be viewed as strengthening and making precise the remarks that I made earlier about R6 being essentially LLE and R8 being Rational Monotonicity in disguise.

**Theorem 9.4.2**    *Suppose that $\vdash_{\mathcal{L}}$ (as used in R5) corresponds to provability in propositional logic.*

(a) *Suppose that $\circ$ satisfies R1–8. Fix a belief set $K$, and define a relation $\to$ on formulas by taking $\phi \to \psi$ to hold iff $\psi \in \mathcal{K} \circ \psi$. Then $\to$ satisfies all the* *properties of* **P** *as well as Rational Monotonicity:*

$$\text{if } \phi \rightarrow \psi_1 \text{ and } \phi \not\rightarrow \neg\psi_2, \text{ then } \phi \wedge \psi_2 \rightarrow \psi_1.$$

*Moreover,* $\phi \rightarrow$ *false iff* $\phi$ *is not satisfiable.*

(b) *Conversely, suppose that* $\rightarrow$ *is a relation on formulas that satisfies the properties of* **P** *and Rational Monotonicity, and* $\phi \rightarrow$ *false iff* $\phi$ *is not satisfiable. Let* $K = \{\psi : true \rightarrow \psi\}$. *Then* $K$ *is a belief set. Moreover, if* $\circ$ *is defined by taking* $K \circ \phi = \{\psi : \phi \rightarrow \psi\}$, *then R1–8 hold for* $K$ *and* $\circ$.

**Proof**   For part (a), suppose that $\circ$ satisfies R1–8. Fix $K$ and define $\phi \rightarrow \psi$ as in the statement of the theorem. The fact that $\rightarrow$ satisfies REF follows immediately from R2. RW and AND both follow from the fact that $K \circ \phi$ is a belief set (i.e., R1). LLE is immediate from R6. The fact that $\phi \rightarrow$ *false* iff $\phi$ is not satisfiable is immediate from R5. It remains to prove OR, CM, and Rational Monotonicity.

For the OR rule, suppose that $\phi_1 \rightarrow \psi$ and $\phi_2 \rightarrow \psi$. Thus, $\psi \in K \circ \phi_1 \cap K \circ \phi_2$. By R2, $\phi_1 \vee \phi_2 \in K \circ (\phi_1 \vee \phi_2)$. Thus, it cannot be the case that both $\neg\phi_1 \in K \circ (\phi_1 \vee \phi_2)$ and $\neg\phi_2 \in K \circ (\phi_1 \vee \phi_2)$. Without loss of generality, suppose that $\neg\phi_1 \notin K \circ (\phi_1 \vee \phi_2)$. By R6, R7, and R8, it follows that

$$K \circ \phi_1 = K \circ ((\phi_1 \vee \phi_2) \wedge \phi_1) = \text{Cl}(K \circ (\phi_1 \vee \phi_2) \cup \{\phi_1\}).$$

Since $\psi \in K \circ \phi_1$, it follows that $\psi \in \text{Cl}(K \circ (\phi_1 \vee \phi_2) \cup \{\phi_1\})$, and so

$$K \circ (\phi_1 \vee \phi_2) \vdash_{\mathcal{L}} \phi_1 \Rightarrow \psi. \tag{9.8}$$

There are now two subcases to consider. First suppose that $\neg\phi_2 \notin K \circ (\phi_1 \vee \phi_2)$. Then the same arguments used to prove (9.8) also show that $K \circ (\phi_1 \vee \phi_2) \vdash_{\mathcal{L}} \phi_2 \Rightarrow \psi$. It follows that $K \circ (\phi_1 \vee \phi_2) \vdash_{\mathcal{L}} (\phi_1 \vee \phi_2) \Rightarrow \psi$. Since $K \circ (\phi_1 \vee \phi_2)$ is a belief set (and thus is closed), it follows that $(\phi_1 \vee \phi_2) \Rightarrow \psi \in K \circ (\phi_1 \vee \phi_2)$. By R2, $(\phi_1 \vee \phi_2) \in K \circ (\phi_1 \vee \phi_2)$. Hence, $\psi \in K \circ (\phi_1 \vee \phi_2)$. On the other hand, if $\neg\phi_2 \in K \circ (\phi_1 \vee \phi_2)$, then since $\phi_1 \vee \phi_2 \in K \circ (\phi_1 \vee \phi_2)$, it follows that $\phi_1 \in K \circ (\phi_1 \vee \phi_2)$. It now again easily follows using (9.8) that $\psi \in K \circ (\phi_1 \vee \phi_2)$. In either case, by definition, $\phi_1 \vee \phi_2 \rightarrow \psi$, so the OR rule holds.

For Rational Monotonicity, note that if $\phi \not\rightarrow \neg\psi_2$, by R7 and R8, $K \circ (\phi \wedge \psi_2) = \text{Cl}(K \circ \phi \cup \{\psi_2\})$. If, in addition, $\phi \rightarrow \psi_1$, then $\psi_1 \in K \circ \phi$, so $\psi_1 \in \text{Cl}(K \circ \phi \cup \{\psi_2\}) = K \circ (\phi \wedge \psi_2)$. Thus, $\phi \wedge \psi_2 \rightarrow \psi_1$. The argument for CM is similar.

For part (b), suppose that $\rightarrow$ satisfies the properties of **P** and Rational Monotonicity, and $K$ and $\circ$ are defined as in the theorem. It follows from AND and RW that $K$ is a belief set. Moreover, for any fixed $\phi$, the same argument shows that $K \circ \phi$ is a belief set, so R1 holds. By REF, R2 holds. R5 holds since $\phi \to false$ iff $\phi$ is not satisfiable. It remains to prove R3, R4, R7, and R8. I leave the proof of R7 and R8 to the reader (Exercise 9.16). The proof of R3 and R4 is similar (and simpler).  ∎

## 9.5    Epistemic States and Iterated Revision

Agents do not change their beliefs just once. They do so repeatedly, each time they get new information. The BCS framework models this naturally, showing how the agent's local state changes as a result of each new observation. It would seem at first that revision operators make sense for iterated revision as well. Given a revision operator ∘ and an initial belief set $K$, it seems reasonable, for example, to take $(K \circ \phi_1) \circ \phi_2$ to be the result of revising first by $\phi_1$ and then by $\phi_2$. However, Example 9.3.6 indicates that there is a problem with this approach. Even if $(K \circ \phi_1) = K$, it may not be desirable to have $(K \circ \phi_1) \circ \phi_2 = K \circ \phi_2$. In Example 9.3.6, revising by $\phi_1$ and then $\phi_2$ is not the same as revising by $\phi_2$, even though the agent has the same belief set before and after revising by $\phi_1$.

The culprit here is the assumption that revision depends only on the agent's belief set. In a BCS, there is a clear distinction between the agent's *epistemic state* at a point $(r, m)$ in $\mathfrak{I}$, as characterized by her local state $s_a = r_a(m)$, and the agent's belief set at $(r, m)$, $\text{Bel}(\mathfrak{I}, s_a)$. As Example 9.3.6 shows, in a system in $\mathcal{REV}$, the agent's belief set does not in general determine how the agent's beliefs will be revised; her epistemic state does.

It is not hard to modify the AGM postulates to deal with revision operators that take as their first argument epistemic states rather than belief sets. Suppose that there is a set of epistemic states (the exact form of the epistemic state is irrelevant for the following discussion) and a function $\text{BS}(\cdot)$ that maps epistemic states to belief sets. There is an analogue to each of the AGM postulates, obtained by replacing each belief set by the beliefs in the corresponding epistemic state. Letting $E$ stand for a generic epistemic state, here are the first three modified postulates:

R1′.    $E \circ \phi$ is an epistemic state.

R2′.    $\phi \in \text{BS}(E \circ \phi)$.

R3′.    $\text{BS}(E \circ \phi) \subseteq Cl(\text{BS}(E) \cup \{\phi\})$.

The remaining postulates can be obtained in the obvious way. The only problematic postulate is R6. The question is whether R6′ should be "if $\vdash_{\mathcal{L}_e} \phi \Leftrightarrow \psi$, then $\text{BS}(E \circ \phi) = \text{BS}(E \circ \psi)$" or "if $\vdash_{\mathcal{L}_e} \phi \Leftrightarrow \psi$, then $E \circ \phi = E \circ \psi$." Dealing with either version is straightforward. For definiteness, I adopt the first alternative here.

There is an analogue of Theorem 9.3.5 that works at the level of epistemic states. Indeed, working at the level of epistemic states gives a more elegant result. Given a BCS $\mathcal{I} \in \mathcal{REV}$, there is a single revision operator $\circ$ that characterizes belief revision in $\mathcal{I}$; it is not necessary to use a different revision operator for each local state $s_a$ in $\mathcal{I}$.

To make this precise, given a language $\mathcal{L}_e$, let $\mathcal{L}_e^*$ consist of all sequences of formulas in $\mathcal{L}_e$. In a BCS, the local states are elements of $\mathcal{L}_e^*$ (although some elements in $\mathcal{L}_e^*$, such as $\langle p, \neg p \rangle$, cannot arise as local states in a reliable BCS). There is an obvious way of defining a revision function $\circ$ on $\mathcal{L}_e^*$: if $E \in \mathcal{L}_e^*$, then $E \circ \phi = E \cdot \phi$.

**Theorem 9.5.1**  *Let $\mathcal{I}$ be a system in $\mathcal{REV}$. There is a function $BS_\mathcal{I}$ that maps epistemic states to belief sets such that*

- *if $s_a$ is a local state of the agent in $\mathcal{I}$, then $Bel(\mathcal{I}, s_a) = BS_\mathcal{I}(s_a)$, and*

- *$(\circ, BS_\mathcal{I})$ satisfies R1′–8′.*

**Proof**  Note that $BS_\mathcal{I}$ must be defined on all sequences in $\mathcal{L}_e^*$, including ones that are not local states in $\mathcal{I}$. Define $BS_\mathcal{I}(s_a) = Bel(\mathcal{I}, s_a)$ if $s_a$ is a local state in $\mathcal{I}$. If $s_a$ is not in $\mathcal{I}$, then $BS_\mathcal{I}(s_a) = Bel(\mathcal{I}, s')$, where $s'$ is the longest suffix of $s_a$ that is a local state in $\mathcal{I}$. The argument that this works is left to the reader (Exercise 9.18).  ∎

At first blush, the relationship between Theorem 9.5.1 and Theorem 9.3.5 may not be so clear. However, note that, by definition,

$$BS_\mathcal{I}(\mathcal{I}, \langle s_a \rangle) \circ \phi_1 \circ \cdots \circ \phi_k) = BS_\mathcal{I}(\mathcal{I}, s_a \cdot \langle \phi_1, \ldots, \phi_k \rangle),$$

so, at the level of epistemic states, Theorem 9.5.1 is a generalization of Theorem 9.3.5.

Theorem 9.5.1 shows that any system in $\mathcal{REV}$ corresponds to a revision operator over epistemic states that satisfies the modified AGM postulates. Is there a converse, analogous to Theorem 9.3.7? Not quite. It turns out that R7′ and R8′ are not quite strong enough to capture the behavior of conditioning given a consistent observation. It is not hard to show that R7′ and R8′ (together with R3′ and R4′) imply that

$$\text{if } \neg\psi \notin BS(E \circ \phi), \text{ then } BS(E \circ \phi \circ \psi) = BS(E \circ (\phi \wedge \psi)) \qquad (9.9)$$

(Exercise 9.17(a)). The following postulate strengthens this:

R9′.  If $\nvdash_{\mathcal{L}_e} \neg(\phi \wedge \psi)$, then $BS(E \circ \phi \circ \psi) = BS(E \circ (\phi \wedge \psi))$.

R9′ says that revising $E$ by $\phi$ and then by $\psi$ is the same as revising by $\phi \wedge \psi$ if $\phi \wedge \psi$ is consistent. This indeed strengthens (9.9), since (given R2′) if $\neg\psi \notin BS(E \circ \phi)$, then

$\nvdash_{\mathcal{L}_e} \neg(\phi \wedge \psi)$ (Exercise 9.17(b)). It is not hard to show that it is a nontrivial strengthening; there are systems that satisfy (9.9) and do not satisfy R9′ (Exercise 9.17(c)).

The following generalization of Theorem 9.5.1 shows that R9′ is sound in $\mathcal{REV}$:

**Theorem 9.5.2**  *Let $\mathcal{J}$ be a system in $\mathcal{REV}$. There is a function $\mathrm{BS}_{\mathcal{J}}$ that maps epistemic states to belief sets such that*

- *if $s_a$ is a local state of the agent in $\mathcal{J}$, then $\mathrm{Bel}(\mathcal{J}, s_a) = \mathrm{BS}_{\mathcal{J}}(s_a)$, and*

- *$(\circ, \mathrm{BS}_{\mathcal{J}})$ satisfies R1′–9′.*

**Proof**   See Exercise 9.18.  ∎

The converse to Theorem 9.5.2 also holds: a revision system on epistemic states that satisfies the generalized AGM postulates and R9′ corresponds to a system in $\mathcal{REV}$. Let $\mathcal{L}_e^{\dagger}$ consist of all the sequences $\langle \phi_1, \ldots, \phi_k \rangle$ in $\mathcal{L}_e^*$ that are consistent, in that $\nvdash_{\mathcal{L}_e} \neg(\phi_1 \wedge \ldots \wedge \phi_k)$.

**Theorem 9.5.3**  *Given a function $\mathrm{BS}_{\mathcal{L}_e}$ mapping epistemic states in $\mathcal{L}_e^*$ to belief sets over $\mathcal{L}_e$ such that $\mathrm{BS}_{\mathcal{L}_e}(\langle\,\rangle)$ is consistent and $(\circ, \mathrm{BS}_{\mathcal{L}_e})$ satisfies R1′–9′, there is a system $\mathcal{J} \in \mathcal{REV}$ whose local states consist of all the states in $\mathcal{L}_e^{\dagger}$ such that $\mathrm{BS}_{\mathcal{L}_e}(s_a) = \mathrm{Bel}(\mathcal{J}, s_a)$ for $s_a \in \mathcal{L}_e^{\dagger}$.*

**Proof**   Let $\mathcal{J} = (\mathcal{R}, \mathcal{PL}, \pi)$ be defined as follows. A run in $\mathcal{R}$ is defined by a truth assignment $\alpha$ to the primitive propositions in $\mathcal{L}_e$ and an infinite sequence $\langle o_1, o_2, \ldots \rangle$ of observations, each of which is true under truth assignment $\alpha$. The pair $(\alpha, \langle o_1, o_2, \ldots \rangle)$ defines a run $r$ in the obvious way: $r_e(m) = \alpha$ for all $m$ and $r_a(m) = \langle o_1, o_2, \ldots, o_m \rangle$. $\mathcal{R}$ consists of all runs that can be defined in this way. The interpretation is determined by $\alpha$: $\pi(r, m) = r_e(m)$. All that remains is to define a prior that ensures that $\mathrm{BS}_{\mathcal{L}_e}(s_a) = \mathrm{Bel}(\mathcal{J}, s_a)$ for all $s_a \in \mathcal{L}_e^{\dagger}$. This is left to the reader (Exercise 9.19).  ∎

To summarize, this discussion shows that, at the level of epistemic states, the AGM postulates are very reasonable (with the possible exception of R5, which perhaps should be modified to R5*) provided that (a) all propositions of interest are static (i.e., their truth values do not change over time), (b) observations are reliable (in that what is observed is true), (c) nothing is learned from observing $\phi$ beyond the fact that $\phi$ is true, and (d) there is a totally ordered plausibility on truth assignments (which by (a) and (c) determines the plausibility on runs). The generality of plausibility measures is not required for (d); using conditional probability measures, ranking functions, possibility measures, or total preference orders will do as well.

Clearly these assumptions are not always appropriate. Nor are they necessary in the BCS framework; it makes perfect sense to consider BCSs that violate any or all of them. For example, it is easy enough to allow partial orders instead of total orders on runs. The effect of this is just that R4 and R8 (or R4′ and R8′) no longer hold. In the next section, I consider a natural collection of BCSs that do not necessarily satisfy these assumptions, based on the Markov assumption discussed in Section 6.5.

## 9.6   Markovian Belief Revision

For the purposes of this section, I restrict attention to BCSs where the prior plausibility measures are algebraic, as defined in Section 3.9. As I observed in Section 6.10, in such systems, the notion of a Markovian plausibility measure on runs makes perfect sense. Not surprisingly, BCSs where the prior plausibility on runs is Markovian are called *Markovian BCSs*. To see the power of Markovian BCSs as a modeling tool, consider the following example:

**Example 9.6.1**   A car is parked with a nonempty fuel tank at time 0. The owner returns at time 2 to find his car still there. Not surprisingly, at this point he believes that the car has been there all along and still has a nonempty tank. He then observes that the fuel tank is empty. He considers two possible explanations: (a) that his wife borrowed the car to do some errands or (b) that the gas leaked. (Suppose that the "times" are sufficiently long and the tank is sufficiently small that it is possible that both doing some errands and a leak can result in an empty tank.)

To model this as a BCS, suppose that $\Phi_e$ consists of two primitive propositions: *Parked* (which is true if car is parked where the owner originally left it) and *Empty* (which is true if the tank is empty). The environment state is just a truth assignment to these two primitive propositions. This truth assignment clearly changes over time, so REV1 is violated. (It would be possible to instead use propositions of the form *Parked$_i$*—the car is parked at time $i$—which would allow REV1 to be maintained; for simplicity, I consider here only the case where there are two primitive propositions.) There are three environment states: $s_{p\bar{e}}$, $s_{pe}$, and $s_{\overline{pe}}$. In $s_{p\bar{e}}$, *Parked* $\wedge$ ¬*Empty* is true; in $s_{pe}$, *Parked* $\wedge$ *Empty* is true; and in $s_{\overline{pe}}$, ¬*Parked* $\wedge$ ¬*Empty* is true. For simplicity, assume that, in all runs in the system, *Parked* $\wedge$ ¬*Empty* is true at time 0 and *Parked* $\wedge$ *Empty* is true at times 2 and 3. Further assume that in all runs the agent correctly observes *Parked* in round 2, and *Empty* in round 3, and makes no observations (i.e., observes *true*) in round 1.

I model this system using a Markovian plausibility on runs. The story suggests that the most likely transitions are the ones where no change occurs, which is why the agent believes at time 2—before he observes that the tank is empty—that the car has not moved and the tank is still not empty. Once he discovers that the tank is empty, the explanation he considers most likely will depend on his ranking of the transitions. This can be captured easily using ranking functions (which are algebraic plausibility measures). For example, the agent's belief that the most likely transitions are ones where no change occurs can be modeled by taking $\tau(s, s) = 0$ and $\tau(s, s') > 0$ if $s \neq s'$, for $s, s' \in \{s_{p\bar{e}}, s_{\overline{pe}}, s_{pe}\}$. This is already enough to make $[s_{p\bar{e}}, s_{p\bar{e}}, s_{p\bar{e}}]$ the most plausible 2-prefix. (Since, for each time $m \in \{0, \ldots, 3\}$, the agent's local state is the same at time $m$ in all runs, I do not mention it in the global state.) Thus, when the agent returns at time 2 to find his car parked, he believes that it was parked all along and the tank is not empty.

How do the agent's beliefs change when he observes that the tank is empty at time 3? As I said earlier, I restrict attention to two explanations: his wife borrowed the car to do some errands, which corresponds to the runs with 2-prefix $[s_{p\bar{e}}, s_{\overline{pe}}, s_{pe}]$, or the gas tanked leaked, which corresponds to the runs with 2-prefix $[s_{p\bar{e}}, s_{pe}, s_{pe}]$ and $[s_{p\bar{e}}, s_{p\bar{e}}, s_{pe}]$ (depending on when the leak started). The relative likelihood of the explanations depends on the relative likelihood of the transitions. He considers it more likely that his wife borrowed the car if the transition from $s_{p\bar{e}}$ to $s_{pe}$ is less likely than the sum of the transitions from $s_{p\bar{e}}$ to $s_{\overline{pe}}$ and from $s_{\overline{pe}}$ to $s_{pe}$, for example, if $\tau(s_{p\bar{e}}, s_{pe}) = 3$, $\tau(s_{p\bar{e}}, s_{\overline{pe}}) = 1$, and $\tau(s_{\overline{pe}}, s_{pe}) = 1$. Applying the Markovian assumption and the fact that $\otimes$ is $+$ for rankings, these choices make $\kappa([s_{p\bar{e}}, s_{\overline{pe}}, s_{pe}]) = 2$ and $\kappa([s_{p\bar{e}}, s_{p\bar{e}}, s_{pe}]) = \kappa([s_{p\bar{e}}, s_{pe}, s_{pe}]) = 3$. By changing the likelihood of the transitions, it is clearly possible to make the two explanations equally likely or to make the gas leak the more likely explanation.  ∎

This example was simple because the agent's local state (i.e., the observations made by the agents) did not affect the likelihood of transition. In general, the observations the agent makes do affect the transitions. Using the Markovian assumption, it is possible to model the fact that an agent's observations are correlated with the state of the world (e.g., the agent's being more likely to observe $p$ if both $p$ and $q$ are true than if $p \wedge \neg q$ is true) and to model unreliable observations that are still usually correct (e.g., the agent's being more likely to observe $p$ if $p$ is true than if $p$ is false, or $p$ being more likely to be true if the agent observes $p$ than if the agent observes $\neg p$; note that these are two quite different assumptions).

These examples show the flexibility of the Markovian assumption. While it can be difficult to decide how beliefs should change, this approach seems to localize the effort in what appears to be the right place: deciding the relative likelihood of various transitions. An obvious question now is whether making the Markovian assumption puts any constraints on BCSs. As the following result shows, the answer is no, at least as far as belief sets go:

**Theorem 9.6.2** *Given a BCS $\mathfrak{I}$, there is a Markovian BCS $\mathfrak{I}'$ such that the agent's local states are the same in both $\mathfrak{I}$ and $\mathfrak{I}'$ and, for all local states $s_a$, $\mathrm{Bel}(\mathfrak{I}, s_a) = \mathrm{Bel}(\mathfrak{I}', s_a)$.*

**Proof** Suppose that $\mathfrak{I} = (\mathcal{R}, \mathcal{PL}, \pi)$. Let $\mathrm{Pl}_{\mathcal{R}}$ be the prior on $\mathcal{R}$ that determines $\mathcal{PL}$. Although the agent's local state must be the same in $\mathfrak{I}$ and $\mathfrak{I}'$, there is no such requirement on the environment state. The idea is to define a set $\mathcal{R}'$ of runs where the environment states have the form $\langle g_0, \ldots, g_m \rangle$, for all possible initial sequences $g_0, \ldots, g_m$ of global states that arise in runs of $\mathcal{R}$. Then $\mathfrak{I}' = (\mathcal{R}', \mathcal{PL}', \pi')$, where $\pi'(\langle g_0, \ldots, g_m \rangle) = \pi(g_m)$ and $\mathcal{PL}'$ is determined by a Markovian prior $\mathrm{Pl}'_{\mathcal{R}}$ on $\mathcal{R}$ that simulates $\mathrm{Pl}_{\mathcal{R}}$. "Simulates" essentially means "is equal to" here; however, since $\mathrm{Pl}'_{\mathcal{R}}$ must be algebraic, equality cannot necessarily be assumed. It suffices that $\mathrm{Pl}'_{\mathcal{R}}([\langle g_0 \rangle, \langle g_0, g_1 \rangle, \ldots, \langle g_0, \ldots, g_m \rangle]) > \mathrm{Pl}'_{\mathcal{R}}([\langle g'_0 \rangle, \langle g'_0, g'_1 \rangle, \ldots, \langle g'_0, \ldots, g'_{m'} \rangle])$ iff $\mathrm{Pl}_{\mathcal{R}}([g_0, \ldots, g_m]) > \mathrm{Pl}_{\mathcal{R}}([g'_0, \ldots, g'_{m'}])$. I leave the technical details to the reader (Exercise 9.20). ∎

# Exercises

**9.1** This exercise shows that the plausibility measures $\mathrm{Pl}_1$ and $\mathrm{Pl}_2$ considered in Section 9.1 can be obtained using the construction preceding Theorem 8.4.12.

(a) Show that $\mathrm{Pl}_1$ is the plausibility measure obtained from the probability sequence $(\mu_1, \mu_2, \mu_3, \ldots)$ defined in Section 9.1, using the construction preceding Theorem 8.4.12.

(b) Define a probability sequence $(\mu'_1, \mu'_2, \mu'_3, \ldots)$ from which $\mathrm{Pl}_2$ is obtained using the construction preceding Theorem 8.4.12.

**9.2** Prove Proposition 9.1.1.

**9.3** Prove Proposition 9.1.2.

**9.4** Prove Proposition 9.1.3.

**9.5** Show that in an SDP system $(\mathcal{R}, \mathcal{PL}_a, \pi)$, if the prior $\mathrm{Pl}_a$ on runs that generates $\mathcal{PL}_a$ satisfies Pl4 and Pl5, then so does the agent's plausibility space $\mathrm{Pl}_a(r, m)$ at each point $(r, m)$.

**9.6**      Show that a BCS is a synchronous system satisfying CONS in which the agent
has perfect recall.

*__9.7__     This exercise expands on Example 9.3.1 and shows that AGM-style belief
revision can be understood as conditioning, using a conditional probability measure.
As in Example 9.3.1, fix a finite set $\Phi$ of primitive propositions and a consequence
relation $\vdash_{\mathcal{L}}$ for $\mathcal{L}^{Prop}(\Phi)$.

   (a) Show that there is a single formula $\sigma$ such that $\vdash_{\mathcal{L}} \phi$ iff $\sigma \Rightarrow \phi$ is a propositional
       tautology.

   (b) As in Example 9.3.1, let $M = (W, 2^W, 2^W - \emptyset, \mu, \pi)$ be a simple conditional
       probability structure, where $\pi$ is such that (i) $(M, w) \models \sigma$ for all $w \in W$ and (ii) if
       $\sigma \wedge \psi$ is satisfiable, then there is some world $w \in W$ such that $(M, w) \models \psi$. Let
       $K = \{\psi : \mu(\llbracket \psi \rrbracket_M) = 1\}$. If $\llbracket \phi \rrbracket_M \neq \emptyset$, define $K \circ \phi = \{\psi : \mu(\llbracket \psi \rrbracket_M | \llbracket \phi \rrbracket_M) = 1\}$;
       if $\llbracket \phi \rrbracket_M = \emptyset$, define $K \circ \phi = Cl(false)$. Show that this definition of revision
       satisfies R1–8.

   (c) Given a revision operator $\circ$ satisfying R1–8 (with respect to $\vdash_{\mathcal{L}}$ and a belief
       set $K \neq Cl(false)$, show that there exists a simple conditional probability space
       $M_K = (W, 2^W, 2^W - \emptyset, \mu_K, \pi)$ such that (i) $K = \{\psi : \mu(\llbracket \psi \rrbracket_M) = 1\}$ and (ii) if
       $K \circ \phi \neq Cl(false)$, then $K \circ \phi = \{\psi : \mu(\llbracket \psi \rrbracket_M | \llbracket \phi \rrbracket_M) = 1\}$.
Note that part (b) essentially shows that every conditional probability measure defines a
belief revision operator, and part (c) essentially shows that every belief revision operator
can be viewed as arising from a conditional probability measure on an appropriate space.

**9.8**      Construct a BCS satisfying REV1 and REV2 that has the properties required in
Example 9.3.3. Extend this example to one that satisfies REV1 and REV2 but violates
R7 and R8.

**9.9**      Show that if BCS1–3 hold and $s_a \cdot \phi$ is a local state in $\mathcal{I}$, then $\mathcal{R}[s_a] \cap \mathcal{R}[\phi] \in \mathcal{F}'$.

**9.10**     Prove Lemma 9.3.4.

**9.11**     Show that $\mathcal{I}_1^\dagger \in \mathcal{REV}$.

*__9.12__    Fill in the missing details of Theorem 9.3.5. In particular, show that the definition
of $\circ_{s,a}$ satisfies R1–8 if $K \neq Bel(\mathcal{I}, s_a)$ or $s_a \cdot \phi$ is not a local state in $\mathcal{I}$, and provide
the details of the proof that R7 and R8 hold if $K = Bel(\mathcal{I}, s_a)$ and $s_a \cdot \phi$ is a local state
in $\mathcal{I}$.

**9.13**     Show that the BCS $\mathcal{I}$ constructed in Example 9.3.6 is in $\mathcal{REV}$.

\***9.14**  Prove Theorem 9.3.7.

 **9.15**  Prove Theorem 9.4.1.

\***9.16**  Complete the proof of Theorem 9.4.2(b) by showing that R7 and R8 hold.

 **9.17**  This exercise relates the postulates and property (9.9).

  (a) Show that (9.9) follows from R3′, R4′, R7′, and R8′.

  (b) Show that if BS satisfies R2′ and $\neg\psi \notin BS(E \circ \phi)$, then $\nvdash_{\mathcal{L}_e} \neg(\phi \wedge \psi)$.

  (c) Describe a system $\mathcal{J}$ that satisfies (9.9) and not R9′.

  (d) Show that R8′ follows from R2′, R4′ and R9′.

\***9.18**  Complete the proof of Theorem 9.5.1. Moreover, show that $(\circ, BS_{\mathcal{J}})$ satisfies R1′–9′, thus proving Theorem 9.5.2.

\***9.19**  Complete the proof of Theorem 9.5.3.

\***9.20**  Complete the proof of Theorem 9.6.2. (The difficulty here, as suggested in the text, is making $Pl'_{\mathcal{R}}$ algebraic.)


# Notes

Belief change has been an active area of study in philosophy and, more recently, artificial intelligence. While probabilistic conditioning can be viewed as one approach to belief change, the study of the type of belief change considered in this chapter, where an agent must revise her beliefs after learning or observing something inconsistent with them, was essentially initiated by Alchourrón, Gärdenfors, and Makinson, in a sequence of individual and joint papers. A good introduction to the topic, with an extensive bibliography of the earlier work, is Gärdenfors's book *Knowledge in Flux* [1988]. AGM-style belief revision was introduced by Alchourrón, Gärdenfors, and Makinson [1985]. However, similar axioms already appear in earlier work by Gärdenfors [1978] and, indeed, also in Lewis's [1973] work on counterfactuals. This is perhaps not surprising, given the connection between beliefs and counterfactuals already discussed in Chapter 8. Interestingly, the topic of belief change was studied independently in the database community; the focus there was on how to update a database when the update is inconsistent with information already stored in the database. The original paper on the topic was by Fagin, Ullman, and Vardi [1983]. One of the more influential axiomatic characterizations of belief change—Katsuno and Mendelzon's notion of *belief update* [1991a]—was inspired by database concerns.

The presentation in this chapter is taken from a sequence of papers that Nir Friedman and I wrote. Section 9.1 is largely taken from [Friedman and Halpern 1997]; the discussion of belief change and the AGM axioms as well as iterated belief revision is largely taken from [Friedman and Halpern 1999] (although there are a number of minor differences between the presentation here and that in [Friedman and Halpern 1999]); the discussion of Markovian belief change is from [Friedman and Halpern 1996]. In particular, Propositions 9.1.1, 9.1.2, and 9.1.3 are taken from [Friedman and Halpern 1997], Theorems 9.3.5, 9.3.7, 9.4.1, 9.5.1, 9.5.2, and 9.5.3 are taken (with minor modifications in some cases) from [Friedman and Halpern 1999], and Theorem 9.6.2 is taken from [Friedman and Halpern 1996]. These papers also have references to more current research in belief change, which is still an active topic. I have only scratched the surface of it in this chapter.

Here are the bibliographic references for the specific material discussed in the chapter. Hansson [1999] discusses recent work on *belief bases,* where a belief base is a finite set of formulas whose closure is the belief set. Thinking in terms of belief bases makes it somewhat clearer how revision should work. The circuit diagnosis problem discussed has been well studied in the artificial intelligence literature (see [Davis and Hamscher 1988] for an overview). The discussion here loosely follows the examples of Reiter [1987b]. Representation theorems for the AGM postulates are well known. The earliest is due to Grove [1988]; others can be found in [Boutilier 1994; Katsuno and Mendelzon 1991b; Gärdenfors and Makinson 1988]. Iterated belief change has been the subject of much research; see, for example, [Boutilier 1996; Darwiche and Pearl 1997; Freund and Lehmann 1994; Lehmann 1995; Levi 1988; Nayak 1994; Spohn 1988; Williams 1994]). Markovian belief change is also considered in [Boutilier 1998; Boutilier, Halpern, and Friedman 1998]. As I said in the text, Ramsey [1931a, p. 248] suggested the Ramsey test.

# Chapter 10

# First-Order Modal Logic

*"Contrariwise," continued Tweedledee, "if it was so, it might be, and if it were so, it would be; but as it isn't, it ain't. That's logic!"*

—Charles Lutwidge Dodgson (Lewis Carroll)

Propositional logic is useful for modeling rather simple forms of reasoning, but it lacks the expressive power to capture a number of forms of reasoning. In particular, propositional logic cannot talk about individuals, the properties they have, and relations between them, nor can it quantify over individuals, so as to say that *all* individuals have a certain property or that *some* individual can. These are all things that can be done in first-order logic.

To understand these issue, suppose that Alice is American but Bob is not. In a propositional logic, there could certainly be a primitive proposition $p$ that is intended to express the fact that Alice is American, and another primitive proposition $q$ to express that Bob is American. The statement that Alice is American but Bob is not would then be expressed as $p \land \neg q$. But this way of expressing the statement somehow misses out on the fact that there is one property—being American—and two individuals, Alice and Bob, each of whom may or may not possess the property. In first-order logic, the fact that Alice is American and Bob is not can be expressed using a formula such as *American(Alice)* $\land \neg$*American(Bob)*. This formula brings out the relationship between Alice and Bob more clearly.

First-order logic can also express relations and functional connections between individuals. For example, the fact that Alice is taller than Bob can be expressed using a formula such as *Taller(Alice, Bob)*; the fact that Joe is the father of Sara can be expressed by a formula such as *Joe = Father(Sara)*. Finally, first-order logic can express the fact that *all* individuals have a certain property or that there is *some* individual who has a certain property by using a universal quantifier ∀, read "for all," or an existential quantifier ∃, read "there exists," respectively. For example, the formula $\exists x \forall y \, Taller(x, y)$ says that there is someone who is taller than everyone; the formula $\forall x \forall y \forall z ((Taller(x, y) \land Taller(y, z)) \Rightarrow Taller(x, z))$ says that the taller-than relation is transitive: if $x$ is taller than $y$ and $y$ is taller than $z$, then $x$ is taller than $z$.

First-order modal logic combines first-order logic with modal operators. As with everything else we have looked at so far, new subtleties arise in the combination of first-order logic and modal logic that do not appear in propositional modal logic or first-order logic alone. I first review first-order logic and then consider a number of first-order modal logics.

## 10.1   First-Order Logic

The formal syntax of first-order logic is somewhat more complicated than that of propositional logic. The analogue in first-order logic of the set of primitive propositions is the *(first-order) vocabulary* $\mathcal{T}$, which consists of *relation symbols, function symbols,* and *constant symbols.* Each relation symbol and function symbol in $\mathcal{T}$ has some *arity,* which intuitively corresponds to the number of arguments it takes. If the arity is $k$, then the symbol is $k$-*ary.* In the earlier examples, *Alice* and *Bob* are constant symbols, *American* is a relation symbol of arity 1, *Taller* is a relation symbol of arity 2, and *Father* is a function symbol of arity 1. Because *American* is a relation symbol of arity 1, it does not make sense to write *American(Alice, Bob)*: *American* takes only one argument. Similarly, it does not make sense to write *Taller(Alice)*: *Taller* has arity 2 and takes two arguments. Intuitively, a relation symbol of arity 1 describes a property of an individual (is she an American or not?), a 2-ary relation symbol describes a relation between a pair of individuals, and so on. An example of a 3-ary relation symbol might be *Parents(a, b, c)*: $a$ and $b$ are the parents of $c$. (1-ary, 2-ary, and 3-ary relations are usually called *unary, binary,* and *ternary* relations, respectively, and similarly for functions.)

Besides the symbols in the vocabulary, there is an infinite supply of *variables,* which are usually denoted $x$ and $y$, possibly with subscripts. Constant symbols and variables are both used to denote individuals. More complicated terms denoting individuals can be formed by using function symbols. Formally, the set of *terms* is formed by starting with variables and constant symbols, and closing off under function application, so that if $f$ is a $k$-ary function symbol and $t_1, \ldots, t_k$ are terms, then $f(t_1, \ldots, t_k)$ is a term. Terms are used in formulas. An *atomic formula* is either of the form $P(t_1, \ldots, t_k)$, where $P$ is a $k$-ary relation symbol and $t_1, \ldots, t_k$ are terms, or of the form $t_1 = t_2$, where $t_1$ and $t_2$ are terms. Just as in propositional logic, more complicated formulas can be formed by closing off under negation and conjunction, so that if $\phi$ and $\psi$ are formulas, then so are $\neg\phi$ and $\phi \wedge \psi$. But first-order logic is closed under one more feature: quantification. If $\phi$ is a formula and $x$ is a variable, then $\exists x \phi$ is also a formula; $\forall x \phi$ is an abbreviation for $\neg\exists x \neg\phi$. Call the resulting language $\mathcal{L}^{fo}(\mathcal{T})$, or just $\mathcal{L}^{fo}$; just as in the propositional case, I often suppress the $\mathcal{T}$ if it does not play a significant role.

First-order logic can be used to reason about properties of addition and multiplication. The vocabulary of *number theory* consists of the binary function symbols $+$ and $\times$, and the constant symbols 0 and 1. Examples of terms in this vocabulary are $1 + (1 + 1)$ and $(1 + 1) \times (1 + 1)$. (Although I use infix notation, writing, for example, $1 + 1$ rather than $+(1, 1)$, it should be clear that $+$ and $\times$ are binary function symbols.) The term denoting the sum of $k$ 1s is abbreviated as $k$. Thus, typical formulas of number theory include $2 + 3 = 5$, $2 + 3 = 6$, $2 + x = 6$, and $\forall x \forall y (x + y = y + x)$. Clearly the first formula should be true, given the standard interpretation of the symbols, and the second to be false. It is not clear whether the third formula should be true or not, since the value of $x$ is unknown. Finally, the fourth formula represents the fact that addition is commutative, so it should be true under the standard interpretation of these symbols. The following semantics captures these intuitions.

Semantics is given to first-order formulas using *relational structures*. Roughly speaking, a relational structure consists of a set of individuals, called the *domain* of the structure, and a way of associating with each of the elements of the vocabulary the corresponding entities over the domain. Thus, a constant symbol is associated with an element of the domain, a function symbol is associated with a function on the domain, and so on. More precisely, fix a vocabulary $\mathcal{T}$. A *relational $\mathcal{T}$-structure* (sometimes simply called a relational structure or just a structure) $\mathcal{A}$ consists of a nonempty domain, denoted $\text{dom}(\mathcal{A})$, an assignment of a $k$-ary relation $P^{\mathcal{A}} \subseteq \text{dom}(\mathcal{A})^k$ to each $k$-ary relation symbol $P$ of $\mathcal{T}$, an assignment of a $k$-ary function $f^{\mathcal{A}} : \text{dom}(\mathcal{A})^k \to \text{dom}(\mathcal{A})$ to each $k$-ary function symbol $f$ of $\mathcal{T}$, and an assignment of a member $c^{\mathcal{A}}$ of the domain to each constant symbol $c$. $P^{\mathcal{A}}$, $f^{\mathcal{A}}$, and $c^{\mathcal{A}}$ are called the *denotations* of $P$, $f$, and $c$, respectively, in $\mathcal{A}$.

For example, suppose that $\mathcal{T}$ consists of one binary relation symbol $E$. In that case, a $\mathcal{T}$-structure is simply a directed graph. (Recall that a directed graph consists of a set of nodes, some of which are connected by directed edges going one from node to another.) The domain is the set of nodes of the graph, and the interpretation of $E$ is the edge relation of the graph, so that there is an edge from $d_1$ to $d_2$ exactly if $(d_1, d_2) \in E^{\mathcal{A}}$. As another example, consider the vocabulary of number theory discussed earlier. One relational structure for this vocabulary is the natural numbers, where 0, 1, $+$, and $\times$ get their standard interpretation. Another is the real numbers, where, again, all the symbols get their standard interpretation. Of course, there are many other relational structures over which these symbols can be interpreted.

A relational structure does not provide an interpretation of the variables. Technically, it turns out to be convenient to have a separate function that does this. A *valuation V* on a structure $\mathcal{A}$ is a function from variables to elements of $\text{dom}(\mathcal{A})$. Recall that terms are intended to represent elements in the domain. Given a structure $\mathcal{A}$, a valuation $V$ on $\mathcal{A}$ can be extended in a straightforward way to a function $V^{\mathcal{A}}$ (I typically omit the superscript $\mathcal{A}$ when it is clear from context) that maps terms to elements of $\text{dom}(\mathcal{A})$, simply by defining $V^{\mathcal{A}}(c) = c^{\mathcal{A}}$ for each constant symbol $c$ and then extending the definition by induction on structure to arbitrary terms, by taking $V^{\mathcal{A}}(f(t_1, \ldots, t_k)) = f^{\mathcal{A}}(V^{\mathcal{A}}(t_1), \ldots, V^{\mathcal{A}}(t_k))$.

I next want to define what it means for a formula to be true in a relational structure. Before I give the formal definition, consider a few examples. Suppose, as before, that *American* is a unary relation symbol, *Taller* is a binary relation symbol, and *Alice* and *Bob* are constant symbols. What does it mean for *American(Alice)* to be true in the structure $\mathcal{A}$? If the domain of $\mathcal{A}$ consists of people, then the interpretation *American*$^{\mathcal{A}}$ of the relation symbol *American* can be thought of as the set of all American people in $\text{dom}(\mathcal{A})$. Thus *American(Alice)* should be true in $\mathcal{A}$ precisely if *Alice*$^{\mathcal{A}} \in$ *American*$^{\mathcal{A}}$. Similarly, *Taller(Alice, Bob)* should be true if Alice is taller than Bob under the interpretation of *Taller* in $\mathcal{A}$; that is, if (*Alice*$^{\mathcal{A}}$, *Bob*$^{\mathcal{A}}$) $\in$ *Taller*$^{\mathcal{A}}$.

What about quantification? The English reading suggests that a formula such as $\forall x American(x)$ should be true in the structure $\mathcal{A}$ if every individual in $\text{dom}(\mathcal{A})$ is American, and $\exists x American(x)$ to be true if some individual in $\text{dom}(\mathcal{A})$ is an American. The truth conditions will enforce this.

Recall that a structure does not give an interpretation to the variables. Thus, a structure $\mathcal{A}$ does not give us enough information to decide if a formula such as *Taller(Alice, x)* is true. That depends on the interpretation of $x$, which is given by a valuation. Thus, truth is defined relative to a pair $(\mathcal{A}, V)$ consisting of an interpretation and a valuation: *Taller(Alice, x)* is true in structure $\mathcal{A}$ under valuation $V$ if $(V(Alice), V(x)) = (Alice^{\mathcal{A}}, V(x)) \in Taller^{\mathcal{A}}$.

As usual, the formal definition of truth in a structure $\mathcal{A}$ under valuation $V$ proceeds by induction on the structure of formulas. If $V$ is a valuation, $x$ is a variable, and $d \in \text{dom}(\mathcal{A})$, let $V[x/d]$ be the valuation $V'$ such that $V'(y) = V(y)$ for every variable $y$ except $x$, and $V'(x) = d$. Thus, $V[x/d]$ agrees with $V$ except possibly on $x$ and it assigns the value $d$ to $x$.

> $(\mathcal{A}, V) \models P(t_1, \ldots, t_k)$, where $P$ is a $k$-ary relation symbol and $t_1, \ldots, t_k$ are terms, iff $(V(t_1), \ldots, V(t_k)) \in P^{\mathcal{A}}$;

$(\mathcal{A}, V) \models (t_1 = t_2)$, where $t_1$ and $t_2$ are terms, iff $V(t_1) = V(t_2)$;

$(\mathcal{A}, V) \models \neg\phi$ iff $(\mathcal{A}, V) \not\models \phi$;

$(\mathcal{A}, V) \models \phi_1 \wedge \phi_2$ iff $(\mathcal{A}, V) \models \phi_1$ and $(\mathcal{A}, V) \models \phi_2$;

$(\mathcal{A}, V) \models \exists x\phi$ iff $(\mathcal{A}, V[x/d]) \models \phi$ for some $d \in \mathrm{dom}(\mathcal{A})$.

Recall that $\forall x\phi$ is an abbreviation for $\neg\exists x\neg\phi$. It is easy to see that $(\mathcal{A}, V) \models \forall x\phi$ iff $(\mathcal{A}, V[x/d]) \models \phi$ for every $d \in \mathrm{dom}(\mathcal{A})$ (Exercise 10.1). $\forall$ essentially acts as an infinite conjunction. For suppose that $\psi(x)$ is a formula whose only free variable is $x$; let $\psi(c)$ be the result of substituting $c$ for $x$ in $\psi$; that is, $\psi(c)$ is $\psi[x/c]$. I sometimes abuse notation and write $(\mathcal{A}, V) \models \phi(d)$ for $d \in \mathrm{dom}(\mathcal{A})$ rather than $(\mathcal{A}, V[x/d]) \models \phi$. Abusing notation still further, note that $(\mathcal{A}, V) \models \forall x\phi(x)$ iff $(\mathcal{A}, V) \models \wedge_{d \in D}\phi(d)$, so $\forall$ acts like an infinite conjunction. Similarly, $(\mathcal{A}, V) \models \exists x\phi(x)$ iff $(\mathcal{A}, V) \models \vee_{d \in D}\phi(d)$, so $\exists x$ acts like an infinite disjunction.

Returning to the examples in the language of number theory, let $\mathbb{N}$ be the set of natural numbers, with the standard interpretation of the symbols 0, 1, $+$, and $\times$. Then $(\mathbb{N}, V) \models 2 + 3 = 5$, $(\mathbb{N}, V) \not\models 2 + 3 = 6$, and $(\mathbb{N}, V) \models \forall x\forall y(x + y = y + x)$ for every valuation $V$, as expected. On the other hand, $(\mathbb{N}, V) \models 2 + x = 6$ iff $V(x) = 4$; here the truth of the formula depends on the valuation. Identical results hold if $\mathbb{N}$ is replaced by $\mathbb{R}$, the real numbers, again with the standard interpretation. On the other hand, let $\phi$ be the formula $\exists x(x \times x = 2)$, which says that 2 has a square root. Then $(\mathbb{R}, V) \models \phi$ and $(\mathbb{N}, V) \not\models \phi$ for all valuations $V$.

Notice that while the truth of the formula $2 + x = 6$ depends on the valuation, this is not the case for $\exists x(x \times x = 2)$ or $2 + 3 = 5$. Variables were originally introduced as a crutch, as "placeholders" to describe what was being quantified. It would be useful to understand when they really are acting as placeholders. Essentially, this is the case when all the variables are "bound" by quantifiers. Thus, although the valuation is necessary in determining the truth of $2 + x = 6$, it is not necessary in determining the truth of $\exists x(2 + x = 6)$, because the $x$ in $2 + x = 6$ is bound by the quantifier $\exists x$.

Roughly speaking, an occurrence of a variable $x$ in $\phi$ is *bound* by the quantifier $\forall x$ in a formula such as $\forall x\phi$ or by $\exists x$ in $\exists x\phi$; an occurrence of a variable in a formula is *free* if it is not bound. (A formal definition of what it means for an occurrence of a variable to be free is given in Exercise 10.2.) A formula in which no occurrences of variables are free is called a *sentence*. Observe that $x$ is free in the formula *Taller*$(c, x)$, but no variables are free in the formulas *American*(*Alice*) and $\exists x$*American*$(x)$, so the latter two formulas are sentences. It is not hard to show that the valuation does not affect the truth of a sentence. That is, if $\phi$ is a sentence, and $V$ and $V'$ are valuations on the structure $\mathcal{A}$, then $(\mathcal{A}, V) \models \phi$ iff $(\mathcal{A}, V') \models \phi$ (Exercise 10.2). In other words, a sentence is true or false in a structure, independent of any valuation.

Satisfiability and validity for first-order logic can be defined in a manner analogous to propositional logic: a first-order formula $\phi$ is *valid* in $\mathcal{A}$, written $\mathcal{A} \models \phi$ if $(\mathcal{A}, V) \models \phi$ for all valuations $V$; it is *valid* if $\mathcal{A} \models \phi$ for all structures $\mathcal{A}$; it is *satisfiable* if $(\mathcal{A}, V) \models \phi$ for some structure $\mathcal{A}$ and some valuation $V$.

Just as in the propositional case, $\phi$ is valid if and only if $\neg \phi$ is not satisfiable. There are well-known sound and complete axiomatizations of first-order logic as well. Describing the axioms requires a little notation. Suppose that $\phi$ is a first-order formula in which some occurrences of $x$ are free. Say that a term $t$ is *substitutable in* $\phi$ if there is no subformula of $\phi$ of the form $\exists y \psi$ such that the variable $y$ occurs in $t$. Thus, for example, $f(y)$ is not substitutable in $\phi = P(a) \wedge \exists y(x, Q(y))$, but $f(x)$ is substitutable in $\phi$. If $f(y)$ is substituted for $x$ in $\phi$, then the resulting formula is $P(a) \wedge \exists y(f(y), Q(y))$. Notice that the $y$ in $f(y)$ is then bound by $\exists y$. If $t$ is substitutable in $\phi$, let $\phi[x/t]$ be the result of substituting $t$ for all free occurrences of $x$. Let $\text{AX}^{fo}$ consist of Prop and MP (for propositional reasoning), together with the following axioms and inference rules:

F1.     $\forall x (\phi \Rightarrow \psi) \Rightarrow (\forall x \phi \Rightarrow \forall x \psi)$.

F2.     $\forall x \phi \Rightarrow \phi[x/t]$, where $t$ is substitutable in $\phi$.

F3.     $\phi \Rightarrow \forall x \phi$ if $x$ does not occur free in $\phi$.

F4.     $x = x$.

F5.     $x = y \Rightarrow (\phi \Rightarrow \phi')$, where $\phi$ is a quantifier-free formula and $\phi'$ is obtained from $\phi$ by replacing zero or more occurrences of $x$ in $\phi$ by $y$.

UGen.  From $\varphi$ infer $\forall x \phi$.

F1, F2, and UGen can be viewed as analogues of K1, K2, and KGen, respectively, where $\forall x$ plays the role of $K_i$. This analogy can be pushed further; in particular, it follows from F3 that analogues of K4 and K5 hold for $\forall x$ (Exercise 10.4).

**Theorem 10.1.1**  $\text{AX}^{fo}$ *is a sound and complete axiomatization of first-order logic with respect to relational structures.*

**Proof**  Soundness is straightforward (Exercise 10.5); as usual, completeness is beyond the scope of this book. ∎

In the context of propositional modal logic, it can be shown that there is no loss of generality in restricting to finite sets of worlds, at least as far as satisfiability and validity are concerned. There are *finite-model theorems* that show that if a formula is satisfiable at all, then it is satisfiable in a structure with only finitely many worlds. Thus, no new axioms are added by restricting to structures with only finitely many worlds. The situation is quite different in the first-order case. While there is no loss of generality in restricting to *countable* domains (at least, as far as satisfiability and validity are concerned), restricting to finite domains results in new axioms, as the following example shows:

**Example 10.1.2**   Suppose that $\mathcal{T}$ consists of the constant symbol $c$ and the unary function symbol $f$. Let $\phi$ be the following formula:

$$\forall x \forall y (x \neq y \Rightarrow f(x) \neq f(y)) \wedge \forall x (f(x) \neq c).$$

The first conjunct says that $f$ is one-to-one; the second says that $c$ is not in the range of $f$. It is easy to see that $\phi$ is satisfiable in the natural numbers: take $c$ to be 0 and $f$ to be the successor function (so that $f(x) = x + 1$). However, $f$ is not satisfiable in a relational structure with a finite domain. For suppose that $\mathcal{A} \models \phi$ for some relational structure $\mathcal{A}$. (Since $\phi$ is a sentence, there is no need to mention the valuation.) An easy induction on $k$ shows that $c^{\mathcal{A}}$, $f^{\mathcal{A}}(c^{\mathcal{A}})$, $f^{\mathcal{A}}(f^{\mathcal{A}}(c^{\mathcal{A}}))$, $\ldots$, $(f^{\mathcal{A}})^k(c^{\mathcal{A}})$ must all be distinct (Exercise 10.6). Thus, dom($\mathcal{A}$) cannot be finite. It follows that $\neg\phi$ is valid in relational structures with finite domains, although it is not valid in all relational structures (and hence is not provable in $\mathrm{AX}^{fo}$). ∎

Are there some reasonable axioms that can be added to $\mathrm{AX}^{fo}$ to obtain a complete axiomatization of first-order logic in finite relational structures? Somewhat surprisingly, the answer is no. The set of first-order formulas valid in finite structures is not *recursively enumerable*, that is, there is no program that will generate all and only the valid formulas. It follows that there cannot be a finite (or even recursively enumerable) axiom system that is sound and complete for first-order logic over finite structures. Essentially this says that there is no easy way to characterize finite domains in first-order logic. (By way of contrast, the set of formulas valid in all relational structures—finite or infinite—is recursively enumerable.)

Interestingly, in *bounded* domains (i.e., relational structures whose domain has cardinality at most $N$, for some fixed natural number $N$), there is a complete axiomatization. The following axiom characterizes structures whose domains have cardinality at most $N$, in that it is true in a structure $\mathcal{A}$ iff dom($\mathcal{A}$) has cardinality at most $N$ (Exercise 10.7):

$\mathrm{FIN}_N.\ \exists x_1 \ldots x_N \forall y (y = x_1 \vee \ldots \vee y = x_N).$

Let $\mathrm{AX}^{fo}_N$ be $\mathrm{AX}^{fo}$ together with $\mathrm{FIN}_N$.

**Theorem 10.1.3**  $AX_N^{fo}$ *is a sound and complete axiomatization of first-order logic with respect to relational structures whose domain has cardinality at most N.*

**Proof**   Soundness is immediate from Exercises 10.5 and 10.7. Completeness is beyond the scope of this book (although it is in fact significantly easier to prove in the bounded case than in the unbounded case).  ∎

Propositional logic can be viewed as a very limited fragment of first-order logic, one without quantification, using only unary relations, and mentioning only one constant. Consider the propositional language $\mathcal{L}^{Prop}(\Phi)$. Corresponding to $\Phi$ is the first-order vocabulary $\Phi^*$ consisting of a unary relation symbol $p^*$ for every primitive proposition $p$ in $\Phi$ and a constant symbol $a$. To every propositional formula $\phi$ in $\mathcal{L}^{Prop}(\Phi)$, there is a corresponding first-order formula $\phi^*$ over the vocabulary $\Phi^*$ that results by replacing occurrences of a primitive proposition $p$ in $\phi$ by the formula $p^*(a)$. Thus, for example, $(p \wedge \neg q)^*$ is $p^*(a) \wedge \neg q^*(a)$. Intuitively, $\phi$ and $\phi^*$ express the same proposition. More formally, there is a mapping associating with each truth assignment $v$ over $\Phi$ a relational structure $\mathcal{A}_v$ over $\Phi^*$, where the domain of $\mathcal{A}_v$ consists of one element $d$, which is the interpretation of the constant symbol $a$, and

$$(p^*)^{\mathcal{A}_v} = \begin{cases} \{d\} & \text{if } v(p) = \textbf{true}, \\ \emptyset & \text{otherwise.} \end{cases}$$

**Proposition 10.1.4**   *For every propositional formula $\phi$,*

   *(a)  $v \models \phi$ if and only if $\mathcal{A}_v \models \phi^*$;*

   *(b)  $\phi$ is valid if and only if $\phi^*$ is valid;*

   *(c)  $\phi$ is satisfiable if and only if $\phi^*$ is satisfiable.*

**Proof**   See Exercise 10.8.  ∎

Given that propositional logic is essentially a fragment of first-order logic, why is propositional logic of interest? Certainly, as a pedagogical matter, it is sometimes useful to focus on purely propositional formulas, without the overhead of functions, relations, and quantification. But there is a more significant reason. As I wrote in Chapters 1 and 7, increased expressive power comes at a price. For example, there is no algorithm for deciding whether a first-order formula is satisfiable. (Technically, this problem is undecidable.) It is easy to construct algorithms to check whether a propositional formula is satisfiable. (Technically, this problem is *NP-complete*, but that is much better than being undecidable!) If a problem can be modeled well using propositional logic, then it is worth sticking to propositional logic, rather than moving to first-order logic.

Not only can propositional logic be viewed as a fragment of first-order logic, but propositional epistemic logic can too (at least, as long as the language does not include common knowledge). Indeed, there is a translation of propositional epistemic logic that shows that, in a sense, the axioms for $K_i$ can be viewed as consequences of the axioms for $\forall x$, although it is beyond the scope of this book to go into details (see the notes to this chapter for references).

Although first-order logic is more expressive than propositional logic, it is certainly far from the last word in expressive power. It can be extended in many ways. One way is to consider *second-order logic*. In first-order logic, there is quantification over individuals in the domain. Second-order logic allows, in addition, quantification over functions and predicates. Second-order logic is very expressive. For example, the induction axiom can be expressed in second-order logic using the language of number theory. If $x$ is a variable ranging over natural numbers (the individuals in the domain) and $P$ is a variable ranging over unary predicates, then the induction axiom becomes

$$\forall P((P(0) \wedge \forall x(P(x) \Rightarrow P(x+1))) \Rightarrow \forall x(P(x))).$$

This says that if a unary predicate $P$ holds for 0 and holds for $n+1$ whenever it holds for $n$, then it must hold for all the natural numbers. In this book, I do not consider second-order logic. Although it is very powerful, the increase in power does not seem that useful for reasoning about uncertainty.

Another way in which first-order logic can be extended is by allowing more general notions of quantification than just universal and existential quantifiers. For example, there can be a quantifier $H$ standing for "at least half," so that a formula such as $Hx\phi(x)$ is true (at least in a finite domain) if at least half the elements in the domain satisfy $\phi$. While I do not consider generalized quantifiers here, it turns out that some generalized quantifiers (such as "at least half") can in fact be captured in some of the extensions of first-order logic that I consider in Section 10.3.

Yet a third way to extend first-order logic is to add modalities, just as in propositional logic. That is the focus of this chapter.

## 10.2   First-Order Reasoning about Knowledge

The syntax for first-order epistemic logic is the obvious combination of the constructs of first-order logic—quantification, conjunction, and negation—and the modal operators $K_1, \ldots, K_n$. The semantics uses *relational epistemic structures*. In a (propositional) epistemic structure, each world is associated with a truth assignment to the primitive propositions via the interpretation $\pi$. In a relational epistemic structure, the $\pi$ function associates with each world a relational structure. Formally, a relational epistemic structure for $n$ agents over a vocabulary $\mathcal{T}$ is a tuple $(W, \mathcal{K}_1, \ldots, \mathcal{K}_n, \pi)$, where $W$ is a set of worlds, $\pi$ associates with each world in $W$ a $\mathcal{T}$-structure (i.e., $\pi(w)$ is a $\mathcal{T}$-structure for each world $w \in W$), and $\mathcal{K}_i$ is a binary relation on $W$.

The semantics of first-order modal logic is, for the most part, the result of combining the semantics for first-order logic and the semantics for modal logic in a straightforward way. For example, a formula such as $K_i American(President)$ is true at a world $w$ if, in all worlds that agent $i$ considers possible, the president is American. Note that this formula can be true even if agent $i$ does not know who the president is. That is, there might be some world that agent $i$ considers possible where the president is Bill, and another where the president is George. As long as the president is American in all these worlds, agent $i$ knows that the president is American.

What about a formula such as $\exists x K_i American(x)$? It seems clear that this formula should be true if there is some individual in the domain at world $w$, say *Bill*, such that agent $i$ knows that *Bill* is American. But now there is a problem. Although *Bill* may be a member of the domain of the relational structure $\pi(w)$, it is possible that *Bill* is not a member of the domain of $\pi(w')$ for some world $w'$ that agent $i$ considers possible at world $w$. There have been a number of solutions proposed to this problem that allow different domains at each world, but none of them are completely satisfactory (see the notes for references). For the purposes of this book, I avoid the problem by simply considering only *common-domain epistemic structures,* that is, relational epistemic structures where the domain is the same at every world. To emphasize this point, I write the epistemic structure as $(W, D, \mathcal{K}_1, \ldots, \mathcal{K}_n, \pi)$, where $D$ is the common domain used at each world, that is, $D = \text{dom}(\pi(w))$ for all $w \in W$.

Under the restriction to common-domain structures, defining truth of formulas becomes quite straightforward. Fix a common-domain epistemic structure $M = (W, D, \mathcal{K}_1, \ldots, \mathcal{K}_n, \pi)$. A *valuation* $V$ on $M$ is a function that assigns to each variable a member of $D$. This means that $V(x)$ is independent of the world, although the interpretation of, say, a constant $c$ may depend on the world. The definition of what it means for a formula $\phi$ to be true at a world $w$ of $M$, given valuation $V$, now proceeds by the usual induction on structure. The clauses are exactly the same as those for first-order logic and propositional epistemic logic. For example,

$(M, w, V) \models P(t_1, \ldots, t_k)$, where $P$ is a $k$-ary relation symbol and $t_1, \ldots, t_k$ are terms, iff $(V^{\pi(w)}(t_1), \ldots, V^{\pi(w)}(t_k)) \in P^{\pi(w)}$.

In the case of formulas $K_i \phi$, the definition is just as in the propositional case:

$(M, w, V) \models K_i\phi$ iff $(M, w', V) \models \phi$ for all $w' \in \mathcal{K}_i(w)$.

First-order epistemic logic is more expressive than propositional epistemic logic. One important example of its extra expressive power is that it can distinguish between "knowing that" and "knowing who," by using the fact that variables denote the same individual in the domain at different worlds. For example, the formula $K_{Alice}\exists x\,(Tall(x))$ says that Alice knows that someone is tall. This formula may be true in a given world where Alice does not know whether Bill or George is tall; she may consider one world possible where Bill is tall and consider another world possible where George is tall. Therefore, although Alice knows that there is a tall person, she may not know exactly who the tall person is. On the other hand, the formula $\exists x\,K_{Alice}(Tall(x))$ expresses the proposition that Alice knows someone who is tall. Because a valuation is independent of the world, it is easy to see that this formula says that there is one particular person who is tall in every world that Alice considers possible.

What about axiomatizations? Suppose for simplicity that all the $\mathcal{K}_i$ relations are equivalence relations. In that case, the axioms K1–5 of $S5_n$ are valid in common-domain epistemic structures. It might seem that a complete axiomatization can be obtained by considering the first-order analogue of Prop (i.e., allowing all substitution instances of axioms of first-order logic). Unfortunately, in the resulting system, F2 is not sound.

Consider the following instance of F2:

$$\forall x\neg K_1(Tall(x)) \Rightarrow \neg K_1(Tall(President)). \qquad (10.1)$$

Now consider a relational epistemic structure $M = (W, D, \mathcal{K}_1, \pi)$, where

- $W$ consists of two worlds, $w_1$ and $w_2$;

- $D$ consists of two elements, $d_1$ and $d_2$;

- $\mathcal{K}_1(w_1) = \mathcal{K}_1(w_2) = W$;

- $\pi$ is such that $President^{\pi(w_i)} = \{d_i\}$ and $Tall^{\pi(w_i)} = \{d_i\}$ for $i = 1, 2$.

Note that $d_1$ is not tall in $w_2$ and $d_2$ is not tall in $w_1$; thus, $(M, w_1) \models \forall x\neg K_1(Tall(x))$. On the other hand, the president is $d_1$ and is tall in $w_1$ and the president is $d_2$ and is tall in $w_2$; thus, $(M, w_1) \models K_1(Tall(President))$. It follows that (10.1) is not valid in structure $M$.

What is going on is that the valuation is independent of the world; hence, under a given valuation, a variable $x$ is a *rigid designator,* that is, it denotes the same domain element in every world. On the other hand, a constant symbol such as *President* is not a rigid designator, since it can denote different domain elements in different worlds.

It is easy to see that F2 is valid if $t$ is a variable. More generally, F2 is valid if the term $t$ is a rigid designator (Exercise 10.9). This suggests that F2 can be salvaged by extending the definition of substitutable as follows. If $\phi$ is a first-order formula (one with no occurrences of modal operators), then the definition of $t$ being substitutable in $\phi$ is just that given in Section 10.2; if $\phi$ has some occurrences of modal operators, then $t$ is substitutable in $\phi$ if $t$ is a variable $y$ such that there are no subformulas of the form $\exists y \psi$ in $\phi$. With this extended definition, the hoped-for soundness and completeness result holds.

**Theorem 10.2.1**  *With this definition of substitutable, S5$_n$ and AX$^{fo}$ together provide a sound and complete axiomatization of first-order epistemic logic with respect to relational epistemic structures where the $\mathcal{K}_i$ relation is an equivalence relation.*

## 10.3   First-Order Reasoning about Probability

There is an obvious first-order extension of the propositional logic $\mathcal{L}_n^{QU}$ considered in Section 7.3. The syntax is just a combination of the syntax for first-order logic and that of $\mathcal{L}_n^{QU}$; I omit the formal definition. Call the resulting language $\mathcal{L}_n^{QU,fo}$. $\mathcal{L}_n^{QU,fo}$ includes formulas such as $\forall x (\ell_1(P(x)) \geq 1/2) \wedge \ell_2(\exists y Q(y)) < 1/3$; quantifiers can appear in the scope of likelihood formulas and likelihood formulas can appear in the scope of quantifiers.

Just as in Chapter 7, the likelihood operator $\ell_i$ can be interpreted as probability (if all sets are measurable), inner measure, lower probability, belief, or possibility, depending on the semantics. For example, in the case of probability, a *relational probability structure* has the form $(W, D, \mathcal{PR}_1, \ldots, \mathcal{PR}_n, \pi)$. (Note that, for the same reasons as in the case of knowledge, I am making the common-domain assumption.) Let $\mathcal{M}_n^{meas,fo}$ consist of all relational (measurable) probability structures. I leave the straightforward semantic definitions to the reader.

If this were all there was to it, this would be a very short section. However, consider the two statements "The probability that a randomly chosen bird will fly is greater than .9" and "The probability that Tweety (a particular bird) flies is greater than .9." There is no problem dealing with the second statement; it corresponds to the formula $\ell(Flies(Tweety)) > .9$. (I am assuming that there is only one agent in the picture, so I omit the subscript on $\ell$.) But what about the first statement? What is the formula that should hold at a set of worlds whose probability is greater than .9?

The most obvious candidate is $\ell(\forall x(Bird(x) \Rightarrow Flies(x)) > .9$. However, it might very well be the case that in each of the worlds considered possible, there is at least one bird that doesn't fly. Hence, the statement $\forall x (Bird(x) \Rightarrow Flies(x))$ holds in none of the worlds (and so has probability 0); thus, $\ell(\forall x (Bird(x) \Rightarrow Flies(x))) > .9$ does not capture the first statement. What about $\forall x (\ell(Bird(x) \Rightarrow Flies(x)) > .9)$ or, perhaps better, $\forall x (\ell(Flies(x) \mid Bird(x)) > .9)$? This runs into problems if there is a constant, say Opus, that represents an individual, say a penguin, that does not fly and is a rigid designator. Then $\ell(Flies(Opus) \mid Bird(Opus)) = 0$, contradicting both $\forall x (\ell(Flies(x) \mid Bird(x)) > .9$ and $\forall x (\ell(Bird(x) \Rightarrow Flies(x)) > .9)$. (It is important here that *Opus* is a rigid designator. The two statements $\forall x (\ell(Flies(x) \mid Bird(x)) > .9)$ and $\ell(Flies(Opus) \mid Bird(Opus)) = 0$ are consistent if *Opus* is not a rigid designator; see Exercise 10.10.)

There seems to be a fundamental difference between these two statements. The first can be viewed as a statement about what one might expect as the result of performing some experiment or trial in a given situation. It can also be viewed as capturing statistical information about the world, since given some statistical information (say, that 90% of the individuals in a population have property $P$), then a randomly chosen individual should have probability .9 of having property $P$. By way of contrast, the second statement captures a *degree of belief*. The first statement seems to assume only one possible world (the "real" world), and in this world, some probability measure over the set of birds. It is saying that, with probability greater than .9, a bird chosen at random (according to this measure) will fly. The second statement implicitly assumes the existence of a number of possible worlds (in some of which Tweety flies, while in others Tweety doesn't), with some probability over these possibilities. Not surprisingly, the possible-worlds approach is well-suited to handling the second statement, but not the first.

It is not hard to design a language appropriate for statistical reasoning suitable for dealing with the first statement. The language includes terms of the form $\|\phi\|_x$, which can be interpreted as "the probability that a randomly chosen $x$ in the domain satisfies $\phi$." This is analogous to terms such as $\ell(\phi)$ in $\mathcal{L}^{QU}$. More generally, there can be an arbitrary set of variables in the subscript. To understand the need for this, suppose that the formula $Son(x, y)$ says that $x$ is the son of $y$. Now consider the three terms $\|Son(x, y)\|_x$, $\|Son(x, y)\|_y$, and $\|Son(x, y)\|_{\{x, y\}}$. The first describes the probability that a randomly chosen $x$ is the son of $y$; the second describes the probability that $x$ is the son of a randomly chosen $y$; the third describes the probability that a randomly chosen pair $(x, y)$ will have the property that $x$ is the son of $y$. These three statements are all quite different. By allowing different sets of random variables in the subscript, they can all be expressed in the logic.

More formally, define a *statistical likelihood term* to have the form $\|\phi\|_X$, where $\phi$ is a formula and $X$ is a set of variables. A *(linear) statistical likelihood formula* is one of the form $a_1 \| \phi_1 \|_{X_1} + \cdots + a_k \| \phi_k \|_{X_k} > b$. Formulas are now formed just as in first-order logic, except that linear statistical likelihood formulas are allowed. In this language, the statement "The probability that a randomly chosen bird will fly is greater than .9" can easily be expressed. With some abuse of notation, it is just $\| Flies(x) \mid Bird(x) \|_x > .9$. (Without the abuse, it would be $\| Flies(x) \wedge Bird(x) \|_x > .9 \| Bird(x) \|_x$ or $\| Flies(x) \wedge Bird(x) \|_x - .9 \| Bird(x) \|_x > 0$.)

Quantifiers can be combined with statistical likelihood formulas. For example, $\forall x (\| Son(x, y) \|_y > .9)$ says that for every person $x$, the probability that $x$ is the son of a randomly chosen person $y$ is greater than .9; $\forall y (\| Son(x, y) \|_x > .9)$ says that for every person $y$, the probability that a randomly chosen $x$ is the son of $y$ is greater than .9. Let $\mathcal{L}^{QU,stat}$ be the language that results from combining the syntax of first-order logic with statistical likelihood formulas.

As with $\ell$, statistical likelihood terms can be evaluated with respect to any quantitative representation of uncertainty. For definiteness, I use probability here. A *statistical* $\mathcal{T}$-*structure* is a tuple $(\mathcal{A}, \mu)$, where $\mathcal{A}$ is a relational structure and $\mu$ is a probability measure on $\text{dom}(\mathcal{A})$. To simplify matters, I assume that all subsets of $\text{dom}(\mathcal{A})$ are measurable, that $\text{dom}(\mathcal{A})$ is finite or countable, and that $\mu$ is countably additive. That means that $\mu$ is characterized by the probability it assigns to the elements of $\text{dom}(\mathcal{A})$. Let $\mathcal{M}^{meas,stat}$ consist of all statistical $\mathcal{T}$-structures of this form.

Statistical structures should be contrasted with relational probability structures. In a statistical structure, there are no possible worlds and thus no probability on worlds. There is essentially only one world and the probability is on the domain. There is only one probability measure, not a different one for each agent. (It would be easy to allow a different probability measure for each agent, but the implicit assumption is that the probability in a statistical structure is objective and does not represent the agent's degree of belief.) An important special subclass of statistical structures (which is the focus of Chapter 11) are structures where the domain is finite and the probability measure is uniform (which makes all domain elements equally likely). This interpretation is particularly important for statistical reasoning. In that case, a formula such as $\| Flies(x) \mid Bird(x) \|_x > .9$ could be interpreted as "more than 90 percent of birds fly."

There are a number of reasons for not insisting that $\mu$ be uniform in general. For one thing, there are no uniform probability measures in countably infinite domains where all sets are measurable. (A uniform probability measure in a countably infinite domain would have to assign probability 0 to each individual element in the domain, which means by countable additivity it would have to assign probability 0 to the whole domain.) For another, for representations of uncertainty other than probability, there is not always an obvious analogue of uniform probability measures. (Consider plausibility measures, for example. What would uniformity mean there?) Finally, there are times when a perfectly reasonable way of making choices might not result in all domain elements being equally likely. For example, suppose that there are seven balls, four in one urn and three in another. If an urn is chosen at random and then a ball in the urn is chosen at random, not all the balls are equally likely. The balls in the urn with four balls have probability 1/8 of being chosen; the balls in the urn with three balls have probability 1/6 of being chosen. In any case, there is no additional difficulty in giving semantics to the case that $\mu$ is an arbitrary probability measure, so that is what I will do. On the other hand, to understand the intuitions, it is probably best to think in terms of uniform measures.

One more construction is needed before giving the semantics. Given a probability measure $\mu$ on $D$, there is a standard construction for defining the *product measure* $\mu^n$ on the product domain $D^n$ consisting of all $n$-tuples of elements of $D$: define $\mu^n(d_1, \ldots, d_n) = \mu(d_1) \times \ldots \times \mu(d_n)$. Note that if $\mu$ assigns equal probability to every element of $D$, then $\mu^n$ assigns equal probability to every element of $D^n$.

The semantic definitions are identical to those for first-order logic; the only new clause is that for statistical likelihood formulas. Given a statistical structure $M = (\mathcal{A}, \mu)$, a valuation $V$, and a statistical likelihood term $\|\phi\|_{\{x_1, \ldots, x_n\}}$, define

$$[\|\phi\|_{\{x_1, \ldots, x_n\}}]_{M,V} = \mu^n(\{(d_1, \ldots, d_n) : (M, V[x_1/d_1, \ldots, x_n/d_n]) \models \phi\}).$$

That is, $[\|\phi\|_{\{x_1, \ldots, x_n\}}]_{M,V}$ is the probability that a randomly chosen tuple $(d_1, \ldots, d_n)$ (chosen according to $\mu^n$) satisfies $\phi$. Then define

$$(M, V) \models a_1\|\phi_1\|_{X_1} + \cdots + a_k\|\phi_k\|_{X_k} > b$$
$$\text{iff } a_1[\|\phi_1\|_{X_1}]_{M,V} + \cdots + a_k[\|\phi_k\|_{X_k}]_{M,V} > b.$$

Note that the $x$ in $\|\phi\|_x$ acts in many ways just like the $x$ in $\forall x$; for example, both bind free occurrences of $x$ in $\phi$, and in both cases the $x$ is a dummy variable. That is, $\forall x \phi$ is equivalent to $\forall y \phi[x/y]$ and $\|\phi\|_x > b$ is equivalent to $\|\phi[x/y]\|_y > b$ if $y$ does not appear in $\phi$ (see Exercise 10.11). Indeed, $\|\cdot\|_x$ can express some of the general notions of quantification referred to in Section 10.1. For example, with a uniform probability measure and a finite domain, $\|\phi\|_x > 1/2$ expresses the fact that at least half the elements in the domain satisfy $\phi$, and thus is equivalent to the formula $Hx\phi(x)$ from Section 10.1.

Of course, statistical reasoning and reasoning about degrees of belief can be combined, by having a structure with both a probability on the domain and a probability on possible worlds. The details are straightforward, so I omit them here.

What about axioms? First consider reasoning about degrees of belief. It is easy to see that F1–5 are sound, as are QU1–3, QUGen, and Ineq from Section 7.3. They are, however, not complete. In fact, there is no complete axiomatization for the language $\mathcal{L}_n^{QU,fo}$ with respect to $\mathcal{M}_n^{meas,fo}$ (even if $n = 1$); the set of formulas in $\mathcal{L}_n^{QU,fo}$ valid with respect to $\mathcal{M}_n^{meas,fo}$ is not recursively enumerable. Restricting to finite domains does not help (since first-order logic restricted to finite domains is by itself not axiomatizable), nor does restricting to finite sets of worlds. But, as in the case of first-order logic, restricting to bounded domains does help.

Let $AX_{n,N}^{prob,fo}$ consist of the axioms and inference rule of $AX_N^{fo}$ together with those of $AX_n^{prob}$ and one other axiom:

IV.     $x \neq y \Rightarrow \ell_i(x \neq y) = 1.$

IV stands for *Inequality of Variables*. It is easy to see that IV is sound, as is the analogous property for equality, called EV.

EV.     $x = y \Rightarrow \ell_i(x = y) = 1.$

EV just follows from the fact that variables are treated as rigid and have the same value in all worlds. EV is provable from the other axioms, so it is not necessary to include it in the axiomatization (Exercise 10.13). In fact, the analogues of IV and EV are *both* provable in the case of knowledge, which is why they do not appear in the axiomatization of Theorem 10.2.1 (Exercise 10.14).

**Theorem 10.3.1** $AX_{n,N}^{prob,fo}$ *is a sound and complete axiomatization with respect to structures in* $\mathcal{M}_n^{meas,fo}$ *with a domain of cardinality at most N for the language* $\mathcal{L}_n^{QU,fo}$.

**Proof**   Soundness is immediate from the soundness of $AX_N^{fo}$ in relational structures of size at most $N$, the soundness of $AX_n^{prob}$ in the propositional case, and the validity of EV, proved in Exercise 10.13. Completeness is beyond the scope of this book.   ∎

Thus, there is a sense in which the axioms of first-order logic together with those for propositional reasoning about probability capture the essence of first-order reasoning about probability.

Much the same results hold for statistical reasoning. Consider the following axioms and rule of inference, where $X$ ranges over finite sets of variables:

PD1.   $\|\phi\|_X \geq 0.$

PD2.   $\forall x_1 \ldots \forall x_n \phi \Rightarrow \|\phi\|_{\{x_1,\ldots,x_n\}} = 1.$

PD3.   $\|\phi \wedge \psi\|_X + \|\phi \wedge \neg\psi\|_X = \|\phi\|_X.$

PD4. $\|\phi\|_X = \|\phi[x/z]\|_{X[x/z]}$, where $x \in X$ and $z$ does not appear in $X$ or $\phi$.

PD5. $\|\phi \wedge \psi\|_{X \cup Y} = \|\phi\|_X \times \|\psi\|_Y$ if none of the free variables of $\phi$ is contained in $Y$, none of the free variables of $\psi$ is contained in $X$, and $X$ and $Y$ are disjoint.

PDGen. From $\phi \Leftrightarrow \psi$ infer $\|\phi\|_X = \|\psi\|_X$.

PD1, PD3, and PDGen are the obvious analogues of QU1, QU3, and QUGen, respectively. PD2 is an extension of QU2. PD4 allows renaming of variables bound by "statistical" quantification. As I mentioned earlier, there is an analogous property for first-order logic, namely $\forall x \phi \Rightarrow \forall y \phi[x/y]$, which follows easily from F2 and F3 (Exercise 10.11). PD5 says that if $\psi$ and $\phi$ do not have any free variables in common, then they can be treated as independent. Its validity follows from the use of the product measure in the semantics (Exercise 10.12).

F1–5 continue to be sound for statistical reasoning, except that the notion of substitutability in F2 must be modified to take into account that $\| \cdot \|_y$ acts like a quantifier, so that $t$ not substitutable in $\phi$ if the variable $y$ occurs in $t$ and there is a term $\| \cdot \|_y$ in $\phi$.

As in the case of degrees of belief, there is no complete axiomatization for the language $\mathcal{L}^{QU,stat}$ with respect to $\mathcal{M}^{meas,stat}$; the set of formulas in $\mathcal{L}^{QU,stat}$ valid with respect to $\mathcal{M}^{meas,stat}$ is not recursively enumerable. And again, while restricting to structures with finite domains does not help, restricting to bounded domains does. Let $AX_N^{stat}$ consist of the axioms and inference rule of $AX_N^{fo}$ together with PD1–5 and PDGen.

**Theorem 10.3.2** $AX_N^{stat}$ *is a sound and complete axiomatization with respect to structures in* $\mathcal{M}^{meas,stat}$ *with a domain of cardinality at most N for the language* $\mathcal{L}^{QU,stat}$.

## 10.4 First-Order Conditional Logic

In Section 8.6 a number of different approaches to giving semantics to conditional logic, including possibility structures, ranking structures, PS structures (sequences of probability sequences), and preferential structures, were all shown to be characterized by the same axiom system, $AX_n^{cond}$, occasionally with C5 and C6 (as defined in Section 8.6) added, as appropriate. This suggests that all the different semantic approaches are essentially the same, at least as far as conditional logic is concerned. A more accurate statement would be that these approaches are the same as far as *propositional* conditional logic is concerned. Some significant differences start to emerge once the additional expressive power of first-order quantification is allowed. Again, plausibility is the key to understanding the differences.

Just as with probabilistic reasoning, for all these approaches, it is possible to consider a "degrees of belief" version, with some measure of likelihood over the possible worlds, and a "statistical" version, with some measure of likelihood on the domain. For the purposes of this section, I focus on the degrees of belief version. There are no new issues that arise for the statistical version, beyond those that already arise in the degrees of belief version. Perhaps the most significant issue that emerges in first-order conditional logic is the importance of allowing structures with not only infinite domains but infinitely many possible worlds.

Let $\mathcal{M}_n^{qual,fo}$, $\mathcal{M}_n^{ps,fo}$, $\mathcal{M}_n^{poss,fo}$, $\mathcal{M}_n^{poss^+,fo}$, $\mathcal{M}_n^{rank,fo}$, $\mathcal{M}_n^{rank^+,fo}$, and $\mathcal{M}_n^{pref,fo}$ be the class of all relational qualitative plausibility structures, PS structures, possibility structures, possibility structures where the possibility measure satisfies Poss3$^+$, ranking structures, ranking structures where the ranking function satisfies Rk3$^+$, and preferential structures, respectively, for $n$ agents. Let $\mathcal{L}_n^{\rightarrow,fo}(\mathcal{T})$ be the obvious first-order analogue of the $\mathcal{L}_n^{\rightarrow}(\Phi)$.

I start with plausibility, where things work out quite nicely. Clearly the axioms of $\text{AX}_n^{cond}$ and $\text{AX}^{fo}$ are sound in $\mathcal{M}_n^{qual,fo}$. To get completeness, it is also necessary to include the analogue of IV. Let $N_i\phi$ be an abbreviation for $\neg\phi \rightarrow_i false$. It is easy to show that if $M = (W, D, \mathcal{PL}_1, \ldots, \mathcal{PL}_n, \pi) \in \mathcal{M}_n^{qual,fo}$, then $(M, w) \models N_i\phi$ iff $\text{Pl}_{w,i}(\llbracket\neg\phi\rrbracket_M) = \bot$; that is, $N_i\phi$ asserts that the plausibility of $\neg\phi$ is the same as that of the empty set, so that $\phi$ is true "almost everywhere" (Exercise 10.15). Thus, $N_i\phi$ is the plausibilistic analogue of $\ell_i(\phi) = 1$. Let $\text{AX}^{cond,fo}$ consist of all the axioms and inference rules of $\text{AX}^{cond}$ (for propositional reasoning about conditional logic) and $\text{AX}^{fo}$, together with the plausibilistic version of IV:

IVPl.   $x \neq y \Rightarrow N_i(x \neq y)$.

The validity of IVPl in $\mathcal{M}^{qual,fo}$ follows from the fact that variables are rigid, just as in the case of probability (Exercise 10.16).

**Theorem 10.4.1** $\text{AX}_n^{cond,fo}$ *is a sound and complete axiomatization with respect to* $\mathcal{M}_n^{qual,fo}$ *for the language* $\mathcal{L}_n^{\rightarrow,fo}$.

In the propositional case, adding C6 to $\text{AX}_n^{cond}$ gives a sound and complete axiomatization of $\mathcal{L}_n^{\rightarrow}$ with respect to PS structures (Theorem 8.6.5). The analogous result holds in the first-order case.

**Theorem 10.4.2** $\mathrm{AX}_n^{cond,fo} + \{\mathrm{C6}\}$ *is a sound and complete axiomatization with respect to* $\mathcal{M}_n^{ps,fo}$ *for the language* $\mathcal{L}_n^{\rightarrow,fo}$.

Similarly, I conjecture that $\mathrm{AX}_n^{cond,fo} + \{\mathrm{C5,C6}\}$ is a sound and complete axiomatization with respect to $\mathcal{M}_n^{poss,fo}$ for the language $\mathcal{L}_n^{\rightarrow,fo}$, although this has not been proved yet.

What about the other types of structures considered in Chapter 8? It turns out that more axioms besides C5 and C6 are required. To see why, recall the lottery paradox (Example 8.1.2).

**Example 10.4.3**   The key characteristics of the lottery paradox are that any particular individual is highly unlikely to win, but someone is almost certainly guaranteed to win. Thus, the lottery has the following two properties:

$$\forall x(true \rightarrow \neg Winner(x)) \tag{10.2}$$

$$true \rightarrow \exists x\, Winner(x). \tag{10.3}$$

Let the formula *Lottery* be the conjunction of (10.2) and (10.3). (I am assuming here that there is only one agent doing the reasoning, so I drop the subscript on $\rightarrow$.)

*Lottery* is satisfiable in $\mathcal{M}_1^{qual,fo}$. Define $M_{lot} = (W_{lot}, D_{lot}, \mathcal{PL}_{lot}, \pi_{lot})$ as follows:

- $D_{lot}$ is a countable domain consisting of the individuals $d_1, d_2, d_3, \ldots$;

- $W_{lot}$ consists of a countable number of worlds $w_1, w_2, w_3, \ldots$;

- $\mathcal{PL}_{lot}(w) = (W_{lot}, \mathrm{Pl}_{lot})$, where $\mathrm{Pl}_{lot}$ gives the empty set plausibility 0, each nonempty finite set plausibility 1/2, and each infinite set plausibility 1;

- $\pi_{lot}$ is such that in world $w_i$ the lottery winner is individual $d_i$ (i.e., $Winner^{\pi_{lot}(w_i)}$ is the singleton set $\{d_i\}$).

It is straightforward to check that $\mathrm{Pl}_{lot}$ is qualitative (Exercise 10.17). Abusing notation slightly, let $Winner(d_i)$ be the formula that is true if individual $d_i$ wins. (Essentially, I am treating $d_i$ as a constant in the language that denotes individual $d_i \in D_{lot}$ in all worlds.) By construction, $[\![\neg Winner(d_i)]\!]_{M_{lot}} = W - \{w_i\}$, so

$$\mathrm{Pl}_{lot}([\![\neg Winner(d_i)]\!]_{M_{lot}}) = 1 > 1/2 = \mathrm{Pl}([\![Winner(d_i)]\!]_{M_{lot}}).$$

That is, the plausibility of individual $d_i$ losing is greater than the plausibility of individual $d_i$ winning, for each $d_i \in D_{lot}$. Thus, $M_{lot}$ satisfies (10.2). On the other hand, $[\![\exists x\, Winner(x)]\!]_{M_{lot}} = W$, so $\mathrm{Pl}_{lot}([\![\exists x\, Winner(x)]\!]_{M_{lot}}) > \mathrm{Pl}_{lot}([\![\neg \exists x\, Winner(x)]\!]_{M_{lot}})$; hence, $M_{lot}$ satisfies (10.3).

It is also possible to construct a relational PS structure (in fact, using the same set $W_{lot}$ of worlds and the same interpretation $\pi_{lot}$) that satisfies *Lottery* (Exercise 10.18). On the other hand, there is no relational ranking structure in $\mathcal{M}_1^{rank^+,fo}$ that satisfies *Lottery*. To see this, suppose that $M = (W, D, \mathcal{RANK}, \pi) \in \mathcal{M}_1^{rank^+,fo}$ and $(M, w) \models Lottery$. Suppose that $\mathcal{RANK}(w) = (W', \kappa)$. For each $d \in D$, let $W_d$ be the subset of worlds in $W'$ where $d$ is the winner of the lottery; that is, $W_d = \{w \in W' : d \in Winner^{\pi(w)}\}$. It must be the case that $\kappa(W' - W_d) < \kappa(W_d)$ (i.e., $\kappa(W' \cap [\![\neg Winner(d)]\!]_M) < \kappa(W' \cap [\![Winner(d)]\!]_M))$, otherwise (10.2) would not be true at world $w$. Let $w_0$ be a world in $W'$ such that $\kappa(w_0) = 0$. (It easily follows from Rk3$^+$ that there must be some world with this property; there may be more than one.) Clearly $w_0 \notin W_d$ for all $d \in D$, for otherwise $\kappa(W_d) = 0 \leq \kappa(W' - W_d)$. That means no individual $d$ wins in $w_0$; that is, $Winner^{\pi(w_0)} = \emptyset$. Thus, $w_0 \in [\![\neg \exists x\, Winner(x)]\!]_M \cap W'$. But that means that

$$\kappa([\![\neg \exists x\, Winner(x)]\!]_M \cap W') \leq \kappa([\![\exists x\, Winner(x)]\!]_M \cap W'),$$

so $(M, w) \not\models true \to \exists x\, Winner(x)$. This contradicts the initial assumption that $(M, w) \models Lottery$.

There is a ranking structure in $\mathcal{M}_1^{rank,fo}$ that satisfies *Lottery*. It is essentially the same as the plausibility structure that satisfies *Lottery*. Consider the relational ranking structure $M_1 = (W_{lot}, D_{lot}, \mathcal{RANK}, \pi_{lot})$, where all the components except for $\mathcal{RANK}$ are the same as in the plausibility structure $M_{lot}$, and $\mathcal{RANK}(w) = (W_{lot}, \kappa)$, where $\kappa(U)$ is 0 if $U$ is infinite, 1 if $U$ is a finite and nonempty, and $\infty$ if $U = \emptyset$. It is easy to check that $M_1$ satisfies lottery, for essentially the same reasons that $M_{lot}$ does.

There is also a relational possibility structure in $\mathcal{M}_n^{poss^+,fo}$ that satisfies *Lottery*. Consider the relational possibility structure $M_2 = (W_{lot}, D_{lot}, \mathcal{POSS}, \pi_{lot})$, where all the components besides $\mathcal{POSS}$ are just as in the plausibility structure $M_{lot}$, $\mathcal{POSS}(w) = (W_{lot}, Poss)$, $Poss(w_i) = i/(i + 1)$, and Poss is extended to sets so that $Poss(U) = \sup_{w \in U} Poss(w)$. (This guarantees that Poss3$^+$ holds.) Thus, if $i > j$, then it is more possible that individual $d_i$ wins than individual $d_j$. Moreover, this possibility approaches 1 as $i$ increases. It is not hard to show that $M_2$ satisfies *Lottery* (Exercise 10.19).

As in Section 2.7 (see also Exercise 2.51), Poss determines a total order on $W$ defined by taking $w \succeq w'$ if $Poss(w) \geq Poss(w')$. According to this order, $\ldots \succ w_3 \succ w_2 \succ w_1$. There is also a preferential structure in $\mathcal{M}_n^{pref,fo}$ that uses this order and satisfies *Lottery* (Exercise 10.20). ∎

Although *Lottery* is satisfiable in $\mathcal{M}_1^{poss^+,fo}$, $\mathcal{M}_1^{pref,fo}$, and $\mathcal{M}_1^{rank,fo}$, slight variants of it are not, as the following examples show:

**Example 10.4.4**   Consider a *crooked lottery,* where there is one individual who is more likely to win than any of the others, but who is still unlikely to win. This can be expressed using the following formula *Crooked*:

$$\neg\exists x(\mathit{Winner}(x) \to \mathit{false}) \land \exists y\forall x((\mathit{Winner}(x) \lor \mathit{Winner}(y)) \to \mathit{Winner}(y)).$$

The first conjunct of *Crooked* states that each individual has some plausibility of winning; in the language of plausibility, this means that if $(M, w) \models \mathit{Crooked}$, then $\mathrm{Pl}(W_w \cap [\![\mathit{Winner}(d)]\!]_M) > \bot$ for each domain element $d$. Roughly speaking, the second conjunct states that there is an individual who is at least as likely to win as anyone else. More precisely, it says if $(M, w) \models \mathit{Crooked}$, $d^*$ is the individual guaranteed to exist by the second conjunct, and $d$ is any other individual, then it must be the case that $\mathrm{Pl}(W_w \cap [\![\mathit{Winner}(d) \land \neg\mathit{Winner}(d^*)]\!]_M) < \mathrm{Pl}(W_w \cap [\![\mathit{Winner}(d^*)]\!]_M)$. This follows from the observation that if $(M, w) \models (\phi \lor \psi) \to \psi$, then either $\mathrm{Pl}(W_w \cap [\![\phi \lor \psi]\!]_M) = \bot$ (which cannot happen for the particular $\phi$ and $\psi$ in the second conjunct because of the first conjunct of *Crooked*) or $\mathrm{Pl}(W_w \cap [\![\phi \land \neg\psi]\!]_M) < \mathrm{Pl}(W_w \cap [\![\psi]\!]_M)$.

Take the crooked lottery to be formalized by the formula *Lottery* $\land$ *Crooked*. It is easy to model the crooked lottery using plausibility. Consider the relational plausibility structure $M'_{lot} = (W_{lot}, D_{lot}, \mathcal{PL}'_{lot}, \pi_{lot})$, which is identical to $M_{lot}$ except that $\mathcal{PL}'_{lot}(w) = (W, \mathrm{Pl}'_{lot})$, where

- $\mathrm{Pl}'_{lot}(\emptyset) = 0$;

- if $A$ is finite, then $\mathrm{Pl}'_{lot}(A) = 3/4$ if $w_1 \in A$ and $\mathrm{Pl}'_{lot}(A) = 1/2$ if $w_1 \notin A$;

- if $A$ is infinite, then $\mathrm{Pl}'_{lot}(A) = 1$.

It is easy to check that $\mathrm{Pl}'_{lot}$ is qualitative, that $M'_{lot}$ satisfies *Crooked*, taking $d_1$ to be the special individual whose existence is guaranteed by the second conjunct (since $\mathrm{Pl}'_{lot}([\![\mathit{Winner}(d_1)]\!]_{M'_{lot}}) = 3/4 > 1/2 = \mathrm{Pl}'_{lot}([\![\mathit{Winner}(d_i)]\!] \cap \neg\mathit{Winner}(d_1)]\!]_{M'_{lot}})$ for $i > 1$), and that $\mathrm{Pl}'_{lot} \models \mathit{Lottery}$ (Exercise 10.21). Indeed, $\mathrm{Pl}'_{lot}$ is a possibility measure, although it does not satisfy Poss3$^+$, so $M'_{lot} \notin \mathcal{M}_n^{poss^+, fo}$. In fact, *Lottery* $\land$ *Crooked* is not satisfiable in either $\mathcal{M}_n^{poss^+, fo}$ or $\mathcal{M}_n^{pref, fo}$ (Exercise 10.22). Intuitively, the problem in the case of possibility measures is that the possibility of $d_1$ winning has to be at least as great as that of $d_i$ winning for $i \neq 1$, yet it must be less than 1. However, the possibility of *someone* winning must be 1. This is impossible. A similar problem occurs in the case of preferential structures. ∎

**Example 10.4.5**    Consider a *rigged lottery,* where for every individual $x$, there is an individual $y$ who is more likely to win than $x$. This can be expressed using the following formula *Rigged*, which just switches the quantifiers in the second conjunct of *Crooked*:

$$\forall x \, \exists y ((Winner(x) \vee Winner(y)) \rightarrow Winner(y)).$$

It is easy to model the rigged lottery using plausibility. Indeed, it is easy to check that the relational possibility structure $M_1$ satisfies *Lottery* $\wedge$ *Rigged*. However, *Rigged* is not satisfiable in $\mathcal{M}_1^{rank, fo}$ (Exercise 10.23). Intuitively, if $M \in \mathcal{M}_1^{rank, fo}$ satisfies *Rigged*, consider the individual $d$ such that $[\![ Winner(d) ]\!]_M$ is minimum. (Since ranks are natural numbers, there has to be such an individual $d$.) But *Rigged* says that there has to be an individual who is more likely to win than $d$; this quickly leads to a contradiction.  ∎

Examples 10.4.3, 10.4.4, and 10.4.5 show that $AX_n^{cond, fo}$ (even with C5 and C6) is not a complete axiomatization for the language $\mathcal{L}_n^{\rightarrow, fo}$ with respect to any of $\mathcal{M}_n^{poss^+, fo}$, $\mathcal{M}_n^{rank, fo}$, $\mathcal{M}_n^{rank^+, fo}$, or $\mathcal{M}_n^{pref, fo}$: $\neg Lottery$ is valid in $\mathcal{M}_1^{rank^+, fo}$, but is not provable in $AX_1^{cond, fo}$ even with C5 and C6 (if it were, it would be valid in plausibility structures that satisfy C5 and C6, which Example 8.1.2 shows it is not); similarly, $\neg(Lottery \wedge Crooked)$ is valid in $\mathcal{M}_1^{poss^+, fo}$ and $\mathcal{M}_1^{pref, fo}$ and is not provable in $AX_1^{cond, fo}$, and $\neg Rigged$ is valid in $\mathcal{M}_1^{rank, fo}$ but is not provable in $AX_1^{cond, fo}$. These examples show that first-order conditional logic can distinguish these different representations of uncertainty although propositional conditional logic cannot.

Both the domain $D_{lot}$ and the set $W_{lot}$ of worlds in $M_{lot}$ are infinite. This is not an accident. The formula *Lottery* is not satisfiable in any relational plausibility structure with either a finite domain or a finite set of worlds (or, more accurately, it is satisfiable in such a structure only if $\bot = \top$). This follows from the following more general result:

**Proposition 10.4.6**    *Suppose that $M = (W, D, \mathcal{PL}_1, \ldots, \mathcal{PL}_n, \pi)$ and either $W$ or $D$ is finite. If $x$ does not appear free in $\psi$, then the following axiom is valid in $M$:*

C9.     $\forall x (\psi \rightarrow_i \phi(x)) \Rightarrow (\psi \rightarrow_i \forall x \phi(x)).$

**Proof**    See Exercise 10.24.  ∎

**Corollary 10.4.7**    *Suppose that $M = (W, D, \mathcal{PL}, \pi)$ and either $W$ or $D$ is finite. Then $M \models \forall x (true \rightarrow \neg Winner(x)) \Rightarrow true \rightarrow \forall x \neg Winner(x)$. Hence $M \models Lottery \Rightarrow (true \rightarrow false)$.*

**Proof**   It is immediate from Proposition 10.4.6 that

$$M \models \forall x(true \rightarrow \neg Winner(x)) \Rightarrow true \rightarrow \forall x \neg Winner(x).$$

Thus, if $(M, w) \models Lottery$, then

$$(M, w) \models true \rightarrow \forall x \neg Winner(x) \wedge true \rightarrow \exists x \, Winner(x).$$

From the AND rule (C2) and right weakening (RC2), it follows that

$$(M, w) \models true \rightarrow false.$$

Thus, $M \models Lottery \Rightarrow (true \rightarrow false)$. ∎

Corollary 10.4.7 shows that if $W$ or $D$ is finite, then if each person is unlikely to win the lottery, then it is unlikely that anyone will win. To avoid this situation (at least in the framework of plausibility measures and thus in all the other representations that can be used to model default reasoning, which can all be viewed as instances of qualitative plausibility measures), an infinite domain and an infinite number of possible worlds are both required. The structure $M_{lot}$ shows that $Lottery \wedge \neg(true \rightarrow false)$ is satisfiable in a structure with an infinite domain and an infinite set of worlds. In fact, $M_{lot}$ shows that $\forall x(true \rightarrow \neg Winner(x) \wedge \neg(true \rightarrow \forall x \neg Winner(x))$ is satisfiable.

Recall that in Section 8.2 it was shown that the definition of $B_i \phi$ in terms of plausibility, as $Pl(\llbracket \phi \rrbracket) > Pl(\llbracket \neg \phi \rrbracket)$ (or, equivalently, defining $B_i \phi$ as $true \rightarrow_i \phi$) is equivalent to the definition given in terms of a binary relation $\mathcal{B}_i$ *provided that the set of possible worlds is finite* (cf. Exercise 8.7). The lottery paradox shows that they are not equivalent with infinitely many worlds. It is not hard to show that $B_i$ defined in terms of a $\mathcal{B}_i$ relation satisfies the property $\forall x B_i \phi \Rightarrow B_i \forall x \phi$ (Exercise 10.25). But under the identification of $B_i \phi$ with $true \rightarrow_i \phi$ this is precisely C9, which does not hold in general.

C9 can be viewed as an instance of an infinitary AND rule since, roughly speaking, it says that if $\psi \rightarrow \phi(d)$ holds for all $d \in D$, then $\psi \rightarrow \wedge_{d \in D} \phi(d)$ holds. It was shown in Section 8.1 that Pl4 sufficed to give the (finitary) AND rule and that a natural generalization of Pl4, Pl4*, sufficed for the infinitary version. Pl4* does not hold for relational qualitative plausibility structures in general (in particular, as observed in Section 8.1, it does not hold for the structure $M_{lot}$ from Example 10.4.3). However, it does hold in $\mathcal{M}_n^{rank, fo}$.

**Proposition 10.4.8**   *Pl4\* holds in every structure in $\mathcal{M}_n^{rank^+, fo}$.*

**Proof**   See Exercise 10.26. ∎

The following proposition shows that C9 follows from Pl4*:

**Proposition 10.4.9**   *C9 is valid in all relational plausibility structures satisfying Pl4\*.*

**Proof**   See Exercise 10.27.   ∎

Propositions 10.4.8 and 10.4.9 explain why the lottery paradox cannot be captured in $\mathcal{M}_n^{rank^+,fo}$. Neither Pl4* nor C9 hold in general in $\mathcal{M}_n^{poss^+,fo}$ or $\mathcal{M}_n^{pref,fo}$. Indeed, the structure $M_2$ described in Example 10.4.3 and its analogue in $\mathcal{M}_1^{pref,fo}$ provide counterexamples (Exercise 10.28), which is why *Lottery* holds in these structures. So why is $\neg(Lottery \wedge Crooked)$ valid in $\mathcal{M}_1^{poss^+,fo}$ and $\mathcal{M}_1^{pref,fo}$? The following two properties of plausibility help to explain why. The first is an infinitary version of Pl4 slightly weaker than Pl4*; the second is an infinitary version of Pl5.

Pl4†.   For any index set $I$ such that $0 \in I$ and $|I| \geq 2$, if $\{U_i : i \in I\}$ are pairwise disjoint sets, and $Pl(U_0) > Pl(U_i)$ for all $i \in I - \{0\}$, then $Pl(U_0) \not< Pl(\cup_{i \in I, i \neq 0} U_i)$.

Pl5*.   For any index set $I$, if $\{U_i : i \in I\}$ are sets such that $Pl(U_i) = \bot$ for $i \in I$, then $Pl(\cup_{i \in I} U_i) = \bot$.

It is easy to see that Pl4† is implied by Pl4*. For suppose that Pl satisfies Pl4* and the preconditions of Pl4†. Let $U = \cup_{i \in I} U_i$. By Pl3, $Pl(U_0) > Pl(U_i)$ implies that $Pl(U - U_i) > Pl(U_i)$. Since this is true for all $i \in I$, by Pl4*, $Pl(U_0) > Pl(U - U_0)$. Therefore $Pl(U_0) \not< Pl(U - U_0)$, so Pl satisfies Pl4†. However, Pl4† can hold in structures that do not satisfy Pl4*. In fact, the following proposition shows that Pl4† holds in every structure in $\mathcal{M}_n^{poss^+,fo}$ and $\mathcal{M}_n^{pref,fo}$ (including the ones that satisfy *Lottery*, and hence do not satisfy Pl4*):

**Proposition 10.4.10**   *Pl4† holds in every structure in $\mathcal{M}_n^{pref,fo}$ and $\mathcal{M}_n^{poss^+,fo}$.*

**Proof**   See Exercise 10.29.   ∎

Pl5* is an infinitary version of Pl5. It is easy to verify that it holds for ranking functions that satisfy Rk3$^+$, possibility measures, and preferential structures.

**Proposition 10.4.11**   *Pl5\* holds in every relational plausibility structure in $\mathcal{M}_n^{rank^+,fo}$, $\mathcal{M}_n^{poss^+,fo}$, and $\mathcal{M}_n^{pref,fo}$.*

**Proof**   See Exercise 10.30.   ∎

Pl5* has elegant axiomatic consequences.

**Proposition 10.4.12**   *The axiom*

   C10.   $\forall x\, N_i \phi \Rightarrow N_i(\forall x \phi)$

*is sound in relational qualitative plausibility structures satisfying Pl5\*; the axiom*

   C11.   $\forall x (\phi(x) \rightarrow_i \psi) \Rightarrow ((\exists x \phi(x)) \rightarrow_i \psi)$, *if $x$ does not appear free in $\psi$,*

*is sound in structures satisfying Pl4$^\dagger$ and Pl5\*.*

**Proof**   See Exercise 10.31. ∎

Axiom C11 can be viewed as an infinitary version of the OR rule (C3), just as C9 can be viewed as an infinitary version of the AND rule (C2). Abusing notation yet again, the antecedent of C11 says that $\wedge_{d \in D}(\phi(d) \rightarrow_i \psi)$, while the conclusion says that $(\vee_{d \in D}\phi(d)) \rightarrow_i \psi$.

When Pl4$^\dagger$ and Pl5\* hold, the crooked lottery is (almost) inconsistent.

**Proposition 10.4.13**   *The formula Lottery $\wedge$ Crooked $\Rightarrow$ (true $\rightarrow$ false) is valid in structures satisfying Pl4$^\dagger$ and Pl5\*.*

**Proof**   See Exercise 10.32. ∎

Since Pl4$^\dagger$ and Pl5\* are valid in $\mathcal{M}_n^{poss^+, fo}$, as is $\neg(true \rightarrow false)$, it immediately follows that *Lottery $\wedge$ Crooked* is unsatisfiable in $\mathcal{M}_n^{poss^+, fo}$.

To summarize, this discussion vindicates the intuition that there are significant differences between the various approaches used to give semantics to conditional logic, despite the fact that, at the propositional level, they are essentially equivalent. The propositional language is simply too weak to bring out the differences. Using plausibility makes it possible to delineate the key properties that distinguish the various approaches, properties such as Pl4\*, Pl4$^\dagger$, and Pl5\*, which manifest themselves in axioms such as C9, C10, and C11.

Conditional logic was introduced in Section 8.6 as a tool for reasoning about defaults. Does the preceding analysis have anything to say about default reasoning? For that matter, how should defaults even be captured in first-order conditional logic? Statements like "birds typically fly" are similar in spirit to statements like "90 percent of birds fly." Using $\forall x (Bird(x) \rightarrow Flies(x))$ to represent this formula is just as inappropriate as using $\forall x (\ell(Flies(x) \mid Bird(x)) > .9)$ to represent "90 percent of birds fly." The latter statement is perhaps best represented statistically, using a probability on the domain, not a probability on possible worlds. Similarly, it seems that "birds typically fly" should be represented using statistical plausibility. On the other hand, conclusions about individual birds (such as "Tweety is a bird, so Tweety (by default) flies") are similar in spirit to statements like "The probability that Tweety (a particular bird) flies is greater than .9"; these are best represented using plausibility on possible worlds.

Drawing the conclusion "Tweety flies" from "birds typically fly" would then require some way of connecting statistical plausibility with plausibility on possible worlds. There are no techniques given in this chapter for doing that; that is the subject of Chapter 11.

## Exercises

**10.1**   Show that $(A, V) \models \forall x \phi$ iff $(A, V[x/d]) \models \phi$ for every $d \in \text{dom}(A)$.

**10.2**   Inductively define what it means for an occurrence of a variable $x$ to be free in a first-order formula as follows:

- if $\phi$ is an atomic formula $(P(t_1, \ldots, t_k)$ or $t_1 = t_2)$ then every occurrence of $x$ in $\phi$ is free;

- an occurrence of $x$ is free in $\neg\phi$ iff the corresponding occurrence of $x$ is free in $\phi$;

- an occurrence of $x$ is free in $\phi_1 \wedge \phi_2$ iff the corresponding occurrence of $x$ in $\phi_1$ or $\phi_2$ is free;

- an occurrence of $x$ is free in $\exists y \phi$ iff the corresponding occurrence of $x$ is free in $\phi$ and $x$ is different from $y$.

Recall that a sentence is a formula in which no occurrences of variables are free.

(a) Show that if $\phi$ is a formula and $V$ and $V'$ are valuations that agree on all of the variables that are free in $\phi$, then $(A, V) \models \phi$ iff $(A, V') \models \phi$.

(b) Show that if $\phi$ is a sentence and $V$ and $V'$ are valuations on $A$, then $(A, V) \models \phi$ iff $(A, V') \models \phi$.

**10.3**   Show that if all the symbols in the formula $\phi$ are contained in $\mathcal{T}' \subseteq \mathcal{T}$ and if $A$ and $A'$ are two relational $\mathcal{T}$-structures such that $\text{dom}(A) = \text{dom}(A')$ and $A$ and $A'$ agree on the denotations of all the symbols in $\mathcal{T}'$, then $(A, V) \models \phi$ iff $(A', V) \models \phi$.

**10.4**   Show that the following two formulas, which are the analogues of K4 and K5 for $\forall x$, are valid in relational structures:

$$\forall x \phi \Rightarrow \forall x \forall x \phi$$
$$\exists x \phi \Rightarrow \forall x \exists x \phi.$$

**10.5**   Show that all the axioms of AX$^{fo}$ are valid in relational structures and that UGen preserves validity.

**10.6**   Show that the domain elements $c^A$, $f^A(c^A)$, $f^A(f^A(c^A))$, ..., $(f^A)^k(c^A)$ defined in Example 10.1.2 must all be distinct.

**10.7**   Show that $A \models FIN_N$ iff $| \, dom(A)| \leq N$.

* **10.8**   Prove Proposition 10.1.4.

**10.9**   Show that F2 is valid if the term $t$ is a rigid designator.

**10.10**   Show that

$$\forall x (\ell(Flies(x) \mid Bird(x)) > .9) \wedge \ell(Flies(Opus) \mid Bird(Opus)) = 0$$

is satisfiable if *Opus* is not a rigid designator.

**10.11**   Show that

$$\forall x \phi \Rightarrow \forall y \phi[x/y], \text{ if } y \text{ does not appear in } \phi,$$

is provable in AX$^{fo}$.

**10.12**   Show that PD5 is valid in $\mathcal{M}^{meas, stat}$.

**10.13**   This exercise and the next consider IV and EV in more detail.

(a)   Show that IV and EV are valid in $\mathcal{M}_n^{meas, fo}$.

(b)   Show that EV is provable in AX$_{n,N}^{prob, fo}$. (Hint: Use QU2, F4, QUGen, and F2.)

* **10.14**   State analogues of IV and EV for knowledge and show that they are both provable using the axioms of S5$_n$. (Hint: The argument for EV is similar in spirit to that for probability given in Exercise 10.13(b). For IV, use EV and K5, and show that $\neg K \neg K \phi \Leftrightarrow K\phi$ is provable in S5$_n$.)

**10.15**   Show that if $M \in \mathcal{M}^{qual, fo}$, then $(M, w) \models N_i \phi$ iff $Pl_{w,i}(\llbracket \neg \phi \rrbracket_M) = \bot$.

**10.16**   Show that every instance of IVPl is valid in $\mathcal{M}^{qual, fo}$.

**10.17**   Show that the plausibility measure $Pl_{lot}$ constructed in Example 10.4.3 is qualitative.

**10.18**   Construct a relational PS structure that satisfies *Lottery*.

**10.19** Show that the relational possibility structure $M_2$ constructed in Example 10.4.3 satisfies *Lottery*.

**10.20** Show that there is a relational preferential structure $M = (W_{lot}, D_{lot}, \mathcal{O}_1, \pi) \in \mathcal{M}_n^{pref,fo}$ such that $M \models$ *Lottery* where $\mathcal{O}_1(w) = (W, \prec)$ and $w_0 \prec w_1 \prec w_2 \prec \dots$.

**10.21** Show that the plausibility measure $Pl'_{lot}$ constructed in Example 10.4.13 is qualitative and that $M'_{lot} \models$ *Lottery* $\wedge$ *Crooked*.

**10.22** Show that *Crooked* $\wedge$ *Lottery* is not satisfiable in either $\mathcal{M}_1^{poss^+,fo}$ or $\mathcal{M}_1^{pref,fo}$.

**10.23** Show that *Rigged* is not satisfiable in $\mathcal{M}_1^{rank,fo}$.

\* **10.24** Prove Proposition 10.4.6.

**10.25** Show that $\forall x \, K_i \phi \Rightarrow K_i \forall x \phi$ is valid in relational epistemic structures.

**10.26** Prove Proposition 10.4.8.

**10.27** Prove Proposition 10.4.9.

**10.28** Show that the structure $M_2$ described in Example 10.4.3 and its analogue in $\mathcal{M}_1^{pref,fo}$ satisfy neither Pl4* nor C9.

**10.29** Prove Proposition 10.4.10.

**10.30** Prove Proposition 10.4.11. Also show that Pl5* does not necessarily hold in structures in $\mathcal{M}^{qual,fo}$ and $\mathcal{M}_n^{ps,fo}$.

**10.31** Prove Proposition 10.4.12.

**10.32** Prove Proposition 10.4.13.

## Notes

The discussion of first-order logic here is largely taken from [Fagin, Halpern, Moses, and Vardi 1995], which in turn is based on that of Enderton [1972]. The axiomatization of first-order logic given here is essentially that given by Enderton, who also proves completeness. A discussion of generalized quantifiers can be found in [Ebbinghaus 1985]. Trakhtenbrot [1950] proved that the set of first-order formulas valid in finite relational structures is not recursively enumerable (from which it follows that there is no complete axiomatization for first-order logic over finite structures). The fact that there is a translation from propositional epistemic logic to first-order logic, as mentioned in Section 10.1, seems to have been observed independently by a number of people. The first treatment of these ideas in print seems to be due to van Benthem [1974]; details and further discussion can be found in his book [1985]. Finite model theorems are standard in the propositional modal logic literature; they are proved for epistemic logic in [Halpern and Moses 1992], for the logic of probability in [Fagin, Halpern, and Megiddo 1990], and for conditional logic in [Friedman and Halpern 1994].

Hintikka [1962] was the first to discuss first-order epistemic logic. The discussion in Section 10.2 on first-order reasoning about knowledge is also largely taken from [Fagin, Halpern, Moses, and Vardi 1995]. Garson [1984] discusses in detail a number of ways of dealing with what is called the problem of "quantifying-in": how to give semantics to a formula such as $\exists x K_i(P(x))$ without the common domain assumption. The distinction between "knowing that" and "knowing who" is related to an old and somewhat murky philosophical distinction between knowledge *de dicto* (literally, "knowledge of words") and knowledge *de re* (literally, "knowledge of things"). See Hintikka [1962] and Plantinga [1974] for a discussion.

Section 10.3 on first-order reasoning about probability is largely taken from [Halpern 1990], including the discussion of the distinction between the two interpretations of probability (the statistical interpretation and the degree of belief interpretation), the axiom systems $AX_{n,N}^{prob,fo}$ and $AX_N^{stat}$, and Theorems 10.3.1 and 10.3.2. The idea of there being two types of probability is actually an old one. For example, Carnap [1950] talks about probability$_1$ and probability$_2$. Probability$_2$ corresponds to relative frequency or statistical information; probability$_1$ corresponds to what Carnap calls *degree of confirmation*. This is not quite the same as degree of belief; the degree of confirmation considers to what extent a body of evidence supports or confirms a belief, along the lines discussed in Section 3.4. However, there is some commonality in spirit. Skyrms [1980] also considers two types of probability, similar in spirit to Carnap although not identical. Skyrms talks about *first-* and *second-order probabilities*, where first-order probabilities represent propensities or frequency—essentially statistical information—while second-order probabilities represent degrees of belief. He calls them first- and second-order probabilities since typically an agent has a degree of belief about statistical information; that is, a second-order probability on a first-order probability.

Bacchus [1988] was the first to observe the difficulty in expressing statistical information using a possible-worlds model; he suggested using the language $\mathcal{L}^{QU,stat}$. He also provided an axiomatization in the spirit of $AX_N^{stat}$ that was complete with respect to structures where probabilities could be nonstandard; see [Bacchus 1990] for details. On the other hand, there can not be a complete axiomatization for either $\mathcal{L}_n^{QU,fo}$ or $\mathcal{L}_n^{QU,stat}$ with respect to $\mathcal{M}_n^{meas,fo}$ or $\mathcal{M}^{meas,stat}$, respectively [Abadi and Halpern 1994].

The material in Section 10.4 on first-order conditional logic is largely taken from [Friedman, Halpern, and Koller 2000], including the analysis of the lottery paradox, the definitions of Pl4*, Pl4$^\dagger$, Pl5*, and all the technical results. Other papers that consider first-order conditional logic include [Delgrande 1987; Brafman 1997; Lehmann and Magidor 1990; Schlechta 1995; Schlechta 1996]. Brafman [1997] considers a preference order on the domain, which can be viewed as an instance of statistical plausibility. He assumed that there were no infinitely increasing sequences, and showed that, under this assumption, the analogue of C9, together with F1–5, UGen, and analogues of C1–4 in the spirit of PD1–4 provide a complete axiomatization. This suggests that adding C5–7 and C9 to the axioms will provide a complete axiomatization of $\mathcal{L}_n^{\rightarrow, fo}$ for $\mathcal{M}_n^{rank^+, fo}$, although this has not yet been proved. Lehmann and Magidor [1990] and Delgrande [1988] consider ways of using conditional logic for default reasoning.

There has been recent work on extending Bayesian networks to deal with relational structures. This is an attempt to combine the representational power given by Bayesian networks and first-order logic. See [Koller and Pfeffer 1998; Friedman, Getoor, Koller, and Pfeffer 1999] for details.

# Chapter 11

# From Statistics to Beliefs

*"In fact, all the complex mass of statistics produced by the sports industry can without exception be produced not only more economically by computer, but also with more significant patterns and more amazing freaks. I take it the main object of organized sport is to produce a profusion of statistics?"*

*"Oh, yes," said Rowe. "So far as I know."*

—Michael Frayn, *The Tin Men*

Section 10.3 shows that, for first-order reasoning about probability, it is possible to put a probability both on the domain and on the set of possible worlds. Putting a probability on the domain is appropriate for "statistical" reasoning, while putting a probability on the set of possible worlds can be viewed as capturing an agent's subjective beliefs. Clearly the two should, in general, be related. That is, if an agent's knowledge base includes statistical information, his subjective probabilities should reflect this information appropriately. Relating the two is quite important in practice. Section 1.1 already has an example of this. Recall that, in this example, a doctor with a patient Eric can see that Eric has jaundice, no temperature, and red hair. His medical textbook includes the statistical information that 90 percent of people with jaundice have hepatitis and 80 percent of people with hepatitis have a temperature. What should the doctor's degree of belief be that Eric has hepatitis? This degree of belief is important because it forms the basis of the doctor's future decision regarding the course of treatment.

Unfortunately, there is no definitive "right" way for relating statistical information to degrees of belief. In this chapter, I consider one approach for doing this that has some remarkable properties (unfortunately, not all of them good). It is closely related to maximum entropy (at least, in the case of first-order language with only unary predicates) and gives insight into default reasoning as well. For definiteness, I focus

395

on probabilistic reasoning in this chapter. Many of the ideas presented here should be applicable to other representations of uncertainty, but to date there has been no work on this topic. I also assume for simplicity that there is only one agent in the picture.

## 11.1    Reference Classes

Before going into the technical details of the approach, it is worth examining in more detail some properties that have been considered desirable for a method for going from statistical information to degrees of belief. This is perhaps best done by considering the traditional approach to the problem, which uses what are called *reference classes*. To simplify matters, assume for the purposes of this discussion that the agent's knowledge base consists of two types of statements: statistical assertions of the form "90 percent of people with jaundice have hepatitis" and "80 percent of people with hepatitis have a temperature" and information about one individual (such as Eric). The problem is to determine appropriate degrees of belief regarding events concerning that individual, given the statistical information and the information about the individual.

The idea of the reference-class approach is to equate the degree of belief in propositions about an individual with the statistics from a suitably chosen *reference class* (i.e., a set of domain individuals that includes the individual in question) about which statistics are known. For example, if the doctor is interested in ascribing a degree of belief to the proposition "Eric has hepatitis," he would first try to find the most suitable reference class for which he has statistics. Since all the doctor knows about Eric is that Eric has jaundice, then the set of people with jaundice seems like a reasonable reference class to use. Intuitively, the reference class is a set of individuals of which Eric is a "typical member." To the extent that this is true, then Eric ought to be just as likely to satisfy a property as any other member of the reference class. Since someone chosen at random from the set of people with jaundice has probability .9 of having hepatitis, the doctor assigns a degree of belief of .9 to Eric's having hepatitis.

While this seems like a reasonable approach (and not far from what people seem to do in similar cases), it is often difficult to apply in practice. For example, what if the doctor also knows that Eric is a baby and only 10 percent of babies with jaundice have hepatitis. What reference class should he use in that case? More generally, what should be done if there are competing reference classes? And what counts as a legitimate reference class?

To understand these issues, consider the following examples. To start with, consider the situation where Eric is a baby and only 10 percent of babies with jaundice have hepatitis. In this case, the standard response is that the doctor should prefer the more *specific* reference class—technically, this means the doctor should use the smallest reference class for which he has statistics. Since the set of babies is a subset of the set of people, this heuristic suggests the doctor ascribe degree of belief .1 to Eric's having hepatitis, rather than .9.

But the preference for the more specific reference class must be taken with a grain of salt, as the following example shows:

**Example 11.1.1**  Consider again the first knowledge base, where the doctor does not know that Eric is a baby. In that case, it seems reasonable for the doctor to take the appropriate reference class to consist of all people with jaundice and ascribe degree of belief .9 to Eric's having hepatitis. But Eric is also a member of the reference class consisting of jaundiced patients without hepatitis together with Eric. If there are quite a few jaundiced patients without hepatitis (e.g., babies), then there are excellent statistics for the proportion of patients in this class with hepatitis: it is approximately 0 percent. Eric is the only individual in the class who may have hepatitis! Moreover, this reference class is clearly more specific (i.e., a subset of) the reference class of all people with jaundice. Thus, a naive preference for the more specific reference class results in the doctor ascribing degree of belief 0 (or less than $\epsilon$ for some very small $\epsilon$) to Eric's having hepatitis! Clearly there is something fishy about considering the reference class consisting of jaundiced patients that do not have hepatitis together with Eric, but exactly what makes this reference class so fishy?  ∎

There are other problems with the reference-class approach. Suppose that the doctor also knows that Eric has red hair but has no statistics for the fraction of jaundiced people with red hair who have hepatitis. Intuitively, the right thing to do in this case is ignore the fact that Eric has red hair and continue to ascribe degree of belief .9 to Eric's having hepatitis. Essentially, this means treating having red hair as irrelevant. But what justifies this? Clearly not all information about Eric is irrelevant; for example, discovering that Eric is a baby is quite relevant.

This discussion of irrelevance should seem reminiscent of the discussion of irrelevance in the context of default reasoning (Section 8.5). This is not an accident. It turns out the issues that arise when trying to ascribe degrees of belief based on statistical information are much the same as those that arise in default reasoning. This issue is discussed in more detail in Section 11.4.

Going back to Eric, while it seems reasonable to prefer the more specific reference class (assuming that the problems of deciding what counts as a reasonable reference class can be solved), what should the doctor do if he has two competing reference classes? For example, suppose that the doctor knows that 10 percent of babies with jaundice have hepatitis but 90 percent of Caucasians with jaundice have hepatitis, and that Eric is a Caucasian baby with jaundice. Now the doctor has two competing reference classes: Caucasians and babies. Neither is more specific than the other. In this case, it seems reasonable to somehow weight the 10 percent and 90 percent, but how? The reference-class approach is silent on that issue. More precisely, its goal is to discover a single most appropriate reference class and use the statistics for that reference class to determine the degree of belief. If there is no single most appropriate reference class, it does not attempt to ascribe degrees of belief at all.

The random-worlds approach that I am about to present makes no attempt to identify a single relevant reference class. Nevertheless, it agrees with the reference-class approach when there is an obviously "most-appropriate" reference class. Moreover, it continues to make sense even when no reference class stands out as being the obviously most appropriate one to choose.

## 11.2   The Random-Worlds Approach

The basic idea behind the random-worlds approach is easy to explain and understand. Fix a finite vocabulary $\mathcal{T}$ and a domain $D_N$ of size $N$; for simplicity, take $D_N = \{1, \ldots, N\}$. Since $\mathcal{T}$ is finite, there are only finitely many possible relational $\mathcal{T}$-structures with domain $D_N$. Since "relational $\mathcal{T}$-structures with domain $D_N$" is a bit of a mouthful, in the remainder of this chapter I call them simply $D_N$-$\mathcal{T}$-structures.

- If $\mathcal{T}$ consists of the unary predicate $P$, there are $2^N$ $D_N$-$\mathcal{T}$-structures: for each subset $U$ of $D_N$, there is a $D_N$-$\mathcal{T}$-structure $\mathcal{A}_U$ such that $P^{\mathcal{A}_U} = U$.

- If $\mathcal{T}$ consists of the unary predicate $P$ and the constant symbol $c$, then there are $2^N N$ $D_N$-$\mathcal{T}$-structures; these can be characterized by pairs $(U, i)$, where $U \subseteq D_N$ is the interpretation of $P$ and $i \in D_n$ is the interpretation of $c$.

- If $\mathcal{T}$ consists of the binary predicate $B$, then there are $2^{N^2}$ $D_N$-$\mathcal{T}$-structures, one for each subset of $D_N \times D_N$.

Given a $D_N$-$\mathcal{T}$-structure $\mathcal{A}$, let $\mu_N^{unif}$ be the uniform probability measure on $D_N$, which gives each element of $D_N$ probability $1/N$. Then $(\mathcal{A}, \mu_N^{unif})$ is a statistical $\mathcal{T}$-structure and can be used to determine the truth of all sentences in $\mathcal{L}^{QU,stat}(\mathcal{T})$. Now consider a simple probability structure $(W_N, \mu)$, where the worlds in $W_N$ are all the pairs of the form $(\mathcal{A}, \mu_N^{unif})$, and $\mu$ is the uniform probability measure on $W_N$. In this probability structure, the conditional probability of a formula $\phi \in \mathcal{L}^{QU,stat}(\mathcal{T})$ given a knowledge base $KB$ consisting of formulas in $\mathcal{L}^{QU,stat}(\mathcal{T})$ is just the fraction of worlds satisfying $KB$ that also satisfy $\phi$. This is what I will take as the degree of belief of $\phi$ given $KB$ (given that the domain size is $N$).

The intuition behind this approach is not hard to explain. If all worlds are originally equally likely (which seems reasonable, in the absence of any other information), then the degree of belief that the agent ascribes to $\phi$ upon learning *KB* should be the conditional probability that $\phi$ is true, given that *KB* is true. Put another way, the degree of belief that the agent ascribes to $\phi$ is just the probability of choosing a world (relational structure) at random that satisfies $\phi$ out of all the worlds that satisfy *KB*. That is why this is called the *random-worlds* approach.

There are two details I need to fill in to make this completely formal. I started by assuming a fixed domain size of $N$. But where did $N$ come from? Why is a particular choice of $N$ the right choice? In fact, there is no obvious choice of $N$. Typically, however, the domain is known to be large. (There are many birds and many people.) One way of approximating the degree of belief for a true but unknown large $N$ is to consider the limiting conditional probability as $N$ grows to infinity. This is what I in fact do here.

The other issue that needs to be dealt with involves some problematic aspects related to the use of the language $\mathcal{L}^{QU,stat}(\mathcal{T})$. To understand the issue, consider a formula such as $\|Hep(x) \mid Jaun(x)\|_x = .9$, which says that 90 percent of people with jaundice have hepatitis. Notice, however, that is impossible for exactly 90 percent of people with jaundice to have hepatitis unless the number of people with jaundice is a multiple of ten. The statistical assertion was almost certainly not intended to have as a consequence such a statement about the number of people with jaundice. Rather, what was intended was almost certainly something like "*approximately* 90 percent of people with jaundice have hepatitis." Intuitively, this says that the proportion of jaundiced patients with hepatitis is close to 90 percent: that is, within some tolerance $\tau$ of .9. To capture this, I consider a language that uses approximate equality and inequality, rather than equality and inequality. The language has an infinite family of connectives $\approx_i$, $\preceq_i$, and $\succeq_i$, for $i = 1, 2, 3 \ldots$ ("*i*-approximately equal" or "*i*-approximately less than or equal"). The statement "80 percent of jaundiced patients have hepatitis" then becomes, say, $\|Hep(x) \mid Jaun(x)\|_x \approx_1 .8$. The intuition behind the semantics of approximate equality is that each comparison should be interpreted using some small tolerance factor to account for measurement error, sample variations, and so on. The appropriate tolerance may differ for various pieces of information, so the logic allows different subscripts on the "approximately equals" connectives. A formula such as $\|Flies(x) \mid Bird\|_x \approx_1 1 \wedge \|Flies(x) \mid Bat(x)\|_x \approx_2 1$ says that both $\|Flies(x) \mid Bird(x)\|_x$ and $\|Flies(x) \mid Bat(x)\|_x$ are approximately 1, but the notion of "approximately" may be different in each case. (Note that the actual choice of subscripts is irrelevant here, as long as different notions of "approximately" are denoted by different subscripts.)

The formal definition of the language $\mathcal{L}^{\approx}(\mathcal{T})$ is identical to that of $\mathcal{L}^{QU,stat}(\mathcal{T})$, except instead of statistical likelihood formulas, inequality formulas of the form $\|\phi \mid \psi\|_X \sim \alpha$ are used, where $\sim$ is either $\approx_i$, $\preceq_i$, or $\succeq_i$, for $i = 1, 2, 3, \ldots .$ (The reason for using *conditional* statistical likelihood terms, rather than just unconditional ones as in $\mathcal{L}^{QU,stat}$, will shortly become clear. The results in this section and the next still hold even with polynomial statistical likelihood terms, but allowing only these simple inequality formulas simplifies the exposition.) Of course, a formula such as $\|\phi\|_X \approx_i \alpha$ is an abbreviation for $\|\phi \mid true\|_X \approx_i \alpha$. Call the resulting language $\mathcal{L}^{\approx}(\mathcal{T})$. As usual, I suppress the $\mathcal{T}$ if it does not play a significant role in the discussion.

The semantics for $\mathcal{L}^{\approx}$ must include some way of interpreting $\approx_i$, $\preceq_i$, and $\succeq_i$. This is done by using a *tolerance vector* $\vec{\tau} = \langle \tau_1, \tau_2, \ldots \rangle$, $\tau_i > 0$. Intuitively $\zeta \approx_i \zeta'$ if the values of $\zeta$ and $\zeta'$ are within $\tau_i$ of each other. (For now there is no need to worry about where the tolerance vector is coming from.) A *statistical-approximation $\mathcal{T}$-structure* is a tuple $(\mathcal{A}, \vec{\tau})$, where $\mathcal{A}$ is a relational $\mathcal{T}$-structure and $\vec{\tau}$ is a tolerance vector. Let $\mathcal{M}^{\approx}(\mathcal{T})$ consist of all statistical-approximation $\mathcal{T}$-structures.

Given a tolerance vector $\vec{\tau}$, a formula $\phi \in \mathcal{L}^{\approx}$ can be translated to a formula $\phi^{\vec{\tau}} \in \mathcal{L}^{QU,stat}$. The idea is that a formula such as $\|\phi \mid \psi\|_X \preceq_i \alpha$ becomes $\|\phi \mid \psi\|_X \leq \alpha + \tau_i$; multiplying out the denominator, this is $\|\phi \wedge \psi\|_X \leq (\alpha + \tau_i)\|\psi\|_X$. Formally, the translation is defined inductively as follows:

- $\phi^{\vec{\tau}} = \phi$ if $\phi \in \mathcal{L}^{fo}$,

- $(\phi_1 \wedge \phi_2)^{\vec{\tau}} = \phi_1^{\vec{\tau}} \wedge \phi_2^{\vec{\tau}}$,

- $(\neg\phi)^{\vec{\tau}} = \neg(\phi^{\vec{\tau}})$,

- $(\|\phi \mid \psi\|_X \preceq_i \alpha)^{\vec{\tau}} = \|(\phi \wedge \psi)^{\vec{\tau}}\|_X \leq (\alpha + \tau_i)\|\psi^{\vec{\tau}}\|_X$,

- $(\|\phi \mid \psi\|_X \succeq_i \alpha)^{\vec{\tau}} = \|(\phi \wedge \psi)^{\vec{\tau}}\|_X \geq (\alpha - \tau_i)\|\psi^{\vec{\tau}}\|_X$,

- $(\|\phi \mid \psi\|_X \approx_i \alpha)^{\vec{\tau}} = (\alpha - \tau_i)\|\psi^{\vec{\tau}}\|_X \leq \|(\phi \wedge \psi)^{\vec{\tau}}\|_X \leq (\alpha + \tau_i)\|\psi^{\vec{\tau}}\|_X$.

This translation shows why conditional statistical terms are taken as primitive in $\mathcal{L}^{\approx}$, rather than taking them to be abbreviations for the expressions that result by clearing the denominator. Suppose that the knowledge base *KB* says

$$(\|Penguin(x)\|_x \approx_1 0) \wedge (\|Flies(x) \mid Penguin(x)\|_x \approx_2 0);$$

that is, the proportion of penguins is very small but the proportion of fliers among penguins is also very small. Clearing the denominator naively results in the knowledge base

$$KB' = (\|Penguin(x)\|_x \approx_1 0) \wedge (\|Flies(x) \wedge Penguin(x)\|_x \approx_2 0 \times \|Penguin(x)\|_x),$$

which is equivalent to

$$(\|Penguin(x)\|_x \approx_1 0) \wedge (\|Flies(x) \wedge Penguin(x)\|_x \approx_2 0).$$

This last formula simply asserts that the proportion of penguins and the proportion of flying penguins are both small, but says nothing about the proportion of fliers among penguins. In fact, the world where all penguins fly is consistent with $KB'$. Clearly, the process of multiplying out across an approximate connective does not preserve the intended interpretation of the formulas.

In any case, using the translation, it is straightforward to give semantics to formulas in $\mathcal{L}^{\approx}$. For a formula $\phi \in \mathcal{L}^{\approx}$

$$(\mathcal{A}, V, \vec{\tau}) \models \phi \text{ iff } (\mathcal{A}, V, \mu_N^{unif}) \models \phi^{\vec{\tau}}.$$

It remains to assign degrees of belief to formulas. Let $W_N(\mathcal{T})$ consist of all $D_N$-$\mathcal{T}$-structures; let $worlds_N^{\vec{\tau}}(\phi)$ be the set of worlds $\mathcal{A} \in W_N(\mathcal{T})$ such that $(\mathcal{A}, \vec{\tau}) \models \phi$; let $\#worlds_N^{\vec{\tau}}(\phi)$ be the cardinality of $worlds_N^{\vec{\tau}}(\phi)$. The degree of belief in $\phi$ given $KB$ with respect to $W_N$ and $\vec{\tau}$ is

$$\mu_N^{\vec{\tau}}(\phi \mid KB) = \frac{\#worlds_N^{\vec{\tau}}(\phi \wedge KB)}{\#worlds_N^{\vec{\tau}}(KB)}.$$

If $\#worlds_N^{\vec{\tau}}(KB) = 0$, the degree of belief is undefined.

Strictly speaking, I should write $\#worlds_N^{\mathcal{T}, \vec{\tau}}(\phi)$ rather than $\#worlds_N^{\vec{\tau}}(\phi)$, since the number also depends on the choice of $\mathcal{T}$. The degree of belief, however, does not depend on the vocabulary. It is not hard to show that if both $\mathcal{T}$ and $\mathcal{T}'$ contain all the symbols that appear in $\phi$ and $KB$, then

$$\frac{\#worlds_N^{\mathcal{T}, \vec{\tau}}(\phi \wedge KB)}{\#worlds_N^{\mathcal{T}, \vec{\tau}}(KB)} = \frac{\#worlds_N^{\mathcal{T}', \vec{\tau}}(\phi \wedge KB)}{\#worlds_N^{\mathcal{T}', \vec{\tau}}(KB)}$$

(Exercise 11.1).

Typically, neither $N$ nor $\vec{\tau}$ is known exactly. However, $N$ is thought of as "large" and $\vec{\tau}$ is thought of as "small." As I suggested earlier, one way of approximating the value of an expression where $N$ is "large" is by considering the limit as $N$ goes to infinity; similarly, I approximate the value of the expression for $\vec{\tau}$ "small" by taking the limit as $\vec{\tau}$ goes to $\vec{0}$. That is, I take the degree of belief in $\phi$ given $KB$ to be $\lim_{\vec{\tau} \to \vec{0}} \lim_{N \to \infty} \mu_N^{\vec{\tau}}(\phi \mid KB)$. Notice that the limit is taken first over $N$ for each fixed

$\vec{\tau}$ and then over $\vec{\tau}$. This order is important. If the limit $\lim_{\vec{\tau} \to \vec{0}}$ appeared last, then nothing would be gained by using approximate equality, since the result would be equivalent to treating approximate equality as exact equality (Exercise 11.2). Note also that the limit of the expression as $\vec{\tau} \to \vec{0}$ may depend on how $\vec{\tau}$ approaches $\vec{0}$. For example, if $\vec{\tau} = \langle \tau_1, \tau_2 \rangle$, then $\lim_{\vec{\tau} \to \vec{0}} \tau_1/\tau_2$ can take on any value from 0 to $\infty$ depending on how $\langle \tau_1, \tau_2 \rangle \to \langle 0, 0 \rangle$. It is not hard to show that, unless the limit is the same no matter how $\vec{\tau}$ approaches $\vec{0}$, then there will be some way of having $\vec{\tau}$ approach $\vec{0}$ for which the limit does not exist at all (Exercise 11.3).

In any case, this limit may not exist, for a number of reasons. An obvious one is that $\mu_N^{\vec{\tau}}(\phi \mid KB)$ is undefined if $\#worlds_N^{\vec{\tau}}(KB) = 0$. It actually is not important if $\#worlds_N^{\vec{\tau}}$ $(KB) = 0$ for finitely many values of $N$; in the limit, this is irrelevant. However, what if $KB$ includes a conjunct such as $\text{FIN}_{100}$, which is true only if $N \le 100$? In that case, $\#worlds_N^{\vec{\tau}}(KB) = 0$ for all $N > 100$, and the limit will certainly not exist. Of course, if the agent is fortunate enough to know the domain size, then this approach (without taking limits) can be applied to domains of that size. However, in this chapter I am interested in the case that there are no known upper bounds on the domain size for any given tolerance. More precisely, I consider only knowledge bases $KB$ that are *eventually consistent*, in that there exists $\vec{\tau}^*$ such that for all $\vec{\tau}$ with $\vec{0} < \vec{\tau} < \vec{\tau}^*$ (where $\vec{\tau} < \vec{\tau}^*$ means that $\tau_i < \tau_i^*$ for all $i$) there exists $N_{\vec{\tau}}$ such that $\#worlds_N^{\vec{\tau}}(KB) > 0$ for all $N > N_{\vec{\tau}}$.

Even if $KB$ is eventually consistent, the limit may not exist. For example, it may be the case that for some $i$, $\mu_N^{\vec{\tau}}(\phi \mid KB)$ oscillates between $\alpha + \tau_i$ and $\alpha - \tau_i$ as $N$ gets large. In this case, for any particular $\vec{\tau}$, the limit as $N$ grows does not exist. However, it seems as if the limit as $\vec{\tau}$ grows small "should," in this case, be $\alpha$, since the oscillations about $\alpha$ go to 0. Such problems can be avoided by considering the *lim sup* and *lim inf*, rather than the limit. The lim inf of a sequence is the limit of the infimums; that is,

$$\liminf_{N \to \infty} a_N = \lim_{N \to \infty} (\inf\{a_i : i > N\}).$$

The lim sup is defined analogously, using sup instead of inf. Thus, for example, the lim inf of the sequence $0, 1, 0, 1, 0, \ldots$ is 0; the lim sup is 1. The limit clearly does not exist. The lim inf exists for any sequence bounded from below, even if the limit does not; similarly, the lim sup exists for any sequence bounded from above (Exercise 11.4).

The lim inf and lim sup of a sequence are equal iff the limit of the sequence exists and is equal to each of them; that is, $\liminf_{N \to \infty} a_n = \limsup_{N \to \infty} a_n = a$ iff $\lim_{N \to \infty} a_n = a$. Thus, using lim inf and lim sup to define the degree of belief leads to a definition that generalizes the one given earlier in terms of limits. Moreover, since, for any $\vec{\tau}$, the sequence $\mu_N^{\vec{\tau}}(\phi \mid KB)$ is always bounded from above and below (by 1 and 0, respectively), the lim sup and lim inf always exist.

**Definition 11.2.1**   If

$$\lim_{\vec{\tau}\to\vec{0}} \liminf_{N\to\infty} \mu_N^{\vec{\tau}}(\phi \mid KB) \quad \text{and} \quad \lim_{\vec{\tau}\to\vec{0}} \limsup_{N\to\infty} \mu_N^{\vec{\tau}}(\phi \mid KB)$$

both exist and are equal, then the *degree of belief in $\phi$ given KB*, written $\mu_\infty(\phi \mid KB)$, is defined as the common limit; otherwise $\mu_\infty(\phi \mid KB)$ does not exist.   ■

Even using this definition, there are many cases where the degree of belief does not exist. This is not necessarily bad. It simply says that the information provided in the knowledge base does not allow the agent to come up with a well-defined degree of belief. There are certainly cases where it is better to recognize that the information is inconclusive rather than trying to create a number. (See Example 11.3.9 for a concrete illustration.)

Definitions cannot be said to be right or wrong; we can, however, try to see whether they are interesting or useful, and to what extent they capture our intuitions. In the next four sections, I prove a number of properties of the random-worlds approach to obtaining a degree of belief given a knowledge base consisting of statistical and first-order information, as captured by Definition 11.2.1. The next three sections illustrate some attractive features of the approach; Section 11.6 considers some arguably unattractive features.

## 11.3   Properties of Random Worlds

Any reasonable method of ascribing degrees of belief given a knowledge base should certainly assign the same degrees of belief to a formula $\phi$ given two equivalent knowledge bases. Not surprisingly, random worlds satisfies this property.

**Proposition 11.3.1**   *If $\mathcal{M}^{\approx} \models KB \Leftrightarrow KB'$, then $\mu_\infty(\phi \mid KB) = \mu_\infty(\phi \mid KB')$ for all formulas $\phi$. ($\mu_\infty(\phi \mid KB) = \mu_\infty(\phi \mid KB')$ means that either both degrees of belief exist and have the same value, or neither exists. A similar convention is used in other results.)*

**Proof**   By assumption, precisely the same set of worlds satisfy $KB$ and $KB'$. Therefore, for all $N$ and $\vec{\tau}$, $\mu_N^{\vec{\tau}}(\phi \mid KB)$ and $\mu_N^{\vec{\tau}}(\phi \mid KB')$ are equal. Therefore, the limits are also equal (or neither exists).   ■

What about more interesting examples; in particular, what about the examples considered in Section 11.1? First, consider perhaps the simplest case, where there is a single reference class that is precisely the "right one." For example, if $KB$ says that 90 percent of people with jaundice have hepatitis and Eric has hepatitis, that is, if

$$KB = \|Jaun(x) \mid Hep(x)\|_x \approx_i .9 \wedge Jaun(Eric),$$

then one would certainly hope that $\mu_\infty(Hep(Eric) \mid KB) = .9$. (Note that the degree of belief assertion uses equality while the statistical assertion uses approximate equality.) More generally, suppose that the formula $\psi(c)$ represents all the information in the knowledge base about the constant $c$. In this case, every individual $x$ satisfying $\psi(x)$ agrees with $c$ on all properties for which there is information about $c$ in the knowledge base. If there is statistical information in the knowledge base about the fraction of individuals satisfying $\psi$ that also satisfy $\phi$, then clearly $\psi$ is the most appropriate reference class to use for assigning a degree of belief in $\phi(c)$.

The next result says that the random-worlds approach satisfies this desideratum. It essentially says that if $KB$ has the form

$$\psi(c) \wedge (\|\phi(x) \mid \psi(x)\|_x \approx_i \alpha) \wedge KB',$$

and $\psi(c)$ is all the information in $KB$ about $c$, then $\mu_\infty(\phi(c) \mid KB) = \alpha$. Here, $KB'$ is simply intended to denote the rest of the information in the knowledge base, whatever it may be. But what does it mean that "$\psi(c)$ is all the information in $KB$ about $c$"? For the purposes of this result, it means that (a) $c$ does not appear in either $\phi(x)$ or $\psi(x)$ and (b) $c$ does not appear in $KB'$. To understand why $c$ cannot appear in $\phi(x)$, suppose that $\phi(x)$ is $Q(x) \vee x = c$, $\psi(x)$ is *true* and $KB$ is the formula $\|\phi(x) \mid true\|_x \approx_1 .5$. If the desired result held without the requirement that $c$ not appear in $\phi(x)$, it would lead to the erroneous conclusion that $\mu_\infty(\phi(c) \mid KB) = .5$. But since $\phi(c)$ is $Q(c) \vee c = c$, and thus is valid, it follows that $\mu_\infty(\phi(c) \mid KB) = 1$. To see why the constant $c$ cannot appear in $\psi(x)$, suppose that $\psi(x)$ is $(P(x) \wedge x \neq c) \vee \neg P(x)$, $\phi(x)$ is $P(x)$, and the $KB$ is $\psi(c) \wedge \|P(x) \mid \psi(x)\|_x \approx_2 .5$. Again, if the result held without the requirement that $c$ not appear in $\psi(x)$, it would lead to the erroneous conclusion that $\mu_\infty(P(c) \mid KB) = .5$. But $\psi(c)$ is equivalent to $\neg P(c)$, so $KB$ implies $\neg P(c)$ and $\mu_\infty(P(c) \mid KB) = 0$.

**Theorem 11.3.2**  *Suppose that KB is a knowledge base of the form*

$$\psi(c) \wedge \|\phi(x) \mid \psi(x)\|_x \approx_i \alpha \wedge KB',$$

*KB is eventually consistent, and c does not appear in $KB'$, $\phi(x)$, or $\psi(x)$. Then* $\mu_\infty(\phi(c)|KB) = \alpha$.

**Proof**  Since $KB$ is eventually consistent, there exist some $\vec{\tau}^*$ such that for all $\vec{\tau}$ with $\vec{0} < \vec{\tau} < \vec{\tau}^*$, there exists $N_{\vec{\tau}}$ such that $\#worlds_N^{\vec{\tau}}(KB) > 0$ for all $N > N_{\vec{\tau}}$. Fix $\vec{\tau} < \vec{\tau}^*$

and $N > N_{\vec{\tau}}$. The proof strategy is to partition $worlds_N^{\vec{\tau}}(KB)$ into disjoint clusters and prove that, within each cluster, the fraction of worlds satisfying $\phi(c)$ is between $\alpha - \tau_i$ and $\alpha + \tau_i$. From this it follows that the fraction of worlds in $worlds_N^{\vec{\tau}}(KB)$ satisfying $\phi(c)$—that is, the degree of belief in $\phi(c)$—must also be between $\alpha - \tau_i$ and $\alpha + \tau_i$. The result then follows by letting $\vec{\tau}$ go to 0.

Here are the details. Given $\vec{\tau}$ and $N > N_{\vec{\tau}}$, partition $worlds_N^{\vec{\tau}}(KB)$ so that two worlds are in the same cluster if and only if they agree on the denotation of all symbols in $\mathcal{T}$ other than $c$. Let $W'$ be one such cluster. Since $\psi$ does not mention $c$, the set of individuals $d \in D_N$ such that $\psi(d)$ holds is the same at all the relational structures in $W'$. That is, given a world $\mathcal{A} \in W'$, let $D_{\mathcal{A},\psi} = \{d \in D_N : (\mathcal{A}, V[x/d], \vec{\tau}) \models \psi(x)\}$. Then $D_{\mathcal{A},\psi} = D_{\mathcal{A}',\psi}$ for all $\mathcal{A}, \mathcal{A}' \in W'$, since the denotation of all the symbols in $\mathcal{T}$ other than $c$ is the same in $\mathcal{A}$ and $\mathcal{A}'$, and $c$ does not appear in $\psi$ (Exercise 10.3). I write $D_{W',\psi}$ to emphasize the fact that the set of domain elements satisfying $\psi$ is the same at all the relational structures in $W'$. Similarly, let $D_{W',\phi\wedge\psi}$ be the set of domain elements satisfying $\phi \wedge \psi$ in $W'$.

Since the worlds in $W'$ all satisfy $KB$ (for the fixed choice of $\vec{\tau}$), they must satisfy $\|\phi(x) \mid \psi(x)\|_x \approx_i \alpha$. Thus, $(\tau_i - \alpha)|D_{W',\psi}| \leq |D_{W',\phi\wedge\psi}| \leq (\tau_i + \alpha)|D_{W',\psi}|$. Since the worlds in $W'$ all satisfy $\psi(c)$, it must be the case that $c^{\mathcal{A}} \in D_{W',\psi}$ for all $\mathcal{A} \in W'$. Moreover, since $c$ is not mentioned in $KB$ except for the statement $\psi(c)$, the denotation of $c$ does not affect the truth of $\|\phi(x) \mid \psi(x)\|_x \approx_i \alpha \wedge KB'$. Thus, for each $d \in D_{W',\psi}$ there must be exactly one world $\mathcal{A}_d \in W'$ such that $c^{\mathcal{A}_d} = d$. That is, there is a one-to-one correspondence between the worlds in $W'$ and $D_{W',\psi}$. Similarly, there is a one-to-one correspondence between the worlds in $W'$ satisfying $\phi(c)$ and $D_{W',\phi\wedge\psi}$. Therefore, the fraction of worlds in $W'$ satisfying $\phi(c)$ is in $[\alpha - \epsilon, \alpha + \epsilon]$.

The fraction of worlds in $worlds_N^{\vec{\tau}}(KB)$ satisfying $\phi(c)$ (which is $\mu_N^{\vec{\tau}}(\phi \mid KB)$, by definition) is a weighted average of the fraction within the individual clusters. More precisely, if $f_{W'}$ is the fraction of worlds in $W'$ satisfying $\phi(c)$, then $\mu_N^{\vec{\tau}}(\phi \mid KB) = \sum_{W'} f_{W'}|W'|/\#worlds_N^{\vec{\tau}}(KB)$, where the sum is taken over all clusters $W'$ (Exercise 11.5). Since $f_{W'} \in [\alpha - \tau_i, \alpha + \tau_i]$ for all clusters $W'$, it immediately follows that $\mu_N^{\vec{\tau}}(\phi \mid KB) \in [\alpha - \tau_i, \alpha + \tau_i]$.

This is true for all $N > N_{\vec{\tau}}$. It follows that $\liminf_{N\to\infty} \mu_N^{\vec{\tau}}(\phi(c) \mid KB)$ and $\limsup_{N\to\infty} \mu_N^{\vec{\tau}}(\phi(c) \mid KB)$ are both also in the range $[\alpha - \tau_i, \alpha + \tau_i]$. Since this holds for all $\vec{\tau} < \vec{\tau}^*$, it follows that

$$\lim_{\vec{\tau}\to\vec{0}} \liminf_{N\to\infty} \mu_N^{\vec{\tau}}(\phi(c) \mid KB) = \lim_{\vec{\tau}\to\vec{0}} \limsup_{N\to\infty} \mu_N^{\vec{\tau}}(\phi(c) \mid KB) = \alpha.$$

Thus, $\mu_\infty(\phi(c) \mid KB) = \alpha$. ∎

Theorem 11.3.2 can be generalized in several ways; see Exercise 11.6. However, even this version suffices for a number of interesting conclusions.

**Example 11.3.3**  Suppose that the doctor sees a patient Eric with jaundice and his medical textbook says that 90 percent of people with jaundice have hepatitis, 80 percent of people with hepatitis have a fever, and fewer than 5 percent of people have hepatitis. Let

$$KB_{hep} = Jaun(Eric) \wedge \|Hep(x) \mid Jaun(x)\|_x \approx_1 .9 \text{ and}$$

$$KB'_{hep} = \|Hep(x)\|_x \preceq_2 .05 \wedge \|Fever(x) \mid Hep(x)\|_x \approx_3 .8.$$

Then $\mu_\infty(Hep(Eric) \mid KB_{hep} \wedge KB'_{hep}) = .9$ as desired; all the information in $KB'_{hep}$ is ignored. Other kinds of information would also be ignored. For example, if the doctor had information about other patients and other statistical information, this could be added to $KB'_{hep}$ without affecting the conclusion, as long as it did not mention Eric.  ∎

Preference for the more specific reference class also follows from Theorem 11.3.2.

**Corollary 11.3.4**  *Suppose that KB is a knowledge base of the form*

$$\psi_1(c) \wedge \psi_2(c) \wedge \|\phi(x) \mid \psi_1(x) \wedge \psi_2(x)\|_x \approx_i \alpha_1 \wedge \|\phi(x) \mid \psi_1(x)\|_x \approx_j \alpha_2 \wedge KB',$$

*KB is eventually consistent, and c does not appear in KB', $\psi_1(x)$, $\psi_2(x)$, or $\phi(x)$. Then $\mu_\infty(\phi(c) \mid KB) = \alpha_1$.*

**Proof**  Set $KB'' = \|\phi(x) \mid \psi_1(x)\|_x \approx_j \alpha_2 \wedge KB'$. Observe that $KB = \psi_1(c) \wedge \psi_2(c) \wedge \|\phi(x) \mid \psi_1(x) \wedge \psi_2(x)\|_x \approx_i \alpha_1 \wedge KB''$ and that $c$ does not appear in $KB''$, so the result follows immediately from Theorem 11.3.2 (taking $\psi = \psi_1 \wedge \psi_2$).  ∎

As an immediate consequence of Corollary 11.3.4, if the doctor knows all the facts in knowledge base $KB_{hep} \wedge KB'_{hep}$ of Example 11.3.3 and, in addition, knows that Eric is a baby and only 10 percent of babies with jaundice have hepatitis, then the doctor would ascribe degree of belief .1 to Eric's having hepatitis.

Preference for the more specific reference class sometimes comes in another guise, where it is more obvious that the more specific reference class is the smaller one.

**Corollary 11.3.5**  *Suppose that KB is a knowledge base of the form*

$$\psi_1(c) \wedge \psi_2(c) \wedge \forall x(\psi_1(x) \Rightarrow$$
$$\psi_2(x)) \wedge \|\phi(x) \mid \psi_1(x)\|_x \approx_i \alpha_1 \wedge \|\phi(x) \mid \psi_2(x)\|_x \approx_j \alpha_2 \wedge KB',$$

*KB is eventually consistent, and c does not appear in* $KB'$, $\psi_1(x)$, $\psi_2(x)$, *or* $\phi(x)$. *Then* $\mu_\infty(\phi(c) \mid KB) = \alpha_1$.

**Proof**   Let $KB_1$ be identical to $KB$ except without the conjunct $\psi_2(c)$. $KB$ is equivalent to $KB_1$, since $\models (\psi_1(c) \wedge \forall x(\psi_1(x) \Rightarrow \psi_2(x))) \Rightarrow \psi_2(c)$. Thus, by Proposition 11.3.1, $\mu_\infty(\phi(c) \mid KB) = \mu_\infty(\phi(c) \mid KB_1)$. The fact that $\mu_\infty(\phi(c) \mid KB_1) = \alpha_1$ is an immediate consequence of Theorem 11.3.2; since $\forall x(\psi_1(x) \Rightarrow \psi_2(x)) \wedge \|\phi(x) \mid \psi_2(x)\|_x \approx_j \alpha_2$ does not mention $c$, it can be incorporated into $KB'$.  ∎

Note that in Corollary 11.3.5 there are two potential reference classes for $c$: the individuals that satisfy $\psi_1(x)$ and the individuals that satisfy $\psi_2(x)$. Since $KB$ implies $\forall x(\psi_1(x) \Rightarrow \psi_2(x))$, clearly $\psi_1(x)$ is the more specific reference class (at least in worlds satisfying $KB$). Corollary 11.3.5 says that the statistical information about the reference class $\psi_1$ is what determines the degree of belief of $\phi$; the statistical information regarding $\psi_2$ is irrelevant.

Example 11.1.1 shows that a preference for the more specific reference class can sometimes be problematic. Why does the random-worlds approach not encounter this problem? The following example suggests one answer:

**Example 11.3.6**   Let $\psi(x) =_{\text{def}} Jaun(x) \wedge (\neg Hep(x) \vee x = Eric)$. Let $KB''_{hep} = KB_{hep} \wedge \|Hep(x) \mid \psi(x)\|_x \approx_4 0$. Clearly $\psi(x)$ is more specific than $Jaun(x)$; that is, $\models \forall x(\psi(x) \Rightarrow Jaun(x))$. Corollary 11.3.5 seems to suggest that the doctor's degree of belief that Eric has hepatitis should be 0. However, this is not the case; Corollary 11.3.5 does not apply because $\psi(x)$ mentions $Eric$. This observation suggests that what makes the reference class used in Example 11.1.1 fishy is that it mentions Eric. A reference class that explicitly mentions Eric should not be used to derive a degree of belief regarding Eric, even if very good statistics are available for that reference class. (In fact, it can be shown that $\mu_\infty(Hep(Eric) \mid KB''_{hep}) = \mu_\infty(Hep(Eric) \mid KB_{hep}) = .9$, since in fact $\mu_\infty(\|Hep(x) \mid \psi(x)\|_x \approx_4 0 \mid KB_{hep}) = 1$: the new information in $KB''_{hep}$ holds in almost all worlds that satisfy $KB_{hep}$, so it does not really add anything. However, a proof of this fact is beyond the scope of this book.)  ∎

In Theorem 11.3.2, the knowledge base is assumed to have statistics for precisely the right reference class to match the knowledge about the individual(s) in question. Unfortunately, in many cases, the available statistical information is not detailed enough for Theorem 11.3.2 to apply. Consider the knowledge base $KB_{hep}$ from the hepatitis example, and suppose that the doctor also knows that Eric has red hair; that is, his knowledge is characterized by $KB_{hep} \wedge Red(Eric)$. Since the knowledge base does not include statistics for the frequency of hepatitis among red-haired individuals, Theorem 11.3.2 does not apply. It seems reasonable here to ignore $Red(Eric)$. But why is it reasonable to ignore $Red(Eric)$ and not $Jaun(Eric)$? To solve this problem in complete generality would require a detailed theory of irrelevance, perhaps using the ideas of conditional independence from Chapter 4. Such a theory is not yet available. Nevertheless, the next theorem shows that, if irrelevance is taken to mean "uses only symbols not mentioned in the relevant statistical likelihood formula," the random-worlds approach gives the desired result. Roughly speaking, the theorem says that if the $KB$ includes the information $\|\phi(x) \mid \psi(x)\|_x \approx_i \alpha \wedge \psi(c)$, and perhaps a great deal of other information (including possibly information about $c$), then the degree of belief in $\phi(c)$ is still $\alpha$, provided that the other information about $c$ does not involve symbols that appear in $\phi$, and whatever other statistics are available about $\phi$ in the knowledge base are "subsumed" by the information $\|\phi(x) \mid \psi(x)\|_x \approx_i \alpha$. "Subsumed" here means that for any other statistical term of the form $\|\phi(x) \mid \psi'(x)\|_x$, either $\forall x(\psi(x) \Rightarrow \psi'(x))$ or $\forall x(\psi(x) \Rightarrow \neg\psi'(x))$ follows from the knowledge base.

**Theorem 11.3.7**    *Let KB be a knowledge base of the form*

$$\psi(c) \wedge \|\phi(x) \mid \psi(x)\|_x \approx_i \alpha \wedge KB'.$$

*Suppose that*

   *(a) KB is eventually consistent,*

   *(b) c does not appear in $\phi(x)$ or $\psi(x)$, and*

   *(c) none of the symbols in $\mathcal{T}$ that appear in $\phi(x)$ appear in $\psi(x)$ or $KB'$, except possibly in statistical expressions of the form $\|\phi(x) \mid \psi'(x)\|_x$; moreover, for any such expression, either $\mathcal{M}^{\approx} \models \forall x(\psi(x) \Rightarrow \psi'(x))$ or $\mathcal{M}^{\approx} \models \forall x(\psi(x) \Rightarrow \neg\psi'(x))$.*

*Then $\mu_\infty(\phi(c) \mid KB) = \alpha$.*

**Proof**    Just as in the proof of Theorem 11.3.2, the key idea involves partitioning the set $worlds_N^{\vec{\tau}}(KB)$ appropriately. The details are left to Exercise 11.7.    ∎

   Note how Theorem 11.3.7 differs from Theorem 11.3.2. In Theorem 11.3.2, $c$ cannot appear in $\psi(x)$ or $KB'$. In Theorem 11.3.7, $c$ is allowed to appear in $\psi(x)$ and $KB'$, but no symbol in $\mathcal{T}$ that appears in $\phi(x)$ may appear in $\psi(x)$ or $KB'$. Thus, if $\phi(x)$ is $P(x)$, then $\psi(x)$ cannot be $(P(x) \wedge x \neq c) \vee \neg P(x)$, because $P$ cannot appear in $\psi(x)$.

From Theorem 11.3.7, it follows immediately that $\mu_\infty(Hep(Eric) \mid KB_{hep} \wedge Red(Eric)) = .9$. The degree of belief would continue to be .9 even if other information about Eric were added to $KB_{hep}$, such as Eric has a fever and Eric is a baby, as long as the information did not involve the predicate *Hep*.

I now consider a different issue: competing reference classes. In all the examples I have considered so far, there is an obviously "best" reference class. In practice, this will rarely be the case. It seems difficult to completely characterize the behavior of the random-worlds approach on arbitrary knowledge bases (although the connection between random worlds and maximum entropy described in Section 11.5 certainly gives some insight). Interestingly, if there are competing reference classes that are essentially disjoint, Dempster's Rule of Combination can be used to compute the degree of belief.

For simplicity, assume that the knowledge base consists of exactly two pieces of statistical information, both about a unary predicate $P$—$\|P(x) \mid \psi_1(x)\|_x \approx_i \alpha_1$ and $\|P(x) \mid \psi_2(x)\|_x \approx_j \alpha_2$—and, in addition, the knowledge base says that there is exactly one individual satisfying both $\psi_1(x)$ and $\psi_2(x)$; that is, the knowledge base includes the formula $\exists! x(\psi_1(x) \wedge \psi_2(x))$. (See Exercise 11.8 for the precise definition of $\exists! x\phi(x)$.) The two statistical likelihood formulas can be viewed as providing evidence in favor of $P$ to degree $\alpha_1$ and $\alpha_2$, respectively. Consider two probability measures $\mu_1$ and $\mu_2$ on a two-point space $\{0, 1\}$ such that $\mu_1(1) = \alpha_1$ and $\mu_2(1) = \alpha_2$. (Think of $\mu_1(1)$ as describing the degree of belief that $P(c)$ is true according to the evidence provided by the statistical formula $\|P(x) \mid \psi_1(x)\|_x$ and $\mu_2(1)$ as describing the degree of belief that $P(c)$ is true according to $\|P(x) \mid \psi_2(x)\|_x$.) According to Dempster's Rule of Combination, $\mu_1 \oplus \mu_2 = \frac{\alpha_1\alpha_2}{\alpha_1\alpha_2+(1-\alpha_1)(1-\alpha_2)}$. As shown in Section 3.4, Dempster's Rule of Combination is appropriate for combining evidence probabilistically. The next theorem shows that this is also how the random-worlds approach combines evidence in this case.

**Theorem 11.3.8** *Suppose that KB is a knowledge base of the form*

$$\|P(x) \mid \psi_1(x)\|_x \approx_i \alpha_1 \wedge \|P(x) \mid \psi_2(x)\|_x \approx_j \alpha_2 \wedge$$
$$\psi_1(c) \wedge \psi_2(c) \wedge \exists! x(\psi_1(x) \wedge \psi_2(x)),$$

*KB is eventually consistent, P is a unary predicate, neither P nor c appears in $\psi_1(x)$ or $\psi_2(x)$, and either $\alpha_1 < 1$ and $\alpha_2 < 1$ or $\alpha_1 > 0$ and $\alpha_2 > 0$. Then $\mu_\infty(P(c) \mid KB) = \frac{\alpha_1\alpha_2}{\alpha_1\alpha_2+(1-\alpha_1)(1-\alpha_2)}$.*

**Proof** Again, the idea is to appropriately partition $worlds_N^{\vec{\tau}}(KB)$. See Exercise 11.9. ∎

This result can be generalized to allow more than two pieces of statistical information; Dempster's Rule of Combination still applies (Exercise 11.10). It is also not necessary to assume that there is a unique individual satisfying both $\psi_1$ and $\psi_2$. It suffices that the set of individuals satisfying $\psi_1 \wedge \psi_2$ be "small" relative to the set satisfying $\psi_1$ and the set satisfying $\psi_2$, although the technical details are beyond the scope of this book.

The following example illustrates Theorem 11.3.8:

**Example 11.3.9**    Assume that the knowledge base consists of the information that Nixon is both a Quaker and a Republican, and there is statistical information for the proportion of pacifists within both classes. More formally, assume that $KB_{Nixon}$ is

$$\|Pac(x) \mid Quak(x)\|_x \approx_1 \alpha \wedge$$

$$\|Pac(x) \mid Repub(x)\|_x \approx_2 \beta \wedge$$

$$Quak(Nixon) \wedge Repub(Nixon) \wedge$$

$$\exists! x (Quak(x) \wedge Repub(x)).$$

What is the degree of belief that Nixon is a pacifist, given $KB_{Nixon}$? Clearly that depends on $\alpha$ and $\beta$. Let $\phi$ be $Pac(Nixon)$. By Theorem 11.3.8, if $\{\alpha, \beta\} \neq \{0, 1\}$, then $\mu_\infty(\phi \mid KB_{Nixon})$ always exists and its value is equal to $\frac{\alpha\beta}{\alpha\beta+(1-\alpha)(1-\beta)}$. If, for example, $\beta = .5$, so that the information for Republicans is neutral, then $\mu_\infty(\phi \mid KB_{Nixon}) = \alpha$: the data for Quakers is used to determine the degree of belief. If the evidence given by the two reference classes is conflicting—$\alpha > .5 > \beta$—then $\mu_\infty(\phi \mid KB_{Nixon}) \in [\alpha, \beta]$: some intermediate value is chosen. If, on the other hand, the two reference classes provide evidence in the same direction, then the degree of belief is greater than both $\alpha$ and $\beta$. For example, if $\alpha = \beta = .8$, then the degree of belief is about .94. This has a reasonable explanation: if there are two independent bodies of evidence both supporting $\phi$, then their combination should provide even more support for $\phi$.

Now assume that $\alpha = 1$ and $\beta > 0$. In that case, it follows from Theorem 11.3.8 that $\mu_\infty(\phi \mid KB_{Nixon}) = 1$. Intuitively, an extreme value dominates. But what happens if the extreme values conflict? For example, suppose that $\alpha = 1$ and $\beta = 0$. This says that almost all Quakers are pacifists and almost no Republicans are. In that case, Theorem 11.3.8 does not apply. In fact, it can be shown that the degree of belief does not exist. This is because the value of the limit depends on the way in which the tolerances $\vec{\tau}$ tend to 0. More precisely, if $\tau_1 \ll \tau_2$ (where $\ll$ means "much smaller than"), so that the "almost all" in the statistical interpretation of the first conjunct is much closer to "all" than the "almost none" in the second conjunct is closer to "none," then the limit is 1. Symmetrically, if $\tau_2 \ll \tau_1$, then the limit is 0. On the other hand, if $\tau_1 = \tau_2$, then the limit is 1/2. (In particular, this means that if the subscript 1 were used for the $\approx$ in both statistical assertions, then the degree of belief would be 1/2.)

There are good reasons for the limit not to exist in this case. The knowledge base simply does not say what the relationship between $\tau_1$ and $\tau_2$ is. (It would certainly be possible, of course, to consider a richer language that allows such relationships to be expressed.) ∎

## 11.4   Random Worlds and Default Reasoning

One of the most attractive features of the random-worlds approach is that it provides a well-motivated system of default reasoning, with a number of desirable properties. Recall that at the end of Chapter 10 I observed that if "birds typically fly" is interpreted as a statistical assertion and "Tweety flies" is interpreted as a statement about a (high) degree of belief, then in order to do default reasoning and, in particular, conclude that Tweety the bird flies from the fact that birds typically fly, there must be some way to connect statistical assertions with statements about degrees of belief. The random-worlds approach provides precisely such a connection.

The first step in exploiting this connection is to find an appropriate representation for "birds typically fly." The intuition here goes back to that presented in Chapter 8: "birds typically fly" should mean that birds are very likely to fly. Probabilistically, this should mean that the probability that a given bird flies is very high. As shown in Section 8.4.1, there are problems deciding how high is high enough: it will not work (in the sense of not giving System **P**) to take "high" to be "with probability greater than $1 - \epsilon$" for some fixed $\epsilon$. One way to deal with that problem, presented in Section 8.4.1, involves using sequences of probabilities. The language $\mathcal{L}^{\approx}$ is expressive enough to provide another approach—using approximate equality. "Birds typically fly" becomes $\|Flies(x) \mid Bird(x)\|_x \approx_i 1$. (The exact choice of subscript on $\approx$ is not important, although if there are several defaults, it may be important to use different subscripts for each one; I return to this issue later.)

This way of expressing defaults can be used to express far more complicated defaults than can be represented in propositional logic, as the following examples show:

**Example 11.4.1**   Consider the fact that people who have at least one tall parent are typically tall. This default can be expressed in as

$$\|Tall(x) \mid \exists y \, (Child(x, y) \wedge Tall(y))\|_x \approx_i 1. \quad ∎$$

**Example 11.4.2**    Typicality statements can have nesting. For example, consider the nested default "typically, people who normally go to bed late normally rise late." This can be expressed using nested statistical assertions. The individuals who normally rise late are those who rise late most days; these are the individuals $x$ satisfying $\|Rises\text{-}late(x, y) \mid Day(y)\|_y \approx_1 1$. Similarly, the individuals who normally go to bed late are those satisfying $\|To\text{-}bed\text{-}late(x, y') \mid Day(y')\|_{y'} \approx_2 1$. Thus, the default can be captured by saying most individuals $x$ that go to bed late also rise late:

$$\left\| \left\| Rises\text{-}late(x, y) \mid Day(y) \right\|_y \approx_1 1 \, \Big| \, \left\| To\text{-}bed\text{-}late(x, y') \mid Day(y') \right\|_{y'} \approx_2 1 \right\|_x \approx_3 1.$$

On the other hand, the related default that "Typically, people who go to bed late rise late (the next morning)" can be expressed as

$$\left\| Rises\text{-}late(x, Next\text{-}day(y)) \, \Big| \, Day(y) \wedge To\text{-}bed\text{-}late(x, y) \right\|_{x,y} \approx_1 1. \quad \blacksquare$$

Representing typicality statements is only half the battle. What about a conclusion such as "Tweety flies"? This corresponds to a degree of belief of 1. More precisely, given a knowledge base $KB$ (which, for example, may include $\|Flies(x) \mid Bird(x)\|_x \approx_i 1$), the default conclusion "Tweety flies" follows from $KB$ if $\mu_\infty(Flies(Tweety) \mid KB) = 1$.

The formula $\phi$ is a *default conclusion from KB*, written $KB \hspace{1pt}\vdash\hspace{-6pt}\sim_{rw} \phi$, if $\mu_\infty(\phi \mid KB) = 1$. Note that it follows immediately from Theorem 11.3.2 that

$$\|Flies(x) \mid Bird(x)\|_x \wedge Bird(Tweety) \hspace{1pt}\vdash\hspace{-6pt}\sim_{rw} Flies(Tweety).$$

That is, the conclusion "Tweety flies" does indeed follow from "Birds typically fly" and "Tweety is a bird." Moreover, if Tweety is a penguin then it follows that Tweety does not fly. That is, if

$$KB_1 = \|Flies(x) \mid Bird(x)\|_x \approx_1 1 \wedge \|Flies(x) \mid Penguin(x)\|_x \approx_2 0 \wedge$$
$$\forall x(Penguin(x) \Rightarrow Bird(x)) \wedge Penguin(Tweety),$$

then it is immediate from Theorem 11.3.2 that

$$KB_1 \hspace{1pt}\vdash\hspace{-6pt}\sim_{rw} \neg Flies(Tweety).$$

(The same conclusion would also hold if $\forall x(Penguin(x) \Rightarrow Bird(x))$ were replaced by $\|Penguin(x) \mid Bird(x)\|_x \approx_3 0$; the latter formula is closer to what was used in Section 8.5, but the former better represents the actual state of affairs.)

In fact, the theorems of Section 11.3 show that quite a few other desirable conclusions follow. Before getting into them, I first establish that the relation $\hspace{1pt}\vdash\hspace{-6pt}\sim_{rw}$ satisfies the axioms of **P** described in Section 8.3, since these are considered the core properties of default reasoning.

**Theorem 11.4.3** *The relation* $\vdash_{rw}$ *satisfies the axioms of* **P**. *More precisely, the following properties hold if KB and KB' are eventually consistent:*

LLE. If $\mathcal{M}^{\approx} \models KB \Leftrightarrow KB'$, then $KB \vdash_{rw} \phi$ iff $KB' \vdash_{rw} \phi$.

RW. If $\mathcal{M}^{\approx} \models \phi \Rightarrow \phi'$, then $KB \vdash_{rw} \phi$ implies $KB \vdash_{rw} \phi'$.

REF. $KB \vdash_{rw} KB$.

AND. If $KB \vdash_{rw} \phi$ and $KB \vdash_{rw} \psi$, then $KB \vdash_{rw} \phi \wedge \psi$.

OR. If $KB \vdash_{rw} \phi$ and $KB' \vdash_{rw} \phi$, then $KB \vee KB' \vdash_{rw} \phi$.

CM. If $KB \vdash_{rw} \phi$ and $KB \vdash_{rw} \phi'$, then $KB \wedge \phi \vdash_{rw} \phi'$.

**Proof** LLE follows immediately from (indeed, is just a restatement of) Proposition 11.3.1. RW is immediate from the observation that $\mu_N^{\vec{\tau}}(\phi \mid KB) \geq \mu_N^{\vec{\tau}}(\phi' \mid KB)$ if $\mathcal{M}^{\approx} \models \phi \Rightarrow \phi'$ (provided that $\#worlds_N^{\vec{\tau}}(KB) \neq 0$). REF is immediate from the fact that $\mu_N^{\vec{\tau}}(KB \mid KB) = 1$, provided that $\#worlds_N^{\vec{\tau}}(KB) \neq 0$. I leave the proof of AND, OR, and CM to the reader (Exercise 11.11). ∎

Not only does $\vdash_{rw}$ satisfy the axioms of **P**, it can go well beyond **P**. Let $KB_1$ be the knowledge base described earlier, which says that birds typically fly, penguins typically do not fly, penguins are birds, and Tweety is a penguin. Then the following are all immediate consequences of Theorems 11.3.2 and 11.3.7:

- red penguins do not fly:

$$KB_1 \wedge Red(Tweety) \vdash_{rw} \neg Flies(Tweety);$$

- if birds typically have wings, then both robins and penguins have wings:

$$KB_1^+ \wedge Robin(Sweety) \vdash_{rw} Winged(Sweety), \text{ and}$$

$$KB_1^+ \vdash_{rw} Winged(Tweety),$$

where $KB_1^+$ is $KB_1 \wedge \|Winged(x) \mid Bird(x)\|_x \approx_3 1 \wedge \forall x(Robin(x) \Rightarrow Bird(x))$;

- if yellow things are typically easy to see, then yellow penguins are easy to see:

$$KB_1^* \wedge Yellow(Tweety) \vdash_{rw} Easy\text{-}to\text{-}see(Tweety),$$

where $KB_1^*$ is $KB_1 \wedge \|Easy\text{-}to\text{-}see(x) \mid Yellow(x)\|_x \approx_4 1$.

Thus, the random-worlds approach gives all the results that were viewed as desirable in Section 8.5 but could not be obtained by a number of extensions of **P**.

The next two examples show how the axioms of system **P** can be combined with Theorems 11.3.2 and 11.3.7 to give further results.

**Example 11.4.4**    Suppose that the predicates $LU$, $LB$, $RU$, and $RB$ indicate, respectively, that the left arm is usable, the left arm is broken, the right arm is usable, and the right arm is broken. Let $KB'_{arm}$ consist of the statements

- $\|LU(x)\|_x \approx_1 1$, $\|LU(x) \mid LB(x)\|_x \approx_2 0$ (left arms are typically usable, but not if they are broken),

- $\|RU(x)\|_x \approx_3 1$, $\|RU(x) \mid RB(x)\|_x \approx_4 0$ (right arms are typically usable, but not if they are broken).

Now, consider

$$KB_{arm} = (KB'_{arm} \wedge (LB(Eric) \vee RB(Eric)));$$

the last conjunct of $KB_{arm}$ just says that at least one of Eric's arms is broken (but does not specify which one or ones). From Theorem 11.3.2 it follows that

$$KB'_{arm} \wedge LB(Eric) \hspace{0.2em}\sim\mkern-9mu\mid_{rw} \neg LU(Eric).$$

From Theorem 11.3.7, it follows that

$$KB'_{arm} \wedge LB(Eric) \hspace{0.2em}\sim\mkern-9mu\mid_{rw} RU(Eric).$$

The AND rule gives

$$KB'_{arm} \wedge LB(Eric) \hspace{0.2em}\sim\mkern-9mu\mid_{rw} RU(Eric) \wedge \neg LU(Eric)$$

and RW then gives

$$KB'_{arm} \wedge LB(Eric) \hspace{0.2em}\sim\mkern-9mu\mid_{rw} (\neg LU(Eric) \wedge RU(Eric)) \vee (\neg RU(Eric) \wedge LU(Eric)).$$

Similar reasoning shows that

$$KB'_{arm} \wedge RB(Eric) \hspace{0.2em}\sim\mkern-9mu\mid_{rw} (\neg LU(Eric) \wedge RU(Eric)) \vee (\neg RU(Eric) \wedge LU(Eric)).$$

The OR rule then gives

$$KB_{arm} \hspace{0.2em}\sim\mkern-9mu\mid_{rw} (\neg LU(Eric) \wedge RU(Eric)) \vee (\neg RU(Eric) \wedge LU(Eric)).$$

That is, by default it follows from $KB_{arm}$ that exactly one of Eric's arms is usable, but no conclusions can be drawn as to which one it is. This seems reasonable: given that arms are typically not broken, knowing that at least one arm is broken should lead to the conclusion that exactly one is broken, but not which one it is. ■

**Example 11.4.5**   Recall that Example 11.4.2 showed how the nested typicality statement "typically, people who normally go to bed late normally rise late" can be expressed by the knowledge base $KB_{late}$:

$$\left\| \Big\| \|Rises\text{-}late(x, y) \mid Day(y)\|_y \approx_1 1 \Big\| \ \|To\text{-}bed\text{-}late(x, y') \mid Day(y')\|_{y'} \approx_2 1 \right\|_x \approx_3 1.$$

Let $KB'_{late}$ be

$$KB_{late} \wedge \|To\text{-}bed\text{-}late(Alice, y') \mid Day(y')\|_{y'} \approx_2 1 \wedge Day(Tomorrow).$$

Taking $\psi(x)$ to be $\|To\text{-}bed\text{-}late(x, y') \mid Day(y')\|_{y'} \approx_2 1$ and applying Theorem 11.3.2, it follows that Alice typically rises late. That is,

$$KB'_{late} \hspace{0.3em}\vdash_{rw} \|Rises\text{-}late(Alice, y) \mid Day(y)\|_y \approx_1 1.$$

By Theorem 11.3.2 again, it follows that

$$KB'_{late} \wedge \|Rises\text{-}late(Alice, y) \mid Day(y)\|_y \approx_1 1 \hspace{0.3em}\vdash_{rw} Rises\text{-}late(Alice, Tomorrow).$$

The CUT Rule (Exercise 11.13) says that if $KB \hspace{0.3em}\vdash_{rw} \phi$ and $KB \wedge \phi \hspace{0.3em}\vdash_{rw} \psi$, then $KB \hspace{0.3em}\vdash_{rw} \psi$. Thus, $KB'_{late} \hspace{0.3em}\vdash_{rw} Rises\text{-}late(Alice, Tomorrow)$: by default, Alice will rise late tomorrow (and every other day, for that matter). ■

Finally, consider the lottery paradox from Examples 8.1.2 and 10.4.3.

**Example 11.4.6**   The knowledge base corresponding to the lottery paradox is just

$$KB_{lottery} = \exists x\, Winner(x) \wedge \|Winner(x)\|_x \approx_1 0.$$

This knowledge base is clearly eventually consistent. Moreover, it immediately follows from Theorem 11.3.2 that $KB_{lottery} \hspace{0.3em}\vdash_{rw} \neg Winner(c)$ for any particular individual $c$. From RW, it is also immediate that $KB_{lottery} \hspace{0.3em}\vdash_{rw} \exists x\, Winner(x)$. The expected answer drops right out.

An objection to the use of the random-worlds approach here might be that it depends on the domain size growing unboundedly large. To simplify the analysis, suppose that exactly one person wins the lottery and that in order to win one must purchase a lottery ticket. Let $Ticket(x)$ denote that $x$ purchased a lottery ticket and let

$$KB'_{lottery} = \exists!x\ Winner(x) \wedge \forall x\ (Winner(x) \Rightarrow Ticket(x)) \wedge Ticket(c).$$

With no further assumptions, it is not hard to show that $KB'_{lottery} \mathrel{\vdash_{rw}} \neg Winner(c)$, that is, $\mu_\infty(Winner(c) \mid KB'_{lottery}) = 0$ (Exercise 11.14(a)).

Now let $KB''_{lottery} = KB'_{lottery} \wedge \exists^N x\ Ticket(x)$, where $\exists^N x\ Ticket(x)$ is the formula stating that there are precisely $N$ ticket holders. (This assertion can easily be expressed in first-order logic—see Exercise 11.8.) Then it is easy to see that $\mu_\infty(Winner(c) \mid KB''_{lottery}) = 1/N$. That is, the degree of belief that any particular individual $c$ wins the lottery is $1/N$. This numeric answer seems just right: it simply says that the lottery is fair. Note that this conclusion is not part of the knowledge base. Essentially, the random-worlds approach is concluding fairness in the absence of any other information. ∎

## 11.5    Random Worlds and Maximum Entropy

The entropy function has been used in a number of contexts in reasoning about uncertainty. As mentioned in the notes to Chapter 3, it was originally introduced in the context of information theory, where it was viewed as the amount of "information" in a probability measure. Intuitively, a uniform probability measure, which has high entropy, gives less information about the actual situation than does a measure that puts probability 1 on a single point (this measure has the lowest possible entropy, namely 0). The entropy function, specifically maximum entropy, was used in Section 8.5 to define a probability sequence that had some desirable properties for default reasoning. Another common usage of entropy is in the context of trying to pick a single probability measure among a set of possible probability measures characterizing a situation, defined by some constraints. The *principle of maximum entropy*, first espoused by Jaynes, suggests choosing the measure with the maximum entropy (provided that there is in fact a unique such measure), because it incorporates in some sense the "least additional information" above and beyond the constraints that characterize the set.

No explicit use of maximum entropy is made by the random-worlds approach. Indeed, although they are both tools for reasoning about probabilities, the types of problems considered by the random-worlds approach and maximum entropy techniques seem unrelated. Nevertheless, it turns out that there is a surprising and very close connection between the random-worlds approach and maximum entropy provided that the vocabulary consists only of *unary* predicates and constants. In this section I briefly describe this connection, without going into technical details.

Suppose that the vocabulary $\mathcal{T}$ consists of the unary predicate symbols $P_1, \ldots, P_k$ together with some constant symbols. (Thus, $\mathcal{T}$ includes neither function symbols nor higher-arity predicates.) Consider the $2^k$ *atoms* that can be formed from these predicate symbols, namely, the formulas of the form $Q_1 \wedge \ldots \wedge Q_k$, where each $Q_i$ is either $P_i$ or $\neg P_i$. (Strictly speaking, I should write $Q_i(x)$ for some variable $x$, not just $Q_i$. I omit the parenthetical $x$ here, since it just adds clutter.) The knowledge base *KB* can be viewed as simply placing constraints on the proportion of domain elements satisfying each atom. For example, the formula $\| P_1(x) \mid P_2(x) \|_x \approx .6$ says that the fraction of domain elements satisfying the atoms containing both $P_1$ and $P_2$ as conjuncts is (approximately) .6 times the fraction satisfying atoms containing $P_1$ as a conjunct. (I omit the subscript on $\approx$, since it plays no role here.) For unary languages (only), it can be shown that every formula can be rewritten in a canonical form from which constraints on the possible proportions of atoms can be simply derived. For example, if $\mathcal{T} = \{c, P_1, P_2\}$, there are four atoms: $A_1 = P_1 \wedge P_2$, $A_2 = P_1 \wedge \neg P_2$, $A_3 = \neg P_1 \wedge P_2$, and $A_4 = \neg P_1 \wedge \neg P_2$; $\| P_1(x) \mid P_2(x) \|_x \approx .6$ is equivalent to $\| A_1(x) \|_x \approx .6 \| A_1(x) \vee A_3(x) \|_x$.

The set of constraints generated by *KB* (with $\approx$ replaced by $=$) defines a subset $S(KB)$ of $[0, 1]^{2^k}$. That is, each vector in $S(KB)$, say $\vec{p} = \langle p_1, \ldots, p_{2^k} \rangle$, is a solution to the constraints defined by *KB* (where $p_i$ is the proportion of atom $i$). For example, if $\mathcal{T} = \{c, P_1, P_2\}$, and $KB = \| P_1(x) \mid P_2(x) \|_x = .6$ as above, then the only constraint is that $p_1 = .6(p_1 + p_3)$ or, equivalently, $p_1 = 1.5p_3$. That is, $S(KB) = \{\langle p_1, \ldots, p_4 \rangle \in [0, 1]^4 : p_1 = 1.5p_3, p_1 + \cdots + p_4 = 1\}$.

As another example, suppose that $KB' = \forall x\, P_1(x) \wedge \| P_1(x) \wedge P_2(x) \|_x \leq .3$. The first conjunct of $KB'$ clearly constrains both $p_3$ and $p_4$ (the proportion of domain elements satisfying atoms $A_3$ and $A_4$) to be 0. The second conjunct forces $p_1$ to be (approximately) at most .3. Thus, $S(KB') = \{\langle p_1, \ldots, p_4 \rangle \in [0, 1]^4 : p_1 \leq .3, p_3 = p_4 = 0, p_1 + p_2 = 1\}$.

The connection between maximum entropy and the random-worlds approach is based on the following observations. Every world $w$ can be associated with the vector $\vec{p}^w$, where $p_i^w$ is the fraction of domain elements in world $w$ satisfying the atom $A_i$. For example, a world with domain size $N$, where 3 domain elements satisfy $A_1$, none satisfy $A_2$, 7 satisfy $A_3$, and $N - 10$ satisfy $A_4$ would be associated with the vector $\langle 3/N, 0, 7/N, (N - 10)/N \rangle$. Each vector $\vec{p}$ can be viewed as a probability measure on the space of atoms $A_1, \ldots, A_{2^k}$; therefore, each such vector $\vec{p}$ has an associated entropy, $H(\vec{p}) = - \sum_{i=1}^{2^k} p_i \log p_i$ (where, as before, $p_i \log p_i$ is taken to be 0 if $p_i = 0$). Define the *entropy* of $w$ to be $H(\vec{p}^w)$. Now, consider some point $\vec{p} \in S(KB)$. What is the number of worlds $w \in W_N$ such that $\vec{p}^w = \vec{p}$? Clearly, for those $\vec{p}$ where some $p_i$ is not an integer multiple of $1/N$, the answer is 0. However, for those $\vec{p}$ that are "possible," this number can be shown to grow asymptotically as $e^{N \times H(\vec{p})}$ (Exercise 11.16). Thus, there are vastly more worlds $w$ for which $\vec{p}^w$ is "near" the maximum entropy point of $S(KB)$ than there are worlds farther from the maximum entropy point. It then follows that if, for all sufficiently small $\vec{\tau}$, a formula $\theta$ is true at all worlds around the maximum entropy point(s) of $S(KB)$, then $\mu_\infty(\theta \mid KB) = 1$.

For example, the maximum entropy point of $S(KB')$ is $\vec{p}^* = \langle .3, .7, 0, 0 \rangle$. (It must be the case that the last two components are 0 since this is true in all of $S(KB')$; the first two components are "as close to being equal as possible" subject to the constraints, and this maximizes entropy (cf. Exercise 3.48).) But now fix some small $\epsilon$, and consider the formula $\theta^\epsilon = \| P_2(x) \|_x \in [.3 - \epsilon, .3 + \epsilon]$. Since this formula certainly holds at all worlds $w$ where $\vec{p}^w$ is sufficiently close to $\vec{p}^*$, it follows that $\mu_\infty(\theta^\epsilon \mid KB') = 1$. The generalization of Theorem 11.3.2 given in Exercise 11.6 implies that $\mu_\infty(P_2(c) \mid KB' \wedge \theta^\epsilon) \in [.3 - \epsilon, .3 + \epsilon]$. It follows from Exercise 11.13 that $\mu_\infty(\psi \mid KB' \wedge \theta^\epsilon) = \mu_\infty(\psi \mid KB')$ for all formulas $\psi$ and, hence, in particular, for $P_2(c)$. Since $\mu_\infty(P_2(c) \mid KB') \in [.3 - \epsilon, .3 + \epsilon]$ for all sufficiently small $\epsilon$, it follows that $\mu_\infty(P_2(c) \mid KB') = .3$, as desired. That is, the degree of belief in $P_2(c)$ given $KB'$ is the probability of $P_2$ (i.e., the sum of the probabilities of the atoms that imply $P_2$) in the measure of maximum entropy satisfying the constraints determined by $KB'$.

This argument can be generalized to show that if (1) $\mathcal{T} = \{P_1, \ldots, P_n, c\}$, (2) $\phi(x)$ is a Boolean combination of the $P_i(x)$s, and (3) $KB$ consists of statistical constraints on the $P_i(x)$s, then $\mu_\infty(\phi(c) \mid KB)$ is the probability of $\phi$ according to the measure of maximum entropy satisfying $S(KB)$.

Thus, the random-worlds approach can be viewed as providing justification for the use of maximum entropy, at least when only unary predicates are involved. Indeed, random worlds can be viewed as a generalization of maximum entropy to cases where there are nonunary predicates.

These results connecting random worlds to maximum entropy also shed light on the maximum-entropy approach to default reasoning considered in Section 8.5. Indeed, the maximum-entropy approach can be embedded in the random-worlds approach. Let $\Sigma$ be a collection of propositional defaults (i.e., formulas of the form $\phi \to \psi$) that mention the primitive propositions $\{p_1, \ldots, p_n\}$. Let $\{P_1, \ldots, P_n\}$ be unary predicates. Convert each default $\theta = \phi \to \psi \in \Sigma$ to the formula $\theta^r = \| \psi^*(x) \mid \phi^*(x) \|_x \approx_1 1$, where $\psi^*$ and $\phi^*$ are obtained by replacing each occurrence of a primitive proposition $p_i$ by $P_i(x)$. Thus, the translation treats a propositional default statement as a statistical assertion about sets of individuals. Note that all the formulas $\theta^r$ use the same approximate equality relation $\approx_1$. This is essentially because the maximum-entropy approach treats all the defaults in $\Sigma$ as having the same strength (in the sense of Example 11.3.9). This comes out in the maximum-entropy approach in the following way. Recall that in the probability sequence $(\mu_1^{me}, \mu_2^{me}, \ldots)$, the $k$th probability measure $\mu_k^{me}$ is the measure of maximum entropy among all those satisfying $\Sigma^k$, where $\Sigma^k$ is the result of replacing each default $\phi \rightarrow \psi \in \Sigma$ by the $\mathcal{L}^{QU}$ formula $\ell(\psi \mid \phi) \geq 1 - 1/k$. That is, $1 - 1/k$ is used for all defaults (as opposed to choosing a possibly different number close to 1 for each default). I return to this issue again shortly.

Let $\Sigma^r = \{\theta^r : \theta \in \Sigma\}$. The following theorem, whose proof is beyond the scope of this book, captures the connection between the random-worlds approach and the maximum-entropy approach to default reasoning:

**Theorem 11.5.1**   *Let c be a constant symbol. Then $\Sigma \models^{me} \phi \rightarrow \psi$ iff*

$$\mu_\infty(\psi^*(c) \mid \Sigma^r \wedge \phi^*(c)) = 1.$$

Note that the translation used in the theorem converts the default rules in $\Sigma$ to statistical statements about individuals, but converts the left-hand and right-hand sides of the conclusion, $\phi$ and $\psi$, to statements about a particular individual (whose name was arbitrarily chosen to be $c$). This is in keeping with the typical use of default rules. Knowing that birds typically fly, we want to conclude something about a particular bird, Tweety or Opus.

Theorem 11.5.1 can be combined with Theorem 11.3.7 to provide a formal characterization of some of the inheritance properties of $\models^{me}$. For example, it follows that not only does $\models^{me}$ satisfy all the properties of **P**, but that it is able to ignore irrelevant information and to allow subclasses to inherit properties from superclasses, as discussed in Section 8.5.

The assumption that the same approximate equality relation is used for every formula $\theta^r$ is crucial in proving the equivalence in Theorem 11.5.1. For suppose that $\Sigma$ consists of the two rules $p_1 \wedge p_2 \rightarrow q$ and $p_3 \rightarrow \neg q$. Then $\Sigma \models^{me} p_1 \wedge p_2 \wedge p_3 \rightarrow q$. This seems reasonable, as there is evidence for $q$ (namely, $p_1 \wedge p_2$) and against $q$ (namely, $p_3$), and neither piece of evidence is more specific than the other. However, suppose that $\Sigma'$ is $\Sigma$ together with the rule $p_1 \rightarrow \neg q$. Then it can be shown that $\Sigma' \not\models^{me} p_1 \wedge p_2 \wedge p_3 \rightarrow q$. This behavior seems counterintuitive and is a consequence of the use of the same $\epsilon$ for all the rules. Intuitively, what is occurring here is that prior to the addition of the rule $p_1 \rightarrow \neg q$, the sets $P_1(x) \wedge P_2(x)$ and $P_3(x)$ are of comparable size. The new rule forces $P_1(x) \wedge P_2(x)$ to be a factor of $\epsilon$ smaller than $P_1(x)$, since almost all $P_1$s are $\neg Q$s, whereas almost all $P_1 \wedge P_2$s are $Q$s. The size of the set $P_3(x)$, on the other hand, is unaffected. Hence, the default for the $\epsilon$-smaller class $P_1 \wedge P_2$ now takes precedence over the class $P_3$.

If different approximate equality relations are used for each default rule, each one corresponding to a different $\epsilon$, then this conclusion no longer follows. An appropriate choice of $\tau_i$ can make the default $\|\neg Q(x) \mid P_3(x)\|_x \approx_i 1$ so strong that the number of $Q$s in the set $P_3(x)$, and hence the number of $Q$s in the subset $P_1(x) \wedge P_2(x) \wedge P_3(x)$, is much smaller than the size of the set $P_1(x) \wedge P_2(x) \wedge P_3(x)$. In this case, the rule $p_3 \to \neg q$ takes precedence over the rule $p_1 \wedge p_2 \to q$. More generally, with no specific information about the relative strengths of the defaults, the limit in the random-worlds approach does not exist, so no conclusions can be drawn, just as in Example 11.3.9. On the other hand, if all the approximate equality relations are known to be the same, the random-world approach will conclude $Q(c)$, just as the maximum-entropy approach of Section 8.5. This example shows how the added expressive power of allowing different approximate equality relations can play a crucial role in default reasoning.

It is worth stressing that, although this section shows that there is a deep connection between the random-worlds approach and the maximum-entropy approach, this connection holds only if the vocabulary is restricted to unary predicates and constants. The random-worlds approach makes perfect sense (and the theorems proved in Sections 11.3 and 11.4 apply) to arbitrary vocabularies. However, there seems to be no obvious way to relate random worlds to maximum entropy once there is even a single binary predicate in the vocabulary. Indeed, there seems to be no way of even converting formulas in a knowledge base that involves binary predicates to constraints on probability measures so that maximum entropy can be applied.

## 11.6   Problems with the Random-Worlds Approach

The previous sections have shown that the random-worlds approach has many desirable properties. This section presents the flip side and shows that the random-worlds approach also suffers from some serious problems. I focus on two of them here: *representation dependence* and *learning*.

Suppose that the only predicate in the language is *White*, and *KB* is *true*. Then $\mu_\infty(White(c) \mid KB) = 1/2$. On the other hand, if $\neg White$ is refined by adding *Red* and *Blue* to the vocabulary and $KB'$ asserts that $\neg White$ is the disjoint union of *Red* and *Blue* (i.e., $KB'$ is $\forall x((\neg White(x) \Leftrightarrow (Red(x) \vee Blue(x)) \wedge \neg(Red(x) \wedge Blue(x))))$, then it is not hard to show that $\mu_\infty(White(c) \mid KB') = 1/3$ (Exercise 11.17). The fact that simply expanding the language and giving a definition of an old notion ($\neg White$) in terms of the new notions (*Red* and *Blue*) can affect the degree of belief seems to be a serious problem.

This kind of representation dependence seems to be a necessary consequence of being able to draw conclusions that go beyond those that can be obtained by logical consequence alone. In some cases, the representation dependence may indicate something about the knowledge base. For example, suppose that only about half of all birds can fly, Tweety is a bird, and Opus is some other individual (who may or may not be a bird). One obvious way to represent this information is to have a language with predicates *Bird* and *Flies*, and take the knowledge base *KB* to consist of the statements $\|Flies(x) \mid Bird(x)\|_x \approx_1 .5$ and *Bird(Tweety)*. It is easy to see that $\mu_\infty(Flies(Tweety) \mid KB) = .5$ and $\mu_\infty(Bird(Opus) \mid KB) = .5$. But suppose that, instead, the vocabulary has predicates *Bird* and *FlyingBird*. Let *KB'* consist of the statements $\|FlyingBird(x) \mid Bird(x)\|_x \approx_2 .5$, *Bird(Tweety)*, and $\forall x (FlyingBird(x) \Rightarrow Bird(x))$. *KB'* seems to be expressing the same information as *KB*. But $\mu_\infty(FlyingBird(Tweety) \mid KB') = .5$ and $\mu_\infty(Bird(Opus) \mid KB') = 2/3$. The degree of belief that Tweety flies is .5 in both cases, although the degree of belief that Opus is a bird changes. Arguably, the fact that the degree of belief that Opus is a bird is language dependent is a direct reflection of the fact that the knowledge base does not contain sufficient information to assign it a single "justified" value. This suggests that it would be useful to characterize those queries that are language independent, while recognizing that not all queries will be.

In any case, in general, it seems that the best that can be done is to accept representation dependence and, indeed, declare that it is (at times) justified. The choice of an appropriate vocabulary is a significant one, which may encode some important information. In the example with colors, the choice of vocabulary can be viewed as reflecting the bias of the reasoner with respect to the partition of the world into colors. Researchers in machine learning and the philosophy of induction have long realized that bias is an inevitable component of effective inductive reasoning. So it should not be so surprising if it turns out that the related problem of finding degrees of belief should also depend on the bias. Of course, if this is the case, then it would also be useful to have a good intuitive understanding of *how* the degrees of belief depend on the bias. In particular, it would be helpful to be able to give a knowledge base designer some guidelines for selecting the "appropriate" representation. Unfortunately, such guidelines do not exist (for random worlds or any other approach) to the best of my knowledge.

To understand the problem of learning, note that so far I have taken the knowledge base as given. But how does an agent come to "know" the information in the knowledge base? For some assertions, like "Tom has red hair," it seems reasonable that the knowledge comes from direct perceptions, which agents typically accept as reliable. But under what circumstances should a statement such as $\|Flies(x) \mid Bird(x)\|_x \approx_i .9$ be included in a knowledge base? Although I have viewed statistical assertions as objective statements about the world, it is unrealistic to suppose that anyone could examine all the birds in the world and count how many of them fly. In practice, it seems that this statistical statement would appear in *KB* if someone inspects a (presumably large) sample of birds and about 90 percent of the birds in this sample fly. Then a leap is made: the sample is assumed to be typical, and the statistics in the sample are taken to be representative of the actual statistics.

Unfortunately, the random-worlds method by itself does not support this leap, at least not if sampling is represented in the most obvious way. Suppose that an agent starts with no information other than that Tweety is a bird. In that case, the agent's degree of belief that Tweety flies according to the random-worlds approach is, not surprisingly, .5. That is, $\mu_\infty(Flies(Tweety) \mid Bird(Tweety)) = .5$ (Exercise 11.18(a)). In the absence of information, this seems quite reasonable. But the agent then starts observing birds. In fact, the agent observes $N$ birds (think of $N$ as large), say $c_1, \ldots, c_N$, and the information regarding which of them fly is recorded in the knowledge base. Let $Bird(Tweety) \wedge KB'$ be the resulting knowledge base. Thus, $KB'$ has the form

$$Bird(c_1) \wedge Flies_1(c_1) \wedge Bird(c_2) \wedge Flies_2(c_2) \wedge \ldots \wedge Bird(c_N) \wedge Flies_N(c_N),$$

where $Flies_i(c_i)$ is either $Flies(c_i)$ or $\neg Flies(c_i)$. It seems reasonable to expect that if most (say 90 percent) of the $N$ birds observed by the agent fly, then the agent's belief that Tweety flies increases. Unfortunately, it doesn't; $\mu_\infty(Flies(Tweety \mid Bird(Tweety) \wedge KB') = .5$ (Exercise 11.18(b)).

What if instead the sample is represented using a predicate $S$? The fact that 90 percent of sampled birds fly can then be expressed as $\|Flies(x) \mid Bird(x) \wedge S(x)\|_x \approx_1 .9$. This helps, but not much. To see why, suppose that $\alpha$ percent of the domain elements were sampled. If $KB''$ is

$$\|Flies(x) \mid Bird(x) \wedge S(x)\|_x \approx_1 .9 \wedge \|S(x)\|_x \approx \alpha \wedge Bird(Tweety),$$

it seems reasonable to expect that $\mu_\infty(Flies(Tweety) \mid KB'') = .9$, but it is not. In fact, $\mu_\infty(Flies(Tweety) \mid KB'') = .9\alpha + .5(1 - \alpha)$ (Exercise 11.18(c)). The random-worlds approach treats the birds in $S$ and those outside $S$ as two unrelated populations; it maintains the default degree of belief (1/2) that a bird not in $S$ will fly. (This follows from maximum entropy considerations, along the lines discussed in Section 11.5.) Intuitively, the random-worlds approach is not treating $S$ as a *random* sample. Of course, the failure of the obvious approach does not imply that random worlds is incapable of learning statistics. Perhaps another representation can be found that will do better (although none has been found yet).

To summarize, the random-worlds approach has many attractive features but some serious flaws as well. There are variants of the approach that deal well with some of the problems, but not with others. (See, e.g., Exercise 11.19.) Perhaps the best lesson that can be derived from this discussion is that it may be impossible to come up with a generic method for obtaining degrees of belief from statistical information that does the "right" thing in all possible circumstances. There is no escaping the need to understand the details of the application.

## Exercises

**11.1**   Show that if both $\mathcal{T}$ and $\mathcal{T}'$ contain all the symbols that appear in $\phi$ and $KB$, then

$$\frac{\#worlds_N^{\mathcal{T},\vec{\tau}}(\phi \wedge KB)}{\#worlds_N^{\mathcal{T},\vec{\tau}}(KB)} = \frac{\#worlds_N^{\mathcal{T}',\vec{\tau}}(\phi \wedge KB)}{\#worlds_N^{\mathcal{T}',\vec{\tau}}(KB)}.$$

**11.2**   Let $\phi^=$ be the result of replacing all instances of approximate equality and approximate inequality (i.e., $\approx_i$, $\preceq_i$, and $\succeq_i$, for any $i$) in $\phi$ by equality and inequality ($=$, $\leq$, and $\geq$, respectively). Show that

$$\lim_{\vec{\tau} \to \vec{0}} \mu_N^{\vec{\tau}}(\phi \mid KB) = \mu_N^{\vec{\tau}}(\phi^= \mid KB^=).$$

Thus, if the order of the limits in the definition of $\mu_\infty(\phi \mid KB)$ were reversed, then all the advantages of using approximate equality would be lost.

**11.3**   Show that unless $\lim_{\vec{\tau} \to \vec{0}} f(\vec{\tau})$ is independent of how $\vec{\tau}$ approaches $\vec{0}$, there will be some way of having $\vec{\tau}$ approach $\vec{0}$ for which the limit does not exist at all.

**11.4**   Show that if $a_0, a_1, \ldots$ is a sequence of real numbers bounded from below, then $\lim\inf_{n \to \infty} a_n$ exists. Similarly, show that if $a_0, a_1, \ldots$ is bounded from above, then $\lim\sup_{n \to \infty} a_n$ exists. (You may use the fact that a bounded increasing sequence of real numbers has a limit.)

**11.5**   Show that, in the proof of Theorem 11.3.2,

$$\mu_N^{\vec{\tau}}(\phi \mid KB) = \sum_{W'} f_{W'}|W'|/\#worlds_N^{\vec{\tau}}(KB),$$

where the sum is taken over all clusters $W'$.

**\*11.6**   Theorem 11.3.2 can be generalized in several ways. In particular,

(a) it can be applied to more than one individual at a time,

(b) it applies if there are bounds on statistical information, not just in the case where the statistical information is approximately precise, and

(c) the statistical information does not actually have to be in the knowledge base; it
just needs to be a logical consequence of it for sufficiently small tolerance vectors.

To make this precise, let $X = \{x_1, \ldots, x_k\}$ and $C = \{c_1, \ldots, c_k\}$ be sets of distinct
variables and distinct constants, respectively. I write $\phi(X)$ to indicate that all of the free
variables in the formula $\phi$ are in $X$; $\phi(C)$ denotes the new formula obtained by replacing
each occurrences of $x_i$ in $\phi$ by $c_i$. (Note that $\phi$ may contain other constants not among
the $c_i$s; these are unaffected by the substitution.) Prove the following generalization of
Theorem 11.3.2:

> Let $KB$ be a knowledge base of the form $\psi(C) \wedge KB'$ and assume that, for all
> sufficiently small tolerance vectors $\vec{\tau}$,
>
> $$\mathcal{M}^\approx \models KB^{\vec{\tau}} \Rightarrow \alpha \leq \|\phi^{\vec{\tau}}(X) \mid \psi^{\vec{\tau}}(X)\|_X \leq \beta.$$
>
> If no constant in $C$ appears in $KB'$, in $\phi(X)$, or in $\psi(X)$, then $\mu_\infty(\phi(C) \mid KB) \in$
> $[\alpha, \beta]$, provided the degree of belief exists.

(Note that the degree of belief may not exist since $\lim_{\vec{\tau} \to \vec{0}} \lim \inf_{N \to \infty} \mu_N^{\vec{\tau}}(\phi \mid KB)$
may not be equal to $\lim_{\vec{\tau} \to \vec{0}} \lim \sup_{N \to \infty} \mu_N^{\vec{\tau}}(\phi \mid KB)$. However, it follows from the
proof of the theorem that both of these limits lie in the interval $[\alpha, \beta]$. This is why the
limit does exist if $\alpha = \beta$, as in Theorem 11.3.2.)

*11.7   Prove Theorem 11.3.7. (Hint: For each domain size $N$ and tolerance vector $\vec{\tau}$,
partition $worlds_N^{\vec{\tau}}(KB^{\vec{\tau}})$ into clusters, where each cluster $W'$ is a maximal set satisfying
the following four conditions:

(a) All worlds in $W'$ agree on the denotation of every symbol in the vocabulary
except possibly those appearing in $\phi(x)$ (so that, in particular, they agree on the
denotation of the constant $c$).

(b) All worlds in $W'$ also agree as to which elements satisfy $\psi_0(x)$; let this set be $A_0$.

(c) The denotation of symbols in $\phi$ must also be constant, except possibly when a
member of $A_0$ is involved. More precisely, let $\overline{A_0}$ be the set of domain elements
$\{1, \ldots, N\} - A_0$. Then for any predicate symbol $R$ or function symbol $f$ of arity
$r$ appearing in $\phi(x)$, and for all worlds $w, w' \in W'$, if $d_1, \ldots, d_r, d_{r+1} \in \overline{A_0}$ then
$R(d_1, \ldots, d_r)$ holds in $w$ iff it holds in $w'$, and $f(d_1, \ldots, d_r) = d_{r+1}$ in $w$ iff
$f(d_1, \ldots, d_r) = d_{r+1}$ in $w'$. In particular, this means that for any constant symbol
$c'$ appearing in $\phi(x)$, if it denotes $d' \in \overline{A_0}$ in $w$, then it must denote $d'$ in $w'$.

(d) All worlds in the cluster are isomorphic with respect to the vocabulary symbols
in $\phi$. (That is, if $w$ and $w'$ are two worlds in the cluster, then there is a bijection

on $\{1, \ldots, n\}$ such that for each symbol $P$ in $\phi$ in the vocabulary, $P^{\pi(w)}$ is isomorphic to $P^{\pi(w')}$ under $f$. For example, if $P$ is a constant symbol $d$, then $f(d^{\pi(w)}) = d^{\pi(w')}$; similarly, if $P$ is a binary predicate, the $(d, d') \in P^{\pi(w)}$ iff $(f(d), f(d')) \in P^{\pi(w')}$.)

Then show that, within each cluster $W'$, the probability of $\phi(c)$ is within $\tau_i$ of $\alpha$.)

**11.8** First-order logic can express not only that there exists an individual that satisfies the formula $\phi(x)$, but that there exists a unique individual that satisfies $\phi(x)$. Let $\exists!x\phi(x)$ be an abbreviation for

$$\exists x\phi(x) \wedge \forall y(\phi(y) \Rightarrow y = x).$$

(a) Show that $(\mathcal{A}, V) \models \exists!x\phi(x)$ iff there is a unique $d \in \operatorname{dom}(\mathcal{A})$ such that $(\mathcal{A}, V[x/d]) \models \phi(x)$.

(b) Generalize this to find a formula $\exists^N\phi(x)$ that expresses the fact that exactly $N$ individuals in the domain satisfy $\phi$.

**\*11.9** Prove Theorem 11.3.8. (Hint: Suppose that $\alpha_1, \alpha_2 > 0$. Consider $\vec{\tau}$ such that $\alpha_i - \tau_i > 0$. Let $\beta_i = \min(\alpha_i + \tau_i, 1)$. For each domain size $N$, partition $worlds_N^{\vec{\tau}}(KB^{\vec{\tau}})$ into clusters where each cluster $W'$ is a maximal set satisfying the following three conditions:

(a) All worlds in $W'$ agree on the denotation of every symbol in the vocabulary except for $P$. In particular, they agree on the denotations of $c$, $\psi_1$, and $\psi_2$. Let $A_i$ be the denotation of $\psi_i$ in $W'$ (i.e., $A_i = \{d \in D : w \models \psi(d)\}$ for $w \in W'$) and let $n_i = |A_i|$).

(b) All worlds in $W'$ have the same denotation of $P$ for elements in $\overline{A} = \{1, \ldots, N\} - (A_1 \cup A_2)$.

(c) For $i = 1, 2$, there exists a number $r_i$ such that all worlds in $W'$ have $r_i$ elements in $A_i$ satisfying $P$.

Note that, since all worlds in $W'$ satisfy $KB^{\vec{\tau}}$, it follows that $\beta_i = r_i/n_i \in [\alpha_i - \tau_i, \alpha_i + \tau_i]$ for $i = 1, 2$. Show that the number of worlds in $W'$ satisfying $P(c)$ is $\binom{n_1-1}{r_1-1}\binom{n_2-1}{r_2-1}$ and the number of worlds satisfying $\neg P(c)$ is $\binom{n_1-1}{r_1}\binom{n_2-1}{r_2}$. Conclude from this that the fraction of worlds satisfying $P(c)$ is $\frac{\beta_1\beta_2}{\beta_1\beta_2+(1-\beta_1)(1-\beta_2)}$.)

**\*11.10** State and prove a generalized version of Theorem 11.3.8 that allows more than two pieces of statistical information.

**11.11** Complete the proof of Theorem 11.4.3.

*  **11.12** This exercise considers to what extent Rational Monotonicity holds in the random-worlds approach. Recall that Rational Monotonicity is characterized by axiom C5 in $AX^{cond}$ (see Section 8.6). Roughly speaking, it holds if the underlying likelihood measure is totally ordered. Since probability is totally ordered, it would seem that something like Rational Monotonicity should hold for the random-worlds approach, and indeed it does. Rational Monotonicity in the random-worlds framework is expressed as follows:

RM.    If $KB \mathrel{|\!\sim}_{rw} \phi$ and $KB \mathrel{|\!\not\sim}_{rw} \neg\theta$, then $KB \wedge \theta \mathrel{|\!\sim}_{rw} \phi$.

Show that the random-worlds approach satisfies the following weakened form of RM:
If $KB \mathrel{|\!\sim}_{rw} \phi$ and $KB \mathrel{|\!\not\sim}_{rw} \neg\theta$, then $KB \wedge \theta \mathrel{|\!\sim}_{rw} \phi$ provided that $\mu_\infty(\phi \mid KB \wedge \theta)$ exists. Moreover, a sufficient condition for $\mu_\infty(\phi \mid KB \wedge \theta)$ to exist is that $\mu_\infty(\theta \mid KB)$ exists.

**11.13** The CUT property was introduced in Exercise 8.42 and shown to follow from **P**. In the setting of this chapter, CUT becomes

CUT.    If $KB \mathrel{|\!\sim}_{rw} \phi$ and $KB \wedge \phi \mathrel{|\!\sim}_{rw} \psi$ then $KB \mathrel{|\!\sim}_{rw} \phi$.

Show directly that CUT holds in the random-worlds approach. In fact, show that the following stronger result holds: If $\mu_\infty(\phi \mid KB) = 1$, then $\mu_\infty(\psi \mid KB) = \mu_\infty(\psi \mid KB \wedge \phi)$ (where equality here means that either neither limit exists or both do and are equal).

*  **11.14** This exercise shows that the random-worlds approach deals well with the lottery paradox.

  (a) Show that $KB'_{lottery} \mathrel{|\!\sim}_{rw} \neg Winner(c)$, where $KB'_{lottery}$ is defined in Example 11.4.6. (Hint: Fix a domain size $N$. Cluster the worlds according to the number of ticket holders. That is, let $W_k$ consist of all worlds with exactly $k$ ticket holders. Observe that $|W_k| = k\binom{N}{k}$ (since the winner must be one of the $k$ ticket holders). Show that the fraction of worlds in $W_k$ in which $c$ wins is $1/k$. Next, observe that

$$| \cup_{k \leq N/4} W_k | = \sum_{k=1}^{N/4} k\binom{N}{k} \leq (N/4) \sum_{k=1}^{N/4} \binom{N}{N/4} = (N/4)^2 \binom{N}{N/4}.$$

Similarly

$$| \cup_{k > N/4} W_k | = \sum_{k=N/4+1}^{N} k\binom{N}{k} > (N/2)\binom{N}{N/2}$$

(since $(N/2)\binom{N}{N/2}$ is just one term in the sum). Show that

$$\lim_{N\to\infty} \frac{(N/4)^2\binom{N}{N/4}}{(N/2)\binom{N}{N/2}} = 0;$$

that is, for $N$ sufficiently large, in almost all worlds there are at least $N/4$ ticket holders. The desired result now follows easily.)

(b) Show that $\mu_\infty(Winner(c) \mid KB''_{lottery}) = 1/N$. (This actually follows easily from the first part of the analysis of part (a).)

**11.15** Show that the random-worlds approach takes different constants to denote different individuals, by default. That is, show that if $c$ and $d$ are distinct constants, then $true \models_{rw} c \neq d$. The assumption that different individuals are distinct has been called the *unique names assumption* in the literature. This shows that the unique names assumption holds by default in the random-worlds approach.

\*  **11.16** Consider a vocabulary $\mathcal{T}$ consisting of $k$ unary predicates $P_1, \ldots, P_k$ and $\ell$ constant symbols. Let $\vec{p} = \langle N_1/N, \ldots, N_n/N \rangle$.

(a) Show that there are

$$N^\ell \binom{N}{N_1, \ldots, N_k} = \frac{N^\ell N!}{N_1! N_2! \ldots N_k!}$$

$D_N$-$\mathcal{T}$-structures $\mathcal{A}$ such that such that there are $N_i$ domain elements satisfying $P_i$ (i.e., $|P_i^{\mathcal{A}}| = N_i$).

(b) *Stirling's approximation* says that

$$m! = \sqrt{2\pi m}\, m^m e^{-m}(1 + O(1/m)).$$

Using Stirling's approximation, show that there exist constants $L$ and $U$ such that

$$\frac{L}{U^k N^k} \frac{N^N \prod_{i=1}^k e^{N_i}}{e^N \prod_{i=1}^k N_i^{N_i}} \leq \frac{N!}{N_1! N_2! \ldots N_k!} \leq \frac{UN}{L^k} \frac{N^N \prod_{i=1}^k e^{N_i}}{e^N \prod_{i=1}^k N_i^{N_i}}.$$

(c) Let $\vec{p} = \langle p_1, \ldots, p_n \rangle$, where $p_i = N_i/N$. Show that

$$\frac{N^N \prod_{i=1}^k e^{N_i}}{e^N \prod_{i=1}^k N_i^{N_i}} = e^{-N \sum_{i=1}^k u_i \ln(u_i)} = e^{N \times H(\vec{p})}.$$

(d) Conclude that

$$\frac{N^{m-k}L}{U^k}e^{N \times H(\vec{p})} \leq |\{w \in W_N : \vec{p}^w = \vec{p}\}| \leq \frac{UN^{m+1}}{L^k}e^{N \times H(\vec{p})}.$$

**11.17** Show that $\mu_\infty(White(c) \mid true) = .5$ and that

$\mu_\infty(White(c) \mid \forall x((\neg White(x) \Leftrightarrow (Red(x) \vee Blue(x))) \wedge \neg(Red(x) \wedge Blue(x))))$
$= 1/3.$

**11.18** This exercise shows that random words does not support sampling, at least not in the most natural way.

(a) Show that $\mu_\infty(Flies(Tweety) \mid Bird(Tweety)) = .5$.

(b) Show that $\mu_\infty(Flies(Tweety) \mid Bird(Tweety) \wedge KB') = .5$ if $KB'$ has the form

$$Bird(c_1) \wedge Flies_1(c_1) \wedge \ldots \wedge Bird(c_N) \wedge Flies_N(c_N),$$

where $Flies_i$ is either $Flies$ or $\neg Flies$ for $i = 1, \ldots, N$.

(c) Show that if

$$KB'' = \|Flies(x) \mid Bird(x) \wedge S(x)\|_x \approx_1 .9 \wedge \|S(x)\|_x \approx \alpha \wedge Bird(Tweety)$$

then $\mu_\infty(Flies(Tweety) \mid KB'') = .9\alpha + .5(1 - \alpha)$.

**11.19** Suppose that $\mathcal{T} = \{P_1, \ldots, P_m, c_1, \ldots, c_n\}$. That is, the vocabulary consists only of unary predicates and constants. Fix a domain size $N$. For each tuple $(k_1, \ldots, k_m)$ such that $0 \leq k_i \leq N$, let $W_{(k_1,\ldots,k_m)}$ consist of all structures $\mathcal{A} \in W_N$ such that $|P_i^{\mathcal{A}}| = k_i$, for $i = 1, \ldots, N$. Note that there are $m^{N+1}$ sets of the form $W_{(k_1,\ldots,k_m)}$. Let $\mu_N$ be the probability measure on $W_N$ such that $\mu_N(W_{(k_1,\ldots,k_m)}) = 1/m^{N+1}$ and all the worlds in $W_{(k_1,\ldots,k_m)}$ are equally likely.

(a) Let $\mathcal{A} \in W_N$ be such that $|P_i^{\mathcal{A}}| = 0$ (i.e., no individual satisfies any of $P_1, \ldots, P_N$ in $\mathcal{A}$). What is $\mu_N(\mathcal{A})$?

(b) Assume that $N$ is even and let $\mathcal{A} \in W_N$ be such that $|P_i^{\mathcal{A}}| = N/2$ for $i = 1, \ldots, N$. What is $\mu_N(\mathcal{A})$?

You should get different answers for (a) and (b). Intuitively, $\mu_N$ does not make all worlds in $W_N$ equally likely, but it does make each possible cardinality of $P_1, \ldots, P_N$

equally likely. For $\phi, KB \in \mathcal{L}^{fo}(\mathcal{T})$, define $\mu'_\infty(\phi \mid KB)$ to be the common limit of

$$\lim_{\vec{\tau} \to \vec{0}} \liminf_{N \to \infty} \mu_N(\phi \mid KB) \text{ and } \lim_{\vec{\tau} \to \vec{0}} \limsup_{N \to \infty} \mu_N(\phi \mid KB),$$

if the limit exists. $\mu'_\infty(\phi \mid KB)$ gives a different way of obtaining degrees of belief from statistical information.

**11.20** Show that the following simplified version of Theorem 11.3.2 holds for $\mu'_\infty$:

$$\mu'_\infty(\phi(c) \mid \|\phi(x) \mid \psi(x)\|_x \approx_i \alpha \wedge \psi(c)) = \alpha.$$

Actually, the general version of Theorem 11.3.2 also holds. Moreover, learning from samples works for $\mu'_\infty$:

$$\mu'_\infty(\textit{Flies}(\textit{Tweety}) \mid \textit{Bird}(\textit{Tweety}) \wedge \|\textit{Flies}(x) \mid \textit{Bird}(x) \wedge S(x)\|_x \approx_i .9) = .9,$$

although the proof of this (which requires maximum entropy techniques) is beyond the scope of the book.

## Notes

The earliest sophisticated attempt at clarifying the connection between objective statistical knowledge and degrees of belief, and the basis for most subsequent proposals involving reference classes, is due to Reichenbach [1949]. A great deal of further work has been done on reference classes, perhaps most notably by Kyburg [1974; 1983] and Pollock [1990]; this work mainly elaborates the way in which the reference class should be chosen in case there are competing reference classes.

The random-worlds approach was defined in [Bacchus, Grove, Halpern, and Koller 1996]. However, the key ideas in the approach are not new. Many of them can be found in the work of Johnson [1932] and Carnap [1950; 1952], although these authors focus on knowledge bases that contain only first-order information and, for the most part, restrict their attention to unary predicates. More recently, Chuaqui [1991] and Shastri [1989] have presented approaches similar in spirit to the random-worlds approach.

Much of the discussion in this chapter is taken from [Bacchus, Grove, Halpern, and Koller 1996]. Stronger versions of Theorems 11.3.2, 11.3.7, and 11.3.8 are proved in the paper (cf. Exercises 11.6 and 11.10). More discussion on dealing with approximate equality can be found in [Koller and Halpern 1992].

Example 11.3.9, due to Reiter and Criscuolo [1981], is called the *Nixon Diamond* and is one of the best-known examples in the default-reasoning literature showing the difficulty of dealing with conflicting information. Example 11.4.4 is due to Poole [1989]; he presents it as an example of problems that arise in Reiter's [1980] *default logic*, which would conclude that both arms are usable.

The connections to maximum entropy discussed in Section 11.5 are explored in more detail in [Grove, Halpern, and Koller 1994], where Theorem 11.5.1 is proved. This paper also provides further discussion of the relationship between maximum entropy and the random-worlds approach (and why this relationship breaks down when there are nonunary predicates in the vocabulary). Paris and Venkovska [1989; 1992] use an approach based on maximum entropy to deal with reasoning about uncertainty, although they work at the propositional level. The observation that the maximum-entropy approach to default reasoning in Section 8.5 leads to some anomalous conclusions as a result of using the same $\epsilon$ for all rules is due to Geffner [1992a]. Geffner presents another approach to default reasoning that seems to result in the same conclusions as the random-worlds translation of the maximum-entropy approach when different approximate equality relations are used; however, the exact relationship between the two approaches is as yet unknown. Stirling's approximation to $m!$ (which is used in Exercise 11.16) is well known; see [Graham, Knuth, and Patashnik 1989].

Problems with the random-worlds approach (including ones not mentioned here) are discussed in [Bacchus, Grove, Halpern, and Koller 1996]. Because of the connection between random worlds and maximum entropy, random worlds inherits some well-known problems of the maximum-entropy approach, such as representation dependence. In [Halpern and Koller 1995] a definition of representation independence in the context of probabilistic reasoning is given; it is shown that essentially every interesting nondeductive inference procedure cannot be representation independent in the sense of this definition. Thus the problem is not unique to maximum entropy (or random worlds). Walley [1996] proposes an approach to modeling uncertainty that is representation independent, using sets of Dirichlet distributions.

A number of variants of the random-worlds approach are presented in [Bacchus, Grove, Halpern, and Koller 1992]; each of them has its own problems and features. The one presented in Exercise 11.19 is called the *random-propensities* approach. It does allow some learning, at least as long as the vocabulary is restricted to unary predicates. In that case, as shown in [Koller and Halpern 1996], it satisfies analogues of Theorem 11.3.2 and 11.3.7. However, the random-propensities method does not extend too well to nonunary predicates.

# Chapter 12

# Final Words

*Last words are for people who haven't said anything in life.*

—Karl Marx

"Reasoning about uncertainty" is a vast topic. I have scratched only the surface in this book. My approach has been somewhat different from that of most books on the subject. Given that, let me summarize what I believe are the key points I have raised.

- Probability is not the only way of representing uncertainty. There are a number of alternatives, each with their advantages and disadvantages.

- Updating by conditioning makes sense for all the representations, but you have to be careful not to apply conditioning blindly.

- Plausibility is a way of representing uncertainty that is general enough to make it possible to abstract the key requirements on the representation needed to obtain properties of interest (like beliefs being closed under conjunction).

- There are a number of useful tools that make for better representation of situations, including random variables, Bayesian networks, Markov chains, and runs and systems (global states). These tools focus on different issues and can often be combined.

- Thinking in terms of protocols helps clarify a number of subtleties, and allows for a more accurate representation of uncertainty.

- It is important to distinguish degrees of belief from statistical information and to connect them.

A number of issues that I have touched on in the book deserve more attention. Of course, many important technical problems remain unsolved, but I focus here on the more conceptual issues (which, in my opinion, are often the critical ones for many real-world problems).

The problem of going from statistical information to degrees of belief can be viewed as part of a larger problem of learning. Agents typically hope to build a reasonable model of the world (or, at least, relevant parts of the world) so that they can use the model to make better decisions or to perform more appropriate actions. Clearly representing uncertainty is a critical part of the learning problem. How can uncertainty best be represented so as to facilitate learning? The standard answer from probability theory is that it should be represented as a set of possible worlds with a probability measure on them, and learning should be captured by conditioning. However, that naive approach often fails, for some of the reasons already discussed in this book.

Even assuming that the agent is willing, at least in principle, to use probability, doing so is not always straightforward. For one thing, as I mentioned in Section 2.1, choosing the "appropriate" set of possible worlds can be nontrivial. In fact, the situation is worse than that. In large, complex domains, it is far from clear what the appropriate set of possible worlds is. Imagine an agent that is trying to decide between selling and renting out a house. In considering the possibility of renting, the agent tries to consider all the things that might go wrong. There are some things that might go wrong that are foreseeable; for example, the tenant might not pay the rent. Not surprisingly, there is a clause in a standard rental agreement that deals with this. The art and skill of writing a contract is to cover as many contingencies as possible. However, there are almost always things that are not foreseeable; these are often the things that cause the most trouble (and lead to lawsuits, at least in the United States). As far as reasoning about uncertainty goes, how can the agent construct an appropriate possible-worlds model when he does not even know what all the possibilities are. Of course, it is always possible to have a catch-all "something unexpected happens." But this is probably not good enough when it comes to making decisions, in the spirit of Section 5.4. What is the utility (i.e., loss) associated with "something unexpected happens"? How should a probability measure be updated when something completely unexpected is observed? More generally, how should uncertainty be represented when part of the uncertainty is about the set of possible worlds?

Even if the set of possible worlds is clear, there is the computational problem of listing the worlds and characterizing the probability measure. Although I have discussed some techniques to alleviate this problem (e.g., using Bayesian networks), they are not always sufficient to solve the problem.

One reason for wanting to consider representations of uncertainty other than probability is the observation that, although it is well known that people are not very good at dealing with probability, for the most part, we manage reasonably well. We typically do not bump into walls, we typically do not get run over crossing the street, and our decisions, while certainly not always optimal, are also typically "good enough" to get by. Perhaps probability is simply not needed in many mundane situations. Going out on a limb, I conjecture that there are many situations that are "robust," in that almost any "reasonable" representation of uncertainty will produce reasonable results. If this is true, then it suggests that the focus should be on (a) characterizing these situations and then (b) finding representations of uncertainty that are easy to manipulate and can be easily used in these situations.

Although I do not know how to solve the problems I have raised, I believe that progress will be made soon on all of them, not only on the theoretical side, but on building systems that use sophisticated methods of reasoning about uncertainty to tackle large, complex real-world problems. It is an exciting time to be working on reasoning about uncertainty.

## Notes

There is a huge literature in economics dealing with unforeseen contingencies. See [Dekel, Lipman, and Rusticchini 1998] for a relatively recent overview and references. Very little seems to exist on the problem of dealing with uncertain domains; the work of Manski [1981] and Goldstein [1984] are two of the few exceptions. There is also a huge literature showing that people are not very good at dealing with probability, largely inspired by the work of Kahneman, Tversky, and their colleagues (see [Kahneman, Slovic, and Tversky 1982]). As I mentioned in the notes to Chapter 5, much work has been done on finding notions of uncertainty and decision rules that are more descriptively accurate (although how successful this work has been is debatable).

# References

Abadi, M. and J. Halpern (1994). Decidability and expressiveness for first-order logics of probability. *Information and Computation 112*(1), 1–36.

Adams, E. (1975). *The Logic of Conditionals*. Dordrecht, Netherlands: Reidel.

Agrawal, M., N. Keyal, and N. Saxena (2002). Primes is in P. Unpublished manuscript.

Alchourrón, C. E., P. Gärdenfors, and D. Makinson (1985). On the logic of theory change: partial meet functions for contraction and revision. *Journal of Symbolic Logic 50*, 510–530.

Allais, M. (1953). Le comportement de l'homme rationel devant le risque: critique de l'école Americaine. *Econometrica 21*, 503–546.

Anderson, A. and N. D. Belnap (1975). *Entailment: The Logic of Relevance and Necessity*. Princeton, N.J.: Princeton University Press.

Anger, B. and J. Lembcke (1985). Infinite subadditive capacities as upper envelopes of measures. *Zeitschirft für Wahrscheinlichkeitstheorie 68*, 403–414.

Arntzenius, F. and D. McCarthy (1997). The two-envelope paradox and infinite expectations. *Analysis 57*, 42–51.

Ash, R. B. (1970). *Basic Probability Theory*. New York: Wiley.

Aumann, R. J. (1976). Agreeing to disagree. *Annals of Statistics 4*(6), 1236–1239.

Bacchus, F. (1988). On probability distributions over possible worlds. In *Proc. Fourth Workshop on Uncertainty in Artificial Intelligence*, pp. 15–21.

Bacchus, F. (1990). *Representing and Reasoning with Probabilistic Knowledge*. Cambridge, Mass.: MIT Press.

Bacchus, F. and A. J. Grove (1995). Graphical models for preference and utility. In *Proc. Eleventh Conference on Uncertainty in Artificial Intelligence (UAI '95)*, pp. 3–11.

435

Bacchus, F., A. J. Grove, J. Y. Halpern, and D. Koller (1992). From statistics to belief. In *Proceedings, Tenth National Conference on Artificial Intelligence (AAAI '92)*, pp. 602–608.

Bacchus, F., A. J. Grove, J. Y. Halpern, and D. Koller (1996). From statistical knowledge bases to degrees of belief. *Artificial Intelligence 87*(1–2), 75–143.

Bacchus, F., H. E. Kyburg, and M. Thalos (1990). Against conditionalization. *Synthese 85*, 475–506.

Balke, A. and J. Pearl (1994). Probabilistic evaluation of counterfactual queries. In *Proceedings, Twelfth National Conference on Artificial Intelligence (AAAI '94)*, pp. 230–237.

Bar-Hillel, M. and R. Falk (1982). Some teasers concerning conditional probabilities. *Cognition 11*, 109–122.

Benthem, J. F. A. K. van (1974). Some correspondence results in modal logic. Report 74–05, University of Amsterdam.

Benthem, J. F. A. K. van (1985). *Modal Logic and Classical Logic*. Naples: Bibliopolis.

Benvenuti, P. and R. Mesiar (2000). Integrals with respect to a general fuzzy measure. In M. Grabisch, T. Murofushi, and M. Sugeno (Eds.), *Fuzzy Measures and Applications—Theory and Applications*, pp. 205–232. Heidelberg: Physica Verlag.

Billingsley, P. (1986). *Probability and Measure*. New York: Wiley, third edition.

Blackburn, P., M. de Rijke, and Y. Venema (2001). *Modal Logic*. Cambridge Tracts in Theoretical Computer Science, No. 53. Cambridge, U.K.: Cambridge University Press.

Blume, L., A. Brandenburger, and E. Dekel (1991a). Lexicographic probabilities and choice under uncertainty. *Econometrica 59*(1), 61–79.

Blume, L., A. Brandenburger, and E. Dekel (1991b). Lexicographic probabilities and equilibrium refinements. *Econometrica 59*(1), 81–98.

Bonanno, G. and K. Nehring (1999). How to make sense of the common prior assumption under incomplete information. *International Journal of Game Theory 28*(3), 409–434.

Boole, G. (1854). *An Investigation into the Laws of Thought on Which Are Founded the Mathematical Theories of Logic and Probabilities*. London: Macmillan.

Borel, E. (1943). *Les Probabilités et la Vie*. Paris: Presses Universitaires de France. English translation *Probabilities and Life*, New York: Dover, 1962.

Borodin, A. and R. El-Yaniv (1998). *Online Computation and Competitive Analysis*. Cambridge, U.K.: Cambridge University Press.

Boutilier, C. (1994). Unifying default reasoning and belief revision in a modal framework. *Artificial Intelligence 68*, 33–85.

Boutilier, C. (1996). Iterated revision and minimal change of conditional beliefs. *Journal of Philosophical Logic 25*, 262–305.

Boutilier, C. (1998). A unified model of qualitative belief change: a dynamical systems perspective. *Artificial Intelligence 98*(1–2), 281–316.

Boutilier, C. and M. Goldszmidt (Eds.) (2000). *Proc. Sixteenth Conference on Uncertainty in Artificial Intelligence (UAI 2000)*. San Francisco: Morgan Kaufmann.

Boutilier, C., J. Y. Halpern, and N. Friedman (1998). Belief revision with unreliable observations. In *Proceedings, Fifteenth National Conference on Artificial Intelligence (AAAI '98)*, pp. 127–134.

Brafman, R. I. (1997). A first-order conditional logic with qualitative statistical semantics. *Journal of Logic and Computation 7*(6), 777–803.

Brandenburger, A. (1999). On the existence of a "complete" belief model. Working Paper 99-056, Harvard Business School.

Brandenburger, A. and E. Dekel (1987). Common knowledge with probability 1. *Journal of Mathematical Economics 16*, 237–245.

Burgess, J. (1981). Quick completeness proofs for some logics of conditionals. *Notre Dame Journal of Formal Logic 22*, 76–84.

Camerer, C. and M. Weber (1992). Recent developments in modeling preferences: uncertainty and ambiguity. *Journal of Risk and Uncertainty 5*, 325–370.

Campos, L. M. de. and J. F. Huete (1993). Independence concepts in upper and lower probabilities. In B. Bouchon-Meunier, L. Valverde, and R. R. Yager (Eds.), *Uncertainty in Intelligent Systems*, pp. 85–96. Amsterdam: North-Holland.

Campos, L. M. de and J. F. Huete (1999a). Independence concepts in possibility theory: Part I. *Fuzzy Sets and Systems 103*(1), 127–152.

Campos, L. M. de and J. F. Huete (1999b). Independence concepts in possibility theory: Part II. *Fuzzy Sets and Systems 103*(3), 487–505.

Campos, L. M. de, M. T. Lamata, and S. Moral (1990). The concept of conditional fuzzy measure. *International Journal of Intelligent Systems 5*, 237–246.

Campos, L. M. de and S. Moral (1995). Independence concepts for sets of probabilities. In *Proc. Eleventh Conference on Uncertainty in Artificial Intelligence (UAI '95)*, pp. 108–115.

Carnap, R. (1946). Modalities and quantification. *Journal of Symbolic Logic 11*, 33–64.

Carnap, R. (1947). *Meaning and Necessity*. Chicago: University of Chicago Press.

Carnap, R. (1950). *Logical Foundations of Probability*. Chicago: University of Chicago Press.

Carnap, R. (1952). *The Continuum of Inductive Methods*. Chicago: University of Chicago Press.

Castillo, E., J. M. Gutierrez, and A. S. Hadi (1997). *Expert Systems and Probabilistic Network Models*. New York: Springer-Verlag.

Charniak, E. (1991). Bayesian networks without tears. *AI Magazine Winter*, 50–63.

Chellas, B. F. (1980). *Modal Logic*. Cambridge, U.K.: Cambridge University Press.

Choquet, G. (1953). Theory of capacities. *Annales de l'Institut Fourier (Grenoble) 5*, 131–295.

Chu, F. and J. Y. Halpern (2003a). Great expectations. Part I: Tailoring generalized expected utility to capture different postulates. In *Proc. Eighteenth International Joint Conference on Artificial Intelligence (IJCAI 2003)*.

Chu, F. and J. Y. Halpern (2003b). Great expectations. Part II: generalized expected utility as a universal decision rule. *Proc. Eighteenth International Joint Conference on Artificial Intelligence (IJCAI 2003)*.

Chuaqui, R. (1991). *Truth, Possibility, and Probability: New Logical Foundations of Probability and Statistical Inference*. Amsterdam: North-Holland.

Cooper, G. F. and S. Moral (Eds.) (1998). *Proc. Fourteenth Conference on Uncertainty in Artificial Intelligence (UAI '98)*. San Francisco: Morgan Kaufmann.

Cousa, I., S. Moral, and P. Walley (1999). Examples of independence for imprecise probabilities. In *Proc. First Intl. Symp. Imprecise Probabilities and Their Applications (ISIPTA '99)*.

Cover, T. M. and J. A. Thomas (1991). *Elements of Information Theory*. New York: Wiley.

Cox, R. (1946). Probability, frequency, and reasonable expectation. *American Journal of Physics 14*(1), 1–13.

Cozman, F. G. (1998). Irrelevance and independence relations in Quasi-Bayesian networks. In *Proc. Fourteenth Conference on Uncertainty in Artificial Intelligence (UAI '98)*, pp. 89–96.

Cozman, F. G. (2000a). Credal networks. *Artificial Intelligence 120*(2), 199–233.

Cozman, F. G. (2000b). Separation properties of setes of probability measures. In *Proc. Sixteenth Conference on Uncertainty in Artificial Intelligence (UAI 2000)*.

Cozman, F. G. and P. Walley (1999). Graphoid properties of epistemic irrelevance and independence. Unpublished manuscript.

Darwiche, A. (1992). *A Symbolic Generalization of Probability Theory*. Ph.D. thesis, Stanford University.

Darwiche, A. and M. L. Ginsberg (1992). A symbolic generalization of probability theory. In *Proceedings, Tenth National Conference on Artificial Intelligence (AAAI '92)*, pp. 622–627.

Darwiche, A. and J. Pearl (1997). On the logic of iterated belief revision. *Artificial Intelligence 89*, 1–29.

Davis, R. and W. Hamscher (1988). Model-based reasoning: troubleshooting. In H. Shrobe (Ed.), *Exploring Artificial Intelligence*, pp. 297–346. San Francisco: Morgan Kaufmann.

Dawid, A. P. (1979). Conditional independence in statistical theory. *Journal of the Royal Statistical Society, Series B 41*, 1–31.

Dawid, A. P. and J. M. Dickey (1977). Likelihood and Bayesian inference from selectively reported data. *Journal of the American Statistical Association 72*(360), 845–850.

de Finetti, B. (1931). Sul significato soggestivo del probabilità. *Fundamenta Mathematica 17*, 298–329.

de Finetti, B. (1936). Les probabilités nulles. *Bulletins des Science Mathématiques (première partie) 60*, 275–288.

de Finetti, B. (1937). La prévision: ses lois logiques, ses sources subjectives. *Annales de l'Institut Henri Poincaré 24*, 17–24. English translation "Foresight: its logical laws, its subjective sources" in H. E. Kyburg, Jr. and H. Smokler (Eds.), *Studies in Subjective Probability*, pp. 93–158, New York: Wiley, 1964.

de Finetti, B. (1972). *Probability, Induction and Statistics*. New York: Wiley.

Dekel, E., B. Lipman, and A. Rusticchini (1998). Recent developments in modeling unforeseen contingencies. *European Economic Review 42*, 523–542.

Delgrande, J. P. (1987). A first-order conditional logic for prototypical properties. *Artificial Intelligence 33*, 105–130.

Delgrande, J. P. (1988). An approach to default reasoning based on a first-order conditional logic: revised report. *Artificial Intelligence 36*, 63–90.

Dellacherie, C. (1970). Quelques commentaires sur les prolongements de capacités. In *Séminaire Probabilités, Strasbourg*, Lecture Notes in Mathematics, Volume 191. Berlin and New York: Springer-Verlag.

Dempster, A. P. (1967). Upper and lower probabilities induced by a multivalued mapping. *Annals of Mathematical Statistics 38*, 325–339.

Dempster, A. P. (1968). A generalization of Bayesian inference. *Journal of the Royal Statistical Society, Series B 30*, 205–247.

Denneberg, D. (2002). Conditional expectation for monotone measures, the discrete case. *Journal of Mathematical Economics 37*, 105–121.

Dershowitz, N. and Z. Manna (1979). Proving termination with multiset orderings. *Communications of the ACM 22*(8), 456–476.

Diaconis, P. (1978). Review of "A Mathematical Theory of Evidence". *Journal of the American Statistical Society 73*(363), 677–678.

Diaconis, P. and S. L. Zabell (1982). Updating subjective probability. *Journal of the American Statistical Society 77*(380), 822–830.

Diaconis, P. and S. L. Zabell (1986). Some alternatives to Bayes's rule. In B. Grofman and G. Owen (Eds.), *Proc. Second University of California, Irvine, Conference on Political Economy*, pp. 25–38.

Doyle, J., Y. Shoham, and M. P. Wellman (1991). A logic of relative desire. In *Proc. 6th International Symposium on Methodologies for Intelligent Systems*, pp. 16–31.

Dubois, D., L. Fariñas del Cerro, A. Herzig, and H. Prade (1994). An ordinal view of independence with applications to plausible reasoning. In *Proc. Tenth Conference on Uncertainty in Artificial Intelligence (UAI '94)*, pp. 195–203.

Dubois, D. and H. Prade (1982). On several representations of an uncertain body of evidence. In M. M. Gupta and E. Sanchez (Eds.), *Fuzzy Information and Decision Processes*, pp. 167–181. Amsterdam: North-Holland.

Dubois, D. and H. Prade (1987). The mean value of a fuzzy number. *Fuzzy Sets and Systems 24*, 297–300.

Dubois, D. and H. Prade (1990). An introduction to possibilistic and fuzzy logics. In G. Shafer and J. Pearl (Eds.), *Readings in Uncertain Reasoning*, pp. 742–761. San Francisco: Morgan Kaufmann.

Dubois, D. and H. Prade (1991). Possibilistic logic, preferential models, non-monotonicity and related issues. In *Proc. Twelfth International Joint Conference on Artificial Intelligence (IJCAI '91)*, pp. 419–424.

Dubois, D. and H. Prade (1998). Possibility measures: qualitative and quantitative aspects. In D. M. Gabbay and P. Smets (Eds.), *Quantified Representation of Uncertainty and Imprecision*, Volume 1 of *Handbook of Defeasible Reasoning and Uncertainty Management Systems*, pp. 169–226. Dordrecht, Netherlands: Kluwer.

Ebbinghaus, H. D. (1985). Extended logics: the general framework. In J. Barwise and S. Feferman (Eds.), *Model-Theoretic Logics*, pp. 25–76. New York: Springer-Verlag.

Ellsberg, D. (1961). Risk, ambiguity, and the Savage axioms. *Quarterly Journal of Economics 75*, 643–649.

Enderton, H. B. (1972). *A Mathematical Introduction to Logic*. New York: Academic Press.

Fagin, R. and J. Y. Halpern (1991a). A new approach to updating beliefs. In P. Bonissone, M. Henrion, L. Kanal, and J. Lemmer (Eds.), *Uncertainty in Artificial Intelligence: Volume VI*, pp. 347–374. Amsterdam: Elsevier.

Fagin, R. and J. Y. Halpern (1991b). Uncertainty, belief, and probability. *Computational Intelligence 7*(3), 160–173.

Fagin, R. and J. Y. Halpern (1994). Reasoning about knowledge and probability. *Journal of the ACM 41*(2), 340–367.

Fagin, R., J. Y. Halpern, and N. Megiddo (1990). A logic for reasoning about probabilities. *Information and Computation 87*(1/2), 78–128.

Fagin, R., J. Y. Halpern, Y. Moses, and M. Y. Vardi (1995). *Reasoning about Knowledge*. Cambridge, Mass.: MIT Press.

Fagin, R., J. D. Ullman, and M. Y. Vardi (1983). On the semantics of updates in databases. In *Proc. 2nd ACM Symp. on Principles of Database Systems*, pp. 352–365.

Fariñas del Cerro, L. and A. Herzig (1991). A modal analysis of possibilistic logic. In *Symbolic and Quantitative Approaches to Uncertainty*, Lecture Notes in Computer Science, Volume 548, pp. 58–62. Berlin/New York: Springer-Verlag.

Farquhar, P. H. (1984). Utility assessment methods. *Management Science 30*, 1283–1300.

Feinberg, Y. (1995). A converse to the Agreement Theorem. Technical Report Discussion Paper #83, Center for Rationality and Interactive Decision Theory.

Feinberg, Y. (2000). Characterizing common priors in the form of posteriors. *Journal of Economic Theory 91*(2), 127–179.

Feldman, Y. (1984). A decidable propositional probabilistic dynamic logic with explicit probabilities. *Information and Control 63*, 11–38.

Feller, W. (1957). *An Introduction to Probability Theory and Its Applications* (2nd ed.), Volume 1. New York: Wiley.

Fine, T. L. (1973). *Theories of Probability*. New York: Academic Press.

Fischer, M. J. and N. Immerman (1986). Foundations of knowledge for distributed systems. In *Theoretical Aspects of Reasoning about Knowledge: Proc. 1986 Conference*, pp. 171–186.

Fischer, M. J. and L. D. Zuck (1988). Reasoning about uncertainty in fault-tolerant distributed systems. Technical Report YALEU/DCS/TR–643, Yale University.

Fonck, P. (1994). Conditional independence in possibility theory. In *Proc. Tenth Conference on Uncertainty in Artificial Intelligence (UAI '94)*, pp. 221–226.

Freund, J. E. (1965). Puzzle or paradox? *American Statistician 19*(4), 29–44.

Freund, M. and D. Lehmann (1994). Belief revision and rational inference. Technical Report TR 94-16, Hebrew University.

Friedman, N., L. Getoor, D. Koller, and A. Pfeffer (1999). Learning probabilistic relational models. In *Proc. Sixteenth International Joint Conference on Artificial Intelligence (IJCAI '99)*, pp. 1300–1307.

Friedman, N. and J. Y. Halpern (1994). On the complexity of conditional logics. In *Principles of Knowledge Representation and Reasoning: Proc. Fourth International Conference (KR '94)*, pp. 202–213.

Friedman, N. and J. Y. Halpern (1995). Plausibility measures: a user's guide. In *Proc. Eleventh Conference on Uncertainty in Artificial Intelligence (UAI '95)*, pp. 175–184.

Friedman, N. and J. Y. Halpern (1996). A qualitative Markov assumption and its implications for belief change. In *Proc. Twelfth Conference on Uncertainty in Artificial Intelligence (UAI '96)*, pp. 263–273.

Friedman, N. and J. Y. Halpern (1997). Modeling belief in dynamic systems. Part I: foundations. *Artificial Intelligence 95(2)*, 257–316.

Friedman, N. and J. Y. Halpern (1999). Modeling belief in dynamic systems. Part II: revision and update. *Journal of A.I. Research 10*, 117–167.

Friedman, N. and J. Y. Halpern (2001). Plausibility measures and default reasoning. *Journal of the ACM 48(4)*, 648–685.

Friedman, N., J. Y. Halpern, and D. Koller (2000). First-order conditional logic for default reasoning revisited. *ACM Trans. on Computational Logic 1(2)*, 175–207.

Fudenberg, D. and J. Tirole (1991). *Game Theory*. Cambridge, Mass.: MIT Press.

Gabbay, D. (1985). Theoretical foundations for nonmonotonic reasoning in expert systems. In K. R. Apt (Ed.), *Logics and Models of Concurrent Systems*, pp. 459–476. Berlin: Springer-Verlag.

Gaifman, H. (1986). A theory of higher order probabilities. In *Theoretical Aspects of Reasoning about Knowledge: Proc. 1986 Conference*, pp. 275–292.

Gärdenfors, P. (1978). Conditionals and changes of belief. *Acta Philosophica Fennica 30*, 381–404.

Gärdenfors, P. (1988). *Knowledge in Flux*. Cambridge, Mass.: MIT Press.

Gärdenfors, P. and D. Makinson (1988). Revisions of knowledge systems using epistemic entrenchment. In *Proc. Second Conference on Theoretical Aspects of Reasoning about Knowledge*, pp. 83–95. San Francisco: Morgan Kaufmann.

Gärdenfors, P. and N. Sahlin (1982). Unreliable probabilities, risk taking, and decision making. *Synthese 53*, 361–386.

Gardner, M. (1961). *Second Scientific American Book of Mathematical Puzzles and Diversions*. New York: Simon & Schuster.

Garson, J. W. (1984). Quantification in modal logic. In D. Gabbay and F. Guenthner (Eds.), *Handbook of Philosophical Logic, Volume II*, pp. 249–307. Dordrecht, Netherlands: Reidel.

Geffner, H. (1992a). *Default Reasoning: Causal and Conditional Theories*. Cambridge, Mass.: MIT Press.

Geffner, H. (1992b). High probabilities, model preference and default arguments. *Mind and Machines 2*, 51–70.

Geiger, D. and J. Pearl (1988). On the logic of causal models. In *Proc. Fourth Workshop on Uncertainty in Artificial Intelligence (UAI '88)*, pp. 136–147.

Geiger, D., T. Verma, and J. Pearl (1990). Identifying independence in Bayesian networks. *Networks 20*, 507–534.

Gilboa, I. and D. Schmeidler (1989). Maxmin expected utility with a non-unique prior. *Journal of Mathematical Economics 18*, 141–153.

Gilboa, I. and D. Schmeidler (1993). Updating ambiguous beliefs. *Journal of Economic Theory 59*, 33–49.

Gill, R. D., M. van der Laan, and J. Robins (1997). Coarsening at random: Characterisations, conjectures and counter-examples. In *Proc. First Seattle Conference on Biostatistics*, pp. 255–294.

Goldberger, A. S. (1972). Structural equation methods in the social sciences. *Econometrica 40*(6), 979–1001.

Goldstein, M. (1984). Turning probabilities into expectations. *Annals of Statistics 12*(4), 1551–1557.

Goldszmidt, M., P. Morris, and J. Pearl (1993). A maximum entropy approach to nonmonotonic reasoning. *IEEE Transactions of Pattern Analysis and Machine Intelligence 15*(3), 220–232.

Goldszmidt, M. and J. Pearl (1992). Rank-based systems: A simple approach to belief revision, belief update and reasoning about evidence and actions. In *Proc. Third International Conference on Principles of Knowledge Representation and Reasoning (KR '92)*, pp. 661–672.

Good, I. J. (1960). Weights of evidence, corroboration, explanatory power, information and the utility of experiments. *Journal of the Royal Statistical Society, Series B 22*, 319–331.

Gordon, J. and E. H. Shortliffe (1984). The Dempster-Shafer theory of evidence. In B. G. Buchanan and E. H. Shortliffe (Eds.), *Rule-based Expert Systems: The MYCIN Experiments of the Stanford Heuristic Programming Project*, pp. 272–292. New York: Addison-Wesley.

Graham, R. L., D. E. Knuth, and O. Patashnik (1989). *Concrete Mathematics—A Foundation for Computer Science*. Reading, Mass.: Addison-Wesley.

Gray, J. (1978). Notes on database operating systems. In R. Bayer, R. M. Graham, and G. Seegmuller (Eds.), *Operating Systems: An Advanced Course*, Lecture Notes in Computer Science, Volume 66. Berlin/New York: Springer-Verlag. Also appears as IBM Research Report RJ 2188, 1978.

Grove, A. (1988). Two modelings for theory change. *Journal of Philosophical Logic 17*, 157–170.

Grove, A. J. and J. Y. Halpern (1997). Probability update: conditioning vs. cross-entropy. In *Proc. Thirteenth Conference on Uncertainty in Artificial Intelligence (UAI '97)*, pp. 208–214.

Grove, A. J. and J. Y. Halpern (1998). Updating sets of probabilities. In *Proc. Fourteenth Conference on Uncertainty in Artificial Intelligence (UAI '98)*, pp. 173–182.

Grove, A. J., J. Y. Halpern, and D. Koller (1994). Random worlds and maximum entropy. *Journal of A.I. Research 2*, 33–88.

Grünwald, P. D. and J. Y. Halpern (2002). Updating probabilities. In *Proc. Eighteenth Conference on Uncertainty in Artificial Intelligence (UAI 2002)*, pp. 187–196.

Hacking, I. (1975). *The Emergence of Probability*. Cambridge, U.K.: Cambridge University Press.

Hagashi, M. and G. J. Klir (1983). Measures of uncertainty and information based on possibility distributions. *International Journal of General Systems 9*(2), 43–58.

Halmos, P. (1950). *Measure Theory*. New York: Van Nostrand.

Halpern, J. Y. (1990). An analysis of first-order logics of probability. *Artificial Intelligence 46*, 311–350.

Halpern, J. Y. (1996). Should knowledge entail belief? *Journal of Philosophical Logic 25*, 483–494.

Halpern, J. Y. (1997a). Defining relative likelihood in partially-ordered preferential structures. *Journal of A.I. Research 7*, 1–24.

Halpern, J. Y. (1997b). On ambiguities in the interpretation of game trees. *Games and Economic Behavior 20*, 66–96.

Halpern, J. Y. (1998a). Characterizing the common prior assumption. In *Theoretical Aspects of Rationality and Knowledge: Proc. Seventh Conference (TARK 1998)*, pp. 133–146.

Halpern, J. Y. (1998b). A logical approach for reasoning about uncertainty: a tutorial. In X. Arrazola, K. Korta, and F. J. Pelletier (Eds.), *Discourse, Interaction, and Communication*, pp. 141–155. Dordrecht, Netherlands: Kluwer.

Halpern, J. Y. (1999a). A counterexample to theorems of Cox and Fine. *Journal of A.I. Research 10*, 76–85.

Halpern, J. Y. (1999b). Cox's theorem revisited. *Journal of A.I. Research 11*, 429–435.

Halpern, J. Y. (1999c). Set-theoretic completeness for epistemic and conditional logic. *Annals of Mathematics and Artificial Intelligence 26*, 1–27.

Halpern, J. Y. (2001a). Conditional plausibility measures and Bayesian networks. *Journal of A.I. Research 14*, 359–389.

Halpern, J. Y. (2001b). Lexicographic probability, conditional probability, and nonstandard probability. In *Theoretical Aspects of Rationality and Knowledge: Proc. Eighth Conference (TARK 2001)*, pp. 17–30.

Halpern, J. Y. (2001c). Substantive rationality and backward induction. *Games and Economic Behavior 37*, 425–435.

Halpern, J. Y. and R. Fagin (1989). Modelling knowledge and action in distributed systems. *Distributed Computing 3*(4), 159–179.

Halpern, J. Y. and R. Fagin (1992). Two views of belief: belief as generalized probability and belief as evidence. *Artificial Intelligence 54*, 275–317.

Halpern, J. Y. and D. Koller (1995). Representation dependence in probabilistic inference. In *Proc. Fourteenth International Joint Conference on Artificial Intelligence (IJCAI '95)*, pp. 1853–1860.

Halpern, J. Y. and Y. Moses (1990). Knowledge and common knowledge in a distributed environment. *Journal of the ACM 37*(3), 549–587.

Halpern, J. Y. and Y. Moses (1992). A guide to completeness and complexity for modal logics of knowledge and belief. *Artificial Intelligence 54*, 319–379.

Halpern, J. Y. and R. Pucella (2001). A logic for reasoning about upper probabilities. In *Proc. Seventeenth Conference on Uncertainty in Artificial Intelligence (UAI 2001)*, pp. 203–210.

Halpern, J. Y. and R. Pucella (2002). Reasoning about expectation. In *Proc. Eighteenth Conference on Uncertainty in Artificial Intelligence (UAI 2002)*, pp. 207–215.

Halpern, J. Y. and M. R. Tuttle (1993). Knowledge, probability, and adversaries. *Journal of the ACM 40*(4), 917–962.

Halpern, J. Y. and M. Y. Vardi (1989). The complexity of reasoning about knowledge and time, I: lower bounds. *Journal of Computer and System Sciences 38*(1), 195–237.

Hammond, P. J. (1994). Elementary non-Archimedean representations of probability for decision theory and games. In P. Humphreys (Ed.), *Patrick Suppes: Scientific Philosopher; Volume 1*. Dordrecht, Netherlands: Kluwer.

Hansson, S. O. (1999). *A Textbook of Belief Dynamics: Theory Change and Database Updating*. Dordrecht, Netherlands: Kluwer.

Harel, D., D. C. Kozen, and J. Tiuryn (2000). *Dynamic Logic*. Cambridge, Mass.: MIT Press.

Harsanyi, J. (1968). Games with incomplete information played by 'Bayesian' players, parts I–III. *Management Science 14*, 159–182, 320–334, 486–502.

Hart, S. and M. Sharir (1984). Probabilistic temporal logics for finite and bounded models. In *Proc. 16th ACM Symp. on Theory of Computing*, pp. 1–13.

Heckerman, D. (1990). Probabilistic similarity networks. Technical Report STAN-CS-1316, Stanford University, Departments of Computer Science and Medicine.

Heitjan, D. and D. Rubin (1991). Ignorability and coarse data. *Annals of Statistics 19*, 2244–2253.

Heyting, A. (1956). *Intuitionism: An Introduction*. Amsterdam: North-Holland.

Hintikka, J. (1962). *Knowledge and Belief*. Ithaca, N.Y.: Cornell University Press.

Hisdal, E. (1978). Conditional possibilities—independence and noninteractivity. *Fuzzy Sets and Systems 1*, 283–297.

Hoek, W. van der (1993). Systems for knowledge and belief. *Journal of Logic and Computation 3*(2), 173–195.

Horn, A. and A. Tarski (1948). Measures in Boolean algebras. *Transactions of the AMS 64*(1), 467–497.

Howard, R. A. and J. E. Matheson (1981). Influence diagrams. In R. A. Howard and J. E. Matheson (Eds.), *The Principles and Applications of Decision Analysis, Volume II (1984)*. Menlo Park, Calif.: Strategic Decisions Group.

Howson, C. and P. Urbach (1989). *Scientific Reasoning: The Bayesian Approach*. La Salle, Ill.: Open Court.

Huber, P. J. (1981). *Robust Statistics*. New York: Wiley.

Hughes, G. E. and M. J. Cresswell (1968). *An Introduction to Modal Logic*. London: Methuen.

Jaffray, J.-Y. (1992). Bayesian updating and belief functions. *IEEE Transactions on Systems, Man, and Cybernetics 22*(5), 1144–1152.

Jaynes, E. T. (1957). Information theory and statistical mechanics. *Physical Review 106*(4), 620–630.

Jeffrey, R. C. (1968). Probable knowledge. In I. Lakatos (Ed.), *International Colloquium in the Philosophy of Science: The Problem of Inductive Logic*, pp. 157–185. Amsterdam: North-Holland.

Jeffrey, R. C. (1983). *The Logic of Decision*. Chicago: University of Chicago Press.

Jelinek, F. (1997). *Statistical Methods for Speech Recognition*. Cambridge, Mass.: MIT Press.

Jensen, F. V. (1996). *Introduction to Bayesian Networks*. New York: Springer-Verlag.

Johnson, W. E. (1932). Probability: The deductive and inductive problems. *Mind 41*(164), 409–423.

Kagel, J. H. and A. E. Roth (1995). *Handbook of Experimental Economics*. Princeton, N.J.: Princeton University Press.

Kahneman, D., P. Slovic, and A. Tversky (Eds.) (1982). *Judgment Under Uncertainty: Heuristics and Biases*. Cambridge/New York: Cambridge University Press.

Kahneman, D. and A. Tversky (1979). Prospect theory: an analysis of decision under risk. *Econometrica 47*(2), 263–292.

Katsuno, H. and A. Mendelzon (1991a). On the difference between updating a knowledge base and revising it. In *Proc. Second International Conference on Principles of Knowledge Representation and Reasoning (KR '91)*, pp. 387–394.

Katsuno, H. and A. Mendelzon (1991b). Propositional knowledge base revision and minimal change. *Artificial Intelligence 52*(3), 263–294.

Keeney, R. L. and H. Raiffa (1976). *Decisions with Multiple Objectives: Preferences and Value Tradeoffs*. New York: Wiley.

Kemeny, J. G. (1955). Fair bets and inductive probabilities. *Journal of Symbolic Logic 20*(3), 263–273.

Kemeny, J. G. and J. L. Snell (1960). *Finite Markov Chains*. Princeton, N.J.: Van Nostrand.

Keynes, J. M. (1921). *A Treatise on Probability*. London: Macmillan.

Kleinbaum, D. (1999). *Survival Analysis: A Self-Learning Text*. Statistics in the Health Sciences. New York: Springer-Verlag.

Klir, G. J. and T. A. Folger (1988). *Fuzzy Sets, Uncertainty, and Information*. Englewood Cliffs, N.J.: Prentice-Hall.

Klir, G. J. and M. Mariano (1987). On the uniqueness of possibilistic measure of uncertainty and information. *Fuzzy Sets and Systems 24*, 197–219.

Knight, F. H. (1921). *Risk, Uncertainty, and Profit*. New York: Houghton Mifflin.

Koller, D. and J. Halpern (1996). Irrelevance and conditioning in first-order probabilistic logic. In *Proceedings, Thirteenth National Conference on Artificial Intelligence (AAAI '96)*, pp. 569–576.

Koller, D. and J. Y. Halpern (1992). A logic for approximate reasoning. In *Proc. Third International Conference on Principles of Knowledge Representation and Reasoning (KR '92)*, pp. 153–164.

Koller, D. and A. Pfeffer (1998). Probabilistic frame-based systems. In *Proceedings, Fifteenth National Conference on Artificial Intelligence (AAAI '98)*, pp. 580–587.

Kouvatsos, D. D. (1994). Entropy maximisation and queueing network models. *Annals of Operations Research 48*, 63–126.

Kozen, D. (1985). Probabilistic PDL. *Journal of Computer and System Sciences 30*, 162–178.

Kraitchik, M. (1953). *Mathematical Recreations* (2nd ed.). New York: Dover.

Kraus, S. and D. Lehmann (1988). Knowledge, belief, and time. *Theoretical Computer Science 58*, 155–174.

Kraus, S., D. Lehmann, and M. Magidor (1990). Nonmonotonic reasoning, preferential models and cumulative logics. *Artificial Intelligence 44*, 167–207.

Kreps, D. (1988). *Notes on the Theory of Choice*. Boulder, Colo.: Westview Press.

Kries, J. von (1886). *Die Principien der Wahrscheinlichkeitsrechnung und Rational Expectation*. Freiburg: Mohr.

Kripke, S. (1963). A semantical analysis of modal logic I: normal modal propositional calculi. *Zeitschrift für Mathematische Logik und Grundlagen der Mathematik 9*, 67–96. Announced in *Journal of Symbolic Logic 24*, 1959, p. 323.

Kullback, S. and R. A. Leibler (1951). On information and sufficiency. *Annals of Mathematical Statistics 22*, 76–86.

Kyburg, Jr., H. E. (1974). *The Logical Foundations of Statistical Inference*. Dordrecht, Netherlands: Reidel.

Kyburg, Jr., H. E. (1983). The reference class. *Philosophy of Science 50*(3), 374–397.

La Mura, P. and Y. Shoham (1999). Expected utility networks. In *Proc. Fifteenth Conference on Uncertainty in Artificial Intelligence (UAI '99)*, pp. 366–373.

Lamarre, P. and Y. Shoham (1994). Knowledge, certainty, belief, and conditionalisation. In *Principles of Knowledge Representation and Reasoning: Proc. Fourth International Conference (KR '94)*, pp. 415–424.

Lambalgen, M. van (1987). *Random Sequences*. Ph.D. thesis, University of Amsterdam.

Laskey, K. and H. Prade (Eds.) (1999). *Proc. Fifteenth Conference on Uncertainty in Artificial Intelligence (UAI '99)*. San Francisco: Morgan Kaufmann.

Lehmann, D. (1989). What does a conditional knowledge base entail? In *Proc. First International Conference on Principles of Knowledge Representation and Reasoning (KR '89)*, pp. 212–222.

Lehmann, D. (1995). Belief revision, revised. In *Proc. Fourteenth International Joint Conference on Artificial Intelligence (IJCAI '95)*, pp. 1534–1540.

Lehmann, D. (1996). Generalized qualitative probability; Savage revisited. In *Proc. Twelfth Conference on Uncertainty in Artificial Intelligence (UAI '96)*, pp. 318–388.

Lehmann, D. (2001). Expected qualitative utility maximization. *Games and Economic Behavior 35*(1–2), 54–79.

Lehmann, D. and M. Magidor (1990). Preferential logics: the predicate calculus case. In *Theoretical Aspects of Reasoning about Knowledge: Proc. Third Conference*, pp. 57–72. San Francisco: Morgan Kaufmann.

Lehmann, D. and M. Magidor (1992). What does a conditional knowledge base entail? *Artificial Intelligence 55*, 1–60.

Lehmann, D. and S. Shelah (1982). Reasoning about time and chance. *Information and Control 53*, 165–198.

Lemmon, E. J. (1977). *The "Lemmon Notes": An Introduction to Modal Logic*. Oxford, U.K.: Basil Blackwell. Written in collaboration with D. Scott; K. Segerberg (Ed.). American Philosophical Quarterly Monograph Series, No. 11.

Lenzen, W. (1978). Recent work in epistemic logic. *Acta Philosophica Fennica 30*, 1–219.

Lenzen, W. (1979). Epistemische betrachtungen zu [S4,S5]. *Erkenntnis 14*, 33–56.

Levi, I. (1985). Imprecision and uncertainty in probability judgment. *Philosophy of Science 52*, 390–406.

Levi, I. (1988). Iteration of conditionals and the Ramsey test. *Synthese 76*, 49–81.

Lewis, C. I. and C. H. Langford (1959). *Symbolic Logic* (2nd ed.). New York: Dover.

Lewis, D. K. (1973). *Counterfactuals*. Cambridge, Mass.: Harvard University Press.

Luce, R. D. (1990). Rational versus plausible accounting equivalences in preference judgments. *Psychological Science 1*, 225–234. Reprinted with minor changes in Ward Edwards (Ed.), *Utility Theories: Measurements and Applications*, pp. 187–206. Boston: Kluwer, 1992.

Luce, R. D. (2000). *Utility of Gains and Losses: Measurement-Theoretical and Experimental Approaches*. London: Lawrence Erlbaum.

Luce, R. D. and H. Raiffa (1957). *Games and Decisions*. New York: Wiley.

Makinson, D. (1989). General theory of cumulative inference. In M. Reinfrank (Ed.), *Non-Monotonic Reasoning: 2nd International Workshop*, Lecture Notes in Artificial Intelligence, Volume 346, pp. 1–18. Berlin: Springer-Verlag.

Manski, C. (1981). Learning and decision making when subjective probabilities have subjective domains. *Annals of Statistics 9*(1), 59–65.

Marek, W. and M. Truszczyński (1993). *Nonmonotonic Logic*. Berlin/New York: Springer-Verlag.

Maurer, S. B. and A. Ralston (1991). *Discrete Algorithmic Mathematics*. Reading, Mass: Addison-Wesley.

May, S. (1976). Probability kinematics: a constrained optimization problem. *Journal of Philosophical Logic 5*, 395–398.

McCarthy, J. (1980). Circumscription—a form of non-monotonic reasoning. *Artificial Intelligence 13*, 27–39.

McDermott, D. and J. Doyle (1980). Non-monotonic logic I. *Artificial Intelligence 13*(1,2), 41–72.

McGee, V. (1994). Learning the impossible. In E. Eells and B. Skyrms (Eds.), *Probability and Conditionals*. Cambridge, U.K.: Cambridge University Press.

McGrew, T. J., D. Shier, and H. S. Silverstein (1997). The two-envelope paradox resolved. *Analysis 57*, 28–33.

Mendelson, E. (1997). *Introduction to Mathematical Logic*. London: Chapman and Hall, fourth edition.

Miller, D. (1966). A paradox of information. *British Journal for the Philosophy of Science 17*, 59–61.

Milne, P. (1996). $\log[p(h/eb)/p(h/b)]$ is the one true measure of confirmation. *Philosophy of Science 63*, 21–26.

Monderer, D. and D. Samet (1989). Approximating common knowledge with common beliefs. *Games and Economic Behavior 1*, 170–190.

Moore, R. C. (1985). Semantical considerations on nonmonotonic logic. *Artificial Intelligence 25*, 75–94.

Morgan, J. P., N. R. Chaganty, R. C. Dahiya, and M. J. Doviak (1991). Let's make a deal: the player's dilemma (with commentary). *The American Statistician 45*(4), 284–289.

Morris, S. (1994). Trade with heterogeneous prior beliefs and asymmetric information. *Econometrica 62*, 1327–1348.

Morris, S. (1995). The common prior assumption in economic theory. *Economics and Philosophy 11*, 227–253.

Moses, Y. and Y. Shoham (1993). Belief as defeasible knowledge. *Artificial Intelligence 64*(2), 299–322.

Mosteller, F. (1965). *Fifty Challenging Problems in Probability with Solutions*. Reading, Mass.: Addison-Wesley.

Nalebuff, B. (1989). The other person's envelope is always greener. *Journal of Economic Perspectives 3*(1), 171–181.

Nayak, A. C. (1994). Iterated belief change based on epistemic entrenchment. *Erkenntnis 41*, 353–390.

Neapolitan, R. E. (1990). *Probabilistic Reasoning in Expert Systems: Theory and Algorithms*. New York: Wiley.

Niehans, J. (1948). Zur preisbildung bei ungewissen erwartungen. *Scbweizerische Zietschrift für Volkswirtschaft und Statistik 84*(5), 433–456.

Nielsen, S. (1998). *Coarsening at Random and Simulated EM Algorithms*. Ph.D. thesis, Department of Theoretical Statistics, University of Copenhagen.

Nilsson, N. (1986). Probabilistic logic. *Artificial Intelligence 28*, 71–87.

Ostrogradsky, M. V. (1838). Extrait d'un mémoire sur la probabilité des erreurs des tribuneaux. *Memoires d'Académie St. Petersbourg, Séries 6 3*, xix–xxv.

Parikh, R. and R. Ramanujam (1985). Distributed processing and the logic of knowledge. In R. Parikh (Ed.), *Proc. Workshop on Logics of Programs*, pp. 256–268.

Paris, J. B. (1994). *The Uncertain Reasoner's Companion*. Cambridge, U.K.: Cambridge University Press.

Paris, J. B. and A. Vencovska (1989). On the applicability of maximum entropy to inexact reasoning. *International Journal of Approximate Reasoning 3*, 1–34.

Paris, J. B. and A. Vencovska (1992). A method for updating justifying minimum cross entropy. *International Journal of Approximate Reasoning 7*, 1–18.

Pearl, J. (1988). *Probabilistic Reasoning in Intelligent Systems*. San Francisco: Morgan Kaufmann.

Pearl, J. (1989). Probabilistic semantics for nonmonotonic reasoning: a survey. In *Proc. First International Conference on Principles of Knowledge Representation and Reasoning (KR '89)*, pp. 505–516. Reprinted in G. Shafer and J. Pearl (Eds.), *Readings in Uncertain Reasoning*, pp. 699–710. San Francisco: Morgan Kaufmann, 1990.

Pearl, J. (1990). System Z: A natural ordering of defaults with tractable applications to nonmonotonic reasoning. In *Theoretical Aspects of Reasoning about Knowledge: Proc. Third Conference*, pp. 121–135. San Francisco: Morgan Kaufmann.

Plantinga, A. (1974). *The Nature of Necessity*. Oxford, U.K.: Oxford University Press.

Pollock, J. L. (1990). *Nomic Probabilities and the Foundations of Induction*. Oxford, U.K.: Oxford University Press.

Poole, D. (1989). What the lottery paradox tells us about default reasoning. In *Proc. First International Conference on Principles of Knowledge Representation and Reasoning (KR '89)*, pp. 333–340.

Popkorn, S. (1994). *First Steps in Modal Logic*. Cambridge/New York: Cambridge University Press.

Popper, K. R. (1968). *The Logic of Scientific Discovery* (2nd ed.). London: Hutchison. The first version of this book appeared as *Logik der Forschung*, 1934.

Puterman, M. L. (1994). *Markov Decision Processes-Discrete Stochastic Dynamic Programming*. New York: Wiley.

Quiggin, J. (1993). *Generalized Expected Utility Theory: The Rank-Dependent Expected Utility Model*. Boston: Kluwer.

Rabin, M. O. (1980). Probabilistic algorithm for testing primality. *Journal of Number Theory 12*, 128–138.

Rabin, M. O. (1982). $N$-process mutual exclusion with bounded waiting by $4 \cdot \log_2 N$-valued shared variable. *Journal of Computer and System Sciences 25*(1), 66–75.

Ramsey, F. P. (1931a). General propositions and causality. In R. B. Braithwaite (Ed.), *The Foundations of Mathematics and Other Logical Essays*, pp. 237–257. London: Routledge and Kegan Paul.

Ramsey, F. P. (1931b). Truth and probability. In R. B. Braithwaite (Ed.), *The Foundations of Mathematics and Other Logical Essays*, pp. 156–198. London: Routledge and Kegan Paul.

Rawlings, P. (1994). A note on the two envelopes problem. *Theory and Decision 36*, 97–102.

Reichenbach, H. (1949). *The Theory of Probability*. Berkeley: University of California Press. Translation and revision of German edition, published as *Wahrscheinlichkeitslehre*, 1935.

Reiter, R. (1980). A logic for default reasoning. *Artificial Intelligence 13*, 81–132.

Reiter, R. (1987a). Nonmonotonic reasoning. In J. F. Traub, B. J. Grosz, B. W. Lampson, and N. J. Nilsson (Eds.), *Annual Review of Computer Science, Volume 2*, pp. 147–186. Palo Alto, Calif.: Annual Reviews Inc.

Reiter, R. (1987b). A theory of diagnosis from first principles. *Artificial Intelligence 32*, 57–95. Reprinted in M. L. Ginsberg (Ed.), *Readings in Nonmonotonic Reasoning*. San Francisco: Morgan Kaufman, 1987.

Reiter, R. and G. Criscuolo (1981). On interacting defaults. In *Proc. Seventh International Joint Conference on Artificial Intelligence (IJCAI '81)*, pp. 270–276.

Rényi, A. (1955). On a new axiomatic theory of probability. *Acta Mathematica Academiae Scientiarum Hungaricae 6*, 285–335.

Rényi, A. (1956). On conditional probability spaces generated by a dimensionally ordered set of measures. *Theory of Probability and its Applications 1*, 61–71. Reprinted as paper 120 in *Selected Papers of Alfred Rényi, I: 1948–1956*, pp. 554–557. Budapest: Akadémia Kiadó, 1976.

Rényi, A. (1964). Sur les espaces simples de probabilités conditionelles. *Annales de l'Institut Henri Poincaré, Nouvelle série, Section B 1*, 3–21. Reprinted as paper 237 in *Selected Papers of Alfred Rényi, III: 1962–1970*, pp. 284–302. Budapest: Akadémia Kiadó, 1976.

Rescher, N. (1969). *Many-Valued Logic*. New York: McGraw-Hill.

Resnik, M. D. (1987). *Choices: An Introduction to Decision Theory*. Minneapolis: University of Minnesota Press.

Rine, D. C. (Ed.) (1984). *Computer Science and Multiple-Valued Logics: Theory and Applications*. Amsterdam: North-Holland.

Rivest, R. L., A. Shamir, and L. Adelman (1978). A method for obtaining digital signatures and public-key cryptosystems. *Communications of the ACM 21*(2), 120–126.

Rosenschein, S. J. (1985). Formal theories of AI in knowledge and robotics. *New Generation Computing 3*, 345–357.

Rosenschein, S. J. and L. P. Kaelbling (1986). The synthesis of digital machines with provable epistemic properties. In *Theoretical Aspects of Reasoning about Knowledge: Proc. 1986 Conference*, pp. 83–97.

Rubin, D. (1976). Inference and missing data. *Biometrika 63*, 581–592.

Ruspini, E. H. (1987). The logical foundations of evidential reasoning. Research Note 408, revised version, SRI International, Menlo Park, Calif.

Samet, D. (1997). Bayesianism without learning. Unpublished manuscript.

Samet, D. (1998a). Common priors and separation of convex sets. *Games and Economic Behavior 24*, 172–174.

Samet, D. (1998b). Quantified beliefs and believed quantities. In *Theoretical Aspects of Rationality and Knowledge: Proc. Seventh Conference (TARK 1998)*, pp. 263–272.

Savage, L. J. (1951). The theory of statistical decision. *Journal of the American Statistical Association 46*, 55–67.

Savage, L. J. (1954). *Foundations of Statistics*. New York: Wiley.

Schlechta, K. (1995). Defaults as generalized quantifiers. *Journal of Logic and Computation* 5(4), 473–494.

Schlechta, K. (1996). A two-stage approach to first order default reasoning. *Fundamenta Informaticae* 28(3–4), 377–402.

Schmeidler, D. (1986). Integral representation without additivity. *Proc. of the Amer. Math. Soc.* 97(2), 255–261.

Schmeidler, D. (1989). Subjective probability and expected utility without additivity. *Econometrica* 57, 571–587.

Scott, A. D. and M. Scott (1997). What's the two-envelope paradox? *Analysis* 57, 34–41.

Segerberg, K. (1968). *Results in Nonclassical Logic*. Lund, Sweden: Berlingska Boktryckeriet.

Shachter, R. D. (1986). Evaluating influence diagrams. *Operations Research* 34(6), 871–882.

Shackle, G. L. S. (1969). *Decision, Order, and Time in Human Affairs* (2nd ed.). Cambridge, U.K.: Cambridge University Press.

Shafer, G. (1976). *A Mathematical Theory of Evidence*. Princeton, N.J.: Princeton University Press.

Shafer, G. (1979). Allocations of probability. *Annals of Probability* 7(5), 827–839.

Shafer, G. (1985). Conditional probability. *International Statistical Review* 53(3), 261–277.

Shafer, G. (1986). Savage revisited. *Statistical Science* 1(4), 463–485.

Shafer, G. (1990). Perspectives on the theory and practice of belief functions. *International Journal of Approximate Reasoning* 4, 323–362.

Shafer, G. and J. Pearl (Eds.) (1990). *Readings in Uncertain Reasoning*. San Francisco: Morgan Kaufmann.

Shannon, C. and W. Weaver (1949). *The Mathematical Theory of Communication*. Urbana-Champaign, Ill.: University of Illinois Press.

Shastri, L. (1989). Default reasoning in semantic networks: a formalization of recognition and inheritance. *Artificial Intelligence* 39(3), 285–355.

Shenoy, P. P. (1994). Conditional independence in valuation based systems. *International Journal of Approximate Reasoning* 10, 203–234.

Shimony, A. (1955). Coherence and the axioms of confirmation. *Journal of Symbolic Logic* 20(1), 1–26.

Shoham, Y. (1987). A semantical approach to nonmonotonic logics. In *Proc. 2nd IEEE Symp. on Logic in Computer Science*, pp. 275–279. Reprinted in M. L. Ginsberg (Ed.),

*Readings in Nonmonotonic Reasoning*, pp. 227–250. San Francisco: Morgan Kaufman, 1987.

Shore, J. E. and R. W. Johnson (1980). Axiomatic derivation of the principle of maximum entropy and the principle of minimimum cross-entropy. *IEEE Transactions on Information Theory IT-26*(1), 26–37.

Skyrms, B. (1980). *Causal Necessity*. New Haven, Conn.: Yale University Press.

Smets, P. and R. Kennes (1989). The transferable belief model: comparison with Bayesian models. Technical Report 89-1, IRIDIA, Université Libre de Bruxelles.

Smith, C. A. B. (1961). Consistency in statistical inference and decision. *Journal of the Royal Statistical Society, Series B 23*, 1–25.

Sobel, J. H. (1994). Two envelopes. *Theory and Decision 36*, 69–96.

Solovay, R. and V. Strassen (1977). A fast Monte Carlo test for primality. *SIAM Journal on Computing 6*(1), 84–85.

Spohn, W. (1980). Stochastic independence, causal independence, and shieldability. *Journal of Philosophical Logic 9*, 73–99.

Spohn, W. (1988). Ordinal conditional functions: a dynamic theory of epistemic states. In W. Harper and B. Skyrms (Eds.), *Causation in Decision, Belief Change, and Statistics*, Volume 2, pp. 105–134. Dordrecht, Netherlands: Reidel.

Stalnaker, R. C. (1968). A theory of conditionals. In N. Rescher (Ed.), *Studies in Logical Theory*, American Philosophical Quarterly Monograph Series, No. 2, pp. 98–112. Oxford, U.K.: Blackwell. Also appears in W. L. Harper, R. C. Stalnaker and G. Pearce (Eds.), *Ifs*. Dordrecht, Netherlands: Reidel, 1981.

Stalnaker, R. C. (1992). Notes on conditional semantics. In *Theoretical Aspects of Reasoning about Knowledge: Proc. Fourth Conference*, pp. 316–328.

Stalnaker, R. C. and R. Thomason (1970). A semantical analysis of conditional logic. *Theoria 36*, 246–281.

Studeny, M. (1994). Semigraphoids are two-antecedental approximations of stochastic conditional independence models. In *Proc. Tenth Conference on Uncertainty in Artificial Intelligence (UAI '94)*, pp. 546–552.

Sutton, R. and A. Barto (1998). *Reinforcement Learning*. Cambridge, Mass.: MIT Press.

Teller, P. (1973). Conditionalisation and observation. *Synthese 26*, 218–258.

Trakhtenbrot, B. A. (1950). Impossibility of an algorithm for the decision problem in finite classes. *Doklady Akademii Nauk SSSR 70*, 569–572.

Uffink, J. (1995). Can the maximum entropy principle be explained as a consistency requirement? *Studies in the History and Philosophy of Modern Physics 26*(3), 223–261.

Ulam, S. (1930). Zur masstheorie in der allgemeinen mengenlehre. *Fundamenta Mathematicae 16*, 140–150.

van Fraassen, B. C. (1976). Representation of conditional probabilities. *Journal of Philosophical Logic 5*, 417–430.

van Fraassen, B. C. (1981). A problem for relative information minimizers. *British Journal for the Philosophy of Science 32*, 375–379.

van Fraassen, B. C. (1984). Belief and the will. *Journal of Philosophy 81*, 235–245.

van Fraassen, B. C. (1987). Symmetries of personal probability kinematics. In N. Rescher (Ed.), *Scientific Enquiry in Philsophical Perspective*, pp. 183–223. Lanham, Md.: University Press of America.

Vardi, M. Y. (1985). Automatic verification of probabilistic concurrent finite-state programs. In *Proc. 26th IEEE Symp. on Foundations of Computer Science*, pp. 327–338.

Verma, T. (1986). Causal networks: semantics and expressiveness. Technical Report R–103, UCLA Cognitive Systems Laboratory.

von Mises, R. (1957). *Probability, Statistics, and Truth*. London: George Allen and Unwin. English translation of third German edition, 1951.

Voorbraak, F. (1991). The theory of objective knowledge and rational belief. In *Logics in AI, European Workshop JELIA '90*, pp. 499–515. Berlin/New York: Springer-Verlag.

vos Savant, M. (Sept. 9, 1990). Ask Marilyn. *Parade Magazine*, 15. Follow-up articles appeared in *Parade Magazine* on Dec. 2, 1990 (p. 25) and Feb. 17, 1991 (p. 12).

Wald, A. (1950). *Statistical Decision Functions*. New York: Wiley.

Walley, P. (1981). Coherent lower (and upper) probabilities. Manuscript, Department of Statistics, University of Warwick.

Walley, P. (1987). Belief function representations of statistical evidence. *Annals of Statistics 18*(4), 1439–1465.

Walley, P. (1991). *Statistical Reasoning with Imprecise Probabilities*, Volume 42 of *Monographs on Statistics and Applied Probability*. London: Chapman and Hall.

Walley, P. (1996). Inferences from multinomial data: learning about a bag of marbles. *Journal of the Royal Statistical Society, Series B 58*(1), 3–34. Discussion of the paper by various commentators appears on pp. 34–57.

Walley, P. (2000). Towards a unified theory of imprecise probability. *International Journal of Approximate Reasoning 24*, 125–148.

Weber, S. (1991). Uncertainty measures, decomposability and admissibility. *Fuzzy Sets and Systems 40*, 395–405.

Weydert, E. (1994). General belief measures. In *Proc. Tenth Conference on Uncertainty in Artificial Intelligence (UAI '94)*, pp. 575–582.

Williams, D. (1991). *Probability and Martingales*. Cambridge, U.K.: Cambridge University Press.

Williams, M. (1994). Transmutations of knowledge systems. In *Principles of Knowledge Representation and Reasoning: Proc. Fourth International Conference (KR '94)*, pp. 619–629.

Williams, P. M. (1976). Indeterminate probabilities. In M. Przelecki, K. Szaniawski, and R. Wojcicki (Eds.), *Formal Methods in the Methodology of Empirical Sciences*, pp. 229–246. Dordrecht, Netherlands: Reidel.

Wilson, N. (1994). Generating graphoids from generalized conditional probability. In *Proc. Tenth Conference on Uncertainty in Artificial Intelligence (UAI '94)*, pp. 583–591.

Wolf, G. (1977). *Obere und untere Wahrscheinlichkeiten*. Ph.D. thesis, ETH, Zurich.

Wright, S. (1921). Correlation and causation. *Journal of Agricultural Research 20*, 557–585.

Yager, R. R. (1983). Entropy and specificity in a mathematical theory of evidence. *International Journal of General Systems 9*, 249–260.

Yates, J. F. (1990). *Judgment and Decision Making*. London: Prentice Hall.

Yemini, Y. and D. Cohen (1979). Some issues in distributed processes communication. In *Proc. of the 1st International Conf. on Distributed Computing Systems*, pp. 199–203.

Zadeh, L. A. (1975). Fuzzy logics and approximate reasoning. *Synthese 30*, 407–428.

Zadeh, L. A. (1978). Fuzzy sets as a basis for a theory of possibility. *Fuzzy Sets and Systems 1*, 3–28.

# Glossary of Symbols

459

# Index